# Communications
# in Computer and Information Science 1503

More information about this series at https://link.springer.com/bookseries/7899

Daniel A. Alexandrov ·
Alexander V. Boukhanovsky ·
Andrei V. Chugunov · Yury Kabanov ·
Olessia Koltsova · Ilya Musabirov ·
Sergei Pashakhin (Eds.)

# Digital Transformation and Global Society

6th International Conference, DTGS 2021
St. Petersburg, Russia, June 23–25, 2021
Revised Selected Papers

Springer

*Editors*

Daniel A. Alexandrov (iD)
National Research University Higher School
of Economics
St. Petersburg, Russia

Andrei V. Chugunov
ITMO University
St. Petersburg, Russia

Olessia Koltsova (iD)
National Research University Higher School
of Economics
St. Petersburg, Russia

Sergei Pashakhin (iD)
National Research University Higher School
of Economics
St. Petersburg, Russia

Alexander V. Boukhanovsky
ITMO University
St. Petersburg, Russia

Yury Kabanov (iD)
National Research University Higher School
of Economics
St. Petersburg, Russia

Ilya Musabirov (iD)
National Research University Higher School
of Economics
St. Petersburg, Russia

ISSN 1865-0929          ISSN 1865-0937 (electronic)
Communications in Computer and Information Science
ISBN 978-3-030-93714-0          ISBN 978-3-030-93715-7 (eBook)
https://doi.org/10.1007/978-3-030-93715-7

This Springer imprint is published by the registered company Springer Nature Switzerland AG
The registered company address is: Gewerbestrasse 11, 6330 Cham, Switzerland

# Preface

The 6th International Conference on Digital Transformation and Global Society (DTGS 2021), hosted by ITMO University (St. Petersburg, Russia) was held during June 23–25, 2021. Due to the COVID-19 pandemic, for the second time the conference was organized in the online format. Despite the challenging circumstances, the virtual format allowed us to organize a full-fledged conference, where the authors could present and discuss their research.

Overall, 95 papers were submitted to the conference this year. For this final post-conference volume, the Program Committee and the Editorial Board carefully evaluated and selected 38 papers, with an acceptance rate of 40 per cent, that fall into the following major sections of the conference:

- eSociety: issues related to social informatics, computational social science, and online media research, as well as the questions of the digital inclusion;
- ePolicy: issues of e-governance and e-participation, including the problems of cyberspace regulation;
- eCity: developments in smart city and digital urban research;
- eHumanities: digital culture and education research;
- eCommunication: research on the online discourses and public sphere;
- eEconomy: issues of e-commerce development, including research on the economic challenges of the COVID-19 pandemic.

This year the session on eSociety was organized in partnership with the Laboratory for Social and Cognitive Informatics at HSE University in St. Petersburg. In addition, HSE University once again co-organized the Youth Forum of the conference. Out of 20 papers submitted by the young scholars, the five best papers were accepted to the final volume based on the evaluation by the Award Committee and substantial revision based on peer-review. Furthermore, the session on eCity was held in partnership with the WeGO Eurasia Regional Office.

We express our gratitude to the members of the Program Committee for their help in selecting the papers for the conference. We would like to thank the Award Committee, including Alena Suvorova, Denis Bulygin, and Alla Loseva from HSE University, Olga Filatova from St. Peterbsurg State University, and Yuri Misnikov from ITMO University.

We are also grateful to the moderators of the sessions including Tatiana Sherstinova from HSE University, Aleksandr Riabushko from the WeGO Eurasia Regional Office, Yuri Misnikov Artem Smolin, and Igor Kuprienko from ITMO University, and Maxim Bakaev from the Novosibirsk State Technical University.

We thank our partners, organizers and hosts, and all those who made this event possible and successful.

June 2021

Daniel A. Alexandrov
Alexander V. Boukhanovsky
Andrei V. Chugunov
Yury Kabanov
Olessia Koltsova
Ilya Musabirov
Sergei Pashakhin

# Organization

## Program Chairs

| | |
|---|---|
| Andrei V. Chugunov | ITMO University, Russia |
| Yury Kabanov (Program Coordinator) | HSE University, Russia |

## Conference and Tracks Chairs

| | |
|---|---|
| Daniel Alexandrov | HSE University, Russia |
| Alexander Boukhanovsky | ITMO University, Russia |
| Olessia Koltsova | HSE University, Russia |
| Ilya Musabirov | HSE University, Russia |
| Sergey Pashakhin | HSE University, Russia |

## Program Committee

| | |
|---|---|
| Thomas Ågotnes | University of Bergen, Norway |
| Roman Amelin | Saratov State University, Russia |
| Dennis Anderson | St. Francis College, USA |
| Francisco Andrade | University of Minho, Portugal |
| Maxim Bakaev | Novosibirsk State Technical University, Russia |
| Svetlana Berezka | HSE University, Russia |
| Alexander Bikkulov | ITMO University, Russia |
| Radomir Bolgov | St. Petersburg State University, Russia |
| Mikhail Bundin | Lobachevsky State University of Nizhni Novgorod, Russia |
| Anna Chizhik | St. Petersburg State University, Russia |
| Sergey Davydov | HSE University, Russia |
| Alexander Fedosov | Russian State Social University, Russia |
| Olga Filatova | St. Petersburg State University, Russia |
| Carlos Gershenson | UNAM, Mexico |
| Christoph Glauser | Institute for Applied Argumentation Research, Switzerland |
| Dimitris Gouscos | University of Athens. Greece |
| Sergei Ivanov | ITMO University, Russia |
| Katerina Kabassi | TEI of Ionian Islands, Greece |
| George Kampis | Eotvos University, Hungary |
| Ilia Karpov | HSE University, Russia |
| Igor Khodachek | RANEPA, Russia |
| Nora Kirkizh | GESIS, Germany |
| Sergei Koltcov | HSE University, Russia |

| Pavel Konyukhonskiy | Herzen State Pedagogical University of Russia, Russia |
| Walter LaMendola | University of Denver, USA |
| Elena Lisanyuk | St. Petersburg State University, Russia |
| Anna Litvinenko | Free University of Berlin, Germany |
| Aleksei Martynov | Lobachevsky State University of Nizhny Novgorod, Russia |
| Harekrishna Misra | Institute of Rural Management Anand, India |
| Sergey Mityagin | ITMO University, Russia |
| Ravil Muhamedyev | International IT University, Kazakhstan |
| Ilya Musabirov | HSE University, Russia |
| Aleksandra Nenko | ITMO University, Russia |
| Olga Nevzorova | Kazan Federal University, Russia |
| Danila Parygin | Volgograd State Technical University, Russia |
| Dmitry Prokudin | St. Petersburg State University, Russia |
| Aleksandr Riabushko | WeGO Eurasia Regional Office, Russia |
| Bogdan Romanov | University of Tartu, Estonia |
| John Magnus Roos | Centre for Consumer Science, Sweden |
| Anna Shirokanova | HSE University, Russia |
| Polina Smirnova | ITMO University, Russia |
| Anna Smoliarova | St. Petersburg State University, Russia |
| Leonid Smorgunov | St. Petersburg State University, Russia |
| Alexander Sokolov | Demidov Yaroslavl State University, Russia |
| Irina Tolstikova | ITMO University, Russia |
| Lyudmila Vidiasova | ITMO University, Russia |
| Arkaitz Zubiaga | Queen Mary University of London, UK |

## Additional Reviewers

Belyi, Vladislav
Bulygin, Denis
Busurkina, Irina
Chuprina, Daria
Kuchin, Yan
Loseva, Alla
Yakunin, Kirill

# Contents

## eCity: Smart Cities and Urban Planning

## eHumanities: Digital Education and Research Methods

## eCommunication: Online Discources and Attitudes

## eEconomy: Challenges of the COVID-19 Pandemic

**eEconomy: E-Commerce Research**

# eSociety: Social Informatics and Digital Inclusion Issues

# What is Fake News? Perceptions, Definitions and Concerns by Gender and Political Orientation Among Israelis

Nili Steinfeld(✉) iD

Ariel University, Ariel, Israel
nilisteinfeld@gmail.com

**Abstract.** "Fake news" is a growing concern among scholars, policymakers and the public. The phenomenon has gained much scholarly attention in recent years, however, most research has been occupied with its manifestation in the United States. To complement on the global nature of the phenomenon, the study evaluates how Israelis perceive its sources and the responsibility of various institutions. The analysis compares trends related to gender gaps and political bias in fake news perception to studies from the US and Europe. Findings illustrate how political orientation correlates with perception of fake news and the main source of false information in the media landscape, such that conservatives associate fake news mostly with mainstream media and journalists, whereas liberals associate politicians and social network users with fake news. Additionally, men and women differ in perceptions, subjective experience of fake news and concerns over the implications of the phenomenon. These trends and their comparison to US and European research contribute to a more complete understanding of fake news as a universal phenomenon.

**Keywords:** Fake news · Conservatives · Liberals · Political orientation · Gender · Social media

## 1 Introduction

"Fake News" is a growing concern among scholars, policymakers and the public [38]. Its potential perceived implications include skewing electoral results [24], promoting postmodern relativism in which facts no longer matter as they once did [30], decreasing trust in institutions [24, 31], and even posing a serious threat to democratic systems [24, 28, 31, 37].

A wealth of solutions and proposals for combating fake news have recently been introduced, from educational through regulatory to algorithmic solutions. However, it seems that we are only getting farther away from a solution to this growing urging problem. Lack of a clear definition and understanding of how it is perceived and engaged with in so many different modes and contexts by a diversity of stakeholders hampers progress in definitively dealing with this phenomenon [34, 39].

© Springer Nature Switzerland AG 2022
D. A. Alexandrov et al. (Eds.): DTGS 2021, CCIS 1503, pp. 3–18, 2022.
https://doi.org/10.1007/978-3-030-93715-7_1

Whereas the vast majority of research on fake news is concentrated on the United States, this study investigates how Israelis experience and define fake news, which factors Israelis perceive as responsible for its spread and prevention, ultimately relating the findings to US and European trends with the aim of characterizing and emphasizing the global nature and importance of fake news. Considering the importance of this phenomenon and its potentially far-reaching consequences, it is valuable to study its characteristics in regions outside the US and Europe. A comparison emphasizing similarities and unique characteristics of the phenomenon is different countries and cultures, under different political and/or social conditions, can shed light on the global nature of misinformation phenomena and external factors influencing and influenced by it.

## 2 Literature Review

### 2.1 What is Fake News?

Fake news is a debatable term, with no single, uniform, widely accepted definition [34, 39]. Although it is hardly a new concept, during the 2016 US presidential election it received global attention following then-candidate Donald Trump's continuous use of the term to describe unflattering mainstream media coverage [25, 26, 28].

A common definition of fake news, widely accepted in the research literature, relates it to fabricated information mimicking news media in form, but not in organizational processes or intent [22, 34]. Often, it incorporates spread of misinformation (false information spread unintentionally) and disinformation (intentional spread of false information [10, 22, 30], although broader definitions include hoaxes, hearsay, rumors [30], and satire [3]. In Tandoc Jr. et al. (2018) systematic fake news literature review, the authors found six types of operationalization: Satire, parody, fabrication, manipulation, propaganda, and advertising.

In the non-academic sphere, fake news is described less as strictly false information masked as news, and more as poor journalism, propaganda by politicians or hyperpartisan sources, and advertising [33]. Furthermore, politicians and authoritative public figures are increasingly using the term tactically to discredit mainstream news outlets [25–28, 34].

### 2.2 Imposing Responsibility

Different fake news definitions naturally lead to differing notions of liability. Often, liability is imposed on social media, criticized for its role in spreading and promoting fake news [8, 15, 26]. The structure of social media platforms, with their integration of news and personal stories, commentaries, and user engagement, in addition to very low gatekeeping, makes differentiating fact from fiction and reliable from misleading content a highly complex undertaking [1, 26]. In addition, tech-savvy users often manipulate social media platforms to promote biased and false content, providing fertile ground for the spread of fake news online [10, 22, 30].

Indeed, social media and messaging boards such as 4chan and 8chan are the main platforms used for spreading fake news and political manipulation [31]. Consequentially, recent efforts have been made by social media companies to reduce the dissemination and visibility of fake news stories on their platforms. Facebook, for example, has flagged disputed posts for US users based on input from fact-checking organizations and tools to tackle the problem of fake news [31]. However, after a period of experimenting with the effectiveness of flagging disputed posts, the company concluded that the flagging might have led to an opposite outcome and directed more attention to such posts, therefore decided to stop flagging content as disputed [6].

But social media is not the only target for criticism. Mainstream media is also facing lower public trust, which can be seen both as cause and consequence of the increase in the spread of fake news [1, 22, 33]. Deeply engaged with social media content, media personalities on television and radio cite and comment on information originating on social media [10]. Additionally, they cover fake news that circulates online, often to debunk it, but in practice legitimating its existence [30].

Overall, the general public tends to perceive fake news as driven by a combination of news media, politicians, and social media platforms [4, 33].

## 2.3 Weaponization of Fake News

"Fake news" as a concept has been exploited as a political weapon [7]. Politicians around the world now use the term against their political enemies. For instance, they accuse journalists of spreading lies with the aim of discrediting individual journalists and news organizations [24, 25]. An example would be Donald Trump's tweet responding to a poll showing worst early approval rating of the president in US history, stating: "Any negative polls are fake news, just like the CNN, ABC, NBC polls in the election" [5]. In more severe cases, they use the accusation of fake news as a pretence to censor media, shutter organizations, imprison reporters, and block public access to news and information [25]. In Tanzania, for example, four independent newspapers and two radio stations have been shut down or suspended during the year 2017 on account of "inaccuracies" in their reporting, according to President Magufuli. In the Philippines, similar accusations have been made as reason for revoking the operating license of the news site Rappler.com [25].

Social media is also weaponized by ideological groups and extremists, such as alt-right movements, and even terrorists, who use it to spread propaganda and disinformation [36, 40]. Its basic architecture enabling viral messaging, algorithmic targeting, automating and favoring of controversial and sensational content, and tools for simplifying mimicking and editing of content all lead to weaponization of false content for maximum impact [24]. Very accurately targeting receptive and pivotal audiences dramatically increases the effectiveness of commercial as well as political advertising in influencing user decisions and behaviors [32].

## 2.4 Implications of Fake News

Media experts are justifiably concerned with the potential of misinformation campaigns to manipulate actions and opinions [36], increase political inefficacy, alienation, and cynicism [3], even skewing electoral results [24]. The use of fake news by politicians to discredit legitimate media threatens freedom of expression [25] and may have serious implications for public trust in established media [25–28]. Fake news may be circulated online with the aim to decrease trust in institutions [24, 31]. As a result, it can be viewed as promoting postmodern relativism, an increasingly prominent strain of thought that insists facts matter less today than in the past [30]. All these processes: Destabilizing the press, democracy's "Watchdog", as an institution; Flooding public discourse with false and misleading information making it difficult for citizens to make rational, educated decisions; Decreasing trust in public institutions which are the foundations of functioning democracies- can thus pose a serious threat to the democratic system in general [24, 28, 31, 37]. As such, governments are increasingly concerned with the implications of fake news, with legislative initiatives proposed in a variety of countries [31].

Less politically informed and engaged populations are at greater risk of fake news influence, and are more inclined to believe false political information [22], whereas individuals with higher levels of understanding of how the news media operates are more likely to suspect and counteract against fabricated headlines, and also more concerned with the chances of encountering disinformation [2]. Indeed, this concern over fake news is not limited to experts and scholars alone. Two thirds of Americans believe that fake news causes high levels of confusion in the general public, distorting perception of basic facts related to current issues [4].

## 2.5 Fake News and Political Orientation

Arguably, the definition, meaning, and perception of fake news depend on individual point of view [7]. Although some research has emphasized that false and misleading information is, and always has been, a weapon used by no single political party or side (28], a number of studies conducted mainly in the US point to a noteworthy ideological gap in definition, perception, and use of fake news. False political content spread online was found to be promoting mostly right ideologies [1, 26]. Correspondingly, conservative, right-wing voters tend to share fake news items more than liberal left-wing voters [16, 29]. This bias is probably linked to the growing distrust in mainstream media, especially among conservatives in the US [35]. In their view, mainstream media is untrustworthy, biased to the left, and responsible for creating and spreading fake news, rather than social media users [43].

## 2.6 Gender Differences in Perception, Opinion, and Identification of Fake News

Some gender differences have been reported regarding perception of fake news liability. Women tend to stress the obligation of the state in actively preventing the spread of fake news, whereas men tend to express more concern over the implications of such intervention leading to excessive state censorship [37]. However, previous research did not find gender differences in confidence [4] or in actual success [13] in identifying fake news, as well as in tendency to share fake news [16].

## 2.7 The Political Media Landscape, Fake News, and Distrust in Israel

As noted, most research on fake news has been conducted in the US [14, 42], largely focusing the US presidential campaign of 2016. However, the phenomenon is now widespread and global [23]. A few recent studies concerned non-US populations such as Korea [42], Singapore [9], European countries [14, 33], and Lebanon [13]. However, little relevant research so far has been published on Israel, although the Israeli media has been excessively preoccupied with the issue of fake news. During three national political campaigns conducted within a year, followed by a political earthquake with the indictment of Prime Minister Benjamin Netanyahu [19] and continuous failing efforts to establish a new government [17], public discourse in Israel has become increasingly polarized [18]. Politicians of all sides accuse mainstream and social media of spreading fake news, although, in fact, they themselves are the agents spreading fake news with data pointing to 62% of opposition and 74% of coalition member posts containing false information during 2018 [20]. Trust in media, as well as in politicians, government and local authorities in Israel, is undergoing dramatic decline [18]. In addition, the PM is consistently attacking mainstream media outlets with accusations of leftist bias and false reporting [41]. All these processes share a resemblance to their fake news counterparts in Europe and the US involving polarized political debates and the rise of populist leaders promoting attacks meant to discredit legitimate mainstream media outlets [24, 25]. For these reasons, looking into how Israelis define, perceive, and engage with fake news offers a valuable contribution to the understanding of its global characteristics and importance, as well as relating Israeli fake news trends to similar reports from the US and other countries.

## 3 Research Questions

This study explores how Israelis define and perceive fake news. It looks at which institutions or factors are perceived as liable for fake news and how trends reported in US studies are reflected in Israeli populations. Therefore, the following research questions are asked:

**RQ1.** How concerned are Israelis about the fake news phenomenon?
**H1.** Consistent with Shin et al. (2018), a majority of Israelis are very concerned with the phenomenon of fake news and its possible implications.
**RQ2.** How do Israelis perceive fake news - what are the differences in perception between liberals and conservatives?

"Liberals" and "conservatives" in this context refer to political orientation, measured on a continuous scale between left-leaning to right-leaning, and religiosity, measured by a categorical variable of four categories: ultra-Orthodox (most conservative), Orthodox, traditional and secular (most liberal). Accordingly, this study hypothesizes:
**H2a.** Liberals (left-leaning voters, secular or traditional) tend to implicate politicians and social network users in the phenomenon of fake news, seeing them as responsible, while the mainstream media is relatively more reliable, consistent with Rainie et al. (2019).
**H2b.** Conservatives (right-leaning voters, Orthodox and ultra-Orthodox) tend to point to mainstream media as the main source of fake news, and, therefore, the most responsible for the phenomenon, in agreement with Tripodi (2018).
**RQ3.** What gender differences exist in perception of fake news and liability of institutions in preventing its spread?

**H3a.** In accordance with Reuter et al. (2019), women tend to impose responsibility on the state and public officials for preventing the spread of fake news, more so than men.
**H3b.** Women in general tend to perceive fake news as more severe than men.

# 4 Method

## 4.1 Questionnaire

A survey questionnaire measured definitions and perceptions of fake news (respondents were asked about "false messages", or "false messages and fake news", to emphasize the narrow definition of fake news as false information). The survey measured its sources, the liability of institutions in preventing its spread, and its implications and severity. In addition, the study assessed political interest, trust, and activism in relation to fake news perception. The questionnaire is composed of questions from several previous studies: [4, 12, 21]. See Appendix A for the complete questionnaire.

## 4.2 Participants

502 respondents (50% female), with ages from 18 to 70 (M = 40.81, Mdn = 39), participated in an online survey distributed by iPanel, a leading Israeli internet data collection service. 50.6% of respondents are secular, 31.7% define themselves as traditional (non-religious), 14.9% as religious (Orthodox) and 2.8% as ultra-Orthodox. In terms of political orientation, on a scale of 1 (most right-leaning) to 10 (most left-leaning), participant average was 4.31 (Mdn = 4, SD = 2.09).

# 5 Results

## 5.1 Concerns Over Fake News

The results of the survey indicate that Israelis are highly concerned over the fake news phenomenon: No less than 80.6% think that false messages leave the public confused about basic facts on topics and events to a large or very large extent. Furthermore, 89.8% think that the implications of the phenomenon are severe to a large or very large extent.

When it comes to responsibility, mainstream media is held most responsible for preventing the spread of false information, with 83.6% of respondents agreeing to a large or very large extent. Second to mainstream media are politicians: 77.8% of respondents impute responsibility to politicians to prevent the spread of false messages to a large or very large extent. They are followed by social networks (68%) and lastly the public (67.2%).

This descriptive data confirms hypothesis H1 and suggests that Israelis are indeed highly concerned with false messages and fake news, its implications, and the responsibility of a variety of stakeholders in combating its spread.

## 5.2 Liberals and Conservatives Define Fake News

Significant differences were found between religious and non-religious respondents, as well as correlations between political orientation and perceptions related to fake news, which suggest that conservatives associate fake news mostly with mainstream media and journalists, whereas liberals tend to associate politicians and social network users with fake news. Several questions measured respondent perceptions and definitions of fake news. Agreement with the statement claiming that a main reason for people's confusion and misperceptions about facts related to their country is politicians misleading the public corelates with political orientation, such that the more left-leaning respondents display greater agreement with the statement ($r = 0.18$, $p < .01$). Significant differences were also found when comparing mean agreement between secular and religious respondents ($F(3,482) = 7.39$, $p < .01$). LSD post-hoc tests reveal that secular ($M = 4.24$, SD = 0.834), traditional ($M = 4.06$, SD = 0.780), and religious ($M = 3.97$, SD = 0.839) respondents agree with the statement to a significantly larger degree than the ultra-Orthodox ($M = 3.29$, SD = 1.267).

The image is reversed with the statement that a main reason for people's confusion is that mainstream media is misleading the public. Here, political orientation corelates with agreement such that the more right-leaning the respondent, the greater the agreement with the statement ($r = -0.33$, $p < 0.01$). One-way ANOVA found significant differences in mean agreement with the statement by religiosity ($F(3,485) = 7.43$, $p < .01$). LSD post-hoc tests reveal significant differences between secular respondents ($M = 3.58$, SD = 1.09) who agree with the statement to a significantly less degree than traditional ($M = 3.87$, SD = .92) and Orthodox (4.14, SD = .79) respondents, who agree significantly more that mainstream media misleading the public is a main reason for people's confusion and misperceptions.

When respondents were asked to select the main source for spreading false messages, significant differences were found in political orientation of those who chose each of the sources ($F(2,486) = 47.281$, $p < .01$). Those who selected politicians and public figures as the main source for spreading false messages were the most left-leaning ($M = 5.47$, SD = 2.09), significantly more than those who chose users on social networks ($M = 4.25$, SD = 1.93) and those who chose journalists and media personas, who are the most right-leaning of respondents ($M = 3.26$, SD = 1.77). In a similar trend, significant differences between secular, traditional, and religious respondents were found on the question of the main source for spreading false messages ($\chi2 = 44.5$, Cramer's V = .17, $p < .001$). Secular respondents perceive social media users (37.8%) and politicians (35.8%) as the main sources for spreading false messages, and less so journalists (22.4%). Traditional respondents mostly point to social media users (48.4%), then journalists (28.9%), and lastly politicians (21.4%), while Orthodox and ultra-Orthodox respondents point mostly to journalists (50.7% and 64.3%, respectively) then social media users (33.3% and 28.6%, respectively) and hardly to politicians (14.7% and 7.1% respectively).

**Table 1.** Results of one-way ANOVA tests for significant differences between liberals and conservatives in views of fake news sources

| Variable | Group | Mean | SD | F | Traditional | Orthodox | Ultra-Orthodox |
|---|---|---|---|---|---|---|---|
| Politicians mislead the public | All | 4.12 | .85 | 7.39** | | | |
| | Secular | 4.24 | .83 | | .04* | .02* | .000*** |
| | Traditional | 4.06 | .78 | | | NS | .001** |
| | Orthodox | 3.97 | .84 | | | | .005** |
| | Ultra-Orthodox | 3.29 | 1.27 | | | | |
| Mainstream media misleads the public | All | 3.76 | 1.01 | 7.43** | | | |
| | Secular | 3.58 | 1.09 | | .004** | .000*** | NS |
| | Traditional | 3.87 | .92 | | | NS | NS |
| | Orthodox | 4.14 | .79 | | | | NS |
| | Ultra-Orthodox | 4.08 | .86 | | | | |
| | | | | | Journalists and media personas | Politicians | None of the above |
| Political orientation (1 = most right to 10 = most left) | All | 4.31 | 2.09 | 32.61 | | | |
| | Users on social media | 4.25 | 1.93 | | .000*** | .000*** | NS |
| | Journalists and media personas | 3.26 | 1.77 | | | .000*** | .001** |
| | Politicians | 5.47 | 2.09 | | | | NS |
| | None of the above | 5.08 | 1.38 | | | | |

These findings support hypotheses H2a and H2b and confirm that liberals (i.e. left-leaning, non-religious respondents) tend to associate politicians and social network users with the phenomenon of fake news, hold them responsible for it, and view the mainstream media as relatively more reliable. In contrast, conservatives (right-leaning, Orthodox and ultra-Orthodox respondents) tend to point to mainstream media and journalists as the primary source of fake news, bearing the most responsibility with hardly any notice of politicians.

Tables 1 and 2 summarize the differences in views of liberals and conservatives on fake news sources.

### 5.3 Gender, Definitions, and Perceptions of Fake News

Gender differences in relation to fake news were also noticeable: in perception, attribution of responsibility, sense of severity, and prior perceived exposure.

No gender differences were found in agreement with the role of politicians or the mainstream media in spreading false messages. However, men tend to agree with the

**Table 2.** Results of chi-square test for differences in view of main source for spreading false messages based on religiosity, $\chi^2 = 44.5$, Cramer's V $= .17$, p $< .001$

|  | Group | N | % |
|---|---|---|---|
| Users on social media | All | 202 | 40.2 |
|  | Secular | **96** | **37.8** |
|  | Traditional | **77** | **48.4** |
|  | Orthodox | 25 | 33.3 |
|  | Ultra-Orthodox | 4 | 28.6 |
| Journalists and media personas | All | 150 | 29.9 |
|  | Secular | 57 | 22.4 |
|  | Traditional | 46 | 28.9 |
|  | Orthodox | **38** | **50.7** |
|  | Ultra-Orthodox | **9** | **64.3** |
| Politicians | All | 137 | 27.3 |
|  | Secular | **91** | **35.8** |
|  | Traditional | 34 | 21.4 |
|  | Orthodox | 11 | 14.7 |
|  | Ultra-Orthodox | 1 | 7.1 |

statement that social media is misleading the public as a source for false messages (M = 3.93, SD = 0.96) significantly more than women (M = 3.73, SD = 0.99) (t(489) = 2.31, p < 0.05).

Women agree more that the government, politicians, and public figures are responsible for preventing the spread of fake news (M = 1.77, SD = 0.95), significantly more than men (M = 2.00, SD = 1.09) (t(494) = 2.59, p < 0.05). Women also agree significantly more than men that social media is responsible for preventing the spread of false messages (M = 1.97, SD = 1.00 for women, M = 2.37, SD = 1.22 for men, 1 = to a very large extent, 5 = to a very small extent) (t(471.02) = 4, p < 0.01).

When requested to choose one main source for spreading false messages, women and men differ significantly ($\chi2 = 8.88$, p < .05). Men slightly tend to point to social media users (35.5%) more than politicians (31.9%) and journalists (31.1%). For women, the culprits are more social media users (45%), journalists (28.7%), and to a lesser degree-politicians (22.7%).

Tables 3 and 4 summarize gender differences in perceptions of fake news sources and responsibility of various stakeholders in preventing the spread of fake news.

**Table 3.** Gender differences in views on sources for fake news and liability of stakeholders

| Variable | Group | N | Mean | SD | t |
|---|---|---|---|---|---|
| Social media misleads the public | All | 491 | 3.83 | .97 | $t_{(489)} = 2.31$, p < 0.05 |
| | Men | 248 | 3.93 | .96 | |
| | Women | 243 | 3.73 | .99 | |
| Government, politicians, and public figures responsible for preventing spread of fake news | All | 496 | 1.89 | 1.03 | $t_{(494)} = 2.59$, p < 0.05 |
| | Men | 248 | 2.00 | 1.09 | |
| | Women | 248 | 1.77 | .95 | |
| Social media responsible for preventing spread of fake news | All | 490 | 2.17 | 1.13 | $t_{(471.02)} = 4$, p < 0.01 |
| | Men | 246 | 2.37 | 1.22 | |
| | Women | 244 | 1.97 | 1.00 | |
| False messages leave the public confused | All | 490 | 1.90 | .90 | $t_{(488)} = 2.46$, p < .05 |
| | Men | 248 | 2.00 | .96 | |
| | Women | 242 | 1.80 | .82 | |
| The implications of false messages on society are severe | All | 489 | 1.70 | .79 | $t_{(453.08)} = 2.61$, p < .01 |
| | Men | 245 | 1.80 | .89 | |
| | Women | 244 | 1.61 | .67 | |

(1 = to a very large extent, 5 = to a very small extent).

Men and women differ in their subjective experience of previously encountering inaccurate or false messages on mainstream media or the internet. Men consistently report encountering such messages more frequently: Men report more frequent prior encounters with inaccurate political messages on the internet (M = 4.19, SD = 1.11) compared to women (M = 3.89, SD = 1.26) (t(500) = 2.82, p < .01), with false political messages on the internet (M = 3.49, SD = 1.27) compared to women (M = 3.25, SD = 1.35) (t(500) = 1.98, p < .05), with inaccurate political messages on mainstream media (M = 3.90, SD = 1.19) compared to women (M = 3.46, SD = 1.31) (t(495.43) = 3.89, p < .001), and with false political messages on mainstream media (M = 3.20, SD = 1.28) compared to women (M = 2.94, SD = 1.42) (t(500) = 2.15, p < .05). Despite reporting less exposure to false messages, women perceive the phenomenon to be more severe than men. On a scale of 1 (to a very large extent) to 5 (to a very small extent), women significantly agree to a larger extent (M = 1.8, SD = .82) than men (M = 2, SD = .96) that false messages leave the public confused about basic facts on topics and events (t(488) = 2.46, p < .05), and also significantly agree to a larger extent (M = 1.61, SD = .67) than men (M = 1.8, SD = .89) that the implications of false messages on society are severe (t(453.08) = 2.61, p < .01).

These findings support hypotheses H3a and H3b and confirm that women tend to perceive the state as responsible for preventing the spread of fake news more than do men,

**Table 4.** Results of chi-square test for differences in view of main source for spreading false messages based on gender, $\chi^2 = 8.88$, p < .05.

|  | Group | N | % |
|---|---|---|---|
| Users on social media | All | 202 | 40.2 |
|  | Men | 89 | 35.5 |
|  | Women | 113 | 45 |
| Journalists and media personas | All | 150 | 29.9 |
|  | Men | 78 | 31.1 |
|  | Women | 72 | 28.7 |
| Politicians | All | 137 | 27.3 |
|  | Men | 80 | 31.9 |
|  | Women | 57 | 22.7 |

although women also perceive social media as responsible more than men. In general, women perceive the phenomenon as severe more than men, although in their subjective experience they have previously encountered false political messages less than men (it is noteworthy that the questions regarding prior encounters with false political messages rely solely on the respondents' own assessments and are, therefore, markers only of respondent subjective experiences and assumptions).

## 6 Discussion and Conclusions

The research focuses on how Israelis perceive, define, and relate to the phenomenon of false information and fake news. Several trends corresponding with findings from previous research conducted mainly in the US, and some in Europe, were examined through an Israeli population.

Academic scholars, policymakers, and mainstream media are increasingly concerned with fake news and its possible implications [38]. These include skewing electoral results [24], promoting postmodern relativism among the public [30], decreasing trust in institutions [24, 31], and even undermining the foundations of democratic systems [24, 28, 31, 37].

Although fake news has been studied mainly in the context of US politics, it is increasingly described as a broader phenomenon on a global scale [23]. The Israeli context is similar to Europe and US, with a relatively unstable political system marked by three national elections in one year, following an unstable government which dissolved after a year. In addition, Israeli public discourse is highly polarized [18], politicians are taking very active roles in creating and pushing false information [20], and the PM is consistently attacking mainstream media outlets with accusations of leftist bias and false reporting [41]. Therefore, an inquiry of how Israelis perceive fake news and how these views relate to global trends is highly relevant.

Indeed, the findings suggest that public perception and conception of fake news in Israel resembles trends reported in previous research conducted in the US and in

Europe. Israelis are highly concerned over the phenomenon and its implications for society. Respondents point to several institutions as liable for preventing and combating fake news. Most liable is the mainstream media, with a solid consensus that it is their role to lead efforts in combating fake news. Politicians are also perceived as responsible, while social networks and the public are by no means "off the hook." From this data emerges a view that fake news is perceived by Israelis as a serious problem with severe implications, and it is up to a variety of stakeholders to fight and contain it.

In Israel, liberals and conservatives differ in their views and perceptions of fake news in ways similar to what is reported in the US: Conservatives blame fake news on the mainstream media more so than social media and politicians. For them, the mainstream media, and hardly politicians, is liable. Liberals see politicians and social network users as responsible, with mainstream media relatively more reliable in their view.

Several gender differences were also found. Women tend to perceive the state and also social media as responsible for preventing the spread of fake news more than men. In general, women express more concern over fake news and its implications for society, although they report less previous encounters with it than men. These gender differences correspond with previous literature reporting similar gender differences on expression of concern over a variety of technological and environmental developments, with women expressing more concern than men [12].

To conclude, the results of this study suggest that fake news is imagined and perceived by Israelis in a manner similar to what is described in US and European-based studies. Israelis are highly concerned with fake news and its social implications, while similar gender and political orientation gaps were found in definition, perception, and concern. These similarities strengthen the claim that we are witnessing a growing global phenomenon.

Focusing research on a specific case, country, or population may be missing the greater picture. Looking at fake news as a global problem, highlighting similarities across cultures and political systems may be a most useful method in developing further understanding of this phenomenon, its trigger mechanisms, consequences, and dynamics. Furthermore, focusing on how politicians as well as citizens, political parties, media outlets, and other institutions around the world engage with fake news may inform and enhance useful tools to navigate, prevent, and combat this ever-growing global challenge.

## Appendix A: Survey Questionnaire

Questions in this questionnaire were inspired, adapted and translated to Hebrew from various sources.

Q1 was adapted from [21].

Q3 was adapted from [12].

Questions Q4–Q12, were inspired by [4].

**Q1.** People often get lots of things wrong about their countries and how they're changing, for example, what proportion of the population are immigrants, or whether crime is going up or down. Please indicate your agreement for each of the following if you think they are a main reason for this: (Answers are on a 5-point Likert scale, with the option to mark "don't know").

- Politicians mislead the public
- Mainstream media misleads the public
- People have biased views, for example, they tend to focus on negative things or think things are getting worse, or generalise from their own experience
- Social media misleads the public
- It's often the figures that are wrong, not people's views
- People are bad with numbers, so they struggle with trying to estimate such things

**Q2.** Recently, claims are made regarding the increase in the spread of "Fake News". Of the following factors, which to your opinion is the main source for spreading false messages and fake news? (Choose one)

- Users on social media
- Journalists and media personas
- Politicians
- None of the above

**Q3.** In politics people sometimes define themselves as left or right. Where would you place yourself on a scale from 1 to 10 where 1 means right and 10 means left?

**Q4.** Over the past year, how often did you come across news stories about politics **online** that you think were not fully accurate?

**Q5.** Over the past year, how often did you come across news stories about politics **online** that you think were almost entirely made-up?

**Q6.** Over the past year, how often did you come across news stories about politics **on mainstream media** (TV, radio, newspapers) that you think were not fully accurate?

**Q7.** Over the past year, how often did you come across news stories about politics **on mainstream media** (TV, radio, newspapers) that you think were almost entirely made-up?

Answers for questions Q4-Q7 were:

1. Never
2. Seldom (once every few months)
3. Sometimes (about once a month)
4. Often (several times a month).

**Q8.** How much responsibility in your opinion do members of the public have in trying to prevent the spread of false messages?

**Q9.** How much responsibility in your opinion do the government, politicians, and elected officials have in trying to prevent the spread of false messages?

**Q10.** How much responsibility in your opinion do social networks and search engines have in trying to prevent the spread of false messages?

**Q11.** How much responsibility in your opinion do mainstream media outlets (TV, Radio, newspapers) have in trying to prevent the spread of false messages?

**Q12.** How much do you think false messages leave the public confused about the basic facts of current issues and events?

**Q13.** How severe are the social implications of the false messages phenomenon in your opinion?

Answers for questions Q8-Q13 were on a 5-point Likert scale.

# References

1. Allcott, H., Gentzkow, M.: Social media and fake news in the 2016 election. J. Econ. Perspect. **31**(2), 211–236 (2017)
2. Amazeen, M.A., Bucy, E.P.: Conferring resistance to digital disinformation: the inoculating influence of procedural news knowledge. J. Broadcast. Electron. Media **63**(3), 415–432 (2019)
3. Balmas, M.: When fake news becomes real: combined exposure to multiple news sources and political attitudes of inefficacy, alienation, and cynicism. Commun. Res. **41**(3), 430–454 (2014)
4. Barthel, M., Mitchell, A., Holcomb, J:. Many Americans believe fake news is sowing confusion. Pew Research Center https://www.journalism.org/2016/12/15/many-americans-believe-fake-news-is-sowing-confusion/
5. Batchelor, T.: Donald Trump says all negative polls about him are fake news. Independent (2017). https://www.independent.co.uk/news/world/americas/donald-trump-negative-polls-fake-news-twitter-cnn-abc-nbc-a7564951.html
6. BBC.: Facebook ditches fake news warning flag. BBC (2017). https://www.bbc.com/news/technology-42438750
7. Berghel, H.: Alt-News and Post-Truths in the "Fake News" Era. Computer **50**(4), 110–114 (2017)
8. Chadwick, A., Vaccari, C., O'Loughlin, B.: Do tabloids poison the well of social media? Explaining democratically dysfunctional news sharing. New Media Soc. **20**(11), 4255–4274 (2018)
9. Chen, X., Sin, S.C.J., Theng, Y.L., Lee, C.S.: Why students share misinformation on social media: motivation, gender, and study-level differences. J. Acad. Librariansh. **41**, 1–10 (2015)
10. Cooke, N. A.: Fake News and Alternative Facts: Information Literacy in a Post-truth Era. American Library Association, Atlanta, GA (2018)
11. Curtice, J., Bryson, C., Schwartz, S., Thomassen, J., van Kersbergen, K., van Waarden, F.: People's underlying value orientations. Chapter 5, 176 (2003). http://www.europeansocials urvey.org/docs/methodology/core_ess_questionnaire/ESS_core_questionnaire_political_iss ues.pdf
12. Davidson, D.J., Freudenburg, W.R.: Gender and environmental risk concerns: a review and analysis of available research. Environ. Behav. **28**(3), 302–339 (1996)
13. El Rayess, M., Chebl, C., Mhanna, J., Hage, R.M.: Fake news judgement: the case of undergraduate students at Notre Dame University-Louaize. Lebanon. Ref. Serv. Rev. **46**(1), 146–149 (2018)
14. Fletcher, R., Cornia, A., Graves, L., Nielsen, R. K.: Measuring the reach of "fake news" and online disinformation in Europe. Reuters institute factsheet (2018)
15. Gil de Zúñiga, H., Chen, H.T.: Digital media and politics effects of the great information and communication divides. J. Broadcast. Electron. Media. **63**(3), 365–373 (2019)
16. Guess, A., Nagler, J., Tucker, J.: Less than you think: prevalence and predictors of fake news dissemination on Facebook. Sci. Adv. **5**(1), 1–8 (2019). https://doi.org/10.1126/sciadv.aau 4586

17. Heller, J., Farrell, S.: Third Israeli election looms after Netanyahu and challenger fail to form government. Reuters (2019). https://www.reuters.com/article/us-israel-politics/third-isr aeli-election-looms-after-netanyahu-and-challenger-fail-to-form-government-idUSKBN1X U1OC

18. Herman, T., Anabi, O., Heller, E., Omar, F.: The Israeli Democracy Index 2018. The Israeli Institute for Democracy, Jerusalem (2018)

19. Holmes, O.: Israeli PM Benjamin Netanyahu indicted for bribery and fraud. The Guardian (2019). https://www.theguardian.com/world/2019/nov/21/israeli-prime-minister-benjamin-netanyahu-indicted-for-bribery-and

20. Ifat media research. Fact or fiction: A study of the factorial discourse in Israel's mainstream media (2019). http://ifat.com/marcom/fairy.pdf

21. IPSOS: Fake news, filter bubbles, post-truth and trust; A study across 27 countries (2018). https://www.ipsos.com/sites/default/files/ct/news/documents/2018-09/fake-news-fil ter-bubbles-post-truth-and-trust.pdf

22. Lazer, D.M.J., et al.: The science of fake news. Science **359**(6380), 1094–1096 (2018). https://doi.org/10.1126/science.aao2998

23. Lees, C.: Fake news: the global silencer: the term has become a useful weapon in the dictator's toolkit against the media. Just look at the Philippines. Index Censorsh. **47**(1), 88–91 (2018). https://doi.org/10.1177/0306422018769578

24. Levi, L.: Real fake news and fake news. First Amend. Law Rev. **16**, 232 (2017)

25. Levinson, P.: Turning the tables: how trump turned fake news from a weapon of deception to a weapon of mass destruction of legitimate news. In: Happer, C., Hoskins, A., Merrin, W. (eds.) Trump's Media War, pp. 33–46. Springer, Cham (2019). https://doi.org/10.1007/978-3-319-94069-4_3

26. Marwick, A.E.: Why do people share fake news? A sociotechnical model of media effects. Georgetown Law Technol. Rev. **2**(2), 474–512 (2018)

27. McGonagle, T.: "Fake news" false fears or real concerns? Netherlands Q. Human Rights **35**(4), 203–209 (2017)

28. McNair, B.: Fake news: Falsehood Fabrication and Fantasy in Journalism. Routledge, Milton Park (2017)

29. Mele, N., et al.: Combating fake news: An agenda for research and action (2017). https://www.hks.harvard.edu/publications/combating-fake-new-agenda-research-and-action. Accessed 17 Oct 2018

30. Mihailidis, P., Viotty, S.: Spreadable spectacle in digital culture: civic expression, fake news, and the role of media literacies in "post-fact" society. Am. Behav. Sci. **61**(4), 441–454 (2017)

31. Morgan, S.: Fake news, disinformation, manipulation and online tactics to undermine democracy. J. Cyber Policy **3**(1), 39–43 (2018)

32. Nadler, A., Crain, M., Donovan, J.: Weaponizing the Digital Influence Machine. Data & Society Research Institute (2018). https://apo.org.au/sites/default/files/resource-files/2018/10/apo-nid197676-1225751.pdf

33. Nielsen, R.K., Graves, L.: "News you don't believe": Audience perspectives on fake news. Reuters Institute for the Study of Journalism (2017). https://reutersinstitute.politics.ox.ac.uk/sites/default/files/2017-10/Nielsen&Graves_factsheet_1710v3_FINAL_download.pdf

34. Quandt, T., Frischlich, L., Boberg, S., Schatto-Eckrodt, T.: Fake news. In: Vos, T.P., Hanusch, F., Dimitrakopoulou, D., Geertsema-Sligh, M., Sehl, A. (eds.) The International Encyclopaedia of Journalism Studies, pp. 1–6. Wiley, Hoboken (2019). https://doi.org/10.1002/978111 8841570.iejs0128

35. Rainie, L., Keeter, S., Perrin, A.: Trust and Distrust in America (2019). https://www.people-press.org/2019/07/22/trust-and-distrust-in-america/

36. Rainie, H., Anderson, J.Q., Albright, J.: The Future of Free Speech, Trolls, Anonymity and Fake News Online. Pew Research Center, Washington, DC (2017)

37. Reuter, C., Hartwig, K., Kirchner, J., Schlegel, N.: Fake news perception in Germany: a representative study of people's attitudes and approaches to counteract disinformation. In: Proceedings of the International Conference on Wirtschaftsinformatik (WI) (2019)
38. Shin, J., Jian, L., Driscoll, K., Bar, F.: The diffusion of misinformation on social media: temporal pattern, message, and source. Comput. Hum. Behav. **83**, 278–287 (2018)
39. Shu, K., Sliva, A., Wang, S., Tang, J., Liu, H.: Fake news detection on social media: a data mining perspective. ACM SIGKDD Explor. Newsl. **19**(1), 22–36 (2017)
40. Smith, C.A.: Weaponized iconoclasm in Internet memes featuring the expression 'Fake News.' Discourse Commun. **13**(3), 303–319 (2019)
41. Stern, I.: Netanyahu Ratchets Up Attack on Production Company, Journalist Reporting His Corruption Probes. Haaretz (2019). https://www.haaretz.com/israel-news/.premium-netany ahu-lashes-out-at-news-company-they-re-doing-harm-to-democracy-1.7772714
42. Tandoc, E.C., Jr., Lim, Z.W., Ling, R.: Defining "fake news" a typology of scholarly definitions. Digit. J. **6**(2), 137–153 (2018)
43. Tripodi, F.: Searching for Alternative Facts: Analyzing Scriptural Inference in Conservative News Practices. Data & Society report (2018)

# A Semi-automated Pipeline for Mapping the Shifts and Continuities in Media Discourse

Anna Shirokanova[1]([✉]) [iD] and Olga Silyutina[2] [iD]

[1] Laboratory for Comparative Social Research, HSE University, Moscow, Russian Federation
a.shirokanova@hse.ru

[2] HSE University, St. Petersburg, Russian Federation

**Abstract.** Mass media are an important actor between the authorities and citizens. Mass media frame the news and set the agenda for public debates. Investigation of this role of media has inspired various techniques for the analysis of media discourse in social and political research. However, manual coding of large corpora takes a long time and is prone to bias. Topic modeling can automate the search for key terms but it can hardly trace the shifts in a debate if the key terms are changing over time. In this paper, we propose a clustering-based pipeline that automates the search of key terms in the media discourse on a given topic and traces their development in time. The proposed technique helps to connect the clusters of unique terms across time periods into 'discursive streams'. Such streams' relative proportions and contents can be compared on a resulting map, a river network. The steps for creating such maps are explained. Two use cases demonstrate the shifts and continuities in the national media discourse about Internet regulation and labor migration in Russia over almost a decade. The analyses are based on more than 5,000 texts coming from the Integrum and Public.ru media archives. The resulting networks show which discussions evolved in the media discourse in the media coverage of these topics; how the key terms changed over time within the same debates; how the discursive streams grew in size and died out. The results are discussed in terms of validity and the applicability of the proposed technique to the study of media coverage of other topics.

**Keywords:** Text analysis · Clustering · Networks · Natural language processing · Media discourse · Internet regulation · Labor migration · Russia

## 1 Introduction

Media discourse can be thought of as a multitude of publicly relevant media discussions of an issue. These discussions frame the issue representations and formulate the key arguments in current debates. Media sources are often compared by the contrasting arguments and points of view of a certain issue. Moreover, the public debate on a topic can evolve over time, shifting the terms but continuing a general line of debate.

Traditionally, an exploratory analysis of large media corpora has set the goal to describe topics (e.g., with topic modeling [1]) and their important covariates (e.g., with structural topic modeling [2]). However, the topics within public discourse do not remain

© Springer Nature Switzerland AG 2022
D. A. Alexandrov et al. (Eds.): DTGS 2021, CCIS 1503, pp. 19–35, 2022.
https://doi.org/10.1007/978-3-030-93715-7_2

intact but evolve over time, so that the debate departs from one hot issue to another while maintaining continuity of the discourse which can be identified by experts or observers. The case has been well argued by Rule et al. [3] where the authors traced the evolution of key terms within more general themes over 200 years of annual presidential addresses to Congress. The starting point of our pipeline is this analysis of State of the Union discourse over 1790–2014 [3]. This analysis not only led to a semantic network of key terms in these addresses but also traced 'master categories' in the discourse over decades and changes in key terms within clusters of semantic networks over long time periods, thus, showing how the appearance of shifting key terms can hide continuities in the discourse.

Our goal is to propose a working instrument that can describe media discourse on a given topic across time, allowing for the keywords within the same topic to change over time and suitable to trace these changes and continuities for a series of years so that there is no need to match the topics manually from year to year. In response to this goal, we propose an easy-to-implement pipeline that (1) defines semantic networks of key terms across the media discourse; (2) can compare the shares of discussion threads ('discourse streams' [3]) within the larger theme across time; (3) can show at what moment the topics went through changes in key terms while staying within the same discussion thread.

The idea of discourse streams comes from an understanding of 'fluidity of discursive categories' [3]. How is a certain topic understood over time? The authors distinguish between topics, i.e., clusters of local semantic networks that are "meaningful from a particular historic standpoint, and not sensitive to semantic changes that occur in subsequent periods", and discourse streams, which represent "the same thing from period to period, although it need not remain one thing … Discourse streams may fork, merge, decline, swell; new streams can always emerge and old ones disappear" [3].

Big political events which are ascribed key changes in historical narratives do not always transform the way societies understand certain tasks in governance or policies—"change in salient contents often masks continuity at a higher level" [3]. One way to disentangle the question about the importance of historical events is to provide arguments for and against them. Another way is to look at the way certain topics were addressed over time and trace the changes through them. The original approach presented in [3] focuses on corpora spanning over long periods of time such as centuries.

We assume that there are some larger streams of discourse or themes that can dwell from one set of key terms to another, while being part of the same public discussion. In what follows, we present and motivate a pipeline that leads to mapping such discursive streams in a network of themes over time. Then we showcase its use, first, on the *Integrum* media corpus about Internet regulation and, second, on the *Public.ru* media corpus about labor migration to Russia. Both studies cover approximately a decade and provide the background, results, and their interpretation. The validity and reproducibility of results are discussed. Finally, we attach a replication code that can be applied to other media corpora.

## 2 Motivation

Our task here is to locate the topics in the discourse and trace their changes and continuities over time. One popular method for extracting topics is the community detection over topic modeling, either as latent Dirichlet allocation (LDA) [1] or as one of its later modifications, such as the topics-over-time algorithm, continuous dynamic topic modeling, or structural topic modeling [2, 4, 5]. These topic modeling approaches include models with time as a covariate so that it is possible to find out how the salience of topics changes over time. Another standard approach uses dictionary-based methods where texts are compared against a pre-defined set of terms [6].

Both approaches have problems when it comes to longitudinal text analysis because of a static set of analyzed terms. In the case of a dictionary, the analyst creates a list of words that can be biased in favor of his or her hypothesis. In addition, some new or old words and their meanings can be lost. In the case of topic modeling, the resulting topics are not always easy to be meaningfully interpreted. Besides, topic models are based on the premise that topics consist of words distributed across texts. Here, words are the semantic units of a topic, even though separate words can change their meanings over time. For example, structural topic modeling allows using categorical covariates such as years of publication. This option creates an opportunity to understand which topics can be described best by a given document from a particular year. However, there is another problem—the number of topics is set by the analyst in advance and it is constant over time [2, 3]. This is a known limitation of all topic modeling techniques. As a result, the documents from one period can be found in a topic mostly composed of documents from another period. Moreover, the model is built on the principle of linear regression so that the more independent variables are used, the harder it is to interpret the results [7].

A different approach would be to look at the words' co-occurrences as terms and then estimate their relationships within the texts. This is the approach adopted here, following [3]. The co-occurrence approach focuses on the interconnections of terms across different units of text. The most important goal it reaches is a better understanding of the context of term use. Understanding the relationships between words is important for tracking the changes between the words over time. In contrast to single words within topic models, terms also make the results directly interpretable. Thus, it is possible to learn about the transformations of particular terms over time, and to find discursive continuities across time even if the key term has changed.

Yet another advantage of this dynamic approach is that the terms do not have to be tied exclusively to one topic over time, in contrast to static approaches. It means that a single term may belong to different topics over time if its relationships with other terms are changing over time. In this study, we propose a more transparent and interpretable approach based on co-occurrences of terms in the text corpora, which are then analyzed with network clustering methods and similarity metrics.

The advantage of the proposed pipeline over original approach is that it can work with shorter texts of varying length and that it involves fewer steps. The proposed pipeline can be placed with a larger direction of studies focusing on tracking topics over time, with a goal to understand their evolution through mutations in key terms [8–10].

## 3  The Analytical Technique

There are six steps in the proposed pipeline:

1. Text Preprocessing
2. Creating a Network of Popular Collocations
3. Clustering semantic networks into several clusters
4. Labeling the Clusters with the Most Specific Collocations
5. Calculating Distances Between Similar Clusters Across years
6. Connecting the most similar clusters into the 'river network' [3] plot (Fig. 1).

These steps were adapted from the original idea by [3] but they use a different set of instruments, they are simpler and easier to apply to any topic of interest.

### 3.1  Text Preprocessing

Since we work with word co-occurrences, first, all the words must be lemmatized in order to take into account all the variations of the same word and bring the words to their initial forms. Stop words are excluded. Then we run a chunking algorithm (from Python's NLTK library) to extract entities for semantic networks.

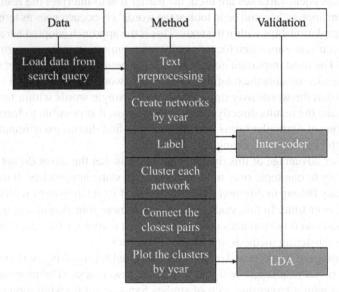

**Fig. 1.** The pipeline for creating a river network of discourse across time

### 3.2  Creating a Network of Popular Collocations

Initially, the chunking algorithm consists of two stages. First, all the words are automatically tagged by their part of speech. Then the researcher manually defines the rules, similar to regular expressions, which can capture the expected grammatical combinations in the documents. In our use cases, we used three types of such entities defined as the combinations of an adjective + a noun, a noun + a noun, or a single noun. These entities were chosen in search of descriptions with characteristics and longer descriptions consisting of several consecutive nouns, which is typical in official Russian texts. This step returns unique terms whose co-occurrence could be interpreted.

The obtained sets of terms are attributed to their documents, while documents are labeled by period. We applied 12-month time buckets for the analyses. The size of each bucket depends on the intensity of publications per period. (If 12-month buckets are further split into smaller buckets, more detailed topics could be obtained, given that there is enough data per period.)

Next, we split the data by the year of publication and calculate the importance metric TFIDF [11] for each entity, which left us with about a hundred relevant and unique terms per year. As the size of media coverage of a topic varied across the years, the TFIDF metric per bucket should be normalized by the size of the bucket.

Each year's set of terms produces a network of co-occurrence. The network is bipartite and consists of terms and documents in which those terms appear. To understand the direct relationships between terms, all networks are then projected on their terms, so that a link between the nodes shows the number of documents where these terms co-occur.

Depending on the number of unique entities per network, either all of them or only those with higher TFIDF can be used for further clustering. The terms with lowest normalized TFIDF can be trimmed in order to filter out the terms commonly used in the topic discussion and relevant to a large number of documents but not specific to any particular topic. This step is adjustable, and several solutions can be tried. The network is then built on the remaining set of terms.

### 3.3 Clustering Semantic Networks into Clusters by Period

In the next step, we apply the fast unfolding Louvain algorithm to cluster these terms into networks [12]. This algorithm is capable of producing a large network and it uses a heuristic based on the maximization of modularity when extracting communities [12]. Modularity 'compares the presence of each intra-cluster edge of the graph with the probability that that edge would exist in a random graph' [13]. A large-scale comparison demonstrated that, as modularity has some limitations such as a resolution limit, it can also be accompanied by conductance, another stand-alone cluster quality metric which shows 'the number of inter-cluster edges for the cluster divided by either the number edges with an endpoint in the cluster or the number of edges that do not have an endpoint in the cluster, whichever is smaller' [13].

### 3.4 Labeling the Clusters with the Most Specific Collocations

Following these steps, we obtained 3–4 clusters per year bucket. Each cluster was then manually labeled by two analysts based on the entities it included. Inter-coder reliability should be applied at this stage for the validity of results. At the very least, the coders should work independently and discuss any mismatches in labeling for further analysis.

When the clusters for each year are ready, a term-cluster matrix of TFIDF measures is created for each term. It takes into account the year in which the term appeared in the corpus. For instance, the term 'Internet regulation' appears in 2011 and it has a different TFIDF in 2012 as we calculate TFIDF measures for each year separately, so that each year has its own proportion of terms. If a term does not occur in a particular cluster, its TFIDF in that cluster is equal to zero. The TFIDF metric is divided by the sum of all TFIDF terms for each time period, which results in the TFIDF normalized by the diversity of discourse in that year.

### 3.5  Calculating Distances Between Similar Clusters Across Years

Hence, for each cluster-year combination, there is a vector of terms arranged by their normalized TFIDF measure. We can compare distances between clusters using cosine similarity. For each cluster, we find the most similar cluster from another year and connect them. Such a combination of the Louvain algorithm and cosine distance has already been used in the literature for similar research tasks [14].

### 3.6  Connecting the Most Similar Clusters into the River Network

After connecting the pairs of clusters closest by cosine distance, we plot the resulting links as paths through the timeline to obtain the overall picture. The result is a 'river network', a plot that represents the texts as 'a series of conversation streams' [3], traces their evolution, and the starting and ending points of particular discussions.

Since cluster quality of Louvain can be debated [13], we conducted additional topic modeling based on LDA [1] with the number of topics $k$ equal to the number of obtained discursive streams. If the resulting topics could be matched to the contents of clusters, we would consider such clustering supported by another method. Despite known problems of topic modeling with choosing the number of topics, this step provided a relatively fast and sound heuristic for validating the results of the pipeline. Therefore, we set $k$ to be the same number as the number of discursive streams in the river network. Topic labeling was carried out by two researchers, again, to make the labels more reliable. The topics from the model were similar to the 'streams' in the network. The results showed that the pipeline could capture not only the topic and their temporal change but also the continuities in the overall discourse.

## 4  Pros and Cons of the Pipeline

The proposed pipeline, from loading the texts to plotting the river network, possesses a number of advantages over the algorithm that inspired it [3]. First, it is a fast, semi-automated method of mapping the key conversations of public debate on a certain topic over years. It requires human intervention at the stage of labeling, which is similar to popular methods such as LDA. Second, it includes a comprehensible set of steps with no black-box algorithms, so that the researcher can trace the process from original texts to resulting clusters and streams. Third, it presents the results in the graphic format in addition to the tables with cluster distances and key terms by period. Having a visualization summary gives an immediate insight to the changes in media discourse over years and can lead to further analysis of the turning points—the shifts and continuities identified at the visualization stage. Fourth, the pipeline can be generalized to describe the development of media discourse on any topic of interest, provided that there are plenty of texts available.

There are three difficulties associated with implementing this pipeline. One problem is that the reliability of labeling depends on human coders who need to have some background in the issue and cannot be agnostic of the context. However, if the analysis is made as part of a research project, minimum necessary expertise will be provided. Another difficulty relates to clustering as a technique with no formal quality benchmarks. However, we rely on the time-tested algorithm [12] and best practices [13, 14] in research to make sure the clustering solution is stable. The last difficulty is the necessity to put all the steps together, from a set of steps carried out in Python and R, to an easy-to-use, one-button instrument.

Next, we will showcase how this pipeline works using two studies covering over 5,000 texts over a range of years. Both topics show significant variance in yearly coverage and relate to the widely debated issues.

## 5   Study 1: Internet Regulation Discourse in Russia

### 5.1   Background

Internet regulation has become commonplace in many countries. Russia is an interesting case to cover. It has an Internet population of over 100 million users and the tightening freedom of press. However, its Internet regulation policy is neither filtering nor censorship. We set out to explore and map how Internet regulation has been discussed in the Russian media in the last decade.

The discourse on Internet regulation is widely politicized. It requires a theoretical perspective with a working model of interdependence between political decisions and media coverage. The Arab Spring of 2011–2012 spurred a possibly largest discussion to date on the interplay of politics and social media. A later analysis demonstrated that, contrary to expectations, 'politics came before media' in these political conflicts [15, 16]. Moreover, the role of media themselves was found to be flexible so that a regime of 'network authoritarianism' [17] could grow its own 'electronic army' of public employees engaged in strategic distraction of the public discourse [18]. In addition, a networked authoritarian state may employ hackers or limit the Internet access for certain social groups or territories [15, 17]. Filtering can also be applied, thus, creating an isolated part of the Internet under surveillance. China is probably the best known example of such policies described in the literature [17, 18]. The case of Russia offers another kind of national Internet regulation, including the Internet media.

The principle of politics-media-politics describes [15, 16] this mechanism. It is based on two points. First, the political environment shapes digital media use, in that order. Second, digital media use is more likely to follow rather than precede political movements. It can be summarized as follows: 'changes in the political environment lead to changes in media performance, which leads to further changes in the environment'

[15]. Thus, mass media serve as a broker between the political system and society, absorbing and articulating different opinions and meanings.

Years 2011–2012 were game-changing for the Internet regulation in Russia. People took to streets in massive after-election rallies starting from December 2011. In mid-2012, a law was passed on protecting children from harmful information on the Internet. It introduced a blacklist of websites and a new regulatory body. It was this law that led to a temporary ban of Wikipedia in Russia in 2015. Each subsequent year, more Internet regulation laws were passed. In 2013, the pre-court blocking and punishment for the online calls for riots were introduced. The 'piracy law' was passed, banning unauthorized reproduction of copyright materials, which some observers saw as a move against the VK, the largest Russian social networking site that had previously denied access to private user data. In 2014, the 'bloggers' law' (revoked in 2017) obliged all bloggers with a monthly audience of over 3,000 visitors to register as a mass media outlet and undertake the liability before the court for defamation. In 2015, another law prescribed the storage of all the personal data of Russian users on the territory of Russia. Many services such as Twitter and Facebook complied, while others, such as LinkedIn, were banned. In 2016, a new set of laws required all the Internet providers to store the communications data of Russian users for up to six months and certain personal data for up to three years and be able to provide them on demand. A criminal punishment was introduced for failing to report on other users engaging others in the street rallies. All messengers using encryption were obliged to share their algorithms with the law enforcement. In 2017, VPNs were banned. These novelties were met with local protests in big cities. The popular Telegram messenger was banned in 2018 (the ban was lifted in 2020 due to its non-efficiency).

What did the media say about Internet regulation in that period? How did the topics evolve over time? Where were the ruptures and continuities in this discourse? Our hypotheses were that (1) media coverage of Internet regulation would be growing steadily as Internet penetration was on the rise and that (2) shifts in the discourse would echo the adoption of Internet regulation laws, causing two shifts, in 2012 (the first Internet regulation laws) and in 2015 (the law on moving the data of Russian citizens to local storage).

## 5.2  Data

We collected the media coverage of the topic in the national newspapers and magazines from 2009 till mid-2017. The data were collected using the *Integrum*, the largest data base of Russian mass media articles from newspapers and magazines, thirty years deep. To retain only the data connected with Internet regulation, a query was used *('(regulat\* OR govern\*) AND (Internet NOT (Internet-site OR Internet-project\*))')* limited to the given time period. It returned 7,240 documents. Most publications came from national daily newspapers covering politics, society, and economics. According to our estimate, about 40% of the involved media sources cover politics regularly.

The largest text corpus belongs to year 2013, the smallest one to 2009. The average yearly corpus is 670 thousand words, while the average text contains 906 words. The number of texts per year grew from 2009 till 2013, reaching a peak in 2013 both by the number of unique terms (over 1,100) and texts related to Internet regulation (over

35,000), and gradually declined to about 30 thousand words per year and 1,000 terms in 2017 (Fig. 2).

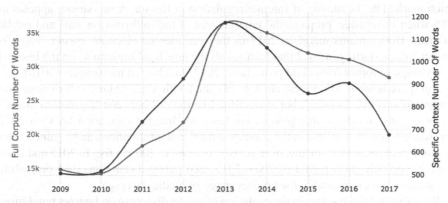

**Fig. 2.** Relation of the full corpus size (left) to Internet regulation media coverage (right)

## 5.3  Results

We implemented the proposed pipeline and obtained the following river network (Fig. 3). We also conducted LDA as a double check on the results.

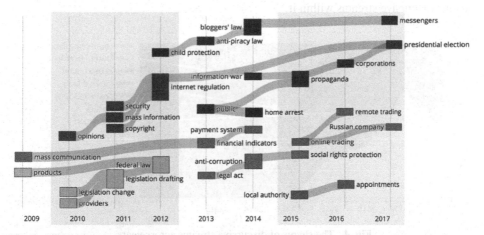

**Fig. 3.** Discursive streams on Internet regulation (2009–2017). Legend: color = discourse stream, line thickness = closeness between clusters, rectangle height = share of discourse

We found out seven distinctive 'discursive streams', i.e. large themes evolving over time and uniting related clusters of entities. Each stream represents a continuing part of discourse.

The longest surviving discursive stream started in 2010 and it focuses on politics. It has forks and merges, starting with a general debate in 2010 and moving on to national security and copyright, and then flowing into the cluster 'Internet regulation' (2012) which marked the beginning of Internet regulation in Russia. A sub-stream appears in 2015 when the cluster 'propaganda' emerges out of the 'information war' and public criticism. Both streams merge in 2017 in the 'presidential election' cluster. There is another stream starting in 2012 that features all the new legal limitations on the Internet with a range of topics from child protection (2012) to a ban on messengers (2018).

But there is more. Of interest are not only the continuities linking sub-streams into greater streams like 'politics', but also shifts, like the one between 'legislation drafts', i.e., proposing and discussing prospective laws, to 'Internet regulation laws' in 2012 representing new, active laws in the country. Additional information can be gained from the number of discursive streams over years, from two in 2009 to five in 2015 and later. In the historically short period of 2009–2017, two public discussions died out, while new streams were born within the broader range of media coverage.

We identified three stages in the evolution of media discourse on Internet regulation. The first stage lasted till the adoption of the first Internet law. The second stage was 2012–2014 when new topics such as 'Internet laws' and related 'law enforcement' gained media attention. The current discourse did not appear until 2015 when two new branches appeared which we labeled 'online trade' (bitcoin included) and 'e-government' ('local authority'). We also estimated the relative weight of each stream in the discourse. More than a third of all the texts belong to the politics stream, which is an additional estimate of how politicized the topic is (Fig. 4). The years 2010, 2013 and 2015 marked in Fig. 4 indicate the years of major changes in the structure of discourse, based on the shares of various discursive streams within it.

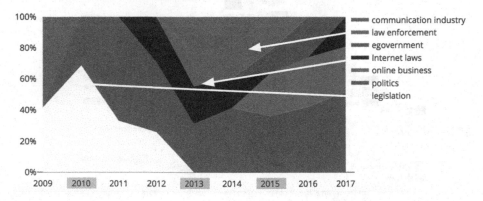

**Fig. 4.** The shares of discursive streams across years

As can be seen, some labels overlap in meaning, which is the result of agreement after the manual labeling by coders. Overlapping labels represent one of the weak points of the proposed pipeline as it depends on the expertise of human interpreters.

As a next step, we conducted LDA on all lemmatized texts from 2009 to 2017 with $k = 7$ topics. The number of topics was equal to the number of discursive streams on the river network. LDA could also potentially catch those topics on the whole corpus. The obvious limitation of this check was that we could not say anything about topic dynamics over time as the method does not provide it (Table 1).

**Table 1.** The results of LDA (k = 7) as a complement to the river network. Topic colors are matched to discursive streams

| Topic | Key terms |
|---|---|
| Politics | Rights, control, government, state, program |
| e-Government | Regulation, control, country, localized, access |
| Law enforcement | Initiative, law, freedom, sales, ban |
| Online business | Company, client, national payment system, market, system |
| Communications industry | Management, project, mass, global, citizen |
| Legislation | Blocking, ban, Internet source, *Roskomnadzor*, amendment |
| Internet laws | International, control, product, ban, development |

Applying the pipeline allowed us to track the point when the focus of debates within the discursive streams shifted from one key term to another, or when new prominent terms appeared following the legislation or major political events.

# 6  Study 2. Anti-immigrant Attitudes in Russia

## 6.1  Background

Russia is a multi-ethnic and multi-religious country, and one of the major five receiving countries in the world for labor migrants. Attitudes to labor migrants who do not share the language and religion of the Russian majority (the majority are Orthodox or atheist, seven percent of Russian citizens are Muslim) have been the topic of media debate since the collapse of communism. Anti-immigrant sentiments often extend to the Russian citizens who fit the image of the 'Other'. Opinion polls conducted in the mid-2010s reported widespread moderate anti-immigrant moods. The media also reported violent anti-immigrant actions in 2007 (rallies against violence to Russians in Karelia), 2010 (nationalist rallies in Moscow), or 2013 (deportation campaigns during Moscow mayor elections). Public fears and risks associated with labor migrants include decrease in public health due to low control and health care protection of illegal migrants, terrorism, and the economic displacement of the local citizens on the labor market.

Media discourse on labor migration in Russia is another interesting case to explore due to the scale and track record of mass labor immigration to Russia which started well before the European migration crisis of the mid-2010s, and the recent policy changes towards migrants in Russia. Up to 2007, the flow of work immigrants to Russia was unlimited. Step by step, country quotas (2007) and language- and income-based work permits (2010) were introduced. Adopted in 2013, a new migration policy prescribed mandatory deportation of illegal migrants. After a few years, following the public debate and the post-war inflow of migrants and refugees from Ukraine, the policy was adjusted to simplify the rules (2018).

Another feature that makes this case interesting to describe is that the predictive power of models explaining anti-immigrant prejudice is lower in Russia as compared to European countries [19]. Neither ethnic competition nor cultural models seem to be meaningful in predicting anti-foreigner sentiment [20]. The theories used in the literature to explain anti-immigrant sentiment in Russia include the group security threat [21, 22] and dissatisfaction with the institutional performance ('state vulnerability' [23]). There also exists a widely shared, informal 'ethnic hierarchy' of tolerance and prestige among the labor migrants in Russia [24]. Ethnicity appears to be the most important predictor of anti-immigrant attitudes, followed by immigration experience, location, religion, and education. Concerns about the impact of immigration on society at large seem to prevail in the anti-immigrant attitudes [19] and, presumably, the public discussion of labor migration.

How does the media coverage extend the existing knowledge on anti-immigrant attitudes? What issues dominated the discourse and how did they change over time?

## 6.2 Data

To investigate this case, we used the *Public.ru*, another large online archive of Russian-language media, twenty-five years deep. Initially, we searched for the media coverage from national print media and Internet media starting from year 2000 but later adjusted the query as the search through years 2000–2010 returned less than fifty documents per year in the database, which would not be representative of the issue. To obtain the coverage of labor immigration to Russia, a query was used ( *'near(labor\*migra\*, immigra\*, migra\* Russia) not (emigra\*, Poland) and near 10 (labor migrants, immigrants, migrants Russia)'*) for 2011–2018. It returned slightly over 5,000 documents.

The largest text corpus belongs to year 2014, the smallest one to 2012. The dynamic of media coverage per year was not linear, reaching the peaks in 2011 (ethnic conflicts) and in 2014–2015 (beginning of the war conflict with Ukraine), both for the Internet media and the national print media (Fig. 5).

## 6.3 Results

We implemented the proposed pipeline and obtained the following river network (Fig. 6). There were eight discursive streams.

The longest surviving stream runs throughout the whole period and focuses on the economic regulation of immigration, including shadow economy and illegal labor migration, remittances, the outflow of migrants following the ruble devaluation of 2014, and the special legal conditions for labor immigrants within the Eurasian Economic Union. This stream became especially prominent in 2015 and after, as shown by the size of rectangles on the map.

The second major stream lasted between 2012 and 2015 and related to the background and implementation of the new immigration policy adopted in 2013. The law came into

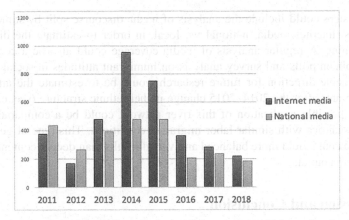

**Fig. 5.**  National Internet media and print media's coverage of labor migration by year

**Fig. 6.**  Discursive streams on labor immigrants (2011–2018)

action in 2014 and was widely discussed at that time. It was shadowed by another stream focusing on the impact of tightening the exams to obtain a work permit for immigrants and their eventual exodus following ruble devaluation in 2014.

The third discursive stream that was also most prominent in 2014–2015 concerned labor migrants from Ukraine. Special rules were created for the hundreds of thousands migrants and refugees who intended to stay in Russia for good.

There are also smaller, and shorter, streams focusing on ethnic-centered discussions about Tajik, Chinese, and Moldovan labor immigrants, but these occupied much smaller shares and lasted for a few years each.

The studied period between 2011 and 2018 can be divided into two parts as there was a major shift around 2015 marking the change in the key terms of conversation. By 2015, the new policy was implemented, and simplified rules were passed for Ukrainians and labor immigrants from the Eurasian Economic Union countries. This shift reflected the changes in legal regulation, international politics, and the economic decline in Russia which followed in late 2014. Since 2015, a new stream has arisen that focuses on international immigrant justice including the fight against terrorism and slavery.

Further steps could include the analysis of media discourse split by some criteria, e.g. print vs. Internet media, national vs. local, in order to estimate the differences in their framing. A regular analysis of media coverage could also be a complement to public opinion polls and survey analysis on immigrant attitudes in social research. Another possible direction for future research would be to estimate the attitudes to labor immigrants after the 2014–2015 change in their ethnic structure (see, e.g., [24]). Yet another possible application of this river network could be a comparative study across the countries with similar labor migration conditions. This type of generalized retrospective could yield more balanced and varied results than deeper content analysis of single media outlets.

## 7 Discussion and Conclusion

Tracing media discourse surrounding politically charged topics in big countries with developed media systems that use non-English languages can help scholars and educators to improve their understanding of key issues in particular discourse and the relationships between such issues in time. This can be particularly relevant for the discourses with changing key terms as those are more difficult to trace using the now popular techniques of topic modeling. This paper proposes and showcases a strategy for mapping out the streams in media discourse over time. The result of the pipeline is a river network showing discursive streams which can continue over years even as the key terms within them are changing.

The two cases described above demonstrate that river networks add details to what is known about the legal and political context of the topic in a given country. In addition, they also help to estimate discursive streams' shares within the media discourse, and their evolution over time. The proposed strategy of analysis can serve as a working tool for semi-automated text analysis in other languages and for longer periods of time. It could be expected to deliver a reasonable number of data-supported streams and to facilitate substantive research of topics within those streams.

Since media discourse does not exist in a vacuum but rather buffers the interactions between the political context and political actions [15], it should be analyzed with those changing conditions in mind. We adapted the analytical approach to studying the change in topics over time [3] and reproduced its logic with our own metrics, obtaining interpretable results that nourish further research hypotheses. A closer look at media coverage using this approach can also provide new evidence on whether 'the leaders who hold authoritarian rule design a type of rule that helps them stay in power' [16].

The proposed pipeline fits into a broader area of approaches to tracking the dynamics of media over time using clusters of networks [8–10]. The papers in this field build more complex models to catch temporal patterns of attention to online content [10], understand the evolution and dynamics of news topics over time [8], or employing massive datasets to track memes, i.e., 'short, distinctive phrases that travel relatively intact through online text', and mutations within such phrases [9]. Given the rich variety of such models and pipelines, we call for their test and comparison across topics and datasets.

The current limitations of the proposed pipeline include manual labeling of clusters and streams, the clarity and reliability of which depends greatly on the expertise of coders. It is up to the researcher to interpret the results and provide the feedback loop to theoretical concepts relevant for analysis. In addition, the quality of clustering has no objective measures and should possibly be complemented with other methods with clear benchmarks for the quality of results. The proposed pipeline is somewhat similar to topic modeling as it 'infers rather than assumes' the content of text clusters [2] and the result is not a supervised categorization which would totally depend on pre-defined topics and concepts as in manual coding [25]. Compared to manual coding, the proposed pipeline is fast in analyzing large datasets across years. Compared to more advanced techniques [3, 9], though, it does not require really large datasets as input and uses time-tested algorithms. However, the pipeline requires a comparable amount of information per time period so as to yield a similar number of clusters. Last, compared to fully automated pipelines, the proposed approach retains more control within the hands of analysts, offering additional sanity checks on cluster labeling. The advantage of this semi-automated approach is then that it can provide a more balanced picture of potentially polarized issues covered in the media and, thus, can be of particular use in the analysis of media discourse in polarized societies, or during conflict events.

The next step for this pipeline is to develop it into an application which could be used by scholars unfamiliar with programming, using the dataset as an input, eliciting labels and producing the river network as the output. An advantage here could be achieved by adding meaningful covariates such as party affiliation of the media outlet, a feature that is already implemented in structural topic modeling [4], or meme-tracking [9]. A more distant perspective would be developing a predictive instrument which could be trained to anticipate the coming changes to discourse or even the expected changes in public opinion surveys. This step would require identifying various patterns of discourse development and projecting further development, given the scale of media coverage and its time span. For the time being, the proposed pipeline could be freely applied to any large corpus on a specific issue over years.

**Acknowledgements.** The paper was prepared within the framework of the HSE University Basic Research Program. We are grateful to Irina Busurkina for assistance with the labor migration study. **Replication code.** https://github.com/olgasilyutina/ic2s2_internet_regulation/.

# References

1. Blei, D.M., Ng, A.Y., Jordan, M.I.: Latent Dirichlet allocation. J. Mach. Learn. Res. **3**, 993–1022 (2003). https://doi.org/10.5555/944919.944937
2. Roberts, M.E., et al.: Structural topic models for open-ended survey responses. Am. J. Polit. Sci. **4**(58), 1064–1082 (2014). https://doi.org/10.1111/ajps.12103
3. Rule, A., Cointet, J.P., Bearman, P.S.: Lexical shifts, substantive changes, and continuity in state of the union discourse, 1790–2014. Proc. Natl. Acad. Sci. **112**(35), 10837–10844 (2015). https://doi.org/10.1073/pnas.1512221112
4. Hong, L., Dom, B., Gurumurthy, S., Tsioutsiouliklis, K.: A time-dependent topic model for multiple text streams. In: Proceedings of the 17th ACM SIGKDD International Conference on Knowledge Discovery and Data Mining, pp. 832–840. ACM, New York (2016). https://doi.org/10.1145/2020408.2020551

5. Wang, C., Blei, D., Heckerman, D.: Continuous time dynamic topic models (2012). arXiv preprint arXiv:1206.3298
6. Grimmer, J., Stewart, B.M.: Text as data: The promise and pitfalls of automatic content analysis methods for political texts. Polit. Anal. **3**(21), 267–297 (2013). https://doi.org/10.1093/pan/mps028
7. Taddy, M.: Multinomial inverse regression for text analysis. J. Am. Statist. Assoc. **108**(503), 755–770 (2013). https://doi.org/10.1080/01621459.2012.734168
8. Krause, A., Leskovec, J., Guestrin, C.: Data association for topic intensity tracking. In: Proceedings of the 23rd International Conference on Machine Learning, pp. 497–504. ACM, New York (2006). https://doi.org/10.1145/1143844.1143907
9. Leskovec, J., Backstrom, L., Kleinberg, J.: Meme-tracking and the dynamics of the news cycle. In: Proceedings of the 15th ACM SIGKDD International Conference on Knowledge Discovery and Data Mining, pp. 497–506. ACM, New York (2009). https://doi.org/10.1145/1557019.1557077
10. Yang, J., Leskovec, J.: Patterns of temporal variation in online media. In: Proceedings of the fourth ACM International Conference on Web Search and Data Mining, pp. 177–186. ACM, New York (2011). https://doi.org/10.1145/1935826.1935863
11. Spärck Jones, K.: IDF term weighting and IR research lessons. J. Document. **5**(60), 521–523 (2004). https://doi.org/10.1108/00220410410560591
12. Blondel, V.D., Guillaume, J.-L., Lambiotte, R., Lefebvre, E.: Fast unfolding of communities in large networks. J. Stat. Mech: Theory Exp. **10**, P10008 (2008). https://doi.org/10.1088/1742-5468/2008/10/P10008
13. Emmons, S., Kobourov, S., Gallant, M., Börner, K.: Analysis of network clustering algorithms and cluster quality metrics at scale. PLoS ONE **11**(7), e0159161 (2016). https://doi.org/10.1371/journal.pone.0159161
14. Koltsova, O., Koltcov, S., Nikolenko, S.: Communities of co-commenting in the Russian LiveJournal and their topical coherence. Internet Res. **26**(3), 710–732 (2016). https://doi.org/10.1108/IntR-03-2014-0079
15. Van Dijk, J.A.G.M., Hacker, K.L.: Internet and Democracy in the Network Society: Theory and Practice Continued. Routledge, New York (2018)
16. Wolfsfeld, G., Segev, E., Sheafer, T.: 2Social media and the Arab spring: politics comes first. Int. J. Press/Polit. **18**(2), 115–137 (2013). https://doi.org/10.1177/1940161212471716
17. MacKinnon, R.: Liberation technology: China's "Networked Authoritarianism." J. Democr. **22**(2), 32–46 (2011). https://doi.org/10.1353/jod.2011.0033
18. King, G., Pan, J., Roberts, M.E.: How the Chinese government fabricates social media posts for strategic distraction, not engaged argument. Am. Polit. Sci. Rev. **111**(3), 484–501 (2017). https://doi.org/10.1017/S0003055417000144
19. Bessudnov, A.: Ethnic hierarchy and public attitudes towards immigrants in Russia. Eur. Sociol. Rev. **32**(5), 567–580 (2016). https://doi.org/10.1093/esr/jcw002
20. Gorodzeisky, A., Glikman, A., Maskileyson, D.: The nature of anti-immigrant sentiment in post-socialist Russia. Post-Soviet Affairs **31**(2), 115–135 (2015). https://doi.org/10.1080/1060586X.2014.918452
21. Alexseev, M.A.: Societal security, the security dilemma, and extreme anti-migrant hostility in Russia. J. Peace Res. **48**(4), 509–523 (2011). https://doi.org/10.1177/0022343311406155
22. Ceobanu, A.M., Escandell, X.: Comparative analyses of public attitudes toward immigrants and immigration using multinational survey data: a review of theories and research. Ann. Rev. Sociol. **36**(1), 309–328 (2010). https://doi.org/10.1146/annurev.soc.012809.102651
23. Gorodzeisky, A., Glikman, A.: Comparative analyses of public attitudes toward immigrants and immigration using multinational survey data: a review of theories and research. Soc. Probl. **65**(4), 543–563 (2018). https://doi.org/10.1093/socpro/spx023

24. Bessudnov, A., Shcherbak, A.: Ethnic discrimination in multi-ethnic societies: evidence from Russia. Eur. Sociol. Rev. **36**(1), 104–120 (2020). https://doi.org/10.1093/esr/jcz045
25. Jacobi, C., Atteveldt, A., Welbers, K.: Quantitative analysis of large amounts of journalistic texts using topic modelling. Digit. J. **4**(1), 89–106 (2016). https://doi.org/10.1080/21670811. 2015.1093271

# Average Nearest Neighbor Degree and Its Distribution in Social Networks

Alexey Grigoriev(ID), Sergei Sidorov(✉)(ID), Sergei Mironov(ID), and Igor Malinskii

Saratov State University, Saratov, Russian Federation
`sidorovsp@sgu.ru`

**Abstract.** The paper is focused on the analysis of average nearest neighbor degree (ANND) in complex social networks. The ANND of nodes with degree $k$ is defined as the average degree of their neighbors over all nodes with degree $k$. ANND is one of the well-established tools for the analysis of degree-degree correlation and assortativity in complex networks. In this paper, we analytically examine the properties of ANND in undirected networks generated by the Barabási-Albert model. First, we prove that for every node, the average degree of its neighbors is increasing logarithmically over time. Then we show that the ANND distribution at each iteration is uniform, i.e. the values of ANND are the same for every $k$, and therefore, Barabási-Albert networks are uncorrelated. Moreover, we compare the ANND distributions in simulated graphs (derived by the Barabási-Albert model) with distributions in real-world social networks (Twitter, Facebook, GitHub and Flickr).

**Keywords:** Social networks · Network analysis · Complex networks · Preferential attachment model · Assortative network · Degree-degree correlation

## 1 Introduction

Graph theory is one of the modern approaches to the analysis of social networks structure. A graph is a set of vertices connected by edges. Similarly, social network such as Facebook or Twitter can be represented as a graph, where the vertices are social objects (user profiles) with different attributes, and the edges are relations between them. Network analysis defines and examines a number of properties with the aim to identify important features of networks. Nodes in networks can represent various types of information (blogs, articles, links). Network analysis solves such critical tasks as community detection [34] and link prediction [25,33]. Moreover, it helps to determine the properties of the network as a whole, as well as specific relations between its objects. Recent papers in

This work was supported by the Ministry of Science and Higher Education of the Russian Federation in the framework of the basic part of the scientific research state task, project FSRR-2020-0006.

the field have been engaged in analysis of different structural and statistical network characteristics including diameter, average degree, clustering coefficient, measure of centrality, small-world effect, community structure, etc.

It is well known that many real-world networks possess degree distributions which follows the power law, i.e. most of networks exhibit the so-called scale-free property [3,14]. Another property that is commonly present in complex social networks is assortativity [5], i.e. whether the nodes prefer to link with nodes which are similar to them. Perhaps, the degree assortativity is the most examined case of assortativity. A network is called assortative if high degree nodes tend to connect to nodes with high degree, while small-degree nodes have a bias towards nodes with small degree. On the contrary, in the networks with degree disassortativity hubs have a tendency to be connected to nodes with small degrees, and vice versa. Networks in similar fields are likely to behave identical in terms of assortativity. Social networks are likely to be assortative, whereas technological or biological networks are disassortative [5,28]. Provided that network is assortative or disassortative, it is said to be correlated. On the other hand, the network is said to have neutral mixing if there is no clear preference.

The average nearest neighbor degree (ANND) is frequently used as a measure to examine degree relations of adjacent vertices, especially in the analysis of degree-degree correlations, which has been the subject of intensive study in recent time. For example, the impact of degree-degree correlations on the spread of diseases in complex networks [6,8,9]. It was shown that disassortative graphs are more accessible for immunization, while in assortative networks any disease takes longer time to spread [1]. The degree-degree correlations have been applied for some problems in the area of neuroscience [16,37]. The recent review [15] shows that if social networks are constructed with the use of group-based methods they demonstrate the tendency to be positively assortative.

One of the measures that aims in estimating the assortativity is the correlation coefficient proposed in [27]. However, it has been shown in [22] that the correlation coefficient might not be appropriate for large networks. By this reason, in this paper we restrict ourselves to the use of the average nearest neighbor degree (ANND) values to quantify the assortativity of networks. Given one or more nodes of degree $k$ exist in a network, the ANND of these nodes is defined as [11,36]

$$\Phi(k) = \sum_{l>0} l P(l|k),$$

where $P(l|k)$ denotes the probability that a node of degree $k$ is connected to a node of degree $l$.

Denote $d_i$ the degree of node $i$. Then $s_i$ would denote the total degree of all neighbors of node $i$:

$$s_i = \sum_{j:\ (i,j)\in E} d_j.$$

Let $\alpha_i$ be the average degree of all neighboring nodes for node $i$ in the network, i.e. the ratio of the total degree of the neighbors of node $i$ to the number of its neighboring nodes, $\alpha_i = \frac{s_i}{d_i}$. Then ANND can be empirically obtained via the following equation:

$$\Phi(k) \sim \frac{1}{|E_k|} \sum_{\{i:d_i=k\}} \alpha_i, \tag{1}$$

where all nodes of degree $k$ contribute to the sum, and $|E_k|$ is the amount of such nodes.

The aim of this paper is to analytically derive the equation describing the properties of the average nearest neighbor degree (ANND) in growth networks constructed with the use of Barabási-Albert model. First, in Sect. 2 we examine the analytical properties of index $\alpha_i$ and obtain the distribution of average nearest neighbor degree in random networks generated by BA model. We derive the equations describing the evolution of the expected value of the average degree of all neighbors of a single node $i$ over time for BA networks. The results also show that $\alpha_i$ follow the logarithmic law over time for all nodes. One arresting corollary of this fact is that the theoretical values of $\Phi(k)$ at an iteration for all degrees $k$ should be the same, on average. Then we compare the ANND distributions in simulated graphs with distributions in real-world networks (Sect. 3). Obtained results are comparable with the results of paper [38].

Another question that is of our interest is how the average degree of neighbors fluctuates among all nodes of a given degree $k$. To quantify such deviations we consider the following quantity

$$\Theta(k) = \frac{1}{|E_k|} \sum_{\{i:d_i=k\}} (\alpha_i - \Phi(k))^2, \tag{2}$$

where the summation takes over all nodes that have degree $k$.

We carry out an empirical analysis of assortativity for some social networks in order to check how the behavior of these real networks differs from the behavior of BA networks (in the sense of degree-degree correlation). Our analysis (presented in Sect. 3) includes four real networks from "Stanford Large Network Dataset Collection" and "Network Repository" [29]:

- 2017 network of a sample of Facebook users [31].
- a follower network of Twitter from 2009 [18].
- 2019 network of a sample of Github users [30];
- 2006 network of photo-sharing social network Flickr from [17].

## 2   Dynamics of the Average Degree of All Neighbors of Node in the Barabási-Albert Growth Networks

### 2.1   Preliminary Analysis

Let $t$ denote the iteration. Then at iteration $t$

- $d_i(t)$ is the degree of node $i$;

- $s_i(t)$ is the total degree of neighbors of $i$;
- $\alpha_i(t)$ is the average of degrees of neighbors of $i$.

Following Barabási–Albert model [3], at each iteration $t$ the network grows with each new node $t$ added and connected to $m$ other nodes in the network, where the probability of being chosen increases with degree (preferential attachment mechanism).

If one looks at the link attachment for a new node as a sequence of $m$ attachments, then as a result each of the attachments may contribute to the values of $d_i(t)$ or $s_i(t)$. It occurs when the new node $t+1$ (with degree $m$) connects:

- to $i$, then $s_i(t+1) = s_i(t) + m$, and $d_i(t)$ is increased by 1;
- to one of the neighbors of node $i$ by one of its edges $j = 1, \ldots, m$, therefore, $s_i(t)$ is increased by 1, while $d_i(t)$ remains unchanged;
- to a neighbor of node $i$ with one of its $m$ edges, while one of the other edges is already linked to the node $i$. In this case the total degree of neighbors of node $i$ is increased by $m+1$, while $d_i$ is increased by 1.

It should be noted that the probability of the third case to occur is an order of magnitude closer to zero compared to the other cases, so we discard this case from the further analysis to gradually simplify the derivation of the equations and thus increase its readability.

Further we shall consider that the random $\xi_{i,j}^{(t+1)} = 1$ if corresponding node $i$ is selected by node $t + 1$ (at iteration $t + 1$) to be linked with one of $j \in \{1, \ldots, m\}$, and, otherwise, $\xi_{i,j}^{(t+1)} = 0$. Similarly, the random $\eta_{i,j}^{(t+1)} = 1$ when the added node $t + 1$ links to one of the nodes already connected to $i$ with one of the links $j \in \{1, \ldots, m\}$, and, otherwise, $\eta_{i,j}^{(t+1)} = 0$. To shorten equations we substitute $\sum_{j=1}^{m} \xi_{i,j}^{(t+1)}$ with $\xi_i^{(t+1)}$ and $\sum_{j=1}^{m} \eta_{i,j}^{(t+1)}$ with $\eta_i^{(t+1)}$.

Since all $m$ attachments are done simultaneously, independently and with the same probability, we get

$$\mathbb{E}(\xi_i^{(t+1)}) = \mathbb{E}\left(\sum_{j=1}^{m} \xi_{i,j}^{(t+1)}\right) = m\frac{d_i(t)}{2mt} = \frac{d_i(t)}{2t} \qquad (3)$$

and

$$\mathbb{E}(\eta_i^{(t+1)}) = \mathbb{E}\left(\sum_{j=1}^{m} \eta_{i,j}^{(t+1)}\right) = m \sum_{j:(j,i)\in E(t)} \frac{d_j(t)}{2mt} = m\frac{1}{2mt}s_i(t) = \frac{1}{2t}s_i(t), \quad (4)$$

## 2.2 Dynamics of $\alpha_i(t)$ in Barabási-Albert Model

In this section we would like to estimate the mean value of $\alpha_i(t)$. Since random variables $s_i(t)$ and $d_i(t)$ might be correlated, the expected value of $\mathbb{E}(\alpha_i(t))$ can not be found as the ratio of the expected value of $s_i(t)$ to the expected number of $d_i(t)$:

$$\overline{\alpha}_i(t) := \mathbb{E}(\alpha_i(t)) = \mathbb{E}\left(\frac{s_i(t)}{d_i(t)}\right) \neq \frac{\mathbb{E}(s_i(t))}{\mathbb{E}(d_i(t))}!$$

Let us write the stochastic equation describing the changes in the value of $\alpha_i(t)$ after inserting a newborn node at iteration $t+1$ with $m$ links connecting the node with other vertices in the network. We have

$$\Delta\alpha_i(t+1) = \alpha_i(t+1) - \alpha_i(t) =$$

$$\xi_i^{(t+1)}\frac{s_i(t)+m}{d_i(t)+1} + \eta_i^{(t+1)}\frac{s_i(t)+1}{d_i(t)} + \left(1 - \xi_i^{(t+1)} - \eta_i^{(t+1)}\right)\frac{s_i(t)}{d_i(t)} - \frac{s_i(t)}{d_i(t)}$$

$$= \xi_i^{(t+1)}\left(\frac{s_i(t)+m}{d_i(t)+1} - \frac{s_i(t)}{d_i(t)}\right) + \eta_i^{(t+1)}\left(\frac{s_i(t)+1}{d_i(t)} - \frac{s_i(t)}{d_i(t)}\right) =$$

$$\xi_i^{(t+1)}\left(\frac{m}{d_i(t)+1} - \frac{1}{d_i(t)+1}\frac{s_i(t)}{d_i(t)}\right) + \eta_i^{(t+1)}\frac{1}{d_i(t)}, \quad (5)$$

where the random $\xi_i^{(t+1)}$ and $\eta_i^{(t+1)}$ are defined above. Then from (3) and (4) we have

$$\Delta\alpha_i(t+1) = \frac{m}{2t} - \frac{1}{2t(d_i(t)+1)} + \alpha_i(t)\frac{1}{2t(d_i(t)+1)}. \quad (6)$$

The approximation to Eq. (6) is the following linear nonhomogeneous differential equation of first order

$$\frac{d(\alpha_i(t)-1)}{dt} = \frac{m}{2t} + (\alpha_i(t)-1)\frac{1}{2t(d_i(t)+1)}. \quad (7)$$

The solution can be expressed as $\alpha_i(t) = u(t)v(t) + 1$, where $v(t)$ is the solution of the differential equation

$$\frac{dv(t)}{dt} = v(t)\frac{1}{2t(d_i(t)+1)} \quad (8)$$

and $u(t)$ is the solution of equation

$$\frac{du(t)}{dt}v(t) = \frac{m}{2t}. \quad (9)$$

The solution of (8) is

$$v(t) = \exp\left(-\int\frac{dt}{2t(d_i(t)+1)}\right). \quad (10)$$

Then the solution of (9) is

$$u(t) = m\int\frac{1}{2t}\exp\left(\int\frac{dt}{2t(d_i(t)+1)}\right)dt + C. \quad (11)$$

We have

$$\alpha_i(t) = u(t)v(t) + 1 =$$

$$m \exp\left(-\int \frac{dt}{2t(d_i(t)+1)}\right)\left(\int \frac{1}{2t}\exp\left(\int \frac{dt}{2t(d_i(t)+1)}\right)dt + C\right) + 1 \sim$$

$$m\left(1 - \int \frac{dt}{2t(d_i(t)+1)}\right)\left(\int \frac{1}{2t}\left(1 + \int \frac{dt}{2t(d_i(t)+1)}\right)dt + C\right) + 1 =$$

$$C + \frac{m}{2}\log t - m\left(C + \frac{1}{2}\log t\right)\int \frac{dt}{2t(d_i(t)+1)} +$$

$$m\int \frac{dt}{4t^2(d_i(t)+1)} - m\left(\int \frac{dt}{4t^2(d_i(t)+1)}\right)^2.$$

$$(12)$$

Since $\int \frac{\kappa_i(x)dx}{x+1} \le \int \frac{\kappa_i(x)dx}{x} \sim \left(\frac{i}{t}\right)^{\frac{1}{2}}$ we get

$$\overline{\alpha}_i(t) := \mathbb{E}(\alpha_i(t)) \sim C + \frac{m}{2}\log t - m\left(C + \frac{1}{2}\log t\right)\int \frac{1}{2t}\int \frac{\kappa_i(x)}{x+1}dxdt$$

$$+ m\int \frac{1}{4t^2}\int \frac{\kappa_i(x)}{x+1}dxdt - m\int \left(\int \frac{dt}{4t^2(x+1)}\right)^2 \kappa_i(x)dx \sim$$

$$C + \frac{m}{2}\log t + \overline{o}(t^{-\frac{1}{2}}), \quad (13)$$

i.e. the average values of neighbor's degree coefficient for all nodes asymptotically behaves as $\frac{1}{2}\log t$.

The dynamics of $\alpha_i(t)$ for three nodes $i = 50, 100, 1000$, obtained as an average of 500 simulations, are plotted in Fig. 1. Both the values and the behaviour of $\alpha_i(t)$ are close to the predictions calculated in Eq. (13).

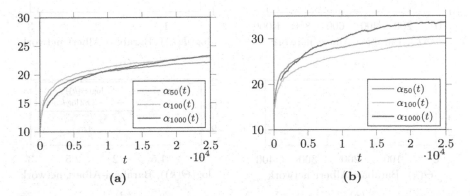

(a)                               (b)

**Fig. 1.** Evolution of $\alpha_i$ for fixed nodes $i = 50, 100, 1000$ for $t$ increasing up to 25000 in synthetic networks based on Barabási–Albert model with (a) $m = 3$ (b) $m = 5$.

## 2.3   ANND Distribution in BA Network

Since the initial value of $\alpha_i(i)$ is $\frac{m}{2}\log i$, we get $C \sim 0$. Therefore, not only do all nodes have the same dynamical behavior, but the expected values of $\alpha_i(t)$ should be the same for all existing nodes at iteration $t$.

One of the main consequences of this fact is that $\Phi(k)$ defined in (1) should fluctuate around the same value $\frac{m}{2}\log t$, for all $k$.

Numerical experiments confirm this observation. We simulated 500 different Barabási-Albert networks of the equal size 25,000 and calculated the values of $\Phi(k)$ for each $k$, and then averaged them for each $k$ over all networks. Figure 2(a) shows the plot of $\Phi(k)$ obtained in this way as the function of $k$. It can be seen that the values of $\Phi(k)$ lie in a very narrow range, i.e. $\Phi(k) \sim const$, with the exception of small degrees. The corresponding log-log plot is shown in Fig. 2(b) and confirms this observation. A slight tendency to a decrease in $\Phi(k)$ with increasing $k$ can be explained by the presence of $o(t^{-\frac{1}{2}})$ in Eq. (13). Thus, the networks produced by the Barabási–Albert model are uncorrelated.

Next, let us check how the values of $\alpha_i$ variate from each other for all nodes $i$ of degree $k$. To do this, we calculate the values of $\Theta(k)$ (defined in Eq. (2)) for each $k$, and average them over 500 different networks of the same size 25,000. The obtained dependence of $\Theta(k)$ on $k$ is shown in Fig. 2(c), while its log-log version is shown in Fig. 2(d). Note that this dependence follows a power law with exponent equal to $-2.82$, i.e. $\Theta(k) \sim k^{-2.82}$.

In the next section, we study various real world social networks to check how these properties of $\Phi(k)$ and $\Theta(k)$ obtained for Barabási-Albert networks are reproduced in these real networks.

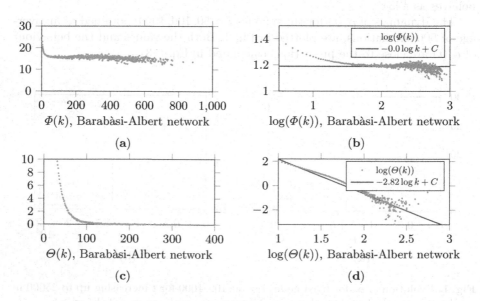

**Fig. 2.** Barabàsi-Albert

# 3   Distribution of ANND in Real Complex Social Networks

Since degree distributions of some real social networks can be simulated with high accuracy by Barabàsi-Albert model, let us observe how average nearest neighbor degree $\Phi$ and deviation $\Theta$ depends on node degree $k$ in real complex networks and compare them to what we obtained for Barabàsi-Albert network. All real networks reflect well-known social networking services, such as Facebook, Twitter, Github and Flickr. Network statistics are shown in Fig. 1. Detailed descriptions and results for each network are listed below. It should be noted that we omit $\Theta_k = 0$ on plots to avoid $\log 0$. Moreover, it is highly unlikely to encounter zero values of $\Theta_k$ outside of cases where there exists only one node in the network.

**Table 1.** Real network statistics

| Network | $|N|$ | $|E|$ |
|---|---|---|
| Facebook artists | 50,500 | 819,000 |
| Twitter followers | 404,700 | 713,300 |
| Github users | 37,700 | 289,003 |
| Flickr users | 514,000 | 3,190,500 |

## 3.1   Facebook

Facebook is one of the most popular international social networking sites with over 2 bln users. The network provides a wide range of features: posting photos; sharing articles and various types of information; text-, audio-, and video messages exchange; live streaming; interest groups and a lot more. Nowadays Facebook is not only a platform used for entertainment, communication and information sharing; it is also a tool, which provides wide opportunities for business promotion and development.

The literature review reveals researchers' great interest to different aspects of this social networking site, which trigger academic discussion. These relate to such issues as: Facebook development trends forecast [21]; Facebook as a forum for discussion and criticism; the use of this social networking site for educational purposes [19,26]; political agenda on Facebook [10]; Facebook audience and clustering analysis [4,7,35]; the degree of the youth involvement in the network [2]; business projects development opportunities provided by Facebook; Facebook as an information resource [12] and other aspects.

Facebook network is based on 50,000 "blue" verified pages on Facebook. Data was collected in 2017 and presented in [31]. Nodes are connected with 820,000 edges in the network if users representing them have mutual likes.

Figures 3(a–b) show the distribution of $\Phi(k)$ on linear (a) and log-log (b) plots. It can be seen that there is neither a grow, nor a fall in values of $\Phi(k)$ for the most part of the plot. However, for small $k$ (up to 100) there is a clear presence of assortativity.

As for $\Theta(k)$ distribution, it follows the power law with exponent $-1.46$. It should be noted that the results are quite close to ones obtained for Barabàsi-Albert network, which once more proves the similarity of modeled networks with real ones, especially for networks based on social interactions.

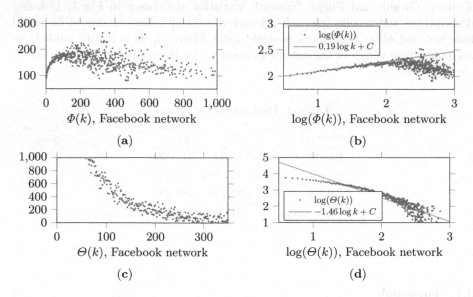

**Fig. 3.** Results for network of Facebook users. (Color figure online)

## 3.2 Twitter

Twitter network represents follower relationships between individuals. Two nodes (users) are linked if one is following another. The network was first used in [18]. It consists of 405,000 nodes and 713,000 edges.

We plot average nearest neighbor degree $\Phi$ on linear and log-log plots on Figs. 4(a) and 4(b) respectively. We observe three distinguishable regimes. For degrees up to 70 and starting from 100 $\Phi(k)$ remains constant, while in the range of 70 to 100 there is negative correlation between the values of $k$ and $\Phi(k)$. In Fig. 4(c) we can see that the deviation is gradually decreasing over time and similarly to $\Phi(k)$ distribution a gap is present, between the nodes with higher deviation and ones that are closer to zero. $\Theta(k)$ distribution follows the power law with exponent $-1.52$.

## 3.3 GitHub

GitHub is a universal service that allows to develop, control and update joint IT projects. GitHub is a repository of project codes that all collaborators can use.

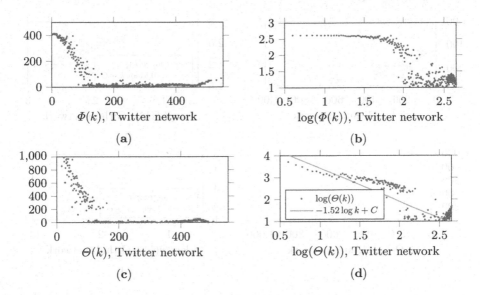

Fig. 4. Results for network of Twitter users.

Developed back in 2008 as a repository, today it is also the largest social network in which like-minded members may work together on important tasks. The tree structure and user-friendly interface make it possible to not only implement software functionality of new developments, but also to follow the news, exchange comments, evaluate the contribution of each collaborator working on the project, and track the communication chains within the network. This service is popular within major IT companies like Yahoo, Google, Facebook, etc.

Recently there has been a growing research interest to GitHub as a web-service for IT-projects and a social network. Many studies have examined different aspects of GitHub operation: analysis of the resource base of GitHub's rivals; GitHub's competitive advantage in providing a platform for IT operations; the benefits of providing joint developments [23]; GitHub projects software quality analysis, which examines the correlation between the quality of projects and the characteristics of team members [20]. There is also some interesting research on some aspects of GitHub user clustering [13,24].

Github network is based on 2019 snapshot of users who have starred (book-marked) at least ten other users [30]. $\Phi(k)$ distribution is shown in Fig. 5(a) and on a log-log plot as well Fig. 5(b). The values in distribution are uniformly decreasing which makes it safe to assume that the network is disassortative. The distribution of $\Theta$ can be seen in Figs. 5(c–d). Unlike the distribution $\Phi$, there are minimal differences between this and all other networks, with a clear power law with exponent $-1.89$. However, as it shown in paper [32] that the GitHub collaboration and membership networks display high values of assortativity with regard to node degree.

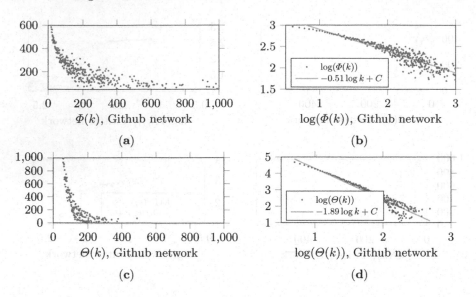

**Fig. 5.** Results for network of developers from Github.

### 3.4  Flickr

Flickr is a popular online community for sharing multimedia content based on social network with millions of registered users. It is interesting to observe, whether photo-oriented social networks differ from more traditional ones. Nodes in the network represent users, while edges connect two nodes if one user follows another. The data was collected using crawling algorithms in 2006 [17]. Flickr network contains 514,000 nodes and 3,190,500 edges.

Figures 6(a–b) show ANND distribution on linear and log-log plots. Surprisingly, the results for this network are greatly reminiscent of ones obtained for Facebook network Fig. 3. Despite having larger degrees overall, the form remains the same with a sharp increase of $\Phi(k)$ for smaller degrees (i.e. assortativity) then the larger degrees remain constant or slightly decrease for the rest of the plot. $\Theta(k)$ plots Fig. 6(c–d) are also similar to most other networks with a distinctive power-law with exponent $-0.85$.

## 4  Conclusion

It is known that many real growing networks use the preferred attachment mechanism in the process of adding new nodes. By this reason, we first study assortativity, which is directly related to the mechanism, for growing networks based on the classical Barabási-Albert model. Using the mean-field method, we show that the dynamics of the expected average degree of the neighbors of each node in the network follows a logarithmic law. The consequence of this fact is that Barabási–Albert networks have no degree-degree correlation.

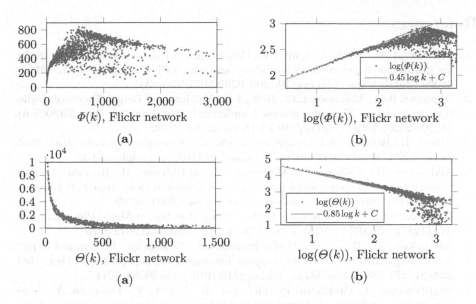

**Fig. 6.** Results for multimedia-sharing social network of Flickr users.

Empirical distributions of ANND for some real social networks are obtained in Sect. 3. The results show that both Facebook and Flickr networks show assortativity only for nodes with low degrees (up to 100), and there is no degree-degree correlation for the rest of the nodes. On the contrary, the Github network turned out to be disassortative over the whole range of degrees, while the Twitter network has three modes: for small (up to 70) and large degrees (over 100), there is no degree-degree correlation, but for nodes with degrees in the range from 70 to 100, there is a clear presence of disassortativity.

However, all considered networks behave the same in the sense of the variation of $\alpha_i$ for nodes with the same degree: the distributions of $\Theta(k)$ obeys a power law both for the BA network and for real networks under consideration.

Thus, the results of comparing ANND distributions for BA graphs and for real networks show that the BA model does not accurately reflect the behavior of real networks in terms of degree-degree correlation. In this regard, the problem of finding such models of network growth is of interest so that the networks generated with their use would have assortativity properties similar to real social networks.

As can be seen from Figs. 2, 3, 4, 5 and 6, constructed for all networks, for small degrees $k$, the values of deviations of $\alpha_i$, calculated as the square roots of $\Theta(k)$, significantly exceed their corresponding average values $\Phi(k)$. This means that statements about the presence of assortativity or disassortability for small $k$ should be done with great caution. However, for sufficiently large degrees, the corresponding values of $\Theta^{\frac{1}{2}}(k)$ are close to zero, and the conclusion about the absence of degree-degree correlation (or the presence of mixed assortativity) do not raise any doubts.

# References

1. Agostino, G.D., Scala, A., Zlatić, V., Caldarelli, G.: Robustness and assortativity for diffusion-like processes in scale-free networks. EPL (Europhys. Lett.) **97**(6), 68006 (2012). https://doi.org/10.1209/0295-5075/97/68006

2. Akpunne, B.C., Akinnawo, E.O., Bello, I.B.: Validation of Bergen Facebook addiction scale among Nigerian university undergraduates. Eur. Sci. Rev. **2020**(5–6), 31–39 (2020). https://doi.org/10.29013/esr-20-5.6-31-39

3. Albert, R., Barabási, A.L.: Statistical mechanics of complex networks. Rev. Mod. Phys. **74**(1), 47–97 (2002). https://doi.org/10.1103/revmodphys.74.47

4. Alkhamees, M., Alsaleem, S., Al-Qurishi, M., Al-Rubaian, M., Hussain, A.: User trustworthiness in online social networks: a systematic review. Appl. Soft Comput. **103**, 107159 (2021). https://doi.org/10.1016/j.asoc.2021.107159

5. Barabási, A.L.: Network science. Philos. Trans. Roy. Soc. A Math. Phys. Eng. Sci. **371**(1987), 20120375 (2013). https://doi.org/10.1098/rsta.2012.0375

6. Barthelemy, M., Barrat, A., Pastor-Satorras, R., Vespignani, A.: Dynamical patterns of epidemic outbreaks in complex heterogeneous networks. J. Theor. Biol. **235**(2), 275–288 (2005). https://doi.org/10.1016/j.jtbi.2005.01.011

7. Bogolyubova, O., Panicheva, P., Tikhonov, R., Ivanov, V., Ledovaya, Y.: Dark personalities on Facebook: harmful online behaviors and language. Comput. Hum. Behav. **78**, 151–159 (2018). https://doi.org/10.1016/j.chb.2017.09.032

8. Boguñá, M., Pastor-Satorras, R., Vespignani, A.: Absence of epidemic threshold in scale-free networks with degree correlations. Phys. Rev. Lett. **90**, 028701 (2003). https://doi.org/10.1103/PhysRevLett.90.028701

9. Boguñá, M., Pastor-Satorras, R.: Epidemic spreading in correlated complex networks. Phys. Rev. E **66**, 047104 (2002). https://doi.org/10.1103/PhysRevE.66.047104

10. Casteltrione, I.: Facebook and political participation: going beyond over-optimistic predictions. In: Northern Lights: Film & Media Studies Yearbook, vol. 15, no. 1, pp. 131–148, June 2017. https://doi.org/10.1386/nl.15.1.131_1

11. Catanzaro, M., Boguñá, M., Pastor-Satorras, R.: Generation of uncorrelated random scale-free networks. Phys. Rev. E **71**, 027103 (2005). https://doi.org/10.1103/PhysRevE.71.027103

12. Chen, J.-S., Lin, C.-B., Yang, C.-Y., Huang, Y.-F.: An efficient Facebook place information extraction strategy. In: You, I., Chen, H.-C., Sharma, V., Kotenko, I. (eds.) MobiSec 2017. CCIS, vol. 971, pp. 131–139. Springer, Singapore (2019). https://doi.org/10.1007/978-981-13-3732-1_10

13. Cohen, E., Consens, M.P.: Large-scale analysis of the co-commit patterns of the active developers in GitHub's top repositories. In: 2018 IEEE/ACM 15th International Conference on Mining Software Repositories (MSR), pp. 426–436. ACM, May 2018. https://doi.org/10.1145/3196398.3196436

14. Dorogovtsev, S.: Lectures on Complex Networks. Oxford University Press, Oxford (2010). https://doi.org/10.1093/acprof:oso/9780199548927.001.0001

15. Fisher, D.N., Silk, M.J., Franks, D.W.: The perceived assortativity of social networks: methodological problems and solutions. In: Missaoui, R., Abdessalem, T., Latapy, M. (eds.) Trends in Social Network Analysis. LNSN, pp. 1–19. Springer, Cham (2017). https://doi.org/10.1007/978-3-319-53420-6_1

16. de Franciscis, S., Johnson, S., Torres, J.J.: Enhancing neural-network performance via assortativity. Phys. Rev. E **83**, 036114 (2011). https://doi.org/10.1103/PhysRevE.83.036114

17. Gleich, D.: Graph of Flickr photo-sharing social network crawled in May 2006, February 2012. https://doi.org/10.4231/D39P2W550
18. Gleich, D.F., Rossi, R.A.: A dynamical system for PageRank with time-dependent teleportation. Internet Math. **10**(1–2), 188–217 (2014). https://doi.org/10.1080/15427951.2013.814092
19. Hall, A.A., Delello, J.A., McWhorter, R.R.: Using Facebook to supplement instruction in online and hybrid courses. Int. J. Innov. Learn. **22**(1), 87–104 (2017). https://doi.org/10.1504/ijil.2017.085250
20. Jarczyk, O., Gruszka, B., Jaroszewicz, S., Bukowski, L., Wierzbicki, A.: GitHub projects. quality analysis of open-source software. In: Aiello, L.M., McFarland, D. (eds.) SocInfo 2014. LNCS, vol. 8851, pp. 80–94. Springer, Cham (2014). https://doi.org/10.1007/978-3-319-13734-6_6
21. Latif, H., Kandemir, A.Ş., Gökkaya, Ö., Karaman, E.: A predictive analysis of Facebook jealousy. Dergi Karadeniz (40), 172–184 (2018). https://doi.org/10.17498/kdeniz.475319
22. Litvak, N., van der Hofstad, R.: Uncovering disassortativity in large scale-free networks. Phys. Rev. E **87**, 022801 (2013). https://doi.org/10.1103/PhysRevE.87.022801
23. Mao, W., Sun, B., Xu, G., Liu, C., Si, C., Wang, W.: Understanding effects of collaborations in developing mobile computing systems: popularity, efficiency, and quality. IEEE Access **7**, 33380–33392 (2019). https://doi.org/10.1109/access.2019.2904333
24. Montandon, J.E., Silva, L.L., Valente, M.T.: Identifying experts in software libraries and frameworks among GitHub users. In: 2019 IEEE/ACM 16th International Conference on Mining Software Repositories (MSR). IEEE, May 2019. https://doi.org/10.1109/msr.2019.00054
25. Nandi, G., Das, A.: An efficient link prediction technique in social networks based on node neighborhoods. Int. J. Adv. Comput. Sci. Appl. **9**(6), 257–266 (2018). https://doi.org/10.14569/ijacsa.2018.090637
26. Naqshbandi, M.M., Ainin, S., Jaafar, N.I., Shuib, N.L.M.: To Facebook or to Face Book? An investigation of how academic performance of different personalities is affected through the intervention of Facebook usage. Comput. Hum. Behav. **75**, 167–176 (2017). https://doi.org/10.1016/j.chb.2017.05.012
27. Newman, M.E.J.: Assortative mixing in networks. Phys. Rev. Lett. **89**, 208701 (2002). https://doi.org/10.1103/PhysRevLett.89.208701
28. Newman, M.E.J.: Mixing patterns in networks. Phys. Rev. E **67**, 026126 (2003). https://doi.org/10.1103/PhysRevE.67.026126
29. Rossi, R.A., Ahmed, N.K.: An interactive data repository with visual analytics. ACM SIGKDD Explor. Newslett. **17**(2), 37–41 (2016). https://doi.org/10.1145/2897350.2897355
30. Rozemberczki, B., Allen, C., Sarkar, R.: Multi-scale attributed node embedding. arXiv e-prints abs/1909.13021 (2019). https://ui.adsabs.harvard.edu/abs/2019arXiv190913021R
31. Rozemberczki, B., Davies, R., Sarkar, R., Sutton, C.: GEMSEC: graph embedding with self clustering. In: Proceedings of the 2019 IEEE/ACM International Conference on Advances in Social Networks Analysis and Mining, ASONAM 2019, pp. 65–72. Association for Computing Machinery, New York (2019). https://doi.org/10.1145/3341161.3342890
32. Safari, H., Sabri, N., Shahsavan, F., Bahrak, B.: An analysis of GitLab's users and projects networks. In: 2020 10th International Symposium on Telecommunications (IST), pp. 194–200 (2020). https://doi.org/10.1109/IST50524.2020.9345844

33. Samanta, S., Dubey, V.K., Sarkar, B.: Measure of influences in social networks. Appl. Soft Comput. **99**, 106858 (2021). https://doi.org/10.1016/j.asoc.2020.106858
34. Sharma, R., Oliveira, S.: Community detection algorithm for big social networks using hybrid architecture. Big Data Res. **10**, 44–52 (2017). https://doi.org/10.1016/j.bdr.2017.10.003
35. Viswanath, B., Mislove, A., Cha, M., Gummadi, K.P.: On the evolution of user interaction in Facebook. In: Proceedings of the 2nd ACM Workshop on Online Social Networks, WOSN 2009, pp. 37–42. ACM Press (2009). https://doi.org/10.1145/1592665.1592675
36. Yao, D., van der Hoorn, P., Litvak, N.: Average nearest neighbor degrees in scale-free networks. Internet Math. **2018**, 1–38 (2018). https://doi.org/10.24166/im.02.2018
37. Zhou, D., Stanley, H.E., D'Agostino, G., Scala, A.: Assortativity decreases the robustness of interdependent networks. Phys. Rev. E **86**, 066103 (2012). https://doi.org/10.1103/PhysRevE.86.066103
38. Zhuang-Xiong, H., Xin-Ran, W., Han, Z.: Pair correlations in scale-free networks. Chin. Phys. **13**(3), 273–278 (2004). https://doi.org/10.1088/1009-1963/13/3/001

# Offline and Online Civic Activity: General and Special

Alexander Sokolov(✉) ⬤, Asya Palagicheva ⬤, and Alexander Frolov ⬤

Demidov P.G, Yaroslavl State University, Yaroslavl, Russia
alex8119@mail.ru

**Abstract.** The article is devoted to the analysis of offline (traditional activity) and online (Internet activity) activity in modern Russia. The article presents the results of a study of civic activity in Russia, which has been conducted by the method of experts' survey (hold on since 2014).

The article focuses on the analysis of differences and similarities of online and offline civic activity. The assessment of the level of development of online and offline civic activity is given. At the moment, there is an uneven development of offline and online activity in the socio-political sphere in Russia. Experts' estimates indicate the superiority of online activity over off-line in terms of popularity and demand. At the same time, the state reacted almost equally to the manifestations of offline and online civic activity. The reasons for the popularity of the Internet, the level of its influence on the socio-political reality are indicated. The analysis of the formation of associations in offline and online coalitions of NGO and civic activists is carried out. The state's attitude to the manifestations of offline and online civic activity is determined.

The results of the study suggest that both real and virtual spaces for the implementation of civic activity are interconnected and unified in nature. Online and offline civic activity do not have clear and serious differences in their manifestations. The spaces themselves have their own specific features of functioning. However, collective actions on the web and in the real world are carried out to implement different forms of civic activity and using the same mechanisms to achieve goals.

**Keywords:** Civic activity · Online civic activity · Offline civic activity · Internet · Collective actions · Protest · E-participation

## 1 Introduction

Digital technologies and the Internet affect social processes, having a transformative effect. New communication mechanisms, tools for the exchange of information, resources and the involvement of citizens in the life of society are emerging. In 2020, the processes of digitalization intensified, new forms of civic activity emerged (online rallies, use of technologies for tracking and monitoring citizens' actions increased).

© Springer Nature Switzerland AG 2022
D. A. Alexandrov et al. (Eds.): DTGS 2021, CCIS 1503, pp. 51–66, 2022.
https://doi.org/10.1007/978-3-030-93715-7_4

At the same time, the impact of new technologies on civic activity is dual. In this regard, G. Asmolov points to researchers who can be divided into groups of cyberoptimists (who emphasize the positive potential of the impact of technology) and cyberpessimists (who focus on the negative aspects of socio-political transformation). Between them is a group of cyber-pragmatists trying to find a balance between the two extremes [1, p. 9].

Civic activity, influenced by online technologies, continues to develop in the real and virtual spaces and has its own specific features in both spaces. Scientists point to the possibility that online civic activity is an imitation of civic activity. At the same time, online participation refers to actions based on network media that are carried out in order to activate strong and weak connections in social network sites to raise awareness of problems or to exert social and political pressure to solve them [2, p. 45]. However, I.A. Bronnikov believes that the existing classical opposition of the political field to the traditional and the network field is unfounded. In the modern post-information society, there is rather a systematic convergence, penetration and co-adaptation of the virtual and physical political space, which creates additional difficulties for the actors [3, p. 278].

In this regard, the purpose of the paper is to highlight the characteristics of civic activity in the offline and online environment, as well as identify common and distinctive characteristics of these processes.

## 2 Theoretical Framework

Civic activity is an essential component of civil society and a model for its dialogue with the State. It is implemented in various forms: online and offline, institutionalized and not, sporadically and constantly. Today, the world is experiencing an increase in the processes associated with the manifestation of civic activity. The reasons are, first of all, the unresolved social and social problems, as well as new forms of information dissemination and citizen participation. Thus, civic activity begins to manifest itself both in the reproduction of new practices of participation, and in the transformation and solution of pressing problems.

S.V. Patrushev distinguishes two types of civic activity: civic participation and civic action. Civic participation is an adaptive public activity that ensures the reproduction of the constitutive values and norms of civil society, established institutional practices, as well as civic identity. At the same time, individuals distinguish between the universal rights of a citizen and their particular restrictions in non-civil spheres (for example, in the economy, politics, etc.). Civic action is a non-adaptive public activity associated with the problems of implementing universal rights and freedoms: ensuring equal civil status, bridging the gap between formal and real rights in everyday life, removing barriers to civic participation, removing restrictions on the exercise of rights in certain areas [4]. X. Wang described two levels of civil participation. The first is the "pseudo" level, where information moves only in one direction to inform citizens about decisions that have already been made. The second is genuine activity, involving citizens' participation in decision-making. Here, citizens are the owners of government and co-producers of public goods [5]. A. Vromen in his research focuses on the process of destroying traditional models of political participation and rebuilding them to solve specific problems [6]. R. Dalton said that the norms of civic participation are moving from the model of debt-based citizenship to the model of active citizenship, which translates new models of citizen participation [7].

According to Russian researcher R.V. Pyrma, "the intensity and frequency of civic and political actions has increased dramatically. The forms of civic activity in the modern world are undergoing drastic changes" [8]. The author believes that new and old forms of civic activity reproduce new practices of participation, increase the number of different forms of expression of one's opinion. The same opinion is shared by S.V. Volodenkov, saying that new technologies transform the public space and political governance, changing the forms and nature of interaction between the state and society [9].

In connection with the development of the Internet, the study of the importance of social network sites as the main digital platform for communication and the organization of collective actions is being updated. The problem of the influence of social network sites on the socio-political discourse through the misinformation of the population is considered in the study of A. Dawson and M. Innes [10]. The authors note that the influence of information in new media has a greater impact on the collective consciousness of users. Other authors note that social network sites influence the motivation of users to participate in various forms of online activity. Proving the influence of the social network site "Twitter" on the signing of an online petition, it is concluded that the speed and ease of distribution of tweets is the basis for the appearance of viral effects (i.e., it significantly increases the speed with which the link to the petition reaches users) [11]. R. Heiss, D. Schmuck and J. Matthes considered the issues of involvement in online activity, studied the formats of posts and posted materials. The authors conclude that emotionally-colored posts attract more users' attention, while mobilization posts negatively affect user activity [12].

Due to the fact that the problems and interests of individuals are quite diverse, civic activity does not represent a clearly structured structure. At the same time, a systematic understanding of civic activity makes it possible to include a large amount of information, increase the participation of different actors in decision-making, and use new means of communication and information transmission.

It often happens that after solving their problems, activists do not continue to spread their positive experience, in such situations it is important to use the Internet. Currently, social network sites, messengers and new media are not only communication platforms for users, but also a digital foundation for active participation of citizens in public and political life. As noted by C. Cohen and J. Kahne, it is impossible not to take into account that the Internet is a special communication space, which, against the background of the crisis of traditional forms of interaction between government and society, makes attempts to reorient itself to new models of interaction and activity [13]. These processes are manifested in the form of the formation of new leaders of public opinion in the Internet, the transition of traditional forms of civic activity to the online environment (Internet petitions, flash mobs, charity, Internet voting, etc.). Changes are also taking place on the part of the state, which translates services into the digital space, accepts electronic appeals from citizens, monitors social network sites on problematic issues with the help of special programs; representatives of legislative authorities hold receptions of citizens online, etc.

## 3 Methods

To collect empirical data for the study, a series of surveys of experts in the subjects of the Russian Federation was conducted. The respondents were experts with the high level of competence, which is associated with their involvement in the regional political process in a particular status. Awareness of research issues became the main criterion for selecting survey participants. The experts of the study were employees of regional and local authorities, scientists, businessmen, members and heads of public organizations, political parties, media representatives, etc. At the same time, the expert is expected to join a certain regional political elite group, as well as have experience in the field that comes into contact with the problems of research (in the field of public policy, in government bodies, local self-government).

The geographical sample annually covers a wide range of regions of the country. According to the methodology, the regions selected for the study include eight federal districts. In 2014, 21 regions were included in the study, in 2015 – 14, in 2017 – 15, in 2018 – 14, in 2019 – 15, in 2020 – 25 (Table 1). Maintaining a significant geographical coverage (even if there is a slight change in the regions included in the sample) in the annual monitoring made it possible to take into account in the collected data the peculiarities of the socio-economic and socio-political situation in different territories of the country, without overestimating each of them.

Thus, all the key expert groups on this topic were covered, which allows us to speak about the validity of the collected data both for the sample as a whole and for individual regions.

Some of the questions during the monitoring were the same every year. They show the dynamics for the observation period. The other part of the questions was updated periodically. This was due to a shift in the focus of the study, the actual aspects in a particular year. Some of the questions involved choosing a qualitative characteristic / judgment, while others involved evaluating the phenomenon/object on a scale from 1 to 10.

The authors sought to maintain a stable sample of regions and respondents from year to year. However, it was not always possible to get the required number of respondents (at least 10). Therefore, there was a change in the regions of the study sample. At the same time, every year we tried to cover different types of regions of Russia (different geographically, economically, politically, ethnically), so that the results could be reliable for the country as a whole.

The survey of experts was conducted using a semi-formal questionnaire and correspondence written data collection. The experts filled out the questionnaires received by e-mail on their own. Statistical data analysis in the SPSS software product was used to process the survey results.

The method of independent characteristics used made it possible to process the collected data in such a way that each described phenomenon received a generalized assessment based on the collected different opinions of independent experts. Within the framework of the study, three stages were implemented. The first stage was to identify and correlate the opinions of experts, the second-to process the collected data using statistical procedures to determine the positions of experts, the third-to formulate conclusions.

**Table 1.** Sample distribution and number of survey respondents.

| Region | 2014 | 2015 | 2017 | 2018 | 2019 | 2020 |
|---|---|---|---|---|---|---|
| Altai Krai | 12 | - | - | 10 | - | - |
| Belgorod region | - | - | - | - | - | 12 |
| Vladimir region | 12 | - | - | - | - | - |
| Vologda region | 11 | - | - | - | - | 11 |
| Voronezh region | 11 | 12 | 11 | 13 | 12 | 12 |
| Zabaikalsky Krai | - | - | - | - | - | 10 |
| Irkutsk region | 14 | 11 | 10 | 11 | 10 | |
| Kabardino-Balkar Republic | - | - | - | - | - | 12 |
| Kaliningrad region | 11 | - | 11 | 10 | 10 | 10 |
| Kemerovo region | - | - | - | 10 | 12 | 14 |
| Kirov region | 13 | 12 | 11 | - | 11 | - |
| Kostroma region | 10 | 11 | 11 | 12 | 11 | 11 |
| Krasnodar Region | 10 | 10 | - | - | - | - |
| Nizhny Novgorod region | 10 | - | - | - | - | - |
| Novosibirsk region | 10 | 15 | - | - | - | 10 |
| Primorsky Krai | - | - | - | - | - | 10 |
| Republic of Adygea | 11 | 11 | 12 | | 11 | 12 |
| Republic of Bashkortostan | 10 | 11 | 10 | 10 | 10 | 10 |
| Republic of Buryatia | - | - | - | - | - | 10 |
| Republic of Dagestan | 12 | 13 | 11 | - | 13 | 13 |
| Republic of Karelia | 11 | - | - | - | - | - |
| Republic of Mari El | - | - | - | - | - | 11 |
| Republic of Mordovia | - | - | - | - | - | 13 |
| Republic of Tatarstan | 10 | 10 | 10 | 11 | 12 | 13 |
| Rostov region | - | - | 14 | 11 | 11 | - |
| Samara region | 10 | 13 | 11 | 13 | 10 | 14 |
| Saratov region | 12 | 14 | 14 | 13 | - | - |
| Sverdlovsk region | - | - | - | - | - | 12 |
| Stavropol Territory | - | - | 10 | 10 | 10 | 12 |
| Tver region | - | - | - | - | - | 13 |
| Ulyanovsk region | 10 | 10 | 10 | 10 | 10 | 11 |
| Khabarovsk region | 10 | - | - | - | - | 10 |

*(continued)*

**Table 1.** (*continued*)

| Region | 2014 | 2015 | 2017 | 2018 | 2019 | 2020 |
|---|---|---|---|---|---|---|
| Chelyabinsk region | - | - | - | - | - | 10 |
| Yaroslavl region | 13 | 12 | 16 | 11 | 12 | 12 |
| Total | 233 | 165 | 172 | 155 | 165 | 288 |

In the course of the study, conclusions were obtained on various thematic blocks of questions.

## 4  Offline and Online Civic Activity: Development, Trends, Features

Civic activity, which is carried out in the real and virtual spaces, is formed in the context of the general state and its institutions. At the same time, in the conditions of the information society, institutions are immersed in the network space, which is characterized by certain rules and behavioral patterns that affect the institutional functioning [14]. Being under the influence of these, as well as many other factors, civic activity is formed, which is expressed in various forms and manifestations.

Civic activity is rarely amorphous. As a rule, it is organized and structured, sometimes these processes occur spontaneously. It has various manifestations and forms, determined by its goals, objectives, orientation, as well as the nature of its "source". Based on the answers of experts, we can say that in Russia today, the most developed institutions of civic activity are volunteerism (the degree of development is 6.57 points, where "1" is the lack of development of the form of civic activity, and "10" is the maximum degree of development of the form of civic activity), public organizations (6.04), discussions on electronic platforms (6.11). It can be assumed that these manifestations of public activity are currently a little more in demand among citizens. It is worth noting that among the most developed forms of civic participation are traditional (offline) institutions and new (online) ones, which are presented in the form of discussions on the Internet.

In addition to these institutions, experts rated charity, public letters (citizens' appeals to the authorities, including in electronic form), educational events, and participation in elections/referendums above average. Civic protests are less developed areas of public activity – the expert assessment was 3.67 points. This fact states that Russian citizens are focused on constructive interaction and building a dialogue with various elements of society, including the authorities.

Now, there is an uneven development of offline and online activity in the socio-political sphere in Russia. Given the speed of development of Internet technologies, the level of its penetration and the activity of accessing it (for reference: the volume of the Internet audience in Russia at the end of August 2020 in Russia was 82%, of which 70% go online every day [15]), it is quite logical to see the assessments of experts who clearly speak about the superiority of online activity over offline in terms of popularity and demand (6.12 points against 4.50).

Citizens are more likely to use online activity on socially important issues due to its accessibility and ease of use. In addition, for citizens, participation in online activity now is not fully connected with the need to be consciously responsible for actions and statements. As with the idea that they are in the focus of the state and their actions (among the crowd of the same Internet users) can be identified and recorded. The real space and the conditions in which civil institutions operate gradually influence the virtual space, creating similar relationships and repertoires of actions of the government and society.

Many factors contribute to the growing popularity of Internet technologies in civic activity, but the main ones are "involving young people in civic activity"(65.6%) and "involving the media in the coverage of civic activity" (47.9%). According to them, the experts' opinion was more consolidated. Of course, each subject of the Russian Federation has its own specifics in this matter. Thus, the inclusion of young people in public activities was not decisive in the activation of Internet technologies in Republic of Dagestan, Kostroma Region, Samara Region, Ulyanovsk Region, Republic of Bashkortostan and Novosibirsk Region. In the rest, this factor determines the role and popularity of online resources of civic activity.

It is interesting that the majority of experts point out that the distinctive feature of the manifestation of civic activity in general is the involvement of young people in civic activity (44.9%). According to the survey, this statement is true for those regions of Russia where young people have become the driving force behind the growing popularity of Internet technologies in the manifestation of civic activity. Another common feature of the manifestation of civic activity in 2020 was the emergence of new subjects of civic activity (the emergence of new conflicts, public campaigns, movements, etc.). Most often, this was said by experts from Yaroslavl Region (81.8%), Kostroma Region (81.8%), Sverdlovsk Region (66.7%), Vologda Region (63.6%) and Khabarovsk Territory (60.0%).

The majority of experts participating in the survey (57.5%) are confident that today Internet technologies continue to gain importance in the issue of civic activity, and sometimes they affect the form of its manifestation. This process is particularly relevant today for Belgorod Region (91.7% of the total number of experts from this subject), Vologda Region (81.8%), Republic of Buryatia (80.0%), Voronezh Region (75.0%), Republic of Bashkortostan (70.0%), Novosibirsk Region (70.0%), Khabarovsk Territory (70.0%) and Zabaikalsky Krai (70.0%). Only 1.0% of experts recorded a decrease in the frequency of using Internet technologies as a way of displaying civic activity. These are representatives of Kemerovo Region (14.3% of the total number of experts from this subject) and Zabaikalsky Krai (10.0%).

## 5  Government Attitudes and Regulation of Online and Offline Civic Activity

Civic activity and its various forms of expression on the Internet and in real life are aimed at influencing and changing any aspects of the socio-political structure of society. The actions of civil society activists cause a certain reaction in the state, which is associated with the need to regulate these processes and their dosed presence in the public discourse in order to maintain a balance. The growing importance of online space for civic activity is changing the perception of online activity. From the rank of peripheral and insignificant sofa activity, it passes into the rank of already more noticed by other political actors, Internet activity acquires subjectivity.

Two-thirds of experts agreed that online civic activity is an important component of the development of society: 18.8% say that it has an unconditional impact on the socio-political reality, 49.3% are sure that the authorities are interested in it. Among the experts, representatives of Republic of Dagestan, Republic of Buryatia, and Kostroma Region spoke more often about the absolute importance of social activity online. 27.1% of the study participants said that the impact of Internet activity on the socio-political sphere was insignificant, while 4.9% said that it was absent. There is not a single region where there would be complete indifference to the manifestations of online activity. In many regions there is no consensus and there are disputes about its impact on the socio-political reality. For example, in Republic of Adygea, Sverdlovsk Region, Zabaikalsky Krai, Vologda Region, Stavropol Krai, and Chelyabinsk Region. The creation of Regional Management Centers (SDGs) in the constituent entities of the Russian Federation can strengthen the role of civic activity online.

Offline civic activity in Russia, which is expressed through traditional forms of participation, is still characterized by the activity of equally active registered associations and formally unregistered organizations. Officially registered public associations and formally unregistered associations of citizens (for example: local groups, social movements, Internet communities, etc.) demonstrate the greatest activity in the subjects of the Russian Federation. This fact has remained unchanged over the past six years (from 2014 to 2020).

Organizers of protest and non-protest actions on Internet agree with the general results of the survey and agree that registered associations and non-registered movements express their activity equally. The organizers of offline protest actions point to the predominance of activity of informal groups, while the leaders of non-protest offline events point to the greatest activity of registered organizations.

The perception of civic activity, which is realized in the real and virtual space, depends on many factors. The attitude of the authorities to the manifestations of civic activity depends largely on the goals and direction of the functioning of the entire of authorities, as well as on the general state of crisis of social processes. In 2020, the state began to slowly change its attitude to the manifestations of offline and online civic activity. On the one hand, small steps have been taken towards establishing a dialogue and interaction with activists, providing them with support, on the other hand, public activists are increasingly faced with ignoring by the state. This is evidenced by the answers of experts. The behavior of the state in relation to civic activists over the past year is also interesting because it reacted almost equally to the manifestations of offline and online civic activity. This fact essentially equates these two forms of manifestation of social activity of citizens. Such a picture is observed for the first time in all the time of observations (since 2017).

The reaction of state authorities to online and offline forms of civic activity "leveled off" and began to manifest itself in approximately the same way in both spaces. This is due to the following dynamics of a number of indicators that have acquired a close value for online and offline activity (data compared to 2019):

- the estimates of experts who say that the government supports online forms of activity, seeing positive results of their work (from 4.9% to 11.9%);

- significantly increased the estimates of experts who say that the government does not notice / does not know about the existence of forms of offline activity (from 4.3% to 9.8%);

- slightly less increased the estimates that show that the government slightly supports forms of online activity (from 21.5% to 25.5%).

The biggest dynamic in the experts' assessments is revealed in the fact that the authorities have become less afraid and avoid interacting with online and offline activists. At the same time, she is less likely to notice civic activity offline and online.

Throughout the entire period of research, there is an increase in the influence of state actions in the sphere of regulating the Internet environment on civic online activity. In 2020, this influence was controversial, as every online activist reacts to the actions of the state based on their beliefs and the external environment. In 2020, according to experts, the number of online activists who fear for their actions has increased, and they have limited their "speeches" on the Internet. This trend is particularly pronounced in Republic of Mordovia, Tver Region, Stavropol Territory and the Vologda Region. There are more and more people who react aggressively to the actions of the state on the Internet, increasing their protest activity online. This reaction is now very common in Republic of Adygea, Sverdlovsk Region and Belgorod Region. In Kaliningrad Region, Ulyanovsk Region, Republic of Buryatia, and Novosibirsk Region, actions to regulate civic activity on the Internet have had virtually no impact on its dynamics over the past year. It is worth noting that the experts' view on the relationship between the state's actions to regulate the Internet and the dynamics of online activity depends on its role and practice in protest and non-protest actions. Thus, the organizers of protest actions (regardless of their form of conduct) say that the state provokes an increase in their activity by its actions. Organizers and participants of non-protest actions, on the contrary, more often than others say that it does not affect the behavior of online activists (the dynamics of Internet activity).

In the Russian segment of the Internet, there is a radicalization of online activists, their posts have increasingly become protest-oriented. This is what the dynamics of expert responses observed since 2017 shows. In the latest survey, 32.5% said that civic activity online has become more protest-oriented and has begun to become radicalized (in previous years, their share did not exceed 27%). 15.7% spoke about increasing the loyalty of online activists, and this point of view is especially widespread among the survey participants from the Khabarovsk Territory and the Stavropol Territory. 51.7% of experts did not notice any changes in the content of the posts of online activists. Based on the data obtained, the dynamics of content and the nature of posts are strongly influenced by the actions of the state authorities of the subjects in the field of Network regulation. At the same time, in different regions, the same management decision can lead to opposite and often not calculated reactions of online activists. For example, an increase in online protest activity is observed in Belgorod Region and Sverdlovsk Region, while in Stavropol Territory, increased control over the Internet has led to an increase in fears among Internet activists and, as a result, a decrease in protest activity on the Internet.

## 6 Online and Offline Coalitions of Civic Associations

Civic activity, which is carried out in the real and virtual world, is carried out based on association of citizens to influence public processes. Civic partnerships play a special role in this process, building the capacity to succeed in their common endeavor.

In 2014, in most cases, the minimum number of NGO joined the coalition: 2–3 partners. In the practice of 2020, it is popular to create larger coalitions – 4–6 partners. In an online environment, it is much easier to find like-minded people and to communicate between public organizations and civic activists geographically remote from each other, for this reason, virtual coalitions are more numerous than those created offline.

In 2020, the activity of mixed coalitions of registered and unregistered associations sharply and significantly decreased, and coalitions of officially registered public associations began to take their place. The opinions of the organizers and participants of public mass protest and non-protest actions on this issue largely converged. Analyzing the answers of experts, we can confidently say that there are specific features in each region. In Kaliningrad Region and Primorsky Territory, there is an extremely high activity of officially registered public associations; in Novosibirsk Region and Republic of Bashkortostan - formally unregistered associations of citizens (for example: local groups, social movements, Internet communities, etc.); in Ulyanovsk Region and Zabaikalsky Krai - coalitions of various officially unregistered associations of citizens.

The regions that have their own specifics in forming coalitions are marked. In Republic of Dagestan, Kemerovo Region, Stavropol Territory, Vologda and Sverdlovsk regions offline coalitions of civic activists are created from numerous partnerships (more than 9), which distinguishes them from others - the national average. There are also regions where online coalitions tend to form a few partnerships, which differs from the all-Russian trend. These regions are: Yaroslavl Region, Republic of Buryatia, and Zabaikalsky Krai. Nevertheless, civic activity in both real and virtual spaces in 2020 shows an overall increase in more numerous partnerships. This may be due to the accumulation of experience of activists in organizing collaborative events and their success in the long run.

The number of partners in a coalition is influenced by the goals and objectives of its creation. Organizers of protest actions in the offline and online environment try to find support and create an alliance with the largest number of like-minded people, participants of non-protest actions have enough 2–3 partners for the successful implementation of their project. It can be assumed that the surge in protest activity recorded in 2020, especially online, contributed to an increase in the number of involved partnerships in order to achieve a common goal. However, it is also worth noting the progressive development of this trend.

The peculiarity of online civic activity is its focus on the most extensive involvement and awareness of citizens in the activities of the association and about the activities of the association, with the help of which it is possible to achieve the goal. Offline activity is characterized by setting and solving tasks that are not necessarily related to the broad involvement of the population in the project.

# 7  Offline and Online Protest Actions in Russian Regions

One of the forms of civic activity that is implemented both on the Internet and through actions and events in the real world is protest. Over the past year, Russia as a whole has seen an increase in the activity of protest actions, especially in the Internet environment. The experts estimated the dynamics of the protest in offline mode by 0.30 points (on a scale from –5 to 5, where " –5 " - a sharp decrease in protest actions, 0 – no dynamics;" 5 " - a sharp increase in protest actions), in online mode-by 1.07 points. Despite the demand for protest by citizens in 2020, it is at the same time the least developed area of public participation.

The analysis of expert assessments of protest activity in Russia allowed us to identify three main groups of regions, depending on the dynamics of its development. The first group-characterized by a general decline in protest potential in 2020. It includes: Kaliningrad Region, Ulyanovsk Region and Tver Region. The second group of regions – with a moderate increase in protest activity. It includes: Samara Region, Stavropol Territory, Yaroslavl Region, Republic of Adygea, Republic of Bashkortostan, Republic of Mari El, Khabarovsk Territory, Chelyabinsk Region, Zabaikalsky Krai, Vologda Region, Primorsky Territory, and Kemerovo Region. The third group of regions – with a high growth in the dynamics of protest activity. It includes: Voronezh Region, Republic of Dagestan, Republic of Tatarstan, Kostroma Region, Republic of Buryatia, Republic of Mordovia, Novosibirsk Region, Belgorod Region, Sverdlovsk Region and Kabardino-Balkar Republic.

In all the studied Russian regions in 2020, there was a surge in online protest activity (the exception is Ulyanovsk region). Some scientists and public figures explain this trend by the spread of coronavirus infection. However, this factor should have led to a weakening of the intensity of traditional protest actions, but this did not happen. Only in the three regions studied during the period under review, there was a decrease in the number of offline protests: Kaliningrad Region, Ulyanovsk Region, and Tver Region.

Representatives of different status and professional groups expressed different opinions on the dynamics of protest actions in online and offline spaces. Representatives of executive authorities, political parties and the media agreed with the overall results of the survey – they were more likely to say that in 2020, there was a decrease in protest activity in offline mode (their ratings are: –0.17, –0.19, –0.30), while online protest actions grew and developed (0.73, 0.65, 0.88). The academic community points to an increase in protest actions in both spaces and assesses the dynamics with the highest scores among other groups of respondents –1.94 points online and 1.18 points offline. Representatives of the legislature noticed protest activity in both spaces at about the same level of growth – 1, 35 points online and 1.00 points offline.

The organizers and participants of the protest and non-protest actions of both sites are unanimous in the opinion that the activists were more active in the network. It is worth noting that the difference between the dynamics of protest activity on the Internet and in reality, which is indicated by the groups – leaders and ordinary participants, was about one point.

The expression of protest by citizens demonstrates the presence of differences in the interests of social groups in society, which often arise between the government and society. The organizers and leaders of the protest unite like-minded people, broadcasting a certain position and goals of the movement, for the opportunity to influence any aspect of social and political life. In 2020, the organizers of online and offline protests were less likely to take into account the interests of the population of the regions than in 2019. This is especially true of traditional forms of protest. Online protests were perceived as focused on public requests and expressing the interests of citizens to a greater extent. However, in our opinion, in general, the difference between the degree of orientation of online and offline protests to the interests of citizens is insignificant, since it is 0.32 points (on a scale from –5 to 5, where " –5 "- are focused only on personal, self-serving goals, 0-find a balance between personal goals and public interests; "5" - act on the basis of public interests).

However, in general, protest activity in 2020 has its own specifics, and it is associated with an increased level of imbalance between the interests of the government and society, as well as an increased level of citizens' distrust of the actions of the government. What happens on the web is a more transparent process for observers, more convenient (fixed) for checking the truthfulness, and moreover-accessible to ordinary citizens, accessible to broad interest groups. In this regard, the online protest in 2020 reflected the interests of civic activists, their dissatisfaction with the socio-political situation. This is also due to mass digitalization and going online.

The dynamics of expert assessments allowed us to determine the presence of a direct correlation between the indicators "orientation of protest organizers in the offline environment to the interests of citizens" and "the degree of influence of protest activity in the offline environment on the socio-political situation in the regions" – the less the organizers of traditional forms of protests are oriented to the interests of citizens, the lower their effectiveness and impact on the development of society. This correlation is absent or extremely weak when it comes to online protests.

In general, in 2020, the degree of influence of protest activity (offline and online) on the socio-political situation in Russia decreased. This was solely due to a decrease in expert assessments of the "value" of offline protests (from 0.66 points in 2019 to 0.25 in 2020, on a scale from –5 to 5, where "–5" - a significant destabilizing influence, "0" - no influence, "5" - a significant stabilizing influence). The impact of online protests during this period, according to experts, on the contrary, increased (from 0.49 points in 2019 to 0.61 points in 2020).

Representatives of the authorities, especially the legislative bodies, note the negative destabilizing effect of offline protest on the socio-political situation and the more positive, but still to a very small extent, calming effect on the society of online protest. Representatives of NGOs do not consider protest activity on the Internet to be more capable of stabilizing the situation than traditional forms of protest. Representatives of the academic community point out the equal influence of protest activity on the Internet and in reality on the stabilization of public relations. Perhaps only the media indicate a more pronounced ability of online protest to influence the socio-political situation in a stabilizing way (including in comparison with offline protest), where the impact of online activity is estimated at 1.31 points against 0.12 points of offline activity.

Because the protest actions in Russia in 2020 were accompanied by forceful methods of demobilization of citizens, the presence of aggression, and as a result of their continued growth of discontent of citizens in connection with dissatisfaction, the offline protest demonstrated an increase in the confrontation of the conflict subjects. Forms of online protest activity did not have such a strong effect of mass confrontation and destabilization, but rather demonstrated civic cooperation and public discussion that contribute to stabilization. Despite the fact that the results of the study indicate a decrease in the ability of offline protests to influence the socio-political situation, in general, the difference in the estimates of online and offline influence is small and amounts to 0.36 points.

Social network sites and Internet technologies in Russia play an important role in the success of protest organizers. The degree of their influence is estimated by experts at 6.40 points (on a scale from 1 to 10, where "1" - no influence, "10" - a very significant influence). Their influence is particularly high in Sverdlovsk Region, Ulyanovsk Region, Khabarovsk Territory, Republic of Mordovia, Republic of Buryatia, Novosibirsk Region, Yaroslavl Region, Samara Region, Republic of Tatarstan, and Kemerovo Region. In many of these subjects, there is an increase in online protest, and relatively high activity of formally unregistered associations of citizens. It can be said that offline civic activity, which is currently carried out unaccompanied in an online environment, causes skepticism.

The perception of real and virtual civic activity tends more and more every year to recognize that together they are one embodiment of collective action. Protest actions on the Internet in 2020 are perceived by the authorities as partially actual protest actions (66.6%), to a lesser extent – as full-fledged protest actions (20.9%). Compared to the previous year in 2019, these indicators have increased. At the same time, there was a 9.4% drop in estimates that the protest in the network is not perceived as an actual protest.

Over the past year, the Russian state has taken small steps towards building dialogue and interaction with civil society activists, but they do not affect the organizers and participants of the protests. Here, quite opposite trends are observed – the transition from a "fragile" peace and "strained" cooperation to countering the public expression of citizens' dissatisfaction both offline and online. In 2019, experts estimated the degree of opposition of authorities to offline and online protests by 0.34 points and 0.28 points, respectively (where " –5 " - opposition to protest activity," 0 " - lack of any impact," 5 " -orientation to cooperation), and in 2020 - by –0.26 points and –0.19 points. Among the subjects presented in the study, the authorities of Zabaikalsky Krai, Belgorod Region, Kemerovo Region, Tver Region, Republic of Mordovia, Voronezh Region and Republic of Tatarstan are particularly active in preventing traditional protest actions. Actively prevents online protests in Republic of Bashkortostan, Belgorod Region, Zabaikalsky Krai and Sverdlovsk Region. In practice, in most cases, excessive enthusiasm in opposing protests leads to their strengthening.

# 8   Discussion

The potential possibilities of the study allow us to understand the qualitative differences in the functioning and interaction of virtual and real spaces in Russia. The data obtained in the course of similar studies provided an opportunity for comparison, which can be interpreted by analyzing the dynamics of the manifestation of different forms of civic activity. The results obtained in this study can be tested in the future in the form of practical recommendations on the use of online and offline forms of civic activity, for actors who initiate a variety of civic campaigns.

The main limitation of such studies is the selection of criteria by which experts give their assessments. On the one hand, reducing the number of criteria allows to focus on specific research tasks, but on the other hand, it sets a framework for which some aspects of the issue under consideration may not be affected at all or may not be taken into account at all. Such a disadvantage can be neutralized by expanding and systematizing the problem field of the given research.

The study of the differences between offline and online civic activity is an important aspect in understanding the algorithm of both group and individual actions in the context of a dialogue between society and the state. Also, we can note the wide coverage of the country's regions, which makes the study reliable for understanding the level of development of civic activity in the country as a whole. However, an increase in the number of regions in the study would allow us to better understand the specifics of the development of the affected problems in the federal districts.

The study provides an ambiguous assessment of the options for the development of civic activity in modern Russia: by increasing the possibilities of "cyber optimism" or increasing the limitations of "cyber pessimism". Taking into account the answers of experts, we can say that both phenomena, according to the current agenda in the country, exist and proceed from the activity of participants in the online discussion and reverse actions on the part of the authorities. It is worth noting that according to the results of the study, it is impossible to say unequivocally about the prevalence of "cyber optimism" or "cyber pessimism" in Russia and vice versa. The study of these aspects is a good basis for conducting new research focused on this problem.

# 9  Conclusions

Summing up, it should be noted that civic activity is usually organized and rarely has a spontaneous nature of appearance and further development. Based on the responses of experts, the following conclusions can be distinguished:

– The most developed forms of civic activity in the online space are discussions on electronic platforms; offline: volunteering and the work of NGOs.
– In the question of the popularity and demand for civic activity, experts highlight the superiority of online activity over offline. The key factors are the simplicity and accessibility of using different Internet technologies. Citizens' lack of awareness of responsibility in expressing their actions online also plays a role.
– One of the determining factors of the growing popularity of Internet technologies is the involvement of young people in civic activity and the involvement of the media in the coverage of civic activity (in particular, the media that represent new media). The participation of young people in various civic actions in general is becoming a trend in 2020.
– In 2020, the state's attitude to the manifestation of civic activity is at the same level in relation to online and offline forms of its manifestation.
– experts note the factors of greater regulation of online activity, which are expressed in two main aspects: the emergence of special structures for monitoring acute social problems (the use of the "Incident Management" system, the formation of separate

structures in the regions "Regional Management Centers" that collect messages and complaints in social network sites and messengers) and the tightening of the legislative framework (the law on "fake news", on "disrespect for the authorities", etc.). One of the reactions to the bans is the radicalization of online activists.

- when it comes to coalitions of online and offline civil associations, we can say that in 2020 the role of the coalition component is increasing. This is primarily reflected in the strengthening of online communications, where it is easier and more accessible to find like-minded people, as well as in increasing the reach of the audience, through the broadcast of successful civil campaigns. At the same time, online activity is more focused on the broad awareness of the population about their activities. Often it is aimed at "calls to action". Offline activity is more focused on solving more specific tasks and is not always aimed at the inclusion of the general public.

- the development of civic activity in the online space along the path of "cyber optimism" (increasing opportunities) or "cyber pessimism" (increasing restrictions) in Russia, based on the answers of experts, is ambiguous. Both trends, according to the current agenda in the country, manifest themselves. At the same time, we can talk about the increasing use of Internet tools in the practices of both civic activists and authorities.

- the year 2020 is marked by an increase in protest activity, especially in the online form. It is possible to emphasize several factors of growth of protest online activity. First, these are the restrictive measures imposed related to the spread of coronavirus infection. Secondly, it is the popularization of social network sites, messengers and video hosting sites, through which socially significant events are increasingly promoted, and discussions of pressing issues are held. This is also the emergence of new and the spread of existing forms of online protest (digital actions on online map platforms, protests in online video games, flash mobs in social network sites, the creation of thematic protest groups, etc.). Another component that experts have identified is the increasing level of imbalance between the interests of the government and society, as well as the increased level of citizens' distrust of the actions of the authorities, which they are trying to express in the online space.

To sum up, we can say that civic activity online and offline does not have clear and serious differences in its manifestations. The types of activity themselves have their own specific features of functioning. However, the mechanisms used by the organizers of these actions are often the same and are increasingly moving to the online format.

**Acknowledgement.** The reported study was funded by the grant from the President of the Russian Federation for state support of young Russian scientists MD-855.2020.6 "Mobilization and demobilization in modern practices of protest activity".

# References

1. Scanning the horizon: the role of information technology in the future of civil society Cogito-Center Publishing House, Moscow (2020)
2. Basheva, O.A.: Digital activity as a new method of civil mobilization // Scientific result. Sociol. Manage. **6**(1), 41–57 (2020)

3. Bronnikov, I.A.: Self-organization of citizens in the age of digital communication. Outlines Global Transform. Polit. Econ. Entitled. **13**(2), 269–285 (2020)
4. Patrushev, S.V.: Civic activity: an institutional approach. Prospects of research. http://www.civisbook.ru/files/File/Patrushev_2009_6.pdf
5. Wang, X.: Assessing public participation in U.S. cities. Public Perform. Manage. Rev. **24**(4), 322–336 (2001)
6. Vromen, A.: Digital Citizenship and Political Engagement. Palgrave Macmillan UK, London (2017). https://doi.org/10.1057/978-1-137-48865-7
7. Dalton, R.: Citizenship norms and the expansion of political participation. Polit. Stud. **56**(1), 76–98 (2008)
8. Pyrma, R.V.: Conceptions of civil activity in the digital space of communications. Vlast **2**, 74–81 (2020)
9. Volodenkov, S.V.: Political communication as an instrument of power distribution in the system of state-society relations. Electron. Bull. **62**, 104–118 (2017)
10. Dawson, A., Innes, M.: How Russia's internet research agency built its disinformation campaign. Polit. Q. **90**(2), 245–256 (2019)
11. Harrison, T., et al.: E-petitioning and online media: The case of #BringBackOurGirls. In: Proceedings of the 18thInternational Conference of the Digital Government Society, pp. 11–20. Staten Island, New York, June 2017 (2017)
12. Heiss, R., Schmuck, D., Matthes, J.: What drives interaction in political actors' Facebook posts? Profile and content predictors of user engagement and political actors' reactions. Inf. Commun. Soc. **22**(10), 1497–1513 (2019)
13. Cohen, C.: Participatory Politics: New Media and Youth Political Action. MacArthur Research Network on Youth and Participatory Politics, Chicago (2012)
14. Kaminchenko, D.I.: Modern political participation online vs offline: new opportunities — former activity? Manage. Consult. **8**, 18–35 (2020)
15. VTsIOM. https://wciom.ru/news/ratings/polzovanie_internetom

# Recognition of Signs and Movement Epentheses in Russian Sign Language

Mikhail Grif$^{(\boxtimes)}$, Alexey Prikhodko, and Maxim Bakaev

Novosibirsk State Technical University, Novosibirsk, Russia
{grif,bakaev}@corp.nstu.ru

**Abstract.** Automated translation from sign languages used by the hearing-impaired people worldwide is an important but so far unresolved task ensuring universal communication in the society. In our paper we propose an original approach towards recognition of Russian Sign Language (RSL) based on extraction of components: handshape and palm orientation, location, path and local movement, as well as non-manual component. We detail the development of the dataset for subsequent training of the artificial neural network (ANN) that we construct for the recognition. We further consider two approaches towards continuous sign language recognition, which are based on sequential search of candidate events for the next sign start and the complete identification of the speech elements – the actual signs, resting state of the signer, combinatorial changes in the parameters of the signs and the epentheses.

**Keywords:** Sign recognition · Neural network · Sign language components · Epenthesis

## 1 Introduction

The development of methods for two-way machine translation of (Russian) text (speech) into sign languages used by the deaf (such as Russian sign language, RSL) in any country of the world is an important social task that contributes to the support of communication between the deaf and the hearing. The urgency of the development of computer sign language interpretation systems for sign languages (from hearer to deaf and vice versa) is due both to the insufficient number of sign language interpreters and in not always desirable mediation (medicine, personal relationships, etc.) in the communication of deaf and hearing citizens [1].

Currently, this task cannot be considered resolved, since there are no known solutions for machine translation of Russian text into RSL and vice versa, which meet the requirements of deaf citizens of Russia. The main requirements of the deaf are the accuracy and quality of the translation (computer character) visualization. The studies carried out among the deaf allow us to establish the requirement towards the accuracy of translation of at least 90% [2] and the quality of visualization must match the level of translation by a human sign language interpreter. These circumstances complicate the communication

D. A. Alexandrov et al. (Eds.): DTGS 2021, CCIS 1503, pp. 67–82, 2022.
https://doi.org/10.1007/978-3-030-93715-7_5

between the hearing and the deaf citizens, which is a serious socio-economic problem. Currently, when translating a Russian text into RSL and vice versa, both machine learning methods and the connection between the grammatical systems of the Russian sounding language and RSL are used. However, the following circumstances hinder the achievement of the required level of translation:

- incomplete description of the RSL grammatical system;
- the lack of "smoothness" in the display of gestures by the RSL avatar-sign language translator, whose control system uses the notation system of the sign languages;
- translation is carried out mainly into tracing sign speech, and not into RSL, which has its own expressive capabilities;
- a high percentage of errors in translating ambiguous words and homonyms into RSL gestures (over 20%);
- the absence of labeled RSL corpuses (datasets) of a significant volume at all levels of analysis (phonological, morphological, lexical, syntactic and discourse) [9] necessary for the implementation of machine translation and natural language processing (NLP) methods based on machine learning;
- lack of reliable methods of recognition, both for individual signs and the whole RSL.

Of particular difficulty is the problem of recognition of continuous sign speech (RSL). For successful recognition, it is not enough just to highlight the individual signs. Their confident selection is necessary, taking into account the combinatorial changes in the parameters of signs, as well as epenthesis. We will dwell on this problem in more detail.

A detailed analysis of the main results for world sign languages can be found in [3]. For recognition, 2D video cameras, digital gloves, bracelets and 3D devices (Kinect sensor) were used. The main applied models are neural networks. Despite the fact that in some cases it was possible to achieve recognition accuracy of 90%, this happened either on a limited set of signs (50–200), or for obviously simple (static) ones. As for solving the problem of epenthesis, methods were used to identify features of the beginning and end of signs, including tracking the speaker's face. However, currently they cannot be recognized as universal and reliable either. It is noted [3] that at present there are no full-fledged systems for recognizing national sign languages.

As for the recognition of RSL itself, the success level is not very high. We can note the works [4, 5], where convolutional neural networks were used to recognize RSL using Kinect sensor. They also developed a dataset for 3D human models [6], which is of interest. However, it should be noted that the dataset was developed for a fairly narrow dialect of RSL (St. Petersburg) and included a small set of signs (about 300).

To recognize individual components of gestures (handshape and palm orientation, as well as non-manual components), a neural network approach was applied in [7, 8]. However, it was more for the study of RSL, and not for its recognition. It should also be noted that the RSL corpus developed by S.I. Burkova [9], however, cannot be applied directly in machine learning to solve the RSL recognition problem.

Thus, we need to admit that at the moment there are no sufficient RSL datasets, recognition methods do not use a full set of sign components, and approaches to the isolation of epenthesis are not universal and reliable. So, the goal of our work is to develop a fairly universal approach to RSL recognition based on machine learning, taking into account all the components of signs and the phenomenon of epenthesis. Although this is a work in progress, we see the main contributions of the current paper as follows:

1. We proposed original approach towards RSL recognition based on identification of the five components.
2. We devised and populated the unprecedented RSL dataset containing over 35,000 images and videos (the number of videos is over 10,000).
3. We proposed the algorithm for recognizing hand gestures based on mediapile holistic library and achieved the accuracy of 85%. The algorithm for the identification of the hand gesture type has achieved the accuracy of 95%.
4. We developed the algorithm for recognition of non-manual components, based on mediapipe module that identifies the conditions of eyes, eyelids, mouth, tongue, and head tilt. There are 16 rules in total.
5. We developed the algorithm for identification of the signs' beginnings and endings in a video stream, with the accuracy of 97%. The work on the dataset for the movement epenthesis continues – currently there are videos for about 100 sentences in RSL in which we label individual signs and epentheses.

## 2 The Development of the Training Dataset

A dataset of Russian sign language is the data that is needed to train neural networks. For the analysis of gestures and RSL recognition, a lot of language-specific data are required, since using a dataset created for another language (e.g., American Sign Language) is largely impossible, due to different grammar. As currently there is no ready-made, universal dataset for RSL recognition, we have created and labeled our own RSL dataset for machine learning. If an unfinished, incomplete dataset is used to develop a recognition system for any sign language, the result will be substandard. In other words, the Dataset, which is the "fuel" for artificial intelligence, created for the purpose of developing machine learning models, needs priority attention. An example from the director of Tesla for artificial intelligence states that it takes a lot of time to develop datasets (75%), and three times less to develop algorithms and machine learning models (25%)[1]. Another quote is from the renowned Andrew Ng[2]: *It's not who has the best algorithm that wins. It's who has the most data.* When developing a dataset, three stages are distinguished: collecting the signs, labeling the signs, cleaning up the dataset.

### 2.1 Sign Language Phonological Description

In linguistics [9] of Russian sign language, five levels of analysis are used: phonological, morphological, lexical, syntactic, and discourse. We focus only on phonological analysis, which deals with the level of elementary units of sign language. As a rule, "Phoneme" is

---

[1] https://cs.stanford.edu/people/karpathy/.
[2] https://www.coursera.org/instructor/andrewng.

defined in sound languages in connection with the acoustic model, and in sign languages – "Five components of Sign Language" in connection with the kinematic model of the hand and body, also with the visual model of facial expressions. This model resides in signing space, the area used by the speaker for articulation. Its vertical border starts just above the head and ends at the waist, and the horizontal border runs from one elbow to the other with the arms free. The five components of Sign Language include: handshape, palm orientation, location, movement, and a non-manual component (Fig. 1).

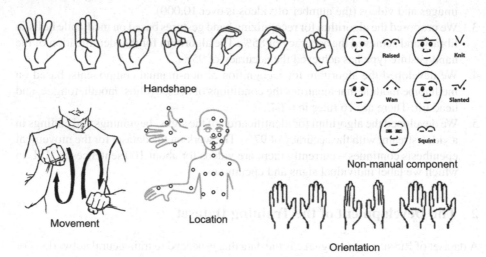

**Fig. 1.** The five components of Sign Language[3].

**Handshape and Palm Orientation.** In Fig. 1, the different "handshapes" are different forms of the hand when performing a sign is demonstrated. Figure 2 shows examples of one word "scissors", where the palm in a gesture is in different handshapes "П" and "Л" - letters of the fingerspelling, but in the same palm orientation. In Fig. 1 different orientations represent the position of the palm in space. The palm of the right or left hand can be turned up, down, right, left, up-right, up-left and in other directions (see symbols in Fig. 3) (see footnote [3]). Figure 4 shows different handshapes[4].

**Location.** In Fig. 1, location of a sign includes two main features – place of articulation and setting. The place of the articulation performance is several large areas within the sign space: the head, face, neck, chest, waist, neutral sign space (the sign is performed without contact of the hand with the body) and the passive hand. The setting is within this large area. For example, place is face, setting is right eye.

**Movement.** In Fig. 1, the "Bicycle" sign is indicated by the arrows as a circle, which denotes the "character" feature of path movement, for example, in a straight line, in a

---

[3] https://aslfont.github.io/Symbol-Font-For-ASL/elements-of-asl.html.
[4] https://slevinski.github.io/SuttonSignWriting/characters/symbols.html#?ui=en&set=fsw.

zigzag, along an arc, etc. And the second feature is "direction" - vertical, horizontal and sagittal. In the second type, "Local movement", the handshape or palm orientation is changed. For example, in the "scissors" gesture (Fig. 2) there is a change in the handshape "Л" and "П".

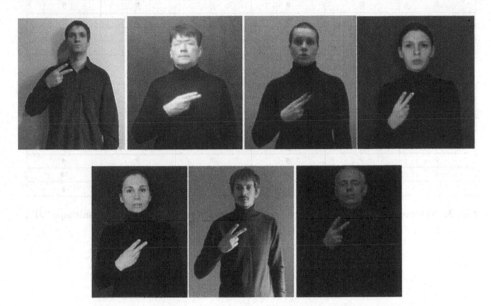

**Fig. 2.** Seven different signers who shown the sign "scissors" in RSL.

**Non-manual Component.** The non-manual components include four articulators: body core, head, shoulders, and facial expressions. In RSL, for many signs, the head, body, facial expressions, mouthing and mouth movements often performed simultaneously, called multi-channel signs. Mouthing is the movement of the lips saying the corresponding word in the speaking language. Mouth gestures are distinct from the mouthing and are not associated with spoken language.

**Types of Signs.** The following classification of signs can be proposed (Fig. 5). There are one-handed and two-handed gestures, static and dynamic, symmetrical and asymmetric, synchronous and alternating.

## 2.2   The Developed RSL Dataset

We have developed the RSL dataset, which includes more than thirty-five thousand elements of common words (images and video files, of which more than ten thousand video files). More than a thousand RSL signs were selected from an online dictionary[5]

---

[5] www.spreadthesign.ru.

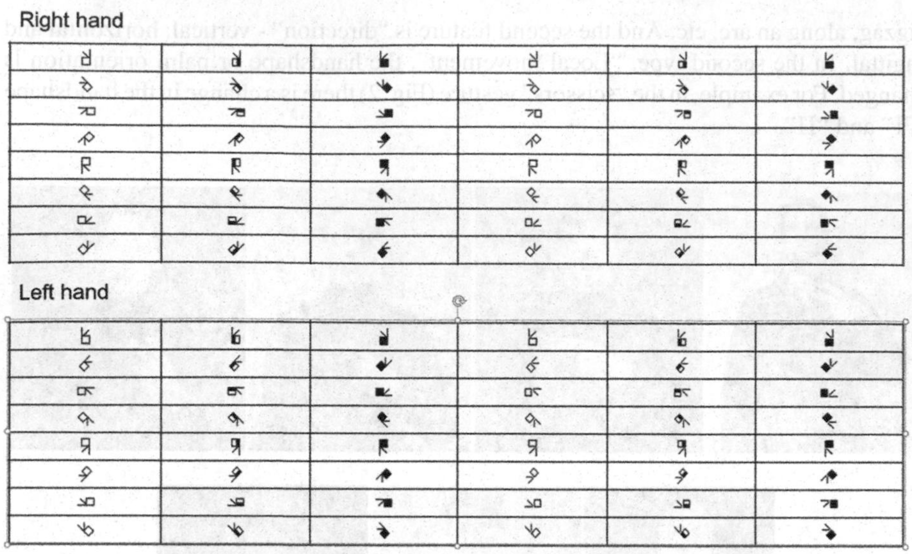

Right hand

Left hand

**Fig. 3.** Symbols of SL writing notation for different palm orientations in one handshape "Л".

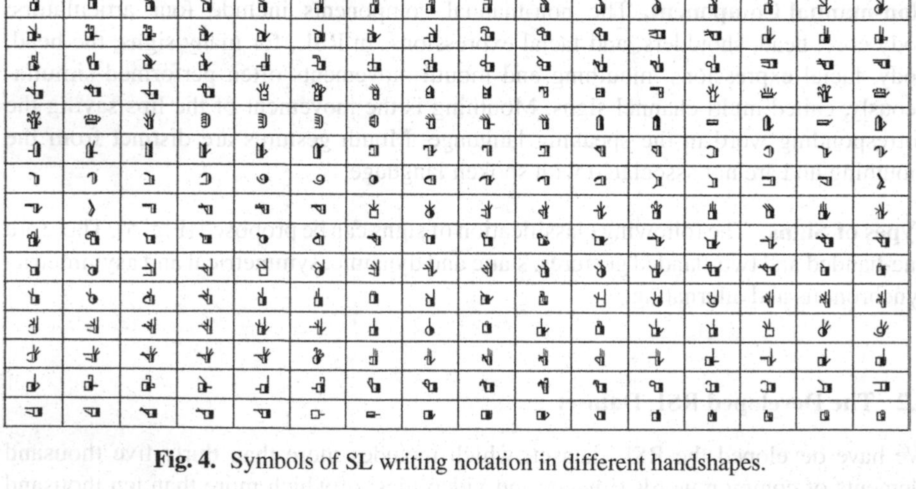

**Fig. 4.** Symbols of SL writing notation in different handshapes.

and a dictionary book [10]. Each sign was performed with 5 repetitions and at least 5 deaf signer of Russian Sign Language from Siberia.

The collection and recording of the Dataset was carried out under the following conditions (requirements):

- against a clear background, the signer in the signing space was wearing a black sweater;
- signs are shown only by native signers of Russian sign language;
- at least 5 repetitions of each sign by each RSL signer;
- at least 20 repetitions of each signs by different signer of RSL;
- before turning on the video recording, the signer is ready to stand and is silent in the signing space, after turning on the video recording, the signer is silent for 2–3 s, then speaks, then is silent for 2–3 s before turning off;
- not less than 1000 reproduced video words;
- the image resolution is not less than 1920x1080 and the frequency is not less than 30 frames per second.

Such actions should provide clean full informative sign examples in the dataset. However, in practice, we were faced with the presence of small phonological habits of signs in signers, which led to inconsistencies with the RSL vocabulary, for example, different handshapes and palm orientations, as well as the setting in the field of sign localization.

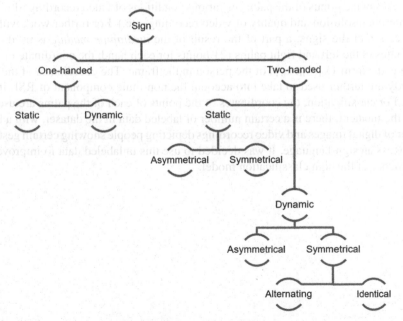

**Fig. 5.** Types of the signs.

The quality of the data labeling depends on the quality of the machine learning markup operator. The sign labeling was carried out in the *Supervisely.ly*[6] and *platform.ai*[7] software systems. The area of the palms and facial elements was highlighted. After collecting the signs, for the convenience of storage, the video file naming system was used, including the numbers of the signs, signer, and repetition, for example, file name *43_3_3.mp4* – gesture number 43, 3rd signer number in the list of informants, and 3rd repetition.

## 3    Methods for Recognizing Individual Signs in RSL

The algorithms are based on an approach to recognizing individual signs by the presence of a certain set of components – handshape-orientations, location, path and local movement, as well as non-manual components.

### 3.1    Recognizing Hand Signs

One of the blocks for creating the sign recognition model is the *mediapipe holistic*[8] library module. This module contains a group of pre-trained neural network algorithms that allow obtaining the coordinates of key points of the body, palms and face of a person in the image.

Using the *mediapipe holistic* module allows solving problems with obtaining the coordinates of the points of the palms in various conditions of video recording (different illumination, resolution and quality of video recording, etc.). For further work with the classification of the signs, a part of the result of the *mediapipe module* is used – the coordinates of the left and right palms (21 points for each hand, the coordinate of each point has the form $\{x_n, y_n, z_n\}$) of the person in the frame. The coordinates of the face and body are further used to take into account the non-mule component of RSL in the model. For classification, the coordinates of the points of each of the palms are used.

At the moment, there is a certain number of labeled data in the dataset, with a large number of digital images and video recordings depicting people showing certain gestures of the Russian sign language. It was decided to use this unlabeled data to improve the performance of the sign classification model.

---

[6] https://supervise.ly/.

[7] https://www.platform.ai/.

[8] https://google.github.io/mediapipe/solutions/holistic.htm.

The first stage of training a classifier model is training a sparse autoencoder, the purpose of which, based on unlabeled data, is to learn to transform the representation of palms in the form of coordinates into a more complex representation for classifying semantically complex feature spaces for palms.

The coordinates of the palms are 21 three-dimensional vectors $[\{x_1, y_1, z_1\} \dots \{x_n, y_n, z_n\}]$, which can be converted into 63 features for input into the neural network. It is worth noting that in addition to the coordinates of the points of the palms, a greater number of features can be distinguished, for example: the connection of the points of the palm, where the point of the fingertip is connected to the end point of the middle phalanx, and that, in turn, to the point of the end of the proximal phalanx of the finger. Another such example is the fact that the point of the base of the finger will always be at a relatively large (relative to the entire palm) distance in three-dimensional space. An even greater number of such examples can be derived from empirical observations of the palms of people, and in particular the positions of the palms in RSL (Fig. 6).

Hypothetically, such additional features can be generated on the basis of a large number of examples of palms, the number of which is about 1 million among the data at our disposal. Due to the regularization of the latent space in the sparse autoencoder, it becomes possible to generate the necessary additional features.

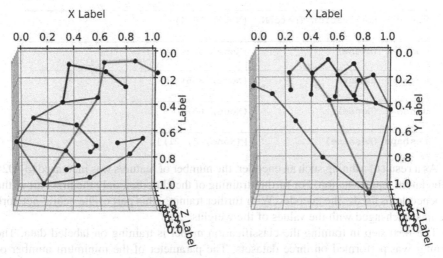

**Fig. 6.** An example of the palms points

Thus, the first stage of training the model is training the autoencoder on the corpus of unlabeled data. Autoencoder training made it possible to achieve 97.5% accuracy. The encoder model has the following structure.

```
Layer  (type)                    Output Shape              Param #
======================================================================

============= ====== Encoder Layers ===================
input_1 (InputLayer)            [(None, 3, 21)]                  0
_____
flatten (Flatten)               (None, 63)                       0
_____
dense (Dense)                   (None, 256)                  16384
_____
dense_1 (Dense)                 (None, 512)                 131584
_____
batch_normalization (BatchNo    (None, 512)         2048
_____
dense_2 (Dense)                 (None, 1024)                525312
_____
================= Decoder Layers ===================
input_2 (InputLayer)            (None, 1024)
_____
dense_3 (Dense)                 (None, 1024)
_____
batch_normalization (BatchNo    (None, 1024)
_____
dense_4 (Dense)                 (None, 512)
_____
dense_5 (Dense)                 (None, 256)
_____
dense_6 (Dense)                 (None, 63)
_____
reshape (Reshape)               [(None, 3, 21)]
```

As a result of training such an encoder, the number of features was increased to 1024 in the latent representation. For further training of the classifier, only the first part of the autoencoder is used – the encoder. With further training, this part of the neural network remains unchanged with the values of the weights.

The next step in training the classification model is training on labeled data. The training was performed on three datasets. The parameter of the minimum number of examples for training has been introduced, taken equal to 40. If the minimum number of class examples is not reached, the class label becomes "0" (does not apply to recognizable gestures). The basic model of the classifier we used is as follows.

```
Layer   (type)                    Output Shape                    Param #
=====================================================================

================= Encoder Layers ===================

input_1 (InputLayer)              [(None, 3, 21)]                 0

flatten (Flatten)                 (None, 63)                               0

dense (Dense)                     (None, 256)                          16384

dense_1 (Dense)                   (None, 512)                         131584

batch_normalization (BatchNo      (None, 512)            2048

dense_2 (Dense)                   (None, 1024)                        525312

================= Classification Layers ===================

dense (Dense)                     (None, 1024)                      1049600

dense_1 (Dense)                   (None, 2048)                      2099200

dense_2 (Dense)                   (None, 1024)                      2098176

batch_normalization (BatchNo      (None, 1024)           4096

dense_3 (Dense)                   (None, 53)                          54325
=====================================================================
```

The accuracy of 85% was achieved on the verification data. In the future, it is necessary to significantly increase the volume of the labeled data.

## 3.2 Recognition of Non-manual Components

Using the *mediapipe holistic* module allows solving problems with obtaining the coordinates of points of a face in various conditions of video recording (different illumination, resolution and quality of video recording, etc.).

To work with the classification of a non-manual component, a part of the result of the mediapipe module is used – the coordinates of the points of the face (468 points of the face, the coordinates of each of the points look like $\{x_n, y_n, z_n\}$) of the person in the frame. The points indicated in red on the image were selected as points of interest to control the movements of the lips and eyes (Fig. 7).

On each frame, the Euclidean distance between the points of the face is calculated. And the fact of movement is revealed empirically. For example, an eyebrow lift is an increase in the distance between the bottom of the eyebrow and the upper eyelid. Thus, a

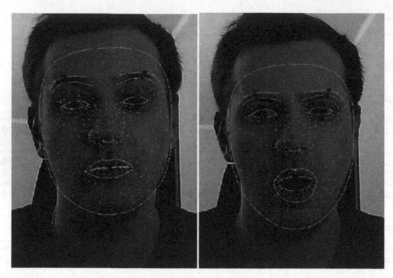

**Fig. 7.** Recognition of the non-manual components

number of rules have been drawn up that correspond to one or another movement of parts of the face. These rules include the conditions of the eyes, eyelids, mouth, tongue, and head tilt. We should note that *mediapipe holistic* does not have built-in identification of tongue points, so we worked with them in an indirect way, via overlap of the lips points. Our further plans involve precise recognition of the tongue with lips as the background.

## 4 Approaches to Isolating Epenthesis and Combinatorial Changes in the Sign Parameters

When recognizing continuous sign speech [11–13], it is necessary to highlight not only epenthesis, but also combinatorial changes in gesture parameters [9].

### 4.1 The Types of Combinatorial Changes in the Sign Parameters

The analysis of continuous speech in Russian sign language made it possible to reveal that in the speech flow in non-verbal languages there are processes of combinatorial changes in sign parameters comparable to combinatorial changes in sounds in the speech flow in the verbal language. So, under the influence of sounds on each other in sound languages, the processes of accommodation (partial adaptation of the articulations of adjacent sounds), assimilation (assimilation of the articulation of sounds), haplology (loss of sounds due to their dissimilation), dissimilation (distribution of the articulation of sounds, loss of common phonetic signs), dieresis (dieresis) (loss of sounds), metathesis (mutual rearrangement of sounds or syllables) and epenthesis (insertion of sounds) [14].

According to studies of RSL [9], continuous Russian sign language is characterized by the following combinatorial changes in gesture parameters.

*Loss of movement* occurs when a combination of signs or repetitive movement is used.

For statements in RSL, *handshape assimilation* and *location assimilation* are characteristic, in which the handshape and location become similar to the corresponding parameters of one of the neighboring gestures.

Statemin RSL are characterized by *perseveration*, i.e. holding by inertia in place of the passive hand instead of returning it to the resting position, which is observed when performing a one-handed sign after showing a two-handed sign.

*Anticipation*, i.e. preparing the passive hand in advance to perform a two-handed sign following a one-handed sign.

RSL is characterized by *metathesis*, i.e. permutation of the initial and final localizations when performing gestures with double localization.

In addition, RSL researchers refer to combinatorial changes in sign parameters as *reduction of movement*, which is execution of a movement with a smaller trajectory.

Taking into account the listed combinatorial changes in gestures is important in order not to mistake the signs with changes for new language units in the process of translating continuous Russian sign speech into Russian verbal language, in order to make the translation more accurate and adequate, to develop a model for teaching neural systems to translate from RSL into Russian sounding language.

## 4.2 Approaches to Continuous Sign Speech Recognition

In [3], an overview of works related to the isolation of epenthesis in world sign languages is given. The main idea is to highlight the signs of the beginning of the next sign or a pause in speech. This can be the state of rest of the signer, the position of the hands, gaze, etc. [15]. Techniques for isolating "fast" and "slow" movements in the video stream are also used. If the process of sign speech is reduced to the analysis of the sequence of identified components, then each such event is a "candidate" for the beginning of recognition of the next sign. In this case, it may turn out that the process of a new search will be launched until the previous one is completed. This approach to sign speech recognition is quite laborious. It seems that it can be modernized with the introduction of a membership function (or some probability) of each event to the beginning of a new sign. In this case, the algorithm for recognizing a new sign can be launched only after some of the most likely events. Another approach is to isolate all the elements of sign speech – the actual signs, the signer's resting state, combinatorial changes in signs and epenthesis. In this case, it is necessary to extend the dataset to recognize signs and other elements associated with combinatorial changes in signs. At the moment it is difficult to estimate the required amount of additions. Given the large number of types of combinatorial gesture changes, it can be significant.

Currently, we have implemented a variant of highlighting the beginning and end of a sign in a video stream based on the mediapipe tool. The trajectories of hand movements are analyzed, the leading and passive hands are highlighted, changes in the intensity of movements are noted. The recognition accuracy of the beginning and end of various types of signs averaged at 91%. An algorithm for recognizing the beginning and end of the display of a non-manual component was also implemented. In this case, mediapipe was also used. The main algorithm was based on the observation that during the display of the non-manual component, the coordinates of the key points of the lower and upper half of the face move away from their average values. The recognition accuracy for a sample of 100 video gests was 97%. To improve the accuracy of sign recognition, an algorithm was developed for highlighting their main types:

- Dynamic one-handed sign;
- Static one-handed sign;
- Dynamic two-handed sign of asymmetric movement;
- Static two-handed sign with asymmetric movement;
- Dynamic two-handed sign of symmetric identical movement;
- Dynamic two-handed sign of symmetric alternate movement;
- Static two-handed symmetric sign.

To solve this problem, the LSTM architecture was chosen [16], which allows processing sequences (Fig. 8).

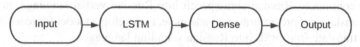

**Fig. 8.** Recognition of the sign types

The trained model for direct recognition of classes showed the probability of correct recognition of 80.3%. To improve the accuracy of determining the types of signs, it was decided to break the solution of the problem into several stages:

- Determine the type between two-handed and one-handed signs;
- Define static or dynamic sign;
- Determine symmetry or asymmetry;
- Determine the synchronicity or identical of movement.

As a result, the accuracy of determining one of the types (of the two) increased to 95%.

Work has begun on the construction of a dataset of movements-epentheses. A video of about 100 sentences for RSL has been formed, and the labeling of individual gestures and epentheses is underway. Upon completion of this work, we will be able to compare the above two approaches. The first relies on the highlighting of features of the beginning and end of signs. And the second is based on the formation of the epenthesis dataset and their isolation in continuous RSL. It should be also possible to combine these two approaches.

## 5   Discussion and Conclusions

The paper proposes an original approach to the recognition of RSL signs on the basis of identifying their components – the handshape and palm orientation, location of gesture display, path and local movement, as well as non-manual component. For the first time in Russia and in the world, the RSL dataset was developed, which includes more than thirty-five thousand elements of general video words (images and video files, of which more than ten thousand video files). More than a thousand RSL signs were selected. Each sign was performed with 5 repetitions and at least 5 deaf users of Russian Sign Language from Siberia.

To recognize hand gestures, the *mediapipe holistic* library module was employed. This module contains a group of pre-trained neural network algorithms that allow obtaining the coordinates of key points of the body, palms and face of a person in the image. An accuracy of 85% was achieved on the verification data. In the future, it is necessary to significantly increase the number of tagged data. To recognize non-manual components, a number of rules were drawn up that correspond to one or another movement of parts of the face. These rules include the conditions of the eyes, eyelids, mouth, tongue, and head tilt.

Two approaches to the recognition of continuous sign speech are considered, associated with a sequential enumeration of candidate events for the beginning of the execution of a subsequent sign and with a complete identification of speech elements – the signs themselves, the signer's resting state, combinatorial changes in sign parameters and epenthesis. A variant of highlighting the beginning and end of a sign in a video stream was implemented based on the mediapipe tool. The trajectories of hand movements are analyzed, the leading and passive hands are highlighted, changes in the intensity of movements are noted. The recognition accuracy of the beginning and end of various types of signs averaged as 91%. An algorithm for recognizing the beginning and end of the display of a non-manual component was also implemented. In this case, mediapipe was also used. The recognition accuracy for a sample of 100 video signs was 97%.

We also began working on the construction of a dataset of movements-epentheses. A video of about 100 sentences for RSL has been formed, marking of individual signs and epentheses is underway.

**Acknowledgment.** The reported study was funded by RFBR and DST according to the research project No. 19–57-45006.

# References

1. Grif, M.G., et al.: Lexical and grammatical aspects of the development of a computer sign language translator for the Russian language: monograph. Publications of NSTU292, p. (2013) .(in Russian)
2. Grif, M.G., Korolkova, O.O., Manueva, Y.S.: Machine translation of Russian sign language for the deaf. In Proceedings of 20th Conference Informatics: Problems, Methods, Technologies, Voronezh, pp. 1591–1597 (2020). (in Russian)
3. Elakkiya, R., et al.: Recognition of Russian and Indian sign languages used by the deaf people. Sci. Bull. NSTU 2–3(79), 57–76 (2020)
4. Gruber, I., Ryumin, D., Hrúz, M., Karpov, A.: Sign language numeral gestures recognition using convolutional neural network. In: Ronzhin, A., Rigoll, G., Meshcheryakov, R. (eds.) ICR 2018. LNCS (LNAI), vol. 11097, pp. 70–77. Springer, Cham (2018). https://doi.org/10. 1007/978-3-319-99582-3_8

5. Konstantinov, V.M., Orlova, Y.A., Rozaliev, V.L.: Development of a 3D model of the human body using MS Kinect. Izvestia VolgGTU: Actual Problems Manage. Comput. Technol. Inf. Techn. Syst. **6**(163), 65–69 (2015)
6. Kagirov, I., et al.: TheRuSLan: database of Russian sign language. In: Proceedings of the Conference on Language Resources and Evaluation (LREC), pp. 6079–6085 (2020)
7. Mukushev, M.A., et al.: Automatic classification of handshapes in russian sign language. In: Proceedings of the LREC 2020 9th Workshop on the Representation and Processing of Sign Languages: Sign Language Resources in the Service of the Language Community, Technological Challenges and Application Perspectives, p. 165–169 (2020)
8. Kimmelman, V., Imashev, A., Mukushev, M., Sandygulova, A.: Eyebrow position in grammatical and emotional expressions in Kazakh-Russian sign language: a quantitative study. PLOS ONE **15**(6), e0233731 (2020). https://doi.org/10.1371/journal.pone.0233731
9. Burkova, S.I., et al.: Introduction to the linguistics of sign languages. Russian sign language: textbook. Publishing house of NSTU, Novosibirsk (2019). 356 p. (in Russian)
10. Bazoev, V.Z.: Dictionary of Russian Sign Language. FLINT, Moscow (2009), 528 p. (in Russian)
11. Athira, P.K., Sruthi, C.J., Lijiya, A.: A signer independent sign language recognition with co-articulation elimination from live videos: an Indian scenario. J. King Saud Univ. Comput. Inf. Sci. (2019). https://doi.org/10.1016/j.jksuci.2019.05.002
12. Joshi, G., Vig, R., Singh, S.: Analysis of Zernike moment-based features for sign language recognition. In: Singh, R., Choudhury, S., Gehlot, A. (eds.) Intelligent Communication, Control and Devices. AISC, vol. 624, pp. 1335–1343. Springer, Singapore (2018). https://doi.org/10.1007/978-981-10-5903-2_140
13. Kumar, D.A., et al.: S3DRGF: spatial 3-D relational geometric features for 3-D sign language representation and recognition. IEEE Signal Process. Lett. **26**(1), 169–173 (2019)
14. Yartseva, V.N.: Linguistic Encyclopedic Dictionary. Soviet Encyclopedia, Moscow (1990), 683 p. (in Russian)
15. Kebets, P.L.: Markers of the transition in the discourse of Russian sign language. In: Proc. 7th Conference on Typology and Grammar for Young Researchers (St. Petersburg), pp. 75–80 (2010). (in Russian)
16. Graves, A., et al.: Speech recognition with deep recurrent neural networks. In: IEEE International Conference on Acoustics, Speech and Signal Processing (ICASSP), pp. 6645–6649 (2013)

# Digital Inclusion Through Sustainable Web Accessibility

Radka Nacheva(✉) [iD]

University of Economics-Varna, 77 Knyaz Boris I Blvd, 9002 Varna, Bulgaria
r.nacheva@ue-varna.bg

**Abstract.** In the age of digitalization, the business environment is changing dynamically due to the growing consumers' demands of the products and services provided. In an effort to respond to rapidly changing market requirements, companies restrict access to their products of certain user groups with special needs due to neglecting of imposed international accessibility standards. This can even lead to disruption of the communication equipment of people with disabilities in the digital environment, which is often the only possible one. The Web remains the largest source of information used by people around the world today. Communication on the Internet is the most common. That is why achieving web accessibility is not an end in itself, but a necessity for digital inclusion of people with special needs. In this regard, the aim of the article is to propose a web accessibility audit approach that follows a well-defined sequence of stages and applies automated tools to study the accessibility issues. The approach has been tested by auditing the accessibility of educational institutions' websites in Russia and Bulgaria.

**Keywords:** Sustainable web accessibility · Web accessibility audit · Web accessibility standards · Digital inclusion · Digitalization

## 1 Introduction

The digital transformation in all business spheres has imposed almost imperative changes in terms of fundamental internal and external organizational processes. The communication channels with customers are changing rapidly. The companies are in constant competition with each other in order to provide competitive digital services, to attract and retain their audience. But in their quest to meet the dynamically changing market demand, they limit the access to their products (both software and hardware) of vulnerable groups in society who have special needs in terms of working with information and communication technologies (ICT). Digital division is observed by violating the fundamental user right to access public services [38] and not reducing inequality between people around the world through their social inclusion [39]. As some authors point out, the term refers to the unequal access of some members of society to information and communication technologies and the uneven acquisition of knowledge and skills related to them [21]. This increases inequality between consumer groups, especially in poor and rural areas, among the elderly and people with disabilities who do not have access to computers or the Internet. On the other hand, people with special needs who have an Internet connection and appropriate software and hardware equipment, also experience difficulties in accessing digital products and services due to non-compliance with basic standards and recommendations.

It is a matter of legal discussion whether ICT should also comply with the legislation specifying the rights of people with disabilities when integrating them into the social environment. For example, the European Commission is defining a European Pillar of Social Rights to build a more inclusive and fairer European Union, set out in twenty key principles [11]. It has 3 main categories: "Equal opportunities and access to the labour market"; "Fair working conditions" and "Social protection and inclusion". Two of the key principles are "Inclusion of people with disabilities" and "Access to essential services", which include digital communications [12].

The cited documents are far from the only ones that direct the attention of business to the construction of "digital bridges" through which to overcome the digital divide with the vulnerable groups of society. They are a starting point that companies can use to implement so-called "digital inclusion". In order for applying it in practice to people with special needs, the accessibility standards and recommendations must be strictly followed. Also, the digital products and services must be developed in accordance with the peculiarities of the computer or mobile assistive technologies.

Referring to the current situation of ICT market share, it can be said that the Web has become a major source of information for people around the world. In 2020, it was estimated that 4.66 billion people or approximately 59% of the world's population had an active connection to the Internet, with 4.28 billion unique mobile Internet users [34]. For the previous 2019, they were 4.48 Internet and 4.07 billion mobile Internet users [33]. In 2019, International Telecommunication Union (ITU) statistics show that Internet users were 51% or approximately 4 billion people worldwide [19]. According to both sources, there is an increase in Internet consumption, which is a prerequisite for increasing competition between companies providing digital products and services. In parallel with these data, the proportional growth of the web presence must be taken into account. As of January 2021, Internet Live Stats states that there are 1.83 billion worldwide websites and that they are constantly growing [41].

On the other hand, it should be borne in mind that for certain groups of people, communication in a digital environment is the only one possible in context of the disabilities they have. The type of disability (e.g., mental, sensory, voice and speech, neuromuscu-loskeletal and movement-related [44], etc.) implies not only compliance with various formal guidelines through which web accessibility is achieved. The use of various computer or mobile assistive technologies should be also taken into account. These are an additional constraint in the development of accessible ICT. In addition, with age, people face many challenges in perceiving information from the environment, controlling their own movements, rejecting methods and techniques that have been applicable in the past [2, 3].

In this regard, the **aim of the article** is to propose a web accessibility audit approach that follows a well-defined sequence of stages and applies automated tools to study the accessibility issues. The following objectives should be achieved:

- examination of international web accessibility frameworks;
- exploration of the theoretical frameworks for web accessibility audit, including evaluation and testing processes.

The approach has been tested by auditing the accessibility of educational institutions' websites in Russia and Bulgaria. The study has potential limitations of the chosen design and collected data. In the first place, they are related to insufficient sample size for statistical measurement and in particular, this is the number of examined websites. They have been used to demonstrate the practical applicability of the accessibility audit approach proposed in this paper. Another limitation of the study is related to instruments used to collect the data - WAVE and HTML_CodeSniffer. They are based on a different number of web content accessibility standards, which results in differences in outputs. If other tools are used, they may show different results from those of the selected ones.

## 2  Literature Review

The efforts of specialists and scientists working in the field of human-computer interaction are mainly aimed at minimizing the barriers between people's mental models in terms of fulfilling their goals and technological support of their tasks. In the paradigm of user-oriented design, the product is designed in accordance with the expectations of its potential users. It should be usable and accessible to a wide range of people with special needs.

The development of user-oriented technologies is related to compliance with the standards [4, 37], recommendations and good practices [32], defined by international and national organizations, as well as by leading IT specialists. The concept of accessibility is quite broad. It can affect a variety of areas, from the arts through transport to computer systems and technologies. To meet the purpose of this article, the author limits the research scope to web accessibility issues. The attention is targeted to the international web accessibility frameworks and guidelines.

International standards set recommendations aimed at eliminating accessibility problems from the point of view of people with various disabilities. There are several benefits of meeting the standards when developing IT products, in particular websites, such as:

- Improving the digital products' quality;
- Compatibility with various specialized assistance technologies;
- Reliability of the digital products, including quality, safety, compatibility with the requirements for international and national regulatory bodies;
- Maintaining customer satisfaction with the company's products;
- Social and digital inclusion of people with special needs;
- Increasing the sustainability of the company by demonstrating social commitment.

The main international organizations that develop accessibility standards for software and hardware products are the International Organization for Standardization (ISO), the European Telecommunications Standards Institute (ETSI) and the World Wide Web Consortium (W3C). Table 1 summarizes the main characteristics of existing web accessibility standards [9, 10, 17, 42].

**Table 1.** Web accessibility standards.

| Standard | Last version | Issuer | Formal approach | Target group | Revision period |
|----------|--------------|--------|-----------------|--------------|-----------------|
| WCAG 2.1 | 2018 | W3C | No | sensory, cognitive, motor, speech disabilities | 10 years |
| ISO 9241–171 | 2008 | ISO | No | physical, sensory and cognitive impairments, elderly people, people with temporary disabilities | 5 years |
| ETSI EG 202 116 | 2009 | ETSI | No | sensory, cognitive, motor, speech disabilities, allergies | - |
| ETSI ES 202 975 | 2015 | ETSI | No | sensory, cognitive, motor, speech disabilities | - |

Source: Own Elaboration

The period of the last revision of the standards is relatively long - between 5 and 10 years. Changes have recently been made to W3C's standard WCAG 2.1 – in 2018, which is practically one of the most used. Each of the standards covers the diverse requirements of a wide range of people with special needs, including the elderly. They are organized into sections according to the type of modalities.

The number of standards is far from limited to those listed in Table 1. Some countries have formalized web accessibility recommendations at the national level. These are: Sect. 508 of USA government, Japanese accessibility standard JIS X 8341, Nordic Council of Ministers' Guidelines for Computer Accessibility, Spain's accessibility standards UNE 139801 and UNE 139804 [13], etc. They are applicable at the local level, but are nevertheless based on international frameworks.

None of these standards offers a formal approach to web accessibility examination, including its evaluation or testing.

A wider range of publications should be studied. Some authors research only the process of web accessibility evaluation [6–8, 16, 24, 25, 28, 35]. Others justify only the testing process [1, 5, 22, 26, 29, 30, 36]. A web accessibility audit process is described in [14, 40], but the stages are not clearly defined. Rather, steps to web accessibility audit are presented, but not a structured, controllable process. No information was found for a clear grouping of the applied methods and tools, which would correspond to their in-stage application.

For this reason, there is a need to approach conceptually, looking for solutions that are aimed at auditing information systems. For example, [23] states that the audit takes place in the following stages:

- Analysis and planning – the main activities are related to liaising with the client, describing the requirements, reviewing reports, files and other sources of information from the organization, creating an audit plan;
- Field work – in this phase a representative sample is selected, subject to audit; tests are conducted and documented; a comparison of the obtained results with the planned ones is made, forming conclusions;
- Creating a report – a final evaluation of the results is prepared; draft of the report, which is discussed with the client; a schedule for resolving the findings is created; a final report is prepared;
- Follow-up activities – the audit is evaluated, including a follow-up report with the actions taken by the client to address the findings in the original report.

Another possible high-level solution is defined by ISO 9001: 2015. This is a process approach that "can be applied to any organization and any management system regardless of type, size or complexity" [18]. As mentioned in [15, 20, 27], it has an important role in managing the quality of IT products. The approach is designed to achieve better coordination and control of the internal organizational environment, documenting processes and setting responsibilities at a horizontal organizational level. Key elements of the process approach are: input; output; resources; process owner; process indicators.

In view of the above, the author considers that the web accessibility audit should be a structured process based on international formal frameworks, with well-founded stages and clearly defined requirements. The next section of the article describes the author's proposal in detail.

## 3   Approach to Web Accessibility Audit

This article proposes a web accessibility audit based on the process approach (Fig. 1) and the main phases of information systems audit described in [23]. It consists of several elements: input data; process stages; result artifacts and constraints.

The input data of the process are the requirements of the users, the objectives of the study and the website or its prototype, which is subject to audit.

This article offers the following audit phases: Designing; Examination; Expert evaluation; Reporting; Follow-up control. The *Audit designing* stage is related to setting audit objectives, resources and indicators. The objectives of the audit derive from the objectives of the study, which are obtained as an input to the process. The resources also come from the objectives of the research. In general, these are technical equipment (both software and hardware), documentation, financial framework. Audit indicators should be in line with the set high-level objectives. They are usually a combination of quantitative and qualitative characteristics of the audit, which are reported through the achieved

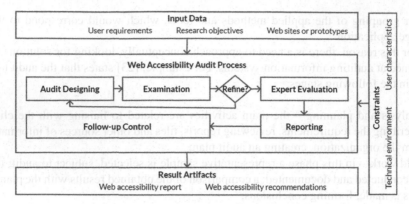

**Fig. 1.** Proposed process approach to web accessibility audit source: own elaboration

final results. These are the number of errors on the website or its prototype, the number of warnings, the availability of additional tools to improve accessibility, adaptable color scheme, assistive technologies' compatibility, etc.

The *Examination* stage is targeted to testing the compliance with established international web accessibility standards based on the extracted unique features of the website. Specialized testing software is used. The phase should be conducted in two sub-stages – preliminary and actual testing, for greater accuracy of the final results. During the preliminary testing, a verification is made for the applicability of the audit plan and indicators. If necessary, refinements are made to those parts of the plan or to indicators that not meet the audit objectives. Then they are reduced to their final form and the actual testing is carried out.

The *Expert evaluation* is conducted by the process owner – the person who is responsible for the final result of the audit. According to [6, 7, 24], the most commonly used methods are Barrier Walkthrough, Conformance Reviews, Screening Techniques. They are based on an expert assessment that takes into account pre-defined accessibility criteria. The criteria depend on the disability group. They can comply with international and / or national accessibility standards or with expert heuristics.

The evaluation results are summarized and moved to the *Reporting* phase. The reports include the final assessment of the web accessibility and recommendations for its improvement. They are usually made in free form, as there is no single established format. It is advisable to refer to the audit plan, indicating whether it has been completed on time and whether the indicators have been met.

By default, as with information systems auditing, this article proposes the *Follow-up control* as a final phase of the web accessibility audit. The purpose is to monitor whether the recommendations for improving the web accessibility are being implemented.

As audit's output artifacts, a report on web accessibility and recommendations for its improvement are obtained.

The process takes place under certain restrictive conditions: the individual characteristics of the users and the technical environment. The latter is the set of assistive technologies and other software and hardware to access the websites, such as browsers, operating systems, network devices. The individual characteristics of people determine the tools that they will use. Each type of disability requires the use of various assistive technologies - software and hardware.

The next section summarizes the results of testing the proposed approach to web accessibility audit.

# 4 Results

To test the process approach to web accessibility audit, 6 Russian and 6 Bulgarian university websites (Table 2). They offer study programmes in Economics. The websites are not a representative sample of Bulgarian and Russian academic sites. They were randomly selected to be used to test the proposed approach.

**Table 2.** Universities' websites list

| University | Code | Website |
|---|---|---|
| Plekhanov Russian University of Economics | PRUE | https://www.rea.ru/en/ |
| South Ural State University | SUSU | https://www.susu.ru/en |
| Lomonosov Moscow State University | LMSU | https://www.msu.ru/en/ |
| Vladivostok State University of Economics and Service | VVSU | https://eng.vvsu.ru/ |
| Saint Petersburg State University of Economics | SPSUE | https://en.unecon.ru/ |
| East Siberian Institute of Economics and Management | VSIEM | http://vsiem.ru/ |
| University of Economics - Varna | UEV | https://www.ue-varna.bg/ |
| University of National and World Economy | UNWE | https://www.unwe.bg |
| D.A. Tsenov Academy of Economics | AEDT | https://www.uni-svishtov.bg |
| Plovdiv university "Paisii Hilendarski" | PHUP | https://uni-plovdiv.bg/ |
| Sofia University "St. Kliment Ohridski" | SUKO | https://www.uni-sofia.bg |
| "Angel Kanchev" University of Ruse | AKUR | https://www.uni-ruse.bg |

Source: Own Elaboration

The audit designing stage requires the setting-up the web accessibility evaluation methodology. In this article it is proposed to include: indicators for assessing accessibility with assigned weight and a formula for calculating websites' accessibility rank; tools for performing automated testing.

The following audit indicators have been identified:

• Number of errors and warnings for non-compliance with the recommendations of the web accessibility standards – they are extracted through web accessibility testing tools;
• Availability of tools to improve the web accessibility – they are included as plug-ins on the websites, which are activated by a keyboard shortcut or a button from the main menu.

Additional criteria may be set to extend the scope of the audit. For example, to assess the compatibility of websites with assistive technologies, if the accessibility for a specific group of users with disabilities is studied. If the object of the study are users who access sites with mobile devices, a mobile-friendly version should be examined. Website speed test is another possible indicator.

Two error testing tools were used to perform the Examination phase of the audit - WAVE and HTML_CodeSniffer. The first one is "a suite of evaluation tools that helps authors make their web content more accessible to individuals with disabilities that can identify many accessibilities and Web Content Accessibility Guideline (WCAG) errors" [43]. "HTML_CodeSniffer is a client-side script that checks HTML source code and detects violations of a defined coding standard < ... > the three conformance levels of the Web Content Accessibility Guidelines (WCAG) 2.1, and the web-related components of the U.S. "Sect. 508" legislation" [31]. A comparison was made between the initial results of the two applications.

The weight of the indicators is determined depending on testing tools' outputs:

- WAVE's weights: errors – 3; contrast errors – 2; alerts – 1;
- HTML_CodeSniffer's weights: errors – 3; warnings – 2; notices – 1.
- Accessibility tools' weight: 4.

A formula for calculating the points of the web accessibility audit is suggested. It is based on the weight of each of the criteria:

$$R = \frac{\sum_{j=1}^{n} i * w_j}{a * w_a + \sum_{j=1}^{n} w_j} \tag{1}$$

Where:

- $i$ – number of web accessibility issues within a certain group;
- $w_j$ – weight of a certain web accessibility issue;
- $a$ – availability of accessibility tools (available - 1, not available - 0);
- $w_a$ – weight of accessibility tools.

The ranking of universities is determined depending on the number of points obtained, arranged in ascending order. The website with the fewest points ranks first, as its test results show that it has the least number of accessibility issues.

The Examination phase requires the application of the testing tools identified at the previous stage. The results of the extracted number of accessibility problems (errors, alerts, notices) serve as a basis for performing the next stage of the audit - the Expert evaluation. The results of using WAVE are summarized in Table 3.

**Table 3.** Websites' rankings based on WAVE's results[1]

| Website Code | Errors | Contrast Errors | Alerts | Accessibility tools | Points | Rank |
|---|---|---|---|---|---|---|
| PRUE | 110 | 7 | 150 | 1 | 49.4 | 12 |
| SUSU | 16 | 8 | 30 | 1 | 9.4 | 5 |
| LMSU | 6 | 0 | 8 | 1 | 2.6 | 1 |
| VVSU | 25 | 31 | 10 | 0 | 24.5 | 8 |
| SPSUE | 17 | 92 | 138 | 1 | 37.3 | 10 |
| VSIEM | 21 | 2 | 4 | 1 | 7.1 | 4 |
| UEV | 8 | 0 | 13 | 0 | 6.17 | 3 |
| UNWE | 22 | 11 | 174 | 0 | 43.67 | 11 |
| AEDT | 4 | 28 | 64 | 0 | 22 | 7 |
| PHUP | 2 | 1 | 45 | 1 | 5.3 | 2 |
| SUKO | 3 | 54 | 89 | 0 | 34.34 | 9 |
| AKUR | 9 | 5 | 29 | 0 | 11 | 6 |

Source: Own Elaboration

The results of the audit show that the most of the examined Russian websites have accessibility tools. They are added as a website plugin, which is activated via a button from the main menu. Only one of the Bulgarian websites has additional accessibility tools - PHUP. The others solve accessibility problems only by reducing the errors number. In the first three places are the websites of LMSU, PHUP and UEV, as the errors according to WCAG 2.1 are the least numerous.

For comparison, it is applied HTML_CodeSniffer to retrieve accessibility issues. The results are summarized in Table 4.

Because HTML_CodeSniffer examines nonconformances with two standards at the same time [31], the results differ from those of WAVE. More errors and warnings are retrieved compared to WAVE. For this reason, the websites' ranking is changing. In the first three places are LMSU, SUSU and PHUP that all support accessibility tools.

The last phase of the web accessibility audit requires a summary of the recommendations for troubleshooting accessibility issues. The most common are related to:

- adding alternative text to images;
- adding title to the links;

---

[1] The websites' issues in the table were retrieved on March 15, 2021.

**Table 4.** Websites' rankings based on HTML_CodeSniffer's results[2]

| Website Code | Errors | Warnings | Notices | Accessibility tools | Points | Rank |
|---|---|---|---|---|---|---|
| PRUE | 161 | 181 | 644 | 1 | 148.9 | 12 |
| SUSU | 17 | 39 | 261 | 1 | 39 | 2 |
| LMSU | 12 | 5 | 102 | 1 | 14.8 | 1 |
| VVSU | 31 | 62 | 228 | 0 | 74.17 | 8 |
| SPSUE | 116 | 76 | 243 | 1 | 74.3 | 9 |
| VSIEM | 94 | 30 | 182 | 1 | 52.4 | 5 |
| UEV | 43 | 53 | 150 | 0 | 64.17 | 6 |
| UNWE | 22 | 68 | 374 | 0 | 96 | 11 |
| AEDT | 3 | 26 | 378 | 0 | 73.17 | 7 |
| PHUP | 4 | 52 | 313 | 1 | 42.9 | 3 |
| SUKO | 45 | 61 | 200 | 0 | 76.17 | 10 |
| AKUR | 13 | 35 | 196 | 0 | 50.84 | 4 |

Source: Own Elaboration

- removing or revising the purpose of blank links;
- reviewing the purpose of the headings and setting the correct hierarchical levels;
- revision of the text sizes;
- form fields should be labelled in some way;
- button elements do not have names available to an accessibility API;
- contrast should be tested when background gradients, transparency, etc. are present;
- a CSS background color that provides sufficient contrast must be defined when a background image is in place.

## 5   Discussion

This paper proposes a process approach to web accessibility audit that would assist usability and accessibility experts, web developers, front-end designers in examining the compatibility of websites with established international standards. The following stages are suggested: Designing; Examination; Expert evaluation; Reporting; Follow-up control. There are integrated automation web accessibility testing tools (WAVE and HTML_CodeSniffer) that retrieve errors, alerts and other specific accessibility issues. The applications are based on international standard WCAG 2.1 and US' Sect. 508. The following indicators have been taken into account when assessing web accessibility: number of errors and warnings for non-compliance with the recommendations of the web accessibility standards; availability of tools to improve the web accessibility.

To test the applicability of the approach, 12 university websites were randomly selected. They were tested in parallel with both tools to compare the results. According

---

[2] The websites' issues in the table were retrieved on March 15, 2021.

to the WAVE's results in the first three places are the websites of LMSU, PHUP and UEV due to the smallest numbers of web accessibility errors and warnings. The application of HTML_CodeSniffer generated a different output. The first three places are taken by LMSU, SUSU and PHUP, all of which have web accessibility tools.

The LMSU's website have the fewest errors and additional accessibility tools are available to users. This secured its first place in the rankings in both tests. The results of the approbation of the approach show that the indicators for assessing web accessibility are not fully met. Most audited Russian sites support accessibility tools, while Bulgarian ones rely on reducing code errors. They follow good programming practices, but not international web accessibility standards and recommendations.

In this way, some people with special needs are restricted in using the relevant web content. For example, web accessibility tools, which integrate five Russian universities and one Bulgarian one, provide:

- alternative color schemes that are suitable for people with color blindness;
- changing the font size, which is useful for visually impaired people;
- changing the distance between the letters and the font type (serif or sans-serif), which helps people with dyslexia to better perceive web content.

Based on the results of the audit, it can be summarized that web accessibility have to be achieved simultaneously by following good coding practices and providing tools to modify web user interfaces. Only in this way should the widest possible range of accessibility issues will be covered.

## 6  Conclusion

Thanks to the rapid development of modern technologies, this user with special needs has equal access to the environment around them, can handle computer resources freely, get opportunities to learn and achieving their better professional realization - their full inclusion in modern dynamic life. In today's conditions of rapid development of information technology and the growing demands of business to employees, web accessibility is not an end in itself, but a necessity and a prerequisite for overcoming barriers between people.

The accessibility issues of digital products and services are becoming more and more topical, especially in moments of social distance. Access to public resources is a fundamental right of people to achieve independence and autonomy. The web space reaches enormous amount of information, much of which is inaccessible to people with disabilities. A better understanding of accessibility issues through the application of audit approaches would contribute to the digital inclusion of a wider range of people. A similar approach is proposed in this paper, which can be used not only in academic websites' accessibility audit, but also in any type of web content.

**Acknowledgments.** The publication is made within project No. 8.2.2.0/18/A/021 "Perfection of the Academic Staff of Liepaja University in the Areas of Strategic Specialization – Natural Sciences, Mathematics and Information Technologies, Art, Social Sciences, Commerce and Law".

# References

1. Abduganiev, S.: Towards automated web accessibility evaluation: a comparative study. Int. J. Inf Technol. Comput. Sci. **9**, 18–44 (2017)
2. Aletdinova, A., Razumnikova, O., Bakaev, M.: Do I Need IT? Russian Pensioners' Engagement with Information and Communication Technologies. CEUR Proceedings of International Conference "Internet and Modern Society" (IMS-2020), p. 199 – 212, St. Petersburg (2020)
3. Bakaev, M., Ponomarev, V., Prokhorova, L.: E-learning and elder people: Barriers and benefits. 2008 IEEE Region 8 International Conference on Computational Technologies in Electrical and Electronics Engineering, pp. 110–113, Novosibirsk, Russia (2008)
4. Bankov, B.: Game design principles in enterprise web applications. 20 conference proceedings of international multidisciplinary scientific geoconference SGEM 2020. Vol. 20. Informatics, Geoinformatics and Remote Sensing. Inform. Geoinform. 161 – 167. STEF 1992 Technology Ltd. (2020)
5. Bogdanova, G., et al.: Accessibility Testing of Digital Cultural Heritage. Conference Proceedings of Digital Presentation and Preservation of Cultural and Scientific Heritage, vol. 10, pp. 213–218. Institute of Mathematics and Informatics – BAS (2020)
6. Brajnik, G.: A comparative test of web accessibility evaluation methods. In Proceedings of the 10th International ACM SIGACCESS Conference on Computers and Accessibility (Assets 2008), pp. 113–120. Association for Computing Machinery, New York, NY, USA (2008). DOI:https://doi.org/10.1145/1414471.1414494
7. Brajnik, G.: Beyond conformance: the role of accessibility evaluation methods. In: Hartmann, S., Zhou, X., Kirchberg, M. (eds.) WISE 2008. LNCS, vol. 5176, pp. 63–80. Springer, Heidelberg (2008). https://doi.org/10.1007/978-3-540-85200-1_9
8. Brajnik, G.: Towards a sustainable web accessibility. https://users.dimi.uniud.it/~giorgio.brajnik/papers/york08.pdf. Accessed 21 Feb 2021
9. ETSI: Human Factors (HF) - Guidelines for ICT products and services - "Design for All" (ETSI EG 202 116: 2009). https://www.etsi.org/deliver/etsi_eg/202100_202199/202116/01.02.02_60/eg_202116v010202p.pdf. Accessed 21 Feb 2021
10. ETSI: Human Factors (HF); Requirements for relay services (ETSI ES 202 975:2015). https://www.etsi.org/deliver/etsi_es/202900_202999/202975/02.01.01_60/es_202975v020101p.pdf. Accessed 21 Feb 2021
11. European Commission: European Pillar of Social Rights. https://ec.europa.eu/info/strategy/priorities-2019-2024/economy-works-people/deeper-and-fairer-economic-and-monetary-union/european-pillar-social-rights_en. Accessed 21 Feb 20211
12. European Commission: The European Pillar of Social Rights in 20 principles, https://ec.europa.eu/commission/priorities/deeper-and-fairer-economic-and-monetary-union/european-pillar-social-rights/european-pillar-social-rights-20-principles_en. Accessed 21 Feb 2021
13. European Commission: Standards: ICT and communication - Accessibility and design for all, https://ec.europa.eu/eip/ageing/standards/ict-and-communication/accessibility-and-design-for-all_en.html, last accessed 2021/02/21
14. Gay, G.: Professional Web Accessibility Auditing Made Easy: Essential Skills for Web Developers, Content Creators, and Designers. Ryerson University Pressbooks (2019)
15. Gazovaa, A., Papulova, Z., Papula, J.: The application of concepts and methods based on process approach to increase business process efficiency. Procedia Econ. Fin. **39**, 197–205 (2016)
16. Giannakoulopoulos, A.: Threefold web accessibility evaluation by the use of an integrated tool. In :Proceedings of the 2nd International Conference on Social and Organizational Informatics and Cybernetics, SOIC 2006, July 20–23, vol. 2, pp. 243–248 (2006)

17. ISO: Ergonomics of human-system interaction — Part 171: Guidance on software accessibility (ISO 9241-171:2008). https://www.iso.org/obp/ui/#iso:std:iso:9241:-171:ed-1:v1:en, Accessed 21 Feb 2021
18. ISO: The Process Approach in ISO 9001:2015. https://www.iso.org/files/live/sites/isoorg/files/archive/pdf/en/iso9001-2015-process-appr.pdf. Accessed 21 Feb 2021
19. ITU: Percentage of Internet users. https://www.itu.int/en/ITU-D/Statistics/Pages/stat/default.aspx. Accessed 21 Feb 2021
20. Jasińska, J.: Hab: the process approach to manage changes in the organization. J. Hotel and Business Manag. **8**, 193 (2019)
21. Kaneva, M.: Digital Divide of the Balkan countries Comparative Statistical Analysis. Izvestia. J. Union. Sci. –Varna. Econ. Sci. Ser, **2**, 158–168 (2017)
22. Kumar, S., JeevithaShree D.V., Biswas, P.: Accessibility evaluation of websites using WCAG tools and Cambridge Simulator. https://arxiv.org/ftp/arxiv/papers/2009/2009.06526.pdf. c
23. Kuyumdzhiev, I.: Audit of Information Systems. Publishing House "Science and Economics", Varna (2018). (In Bulgarian)
24. Lang, T.: Comparing website accessibility evaluation methods and learnings from usability evaluation methods. http://www.peakusability.com.au/about-us/pdf/website_accessibility.pdf. Accessed 21 Jan 2021/01/21
25. Litman, T.: Evaluating accessibility for transport planning evaluating accessibility for transportation planning. Victoria Transp. Policy Inst. **49**, 1–10 (2008). https://doi.org/10.1016/j.jth.2017.05.359
26. Martín, Y.-S., Yelmo, J.: Guidance for the development of accessibility evaluation tools following the unified software development process. Proc. Comput. Sci. **27**, 302–311 (2014)
27. Pavlov, P.: Methods of improving the process approach in assessing the efficiency of university quality management systems. Int. J. Inf. Models Anal. **7**(2), 142–151 (2018)
28. Salvador-Ullauri, L., Acosta-Vargas, P., Gonzalez, M., Luján-Mora, S.: A heuristic method for evaluating accessibility in web-based serious games for users with low vision. Appl. Sci. **10**(24), 8803 (2020). https://doi.org/10.3390/app10248803
29. Sánchez-Gordón, M.-L., Moreno, L.: Toward an integration of Web accessibility into testing processes. Proc. Comput. Sci. **27**, 281–291 (2014)
30. Shawar, B.: Evaluating web accessibility of educational websites. Int. J. Emerg. Technol. Learn. (iJET) **10**(4), 4–10 (2017)
31. Squiz: HTML_CodeSniffer. http://squizlabs.github.io/HTML_CodeSniffer/. Accessed 2 Feb 2021
32. Stancu, A., Cristescu, M., Stoyanova, M.: Data mining algorithms for knowledge extraction. In: Fotea, S.L., Fotea, I.Ş, Văduva, S.A. (eds.) GSMAC 2019. SPBE, pp. 349–357. Springer, Cham (2020). https://doi.org/10.1007/978-3-030-43449-6_20
33. Statista.com: Global digital population as of October 2019 (in millions). https://www.statista.com/statistics/617136/digital-population-worldwide/. Accessed 2 Feb 2021
34. Statista.com: Global digital population as of October 2020 (in billions). https://www.statista.com/statistics/617136/digital-population-worldwide/. Accessed 2 Feb 2021
35. Tanaka, E., Bim, S., Vieira da Rocha, H.: Comparing accessibility evaluation and usability evaluation in HagáQuê. In: Proceedings of the 2005 Latin American conference on Human-computer interaction (CLIHC 2005), pp. 139–147. Association for Computing Machinery, New York, NY, USA (2005)
36. Timbi-Sisalima, C., et.al.: Comparative analysis of online web accessibility evaluation tools. In: Proceedings of 25TH International Conference on Information Systems Development (ISD2016 Poland), pp. 562–573 (2016)
37. Todoranova, L., Penchev, B.: A conceptual framework for mobile learning development in higher education. In: Proceedings of the 21st International Conference on Computer Systems and Technologies 2020, pp. 251–257. Association for Computing Machinery (2020)

38. United Nations: Universal Declaration of Human Rights. https://www.un.org/en/universal-declaration-human-rights/index.html. Accessed 2 Feb 2021
39. United Nations: Reduce inequality within and among countries. https://sdgs.un.org/goals/goal10. Accessed 2 Feb 2021
40. Vorozheykina, O.: Web accessibility audit: a case study. University of Applied Sciences Haaga-Helia (2019)
41. W3C: Internet Live Stats. https://www.internetlivestats.com/. Accessed 21 Feb 2021
42. W3C: Web Content Accessibility Guidelines (WCAG 2.1:2018). https://www.w3.org/TR/WCAG21/. Accessed 21 Feb 2021
43. WebAIM: WAVE Web Accessibility Evaluation Tool. https://wave.webaim.org/. Accessed 21 Feb 2021
44. Flaherty, L., Zimmerman, D., Hansen, T.H.: Further serological analysis of the Qa antigens: analysis of an anti-H-2.28 serum. Immunogenetics 6(1), 245–251 (1978). https://doi.org/10.1007/BF01563914

# Lövheim Cube-Backed Emotion Analysis: From Classification to Regression

Anastasia Kolmogorova(✉) ⓘ, Alexander Kalinin ⓘ, and Alina Malikova ⓘ

Siberian Federal University, 82a Svobodny Avenue, 660041 Krasnoyarsk, Russian Federation

**Abstract.** Nowadays sentiment and emotion analyses are widespread methodologies. However, most of all related tasks in classification manner use discrete classes as target variables: Positive vs Negative (sometimes accompanied by Neutral class), or discrete emotion classes (as Anger, Joy, Fear, etc.). Nonetheless, it is more likely that emotion is not discrete. In this paper, we argue that regression is more natural way to evaluate and predict emotions in text and apply regression framework in study of using Lövheim Cube emotional model for emotion analysis. A regression approach for predicting a point in 3-d space or a configuration of its diagonals can provide us with detailed analytics from an emotional diversity perspective. The preliminary results on regression values prediction performed by five different models demonstrate the need of optimization in regard to a precision. The additional conclusion is that the accuracy of classification is not affected significantly by the target variable type.

**Keywords:** Classification · Emotion Analysis · Lövheim Cube · Non-discrete emotion · Regression

## 1 Introduction

The paper continues the discussion on the field of Emotional Text Analysis – a recently emerged branch of Affective Computing that goes beyond the classical Sentiment Analysis tasks and explores not sentiment, but emotions in text data.

Our project aims to develop a theoretical framework for analyzing emotions in the internet-texts in Russian and collect appropriate data and implement approaches in code as artifacts of the project. For the task of modeling emotions, we apply Lövheim Cube concept; to annotate our training set we have elaborated an interface for non-discrete emotion assessment procedure. At the current step of the work, we are searching for an adequate computational model, algorithm, which would be coherent to both – theoretical dimensional model of emotions and data obtained in a non-discrete way. Our aspiration is to find a development approach (ML models and data-processing pipelines), which could not only perform well, but would do it in an ecological way regarding the whole logic of the project.

This paper aims to share the results of our experimentations with five models based on regression (Decision Tree Regressor, Extra Tree Regressor, K-Neighbors Regressor, Random Forest Regressor, MLP Regressor). Although the obtained results are far from

© Springer Nature Switzerland AG 2022
D. A. Alexandrov et al. (Eds.): DTGS 2021, CCIS 1503, pp. 97–107, 2022.
https://doi.org/10.1007/978-3-030-93715-7_7

being satisfactory either sufficient, they provide us with some specific knowledge about our data and technics and suggest some new tracks for the further work.

Thus, in Sect. 2 we will give an overview of the two types of models used to conceptualize and to represent emotions – categorical and dimensional. We will specially focus on the latter because we implement one of this type of model in our research. In Sect. 3 we analyze the related works in Sentiment Analysis and Emotional Text Analysis where the regression model has already been successfully applied. Section 4 gives a detailed description of our dataset while in Sect. 5 we compare the performance of five models based on regression and used to predict emotions in the internet texts in Russian after having been trained on our data. Sections 6 and Conclusion section propose our reflections on experiment evidences and ideas for further work.

## 2 Continuum in Emotion Analysis

The emotion has always been a puzzling question for researchers because of its doubly grounded character: it is both biologically based and socially rooted. As phenomena afforded by a sophisticated interplay of a number of neural substrates, emotions represent continuum with dimensions. On the contrary, being viewed from the social perspective, the emotions are more similar to a map where all territories have boundaries and labels – they are considered as discrete categories in Aristotelian sense.

Thus, to describe emotions the scholars operate either dimensional or categorical models [1].

As for the latter, they are quite numerous and include different number of emotional classes: from 6 categories in Ekman's classification [2], via 9 – in Tomkins affect typology [3] and, finally, towards famous Plutchik's wheel of emotions [4]. Many projects in Affective Computing exploit the aforementioned emotional systems or their parts to perform the task in Emotion Detection, Emotion Recognition and Emotional Text Analysis [5–7].

Among dimensional models, three conceptions are particularly worth to be mentioned. The first is VAD model [8], which uses three orthogonal dimensions: Valence (polarity), Arousal (a calm-excited scale) and Dominance (perceived degree of control in social situation). Its simplified version with only two dimensions (Valence and Arousal) is also known as VA model [9]. Another dimensional model, which is welcome in research of emotions in text, is Osgood's multi-dimensional scaling (MDS) [10] modelling emotions on three scales: evaluation, potency, and activity. One of the most recent achievements in this domain – the three-dimension model of H. Lövheim well-known as Lövheim Cube. It takes into account three neurotransmitters that are supposed to trigger emotions – serotonin, noradrenaline and dopamine [11]. Our project in Emotional Text Analysis relies on this continual emotional representation.

In research practice, the dimensional models are not often applied to deal with emotions by using automatized methods or tools. Therefore, in the overview presented by H. Gunes and M. Pantic [12] approximately ten projects in this line are referred. In reported works, the researchers prefer a variety of "classical" methods to run the classification: support vector machine method, neural networks algorithms (LSTM, recurrent network), etc. However, a common observation deduced from the analysis of these cases is that such models are more appropriate for classifiers based on categorical emotion representations. On the contrary, when they are applied to assign emotions along a continuum, there are used ecologically. It seems that another fashion to analyze automatically an emotion is the regression model.

## 3 Previous Work on Regression in Sentiment and Emotion Analyses

The last five years the number of works using regression to process text data containing emotions grows in permanence.

For example, in [13] the research team addresses the problem of using regression to perform classification task in Sentiment Analysis. Based on the Twitter short texts about the weather, the experiments were particularly focused on testing the hypothesis that regression analysis, using class confidence scores, performs better than classification methods like SVM and K-Nearest Neighbor based on the discrete labels. The researchers operated a systemic comparison of accuracy values obtained in 5 (negative/positive/neutral/irrelevant/unknown), 3 (negative/positive/neutral) and 2 (negative/positive) class classification and concluded that, in general, there is no significant difference between these two fashions to assign the sentiment to text. The plausible explanation of this fact may be that the regression model fits better to classification tasks demanding more nuanced, multi-label and fine-grained analysis supposed to compute numerous heterogeneous features.

In the frame of sentiment extraction, the insightful example of this kind is described in [14] where the score regression is applied to experiments on unimodal (verbal or vocal or visual or human) vs multimodal (verbal & vocal & visual & human) and unitask (sentiment or polarity or intensity) vs multitask (sentiment & polarity; sentiment & polarity & intensity) learning models. The conclusion made by authors is that the majority of tested unimodal and multimodal models "benefits from multi-task learning" [ibid: 44]. The evidence, which could be deduced from this statement, is that regression methods seem to be more sensitive to multiplicity and complexity of parameters involved in prediction algorithms.

In the field of Emotion Analysis, it was shown that the logistic regression model outperforms the methods of SVM and KNN showing the F-score equal to 84% [15].

When dealing with non-discrete properties, such as emotion intensity within a given emotion category, the linear regression model demonstrates its ability to make reliable predictions, for example, for four-class emotional classification of short texts from Social Media [16].

The regression model performs even better than neural network models (LSTM, CNN, GRU) in emotion intensity prediction task, showing the highest values of Pearson coefficient for predicted vs real intensity [17].

Generally, it is a noticeable fact that the number of articles covering emotion (and sentiment) analysis as classification task greatly outnumbers articles that describes regression approaches in this domain. The most possible explanation to this imbalance is a shortage of appropriate publicly available data. Continuous annotation of text is a very cost-demanding operation that requires manual annotation and very specialized ad-hoc scenarios to be the reason to get such a dataset. That makes such non-discrete datasets to be a non-disclosed asset. While discretely annotated data can be very easily collected (using hashtags like in Twitter Corpus or user response like in IMDB dataset), published and serve a data source for many experiments.

Thus, the main evidence obtained via our preliminary research literature analysis is that even if the regression model does not belong to the pull of largely used methods to perform Emotion Analysis, however, in recent works it is estimated as a very appropriate tool for complex classification tasks dealing with non-discrete properties. Our hypothesis consists in that using the regression will permit us to develop the classification model fitting in the best way to our data obtained from the non-discrete procedure of emotion assessment.

## 4   Dataset

Due to absence of datasets annotated in an appropriate continuous way, we had to obtain data by ourselves. We used Yandex Toloka crowdsourcing engine, which provides pools of Russian speaker assessment, tools for organizing user-interface for annotation tasks and orchestrating acquisition process. Since it was quite difficult to make the assessor specify the point in 3-d space, we went another way – the use of cube diagonals as scales along which the estimation was performed [see Fig. 1]. The default position was a center of the cube, which was treated as neutral configuration. Assessors were adjusting the positions of the point on the diagonals to specify the "presence" or intensity of a given emotion.

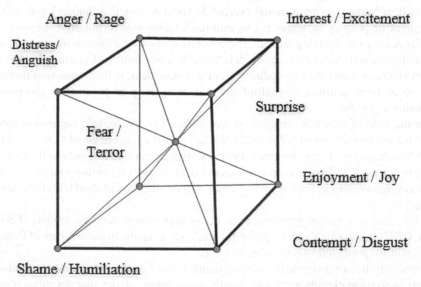

**Fig. 1.** Cube diagonals (modified version of Lövheim Cube published in [18])

In this way, some of the data could be lost, that is why it was a compromise between the dataset quality, the number of annotated texts and the speed of annotation. A sample of user interface (UI) for the task assessment is presented on the Fig. 2.[1]

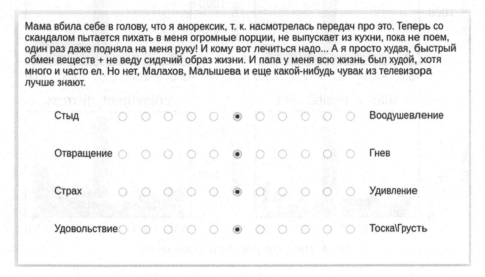

**Fig. 2.** Example of annotation UI designed by our team using Yandex Toloka platform [18]

As a result, we had a mapping of texts and 4 corresponding vectors with angle derived from diagonal vector and magnitude derived from user estimation scalar. To transform users' answers into Lövheim Cube entities (point described by neurotransmitters' values) we used a pooling technique of averaging of all 4 vectors. In this way, we could transform terms of emotions and their intensity into coordinates resembling 3 neurotransmitters. This part is more thoroughly explained in our previous work [18].

Regarding target variables, we faced a dilemma – whether to use pooled Cube coordinates derived from diagonals in terms of neurotransmitter values or to choose diagonals assessment values "per se". From the point of view of following Lövheim Cube ideology it is better to operate in neurotransmitter space to provide "neurobiological coordinates", but raw assessment values are more interpretable from human point of view. Thus, in our preliminary stage we decided to experiment both with 3-d coordinates and raw values.

On the Fig. 3 you can see histogram plots for diagonal values. As you can see the most probable version is a neutral position due to the design of annotation tool. Despite 0.0 value being the densest all other values are U-like distributed, i.e. extreme values of diagonals are more preferable than modest ones.

---

[1] *Mum has got it into her head that I'm an anorexic, since she has been seeing a lot of TV shows about it. Now she makes a scene forcing me to eat huge portions, doesn't let me out of the kitchen till I finish eating, once she even raised her hand on me! And who needs to be treated after that... I'm just thin, fast metabolism + I don't lead a sedentary life. And my dad has always been thin, although he has eaten a lot and often. But no, Malakhov, Malysheva and some other guy from TV know better.* Shame _ Excitement. Disgust _ Anger. Fear _ Surprise. Enjoyment _ Distress\Anguish.

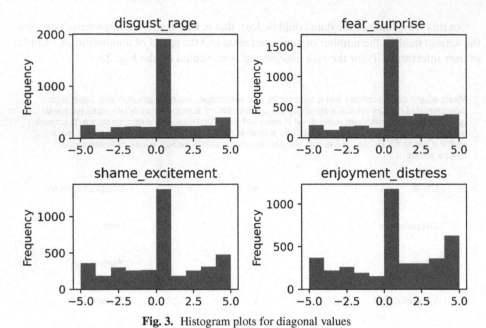

**Fig. 3.** Histogram plots for diagonal values

Figure 4 shows histograms for neurotransmitters. Data values are mostly normally distributed that allow us to use some parametric statistics.

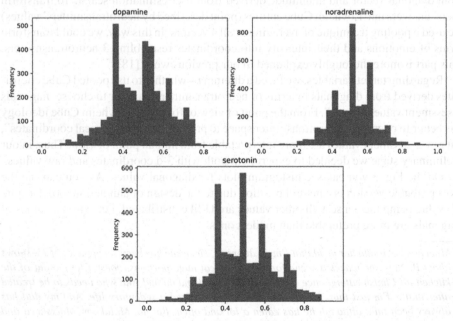

**Fig. 4.** Histogram plots for neurotransmitters

# 5 ML Approaches for Emotional Regressor

Having refined the questions with target variables we have started experimenting with different ML models and approaches for our task. For a given task, we used conventional ML approaches and avoided using deep learning techniques. The reason is that at a current stage of our project we want to rapidly check the applicability of ML approaches, which is not compatible with verbosity and complications of deep learning approaches. Overall, we had 3421 samples in the training set and 1143 in the validation one.

First question we have to resolve while working with text is an approach for vectorization of textual data. Nowadays there is a huge amount of already pretrained language models like BERT, RoBERTa, GPT-2, XLNet and other transformer-based embeddings. However, in this article we avoid using them preferring conventional Bag-of-words for the following reasons:

- Insufficient pooling facilities. Transformer embeddings are dense vectors mapped to tokens from text, thus, in order to use them for describing the whole text, we have to aggregate them. Simple averaging is not the best approach because a lot of data is lost. CLS token is also not a good candidate as it was trained for classification task, however we pursue regression.
- Bad support for Russian language. Despite the fact that BERT has a multilingual version and there is specially trained RuBERT we do not use them, as the original dataset used for multi-language support is a Wikipedia dump which is totally different from the data-source we are working with (personified emotionally intense texts from social media).
- Heavy-weights. This is the main drawback. Even the tiniest version of transformers starts from 100 MB, which is not efficient especially on the proof-of-concept stage, when the main goal is to assemble the most viable and lightweight solution and develop it further if necessary.

Due to these reasons we decided to go with the Bag-of-words approach with TF-IDF weighting available from Scikit-learn tool box. We used the following set of models – Decision Tree Regressor, Extra Tree Regressor, Multilayer Perceptron Regressor, Random Forest Regressor, K-Neighbor Regressor. This set of models has been selected due to inherent support of multi output for regression operations.

A family of tree models (Decision Tree Regressor, Extra Tree Regressor, Random Forest Regressor) is usually a good starting point for any data with high nonlinearity (which includes texts downstream tasks) and provides good baselines for initial trials. Also, they are quite light-weight and provide fast convergence. Their drawback is a tendency towards overfitting: when a model performs great on a training set but performs very poorly on a validation set of previously unseen samples.

K-Neighbor Regressor was spotted because our target variables deal with spatial features – a point on diagonal and a point in 3-d neurotransmitters state. Just because this model is resistant for overfitting and resembles spatial nature of the target variables, we decide to experiment with it.

A Multilayer Perceptron Regressor was selected to see how good a deep learning approach would work if we proceed further with "neural networks" and use more complex models.

As a vectorization approach we used the Bag-of-words approach with TF-IDF weighting. The reason is similar to model's selection – easy to vectorize and combine with models.

All parameters of the estimators were default sklearn settings. For metrics we used R Squared, mean absolute error (MAE) and mean squared error (MSE).

The dataset was randomly split into training and validation. The results of the training of the regression models for diagonal values are presented in Table 1.

**Table 1.** Regression results for diagonal values prediction

| Model name | R Squared | MAE | MSE |
|---|---|---|---|
| DecisionTreeRegressor | – 0.635 | 2.429 | 10.973 |
| ExtraTreeRegressor | – 0.528 | 2.342 | 10.333 |
| KNeighborsRegressor | – 0.073 | 2.080 | 7.211 |
| RandomForestRegressor | 0.097 | 1.816 | 6.047 |
| MLPRegressor | 0.055 | 1.951 | 6.332 |

As we can see, the best model performed during trials was Random Forest Regression which represents an ensemble of separate learners (Decision Tree Regressor) which decisions are pooled for final prediction. Performance superiority can be explained by the ability of tree models to learn highly nonlinear functions, and bagging learners into ensembler protects models from overfitting. However, MLP Regressor has shown comparable results without using ensembling and we think it is a clue that neural network approach would be very effective if we proceed further.

The same approach including spilt of test-train data and set of regressors was used for neurotransmitters coordinate target values. The results are presented in Table 2.

**Table 2.** Regression results for neurotransmitters regression

| Model name | R Squared | MAE | MSE |
|---|---|---|---|
| DecisionTreeRegressor | – 0.612 | 0.135 | 0.030 |
| ExtraTreeRegressor | – 0.613 | 0.134 | 0.030 |
| KNeighborsRegressor | – 0.067 | 0.111 | 0.019 |
| RandomForestRegressor | 0.093 | 0.101 | 0.016 |
| MLPRegressor | – 0.253 | 0.122 | 0.024 |

The results are very similar to Table 1 – they are visualized in comparison on the Fig. 5. It can be explained that coordinates values are derived from diagonals values in a functional manner, so they are mimicking the same distribution. An interesting fact is that KNN regressor performed better than MLP, and it is probably an effect of spatial nature of target values (Cube 3-d coordinates). Also, as target values are presented in range from 0 to 1, MSE metric seems not relevant here as it does not show dispersion of the performance.

Code and links to the dataset are presented in Colab notebook [19].

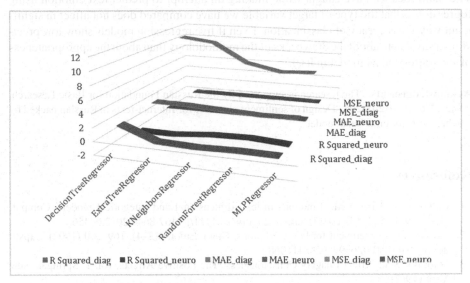

**Fig. 5.** The measure values deviation regarding type of model and type of target variable

## 6 Further Work and Discussion

As we can see, a regression approach for predicting either point in 3-d space or a configuration of diagonals can provide fruitful insights into emotional estimation of texts and give nuanced analytics from an emotional diversity perspective.

However, our preliminary results of applying regression models are not that perfect. For diagonals range of values is from −5 to + 5, consequently, having 1.8 as mean absolute error along 4 axes is an evidence of low precision of models. We would be satisfied by a MAE of 0.5 for diagonals and MAE of 0.05 for coordinates, so there is a lot of space for improvements.

The non-satisfactory results could be explained by inefficient vectorization techniques – BoW with TF-IDF – and insufficient complexities of estimators. Our future plans are to continue research in regression with transformer-based embeddings like RuBERT or multi-language RoBERTa, and to substitute conventional ML models with deep learning approaches. Also, we plan to organize human estimation during which assessors will have to decide how good is prediction from an intuitive point of view.

The last question to be discussed is how to treat bias in data and annotation. Whether or not such smoothing can be done during the annotation and data collection, or whether the bias in affective computation is inevitable and should be left as it is.

# 7 Conclusion

The main idea we have caught while making an attempt to predict text emotion using regression is that the type of target variable we have compared does not affect in significant way the accuracy of classification. Even if five regression models show low precision, it says more about the drawbacks of the methodology than about the appropriateness of the regression as model in itself.

**Acknowledgements.** The research is supported by the Russian Foundation for Basic Research, project No. 19–012-00205 "Design of sentiment classifier for Internet-texts in Russian backed by Lövheim's Cube emotional model".

# References

1. Calvo, R.A., Kim, S.M.: Emotions in text: dimensional and categorical models. Comput. Intell. **29**(3), 527–543 (2013). https://doi.org/10.1111/j.1467-8640.2012.00456.x
2. Ekman, P.: An argument for basic emotions. Cogn. Emot. **6**(3–4), 169–200 (1992). https://doi.org/10.1080/02699939208411068
3. Tomkins, S.S.: Affect Imagery Consciousness. The Positive Affects, vol. 1. Springer, New York (1962)
4. Plutchik, R.: Emotions: a general psychoevolutionary theory. In: Scherer, K., Ekman, P. (eds.) Approaches to emotion, pp. 197–219. Lawrence Erlbaum Associates, Hillsdale (1984). https://doi.org/10.4324/9781315798806
5. Bhowmick, P.K., Basu, A., Mitra, P.: Reader perspective emotion analysis in text through ensemble based multi-label classification framework. Comput. Inf. Sci. **2**(4), 64–74 (2009). https://doi.org/10.5539/cis.v2n4p64
6. Alm, C.O., Rot, D., Sproat, R.: Emotions from text: Machine learning for text-based emotion prediction. In: Raymond, J. (ed.) Proceedings of Human Language Technology Conference and Conference on Empirical Methods in Natural Language Processing, pp. 579–586. Association for Computational Linguistics, Vancouver (2005)
7. Volkova, E., Mehler, B., Meurers, W.D., Gerdemann, D., Bülthoff, H.: Emotional perception of fairy tales: achieving agreement in emotion annotation of text. In: Inkpen, D., Strapparava, C. (eds.) Proceedings of the NAACL HLT 2010 Workshop on Computational Approaches to Analysis and Generation of Emotion in Text, pp. 98–106. Association for Computational Linguistics, Los Angeles (2010)
8. Barrett, L.F.: Are emotions natural kinds? Perspect. Psychol. Sci. **1**(1), 28–58 (2006). https://doi.org/10.1111/j.1745-6916.2006.00003.x
9. Russell, J.A.: A circumplex model of affect. J. Pers. Soc. Psychol. **39**(6), 1161–1178 (1980). https://doi.org/10.1037/h0077714
10. Osgood, C.E., May, W.H., Miron, M.S.: Cross-Cultural Universals of Affective Meaning. University of Illinois Press, Urbana (1975)
11. Lövheim, H.: A new three-dimensional model for emotions and monoamine neurotransmitters. Med. Hypotheses **78**, 341–348 (2012). https://doi.org/10.1016/j.mehy.2011.11.016

12. Gunes, H., Pantic, M.: Automatic, dimensional and continuous emotion recognition. International Journal of Synthetic Emotions **1**(1), 68–99 (2010). https://doi.org/10.4018/jse.2010101605

13. Önal, I., Ertuğrul, A.M.: Effect of using regression in sentiment analysis. In: 22nd Signal Processing and Communications Applications Conference (SIU), pp. 1822–1825. IEEE, Trabzon (2014). https://doi.org/10.1109/SIU.2014.6830606

14. Tian, L., Lai, C., Moore, J.D.: Polarity and intensity: the two aspects of sentiment analysis. In: Zadeh, A., Liang, P.P., Morency, L.-Ph., Poria, S., Cambria, E., Scherer, S. (eds.) Proceedings of Grand Challenge and Workshop on Human Multimodal Language (Challenge-HML), pp. 40–47. Association for Computational Linguistics, Melbourne (2018). https://doi.org/10.18653/v1/W18-3306

15. Alotaibi, F.M.: Classifying text-based emotions using logistic regression. VAWKUM Trans. Comput. Sci. **7**(1), 31–37 (2019). https://doi.org/10.21015/vtcs.v16i2.551

16. Mashal, S.X., Asnani, K.: Emotion intensity detection for social media data. In: Proceedings of the 2017 International Conference on Computing Methodologies and Communication (ICCMC), pp. 155–158. IEEE, Erode (2017). https://doi.org/10.1109/ICCMC.2017.8282664

17. Akhtar, M.S., Ekbal, A., Cambria, E.: How intense are you? Predicting intensities of emotions and sentiments using stacked ensemble. IEEE Comput. Intell. Mag. **15**(1), 64–75 (2020). https://doi.org/10.1109/MCI.2019.2954667

18. Kolmogorova, A., Kalinin, A., Malikova, A.: Non-discrete sentiment dataset annotation: case study for Lövheim Cube emotional model. In: Alexandrov, D.A., et al. (eds.) DTGS 2020. CCIS, vol. 1242, pp. 154–164. Springer, Cham (2020). https://doi.org/10.1007/978-3-030-65218-0_12

19. Kalinin, A., Kolmogorova, A., Malikova, A.: Non-discrete sentiment annotation for Lövheim Cube. Google Colab Notebook (2021). https://colab.research.google.com/drive/15_0q1ff7_2fuldHoC1qzh4U7av16qM1V

# Anti-vaccination Movement on VK: Information Exchange and Public Concern

Igor Petrov[✉] (iD)

National Research University Higher School of Economics, Saint Petersburg, Russia

**Abstract.** Vaccination is a simple but effective way to control the spread of communicable diseases. However, an increasing number of people express their distrust in the immunization process and refuse to vaccinate themselves and their children. One explanation suggests that doubtfulness is maintained through widespread misinformation available on social media. This research takes an exploratory approach to the anti-vaccination communities in the Russian social network – VK. It applies network analysis to identify patterns in the dissemination of information and text mining to capture general public concern shown through the language of the posts published. In total, the digital fields of 135 open communities were analyzed. Textual data, public information about communities as well as reposts were collected using API technology. The results showed that the network of the communities can be characterized by a hierarchical structure, meaning that big and active communities control the information exchange within the network. At the same time, the public concern on the vaccination is associated with vaccine complications, parental worries, and uncertainty on the effects on the body.

**Keywords:** Social media · Vaccine hesitancy · Networks · Text analysis

## 1 Introduction

Vaccination is a tremendous medical achievement that contributes to lowering the presence of communicable diseases in the population. Despite the scientifically proven effectiveness and the safety of immunization, vaccine hesitancy tends to affect more and more people [1]. Some studies explain the tendency by proposing that social media plays an important role in conveying anti-vaccination messages [2, 3]. Notably, reliance on online media for health information determines a rapid spread of misinformation [3]. Thus, understanding individuals' engagement in the immunization debate becomes necessary. In particular, it is in social scientists' interest to analyze how this debate is held through a communication channel that is crucial at a national level.

In Russia, the research upon the impact of social media on vaccination behavior is not as extensive as in the Western academic community. However, some progress has been made in recent years. For instance, the largest social media platform in Russia, Vkontakte, started to warn users about potentially misleading information in anti-vaccination communities, drawing researchers' attention to the topic.

D. A. Alexandrov et al. (Eds.): DTGS 2021, CCIS 1503, pp. 108–121, 2022.
https://doi.org/10.1007/978-3-030-93715-7_8

This research looks at these communities and utilizes text mining and network analysis methods to gain insight into the country's anti-vaccination movement. Specifically, we try to understand the peculiarities of information exchange and identify topics in anti-vax conversations to see public concerns that form the exchange basis in the VK communities.

This paper contributes to understanding the anti-vaccination phenomenon in Russia and social media's role in its development. Furthermore, we believe that the results can elaborate on communicating strategies to eliminate peoples' fears and misconceptions. Finally, from a global perspective, we assume that research of this kind can help acknowledge that digitalization takes its place in spreading misinformation, which should be seen as one of the determinants of lowered vaccine uptake in both developed and developing countries.

## 2 Literature Review

### 2.1 Social Media and Anti-vaccination

Public perception of the risks of vaccine-preventable diseases has experienced a notable decline, while public concern for immunization has increased [4]. Predictably, increased distrust contributed to the rise of vaccine hesitancy in the developed countries [4]. Social media is often at the heart of the hesitancy transmission, acting as a tool that provides opportunities for sharing information about actual or perceived risks of vaccination [5]. The primary concern is that social networking service does not provide moderation by the expert community, meaning that this information can be deceptive [6, 7]. More importantly, social media is commonly associated with negative attitudes towards vaccination [8, 9]. For instance, two US studies determined a positive relationship between social media usage and parents' negative perception of vaccines [10, 11]. An overview showed that those parents who used social networking sites and online blogs as the primary source of information tended to express doubt about vaccine benefits more often than those who used magazines and newspapers [11]. Therefore, analyzing how vaccination is depicted in social media can reveal the cause of distrust in the immunization process.

### 2.2 Rumor Theory and Spread of Misinformation

Concerns about the transmission of inaccurate information have rapidly grown in recent years [12]. The prior literature with a subject of online information dissemination usually refers to the concept of *rumor*. The term can be defined as "an unverified information proposition for belief that bears topical relevance for persons actively involved in its dissemination."[1] Thus, rumor as a unit of information is characterized by a lack of authenticity and importance for interpersonal communication. It is also crucial to note that rumors possess the hypothesis-like characteristic, which defines their principal function in the transmission process, namely sense-making [13]. In that respect, by spreading rumors, individuals close the information gap and eliminate the feeling of uncertainty

---

[1] Rosnow, R.L., Kimmel, A.J.: Rumor. In: A. E. Kazdin (Ed.), Encyclopedia of psychology, Vol. 7. pp. 122–123. Oxford University Press, New York (2000).

[14, 15]. Given the connectedness of social networks, these sense-making rumors spread quickly, affecting many people [16].

In vaccination conversation, the transmission of rumors is also characterized by the fact that anti-vaccination expressions are accepted by the public quickly. In the literature, this phenomenon is associated with the fact that rumors often describe situations that coincide with the previously held attitude [17]. In other words, those who encounter a rumor that supports their beliefs or experience are likely to share it with other users without questioning its accuracy. Since social media is based on information cascades – one posts and others can repost, rumor transmission becomes much easier [18].

In the psychological dimension, the tendency can be also explained by the fact that information exchange on the Internet usually occurs at the microgroup level. In that regard, the collective discussion of information by members of a temporary microgroup leads to the point in which agents gain access to knowledge and life experience of each other. This, in turn, can affect the subjective assessment of rumor's reliability [19]. Therefore, the conversation about studying the online information channel is more than meaningful.

## 2.3  Linguistic Approach

In the field of anti-vaccination research, the usage of Natural Language Processing finds its application in many tasks, including tracking negative attitudes in social media. Furthermore, researchers suggest that text mining can be an advantageous technique to explore people's views towards vaccination [20]. Specifically, the scope of research on this topic reports that the method can be successfully used to describe how language differs between individuals who support vaccination and those who oppose it [21, 22]. For example, one study showed that opponents often used words of causation and made references to health and body in their entities, while supporters were more tentative in their expressions and frequently referenced family and society [22]. Another study considered anti-vaccination on VK and applied sentiment analysis as well as SVM algorithms [23]. As a result, researchers found that 59% of posts contained negative sentiment on vaccination and that the most prevalent topic in pro- and anti-vaccination communities was children's health.

## 3    Problem and Research Questions

The digital anti-vaccination movement in Russia has little coverage in academic papers, which creates a noticeable gap in the research field. Those studies that consider anti-vaccination in Russia and analyze country-specific social networking sites explore the phenomenon using classification tasks and sentiment analysis, which helps to compare pro- and anti-vaccination beliefs [23]. However, some of the questions, including network structure and information exchange, are still being uncovered. This research intends to examine these questions, contributing to the existing examination of the topic.

Therefore, our research questions are: 1) How is the information exchange network among anti-vaccination communities organized on VK? 2) What are the peculiarities of anti-vaccination discourse from the perspective of language usage? 3) What are the main topics of posts that circulate in the studied anti-vaccination environment?

# 4  Methodology

## 4.1  Initial Data

In 2019 VK started to put a warning about potentially inaccurate information in the anti-vaccination communities. Each time a user visits the page, a warning window appears with a link to an article on vaccination prepared by World Health Organization. At the moment, the list comprises 161 public pages that we used as an initial source of data. The list has both open and restricted communities. Precisely, 26 of them had limited access. Since it was impossible to enter those communities, we did not consider them during the analysis. Overall, the resulting list had 135 VK pages. We used parsing services and API to collect detailed information about the communities and their content. Specifically, we gathered information about the geographical position, the number of subscribers, publication activity, and subscriber's functionality, including the opportunity to write their posts.

## 4.2  Methods of Network Analysis

For this inquiry, we looked at the first 2000 posts in each of the 135 communities.[2] Among these posts, we have collected reposts made by each public page in our database. Since we aimed to analyze the information exchange on the communities' level, posts written by VK users were excluded from the search. In total, we managed to collect 6095 entities from 67 communities. Other 68 communities that were included in the database did not have reposts.

The mined data was presented as an edge list with weights. The first column denoted the community that made the repost, the second showed the source of the repost, while the third one the total number of reposts that the community made from the source. Using this data and Gephi, we have constructed and analyzed the overall network of communities using fundamental concepts of network theory.

Precisely, we have calculated several centrality measures to explore key relationships between vertices and conclude on the most influential units. Firstly, we referred to the concept of degree centrality. This notion differentiates between *in-degree* and *out-degree:* the first denotes how many incoming edges a vertex has while the second one shows the number of outgoing edges. In that sense, *in-degree* can be referred to as a measure of popularity and *out-degree* as a measure of influence [24]. Secondly, we described network structure through diameter and graph density and identified information bridges using *betweenness* centrality. Finally, to identify the portion of a directed graph in which each vertex can reach another one, we made a partition by Strongly Connected Components (SCC).

## 4.3  Text Analysis

For text analysis, we decided to continue with reposts. Similar to network analysis, we have looked at the first 2000 posts in each community and then collected reposts. Here

---

[2] The specific number of posts is due to VK restrictions on collecting information using API.

we also included reposted entities written by the communities outside of our database. This allowed us to consider more vaccine-related information, which was especially beneficial for text mining.

The raw text dataset included 8851 posts in Russian only. We have applied basic preprocessing procedures to eliminate useless elements, including Latin words, numbers, emoticons, and stop-words. Also, we excluded posts containing less than 50 words and more than 1000 words because these "outliers" could produce misleading results. Finally, we used lemmatization to combine various cases of Russian words and then tokenized posts for further analysis. After all manipulations, the dataset included texts of 5403 posts with a mean length of 281 words.

As for the method, we used topic modeling technique to analyze the peculiarities of the anti-vaccination discourse on VK. Specifically, we built a document-term matrix and decided on sparsity reduction, identified the rational number of topics and ran Latent Dirichlet Allocation (LDA) model. Finally, we calculated coherence and prevalence to evaluate highlighted topics.

## 5   Analysis and Results

### 5.1   Description of the Digital Field

**Geography of Anti-vaccination Communities**
When creating a community, VK asks users to indicate the page's territorial affiliation, including the country and city. That is an optional step that the user can skip. However, most tend to provide the named data. In our case, only 19 communities did not indicate the country in the description. In addition to the expected prevalence of communities created in Russia, we noticed that some public pages belonged to other regions, namely Ukraine, Kazakhstan, Belarus, and Moldova. Despite different affiliations, the content in all communities was written in Russian. The exact distribution of communities by country can be seen in Table 1.

**Table 1.** Distribution of the communities by country

| Country | Number of the communities |
| --- | --- |
| Russia | 89 |
| Ukraine | 22 |
| Not stated | 19 |
| Belarus | 2 |
| Kazakhstan | 2 |
| Moldova | 1 |

For Russia, we also looked at the distribution of communities within the country. As a result, anti-vaccination pages were found in 45 cities. Interestingly, most of the communities belong to territorial units, the population of which is less than 500 thousand. Specifically, we found that anti-vaccination communities were seen in the 33 small cities, while the other 12 were established in cities with over a million people. Furthermore, we identified centers with most of the communities – St. Petersburg and Moscow were absolute leaders with 13 and 8 communities, respectively. Considering the big population size and increased digital accessibility in the named cities, this dominance in the number of public pages is expected. The general conclusion is that the VK anti-vaccination movement is scattered across the country.

**Small and Big Communities**
Based on the number of subscribers, we found that most of the communities were characterized by a small audience (trimmed mean $= 351.48$), making them important only at the local level. Large communities were also present in the database. Here the number of subscribers varied from 20315 to 103268. Content from these pages often appeared in small communities in the form of reposts and unquoted references. We discovered that in large communities, the subscribers did not have the opportunity to write their posts. Also, the names of the pages differed among the communities. Specifically, pages with a small number of subscribers tended to include territorial affiliation and targeted terms such as "parents," "mothers". In contrast, the names of big pages comprised general terms such as "vaccine," "risks," and "truth".

## 5.2 Network Analysis

**Overall Network Structure**
The resulting network of the communities by reposts was constructed with the help of the Gephi engine, which also helped us calculate the basic graph metrics. Overall, the network comprises 82 distinct nodes and 368 edges among them. Figure 1 represents the overall networked data and summarizes the graph metrics. Specifically, we have identified diameter or the greatest distance between any pair of vertices that turned out to be 7. We have calculated the graph density that showed that only 5% of the possible edges were present in the graph and found an average diameter that was equal to 2.54. To be more indicative, we also used color and size to show how vertices differ in the graph. Specifically, the color shows out-degree centrality, while size in-degree centrality. Also, we would like to emphasize that the reposts that we have used for this network were written only on behalf of the community.

**Degree Centrality**
Firstly, we have identified the most popular communities by referring to the concept of in-degree. As a result, we distinguished top-3 vertices with most of the incoming edges. Namely, community №47 with an in-degree of 57, community №71 with an in-degree of 47, and community №72 with an in-degree of 39. Interestingly, all of the mentioned vertices possess a big audience that exceeds 20000. Since incoming links denote the commonly referenced vertices, this observation suggests that a rather hierarchical structure characterizes the anti-vaccination environment of VK. By this we mean that communities with the vast audience are major sources of information in

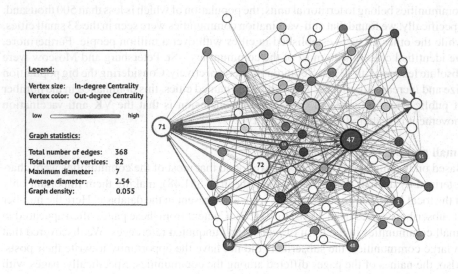

**Fig. 1.** Summarizing network of VK communities by reposts

the network. That is, huge communities post information that is picked up by smaller communities and then disseminated through the network. In that regard, the prominent information exchange between small and large communities that we see in the network contributes to the spread of misinformation and acts as a mechanism of audience reach. It means that subscribers of smaller communities can be exposed to bigger misinformation channels while reading reposts. Separate distribution of in-degree shown through vertex size can be seen in Fig. 2 (A).

Secondly, we looked at out-degree to identify the most influential units in a network. For our case, the higher the value of out-degree, the more reposts the community makes. The analysis showed that several communities could be classified as the most active in terms of reposting. Specifically, these vertices are community №36 with an out-degree of 18, community №59 with an out-degree of 17, and communities №1, №48, №51 with an out-degree of 15. The number of subscribers in these communities ranges from 418 to 9148 with a mean of 3177. Interestingly, most of these communities clearly state a territorial affiliation and incorporate targeted terms in their names, which leads us to the assumption that the most influential communities are commonly presented as platforms for discussion among specific social groups connected by their location in the country. Figure 2 (B) represents a separate distribution of out-degree shown through vertex size, while Table 2 summarizes the in-degree and out-degree centrality of the network.

**Betweenness Centrality**
Betweenness centrality is the widely used measure that makes it possible to identify a vertex's role in the process of information dissemination. Specifically, the metric shows which communities can be considered mediators or key bridges between different parts of the graph. The higher the measure's value, the more information passes through the

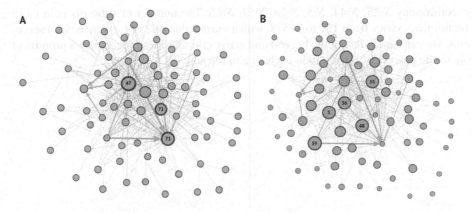

**Fig. 2.** Network by in-degree and out-degree (A – in degree, B – out-degree)

**Table 2.** In-degree and out-degree centrality of the network

| Statistic | In-degree | Out-degree |
|-----------|-----------|------------|
| Maximum   | 57        | 18         |
| Minimum   | 0         | 0          |
| Average   | 4.487805  | 4.487805   |

vertex studied, which also explains why betweenness centrality can be seen as a measure of influence. For the case of our network, we have identified three prominent mediators: community №47 with betweenness 758, community №36 with betweenness 410, and community №48 with betweenness 290. These results coincide with the discussion on degree centrality above and show that the highest betweenness centrality is held by the biggest community in the network and then followed by communities with the biggest number of outgoing edges. These findings support the conclusion on the network's structure and suggest that the biggest and active communities have more control over the network or act as information gatekeepers.

**Strongly Connected Components**
Since reposting is a dynamic process that we present in a directed graph, we can identify strongly connected components that show us a set of vertices in which each vertex is reachable in both directions from any other vertex in the same set. In our case, we were able to highlight 68 strongly connected components in the graph: one component comprises 15 vertices, making up about 18% of the total number of vertices. In contrast, each of 67 other components includes only one vertex. Figure 3 depicts the stressed sub-networks using color. The largest component is also underscored with borders. Interestingly, the biggest SCC consists of all information gatekeepers that we have identified in the previous step, as well as the communities with the highest in-degree and out-degree. Also, we can see communities that were not emphasized previously

— community №25, №44, №5, №49, №57, №66. The number of subscribers in these communities varies from 127 to 27578, with a mean value of 2599. given these observations, we can conclude that the biggest and active communities indeed play a prominent role in the process of information exchange in the network.

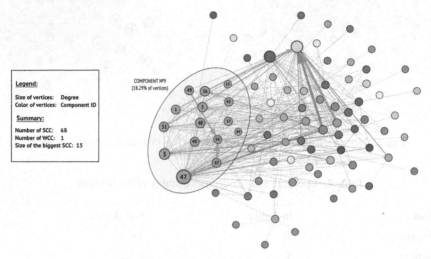

**Fig. 3.** Strongly connected components

### 5.3   Topic Modeling

Topic modeling is used to identify hidden patterns in textual data. One of the widely spread modeling techniques is Latent Dirichlet Allocation (LDA), a method that is based on semantic similarity [25]. Specifically, LDA uses a document-term matrix to generate probabilistic models, detecting features or trends of the textual data [25]. In this research, we used LDA to identify topics in reposts that were made by anti-vaccination communities.

**Document-Term Matrix and Number of Topics**

A document-term matrix shows the number of times a term $t$ appears in a document $D$. Initial matrix had 45016 terms, 5403 documents, and 242501000 sparse entities (sparsity: 100%), indicating that the matrix consists mainly of zero elements. The high sparsity can affect the results of the topic modeling algorithm, so it is advisable to filter out the matrix values before modeling. In our case, we removed terms that appeared in less than two documents and terms that were in 90% of the posts. The resulting matrix had 24911 terms and 133920589 sparse entities (sparsity: 99%).

The number of topics is a key parameter of the LDA model, which should be reasonably related to the number of terms and documents. That is, for small corpora, a large number of topics will lead to meaningless results. In our case, we have built the fitting model, which showed coherence of the algorithm for models that incorporated

20, 30 and 40 topics. As a result, the highest coherence was identified for 40 topics (coherence $= 0.149$). Considering the absence of apparent differences among the results of the constructed models and the general repetitiveness of some topics in the model with 40 topics, we decided to stick with a smaller parameter, namely 20.

**Phi, Coherence and Prevalence**
The major parameter that is used in the interpretation of LDA results is *Phi*. Phi represents a probability distribution of terms over topics. The higher the Phi value, the greater the probability that a particular topic will contain the term. Based on the model assignment, we named each topic with summarizing label. Figure 4 shows the resulting table with top-10 terms by Phi in each topic.

To identify topics that should be analyzed deeply, we calculated coherence and prevalence. To be precise, coherence differentiates between semantically interpretable topics and topics that include poorly related terms. Technically, this concept is a measure of algorithmic efficiency. The prevalence, in turn, shows the most frequent topics in the corpus. In that regard, this measure denotes topics that commonly occur in reposts, and therefore can be seen as the most widespread subjects in information exchange. As a result, we highlighted three topics by coherence and three topics by prevalence. For coherence those are *Biochemistry (T3)* with coherence of 0.24, *Tuberculosis (T6)* with coherence of 0.22 and *Rights (T13)* with coherence of 0.19. As for the prevalence, the topics are *Unidentified (T14), Immunity (T19)* and *Legislation (T12)* with prevalence of 9.7, 8.1 and 8, respectively. Interestingly, the most prevalent topic – Topic 14 comprises terms that semantically are poorly connected. By considering this topic in more detail, we found that it consists of multiple verbs and other parts of speech that cannot be connected with a single topic. Since it was impossible to draw a meaningful conclusion on the content of this topic, we did not consider it in the analysis.

**Interpretation**
One of the major observations that can be drawn from the modeled topics is that health-related issues are common for anti-vaccination information exchange (T4, T6, T7, T8, T19). Almost in each subject, we can detect terms that directly relate to the medicine or body, supporting the suggestion that social media is often used as a source of health-related information. As we saw earlier, even the most coherent and prevalent topics are associated with the medical discussion. This leads us to think that when it comes to the point in which the community decides what information to repost, the choice falls to entities that embrace professional or science-specific information, which can create an illusion of reliable information when, in nature, it is often being misinterpreted or purposefully distorted. In that regard, we can also imply that notable concerns of anti-vaxxers are medical.

Another observation is that topics include terms related to family, children, and legislation (T9, T12, T16), meaning that most of the information that passes through communities is targeted at particular social groups and intends to alienate children from vaccination, especially in educational institutions. As our analysis has shown, publications fitting into these topics discuss the disadvantageous position in which the modern child is seen, arguing that the state and official medicine are aimed at worsening the younger generation's health, forcing parents to perform "dangerous" practices — for

| Nutrition (T1) | Information (T2) | Biochemistry (T3) | Complications (T4) | Russia (T5) |
|---|---|---|---|---|
| вода (water) | наш (our) | вирус (virus) | заболевание (disease) | русский (Russian) |
| продукт (product) | правда (truth) | клетка (cell) | вызывать (to cause) | наш (our) |
| питание (nutrition) | информация (information) | ртуть (mercury) | мозг (brain) | народ (nation) |
| масло (oil) | фильм (movie) | организм (organism/body) | развитие (development) | страна (country) |
| день (day) | книга (book) | алюминий (aluminum) | рак (cancer) | россия (Russia) |
| кожа (skin) | сайт (site) | содержать (to contain) | препарат (a drug) | класс (grade) |
| витамин (vitamin) | материал (material) | вещество (substance) | исследование (research) | женщина (woman) |
| молоко (milk) | научный (scientific) | вызывать (to cause) | осложнение (complication) | школа (school) |
| пища (food) | тема (topic) | акдс (DPT vaccine) | система (system/body) | становиться (to become) |
| алкоголь (alcohol) | видео (video) | ткань (tissue) | случай (case) | программа (program) |

| Tuberculosis (T6) | Infections (T7) | Death (T8) | Vaccine refusal (T9) | Digitalization (T10) |
|---|---|---|---|---|
| туберкулез (tuberculosis) | корь (measles) | врач (doctor) | врач (doctor) | электронный (digital) |
| манту (Mantoux test) | заболевание (desease) | больница (hospital) | сделать (to make) | данные (data) |
| проба (sample) | случай (case) | девочка (girl) | прививать (to vaccinate) | семья (family) |
| бцж (BCG vaccine) | грипп (flu) | день (day) | осложнение (complication) | наш (our) |
| россия (Russia) | против (against) | становиться (to become) | родитель (parent) | цифровой (digital) |
| тест (test) | полиомиелит (polio) | сделать (to make) | говорить (to talk) | против (against) |
| реакция (reaction) | инфекция (infection) | смерть (death) | отказываться (to refuse) | защита (protection) |
| фтизиатр (phthisiatrician) | прививать (to vaccinate) | мама (mother) | каждый (each) | законопроект (law) |
| диагностика (diagnostics) | болезнь (desease) | родитель (parent) | болезнь (desease) | персональный (personal) |
| диаскинтест (Diaskintest) | вирус (virus) | умирать (to die) | очень (very) | адрес (address) |

| USA influence (T11) | Legislation (T12) | Rights (T13) | Unidentified (T14) | Cities and COVID (T15) |
|---|---|---|---|---|
| коронавирус (COVID) | семья (family) | медицинский (medical) | очень (very) | область (region) |
| против (against) | родитель (parent) | право (right) | просто (simple) | россия (Russia) |
| компания (company) | право (right) | гражданин (citizen) | говорить (to talk) | маска (face mask) |
| здравоохранение (health care) | россия (Russia) | закон (law) | ваш (your) | регион (region) |
| сша (USA) | наш (our) | рф (Russian Federation) | знать (to know) | москва (Moscow) |
| также (also) | общественный (public) | документ (document) | делать (to do) | республика (republic) |
| новый (new) | закон (law) | федеральный (federal) | хотеть (to want) | город (city) |
| препарат (a drug) | вопрос (question) | руб (ruble) | понимать (to understand) | власть (authority) |
| страна (country) | рф (Russian Federation) | российский (Russian) | мама (mother) | режим (regime) |
| получать (to receive) | защита (protection) | статья (article) | наш (our) | коронавирус (COVID) |

| Schools (T16) | Female Support (T17) | Medical knowledge (T18) | Immunity (T19) | Research (T20) |
|---|---|---|---|---|
| школа (school) | помогать (to help) | врач (doctor) | система (system/body) | исследование (research) |
| родитель (parent) | женщина (woman) | иммунитет (immunity) | иммунитет (immunity) | прививать (to vaccinate) |
| право (right) | помощь (assistance) | дело (case) | болезнь (desease) | болезнь (desease) |
| суд (court) | наш (our) | знать (to know) | самый (very) | непривитый (unvaccinated) |
| детский (for children) | очень (very) | самый (very) | являться (to be) | получать (to receive) |
| отказ (refusal) | группа (community) | детский (for children) | наш (our) | здоровье (health) |
| сад (kindergarten) | рубль (ruble) | вакцинировать (to vaccinate) | время (time) | аутизм (autism) |
| образование (education) | время (time) | профессор (professor) | иммунный (immune) | врач (doctor) |
| учреждение (institution) | аборт (abortion) | родитель (parent) | иметь (to have) | заболевание (desease) |
| прокуратура (prosecutor) | друг (friend) | институт (institution) | организм (organism/body) | иммунитет (immunity) |
| новый (new) | закон (law) | федеральный (federal) | хотеть (to want) | город (city) |
| препарат (a drug) | вопрос (question) | руб (ruble) | понимать (to understand) | власть (authority) |
| страна (country) | рф (Russian Federation) | российский (Russian) | мама (mother) | режим (regime) |
| получать (to receive) | защита (protection) | статья (article) | наш (our) | коронавирус (COVID) |

**Fig. 4.** Top-10 terms in each topic by phi

example, vaccinating children before entering kindergarten or school. In this discourse, the argument is that the parent's main task is to provide adequate protection from external incentives, including vaccination.

Finally, we should remark on topics that incorporate coronavirus, external influence, and digitalization (T10, T11, T15). Some of the reposts that fall into these topics tend to criticize restrictions introduced due to the coronavirus pandemic and deny the virus existence, which backs up overall skepticism towards medical knowledge among opponents of vaccination. Furthermore, anti-vaxxers tend to possess conspiracy thinking. For instance, topic 11 includes publications suggesting that vaccines and medications are produced in the USA and used to control the Russian population. The general conclusion is that anti-vaccination conversation can be characterized by overall information illiteracy and intolerance of uncertainty, which is conducive to the ingraining of false information in individuals' minds.

# 6    Conclusion

Overall, the results of the examination show promising prospects for research development. First, we utilized exploratory analysis and identified that anti-vaccination on VK is a well-established phenomenon that attracts more and more people. Communities that we subjected to analysis were scattered across the country and possessed a considerable number of subscribers. This, in turn, confirmed research's relevance and suggested the need for further investigation. Second, we applied fundamental concepts of network analysis and built a graph denoting information exchange among the anti-vaccination communities manifested in reposting. We have found that the network can be characterized by the fact that big and active communities are information gatekeepers, meaning that these network units can be seen as a primary source of information. In that sense, smaller communities adopt messages from big and active ones, which can be a determining factor in the informational development of the field. That is, the prevailing type and subject of information are partly defined by the gatekeepers mentioned earlier. In practical terms, the results highlight the central channels of misinformation on VK, which can help healthcare representatives develop precise actions in controlling the dissemination of information. Third, we implemented topic modeling and saw that VK's anti-vaccination discourse is delineated by topics related to general health issues, legislation, parental position, and conspiracy thinking. In that sense, we also suggested that these issues can be perceived as a part of peoples' concern on vaccination, which is critical to consider in formulating communicating strategies targeted to eliminate general misconceptions.

The study has several limitations. Firstly, we were unable to enter the communities with restricted access, meaning that the potentially beneficial information was not considered during the analysis. Secondly, VK allows users to collect a limited amount of data through API, putting restrictions on analytical purposes and implementations. Thirdly, this paper analyzed only reposts, which is definitely only a tiny part of all posts published by the communities.

For further research, we aim to extend the analytical field by adding all publications available in the communities studied as well as utilizing text mining techniques, including structural topic modeling and sentiment analysis. Besides, it is necessary to analyze subscribers' socio-demographic characteristics and draw up a social portrait of a typical anti-vaxxer. Finally, we want to expand network analysis by creating a network of communities by mutual subscribers to make a more elaborated conclusion on the structure of the field.

# References

1. Tafuri, S., Gallone, M.S., Cappelli, M.G., Martinelli, D., Prato, R., Germinario, C.: Addressing the anti-vaccination movement and the role of HCWs. Vaccine **32**, 4860–4865 (2014). https://doi.org/10.1016/j.vaccine.2013.11.006
2. Keelan, J., Pavri, V., Balakrishnan, R., Wilson, K.: An analysis of the human papilloma virus vaccine debate on MySpace blogs. Vaccine **28**, 1535–1540 (2010). https://doi.org/10.1016/j.vaccine.2009.11.060

3. Kata, A.: A postmodern Pandora's box: anti-vaccination misinformation on the Internet. Vaccine **28**, 1709–1716 (2010). https://doi.org/10.1016/j.vaccine.2009.12.022
4. Featherstone, J.D., Ruiz, J.B., Barnett, G.A., Millam, B.J.: Exploring childhood vaccination themes and public opinions on Twitter: a semantic network analysis. Telemat. Inform. **54**, 101474 (2020). https://doi.org/10.1016/j.tele.2020.101474
5. Betsch, C., Sachse, K.: Dr. Jekyll or Mr. Hyde? (How) the Internet influences vaccination decisions: Recent evidence and tentative guidelines for online vaccine communication. Vaccine **30**(25), 3723–3726 (2012). https://doi.org/10.1016/j.vaccine.2012.03.078
6. Broniatowski, D.A., et al.: Weaponized health communication: Twitter bots and Russian trolls amplify the vaccine debate. Am. J. Public Health. **108**, 1378–1384 (2018). https://doi.org/10.2105/AJPH.2018.304567
7. Guidry, J.P.D., Carlyle, K., Messner, M., Jin, Y.: On pins and needles: how vaccines are portrayed on Pinterest. Vaccine **33**, 5051–5056 (2015). https://doi.org/10.1016/j.vaccine.2015.08.064
8. Betsch, C., Renkewitz, F., Betsch, T., Ulshöfer, C.: The influence of vaccine-critical websites on perceiving vaccination risks. J. Health Psychol. **15**, 446–455 (2010). https://doi.org/10.1177/1359105309353647
9. Kim, J.: The relationship of health beliefs with information sources and HPV vaccine acceptance among young adults in Korea. Int. J. Environ. Res. Public Health **15**(4), 673 (2018). https://doi.org/10.3390/ijerph15040673
10. Luisi, M.: Kansan guardian perceptions of HPV and the HPV vaccine and the role of social media. Kansas J. Med. **13**(1), 9–18 (2020). https://doi.org/10.17161/kjm.v13i1.13397
11. Hwang, J., Shah, D.V.: Health information sources, perceived vaccination benefits, and maintenance of childhood vaccination schedules. Health Commun. **34**, 1279–1288 (2019). https://doi.org/10.1080/10410236.2018.1481707
12. Chua, A.Y.K., Banerjee, S.: To share or not to share: the role of epistemic belief in online health rumors. Int. J. Med. Inf. **108**, 36–41 (2017). https://doi.org/10.1016/j.ijmedinf.2017.08.010
13. DiFonzo, N., Bordia, P.: Rumor Psychology: Social and Organizational Approaches. American Psychological Association, Washington (2007). https://doi.org/10.1037/11503-000
14. DiFonzo, N., Bordia, P.: A tale of two corporations: managing uncertainty during organizational change. Hum. Resour. Manage. **37**, 295–303 (1998). https://doi.org/10.1002/(SICI)1099-050X(199823/24)37:3/4%3c295::AID-HRM10%3e3.0.CO;2-3
15. Bordia, P., Difonzo, N.: Problem solving in social interactions on the internet: rumor as social cognition. Soc. Psychol. Q. **67**, 33–49 (2004). https://doi.org/10.1177/019027250406700105
16. Chua, A.Y.K., Tee, C.-Y., Pang, A., Lim, E.-P.: The retransmission of rumor and rumor correction messages on Twitter. Am. Behav. Sci. **61**, 707–723 (2017). https://doi.org/10.1177/0002764217717561
17. Ambrosini, P.J.: Clinical assessment of group and defensive aspects of rumor. Int. J. Group Psychother. **33**, 69–83 (1983). https://doi.org/10.1080/00207284.1983.11491745
18. Vosoughi, S., Roy, D., Aral, S.: The spread of true and false news online. Science **359**, 1146–1151 (2018). https://doi.org/10.1126/science.aap9559
19. Gorbatov, D.S.: Rumors: about the problem of definition in social psychology (in Russian). Siber. J. Psychol. **35**, 47–51 (2010). (UDC: 16.454.52)
20. Agarwal, A., Biadsy, F., McKeown, K.R.: Contextual phrase-level polarity analysis using lexical affect scoring and syntactic n-grams. In: Proceedings of the 12th Conference of the European Chapter of the ACL (EACL 2009), pp. 24–32. Association for Computational Linguistics, Athens, Greece (2009)
21. Xu, Z., Guo, H.: Using text mining to compare online pro- and anti-vaccine headlines: word usage, sentiments, and online popularity. Commun. Stud. **69**, 103–122 (2018). https://doi.org/10.1080/10510974.2017.1414068

22. Faasse, K., Chatman, C.J., Martin, L.R.: A comparison of language use in pro- and anti-vaccination comments in response to a high profile Facebook post. Vaccine **34**, 5808–5814 (2016). https://doi.org/10.1016/j.vaccine.2016.09.029
23. Tserkovnaya, D., Larson, H.: Vaccine confidence in Russia: digital analysis of the online behavior and attitudes of the Russian speaking internet users. In: Proceedings of the 9th International Conference on Digital Public Health, pp. 135–136. Association for Computing Machinery, New York, NY, USA (2019). https://doi.org/10.1145/3357729.3357763
24. Miller, P.R., Bobkowski, P.S., Maliniak, D., Rapoport, R.B.: Talking politics on Facebook: network centrality and political discussion practices in social media. Polit. Res. Q. **68**, 377–391 (2015). https://doi.org/10.1177/1065912915580135
25. Blei, D.M., Ng, A.Y., Jordan, M.I.: Latent Dirichlet allocation. J. Mach. Learn. Res. **3**, 993–1022 (2003)
26. Rosnow, R.L., Kimmel, A.J.: Rumor. In: Kazdin, A.E. (ed.) Encyclopedia of Psychology, vol. 7, pp. 122–123. Oxford University Press, New York (2000)

# Transformer Models for Question Answering on Autism Spectrum Disorder QA Dataset

Victoria Firsanova[✉]

Saint Petersburg State University, University Embankment 7/9,
St. Petersburg 199034, Russia
st085687@student.spbu.ru
https://github.com/vifirsanova

**Abstract.** Question answering (QA) Transformer-based models might become efficient in inclusive education. For example, one can test and tune such models with small closed-domain datasets before the implementation of a new system in an inclusive organization. However, studies in the sociomedical domain show that such models can be unpredictable. They can mislead a user or evoke aversive emotional states. The paper addresses the problem of investigating safety-first QA models that would generate user-friendly outputs. The study aims to analyze the performance of SOTA Transformer-based QA models on a custom dataset collected by the author of the paper. The dataset contains 1 134 question-answer pairs about autism spectrum disorders (ASD) in Russian. The study presents the validation and evaluation of extractive and generative QA models. The author used transfer learning techniques to investigate domain-specific QA properties and suggest solutions that might provide higher QA efficiency in the inclusion. The study shows that although generative QA models can misrepresent facts and generate false tokens, they might bring diversity in the system outputs and make the automated QA more user-friendly for younger people. Although extractive QA is more reliable, according to the metric scores presented in this study, such models might be less efficient than generative ones. The principal conclusion of the study is that a combination of generative and extractive approaches might lead to higher efficiency in building QA systems for inclusion. However, the performance of such combined systems in the inclusion is yet to be investigated.

**Keywords:** Question answering · Dialogue system · Transformer

## 1 Introduction

Closed-domain question answering (CDQA) systems might find an application in the sphere of inclusive education by providing information about inclusion

D. A. Alexandrov et al. (Eds.): DTGS 2021, CCIS 1503, pp. 122–133, 2022.
https://doi.org/10.1007/978-3-030-93715-7_9

and people with special needs in a user-friendly way. In general, CDQA is a challenging task due to the volume limitations of available datasets. In the past few years, much research has focused on the abilities of the Transformer-based [1] models that can achieve state-of-the-art (SOTA) results on various NLP tasks [2], including generative [3] and extractive question answering [4], even with limited training data.

Neural approaches allow us to achieve high metric scores. Nevertheless, the evaluation of the safety level of a built model remains unclear. The safety evaluation should help us to ensure the model does not misrepresent the data or generate false facts. Understanding how to evaluate and achieve the safety of a CDQA model for inclusive education is essential. A new app must not give misleading information, cause anxiety or negative emotions. One of the possible solutions might lie in the structure of a training dataset. For example, one can use or build a dataset containing different types of questions [5] or special keywords [6].

The purpose of the study was to explore the properties of state-of-the-art (SOTA) Transformer-based CDQA models fine-tuned for the autism spectrum disorder domain by comparing results of training extractive and generative QA systems on a dataset compiled by the author of the paper with results of other open- or medical (COVID-19 question answering) domain studies. The dataset presented in the study focuses on providing objective information about autism spectrum disorder and Asperger syndrome in the form of sets of reading passages and corresponding question-answer pairs [7]. The principal findings based on the comparison of Transformer models concern the analysis of extractive and generative QA performance. The author also looks forward to combining two approaches in the context of inclusive education. The novelty of the research is that the author tries to find out if the results of the SOTA models would be similar in the autism spectrum disorder, open- or medical domains.

The author of the paper consulted with psychiatrists from Russia. They have described to her during the interview the main features of apps for autistic people. According to experts, many people with special needs find it difficult to perceive new information by ear. The perception of visual information is more comfortable for many people with autism (but this is not true for everyone). The adapted information should be clear, unambiguous, unloaded from unnecessary details. The author of the paper considered these domain-specific features during the dataset compilation described in Sect. 3.

## 2    Related Work

Applying natural language technologies to teaching, diagnostics, rehabilitation of people with autism spectrum disorder is an extensively discussed topic. For example, in the 2000s, Boris Galitsky proposed a question answering system for autistic children [9]. His model aimed to teach patients reasoning about mental states. The online agent asked a user about mental states of characters from given scenarios. Some later studies proposed using systems based on closed-domain question answering to diagnose autism spectrum disorder. For example, the Aquabot, developed in 2017, has a psychiatrist mode that asks a user questions to predict possible achluophobia or autism [10]. Another example is the Autism AI mobile app developed in 2020 that is based on a convolutional classifier and sets of questionnaires and can be used to predict possible autism spectrum disorder [11].

The research has focused on issues of building Conversational AI (ConvAI) models. ConvAI approaches are closely related to the development of natural language interfaces and human-machine interaction. Question answering, as one of the fundamental ConvAI tasks, copes with input questions within one or several domains by generating, extracting, or retrieving an answer based on the information from a data or knowledge base [8].

Closed-domain ConvAI systems have their roots in the 1960s. For instance, ELIZA [12], a closed-domain imitator of a psychotherapist session and the forerunner of modern chatbots, could generate dialogue lines by pattern matching and memory accessing. Another example is LUNAR [13], a closed-domain question answering system on moon geology and the forerunner of natural language interfaces based on syntax and semantic analyzers [14]. The parser of LUNAR was built with an augmented transition network (ATN), an automaton that changes states while moving from one word to another in a parsed piece of text.

Recent advances in natural language processing show that Transformer architecture based solely on attention mechanisms [1] allows achieving high metric scores on a wide range of tasks by transferring knowledge gained during the model training from one task to another through so-called fine-tuning [15]. For example, models based on Bidirectional Encoder Representations from Transformers (BERT) [27] fine-tuned for question answering, in fact, deal with Machine Reading Comprehension (MRC) task, which is to extract an answer from a given reading passage. In turn, QA models based on Generative Pre-trained Transformer [16] use zero-shot learning (a model learns to predict the data it has never seen before) to memorize the data and predict possible answers to questions.

According to the empirical findings from a study on applying GPT-2 [17] and GPT-3 [18] in building medical closed-domain question answering (CDQA) models, generative Transformer-based models might become harmfully biased [19] and, as a result, misrepresent information and cause negative emotions. On the contrary, extractive and retrieval-based approaches might be more reliable. Such models have already found their practical implementation in medical natural language processing tasks. Those are safety-first tasks [20].

The author of the paper has considered these hypotheses about generative and extractive question answering. To prove or disprove them, she has built and evaluated several CDQA models based on Transformer architecture using her custom dataset [7]. She aimed to find out domain-specific features of closed-domain question answering applied to the sphere of inclusive education. Although there are many domain-specific studies on medical natural language processing, the applicability of the existing approaches in inclusive education is not well investigated. That indicates a research gap which might be closed by further studies of the abilities and interpretability of Transformer-based models.

```
[
"title": "синдром Аспергера и РАС — общие сведения",
"paragraphs": [
    {
        "qas": [
            {
                "question": "Аутизм лечится?",
                "answers": [
                    {
                        "text": "Аутизм является пожизненным
                        "answer_start": 224,
                        "answer_end": 262
                    }
                ],
                "is_impossible": false
            },
        ],
        "context": "Этот текст подготовила группа аутичных в:
    },
```

**Fig. 1.** A dataset sample.

## 3   Dataset

The Autism Spectrum Disorder Question Answering (ASD QA) [7] is a dataset compiled by the author of the paper for the present study. The dataset contains data from the online information resource for individuals with autism spectrum disorders (ASD) and Asperger syndrome [21], totaling 1 134 answered questions. One can use question-answer pairs and metadata from the dataset for training or fine-tuning models for machine reading comprehension (MRC), question answering (QA), text generation, etc.

The Stanford Question Answering Dataset (SQuAD) [22,23] was the source of inspiration for the ASD QA dataset [7]. Figure 1 presents a dataset sample. On the Fig. 1, *Title* denotes the name of a thematic cluster. The dataset includes three clusters. The first cluster comprises general information on autism spectrum disorder and Asperger syndrome. The second cluster contains facts about interaction and communication with people with special needs. The third cluster includes practical guidelines for parents. The block *Paragraphs* on the Fig. 1 denotes pairs of questions and answers (see *qas* on the Fig. 1) along with reading passages containing the corresponding information (see *context* on the Fig. 1). The dataset comprises 96 reading passages. The volume of the reading passages is 45 400 symbols, 6 578 words. The maximum length of a reading passage in the dataset is 512 symbols.

Each set of question-answer (QA) pairs (*qas*) includes one *question* and one *answer*. The volume of QA-sequences is 179 174 symbols, 26 269 words. Each set of *answers* includes their *texts* and metadata: (1) the numeric representation of an answer span in a corresponding *context* with its first symbol (*answer_start*)

**Table 1.** The dataset statistics.

|  | Train | Val | Test |
|---|---|---|---|
| Number of reading passages (E) | 67 | 15 | 14 |
| % of unanswerable questions (E) | 5.8 | 3.95 | 4.35 |
| Number of QA pairs | 802 | 158 | 174 |
| Number of tokens (word-level) in questions | 5,524 | 1,204 | 1,381 |
| Maximum length of a question (word-level) | 20 | 15 | 15 |
| Minimum length of a question (word-level) | 2 | 2 | 2 |
| Number of tokens (word-level) in answers | 12,252 | 2,795 | 3,113 |
| Maximum length of an answer (word-level) | 45 | 50 | 42 |
| Minimum length of an answer (word-level) | 2 | 3 | 5 |
| Maximum length of a reading passage (E) | 512 | 512 | 512 |
| Vocabulary size (E) | 30,522 | 30,522 | 30,522 |
| Out-of-vocabulary rate (E), mBERT | 31.38 | 29.3 | 29.85 |
| Out-of-vocabulary rate (E), mDBERT | 0 | 0 | 0 |
| Out-of-vocabulary rate (E), XLM-R | 32.48 | 30.65 | 31.21 |
| Out-of-vocabulary rate (E), ruBERT | 0 | 0 | 0 |
| Vocabulary size (G) | 50,257 | 50,257 | 50,257 |
| Out-of-vocabulary rate (G), GPT-2 | 0 | 0 | 0 |

and its last symbol (*answer_end*), and (2) a tag *is_impossible* that shows if a question can have a coherent answer. All the unanswerable questions in the ASD QA dataset are provided with the following plausible answer in Russian: *I cannot answer this question.*

The ASD QA dataset was shuffled and split into (1) a training set containing around 70% of total data, (2) a validation set that comprises around 15% of the data, and (3) a test set with around 15% of the data. The data was split with *train_test_split* method from Scikit-learn library [24]. Table 1 presents statistics on the split dataset. The table also shows specifications for extractive and generative question answering. *(E)* and *(G)* on the Table 1 denote respectively specific features of the dataset transformed for extractive and generative QA models. The table displays the out-of-vocabulary (OOV) rate separately for each Transformer-based model used in the study.

The ASD QA is a machine reading comprehension (MRC) dataset ready for building extractive QA models. The author has transformed the dataset for generative question answering: questions and answers were retrieved without metadata, and QA-pairs were supplemented with *start-* and *end-of-sentence* tags. The dataset was converted into a Python list object where each element represented a QA-pair. Figure 2 shows a dataset sample transformed for the training of generative QA models. ⟨s⟩ and ⟨/s⟩ denote start- and end-of-sentence tags respectively.

```
<s> Расскажи мне сказку? Я не могу ответить на этот вопрос. </s>
<s> Что развивают у детей с аутизмом совместные игры с родителями? Если вы делаете :
<s> Сможет ли мой ребенок с РАС заниматься спортом наравне с другими детьми? многие
<s> Что такое любовь? Я не могу ответить на этот вопрос. </s>
<s> Нужно ли бояться эпидемии аутизма. Нет никакой эпидемии аутизма. </s>
<s> Какими спортивными активностями можно заниматься вместе с ребенком с РАС? Забраc
<s> Если я обижу аспи, она простит меня? Большинство Аспи могут легко прощать. </s>
```

**Fig. 2.** A dataset sample transformed for generative QA models training.

## 4    Models and Learning Configuration

Transformer architecture chosen for the experiments was described in [1]. This architecture is based solely on attention mechanisms with a fully connected feed-forward network (*FFN*). The position-wise FFN in the Transformer takes a vector $x$ and passes it through the matrices *W1* and *W2* and bias vectors *b1* and *b2*:

$$FFN(x) = max(0, xW_1 + b_1)W_2 + b_2 \qquad (1)$$

The unit of a multi-head self-attention mechanism $A$ in the Transformer takes key-value pairs ($K$, $V$) as input. The keys are of dimension $dk$, and the values are of dimension $dv$. The attention function is multiplied by a matrix $Q$, and a *softmax* function is applied for the computation of the scaled dot-product attention described in [1]:

$$A(Q, K, V) = softmax(\frac{QK^T}{\sqrt{dk}})V \qquad (2)$$

The Transformer-based models were fine-tuned using PyTorch [25] and HuggingFace [26] tools. Four models chosen for the experiments were pre-trained for masked language modeling (MLM) [27]. The author used these models for extractive QA. The list of models is as follows: Bidirectional Encoder Representations from Transformers multilingual (BERT, mBERT) base model (cased) [27], distilled version of BERT base multilingual (DBERT, mDBERT) model (cased) [28], Unsupervised Cross-lingual Representation Learning at Scale (XLM-RoBERTa, XLM-R) base model [29] and BERT base model for Russian (cased) fine-tuned by Geotrend (ruBERT) [30]. One of the models chosen for the experiments was pre-trained for traditional language modeling. The author used this model for generative QA. This model was Generative Pre-trained Transformer 2 [17].

The training data and model weights were stored on Google Cloud Storage [31]. The training was performed on Google Collaborative Environment [32] with Nvidia Tesla T4 graphics processing unit (GPU) [33]. During the experiments, the training time for each model was recorded in minutes. During the hyperparameters optimization, the author tuned batch size, learning rate, and the number of epochs. Each model was retrained ten times with different parameters.

The BERT-, DistilBERT- and XLM-RoBERTa-based models were retrained for 5, 10, 15, and 20 epochs with 1e−5, 3e−5, and 5e−5 learning rate. The optimal batch size for all those models was 1. The GPT-2-based model was retrained for 15, 20, and 30 epochs with 1e−5, 3e−5, and 5e−5 learning rate. The optimal batch size for this model is 16. The optimal parameters are presented in the next section in Table 3 in the next section. Table 2 presents models' configurations.

**Table 2.** Models' configurations.

| Parameter | BERT | DBERT | XLM-R | GPT-2 |
|---|---|---|---|---|
| Dropout rate | 0.1 | 0.1 | 0.1 | 0.1 |
| Activation function | GELU | GELU | GELU | GELU |
| Hidden layers | 12 | 6 | 12 | 12 |
| Embeddings | 512 | 512 | 512 | 768 |
| Attention heads | 12 | 12 | 12 | 12 |
| Vocabulary size | 30,522 | 30,522 | 30,522 | 50,257 |
| Model parameters | 110M | 66M | 125M | 117M |

## 5    Experiments and Results

One of the issues identified during the training is the "weight" of the latest natural language processing models. Even a small version of GPT-2 with 117 million parameters and BERT-based models with 110 million parameters necessitate high computation power to run training sessions. The issue was solved by using smaller batch sizes and applying a Python garbage collector. The garbage collector for the automatic memory allocation management prevented the crash of sessions caused by using all Random-Access Memory.

The next issue was related to the metric scores. The models mostly showed high precision and low recall, which means that the models were outputting very few but frequently correct answers. The problem was solved by increasing the dataset volume. During the experiments, it was found that shorter reading passages lead to better results. The reduction of reading passages' maximum length from 1 024 to 512 symbols increased the average model performance (F1-Score and Exact Match) by around 10%.

**Table 3.** Results obtained on ASD QA (extractive and generative question answering).

| Model name | Time (minutes) | Number of epochs | Learning rate | Batch size | EM | F1 |
|---|---|---|---|---|---|---|
| mBERT | 22 | 10 | 3e−5 | 1 | 0.29 | 0.40 |
| mDBERT | 11 | 20 | 1e−5 | 1 | 0.32 | 0.42 |
| XLM-R | 10 | 10 | 3e−5 | 1 | **0.39** | **0.48** |
| ruBERT | 10 | 10 | 5e−5 | 1 | 0.30 | 0.39 |
| GPT-2 | 30 | 30 | 3e−5 | 16 | **0.41** | **0.53** |

The final issue is the choice of models. The investigation of the HuggingFace Transformers repository showed that models pre-trained on masked language modeling (MLM) and traditional language modeling (LM) are more flexible than narrow models pre-trained for question answering or machine reading comprehension (MRC). Narrow models could allow achieving higher metric scores after the fine-tuning. However, such models do not have zero-shot learning capabilities and have more dataset requirements. During the experiments, it was found that with low-resource closed-domain datasets models pre-trained on a target language data do not achieve higher results than multilingual ones. Table 3 shows the models' results.

# 6   Discussion

The author has compared the achieved metric scores (see Sect. 5) with the results of some similar studies. Table 4 is a comparison table of metric scores of Transformer-based models trained on open- and medical domain datasets. The properties of the dataset used in this study should differ from the features of the medical domain because texts about autism spectrum disorder (ASD) from the dataset are not professional. Such texts are usually being adapted for parents of people with ASD, neurotypical adults, adults with special needs, etc. In turn, medical texts that address professionals include more special vocabulary. Authors of such documents usually do not adapt their texts for non-professionals. Nevertheless, these domains have a lot in common because they both cover various medical topics. That is why the author decided to compare her results with the results of similar models trained on the medical COVID-19 Open Research Dataset (CORD-19) [34].

**Table 4.** Results obtained on open-domain and medical COVID-19 benchmarks.

| Model name | Dataset | EM | F1 |
|---|---|---|---|
| BERT | CORD-19 (medical, COVID-19) | 81.5 | 88.3 |
| DBERT | CORD-19 (medical, COVID-19) | 80.6 | 87.3 |
| BERT | SQuAD 1.1 dev (open, English) | 81.3 | 88.7 |
| DBERT | SQuAD 1.1 dev (open, English) | 80.1 | 87.5 |
| XLM-R | MKQA (open, multilingual) | – | 46.0 |
| mBERT | MKQA (open, multilingual) | – | 44.1 |
| mT5 (generative QA) | MKQA (open, multilingual) | – | 38.5 |

Table 4 includes metric scores given in a paper describing COBERT, a BERT-based COVID-19 question answering system [35]. The authors of the COBERT compared the results of BERT-[27] and DistilBERT-based [28] models obtained on CORD-19 and open-domain SQuAD 1.1 [22] datasets in English. The results of multilingual BERT- and DistilBERT-based models obtained on the ASD QA dataset presented in this study differ. BERT showed slightly better results than

DistilBERT for both CORD-19 and SQuAD. In this study, a multilingual version of DistilBERT became more efficient than multilingual BERT on the ASD QA dataset (see Table 3).

The table of comparison includes F1 scores achieved by multi- and crosslingual Transformer-based models trained on Multilingual Open Domain Question Answering dataset (MKQA) [36]. The results presented in the MKQA paper allow us to compare the efficiency of generative and extractive question answering. The MKQA authors have chosen a multilingual version of T5 [37] Transformer-based model to implement the generative approach. They have also compared the efficiency of XLM-RoBERTa [29] and multilingual BERT. XLM-RoBERTa became the most powerful model. That is consistent with the results obtained on the ASD QA dataset. In this study, XLM-RoBERTa showed the highest metric scores among all the models chosen for the extractive approach implementation. In the MKQA case, the generative model achieved lower metric scores, whereas the same approach allowed the author to get the best results in this study.

## 7    Conclusion

Overall, in the study, the author compares SOTA Transformer-based question answering models' performance in the autism spectrum disorder domain with their performance in the open- or medical domain. The hypothesis that extractive models would cope with the task significantly better due to their reliability did not confirm according to the metric scores of the models and the analysis of the models' outputs obtained on the test data. The traditional language model fine-tuned for generative question answering showed higher results than any other model for extractive question answering used in the study.

Among the extractive QA models, the most effective became XLM-RoBERTa. Supposedly, the number of model parameters is the reason for that. The number of parameters is the highest for XLM-RoBERTa. It is also high for GPT-2. Apart from that, the number of embeddings is the highest for GPT-2. Out-of-vocabulary (OOV) rate linked to the vocabulary size did not play a crucial role (for example, XLM-RoBERTa had the highest OOV rate, but this model showed the highest performance among all the extractive models from the study). The author hasn't noticed any significant advantages of ruBERT model pre-trained on Russian (target language) data over multilingual ones.

A large number of unsuccessful outputs produced by trained systems shows that generative and extractive models are both yet far from the first trials of their integration into the education processes. One of the possible reasons for some unsuccessful outputs is the vocabulary of texts about autism spectrum disorders. Texts from the dataset used in the study contain specific words from the medical domain. For example, such texts comprise designations of mental, neurodevelopmental, generic, and other disorders (Asperger's syndrome, intellectual disability, Down's syndrome). They also include other medical terms (diagnosis, hypersensitivity, etc.). Those terms are mixed in the dataset with everyday vocabulary about childhood and adolescence, for example, names of games and school-related words. Due to the topics' narrowness, the sentences in the dataset have a similar structure and are not lexically diverse.

Extractive models are considered to be more reliable than generative ones. They do not generate a new answer but extract one from a given piece of text. However, the study showed that such models could give misleading answers as often as generative models while being trained on a low-resource closed-domain dataset. The reason for that is that such models can shift the answer by extracting the right sentence from the reading passage but the wrong word or phrase due to the lexical similarities and little diversity in the dataset vocabulary. This problem can be solved by providing the dataset with shorter answers consisting of one or two words so that models would be able to learn to extract specific unique text pieces.

Generative models could generate correct information based on the knowledge from their memory not answering a user's question. The issue was caused by the large number of similar terms repeated in different reading passages and question-answer pairs. The models were so to say confused by a large amount of repeating vocabulary. Possibly, the problem can be solved by enriching the dataset with texts on different topics with a more diverse vocabulary.

In the longer term, the author decided to continue experimenting with the dataset transformations. In particular, the author plans to add more answers to each question and investigate the effect of the length of answers and questions on system performance. The author also intends to find out how various Transformer-based models deal with unanswerable questions and which techniques might lead to higher efficiency in solving this task.

# References

1. Vaswani, A., et al.: Attention is all you need. In: Proceedings of the 31st International Conference on Neural Information Processing Systems (NIPS 2017), pp. 6000–6010. Curran Associates Inc., Red Hook (2017). https://doi.org/10.5555/3295222.3295349
2. He, X., Zhao, K., Chu, X.: AutoML: a survey of the state-of-the-art. Knowl.-Based Syst. **212**, 1–27 (2021)
3. Li, S., et al.: Zero-shot generalization in dialog state tracking through generative question answering, pp. 1–11. CoRR abs/2101.08333 (2021)
4. Chakravarti, R., Sil, A.: Towards confident machine reading comprehension, pp. 1–8. arXiv e-prints 2101.07942 (2021)
5. Vargas-Vera, M., Lytras, M.D.: AQUA: a closed-domain question answering system. Inf. Syst. Manag. **27**(3), 217–225 (2010). https://doi.org/10.1080/10580530.2010.493825
6. Kamdi, R.P., Agrawal, A.J.: Keywords based closed domain question answering system for Indian penal code sections and Indian amendment laws. Int. J. Intell. Syst. Appl. **7**(12), 57–67 (2015)
7. ASD QA dataset. https://figshare.com/articles/dataset/Autism_Spectrum_Disorder_and_Asperger_Syndrome_Question_Answering_Dataset_1_0/13295831. Accessed 25 July 2021

8. Gao, J., Galley, M., Li, L.: Neural approaches to conversational AI. Found. Trends® Inf. Retrieval **13**(2–3), 127–298 (2016). https://doi.org/10.1561/1500000074

9. Galitsky, B.: Question-answering system for teaching autistic children to reason about mental states. Center for Discrete Mathematics Theoretical Computer Science (2000). https://doi.org/10.5555/868301

10. Mujeeb, S., Javed, M.H., Arshad, T.: Aquabot: a diagnostic chatbot for achluophobia and autism. Int. J. Adv. Comput. Sci. Appl. (IJACSA) **8**(9), 209–216 (2017). https://doi.org/10.14569/IJACSA.2017.080930

11. Shahamiri, S.R., Thabtah, F.: Autism AI: a new autism screening system based on artificial intelligence. Cogn. Comput. **12**(4), 766–777 (2020). https://doi.org/10.1007/s12559-020-09743-3

12. Weizembaum, J.: ELIZA - a computer program for the study of natural language communication between man and machine. Commun. Assoc. Comput. Mach. **9**(1), 36–45 (1965)

13. Woods, W.: Progress in natural language understanding: an application to lunar geology. In: Proceedings of the National Computer Conference, AFIPS 1973, New York, pp. 441–450. ACM, New York (1973)

14. Vassallo, G., Pilato, G., Augello, A., Gaglio, S.: Phase coherence in conceptual spaces for conversational agents. In: Semantic Computing, pp. 357–371. IEEE/Wiley (2010)

15. Ruder, S., Peters, M., Swayamdipta, S., Wolf, T.: Transfer learning in natural language processing. In: Conference: Proceedings of the 2019 Conference of the North, pp. 15–18 (2019). https://doi.org/10.18653/v1/N19-5004

16. Radford, A., Narasimhan, K., Salimans, T., Sutskever, I.: Improving language understanding by generative pre-training. Preprint (2018)

17. Radford, A., Wu, J., Child, R., Luan, D., Amodei, D., Sutskever, I.: Language models are unsupervised multitask learners. OpenAI (2019)

18. Brown, T.B., et al.: Language models are few-shot learners. In: Advances in Neural Information Processing Systems (NeurIPS 2020), vol. 33, pp. 1–75 (2020)

19. Logé, C., et al.: Q-Pain: a question answering dataset to measure social bias in pain management (version 1.0.0). PhysioNet 1–13 (2021). https://doi.org/10.13026/2tdv-hj07

20. Zhang, E., Gupta, N., Nogueira, R., Cho, K., Lin, J.: Rapidly deploying a neural search engine for the COVID-19 open research dataset. In: Proceedings of the 1st Workshop on NLP for COVID-19 at ACL 2020. Association for Computational Linguistics (2020). Online

21. Autistic City. http://aspergers.ru/. Accessed 4 Apr 2021

22. Rajpurkar, P., Zhang, J., Lopyrev, K., Liang, P.: SQuAD: 100,000+ questions for machine comprehension of text. In: Proceedings of the 2016 Conference on Empirical Methods in Natural Language Processing, pp. 2383–2392. Association for Computational Linguistics, Austin (2016). https://doi.org/10.18653/v1/D16-1264

23. Rajpurkar, P., Jia, R., Liang, P.: Know what you don't know: unanswerable questions for SQuAD. In: Proceedings of the 56th Annual Meeting of the Association for Computational Linguistics (Volume 2: Short Papers), pp. 784–789. Association for Computational Linguistics, Melbourne (2018). https://doi.org/10.18653/v1/P18-2124

24. Scikit-learn: machine learning in Python. https://scikit-learn.org/. Accessed 6 Apr 2021

25. PyTorch. https://pytorch.org/. Accessed 6 Apr 2021
26. Hugging Face - The AI community building the future. https://huggingface.co/. Accessed 6 Apr 2021
27. Devlin, J., Chang, M.-W., Lee, K., Toutanova, K.: BERT: Pre-training of deep bidirectional transformers for language understanding, pp. 4171–4186. Association for Computational Linguistics, Minneapolis (2019). https://doi.org/10.18653/v1/N19-1423
28. Sanh, V., Debut, L., Chaumond, J., Wolf, T.: DistilBERT, a distilled version of BERT: smaller, faster, cheaper and lighter. In: 5th Workshop on Energy Efficient Machine Learning and Cognitive Computing - NeurIPS, pp. 1–5 (2019)
29. Conneau, A., et al.: Unsupervised cross-lingual representation learning at scale. In: Proceedings of the 58th Annual Meeting of the Association for Computational Linguistics, pp. 8440–8451. Association for Computational Linguistics (2020). https://doi.org/10.18653/v1/2020.acl-main.747
30. Geotrend - One click for intelligent data. https://www.geotrend.fr/. Accessed 6 Apr 2021
31. Cloud Storage—Google Cloud. https://cloud.google.com/storage. Accessed 8 Apr 2021
32. Google Colab. https://colab.research.google.com/. Accessed 8 Apr 2021
33. Cloud GPUs (Graphics Processing Units)—Google Cloud. https://cloud.google.com/gpu. Accessed 8 Apr 2021
34. CORD-19: COVID-19 Open Research Dataset. https://www.semanticscholar.org/cord19. Accessed 6 Sept 2021
35. Alzubi, J.A., Jain, R., Singh, A., et al.: COBERT: COVID-19 question answering system using BERT. Arab. J. Sci. Eng. (2021). https://doi.org/10.1007/s13369-021-05810-5
36. Longpre, S., Lu, Y., Daiber, J.: MKQA: a linguistically diverse benchmark for multilingual open domain question answering. arXiv e-prints 2007.15207 (2020)
37. Raffel, C., et al.: Exploring the limits of transfer learning with a unified text-to-text transformer. arXiv e-prints 1910.10683 (2020)

# ePolity: E-Governance and Regulation

# What Drives Adoption of E-Services in Russia?

Elena Dobrolyubova[✉] ⓘ and Alexandra Starostina ⓘ

Russian Presidential Academy of National Economy and Public Administration (RANEPA),
Vernadskogo pr. 84, 119571 Moscow, Russia
dobrolyubova-ei@ranepa.ru

**Abstract.** The expectations from digital government transformation are remarkably high, especially in public service delivery. However, the recent research points to the fact that often such impacts are overestimated, and the actual results of public administration digitalization are more modest than expected. One of the reasons for that is insufficient adoption of digital public service delivery channels especially in the countries like Russia where digital by default principle has not been established. The significant variance in regional development makes Russia an interesting case for research and comparison both for developed and developing nations.

This paper aims at identifying the factors influencing citizen adoption of digital public service delivery channels in Russian regions. Based on the review of theoretical and empirical literature, we selected 11 possible factors that could be related to the extent of adoption of electronic public services at the regional level. While statistically significant correlation was found with most variables considered, no such interrelation was confirmed for age and information security risks indicators. The results of regression analysis suggest that quality of public service supply in electronic form, education, and per capita income determine the extent of digital public services adoption.

Our findings demonstrate that social aspects of digital divide are more important than variations in ICT infrastructure development and should be accounted for in the ongoing and future government digital transformation initiatives.

**Keywords:** Adoption · Digital divide · Digital government · Digital interaction · Electronic public services · Factors

## 1 Introduction

Both international organizations [54] and national governments (see, for instance, [5, 45, 46]) set high expectations from government digital transformation. As predicted by multiple stage digital maturity models [36], unleashing the potential of digital technologies in the public administration is expected to optimize the public value of government services for citizens [7], increase efficiency of government functions [24] and develop new bureaucratic culture [34], support citizen participation [33] and client engagement in public value co-production and co-creation [11]. Government digitalization is expected to significantly reduce administrative costs [48] and improve business environment [26].

© Springer Nature Switzerland AG 2022
D. A. Alexandrov et al. (Eds.): DTGS 2021, CCIS 1503, pp. 137–151, 2022.
https://doi.org/10.1007/978-3-030-93715-7_10

While the readiness to digital transformation in Russia is debated [15], digitalization has become one of the key national objectives till 2030 (as per Presidential Decree No. 474 dated July 21, 2020, *On the Russian Federation National Development Objectives till 2030*). Achieving digital maturity in various sectors, including public governance, making 95% of in-demand socially significant public services available in electronic format, and improving broadband connection to Internet are among performance indicators used for achieving this objective. A recent set of digital maturity performance indicators approved by the RF Ministry of Digital development suggests that digital transformation in public administration should result in a threefold decrease of the time required to obtain the results of public services and lead to 90% level of uptake of digital channels in public service delivery (for services which do not require mandatory personal visits)[1]. Thus, the ambitions related to government digital transformation in Russia are also quite high.

However, the recent review suggests that, at least in the early e-government maturity models, the outcomes of public administration digitalization have been overestimated, though digital technologies did bring about some improvements in public administration practices [6]. While there are various constraints [38] and enablers of digital transformation in the public sector, digital divide and variation in adoption of digital interaction channels by citizens and businesses are considered among the most common [22].

Significant variations in digital services uptake are confirmed by the recent empirical studies in the EU [55] and in Russia [32]. Such variation is often related to infrastructure constraints. Indeed, some recent research suggests that 'a high level of e-Government maturity can be attained purely through investment in ICT infrastructure, without substantial changes to human capital or governance' [13]. Other studies emphasize the importance of perceived usefulness of digital services [8], citizen e-readiness [20], and other factors.

It is highly likely that significance of various factors influencing digital government services uptake by citizens may vary depending both on the country context and on the stage of digital maturity. Such variations may be especially high in the countries where digital by default principle of public service delivery has not been adopted and multiple (offline and digital) channels of service provision are supported, which is the case in Russia. Therefore, identifying the factors influencing interregional variations in digital public services uptake in Russia and developing adequate policy solutions appears an important task for achieving national digital government transformation objectives. The outcomes of this study may also be of interest for other countries, especially those with high interregional development disparities.

## 2  Objective

The objective of this paper is to identify the factors influencing citizen adoption of digital public service delivery channels in Russian regions.

To achieve this objective, we need to:

---

[1] Order of RF Ministry of Digital Development No. 601 dated November 18, 2020.

1. review the existing literature on factors enabling and constraining digital public services adoption,
2. based on the literature review, select possible list of factors influencing digital public services adoption,
3. perform correlation and regression analyses to identify factors influencing citizen adoption of digital public service delivery channels in Russian regions and evaluate significance of such factors.

The study is based on official statistical data on adoption of digital public services in Russia as well as official assessment of e-readiness of public services by the RF Ministry of Economic Development.

## 3 Methodology

### 3.1 Literature Review

Theoretical and empirical studies of the factors affecting citizen uptake of digital public services (and e-government institutes as a whole) form a popular area of digital government research [4]. The approaches based on innovation diffusion theory [42] suggest that social and demographic factors, such as age, education, and income play a significant role in adopting innovations, including digital public services. Empirical studies have confirmed the importance of these factors both at the national level [53] and for explaining cross-country variations [17].

Social and demographic factors may influence public perceptions of the ease of use and technology usefulness which constitute the two critical factors of Technology Acceptance Model (TAM) proposed by F. Davis [14]. The model is still universally used in research [3, 12, 27, 31] with several proposed extensions.

One of such extensions known as Unified Theory of Acceptance and Use of Technology (UTAUT) was proposed in 2003. UTAUT accounts both for factors related to performance expectancy and effort expectancy along with social influence and facilitating conditions [49]. The model accounts for some demographic factors, such as gender and age, while other important characteristics such as education, income, and territorial factors (i.e., rural, or urban population) are not included creating a basis for critique and further model extension [1].

To explain the variations in digital government adoption, some additional factors extending TAM and UTAUT models were proposed and tested in literature. Thus, some authors argued for accounting for public value including environmental sustainability of digitization [39]. Others point to the need to incorporate such factors as trust [12, 23], which includes both trust to government and trust to Internet-based technology (digital trust) [29, 30], as well as transparency [50]. Another proposed factor related to both trust and transparency is perceived risk of electronic interaction as opposed to traditional offline channels [18, 19, 22]. In some studies, this factor is complemented by other parameters measuring relative benefits from switching from offline to online interaction (i.e., geographic proximity of public offices [44]). Empirical research conducted in some countries highlighted the need to account for such factors as the level of urbanization and employment [43], IT capabilities [2], as well as cultural issues and habitual patterns

[10]. Finally, some authors argue that there is a need to account for behavioral aspects of technology acceptance, such as attitude to technology which is closely correlated with performance and effort expectancy, social influence, and perceived risk [18].

Noteworthy, some studies are focused not on the factors enabling digital interaction and e-services adoption, but on the factors constraining adoption of digital services or fostering resistance thereto. Such factors include inertia [41] and costs of switching from offline to online interaction [38].

Since digital transformation is not a one-time event but an evolving process of change both within public administration and in society at large, the factors affecting digital public services adoption are likely to change with time. Therefore, identifying both enablers and inhibitors for digital interaction with public administration is a relevant task for various stages of government digital transformation.

Most empirical studies analyzed in this section were based on sociological surveys, often with limited samples, while the research at the national and international level is less common. An example of such recent research conducted for the EU countries suggests that digital public services adoption in this region depends both on social and demographic characteristics and on the level of e-government development as well as trust in government [40].

In Russia, both the issues of digital divide (see for instance [35, 37]) and managerial and technological factors of e-government development [25] have been studied extensively. However, the research of digital government adoption factors has been limited to selected population groups (i.e., rural population [9]) and selected territories [51]. This article attempts to fill this gap and identify the key factors influencing adoption of digital interaction by citizens in the Russian regions.

## 3.2 Methodic Approach

The literature review presented in Sect. 3.1 allows to identify 11 potential factors that may influence the adoption of digital public services including social and demographic factors (age, education, urbanization, employment, average income and poverty level), availability and quality of e-services (quality of e-services at the regional level and citizen satisfaction), ICT infrastructure (households with broadband access to Internet), experience in facing Internet-related risks and using Internet technology for other purposes (Table 1). Most factors are based on official statistics, including the results of the federal statistical survey on the use of information technology by the population in 2019[2]. Quality of regional e-service delivery is based on expert evaluation published by the RF Ministry of Economic Development[3].

Noteworthy, given the lack of up-to-date data on citizen trust in government (or citizen evaluation of public administration performance) by region, this factor was not included into the analysis.

In Russia, adoption of digital public services is traditionally measured by a percentage of citizens using Internet to obtain state and municipal services out of the total number of citizens that applied for such services. According to Rosstat, this percentage is quite

---

[2] https://gks.ru/free_doc/new_site/business/it/ikt20/index.html (accessed on June 16, 2021).

[3] https://ar.gov.ru/ru-RU/menu/default/view/21 (accessed on February 25, 2021).

**Table 1.** Possible factors of digital public service adoption by citizens

| Possible factor | Description | Related factors analyzed in other studies |
|---|---|---|
| Quality of e-services at the regional level (X1) | Quality of regional e-service delivery is evaluated annually by the RF Ministry of Economic Development[a]. The evaluation is related only to the services delivered at the regional level (i.e., social protection) and does not include federal level services (i.e., property and vehicle registration, tax filing, etc.) | Perceived usefulness and perceived ease of use (TAM); level of e-government development [40] |
| Citizen satisfaction (X2) | Percentage of citizens fully satisfied with quality of public service delivery in electronic form (Source: Rosstat*) | Perceived usefulness (TAM); expected performance, effort expectancy (UTAUT) |
| Age (X3) | Percentage of population above working age (Source: Rosstat**) | Age [17, 40, 53] |
| Urbanization (X4) | Percentage of urban population (Source: Rosstat **) | Urbanization [40, 43] |
| Per capita income (X5) | Per capita income (Source: Rosstat**) | Income [40, 53] |
| Income distribution (X6) | Percentage of population with income below poverty level (Source: Rosstat**) | Income [40, 53] |
| Education (X7) | Percentage of employed population with professional education (Source: Rosstat**) | Education [17, 40, 53] |
| Employment (X8) | Percentage of employed population, 15 years old and above (Source: Rosstat) | Employment [43] |
| ICT infrastructure (X9) | Percentage of households with broadband access to Internet (Source: Rosstat***) | ICT infrastructure [13], switching costs [38], facilitating conditions (UTAUT) |
| Internet-related risks (X10) | Percentage of Internet users facing information security problems (Source: Rosstat*) | Perceived risk [19, 22] |

*(continued)*

**Table 1.** (*continued*)

| Possible factor | Description | Related factors analyzed in other studies |
|---|---|---|
| Experience in digital interactions for other purposes (X11) | Percentage of population using Internet to order goods and/or services (Source: Rosstat*) | ICT capabilities [2], Perceived usefulness (TAM) Expected performance, effort expectancy (UTAUT) |

[a]https://ar.gov.ru/ru-RU/menu/default/view/21 (accessed on February 25, 2021).
*https://gks.ru/free_doc/new_site/business/it/ikt20/index.html (accessed on June 16, 2021).
**https://gks.ru/bgd/regl/b20_13/Main.htm (accessed on June 16, 2021).
***https://rosstat.gov.ru/folder/14478 (accessed on June 16, 2021).

high: in 2019, some 77.6% of citizens that applied for public services used Internet. However, in many cases, citizens used Internet not to apply for a service or to obtain a result of such service, but for getting information about the service procedure (72.7%), scheduling a visit to a public authority or one stop shop of public services (60.4%), paying taxes and fees (60.4%). Only some 26.9% of citizens that applied for public services used Internet to send relevant forms. Some 26.5% of citizens obtained a result of public service in electronic form. In this respect Russia lags the EU where, on average, 64.3% of citizens send filled forms to apply for a public service electronically.

Therefore, to evaluate the extent of digital public service adoption, it seems important to account not only for the level of Internet usage in the process of service delivery, but also for the fact of digital interaction with public administration, including filing forms (applying for public services) and obtaining public service result electronically.

Hence, in our analysis we consider three dependent variables reflecting various stages of digital public service delivery adoption:

- percentage of citizens using Internet to obtain state and municipal services, out of total number of citizens who applied for such services (Y1),
- percentage of citizens using Internet to file forms to obtain public services, out of total number of citizens who applied for such services (Y2), and
- percentage of citizens that received results of public services in electronic form, out of total number of citizens who applied for such services (Y3).

For dependent variables Rosstat data[4] for 2019 was used.

Our sample included all Russian regions (N = 85). The data for 2019 aggregated at the regional level was used for the analysis. Both correlation and multiple regression analyses were conducted.

## 4   Results

Descriptive statistics of potential factors included in the analysis as well as the extent of digital public services adoption demonstrate significant interregional variations (Table

---

[4] https://gks.ru/free_doc/new_site/business/it/ikt20/index.html (accessed on June 16, 2021).

2). Thus, while the average quality of regional e-service delivery was rated by the RF Ministry of Economic Development at 44.2 points on 0–100 scale, the highest quality of e-service delivery was observed in Moscow (98.36), while the lowest score (7.71) was assigned to Ingushetia. Citizen satisfaction with quality of public service delivery in electronic form also varied significantly: from 93.4% in Adyghea Republic to 26.1% in Magadan oblast. There is significant interregional variation in social and demographic indicators included in the study as well as in ICT infrastructure development, frequency of risks related to information security as well as in experience in using Internet technology for ordering goods and services.

**Table 2.** Descriptive statistics for potential factors of digital public services adoption in 2019

| Variable | Average | Minimum | Maximum | Standard Deviation |
|----------|---------|---------|---------|--------------------|
| X1 | 44.20 | 7.71 | 98.36 | 19.75 |
| X2 | 71.07 | 26.10 | 93.40 | 12.32 |
| X3 | 25.11 | 10.80 | 31.30 | 4.65 |
| X4 | 70.68 | 29.20 | 100.00 | 13.07 |
| X5 | 32069.02 | 16413.00 | 84135.00 | 13873.12 |
| X6 | 14.28 | 5.60 | 34.70 | 5.15 |
| X7 | 77.58 | 43.30 | 92.80 | 6.54 |
| X8 | 58.5 | 47.5 | 76.7 | 5.1 |
| X9 | 71.64 | 50.60 | 93.90 | 8.30 |
| X10 | 21.30 | 3.60 | 70.60 | 10.56 |
| X11 | 39.32 | 13.10 | 79.50 | 11.78 |

Source: calculated by authors based on RF Ministry of Economic Development and Rosstat data

The results of the analysis suggest that statistically significant correlation was found with most of the variables included into the analysis (Table 3).

Thus, there is statistically significant correlation between the level of education (x7) and digital service adoption, especially as far as filing electronic forms to obtain public services is concerned (y2) (Fig. 1). Better educated citizens find it easier to interact with public administration digitally, hence, the level of digital service adoption in regions with larger percentage of employed population with tertiary education is higher than in those where the education level is lower.

Quality of regional e-service delivery (x1) as well as experience of digital interactions for other purposes (x11) are also statistically significant variables correlating with all stages of digital public services adoption. The first variable (x1) demonstrates the importance of supply factors for digital public services adoption: the more services are available at the regional level, the more they correspond to the quality standards, the higher is the digital public service adoption. The interrelation of digital public services adoption with the experience of digital interactions for other purposes suggests that

**Table 3.** Pearson correlation coefficients

| Variable | Y1 | Y2 | Y3 |
|---|---|---|---|
| X1 | .443** | .278* | .238* |
| X2 | .254* | .084 | .098 |
| X3 | .095 | .010 | − .074 |
| X4 | .102 | .360** | .281** |
| X5 | .039 | .398** | .402** |
| X6 | − .168 | − .416** | − .312** |
| X7 | .305** | .403** | .384** |
| X8 | .105 | .369** | .332** |
| X9 | .233* | .165 | .168 |
| X10 | .064 | .035 | .041 |
| X11 | .230* | .420** | .348** |

*correlation valid at p = 0.05 (two-tailed); ** correlation valid at p = 0.01 (two-tailed).* Source: calculated by authors based on RF Ministry of Economic Development and Rosstat data.

experience and relevant skills used for ordering goods and services via Internet help citizens to use the technology for interacting with public administration.

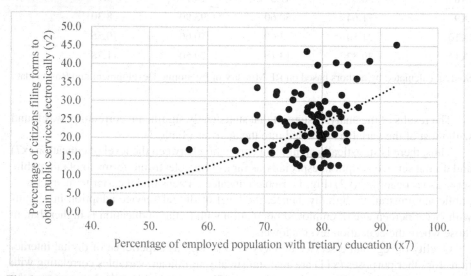

**Fig. 1.** Correlation of education and adoption of e-services in Russian regions in 2019. Source: calculated by authors based on Rosstat data.

Correlation of other factors with indicators of digital public service delivery adoption varies depending on the extent the technology is used.

For instance, urbanization (x4), employment (x8) and income indicators (x5, x6) are correlated with the indicators assuming some level of engagement in digital interaction with public administration (i.e., filing forms and receiving service results electronically). However, these variables demonstrate no statistically significant correlation with the use of Internet technologies in a broad sense, i.e., for information and other purposes.

On the contrary, broadband access to Internet (x9) and citizen satisfaction with quality of public service delivery in electronic form (x2) are correlated with the percentage of citizens using Internet for obtaining public services but demonstrate no correlation when actual digital interaction indicators (y2 and y3) are used.

Such situation may be partially explained by the fact that the share of citizens filing forms electronically is still quite low in Russia. Moreover, filing forms electronically, let alone the option of getting public service results electronically, is not always available for the most in-demand public services. For instance, such services as getting a passport, registering vehicles, etc., require personal visits to public bodies or multifunctional centers (public service delivery one stop shops, or MFCs).

We found no statistically significant correlation between the share of older population in the region and the extent of e-services adoption. Notably, similar findings were presented in the recent research of e-government adoption factors in the EU where no correlation between age and e-services adoption was found [40].

To evaluate the significance of various factors for predicting the adoption of digital public services, three multiple regression models were developed, one for each dependent variable: percentage of citizens using Internet to obtain state and municipal services (y1), percentage of citizens using Internet to file forms to obtain public services (y2), and percentage of citizens that received results of public services in electronic form (y3). For regression purposes, only the variables with correlation coefficients significant at p = 0.01 were used as predictors.

The regression results (Table 4) demonstrate that the only significant factor in the first model is the quality of e-services at the regional level (x1). Thus, the use of Internet for obtaining public services in Russia in a broad sense is supply driven. The significant factors determining the use of Internet to file forms to obtain public services and to obtain results of such services in electronic form include per capita income (x5) and education (x7). Other factors proved insignificant based on regression analysis.

**Table 4.** Regression analysis summary

| Factors | β-coefficients (significance) | | |
|---------|------|------|------|
| | Y1 | Y2 | Y3 |
| X1 | **.396 (.000)** | - | - |
| X4 | - | .158 (.189) | .099 (.364) |
| X5 | - | **.381 (.000)** | **.485 (.000)** |

(*continued*)

**Table 4.** (*continued*)

| Factors | β-coefficients (significance) | | |
|---|---|---|---|
| | Y1 | Y2 | Y3 |
| X6 | - | − .176 (.159) | − .032 (.780) |
| X7 | .158 (.146) | **.294 (.004)** | **.318 (.000)** |
| X8 | - | .146 (.341) | .062 (.657) |
| X11 | - | .170 (.169) | .090 (.419) |
| Adjusted R2 | .207 | .282 | .417 |
| Standard Err | 10.343 | 6.690 | 6.670 |
| F-statistics | 11.314 | 16.545 | 29.195 |
| Durbin-Watson | 1.886 | 2.214 | 2.128 |

Noteworthy, the value of adjusted $R^2$ in all three models is quite low. The factors included in all three models explain less than a half of interregional variation in digital public services adoption. Therefore, other factors not included in the models may have significant influence on the adoption of digital public services.

## 5 Discussion

The results of analysis presented in this paper suggest that digital public service adoption correlates with several variables related to social and demographic characteristics (such as the level of education, urbanization, income, and employment), experience in using Internet-based technology for other purposes (i.e., for ordering goods and services), and quality of public services (measured based on user satisfaction and on the results of the expert assessment of quality of e-service delivery at the regional level).

However, based on regression analysis, the determinants of digital public service adoption are limited. Thus, the interregional variation in the use of Internet for obtaining public services (regardless the objective of such use), depends on availability and quality of supply of such services in various regions. More advanced stages of digital public services adoption (i.e., filing e-forms and obtaining results in e-format) are determined by social and economic factors, i.e., average per capita income and education.

The difference in factors determining various stages of digital public service adoption supports the point made by some other studies (see for instance [29]) that digital government adoption enablers change depending on the extent of digital maturity.

Due to continuous improvement in broadband access to Internet and significant growth in the use of smartphones for digital transactions the factor of household access to broadband Internet does not have a significant influence on citizen adoption of digital channels for interacting with the public administration. This finding challenges the point made by A. Das et al. that digital government maturity does not require human capital development and may rely only on development of ICT infrastructure [13].

The study results confirm the significance of some of the factors of digital public services adoption identified in earlier studies, such as education [17, 40, 53], income [40, 53], and quality of digital public services [40]. However, other factors, identified as significant based on studies in other countries, such as urbanization [40, 43] and employment [43], proved insignificant in our regression models. This situation can be explained by the mutual correlation between these factors in the Russian context. For instance, the level of urbanization is correlated with education (Pearson correlation coefficient is 0.539). The level of employment is strongly correlated with per capita income (Pearson correlation coefficient is 0.783).

Overall, our findings confirm the propositions of innovation diffusion theory. However, the fact that no statistical correlation between age factor and digital public service delivery adoption was found challenges some theoretical approaches and questions the need to account for the age factor when applying innovation diffusion theory and its practical models, such as UTAUT [49], to digital public service delivery uptake.

Noteworthy, no statistical interrelation was found between the frequency of facing information security risks on the Internet and the extent of public e-services adoption. Such results suggest that so far information security risks do not affect technology adoption, at least in public services. However, with increase of digital interaction with public administration this factor is likely to become more significant, given that only some 30% of Russian citizens find that their personal data and privacy is sufficiently protected from risks, as the recent sociological survey demonstrates [16].

Relatively low value of determination coefficient ($R^2$) suggests that there are other factors determining digital public service adoption in Russian regions. Such factors may include trust in government, digital trust, and cultural differences which, due to the lack of data, were not considered in this paper.

Another limitation of this paper is related to using aggregate data at the regional level for modelling which does not allow to differentiate factors by the type of public service and does not account for intra-regional variations which may be significant. At present, there is no data available to account for intra-regional and service type variations, so such analysis is rather a subject of possible future research.

## 6  Conclusion and Recommendations

The study suggests that adoption of digital public services in Russia is driven by the quality of such services supplied and, at later stages of digital adoption, on income and education. Other factors, not accounted for in this analysis due to the lack of data, include trust in government, digital trust, and cultural differences, as well as possible intra-regional and type of service variations.

Notably, access to infrastructure is only weakly associated with the use of Internet to obtain public services. Therefore, measuring the digital divide among the regions based only on variations in ICT infrastructure availability (such practice is inter alia used for estimating the indicator on differentiation of Russian regions based on integral indicators of information development) seems insufficient. Digital divide measurement should incorporate social component accounting for variations in the extent of education and skills, as well as income.

The fact that the extent of e-services adoption depends on social and demographic factors means that rapid switch to digital interactions may have negative effects on some social groups, such as the poor and less educated citizens. The recent experience of coronavirus pandemic has highlighted this risk, especially in distance learning [21], but also in other areas.

Therefore, increasing the adoption of digital public services in Russia would call for a set of measures both aiming at developing ICT skills among various groups of population and reducing requirements to citizens related to providing data and documents to the public administration while applying for a public service (i.e., making digital interaction with public administration simpler and therefore less skill-dependent). To this end, the recent decision to eliminate the requirements on providing documental proofs for citizens applying for welfare payments is an important step in the right direction.

Coronavirus pandemic and the restrictions imposed to limit the infection spread have become an important incentive for digitalizing public services and have boosted adoption of e-services in Russia. The number of users of the Unified identification and authentication system (citizens and businesses with digital IDs) has grown from 103 million at the end of 2019 to 132,9 million by end-February, 2021[5]. During the peak periods in May 2020, the weekly number of public services requested through the single public service delivery portal exceeded 12.6 million (which is about three times higher than the usual pre-pandemic level).

However, after the restrictions on offline public service delivery were lifted, the number of offline public service requests through the network of one stop shops (MFCs) reached the pre-pandemic levels. Thus, while the pandemic restrictions helped citizens to gain some experience in digital interaction with the public administration, they also demonstrated important limitations and lack of readiness to fully digital interactions both on the side of public administration and on the side of citizens themselves.

This situation can be partially explained by a habit of applying to MFCs when this offline service delivery channel is perceived as a simpler and more reliable way of interaction with public administration. Similar effects were observed in other countries with a broad network of one stop shops, i.e., Latvia [47] and Greece [52].

However, as confirmed by this analysis, the supply side (i.e., availability and quality of public services delivered digitally) also plays an important role in promoting digital adoption. To this end, partial digitalization of public services when only some service-related procedures are available digitally while others require personal visits, limits the effects of digital transformation especially in the circumstances when digital interactions become a preferred if not the only possible service delivery channel. Thus, the increase of personal visits to MFCs and public administration bodies illustrate the fact that many in-demand public services are simply not available online. Therefore, increasing adoption of electronic public services by citizens calls for deeper and more comprehensive digital transformation in the public administration.

**Acknowledgment.** The paper was written on the basis of the RANEPA state assignment research program.

---

[5] https://sc-new.minsvyaz.ru/ (accessed on February 27, 2021).

# References

1. Alghamdi, S., Beloff, N.: Towards a comprehensive model for e-Government adoption and utilisation analysis: the case of Saudi Arabia. In: 2014 Federated Conference on Computer Science and Information Systems, pp. 1217–1225. Warsaw (2014)
2. Alshaher, A.: IT capabilities as a fundamental of electronic government system success in developing countries from users perspectives. Transf. Govern. People Process Policy **15**(1), 129–149 (2020). https://doi.org/10.1108/TG-05-2020-0080
3. Amanbek, Y., Balgayev, I., Batyrkhanov, K., Tan, M.: Adoption of e-government in the Republic of Kazakhstan. J. Open Innov. Technol. Mark. Complex. **6**(3), 46 (2020). https://doi.org/10.3390/joitmc6030046
4. Arias, M.I., Serra, F., Guerrazzi, L., Ferreira, M.P.: Intellectual foundations and mainstream research of e-government in public administration. Manage. Res. **17**(1), 89–115 (2019)
5. Australia Digital Transformation Strategy (2018). https://dta-www-drupal-201801302 15411153400000001.s3.ap-southeast-2.amazonaws.com/s3fs-public/files/digital-transform ation-strategy/digital-transformation-strategy.pdf. Accessed 25 Feb 2021
6. Bannister, F., Connolly, R.: The future isn't what it used to be: forecasting the impact of ICT on the public sphere. Gov. Inf. Q. **37**, 1 (2020)
7. Bannister, F., Connolly, R.: ICT, public values and transformative government: a framework and programme for research. Gov. Inf. Q. **31**(1), 119–128 (2014)
8. Blagoeva, K.T., Mijoska, M., Trenovski, B.: Determinants of the citizens' usage of electronic public services in the Republic of Macedonia. Electron. Gov. **16**(4), 410–425 (2020)
9. Bylina, S.G.: Regional characteristics and determinants of using electronic services among rural population. Probl. Territory's Dev. **5**(97), 84–98 (2018). (in Russian)
10. Cabinakova, J., Kroenung, J., Eckhardt, A., Bernius, S.: The importance of culture, trust, and habitual patterns - Determinants of cross-cultural e-government adoption ECIS. In: 2013 - Proceedings of the 21st European Conference on Information Systems (2013)
11. Cordella, A., Paletti, A.: ICTs and value creation in public sector: manufacturing logic vs service logic. Inf. Polity **23**(2), 1–17 (2018)
12. Dahi, M., Ezziane, Z.: Measuring e-government adoption in Abu Dhabi with technology acceptance model (TAM). Int. J. Electron. Govern. **7**(3), 206–231 (2015)
13. Das, A., Singh, H., Joseph, D.: A longitudinal study of e-government maturity. Inf. Manage. **54**(4), 415–426 (2017)
14. Davis, F.D.: Perceived usefulness, perceived ease of use, and user acceptance of information technology. MIS Q. **13**(3), 319–340 (1989). https://doi.org/10.2307/249008
15. Dobrolyubova, E., Alexandrov, O., Yefremov, A.: Is Russia ready for digital transformation? In: Alexandrov, D.A., Boukhanovsky, A.V., Chugunov, A.V., Kabanov, Y., Koltsova, O. (eds.) DTGS 2017. CCIS, vol. 745, pp. 431–444. Springer, Cham (2017). https://doi.org/10.1007/978-3-319-69784-0_36
16. Dobrolyubova, E., Yuzhakov, V., Pokida, A., Zybunovskaya, N.: How citizens evaluate safety from state-controlled risks and why. Sotsiologicheskie issledovaniya **7**, 70–81 (2020). https://doi.org/10.31857/S013216250009316-0(inRussian)
17. Domínguez, L.R., Sánchez, I.M., Alvarez, I.G.: Determining factors of e-government development: a worldwide national approach. Int. Public Manag. J. **14**(2), 218–248 (2011). https://doi.org/10.1080/10967494.2011.597152
18. Dwivedi, Y.K., Rana, N.P., Janssen, M., Lal, B., Williams, M.D., Clement, M.: An empirical validation of a unified model of electronic government adoption (UMEGA). Gov. Inf. Q. **34**(2), 211–230 (2011). https://doi.org/10.1016/j.giq.2017.03.001
19. Fakhruzzaman, M.N., Dimitrova, D.V.: Factors influencing e-government adoption in Indonesia: the importance of perceived risk. J. Adv. Res. Dyn. Control Syst. **12**(6), 125–131 (2020)

20. Ghosh Roy, S., Upadhyay, P.: Does e-readiness of citizens ensure better adoption of government's digital initiatives? A case based study. J. Enterp. Inf. Manag. **30**(1), 65–81 (2017)
21. Goncharova, N., Zaitseva, E.: Responses of Russian universities to the challenges of Covid-19 pandemic. In: Proceedings of the European Conference on e-Learning, ECEL, 2020-October, pp. 221–228. (2020). https://doi.org/10.34190/EEL.20.140
22. Israel, D., Tiwari, R.: Empirical study of factors influencing acceptance of e-government services in India. In: ACM International Conference Proceeding Series, pp. 141–146 (2011)
23. Jacob, D.W., Mohd Farhan, M., Fudzee, M.A., Salamat, S.K., Mahdin, H., Ramli, A.A.: Modelling end-user of electronic-government service: the role of information quality, system quality and trust. IOP Conf. Ser. Mater. Sci. Eng. **226**, 012096 (2017). https://doi.org/10.1088/1757-899X/226/1/012096
24. Janssen, M., Estevez, E.: Lean government and platform-based governance -doing more with less. Gov. Inf. Q. **30**, 1–8 (2013)
25. Kabanov, Y., Sungurov, A.: E-government development factors: evidence from the Russian regions. In: Chugunov, A.V., Bolgov, R., Kabanov, Y., Kampis, G., Wimmer, M. (eds.) DTGS 2016. CCIS, vol. 674, pp. 85–95. Springer, Cham (2016). https://doi.org/10.1007/978-3-319-49700-6_10
26. Kästik, T.: The impact of digital governance on the business environment: the case of Estonian tax and customs board. In: ACM International Conference Proceeding Series, Part F148155, pp. 472–4742019. https://doi.org/10.1145/3326365.3326430
27. Khamis, M., Van der Weide, T.: Conceptual framework for sustainable e-government implementation in low infrastructure situation. In: Proceedings of the European Conference on e-Government, ECEG, 2016-January, pp. 283–290 (2016)
28. Khvatov, A.E., Vatoropin, A.S.: Factors preventing the public from receiving public services in electronic form. Manage. Issues. **3**(46), 53–61 (2017). (in Russian)
29. Kumar, R., Sachan, A.: Empirical study to find factors influencing e-Filing adoption in India. ACM Int. Conf. Proc. Ser. Part **F127653**, 52–57 (2017)
30. Kurfalı, M., Arifoğlu, A., Tokdemir, G., Paçin, Y.: Adoption of e-government services in Turkey. Comput. Hum. Behav. **66**, 168–178 (2017)
31. Lean, O.K., Zailani, S., Ramayah, T., Fernando, Y.: Factors influencing intention to use e-government services among citizens in Malaysia. Int. J. Inf. Manage. **29**(6), 458–475 (2009)
32. Litvintseva, G.P., Shmakov, A.V., Stukalenko, E.A., Petrov, S.P.: Digital component of people's quality of life assessment in the regions of the Russian Federation. Terra Econ **17**(3), 107–127 (2019). (in Russian)
33. Luna-Reyes, L.F.: Opportunities and challenges for digital governance in a world of digital participation. Inf. Polity **22**(2–3), 197–205 (2017). https://doi.org/10.3233/IP-170408
34. Mergel, I., Edelmann, N., Haug, N.: Defining digital transformation: Results from expert interviews. Govern. Inf. Q. **36**(4), 101385 (2019). https://doi.org/10.1016/j.giq.2019.06.002
35. Miroliubova, T.V., Radionova, M.V.: ICT sector role and digital transformation factors in the regional economy in the context of public governance. Perm University Herald. Econ. **15**(2), 253–270 (2020). (in Russian)
36. Normann Andersen, K., Lee, J., Mettler, T., Moon, M.J.: Ten misunderstandings about maturity models. In: ACM International Conference Proceeding Series, pp. 261–266 (2020)
37. Nosonov, A.M.: Formation of information society in Russian regions. Russian J. Reg. Stud. **4**, 114–126 (2016). (in Russian)
38. Ochara, N.M., Mawela, T., Odhiambo, J.N.: Citizen resistance to e-government adoption. In: Proceedings of the European Conference on e-Government, ECEG, 2016-January, pp. 122–132 (2016)

39. Perez, S., Cabrera, J., Rodriguez, J., Raymundo, C.: E-Government adoption model extended with public value in Peru. In: Proceedings of 2019 8th International Conference on Industrial Technology and Management, ICITM 2019, pp. 338–342. (2019). https://doi.org/10.1109/ICITM.2019.8710646
40. Pérez-Morote, R., Pontones-Rosa, C., Núñez-Chicharro, M.: The effects of e-government evaluation, trust and the digital divide in the levels of e-government use in European countries. Technol. Forecast. Soc. Change **154**, 119973 (2020). https://doi.org/10.1016/j.techfore.2020.119973
41. Rey-Moreno, M., Felício, J.A., Medina-Molina, C., Rufín, R.: Facilitator and inhibitor factors: adopting e-government in a dual model. J. Bus. Res. **88**, 542–549 (2018)
42. Rogers, E.M.: Diffusion of Innovations. Free Press, New York (2003)
43. Sanmukhiya, C.: Predicting e-government use in Mauritius: non-parametric procedures. Int. J. Recent Technol. Eng. **8**(2), 535–549 (2019)
44. Seo, D., Bernsen, M.: Comparing attitudes toward e-government of non-users versus users in a rural and urban municipality. Gov. Inf. Q. **33**(2), 270–282 (2016)
45. Singapore Government. Digital Government Blueprint (2018). https://www.tech.gov.sg/files/media/corporate-publications/dgb-public-document_30dec20.pdf. Accessed 25 Feb 2021
46. UK. UK Digital Strategy (2017) https://www.gov.uk/government/publications/uk-digital-strategy. Accessed 25 Feb 2021
47. Van De Walle, S., Zeibote, Z., Stacenko, S., Muravska, T., Migchelbrink, K.: Explaining non-adoption of electronic government services by citizens: a study among non-users of public e-services in Latvia. Inf. Polity **23**(4), 399–409 (2018)
48. Veiga, L., Janowski, T., Soares Barbosa, L.: Digital government and administrative burden reduction. In: ACM International Conference Proceeding Series 01–03-March-2016, pp. 323–326 (2016)
49. Venkatesh, V., Morris, M., Davis, G., Davis, F.: User acceptance of information technology: toward a unified view. MIS Q. **27**(3), 425–478 (2003)
50. Venkatesh, V., Thong, J.Y.L., Chan, F.K.Y., Hu, P.J.H.: Managing citizens' uncertainty in e-government services: the mediating and moderating roles of transparency and trust. Inf. Syst. Res. **27**(1), 87–111 (2016)
51. Vidiasova, L.A., Chugunov, A.V.: Citizens' awareness and satisfaction with public services' portals (the case of Saint Petersburg)]. Public Admin. Issues **2**, 165–185 (2017). (in Russian)
52. Voutinioti, A.: Critical factors of e-government adoption in Greece. In: Proceedings of the European Conference on e-Government, ECEG, 2018-October, pp. 240–248 (2018)
53. Williams, M., Dwivedi, Y.: The influence of demographic variables on citizens' adoption of e-government. In: Association for Information Systems - 13th Americas Conference on Information Systems, AMCIS 2007: Reaching New Heights. 1. 309 (2007). http://aisel.aisnet.org/amcis2007/309
54. World Bank. Digital Dividends. World Development Report (2016). http://documents.worldbank.org/curated/en/896971468194972881/pdf/102725-PUBReplacement-PUBLIC.pdf. Accessed 05 Feb 2021
55. Yera, A., Arbelaitz, O., Jauregui, O., Muguerza, J.: Characterization of e-government adoption in Europe. PLOS ONE **15**(4), e0231585 (2020). https://doi.org/10.1371/journal.pone.0231585

# Institutional Factors for Building Trust in Information Technologies: Case-Study of Saint Petersburg

Evgenii Vidiasov⬭, Lyudmila Vidiasova(✉) ⬭, and Iaroslava Tensina⬭

ITMO University, Saint Petersburg, Russia
vidyasov@lawexp.com

**Abstract.** The paper is devoted to finding the factors that influence on citizen' trust in information technologies. Research has been proposed to identify which institutional factors affect the establishment of trust in information technology. Saint Petersburg was selected as a research case. The survey applied SCOT approach in assessment citizens' use and attitudes towards new technologies. The study was conducted in two phases: pilot and main survey. In the second phase of the study, 800 respondents took part in the survey. According to the data of conducted surveys, factor analysis was carried out. The study shows that institutional trust reflected in attitudes towards organizations on the Internet is important for building trust in information technologies. People who are more inclined to trust government institutions are also more inclined to trust interactions in the Internet space.

**Keywords:** Social trust · Information technology · Institutions · Survey

## 1 Introduction

Nowadays, social trust is an essential element of building the information society. Trust significantly influences the adoption of innovations and changes, as well as motivation for using technologies. At the same time, diversity and expansion of new technologies lead to an increase in negative trends in relation to new information technologies and content posted on the Network.

Modern research demonstrates the complexity and multidimensionality of trust in information technology: it is not constant and varies depending on the sphere and technology itself. In modern conditions, it becomes obvious that there is a whole complex of elements that can have an impact on trust relationship in new technologies. The penetration of information technologies into people's lives introduces new forms of communication and the establishment of relationships, as their wider penetration, new social norms arise and are established. In essence, there is a process of institutionalization of new structures and processes. At the same time, the role of institutional factors and mechanisms affecting trust remains insignificantly studied.

In this paper we present the 2-waves research took place in Saint Petersburg. In order to identify institutional factors affecting trust in information technology, the team

© Springer Nature Switzerland AG 2022
D. A. Alexandrov et al. (Eds.): DTGS 2021, CCIS 1503, pp. 152–162, 2022.
https://doi.org/10.1007/978-3-030-93715-7_11

of authors conducted a two-phase study. The purpose of the annual survey was to detect new factors and to reveal some changes in respondents' attitudes in 2-year dynamic.

The paper has the following structure: literature review sheds a light on the previous research findings. Methodology section gives an overview of the applied approach and questionnaire development. The findings draw a picture of the dynamic of citizens' opinions. Finally, conclusion and discussion section underlines the important issues for further consideration.

## 2   Literature Review

The scientific interest in trust is mainly related to its role in the formation of social capital. Trust forms a basis of social capital in sociological and economic research. F. Fukuyama believed that it is the development of trust relations determines the development of society as a whole [8]. R. Putnam considered trust, norms, and social ties as elements of social capital that increase the effective functioning of modern society [24]. According to N. Luhmann, trust provides favorable social relations, as it introduces elements of certainty and predictability into them [15]. Most studies of the phenomenon of trust concern precisely the sphere of interpersonal relations [1, 14, 15, 19].

In recent years, trust in information technology is gaining special relevance. Despite the different object of trust, trust in technology is similar to trust in interpersonal relationships [15]. It is most often considered in the context of automation where the object of trust is a specific technology [13, 23]. According to A. Kiran and P. Verbeek, complex connections between people and technology encourage active trust in technology, instead of mistrust [11].

Trust in technology is often related to users attitude and willingness to use some technologies [9, 25]. Research in this field separates into several directions counting trust in electronic communication in bank services [4, 25], and governmental services as well [5, 26]. Trust in technology is determines acceptance or rejection of a certain technology, and in terms of over and under reliance in technology [2].

While usage of new and even unknown technologies is connected with certain risks, establishment of trust relations could help to overcome such risks [17]. Several studies have examined the relationship between institutional trust and the use of technology in online services such as e-government [26] and mobile banking [21]. Thus, Reid and Levy in their study identified the connection between trust in an organization (institution) that uses technology and user behavior [25].

Trust in technology is associated with a propensity to trust technology and institutional trust [17]. Institutional trust is defined through the attitude to existing rules and norms within social institutions [18].

Some studies underline a complex of parameters that determine trust in technologies [12]. According to Montague and Asan, there are several layers of trust that could affect each other and reflect into users' relationships with technologies [20].

Special attention is paid to studying trust in government e-services that involves not just trust in technological side but in government as an institution as well [3, 22, 26]. M. Smith identified the relationship between trust in public electronic services and trust in public institutions [26]. The special role of trust in the choice of electronic services was noted by D. Moe, D. Shin and D. Cohen [22]. They fixed on a case of Lebanon, that low usage of services hindered their promotion. As a solution, the authors note the importance of increasing trust in government, the Internet, and technology.

Thus, current studies demonstrate the connection between institutional trust and trust in technology. Identification of specific institutional factors can help to establish trust in technology and innovations.

Theoretical framework shows the importance of the influence of the institutional factor on the implementation of any innovation. At the same time, the category "institutional trust" has different interpretations and interpretations in relation to the assessment of the application of information technologies. A particularly important task is to find the variables that make up the institutional trust in information technology, which is currently not disclosed in the literature. This served as a prerequisite for starting our research. For the research the following research question was stated: which institutional factors affect the establishment of trust in information technology among residents of St. Petersburg, and how did they change in the dynamic period?

## 3  Methodology

### 3.1  Research Design

The research was conducted in accordance to SCOT approach, that means a focus on combination of experience detection, as well as attitudes assessment towards new technologies.

The research focus covered the determination of institutional factors that affect the establishment of trust in information technology. The study was conducted in Saint Petersburg, Russia. The findings demonstrate the picture of the city residents on the selected territory. In this study, we consider trust in information technology, defining it as a state of confidence in the unambiguous behavior of a digital system, as well as a belief in the reliability of its operation and predictability.

St. Petersburg was chosen as a research site because it is one of the leaders in the development and use of IT. Therefore, this long-term use of IT is preferable to discover new norms and institutional linkages.

There was a 2-years cycle of research. We conducted survey in 2019–2020 annually. In 2019 the survey was conducted in 6 multifunctional centers (MFCs) that provide municipal and government services using a personal questionnaire method. MFCs represented different districts of the city [28]. The interviewers asked 600 respondents [29]. The distribution of the polls' participants was representative. There were 15% of younger category (18–25 y.o.), 19% of people of 26–35 y.o., 17% belonged to the group of 36–45 y.o., 18% of citizens of 46–55 y.o., 16% of 56–65 y.o., and the rest 16% belonged to the oldest group (65 +). The respondents' occupation showed the prevalence of employees/specialists (45%) and non-working pensioners (16%). Businessmen and top-managers occupied 11%, as well as the students. The group of workers, drivers and guards presented 8%, and the rest of the sample belonged to the temporary unemployed, housewives and others [29].

In 2020, the survey scale covered 800 respondents. The questionnaire was corrected in several blocks due to the results of the first wave. The study was carried out during a global pandemic, therefore it was decided to conduct the survey in an online format. The Anketolog service and the anonymous database of respondents provided by it were used. All respondents in the database undergo a mandatory identification procedure during initial registration, their data is also confirmed by passport data. All necessary checks are carried out by the staff of the Anketolog service.

The sample in 2020 covered 54% of women and 46% of men. Among the respondents 22% belonged to the youngest group (18–30 y.o), 29% for a group of 31–40 y.o., 29% for citizens of 41–50 y.o., and 20% were older than 51 years. The majority in the sample were employees, also 14% represented the managerial positions, and 11% were occupied by the workers of the third range.

We used the Likert-scale to range the respondents' responses to a set of questions. The questionnaire consisted of a list of statements with which the respondents could express their agreement on 1 to 5 scale [28, 29]. The extent of the agreement/ disagreement showed their experience in using information technologies.

### 3.2  Variables of Institutional Factors Influencing Trust in IT

Assessing the level of citizens' trust in information technologies is impossible without taking into account the fact that the level of trust varies from one sphere to another, as well as in various situations of online interaction. According to the data of conducted surveys, factor analysis was carried out. This allowed us to reduce the data dimensions and to present the structure of trust in information technology through several key hidden factors.

At the first stage, 13 variables from the pilot survey were selected for certain aspects of trust in information technology. The method of principal components was used as a method of factor analysis. The eigenvalue according to the Kaiser criterion is used as a criterion for selecting components: only factors with an eigenvalue above one are selected for analysis. The orthogonal Varimax method is used as a rotation technique. In the survey Kaiser-Meyer-Olkin (KMO) sample adequacy measure, as well as the Bartlett sphericity criterion were used.

A factor analysis revealed 3 main factors: institutional, transactional and information. Each of them belonged to trust in different areas: attitudes towards institutions, operations with other actors online, and information services quality. These factors cover 64.4% of the sample, which is a fairly high indicator: the institutional factor covers 24.7% of the sample, transactional –23%, and informational –16.5%.

The institutional trust factor groups variables related to their confidence about specific organizations involved in IT communication, such as government, Internet providers, as well as administrators of networks.

The pilot factorial model made it possible to identify some theoretical expectations regarding the components of trust in information technologies and the significant role of the institutional factor.

## 4  Findings

### 4.1  Assessment of IT Use by Respondents

As the research has shown, in St. Petersburg residents are quite active Internet users (81%). In addition, 42% can call themselves skillful users, they are not afraid to master new information technologies. Almost every second respondent said that their confidence in the security of electronic communications contributes to the expansion of IT penetration into their lives. Also, every third respondent is motivated to use IT by reducing time costs in comparison with traditional communication methods.

According to the survey, 65% of city residents often use electronic government services. Almost every second respondent uses various electronic channels to contact the authorities. As the survey results show, in most cases city residents regard such practical cases as positive (distribution from 58% to 64%).

Also, every second respondent said about their confidence in the security of data and their exchange when interacting with government agencies. In general, residents of St. Petersburg demonstrated a fairly high level of trust in interacting with the government when receiving electronic services, going through personal identification procedures on portals (65%) (Fig. 1).

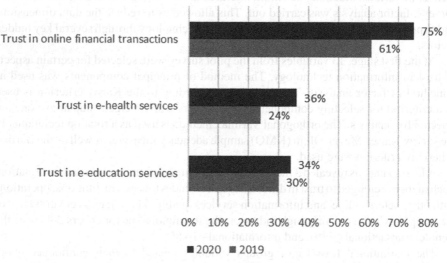

**Fig.1.** Dynamics of trust in information technology when used in various fields

According to 70% of St. Petersburg residents who took part in the survey, Internet communication has a positive effect on the general level of awareness of the population about what the authorities are doing. Half of the respondents believe that this awareness helps them understand causal relationships and explain management decisions made by the city government. Every third respondent agreed that Internet interaction allows citizens to be really involved in making decisions about urban development and governance.

However, the respondents were rather cautious when expressing their opinion about the prospects of electronic voting in the country as a whole. Only a third of the respondents consider this method of collecting votes to be effective and truthful. Also, almost a third of the respondents (28%) use non-governmental, alternative resources for collecting votes.

Certain positive trends were noted by the respondents over the course of two years of research. In particular, a third of the city's residents already now note more attention to the problems of residents on the part of officials and politicians. The respondents associate this state of affairs with the penetration of the Internet, the publicity of sufficiently important social and urban problems. However, there is also a group of pessimistic residents (72%) who believe that the opinions of residents are not taken into account when making decisions on serious issues. In general, the city recorded a level of trust in the authorities of 26%.

The study included questions about the distribution of responsibility for the security of electronic communications. Almost half of the surveyed residents of the city (43%) believe that ensuring security should fall on the shoulders of the authorities.

Almost every third respondent believes that the current Internet interaction is sufficiently safe and provided by the state with all necessary measures. But this raises a complex issue related to the boundaries of freedom on the Internet and security. Thus, 78% of the city residents surveyed believe that in no case should the freedom of speech and expression on the Internet be sacrificed in favor of enhancing security.

## 4.2 Dynamic of Trust

The results of the study over two years have shown positive dynamics in the use of electronic forms of communication with the government, as well as an increase in demand for electronic government services. Of course, these trends were also influenced by the global pandemic, when residents were forced to receive electronic services.

In general, the share of St. Petersburg residents who applied for electronic services and who regard this experience as positive has increased by 17% in the last city. Also, the share of respondents submitting online appeals to the authorities and assessing this experience as positive has also increased by a quarter.

The percentage of St. Petersburg residents who generally trust electronic identification systems and consider the exchange of data with the state safe has increased by 13%.

The share of respondents who believe in the positive ability of the Internet to involve residents in city management increased by 18%. Their voices can be heard by the government as their internet presence expands. Also, the share of those who rate the authorities' attentiveness to the problems of residents has increased by 10%. The share of those who believe in a real opportunity to influence political decisions through Internet communications has grown slightly less.

Over the past year, the share of residents who trust government online services has increased by 15%. At the same time, the overall level of trust in regional and local authorities has decreased by 3% over the past year. On the whole, the last year was not easy enough, many government decisions were made, so it is impossible to unequivocally assess what is the reason for the negative trend towards decreasing trust. During the period 2019–2020, there has been a trend towards an increase in trust in communication on social networks (by 8%). In general, users began to better assess the security of data exchange when interacting with authorities through social networks (Fig. 2).

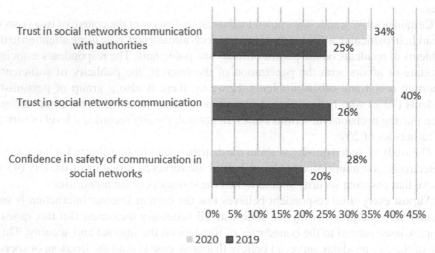

**Fig. 2.** The dynamics of trust in communication in social networks

The number of residents closely following the discussions of socially and politically important issues increased by 17% in 2020. It is important to note that the share of involved respondents who actively participate in discussions (commenting on posts, creating posts, etc.) has doubled.

### 4.3 Institutional Factors Influencing Trust in IT

At the second stage of the study, 20 variables were selected for factor analysis, represented by a Likert scale of 1 to 5. The estimated parameters in 2020 involved trust in the services of the platform economy (taxi, ordering food from restaurants, ordering food from stores and ordering goods), as well as questions about the credibility of information on the Internet (on the websites of news agencies and on social networks) in addition to 2019 list.

EFA and PCA were used as analytical tools for determination of factor model. The first method is better suited for identifying latent factors, while the second allows us to reduce the dimension of the data and get fewer variables for further analysis. The analysis was performed with R software package. Based on the comparison of eigenvalues and the scree method, six factors were identified within the EFA and five factors within the PCF. The EFA was performed using Oblimin oblique rotation allowing for correlation of factors. PCA was performed using Varimax orthogonal rotation.

As a result of factor analysis using the PCA method, 5 factors were identified: institutional, service, platform, transactional, and informational types of trust. In the context of this study 3 factors were considered: institutional, transactional and informational trust.

We applied Varimax orthogonal rotation for factor loading matrix (see Table 1). Bold type indicates the largest factor loadings for each factor.

**Table 1.** Factor loadings matrix

|  | Institutional | Informational | Transactional |
|---|---|---|---|
| Trust_E_Identification | 0.22 | 0.08 | **0.78** |
| Online_Trust_Gov | 0.12 | 0.25 | **0.77** |
| SocMedia_Trust_People | 0.33 | **0.56** | 0.27 |
| SocMedia_Trust_Gov | 0.21 | **0.46** | **0.58** |
| Online_Trust_Payment | 0.29 | 0.11 | **0.56** |
| Trust_Provider | **0.61** | 0.25 | 0.37 |
| Trust_Rus_Companies | **0.73** | 0.19 | 0.26 |
| Trust_Foreign_companies | **0.76** | 0.09 | 0.11 |
| _Trust_Rus_SocMedia | **0.67** | 0.34 | 0.28 |
| _Trust_Foreign_SocMed | **0.75** | 0.20 | 0.02 |
| _Trust_InformationSocMed | 0.18 | **0.83** | 0.06 |
| _Trust_Information_Websites | 0.15 | **0.74** | 0.23 |
| _Trust_OnlineInfo_General | 0.20 | **0.75** | .10 |

Informational trust reflects the variables that assess the quality of information exchange. Transactional trust includes trust in electronic identification when interacting or communicating with government authorities, and trust in online payments.

The identified factor of institutional trust groups variables that fix trust in certain cyberspace actors includes the following: Internet providers, Russian and international companies who provide their services in the Internet, social networks administration as well. This factor reflects trust in organizations on the Internet that corresponds to a classical meaning of trust in social institutions as "perceived reliability of a system or institution", or as trust to a third party that has a corresponding "reputation".

Correlation analysis also showed a strong connection between respondents' perceptions of themselves as active and advanced Internet users, as well as active users of social networks These three variables are significantly correlated with age: younger respondents consider themselves to be more active and advanced users. The perception of the Internet as a space of more harm than good also increases with age. Women are more likely to perceive themselves as more active users of social networks, and more positively assess their experience of interacting with some online tools. At the same time, the level of education positively and significantly correlates only with the "advancedness" of the user, but not with the active use of the Internet. In addition, it is worth noting the significant correlation between generalized and institutional trust. Variables reflecting the experience of interacting with various online tools also show a high degree of correlation with each other, as well as significant correlations with the level of generalized and institutional trust and the activity of Internet use.

The results of the analysis draw attention to the importance of variables related to trust in traditional institutions in constructing a factor model. In particular, it is about trust in organizations and government. In general, people who are more inclined to trust people and government institutions are also more inclined to trust interactions in the Internet space.

## 5   Conclusions and Discussion

The study revealed some theoretical expectations of what constitutes online trust, in addition to trust in technology itself or the degree of ownership of it. We can attribute to such a component (1) institutional trust in organizations operating on the Internet; (2) transactional trust in interaction with other online actors (first of all, in the state); (3) informational trust in services and information quality.

The revealed data demonstrated that the factor of institutional trust significantly influenced social trust in information technology. According to conducted factor analysis, variables of institutional factor occupy the major place by weight compared to other factors. These group describes the citizens' attitude towards companies that provide services in the Internet (including connection to the Internet itself).

Trust in institutions determines the choice in favor of using or not using various technologies. Continuing the positive experience of using and trusting organizations providing online services increases confidence in the security of electronic exchange and reduces the level of perceived risks in electronic communications.

The research results are of practical importance in the development and implementation of various innovative IT services. The presented findings indicate the importance of establishing a positive image of the organization implementing the service itself, which will have a positive effect on the use of the proposed new products and services.

In recent studies there are also some evidences that citizens prefer chatbots over the real people providing online services [30]. From this perspective, authorities should also pay attention to feedback from users of government portals and services. When trust is established, constructive dialogue and citizen involvement in the management of urban areas through electronic mechanisms and channels is possible.

The limitations of the study are related to its focus on a particular city and its inhabitants. In addition, conducting the second wave of the survey in 2020 online may have contributed to a slight bias in the results towards respondents who are clearly using information technology. In this regard, after the end of the isolation policy, it makes sense to conduct a third wave of the survey. However, one should not ignore the fact that the global pandemic has forced a large number of people to join the online format. Thus, the distortion can be partially compensated for by events and processes caused by the global pandemic.

Also it is important to have comparable research data in other territories, and more importantly, in other countries. At the same time, factor analysis showed the applicability of the selected variables, and the research questionnaire can be used for other objects of study of trust in information technology.

**Acknowledgements.** The study was performed with financial support by the grant from the Russian Foundation for Basic Research (project №19-311-90031): "E-participation in the city management: the case of Saint Petersburg".

# References

1. Arrow, K.: The Limits of Organization. Norton & Company, New York (2016). https://doi.org/10.1177/000271627541700157
2. Bahner, J., Hüper, A., Manzey, D.: Misuse of automated decision aids: complacency, automation bias and the impact of training on experience. Int. J. Hum Comput Stud. **66**(9), 688–699 (2008). https://doi.org/10.1016/j.ijhcs.2008.06.001
3. Benoit, A., Fakhoury, R.: Citizenship, trust, and behavioral intentions to use public e-services: the case of Lebanon. Int. J. Inf. Manage. **35**(3), 346–351 (2015). https://doi.org/10.1016/j.ijinfomgt.2015.02.002
4. Blank, G., Dutton, W.: Age and trust in the internet: the centrality of experience and attitude towards technology in Britain. Soc. Sci. Comput. Rev. **30**(2), 135–151 (2011). https://doi.org/10.1177/0894439310396186
5. Carter, L., Bélanger, F.: The utilization of e-government services: citizen trust, innovation and acceptance factors. Inf. Syst. J. **15**(1), 5–25 (2005)
6. Ejdys, J.: Trust in technology in case of humanoids used for the care for the senior persons. Multidiscip. Aspects Prod. Eng. **1**(1), 875–881 (2018). https://doi.org/10.2478/mape-2018-0110
7. Factors: The Journal of the Human Factors and Ergonomics Society. 46, 50 – 82
8. Fukuyama, F.: Trust: The Social Virtues and the Creation of Prosperity. Free Press, NY (1995)
9. Gefen, D., Karahanna, E., Straub, D.W.: Trust and TAM in online shopping: an integrated model. MIS Q. **27**(1), 51–90 (2003)
10. Gibb, J.R.: Trust: A New View of Personal and Organizational Development. The Guild of Tutors Press, Los Angeles (1978)
11. Kiran, A.H., Verbeek, P.P.: Trusting ourselves to technology. Knowl. Technol. Policy **23**(3–4), 409–427 (2010). https://doi.org/10.1007/s12130-010-9123-7
12. Kuriyan, R., Kitner, K., Watkins, J.: ICTs, development and trust: an overview. Inf. Technol. People **23**(3), 216–221 (2010). https://doi.org/10.1108/09593841011069130
13. Lee, J.D., See, K.A.: Trust in automation: designing for appropriate reliance. Human Fact. J. Human Fact. Ergon. Soc. **46**(1), 50–80 (2004). https://doi.org/10.1518/hfes.46.1.50.30392
14. Lipset, S.M., Scheider, W.: The Confidence Gap: Business, Labour and Government in the Public Mind. The Free Press, New York (1983)
15. Grimm, R., Maier, M., Rothmund, T.: Vertrauen. Datenschutz und Datensicherheit - DuD **39**(5), 283–288 (2015). https://doi.org/10.1007/s11623-015-0414-8
16. Mayer, R.C., Davis, J.H., Schoorman, F.D.: An integrative model of organizational trust. Acad. Manage. Rev. **20**(3), 709–734 (1995)
17. McKnight, D.G., Carter, M., Thatcher, J.B., Clay, P.F.: Trust in a specific technology: an investigation of its components and measures. ACM Trans. Manage. Inf. Syst. **2**(2), 12–32 (2011)
18. McKnight, D.H., Cummings, L., Chervany, N.: Initial trust formation in new organizational relationships. Acad. Manag. Rev. **23**(3), 473–490 (1998). https://doi.org/10.5465/AMR.1998.926622
19. Misztal, B.: Trust in Modern Societies. Polity Press, Cambridge (1986)

20. Montague, E., Asan, O.: Trust in technology-mediated collaborative health encounters: constructing trust in passive user interactions with technologies. Ergonomics **5**(7), 752–761 (2012). https://doi.org/10.1080/00140139.2012.663002
21. Morawszynski, O., Miscione, G.: Examining trust in mobile banking transactions: The case of M-Pesa in Kenya. In: Avgerou, C., Smith, M.L., van den Besselaar, P. (Eds.) Social Dimensions of Information and Communication Technologies Policy, pp. 287–298. Springer, New York, NY (2008)
22. Mou, J., Shin, D.-H., Cohen, J.F.: Trust and risk in consumer acceptance of e-services. Electron. Commer. Res. **17**(2), 255–288 (2017). https://doi.org/10.1007/s10660-015-9205-4
23. Muir, B.M.: Trust between humans and machines, and the design of decision aids. Int. J. Man Mach. Stud. **27**(5–6), 527–539 (1987). https://doi.org/10.1016/S0020-7373(87)80013-5
24. Putnam, R.D.: Bowling alone: The Collapse and Revival of American Community. Simon & Schuster, New York (2000)
25. Reid, M., Levy, Y.: Integrating trust and computer self-efficacy with TAM: an empirical assessment of customers' acceptance of banking information systems (BIS) in Jamaica. J. Internet Bank. Commer. **12**(3), 1–18 (2008)
26. Smith, M.: Building institutional trust through e-government trustworthiness cues. Inf. Technol. People **23**(3), 222–246 (2010). https://doi.org/10.1108/09593841011069149
27. Song, R., Korba, L., Yee, G.: Trust in e-services: technologies. Pract. Chall. IGI Global (2007). https://doi.org/10.4018/978-1-59904-207-7
28. Vidiasova, L., Kabanov, Y.: Online trust and ICTs usage: findings from St. Petersburg, Russia. In: Proceedings of the 13th International Conference on Theory and Practice of Electronic Governance, pp. 847–850 (2020)
29. Vidiasova L.A., Vidiasov E.Y., Tensina I.D.: A study of social trust in information technology in the provision of electronic public services and the use of electronic participation portals (Case Study of St. Petersburg, Russia). Monitor. Public. Opin. Econ. Soc. Changes. **5**, 43–57 (2019). https://doi.org/10.14515/monitoring.2019.5.03
30. Zierau, N., Flock, K., Janson, A., Söllner, M., Leimeister, J.M.: The influence of AI-based chatbots and their design on users trust and information sharing in online loan applications. In: Proceedings of the 54th Hawaii International Conference on System Sciences- 2021, pp. 5483–5492 (2021). https://doi.org/10.24251/HICSS.2021.666

# Main Regulatory Plans in European Union's New Digital Regulation Package

Kristina Cendic[1]([✉]) [iD] and Gergely Gosztonyi[2] [iD]

[1] Faculty of Law, University of Zenica, Zenica, Bosnia and Herzegovina
[2] Faculty of Law, Eötvös Loránd University (ELTE), Budapest, Hungary
gosztonyi@ajk.elte.hu

**Abstract.** It seems clear that the Internet, as highlighted by the European Court of Human Rights in Cengiz and Others v. Turkey, "has now become the primary means by which individuals exercise their freedom to receive and impart information and ideas". As a result, in many countries worldwide, regulating the Internet has become one of the top priorities on the political agenda, albeit with different solutions, from Australia through Germany and Canada to Poland and Hungary. The world has become acquainted with 'fake news', 'deepfake', 'dis- and misinformation' in recent years. Digital platforms providing services worldwide have so far not devoted significant resources – for the sake of their well-conceived business interest – to prevent these from spreading. Two proposals are on the table since December 2020 in the European Union: Digital Services Act and Digital Markets Act. Both want to set an exemplary approach to regulating tech companies and have several advantages and disadvantages. The article intends to show them all in an explanatory manner.

**Keywords:** Freedom of expression · Media · Digital services act · Digital markets act · Advantages · Disadvantages · Competition · Regulation

## 1 Introduction

"By 2030, more than just enablers, digital technologies including 5G, the Internet of Things, edge computing, Artificial Intelligence, robotics and augmented reality will be at the core of new products, new manufacturing processes and new business models based on fair sharing of data in the data economy. In this context, the swift adoption and implementation of the Commission's proposals for the Digital Single Market and Shaping Europe's digital future strategies will enhance the digital transformation of businesses and ensure a fair and competitive digital economy." [1] – stated the European Commission in March 2021. The future is already here, it seems.

But this is not the case if one examines the field of the current regulation. Twenty years have passed since 8 June 2000, when the Directive on electronic commerce [2] (hereinafter e-comm directive), which regulates digital services to date, was adopted. In a such a rapidly changing market those regulatory solutions that seemed forward in 2000 have now lost their relevance. All this became crystal-clear in practice when – following

D. A. Alexandrov et al. (Eds.): DTGS 2021, CCIS 1503, pp. 163–176, 2022.
https://doi.org/10.1007/978-3-030-93715-7_12

the United States' and other countries' attempts – the European Union (EU) also took actions against the perceived or real dominance of the digital giants. For example, in 2017, a fine of €110 million was imposed on Facebook [3], a record fine of a total of €8.2 billion [4] was imposed on Google between 2017 and 2019 for regular and systemic infringements of competition rules [5], and proceedings against Amazon were launched at the very end of 2020, alleging a breach of antitrust rules [6]. The fact of these fines is a good indication that – typically American – big-tech companies, previously thought to be untouchable have paddled into waters that are considered dangerous not only legally but also politically [7]. Although fines represent only a fraction of their annual revenues, the path taken by several countries around the world clearly shows the politicians will try to regulate the digital services.

It seems clear that the Internet, as highlighted by the European Court of Human Rights (ECtHR) in Cengiz and Others v. Turkey, "has now become the primary means by which individuals exercise their freedom to receive and impart information and ideas" [8]. As a result, in many countries worldwide, regulating the Internet has become one of the top priorities on the political agenda, albeit with different solutions, from Australia [9] through Germany [10] and Canada [11] to Poland [12] and Hungary [13]. As Goldstein and Grossman stated in 2021: "governments work to develop responses, (and) it is imperative to begin with an understanding of how these operations work in practice (…)." [14].

Digital platforms providing services worldwide have so far not devoted significant resources – for the sake of their well-conceived business interest – to prevent these from spreading. Once again, quoting the ECtHR, "the Internet plays an important role in promoting public access to news and the dissemination of information in general [15]. The expressive activities generated by users on the Internet are an unprecedented platform for exercising freedom of expression" [16]. Moreover, the changed political climate was also perceived by big tech-giants and they took steps to change the situation: on 6 May 2020, Facebook announced that it would set up an Oversight Board of recognized experts to address inappropriate content to help the company. The first decisions had already been made in early 2021, and in four of the first five cases, the Board ruled against Facebook's moderation decision [17].

## 2 Theoretical Framework

In these years, the new media have "a much more immediate and powerful effect" [18], than e.g., print media. There are several indicators in the Recommendation [19] that clarify this question: "self-categorization as a media outlet, membership in professional media organizations, working methods analogue to those typical of media organizations, and, in the new media environment, the capacity and the availability of technical means (e.g. platform or bandwidth) to disseminate content to large audiences online." [20] The crucial article for freedom of expression of the the European Convention on Human Rights (ECHR) is Article 10 which in its paragraph 1 states that "Everyone has the right to freedom of expression. This right shall include freedom to hold opinions and to receive and impart information and ideas without interference by public authority and regardless of frontiers." On the other hand, paragraph 2 explains the restrictions that may be imposed on freedom of expression in certain circumstances.

Paragraph 2 of Article 10 is applicable not only to information or ideas that are favorably received or regarded as inoffensive or as a matter of indifference, but also to those that "offend, shock, or disturb the State or any sector of the population" [21]. The demands of the pluralism, tolerance, and broadmindedness are the aims here without which there is no democratic society. As the European Court of Human Rights stated in the case of Handyside v. The United Kingdom, this primarly means that every 'formality', 'condition', 'restriction' or 'penalty' imposed in this sphere must be proportionate to the legitimate aim pursued. [22] It is also important to underline that any limitations of freedom of expression in line with Article 10 are to be applied vigorously restrictively.

At the same time, we must not forget that the basic problems can be seen in determining the levels of responsibility, as in many cases, these huge platforms acted as quasi-states [23] and acted as quasi-independent legislative powers only based on their own Terms of Services. All this is further underlined by the fact that the case-law of the European Court of Human Rights and the Court of Justice of the European Union (ECJ) is far from being consistent [24]. It is therefore necessary to underline the differences between the two courts. First, when the national legal remedies are exhausted, the cases come before international courts. European Court of Human Rights relies on European Convention on Human Rights and focuses on the 47 member states of the Council of Europe. On the other hand, the European Court of Justice follows the European Union law and focuses on European Union member states. The difference between the courts is that "the ECJ can be seen as an integrative agent, striving for further EU harmonization" while "the ECtHR's mandate is that of providing minimum human rights standards protection, beyond which wider scope is left for pluralism and national sovereignty within the EU." [25] More specifically, "ECtHR ruling will result in a "more gradual (and perhaps less politically costly) implementation" of the decision than in the case of an adverse ECJ ruling." [See 25] These courts consider each other's judgments referring to human rights' violations, with a note that "the case law of the ECJ shows that where fundamental rights come into conflict with the economic Treaty freedoms, the economic freedoms may sometimes prevail over fundamental rights." [27].

## 3   Proposal for a Regulation on Digital Services [28]

With the General Data Protection Regulation (commonly known as the GDPR) [29] set by the European Union as an excellent path to follow, it is no wonder that it also wants to set an exemplary approach to regulating tech companies. The first striking legal difference from previous legislation in this area is that, by analogy with the GDPR solution, the European Union intends to implement it not as a directive but as a regulation [30]. The legislator explained this in the proposal (hereinafter DSA):" The Commission has decided to put forward a proposal for a Regulation to ensure a consistent level of protection throughout the Union and to prevent divergences hampering the free provision of the relevant services within the internal market, as well as guarantee the uniform protection of rights and uniform obligations for business and consumers across the internal market. This is necessary to provide legal certainty and transparency for economic operators and consumers alike. The proposed Regulation also ensures consistent monitoring of the rights and obligations, and equivalent sanctions in all Member States, as well as effective cooperation between the supervisory authorities of different Member States and at Union level" [31]. However, the solutions in other articles in the draft regulation show the real intention without question: "by its nature cross-border, the legislative efforts at national level referred to above hamper the provision and reception of services throughout the Union" [See 31], intending to "empowering citizens and building more resilient democracies" [33].

It is worth noting that the draft regulation cannot replace the e-comm directive in its entirety, instead of building on its legal solutions. However, certain sections of the e-comm directive may be supplemented, as appropriate, by new provisions (such as Articles 12 to 15, including 'mere conduit','caching', hosting and the non-obligation to general monitoring). It should already be noted here that the new proposal for a regulation, the Directive on electronic commerce and some of the rules of the Audiovisual Media Services Directive [34] (hereinafter AVMSD) do not appear to be harmonised [35], so standardising and summarising them will be also an important task in the future. This is so, as according to the most optimistic expectations, the proposal for a regulation will not be adopted before the end of 2022 or the beginning of 2023 [36].

The communication on the proposal for a regulation on Digital Services summarises the main changes as:

1) Benefits for citizens

   - More choice, lower prices
   - Less exposure to illegal content
   - Better protection of fundamental rights

2) Benefits for providers of digital services

   - Legal certainty, harmonisation of rules
   - Easier to start-up and scale-up in Europe

3) Benefits for business users of digital services

   - More choice, lower prices
   - Access to EU-wide markets through platforms
   - Level-playing field against providers of illegal content

4) Benefits for society at large

   - Greater democratic control and oversight over systemic platforms
   - Mitigation of systemic risks, such as manipulation or disinformation" [37]

All this is expected to lead to the strengthening of human rights, equality, legal certainty, freedom and democracy; in short, the rule of law, as uniform liability rules, transparency and predictability in the online environment could stifle the false news discussed above, and misinformation problems.

## 3.1  Pros of the Proposed Regulation

The proposal's main advantage is that it seeks to put on a new footing the regulatory environment that has been essentially unchanged for twenty years, over which time, technological development have already taken place. It should be noted that it creates a category of so-called trusted flaggers [38], i.e. it would bring the fight against illegal content online back to the field of reliability and predictability. It would also give users stronger tools, as they would have the opportunity to challenge the moderation decisions of the platforms and appeal against them, contrary to current practice [39].

To increase transparency, the regulation would also put one of the most controversial issues, the algorithms of the platforms, on a new basis, as it would also provide access to them for independent auditors and researchers [40]. In order to address systemic risks, the regulation would introduce a new category called very large online platforms [41], which, unlike at present, would not be subject to an uniform, but specifically different, liability rules [42]. This category includes those who "provide their services to a number of average monthly active recipients of the service in the Union equal to or higher than 45 million" [43]. In this context, Member States must designate one of their competent authorities (digital service coordinator) to carry out all tasks related to the application and enforcement of the Regulation in that Member State [44]. It is important to note that "The DSA would apply to all online intermediary service providers as long as their users (businesses or individuals) have their place of establishment or residence in the EU" [45], which means that the DSA the DSA goes back to the GDPR's extraterritorial solution. In addition, the DSA „reaffirms the negligence-based model of liability for service providers" [46] and the liability rules (known as the 'safe harbor model') that were set out in the e-comm directive would be transferred to the DSA. It is particularly important that the DSA also confirms the ban on requiring general monitoring.

Given the real and comprehensible fines of previous years, it is not surprising that if an online giant platform infringes the regulation, the Commission may impose a fine of up to 6% of the platform's total turnover in the preceding financial year [47]. However, the use of so-called interim measures (such as temporary suspension of service) has been included in the text as a real method of enforcement, as "where there is an urgency due to the risk of serious damage for the recipients of the service, the Commission may, by decision, order interim measures against the very large online platform concerned on the basis of a prima facie finding of an infringement." [48].

## 3.2  Cons of the Proposed Regulation

In terms of liability, the regulation would follow the path taken by national regulations (such as the German NetzDG [49], the French Avia Act [50] or the Austrian Anti-Hate Speech Act [51]) which force platforms – to avoid fines – constantly police and monitor their user's content [52]. This could result in excessive – censored – measures, i.e., as the European Court of Human Rights has stated, „the organization will take action to exclude its own liability (and thus erroneously remove content) instead of protecting freedom of expression." [53] The most recent outbreak of Covid-19 caused a great shift to the online sphere and brought digital rights into the spotlight more than ever before [54], and therefore the concept of digital media, too. There have been censorships and arrests of citizens and journalists, breaches of privacy and problems with free access to information, too, which curbed the basic human rights. On the World Press Freedom Day, the High Representative on behalf of the European Union issued a Declaration stating that: „Journalists continue to experience harsh working conditions with increasing financial and political pressure, surveillance, arbitrary prison sentences or violence for doing their work. According to the UNESCO Observatory, 76 journalists were killed since 2020, while many more were arrested, harassed or threatened worldwide. Of particular concern is gender-based violence targeting women journalists." [55].

Some authorities created a type of information monopoly insisting on state-approved sources to be the only ones sharing information about the virus, press conferences were either open only to media "in favour", or closed altogether, etc. [56] Finally, even though health information is certainly a matter of public interest, in some cases, the right to free access to information suffered because the media, as public watchdogs, were unable to get accurate information from the authorities [57]. All these negative patterns brought not only a chilling effect among citizens and media in some countries, but also intensified the lingering problems. However, the state intervention in online sphere should not be stricter than the one in offline sphere and "freedom of expression, information and communication... should not be subject to restrictions other than those provided for in Article 10 of the ECHR, simply because communication is carried in digital form." [58] Instead, the states are encouraged to "promote frameworks for self- and co-regulation by private sector...(as well as)... interoperable technical standards in the digital environment, including those for digital broadcasting, that allow citizens the widest possible access to content." [See 58].

The internet did open numerous possibilities for freedom of expression to flourish, and "as a guiding principle, it has been established that communication happening on the Web should not be subject to any stricter content rules or restrictions than any other medium." [60] The very nature of the internet brought new categories of media, journalists and media actors in general with a note that "state interventions into the right to freedom of expression and media freedoms in particular should be guided by similar general regulatory principles irrespective whether or not professional media outlets, intermediaries or individual users are involved" [61]. In fact, the Council of Europe therefore stated that instead of restricting freedom of expression online the states should turn to "embracing a notion of media which is appropriate for such a fluid and multi-dimensional reality" [19].

However, the lack of a distinction and definition of illegal and harmful online content has turned out to be a particularly problematic issue: according to the Euractiv, Patrik Tovaryš (Head of Information Society Services Unit of the Czech Ministry of Industry and Trade) pointed out that „there is an absolute need to distinguish between the notion of illegal content and legal but harmful content. This is imperative as there usually is a distinction between criminal conduct such as sharing terrorist content and sharing disinformation, which many users share with faith it is true" [62]. One can assume that this question would be replaced by the concepts of the European Union's Code of Practice on Disinformation from 2018. [63] We should point out that the Code applies only to signatories, and although it has been signed by Facebook, Google, Twitter and Mozilla (then Microsoft in 2019 and TikTok in 2020), in legal terms, its usage is very questionable. As Monti stated: "the vital task of fighting disinformation online cannot be delegated entirely to Internet platforms in the way that the Code provides: the risks that dwell in the privatisation of censorship (in this case, the removal of politically oriented content instead of fake news, or the prioritisation of conservative news over progressive news or vice versa) are too big to be ignored." [64].

Beside all these, the use of terms in the DSA and the DMA and the definition set of the current e-comm directive and the AVMSD, are not fully harmonized. About the issue of extraterritorial scope Joan Barata raised the question that „this would violate the international law principles of comity and reciprocity and open the door to the possibility that other countries with a more restrictive conception of the right to freedom of expression may be able to legitimately extend to the territory of the European Union (and globally) similar remedies based on their national law." [65] Some also emphasized that the necessary rules had already been put in place, so the European Union should focus on complying with them rather than adopting new legislation [66].

# 4 Proposal for a Regulation on Digital Markets [67]

The other element of the package (hereinafter DMA) would regulate digital markets, and President of the European Commission Ursula von der Leyen said at the 2020 Web Summit [68] that the European Union would seek to control the power of big technology players much more firmly. In this context, she emphasized that these giants were to be regulated not only in terms of content but also in terms of technology.

The proposed regulation's key concept is the implementation of the notion of gate-keepers [69], which covers service providers with a significant impact on the internal market, a stable and lasting position, and at least one core platform service. Such core platform services mean any of the following:

- "online intermediation services (including, for example, marketplaces, application stores and online intermediation services in other sectors such as mobility, transport or energy);
- online search engines;
- online social networking services;
- video-sharing platform services;
- number-independent interpersonal communication services;
- operating systems;
- cloud computing services;
- advertising services, including any advertising networks, advertising exchanges and any other advertising intermediation services, provided by the above." [70]

The legislature states that "a small number of large providers of core platform services have emerged with considerable economic power. (...) The combination of those features of gatekeepers is likely to lead in many cases to serious imbalances in bargaining power and, consequently, to unfair practices and conditions for business users as well as end-users of core platform services provided by gatekeepers, to the detriment of prices, quality, choice and innovation therein." [71] Based on all this, in order to ensure the conditions of fair competition, a much stricter system of conditions and sanctions is established for the tech-giants. Moreover, as these providers are international in nature, so individual national regulations can only achieve partial results against them. [72] According to the plans, the European Commission will classify a service provider if it meets three conditions altogether: the number of users reached, the amount of annual turnover and the duration of the operation. In details that means:

- "achieveing an annual EEA turnover equal to or above EUR 6.5 billion in the last three financial years;
- having more than 45 million monthly active end-users established or located in the Union and more than 10 000 yearly active business users established in the Union in the last financial year;
- the above thresholds were all met in each of the last three financial years" [73].

### 4.1 Pros of the Proposed Regulation

Ursula von der Leyen put it at the Web Summit above [See 69] that with great power comes great responsibility. One should already hail the tries to regulate the gatekeepers. Concerning all the technological constraints, the key phrase should be found in the explanatory memorandum to the proposed regulation, which states: "the conduct of combining end-user data from different sources or signing in users to different services of gatekeepers gives them potential advantages in terms of accumulation of data, thereby raising barriers to entry." [75] In other words, the regulation seeks to strengthen the possibility of entering the market for new service providers and services and to protect the data and opportunities of end-users. Such technological restrictions under Article 5 may include, but are not limited to [76]:

- refrain from aggregating personal data from multiple locations;
- refrain from signing in end-users to other services of the gatekeeper [77];
- allow business users to offer the same products or services to end-users through third party online intermediation services at prices or conditions that are different from those offered through the online intermediation services of the gatekeeper;
- refrain from preventing or restricting business users from raising issues with any relevant public authority relating to any practice of gatekeepers;
- refrain from requiring business users to use, offer or interoperate with an identification service of the gatekeeper in the context of services offered by the business users using the core platform services of that gatekeeper (lock-in);
- refrain from requiring business users or end-users to subscribe to or register with any other core platform services [78].

Gatekeepers should also ensure the effective portability of data generated by business and end-user activities, and in particular, provide end-users with tools that facilitate the exercise of data portability, including through continuous and real-time access. [79] Like the DSA rules, violators of key rules can be severely sanctioned: the Commission can impose fines of up to 10% of its total turnover in the preceding financial year [80]. The interim measures has also been included in this proposal [81].

## 4.2  Cons of the Proposed Regulation

Although stated by the European Commission that „some platforms have acquired significant scale, which effectively allows them to act as private gatekeepers to markets, customers and information. We must ensure that the systemic role of certain online platforms and the market power they acquire will not put in danger the fairness and openness of our markets." [82], the above-mentioned conceptual inconsistency should also be handled here. However, the most serious criticisms have been made by many regarding the classification as a gatekeeper under Article 3 of the DMA. Based on the regulation, the Commission may declare a service provider to be a gatekeeper even in the absence of the criteria discussed above. The methodology of this process is yet alarmingly uncertain.

It is yet also unclear that to what extent the criteria set out in Article 3 (6) should the Commission take into account during an investigation. Similarly, it is not obvious whether there is an order of priority between the three main conditions, and according to the procedure, the burden of proof of non-compliance lies with the service provider. There is also a lack of precise rules for business and end-user data transmission, so it is technically inconceivable in the current context whether it will offer real help and a solution to the practical problems that have arisen.

The future will tell in this context how the Commission "will further explore, in the context of the Digital Services Act package, ex ante rules to ensure that markets characterised by large platforms with significant network effects acting as gatekeepers, remain fair and contestable for innovators, businesses, and new market entrants." [83].

## 5  Conclusion

The need for stricter regulation than the current one does not seem to be in doubt. Moreover, that is a question that all actors in our politically polarised world – whether on the right or the left side – seem to agree. The Internet, as such, is nothing more than a vast ecosystem [84]. And like all of these: complex, ever-changing, and diverse. The intention to welcome the regulation of this vast ecosystem on a new footing is to be welcomed, but the devil is always hiding in the details.

In the United Stated of America „for good reason, long-neglected tech issues—from privacy to political ads to disinformation—are finally penetrating the public's attention. The issue of antitrust has specifically gotten more and more attention of late, with much of the interest focused on Amazon, Apple, Facebook, and Google. The four CEOs of those companies—Jeff Bezos, Tim Cook, Mark Zuckerberg, and Alphabet's Sundar Pichai, who runs Google—testified (…) in July 2020." [85] One of the key issue was the use and abuse of Sect. 230 of the Communication Decency Act (CDA) [86]. It is not a big surprise that the European Union found also a perfect time to deal with these questions: the real power of the big tech-giants. Also their liability for the contents posted onto their services, their actions toward the questionable contents and their market behaviours.

Although the new European regulation proposals seem to be in line with (most of the) Member States' political aspirations and regulatory orientations, much will depend on the negotiations in the coming years. According to Politico, „Paris (already) plans to rework the EU's content moderation bill so that it doesn't have to rely on other countries' regulators to police—and if required, punish—the biggest platforms." [87] It does really matter what parts will'fall' during the negotiations and whether all the Member States would accept the above-mentioned goal of "building more resilient democracies" [See 32]. What is certain is that the two proposals for regulations have several advantages, and fortunately, there seems to be a consensus on the issue of making the integration of the experience of the last twenty years a priority. In addition, regulation is planned to be monitored regularly, so, likely, we will not have to wait another two decades for another Internet evolutionary step. Regulators, tech-giants and end-users all should hope that the regulation will be able to follow changes in market practice much better than at the present time.

# References

1. 2030 Digital Compass: the European way for the Digital Decade, COM/2021/118 final, pp. 8–9, 9 March 2021. https://eur-lex.europa.eu/legal-content/en/TXT/?uri=CELEX%3A5 2021DC0118
2. Directive 2000/31/EC of the European Parliament and of the Council of 8 June 2000 on certain legal aspects of information society services, in particular electronic commerce, in the Internal Market ('Directive on electronic commerce'), OJ L 178, 17.7.2000, 1–16
3. Mergers: Commission fines Facebook €110 million for providing misleading information about WhatsApp takeover, 18 May 2017, <https://ec.europa.eu/commission/presscorner/det ail/en/IP_17_1369>
4. For more details see: Polyák, G., Pataki, G.: Google Shopping: a 2017-es versenyjogi "gigabírság" elemzése, avagy milyen tanulságokkal szolgált a keresőmotorra kiszabott rekordbüntetés (Google Shopping: Analysis of the 2017 competition "gigantic fine" or lessons learned from the record-breaking penalty imposed on a search engine). In: Polyák, G. (ed.): Algoritmusok, keresők, közösségi oldalak és a jog: A forgalomirányító szolgáltatások szabályozása (Algorithms, search engines, social sites, and law: Regulating traffic management services). pp. 273–288. HVG-ORAC Lap- és Könyvkiadó Kft., Budapest (2020)
5. Weissmann, C. G.: Google hit with another EU antitrust fine: The grand total now comes to €8.2B. Fastcompany, 20 March 2019. https://www.fastcompany.com/90322678/google-hit-with-another-eu-antitrust-fine-the-grand-total-now-comes-to-e8-2b
6. AT.40462, Amazon.com, Inc.; Amazon Services Europe SARL; Amazon EU SARL; Amazon Europe Core SARL. https://ec.europa.eu/competition/elojade/isef/case_details.cfm?proc_c ode=1_40462
7. Klobuchar, A.: Antitrust: Taking on Monopoly Power from the Gilded Age to the Digital Age. Alfred A. Knopf, New York (2021)
8. Cengiz and Others v. Turkey App nos 48226/10 and 14027/11 (ECtHR, 1 December 2015), 49
9. Stelter, B.: What Australia's new law might mean for the news you see in the future. CNN, 1 March 2021. https://edition.cnn.com/2021/02/27/media/australia-facebook/index.html
10. Toor, A.: Germany passes controversial law to fine Facebook over hate speech. The Verge, 30 June 2017. https://www.theverge.com/2017/6/30/15898386/germany-facebook-hate-speech-law-passed
11. Meyer, C.: Canada looks at Australia's experience regulating social media. Canada's National Observer, 1 Feb 2021. https://www.nationalobserver.com/2021/02/01/news/canada-looking-australias-experience-regulating-social-media
12. Easton, A.: Poland proposes social media 'free speech' law. BBC, 15 Jan 2021. https://www.bbc.com/news/technology-55678502

13. Huszák, D.: Bejelentették: szabályozza Magyarország a Facebookot és a nagy techcégeket (It has been announced: Hungary regulates Facebook and large tech companies). Portfolio.hu, 26 Jan 2021. https://www.portfolio.hu/uzlet/20210126/bejelentettek-szabalyozza-magyarors zag-a-facebookot-es-a-nagy-techcegeket-466858

14. Goldstein, J. A., Grossman, S.: How disinformation evolved in 2020. TechStream, 4 January 2021. https://www.brookings.edu/techstream/how-disinformation-evolved-in-2020

15. More details: Gosztonyi, G.: The European Court of Human Rights and the access to Internet as a mean to receive and impart information and ideas. In: International Comparative Jurisprudence 2020/2, pp. 134–140 (2020)

16. Cengiz and Others v. Turkey App nos 48226/10 and 14027/11 (ECtHR, 1 December 2015), 52

17. Excellent analysis about the decisions: Szikora, T.: A Facebook Oversight Board első döntései – meglepetések helyett „papírforma"? (First decisions of the Facebook Oversight Board – no surprises just the same old routine), Ludovika Blog, 5 Feb 2021. https://www.ludovika.hu/blogok/itkiblog/2021/02/05/a-facebook-oversight-board-elso-dontesei-meglepetesek-helyett-papirforma/

18. McGonagle, T., Voorhoof, D.: Freedom of Expression, the Media and Journalists: Case-law of the European Court of Human Rights. European Audiovisual Observatory, Strasbourg (2013)

19. Recommendation CM/Rec(2011)7 of the Committee of Ministers to member states on a new notion of media, adopted on 21 September 2011. https://search.coe.int/cm/Pages/result_det ails.aspx?ObjectID=09000016805cc2c0

20. Cendic, K., Gosztonyi, G.: Freedom of expression in times of Covid-19: chilling effect in Hungary and Serbia. Journal of Liberty and International Affairs 2020/6, 16 (2020)

21. Wildhaber, L.: The right to offend, shock or disturb? – aspects of freedom of expression under the european convention on human rights. Irish Jurist **36**, 17–31 (2001)

22. Handyside v. The United Kingdom App no. 5493/72 (ECtHR, 7 December 1976)

23. Kim, N.S., Telman, D.A.J.: Internet giants as quasi-governmental actors and the limits of contractual consent. 80 Missouri Law Rev. **723**, 725–770 (2015)

24. In support of all this, it is worth following the decision and contradiction of the ECtHR on the issue of liability of content providers: Delfi AS v. Estonia App no. 64569/09 (ECtHR, 16 June 2015), Magyar Tartalomszolgáltatók Egyesülete and Index.hu Zrt v. Hungary App no. 22947/13 (ECtHR, 2 February 2016), Pihl v. Sweden App no. 74742/14 (ECtHR, 9 March 2017), Tamiz v. United Kingdom App no. 3877/14 (ECtHR, 19 September 2017), Magyar Jeti Zrt. v. Hungary App no. 11257/16 (ECtHR, 4 December 2018), Høiness v. Norway App no. 43624/14 (ECtHR, 19 March 2019)

25. Imbarlina, E.: The Roles and Relationship between the Two European Courts in Post-Lisbon EU Human Rights Protection, 12 September 2013. http://www.jurist.org/dateline/2013/09/ elena-butti-lisbon-treaty.php

26. see: [25]

27. Vries, S.A.: Editorial EU and ECHR: conflict or harmony? Utrecht Law Rev. **9**(1), 78–79 (2013)

28. Proposal for a regulation of the European Parliament and of the Council on a Single Market for Digital Services (Digital Services Act) and amending Directive 2000/31/EC, COM/2020/825 final

29. Regulation (EU) 2016/679 of the European Parliament and of the Council of 27 April 2016 on the protection of natural persons with regard to the processing of personal data and on the free movement of such data and repealing Directive 95/46/EC (General Data Protection Regulation), OJ L 119, pp. 1–88, 4.5.2016

30. de Witte, B.: Legal Instruments and Law-Making in the Lisbon Treaty. In: Griller, S., Ziller, J. (eds.): The Lisbon Treaty. Schriftenreihe der Österreichischen Gesellschaft für

Europaforschung (ECSA Austria)/European Community Studies Association of Austria Publication Series, vol. 11, pp. 79–108. Springer, Vienna (2008)

31. DSA, Explanatory Memorandum, 2
32. see: [31]
33. DSA, Explanatory Memorandum, 1
34. Directive 2010/13/EU of the European Parliament and of the Council of 10 March 2010 on the coordination of certain provisions laid down by law, regulation or administrative action in Member States concerning the provision of audiovisual media services (Audiovisual Media Services Directive), OJ L 95, pp. 1–24, 15.4.2010
35. Cauffman, C., Goanta, C.: A new order: the digital services act and consumer protection. Eur. J. Risk Regul. First View, pp. 3–4 (2021). https://www.cambridge.org/core/journals/eur opean-journal-of-risk-regulation/article/new-order-the-digital-services-act-and-consumer-protection/8E34BA8A209C61C42A1E7ADB6BB904B1
36. Although not a European survey, interestingly, a simultaneous online survey of twelve countries found that 67% of the population said legislators did not understand enough about how the Internet and digital services work to realistically judge the regulatory governance needed. Internet Way of Networking: Two Thirds of People Worldwide Are Not Confident in Politicians Regulating the Internet. Internet Society, 9 Dec 2020. https://www.internetsociety.org/news/press-releases/2020/two-thirds-of-people-worldwide-are-not-confident-in-politicians-regulating-the-internet
37. https://ec.europa.eu/info/strategy/priorities-2019-2024/europe-fit-digital-age/digital-ser vices-act-ensuring-safe-and-accountable-online-environment_en
38. DSA, Article 19
39. DSA, 42: "provider should inform the recipient of its decision, the reasons for its decision and the available redress possibilities to contest the decision"
40. DSA, Article 31
41. DSA, Chapter III, Section 4
42. DSA, Chapter II
43. DSA, Article 25 (1)
44. DSA, Article 38 (2)
45. Van Canneyt, T.: The proposed DSA – part 1 – Transforming the delivery of online services through EU regulation. fieldfisher, 12 Jan 2021. https://www.fieldfisher.com/en/services/tec hnology-outsourcing-and-privacy/technology-and-outsourcing-blog/the-digital-services-act
46. Golunova, V.: The Digital Services Act and freedom of expression: triumph or failure? Maastricht University Blog, 8 March 2021. https://www.maastrichtuniversity.nl/blog/2021/03/dig ital-services-act-and-freedom-expression-triumph-or-failure
47. DSA, Article 59 (1)
48. DSA, Article 55 (1)
49. On April 1, 2020, Germany's federal government published a new draft bill to amend the German Hate Speech Act (Netzwerkdurchsetzungsgesetz, NetzDG)
50. Although it was declared unconstitutional by the French Constitutional Council on 18 June 2020
51. Kommunikationsplattformen-Gesetz (KoPl-G)
52. About the 'new school speech regulation' see: Balkin, J. M.: Old School/New School Speech Regulation. Harvard Law Rev. 127, 2296–2306 (2014)
53. Delfi AS v. Estonia App no. 64569/09 (ECtHR, 16 June 2015), Joint dissenting opinion of Judges Sajó and Tsotsoria, 19
54. More details: Cendic, K., Gosztonyi, G.: Freedom of expression in times of Covid-19: chilling effect in Hungary and Serbia. J. Liber. Int. Affairs 2020/6, 14–29 (2020)

55. World Press Freedom Day: Declaration by the High Representative on behalf of the EU, 2 May 2021. https://www.consilium.europa.eu/en/press/press-releases/2021/05/02/world-press-freedom-day-declaration-by-the-high-representative-on-behalf-of-the-eu

56. Wiseman, J.: Crisis point: Covid-19 intensifies challenge for independent media in Hungary, International Press Institute, 18 May 2020. https://ipi.media/crisis-point-covid-19-intensifies-challenge-for-independent-media-in-hungary

57. OECD: The COVID-19 crisis and state ownership in the economy: Issues and policy considerations. Updated 25 June 2020. https://www.oecd.org/coronavirus/policy-responses/the-covid-19-crisis-and-state-ownership-in-the-economy-issues-and-policy-considerations-ce417c46

58. Voorhoof, D.: European Media Law Collection of Materials 2015–2016. http://www.mijnwetboek.be/en/producten/European-Media-Law-2015-2016

59. see: [58]

60. Declaration on freedom of communication on the Internet, adopted on 28 May 2003. https://search.coe.int/cm/Pages/result_details.aspx?ObjectId=09000016805dfbd5

61. Irion, K., Cavaliere, P., Pavli, D.: Comparative study of best European practices of online content regulation. Law and policy of online content regulation, in particular defamation online, in the light of Albanian legislative proposals. Council of Europe, Amsterdam/ Edinburgh/Tirana, 14 (2014)

62. Yar, L., Hendrych, L., Strzałkowski, M., Szicherle, P.: Visegrad Four want to distinguish between 'illegal' and 'harmful' content in Digital Services Act. 2 Nov 2020. https://www.euractiv.com/section/digital/news/visegrad-four-want-to-distinguish-between-illegal-and-harmful-content-in-digital-services-act

63. EU Code of Practice on Disinformation. https://ec.europa.eu/newsroom/dae/document.cfm?doc_id=54454

64. Monti, M.: The Eu Code of Practice on Disinformation and the Risk of the Privatisation of Censorship. In: Giusti, S., Piras, E. (eds.): Democracy and Fake News. Information Manipulation and Post-Truth Politics, pp. 214–225. Routledge, London and New York (2021)

65. Barata, J.: The Digital Services Act and Its Impact on the Right to Freedom of Expression: Special Focus on Risk Mitigation Obligations. Plataforma en Defensa de la Libertad de Información, 22 June 2021, 5. https://libertadinformacion.cc/wp-content/uploads/2021/06/DSA-AND-ITS-IMPACT-ON-FREEDOM-OF-EXPRESSION-JOAN-BARATA-PDLI.pdf

66. Mussard, H.: Digital Advertising Industry Warns Against Misguided EU Regulation. IAB Europe, 29 Sep 2020. https://iabeurope.eu/all-news/digital-advertising-industry-warns-against-misguided-eu-regulation

67. Proposal for a regulation of the European Parliament and of the Council on contestable and fair markets in the digital sector (Digital Markets Act), COM/2020/842 final

68. <https://www.youtube.com/watch?v=jgOBZv2nHjA>

69. DMA, Article 3 (1)

70. DMA, Article 2 (2)

71. DMA, 3–4

72. See: DMA, Explanatory Memorandum, 2: "Almost 24% of total online trade in Europe is cross-border."

73. DMA, Article 3 (2)

74. see: [69]

75. DMA, 36

76. DMA, Article 5

77. That is, for example, logging in to one's Gmail account will not automatically sign in to one's YouTube account

78. That is, for example, allow the Apple's App Store to be used from non-Apple devices

79. DMA, Article 6 (1) h)

80. DMA, Article 26 (1)
81. DMA, Article 22
82. Communication: Shaping Europe's digital future, 19 February 2020, 5, <https://ec.europa.eu/info/sites/default/files/communication-shaping-europes-digital-future-feb2020_en_4.pdf>
83. see: [83]
84. Ma, R.T.B., Lui, J.C.S., Misra, V.: Evolution of the internet economic ecosystem. IEEE/ACM Trans. Netw. **23**(1), 85–98 (2015)
85. Klobuchar, A.: Antitrust: Taking on Monopoly Power from the Gilded Age to the Digital Age. **369** Alfred A. Knopf, New York (2021)
86. Dreeben, M., Drummond Hansen, M. et al.: CDA Section 230: Its Past, Present, and Future. https://www.omm.com/omm_distribution/momentum/CDA_Section_230.pdf
87. Kayali, L.: France's plan to rein in Big Tech (and Ireland and Luxembourg), Politico, 27 May 2021. https://www.politico.eu/article/france-ireland-luxembourg-big-tech-regulation-apple-amazon-facebook-google-digital-services-act-digital-markets

# Lex Informatica: Information Technology as a Legal Tool

Roman Amelin[1]([⊠]), Sergey Channov[2]([⊠]), and Eduard Lipatov[2]([⊠])

[1] National Research Saratov State University Named After N. G. Chernyshevsky, 83
Astrakhanskaya Street, Saratov 410012, Russia
[2] The Russian Presidential Academy of National Economy and Public Administration, 23/25
Sobornaya Street, Saratov 410031, Russia

**Abstract.** In the era of the fourth technological revolution, the implementation
of social relations depends on information technology and software systems. The
program code that controls the operation of these systems begins to play the role of
a regulator of social relations, since it de facto sets the boundaries of capabilities
and imposes requirements on user behavior.

The paper opened a discussion about what conditions are important for the
program code to receive scientific recognition as a source of law. Three features
are proposed to be considered necessary conditions. First, the program code must
have an impact on social relations. Secondly, he must establish special rules for
the participants in these relations, which are absent in legal acts, moreover, these
rules de facto receive the status of mandatory if the information system (computer
program, other tool) is the only way to exercise certain rights and/or responsibilities
of the subject. Finally, users and other actors should accept these rules as a given,
and consider opposition to them as an undesirable exception.

A separate and very important issue is the attitude of the state - it must at least
recognize and support the rules laid down in the code as the natural order of things
in the corresponding social relations (if the state takes on the role of guarantor of
such rules, for example, obliging the subjects of the right to use certain software,
then the program code de facto begins to play the role of a source of law).

**Keywords:** Legal norms · Program code · Source of law · Lex informatica ·
State information systems · Digital transformation · Code legitimacy

## 1 Introduction

The concept of the source (form) of law is one of the fundamental in the theory of law.
The metaphor "source of law" belongs to the Roman historian Titus Livy, who called
the Laws of the XII tables "the source of all public and private law" (fons omni publice
privatique iuris) [1]. Philosophers such as John Locke and Thomas Hobbes developed

The study was conducted within the grant project 20-011-00355 from the Russian Foundation for
Basic Research.

© Springer Nature Switzerland AG 2022
D. A. Alexandrov et al. (Eds.): DTGS 2021, CCIS 1503, pp. 177–189, 2022.
https://doi.org/10.1007/978-3-030-93715-7_13

the doctrine of the forms of law and formulated the general principle that in order to apply, the law must be recorded and communicated to the public.

Legal theorists offer definitions that are quite similar in content. Aleksandrov called the type of activity of the state, which consists in the establishment of legal norms or in the recognition of other social norms as a legal source of law [2, pp. 49, 51]. According to Malko, the forms of law are a way of expressing outside the state will, legal rules of conduct [3, p. 281]. Vengerov defined the form of law as an objectified consolidation and manifestation of the content of law in certain acts of state bodies, court decisions, contracts, customs and other sources [4, p. 279]. Nersesyants referred to sources of law as sources of information about law, as well as social factors that determine the content of legal norms and the state as the force that creates law [5]. Alekseev considered the source of law to be documentary ways of expressing and securing the norms of law, emanating from the state or officially recognized by it [6, p. 76].

Voplenko divides all known forms of law into three groups according to their status: 1) forms of law officially recognized by the state (legal custom, normative legal act, agreement with normative content); 2) forms of law that are not officially recognized by the state (religious texts, legal doctrine, individual legal acts, individual contractual acts, legal awareness, legal culture) and 3) forms of law, the legal status of which is not officially determined (legal precedent, legal practice, acts of interpretation rights, generally recognized principles and norms of international law) [7, p. 5]. Although this classification will differ for states from different legal families, in general, the approach can be considered universal. The evolution and transformation of forms of law is largely associated not only with the emergence of new, but also with the official recognition by the state of previously existing forms.

The role and place of individual sources (forms) of law change with the development of social relations. Thus, legal customs were superseded by legislation and other normative legal acts and acquired a subsidiary character [8, p. 110]. Such processes usually took centuries: the forms of law, not without reason, can be considered one of the most conservative elements of the legal system. But under the influence of modern digital technologies, ideas about the forms of law are beginning to undergo a significant transformation.

Lawrence Lessig was the first to express the definite opinion that software code can replace laws. Discussing the fundamental difference between legal regulation in cyberspace and in the real world, he emphasized the importance of the fact that the very structure of the real world sets a limitation not only for regulation, but also for the behavior that must be regulated. A fundamentally different structure of "cyberspace" requires special legal norms to regulate the relations arising in it. At the same time, "cyberspace does not have such an architecture that could not be changed, its architecture is derived... from the code. Such a code can change either because it develops differently, or because the state and business somehow influence it" [9]. Thus, Lessig formulated the thesis that the main regulator of relations realized in the virtual space will be the program code, which directly sets the boundaries of what is proper and possible for participants in legal relations interacting only through software.

Apart from massively multiplayer online games and similar virtual worlds, today there are very few examples of social relations that take place entirely in "cyberspace".

However, with the development of digital technologies and their penetration into all types of human life, a huge number of traditional legal relations began to be implemented using such technologies, to the point that their implementation becomes impossible without the mediation of software systems and information systems at some stages. And at these stages, the program code that embodies certain algorithms absolutely rigidly sets the boundaries of what is necessary and possible for the participants in such legal relations.

This situation is especially pronounced in cases where the use of information systems and individual programs is sanctioned by the state or even established by the state as a prerequisite. This is a phenomenon that, for historical reasons, turned out to be characteristic of the Russian Federation. For accounting and control purposes, state information systems are being created on the basis of laws. The same laws impose the obligation on controlled entities to transfer information to state bodies using this system, post certain information in the system or use the system for information interaction with other entities. In some cases, the state information system becomes the only source of official information. We have repeatedly written about a trend that began to form in Russian lawmaking in the early 2010s - instead of adopting a detailed draft law regulating certain relations, the authorities make a legislative decision on the implementation and use of a new state information system [10]. Subsequently (usually after the creation of the system), the details of interaction with it are regulated by subordinate normative acts, but it is axiomatic that no normative act can set requirements for information interaction in more detail than the actual program code of the information system. As has been repeatedly noted in our works, although the requirements for state information systems are formally enshrined in regulatory legal acts of various levels, the developer, even if he does not allow deviations from legal norms, in any case, at least, specifies them until they are fully implemented in software. Thus, in reality there are generally binding rules (norms) that are contained exclusively in the program code of the system. Moreover, information systems used in the field of public administration may contain non-obvious, manifested in very specific cases, discrepancies with legal documents [11].

The program code of multi-user information systems created and maintained by private companies deserves no less attention. These systems are not mandatory for use, do not receive a special status from the state, and the restrictions and requirements imposed by them on the behavior of users do not have any official status. However, large social groups if they interact through these information systems (technologies, platforms, protocols) and accept their capabilities and limitations, it is legitimate to say that such systems objectively express pro-legal requirements [7, p. 10]. It is quite obvious that the Internet in general, large social networks (such as Facebook), online platforms (eBay, Amazon), Google services, etc. have a large-scale impact on the behavior of their members.

## 2 Formulation of the Problem

The purpose of this article is to identify the necessary and sufficient conditions for the program code and algorithms of computer systems to act as sources (forms) of law.

Boshno quite exhaustively singled out the signs of forms of law that allow them to play the role of a regulator of social relations: a) certainty of the content; b) the duration of existence; c) common knowledge; d) obligation; e) universality; f) clarity of external expression; g) rationality; h) justice; i) recognition by subjects of law [12, p. 46].

The code embedded in the program, which is widely used by people, a priori has such properties as the certainty of the content, the duration of existence and (with some reservations) the clarity of external expression. The rest of the signs need some clarification, taking into account the specifics of the program code. As a first approximation, intended to start a discussion about the role of code as a source of law, we propose to consider the following three features that, in our opinion, claim to be necessary and sufficient conditions:

1. The code mediates social relations.
2. The rules established by the de facto code are absent in other sources of law.
3. Legitimacy of the code.

## 3    Program Code as a Means of Implementing Social Relations

First of all, speaking about the very essence of law, it should be noted that it regulates the activities of people, their behavior and relationships. A legal norm is a form of realization and consolidation of the rights and obligations of participants in social relations [13].

Not any program code (speaking of program code, of course, we do not mean individual lines or other code fragments, but an integral application or information system) directly affects human activity. There are many programs that perform utility functions. A utility that provides synchronization with world time, a tool for automatic diagnostics of the device's health, signal conversion protocols for transmission over communication channels - although these applications interact with others and contribute to the operation of a complex of systems, their functions do not directly affect human activity and do not have any impact on it.

If the user interacts with the application directly, for example, specifies commands for execution, receives information about their results, etc., we can say that the program code affects his activities. Moreover, it is the program code that will determine the boundaries of a person's capabilities within the framework of interaction with this application, and the information obtained as a result of the work of the code can determine the further behavior of a person already as a member of society. Nevertheless, we can talk about the legal or at least quasi-legal nature of this impact only if it affects social relations, and contributes to the consolidation or implementation of the rights and obligations of these relations' subjects.

Indeed, the fundamental difference between legal norms and other ways of regulating human activity (such as customs, religion, morality, corporate ethics, etc.) is that the boundaries of proper and possible behavior established by these norms are formalized in the form of legal rights and legal obligations of the subjects of social relations.

Legal obligation is a statutory measure of due socially necessary behavior, as well as a type (line) of behavior [14]. It is a measure of proper behavior towards other subjects. According to the International Covenant on Civil and Political Rights, "the individual has responsibilities towards other people and the community to which he belongs" [15]. The Universal Declaration of Human Rights states that "everyone has responsibilities to society, in which only the free and full development of his personality is possible" [16]. Legal right, closely and bilaterally related to legal obligation, is a measure of possible behavior in society, in the framework of interaction with other subjects.

Any program code naturally determines the range of user actions that are possible when working with the corresponding application or information system. The use of the application is subject to legal regulations (primarily in the field of intellectual property - regulating the relationship between the user and the software manufacturer, as well as in the field of communications, financial and other areas). However, one should distinguish between the capabilities provided by a local single-user application, no matter how complex and multifunctional it may be (from a text editor to a decision support system based on big data) and applications designed for information interaction between several participants.

If the program code mediates the processes of information interaction, a group of mutual rights and obligations arises, the implementation of which is possible only according to the rules laid down in the program.

Using social networks or other tools of network communication, the user has the right to send a message to another subject, hoping that it will be delivered, and the recipient will be informed about the delivery of the message. The recipient, in turn, has the right to reply to the message, ignore or block it. If the functionality of the system provides for the possibility of moderation, any message can be read, blocked or deleted by the administrator - thus, the program code consolidates the ability to restrict the rights of participants in information interaction (in most cases, they are aware of this and actually give their consent using this system). In some cases, restriction of rights occurs automatically based on programmatically established rules. The impossibility of sending a message or posting information on the site due to not filling in the required fields, violation of the requirements for the format or size of files can hardly be regarded as a significant limitation. But the automatic censoring of messages based on stop words and expressions (which can consist of replacing such words or completely blocking the message and even the entire account) is already an explicit restriction of rights enshrined in the program code. It can also be interpreted as a duty to refrain from certain actions that are socially harmful (at least from the point of view of software developers, although this point of view is most likely due to other norms existing in society, primarily legal ones), the violation of which follows programmed sanctions. Youtube and other sites that post user-generated content actively use means of automatic copyright detection and automatically block content that is marked by the algorithm as belonging to a different copyright holder [17, 18]. The time is not far off when journalistic content will also be automatically rejected by anti-plagiarism systems. An attempt to "cheat" a multiplayer computer game (more precisely, those actions of the user that violate the user agreement from the point of view of the algorithm) leads to the automatic blocking of the account.

Thus, the program code, through which the information interaction of various participants occurs, not only ensures the possibility of realizing their mutual rights and obligations, but can also set the boundaries of these rights when using the application (information system), as well as establish rigid causal relationships between certain socially significant actions of the participants and socially significant consequences that will follow as a result of these actions - including those that can be considered as sanctions for the commission of prohibited actions.

## 4    Program Code as the Only Way to Implement Rights or Obligations

The law sets standards for socially acceptable human behavior. The program code sets the boundaries of human behavior in the process of using the appropriate software and hardware tools.

At first glance, it seems that the program code is more appropriate to compare with such tools as a drill or a telegraph, which also require a person to perform a certain sequence of actions if he wants to achieve the desired result. But the program code embedded in the application takes on a completely different meaning if this application is the only way to implement certain rights and/or obligations of the subject.

For example, a social network in modern society may be the only way to convey your position to a certain circle of people. While there are certainly many other means of communication, social media today play a special role in organizing distributed communities. Just as in the past millennia, the media fundamentally differed from other means of communication (and these distinctive features of the media required special legal regulation of this area), social networks are fundamentally different from other means of communication by the possibility of simultaneous mass and targeted dissemination of information. It is no coincidence that the blocking of Trump's Facebook and Twitter accounts in January 2021 caused such a heated public debate [19]. The essence of this precedent comes down not so much to the rights of individual communication platforms to establish their own rules and restrictions on the communication of participants and, accordingly, the question of whether such a restriction will constitute censorship. Subsequent events, namely, the transition of Trump's supporters to other social networks, pressure on these networks, including from companies that provide their technical infrastructure (the closure of the Parler site), led to an almost complete blocking of Trump's ability to quickly and massively communicate his position to his supporters [20].

Of course, in an ecosystem that includes many competing social networks, such a situation is rather an exception and requires the concerted action of a large number of actors. The software and hardware that block individual users play here a purely auxiliary, instrumental role. The very right to disseminate information using a social network is currently not considered a special subjective right - accordingly, blocking in a particular social network is not a prohibition on the dissemination of information. Although in the future we can predict the isolation of such a right and the emergence of sanctions in the form of its deprivation/restriction based on a court decision for committing certain offenses - precisely because of the special public importance of the information that public figures disseminate among certain communities through social networks.

However, even now it is pertinent to say that the dissemination and receipt of information through a specific social network is a particular commons. Each social network is unique, first of all, by the range of active users, for whom it is the preferred method of communication or the main source of information, and secondly by the set of available services. By distributing information through a specific social network and using its services, the user exercises a right different from the general right to information - the right to disseminate and receive information through this particular social network that is especially important for him for some reason. And the implementation of this right depends not only on legal and political decisions that can be made in relation to the user by the administration of the social network or law enforcement agencies, but also on the algorithms embedded in the program code of the platform.

The right to disseminate information through a social network will be limited by filters that automatically cut off obscene and politically incorrect messages, and respond to potential copyright violations or other requirements. In addition, the range of addressees of the distributed message will depend on the search and ranking algorithms. In the conditions of an excess of information and overwhelming information noise, each message that does not have a specific addressee is experiencing strong competition. Only the program code of the social network will determine which messages a particular user will see in his news feed. The same algorithms will affect the right to receive information by the user, by forming his news feed based on a combination of user settings, analysis of preferences and rating of publications (adjusted for the paid service of increasing such rating) [21].

Not a single legal act will fully enshrine all the rules according to which a social network must deliver information to the user or distribute his information. Even when the filters mentioned above are configured to block illegal information, they cannot replace the law enforcement officer - the result of the filter's work will not always correspond to the result of a judicial or administrative procedure carried out in strict accordance with the law. It should be noted that the implementation of this right is influenced by artificial intelligence algorithms. Their parameters are constantly changing during training, and the logic of decision-making is described by mathematical models that depend on data, completely different from the causal logic of "human" rules. Therefore, even theoretically, going in the opposite direction "from the code", it is impossible to formalize these de facto rules and restrictions in the form of a legal act expressed in natural language [22].

Thus, in a number of cases, the information system (computer program) is the only way to exercise certain rights and/or obligations of the subject, even if very narrow and specific. And at the same time, the rules established de facto by the program code are absent in other sources of law.

There is another important caveat to be made. Even if a software application is not the only way to exercise the rights or obligations of participants in certain public relations (for example, the obligation to provide information to a counterparty can be performed both orally and using traditional paper forms of information transfer, or maybe through any of the many electronic communication tools), it still imposes its own special rules, restrictions and opportunities that affect the implementation of rights and obligations, subject to the choice of this instrument. For example, some programs and information systems can guarantee anonymity, others - confidentiality (even if this confidentiality is contrary to the legal requirements in force in a particular country [23]), and still others - strict authentication of communication participants and the integrity of the message itself, provided they follow a certain protocol. Thus, the variability available in the software ecosystem is analogous to how traditional forms of law can enshrine alternative ways of enforcing legal rights and obligations.

## 5   The Legitimacy of the Rules Enshrined in the Program Code

In order for the possibilities and limitations that the program code establishes to be considered as regulators of behavior, and in the long term - as legal norms, it is necessary to observe such an important feature as their recognition by subjects of law.

This feature is best defined through the concept of legitimacy, which should be distinguished from the concept of legality close to it. Legality is understood as the legal rightness of the emergence, organization and activity of power, while legitimacy means the actual recognition of the power, its actions by the population, the degree of their approval. Thus, S.I. Nosov, "if legality means legal justification, strict adherence to the established procedure for the formation of power, the adoption of a legislative or other normative act, then legitimacy is trust in the government, approval of the adopted legislative or other legal act, voluntary recognition of the power of the right to make binding decisions" [24, p. 44].

At the same time, the author notes, "there may be cases when legal acts that meet the requirements of legality do not have legitimacy and, on the contrary, acts that do not meet the requirements of legality (for example, acts adopted by an improper entity and in violation of the established procedure) subsequently become legitimate. Thus, not every legal norm contained in a legal act can be legitimate from the point of view of its perception by public opinion, the general population, just as not every legitimate legal act can be legal from the point of view of the order of adoption" [24, p. 47].

The software code, if it is not approved in a special manner by specially authorized state entities (which is the case in extremely rare cases), cannot be legal in the same sense as a legal act. Therefore, in this case, the property of legitimacy is of particular importance.

Just as a rule of law, being legal by definition, can be illegitimate, software code legally protected by laws and user agreements can be disapproved and even challenged by users. An example is the famous scandal of 2005, when Sony introduced a rootkit on its DVDs, which penetrates deeply into the user's system without his knowledge in order to subsequently monitor the copyright of Sony films and applications. It triggered a public uproar that ultimately led to recall of millions of discs. As a result of a wide public campaign, Sony was forced to apologize, and antiviruses began to classify the rootkit as malware [25]. In the spring of 2020, the Moscow government, in order to counter the spread of the coronavirus epidemic, developed the Social Monitoring application, designed to monitor citizens' compliance with the isolation regime. The first version of the application was automatically removed from the App Store platform after Muscovites, dissatisfied with the features of the application, dropped its rating on this platform beyond the minimum acceptable value [26].

On the other hand, software systems and the actions they allow that are legally prohibited in a particular jurisdiction can enjoy the recognition and support of a significant part of society - cryptocurrency mining and circulation, using torrents to distribute unlicensed content, bypassing content blocking tools using anonymizers, and WPN etc.

If the legitimacy of legal acts is largely ensured by their legality, namely the powers of the receiving bodies, the observance of the procedure for adoption and publication, then the legitimacy of the program code primarily stems from the rationality of the requirements laid down in it for participants in public relations.

If the law does not demonstrate an egregious degree of unreasonableness, the majority tacitly agrees with the order it establishes, and the minority (first of all, those who believe that the law infringes on their interests) chooses the way of combating it in legal (participating in political activities, organizing public campaigns or addressing complaints to the appropriate courts and authorities) or illegal (breaking the law) methods. Likewise, if an application is clearly not beyond reason, most users tend to put up with the specifics of its operation, and a disaffected minority can protest in various ways (in many cases - by choosing other applications, and if there are no alternatives, using the same ways - public campaigns for pressure on developers, judicial and administrative measures - or bypassing the requirements by hacking the application as a cardinal method of countering the established order).

Thus, an application, the algorithm of which reasonably and adequately corresponds to its tasks, will have legitimacy, that is, recognition from the majority of users. As a result, users consciously (or at least without resistance) accept the requirements and restrictions imposed by the program code and affecting the exercise of their rights or obligations in the process of using such an application.

## 6   Protection of the Rules Enshrined in the Program Code

The features listed above are quite enough for a program code that satisfies them to act as a regulator of social relations, which are implemented using the appropriate software. But the fundamental difference between a legal norm is such a characteristic feature as the provision of the power of state coercion. It is this feature that makes the rule/requirement a legal norm, it is for this reason that state and law are closely related and mutually conditioned phenomena.

The program code, due to its immanently inherent features, in principle, does not need external support. A mandatory norm established in a legal act can be fulfilled or ignored by the subject of law. To prevent the latter case or eliminate its consequences, the mechanism of state coercion is used. A user working with a computer program, in principle, is not able to perform actions that are not included in the algorithm of the program. (Speaking about the algorithm of the program, we mean the objectively given program code - with all errors and undocumented features, and not the ideal image that may be present in the imagination of its owners and developers.)

However, the state continues to play an important role.

Some applications are specially sanctioned by the state. Their use is mandatory for established entities in the implementation of certain activities. The requirements laid down in the program code of these applications are de facto mandatory for execution under the threat of legal liability - even if they are not enshrined in other legal acts. Thus, such applications are actually sources of law. This category includes, for example, state and municipal information systems that have a special legal regime in the Russian Federation - we have repeatedly investigated this phenomenon in our publications [10, 30].

As for the information systems developed by private companies, at present their future as a legal instrument is not fully defined. On the one hand, states closely monitor large information systems and impose many special requirements on the algorithms for their work. So, in the Russian Federation, information systems that provide targeted transmission of messages between users are required to store these messages for a certain time, as well as to analyze them in accordance with the needs of special services or law enforcement agencies. In China, a large-scale experiment is underway to introduce a social rating - multi-user systems must provide the data necessary to calculate such a rating, and in the near future - restrict the user in opportunities (or, conversely, provide preferences) based on it. On the other hand, the state does not regulate (and, as shown above, cannot regulate) all the details of the functioning of such systems. However, the state can assume the role of arbiter in the relevant public relations. It can establish that if the operation of a multi-user information system is authorized by the state, then the rules laid down in its algorithms are mandatory for users. In this case, the program code of the system becomes a full-fledged source of law. Of course, it is more likely that most states will limit themselves to establishing some general requirements - and then the algorithms of the system's operation and their results will not be binding and may be subject to challenge both in court and in other ways, including public pressure on the owners of multi-user systems.

In the latter case, the area where the software code and the legal sphere are interfaced is of particular importance - the point of transition of social relations from the area where they are subject exclusively to the logic embedded in the algorithms of software systems to the area where they come under the influence of traditional legal norms.

Everything that happens during the operation of the application is safely regulated by the application itself. However, if there is a violation of the logic of the application as a result of external interference - hacking, such self-regulation loses its meaning. For the stability of such relations, software and technical measures to protect the program are not enough; legal measures supported by the state are important, for example, criminal liability for unauthorized disruption of the system's operation.

Moreover, the work of any program code is reduced to the processing of information and, accordingly, the result of the work will always be the transfer to the final addressee of information received from the source or created as a result of the application. This is a fairly narrow category of social relations. They are of particular importance when they are part of a more complex complex legal relationship. For example, the provision of information to authorized bodies by a controlled entity using a state information system or simply a postal application for these purposes is part of a complex relationship of state control over the activities of this entity, within which the transferred information acquires special legal significance, and its receipt by an authorized body is a legal force. Fact, entailing legal consequences. Likewise, information stored in a public registry, on an open blockchain or simply on a private website page will have different legal force and lead to different legal consequences depending on the provisions of the regulations enforced by the state.

Special mention should be made of the situation when the information obtained as a result of the work of the program code has the character of a control action and directly affects the operation of a complex mechanism, for example, a production complex or a robot, acting in the real world and producing relations by its actions, in which various participants are involved and which are no longer limited to purely informational ones. The legal status of a robot, the legal significance of its actions and responsibility for the result of these actions is one of the most difficult and debatable issues in modern legal thought.

The closest analogy to the ecosystem of requirements inherent in the code of software products is the medieval system of commercial law lex mercatoria, some elements of which are still preserved in international practice. As noted by Majorina, this right was distinguished, first, by the fact that it was not generated by a law or other authoritative official act; secondly, it existed in a sense autonomously and in addition to the law [27]. By analogy with this construct, a number of researchers speak of the emergence of a special sphere of autonomously emerging legal regulation - lex informatica. "In the age of networking and communication technologies, users traveling through information infrastructure are faced with an unstable and uncertain environment of numerous legal acts, changing national rules and conflicting regulations. For the information infrastructure, the default basic rules are as essential to users in the information society as lex mercatoria was to merchants hundreds of years ago" [28].

Thus, the role of the program code as a regulator of social relations is by no means diminished, even if it is not supported by the mechanism of state coercion. But taking into account the fact that its execution does not take place in a vacuum, the still insufficiently studied issue of the relationship between lex informatica and positive legal regulation acquires special significance. Summarizing the positions of scientists, Majorina draws attention to two approaches: competition with law ("if in the legal regime the content of norms is determined by law and court decisions, in lex informatica the rules of conduct are determined by technical capabilities and the practice of applying technologies" [29]) and equivalence. It seems that in both cases the role of the program code as a source of law is quite explicit and conditioned by the features identified and discussed above.

## 7   Conclusion and Prospects

Today, the program code has a weak regulatory effect on social relations and relatively harmoniously coexists with law, occupying an undoubtedly subordinate role in relation to the latter. However, the qualitative transition of processes and relations in all spheres of human activity to forms tied to digital technologies, as well as the development of other trends associated with the development of digital technologies, will undoubtedly lead to the fact that the program code will act as a special technological regulator of social relations. At the same time, both coexistence (harmonious or competitive, when digital technologies will provide ways to circumvent legal norms) of law and program code, and the emergence of code as a new kind of sources of law, fully implemented into the legal system, are possible.

With this paper, we would like to open a discussion about what conditions are important for the program code to receive scientific recognition as a source of law. Three features are proposed to be considered necessary conditions. First, the program code must have an impact on social relations. Secondly, he must establish special rules for the participants in these relations, which are absent in legal acts, moreover, these rules de facto receive the status of mandatory if the information system (computer program, other tool) is the only way to exercise certain rights and/or responsibilities of the subject. Finally, users and other actors should accept these rules as a given, and consider opposition to them as an undesirable exception. A separate and very important issue is the attitude of the state - it must at least recognize and support the rules laid down in the code as the natural order of things in the corresponding social relations (if the state takes on the role of guarantor of such rules, for example, obliging the subjects of the right to use certain software, then the program code de facto begins to play the role of a source of law).

Recognition of the software code as a source of law not only opens up opportunities for the development of the legal system in the era of the fourth technological revolution, but also allows to ensure the protection of the rights of users, which are influenced by the possibilities and restrictions that the software code constructs. In particular, these rules may be subject to the establishment and challenge mechanisms typical of legal norms, including judicial and administrative procedures. These questions are the subject of further in-depth research.

# References

1. Rubanov, A.: The concept of a source of law as a manifestation of the metaphoric nature of ancient consciousness. Judicial practice as a source of law, Moscow, pp. 45–46 (1977)
2. Alexandrov, N.: Concept of the source of law. VYUN scholarly notes. Issue VIII, Moscow, pp. 49–71 (1946)
3. Matuzov, N., Malko, A.: Theory of State and Law. Publishing House "Delo" RANEPA, Moscow (2016)
4. Vengerov, A.: Theory of State and Law. Omega-L, Moscow (2009). 607 p.
5. Nersesyants, V. (ed.): Problems of the general theory of law and state. Moscow (1999)
6. Alekseev, S.: Law: ABC - Theory - Philosophy. Comprehensive Research Experience, Moscow (1999)
7. Voplenko, N.: Sources and Forms of Law. VolSU Publishing House, Volgograd (2004)
8. Laptev, V.: Local legal custom as a source of regulation of business relations. Lex russica 4, 110–119 (2017)
9. Lessig, L.: The Law of the Horse: What Cyberlaw Might Teach. Harv. Law Rev. 113(2), 501–549 (1999)
10. Amelin, R., Channov, S.: State information systems in e-government in the Russian Federation: problems of legal regulation. In: Proceedings of the 2nd International Conference on Electronic Governance and Open Society: Challenges in Eurasia (EGOSE 2015), pp. 129–132. ACM, New York (2015)
11. Amelin, R., Channov, S.: Automated information system as a "source of law." Inf. Law 2, 23–27 (2008)
12. Boshno, S.: Form of law: theoretical and legal research. Author's abstract of PhD thesis. Moscow (2005)
13. Kelsen, H., Hartney, M.: General Theory of Norms. Oxford University Press, Oxford (1991). https://doi.org/10.1093/acprof:oso/9780198252177.003.0001
14. Green, L.: Legal Obligation and Authority. Stanford Encyclopedia of Philosophy (2003). https://plato.stanford.edu/entries/legal-obligation/

15. International Covenant on Civil and Political Rights. Adopted and opened for signature, ratification and accession by General Assembly resolution 2200A (XXI) of 16 December 1966 entry into force 23 March 1976, in accordance with Article 49. https://www.ohchr.org/en/professionalinterest/pages/ccpr.aspx
16. Universal Declaration of Human Rights. https://www.un.org/en/about-us/universal-declaration-of-human-rights
17. Spoerri, T.: On Upload-Filters and other Competitive Advantages for Big Tech Companies under Article 17 of the Directive on Copyright in the Digital Single Market. J. Intellect. Prop. Inf. Technol. Electron. Commerce Law 2, 173–186 (2019). https://www.jipitec.eu/issues/jipitec-10-2-2019/4914/JIPITEC_10_2_2019_173_Spoerri
18. The impact of algorithms for online content filtering or moderation. Study Requested by the JURI committee (2020). https://www.europarl.europa.eu/RegData/etudes/STUD/2020/657101/IPOL_STU. 657101_EN.pdf
19. Floridi, L.: Trump, Parler, and regulating the infosphere as our commons. Philos. Technol. 34(1), 1–5 (2021). https://doi.org/10.1007/s13347-021-00446-7
20. Crichton, D.: The deplatforming of President Trump - a review of an unprecedented and historical week for the tech industry. TechCrunch (2021)
21. Cotter, K., Cho, J., Rader, E.: Explaining the news feed algorithm: an analysis of the "News Feed FYI" blog. In: CHI 2017 Extended Abstracts, 06–11 May 2017, Denver (2017). https://doi.org/10.1145/3027063.3053114
22. Mayer-Schönberger, V., Cukier, K.: Big Data: A Revolution That Will Transform How We Live, Work, and Think. An Eamon Dolan Book, Houghton Mifflin, Mariner Books (2014)
23. Akbari, A., Gabdulhakov, R.: Platform surveillance and resistance in Iran and Russia. Surveill. Soc. 17(1/2), 223–231 (2017)
24. Nosov, S.: Legitimacy and legality as legal categories. Lawyer, no. 8 (2020)
25. Halderman A., Felten, E.: Lessons from the Sony CD DRM episode. In: Proceedings of the 15th USENIX Security Symposium (2006). https://jhalderm.com/pub/papers/rootkit-sec06-full.pdf
26. Kovaleva, N. (ed.): Problems and Challenges of Digital Society: Trends in the Development of Legal Regulation of Digital Transformations, vol. 2. Saratov State Law Academy, Saratov (2020)
27. Majorina, M.: On the conflict of law and "wrong", lex mercatoria renovation, smart contracts and blockchain arbitration. Lex russica 7, 93–107 (2019)
28. Reidenberg, J.R.: Lex informatica: the formulation of information policy rules through technology. Texas Law Rev. 3, 553–593 (1998)
29. Voynikanis, E.: Intellectual Property Law in the Digital Age: A Paradigm of Balance and Flexibility. Jurisprudence, Moscow (2013)
30. Amelin, R.: State and Municipal Information Systems in Russian Information Law: Theoretical and Legal Analysis. GrossMedia, Moscow (2018)

# eCity: Smart Cities and Urban Planning

# Detection the Relevance of Urban Functions for Value-Based Smart City Management

Olga Tikhonova, Ilya Yakimuk, and Sergey A. Mityagin[✉] [iD]

ITMO University, Kronverkskiy pr. 49, Saint-Petersburg 197101, Russia
mityagin@itmo.ru

**Abstract.** The article deals with the issue of value-based city management. Value-based management is one of the most important attributes of the concept of smart cities of the new generation. It relates to the transition from the technological understanding of a smart city to the concept of a city adapted to a person to create a new quality of life and create new opportunities for development. At the same time, the most important problem of implementing a value-based approach is the difficulty in quickly identifying the values and needs of citizens. Traditional methods based on sociological research do not provide the necessary speed and coverage, in addition, their results require additional adaptation for management tasks. This requires the development of new approaches to determining the significance of urban functions for citizens based on data that has operational specifics. One of the sources of such data can be social networks on the Internet. The article suggests an approach to clarifying the structure of values and needs of citizens based on the analysis of social network data.

**Keywords:** Machine learning · Text mining · Natural language processing · Value-based management · Smart city

## 1 Introduction

Since its appearance at the end of the 20th century, the concept of a smart city has evolved and adapted to the specifics of each city [1, 2, 4]. The understanding remained unchanged that a smart city is primarily a tool for overcoming current barriers and problems of cities through modern technologies to ensure the sustainable development of the city in the long term [3]. At the same time, both the barriers and the technologies that allow them to be overcome have changed over time. Different cities, being at different stages of development, readiness for the introduction of technologies, or as it is now commonly called, the level of digital transformation, differently organized the processes of implementing elements of a smart city and differently evaluated the effectiveness of this activity.

Modern smart cities are forced to focus on modern challenges, among which the most significant are the change of the value paradigm, the transition from materialistic to post-materialistic values [5] and the associated emergence of new types of economic activity and production [6]. The creative economies, the innovation economies, the knowledge

© Springer Nature Switzerland AG 2022
D. A. Alexandrov et al. (Eds.): DTGS 2021, CCIS 1503, pp. 193–206, 2022.
https://doi.org/10.1007/978-3-030-93715-7_14

economy, and the digital economy are prominent representatives. For these types of economy, a distinctive feature is the prevailing importance of the individual and creative communities over production collectives [5]. This situation has created new requirements for the organization of human interaction with the city, for the organization and quality of the urban environment and life in the city itself.

For smart cities, this required the development of new approaches to management. One of them is the value-based management of the city [7]. Value-based management involves understanding and considering the values and needs of citizens in decision-making to create new opportunities and a new quality of life [8, 9].

However, one of the actual problems of practical implementation of value-based management is the difficulty in restoring the actual structure of values and needs of citizens. Traditional methods based on sociological research have several typical disadvantages:

they are limited in both the sample size and the measurement volume;
they become obsolete almost immediately after the survey is completed;
they do not have the nature of operational monitoring.

One of the solutions to this problem can be the modeling of values and needs, combining data from traditional methods of sociological research and methods of processing operational data generated by citizens to refine estimates.

In this article, we will consider an approach to modeling the structure of the significance of urban functions based on combining data from traditional surveys and data from users of social networks on the Internet. And the application of this model in the task of value-based management.

## 2 Methodological Background in the Field of Natural Language Analysis

### 2.1 Methods and Models of Natural Language Analysis

According to several studies [10], the publications of users of social networks can be considered as a reflection of people's ideas about what is significant and valuable. Thus, one of the approaches to assessing the value or significance of urban functions and objects of the urban environment for citizens can be the analysis of sources where the main way of expressing citizens is in writing (messages, appeals, posts, questions, and judgments, etc.). To analyze this kind of data, it is necessary to use the most effective tools and technologies for processing and analyzing large volumes of unstructured text data.

The solution of this problem is considered within the framework of the discipline of computational linguistics, which is based on the development of algorithms and application programs for processing language information. The greatest popularity and development in this area is occupied by such a direction as Natural Language Processing (hereinafter referred to as NLP) [11].

NLP includes a set of methods aimed at understanding and analyzing human language by a computer program. NLP lies at the intersection of such areas as artificial intelligence and computer (mathematical) linguistics [12]. The emergence of this trend is due to several reasons and is discussed in detail in [13] by Christopher D. Manning.

The two main methods used in natural language processing (NLP) are syntactic and semantic analysis [11–13].

The solution to the problem of assessing the significance of urban objects and urban functions for users of social networks can be achieved by means of a semantic analysis and correlation of user publications to the relevant topics related to the urban function or object of the urban environment.

Thus, NLP is used directly in the task of classifying user texts when evaluating the significance of city functions. At the same time, the choice of tools is determined by metrics [13], which show how well the machine learning method copes with the task.

Modern approaches to NLP are based on deep learning, a type of AI that learns and uses patterns in data to improve program understanding [14]. In [15–17], the authors also evaluate the main methods of machine learning in tasks for determining the text's tonality and for correlating the text to specified categories. Artificial neural networks (ANN) also showed the best results in accuracy, completeness, and F-measure, outperforming other methods by 7–9%. The results were also presented for different types of artificial neural network architectures, for example, for convolutional neural network (CNN) and recurrent neural network with LSTM blocks (long/short-term memory blocks), which also showed good performance, reaching 80–90% of the F-measure on each class.

As a result of this analysis of the works, we can conclude that the class of artificial neural networks (ANN) is the most successful with the task of classifying texts into different categories.

The NLP framework spaCy was chosen as a tool for implementing the classification model of user publications [18, 19]. This choice was made based on a comparison of similar NLP frameworks, such as StanfordNLP [20], where the spaCy model showed the most accurate results on both standard and pre-trained implementations [21, 22].

To solve the problems of natural language processing and machine learning of the classifier of the language model, it was decided to use the spaCy library [14]. This is an open-source library in the Python programming language, which has the following advantages for the task being solved:

- SpaCy language models have a built-in text classification component and tools for learning it.
- The standard Language Processing Pipeline of the spaCy model has built-in components for tokenization (tokenizer), morphological markup (part-of-speech tagger), definition of grammatical dependencies (dependency parser) and allocation of named entities (entity recognizer), and the library provides tools for working with them [18].
- A model of the Russian language has been developed for the library, which is available under the open MIT license [28] and has the standard pipeline components in front of the trained ones.

## 2.2 Source Data

For high-quality training and subsequent evaluation of the components of the neural network model, it is necessary to use a sufficient amount of data that is representative of the data to which the trained model is supposed to be applied, and relevant to the task [27].

Extracting information about the significance of urban functions for citizens from the data of users of social networks on the Internet requires the use of a natural language analysis tool. At the same time, it is necessary to consider the peculiarities of publications in such sources, which may differ from the classical language.

With all the variety of public platforms for discussion on the Internet, not all of them can show a certain cross-section of public opinion on a particular topic. The problem statement imposes increased requirements for data preparation. Since the names of the objects of the urban environment can be given in a general form:

- geographical localization of the text is required;
- high intensity of updates (relevance);
- completeness of text messages (contain from one to several sentences)
- the availability of data.

These requirements must be considered when choosing a data source. Users of social networks usually indicate their social and territorial affiliation, which is an advantage of social networks as data sources.

In this case, it is convenient to use anonymized publications from open thematic communities in social networks as a source of discussion. Social networks in general are a representative source of opinions of their users, and thematic communities allow for selective access to publications of specific population groups. It can be argued that users of social networks independently declare their belonging to certain groups of the population by joining thematic communities.

Facebook Instagram [23, 24], Facebook [25], VKontakte [26] are the largest of them. However, Instagram does not have a feature of thematic communities, and most of the published content is visual, entertaining, and accompanied by monosyllabic comments that are reduced to the simplest expression of emotions (for example, "emoji").

From the point of view of this study, the social networks Facebook and VKontakte are similar in their characteristics, as they have tools for both customizing users' personal pages, and for creating and maintaining thematic communities, including those dedicated to urban topics.

For the demonstration, the VKontakte social network was chosen as superior in terms of the number of users for the selected territory of St. Petersburg (Russia).

## 3  A Method for Assessing the Structure of the Significance of Urban Functions Through Text Analysis of Publications in Social Networks

The method is based on the assumption that the more often a group of people discusses the topic of a certain urban function, the higher the significance of this urban function for this group of people. The task of obtaining the structure of the significance of urban functions for a population group can be reduced to determining the frequency of publications on the topic of different urban functions in a certain relevant sample of publications in social networks.

The general scheme of using natural language analysis methods to assess the significance of city functions is shown in Fig. 1.

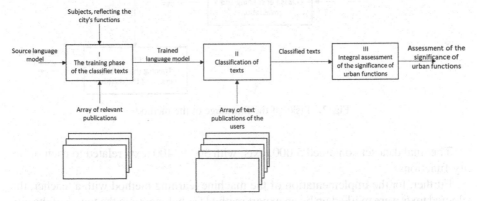

**Fig. 1.** The main stages of the method of assessing the significance of urban functions.

The presented method includes three stages. The first stage involves training the source text model on the selection of user publications from the corresponding source. This stage is included in the light of publications [21, 22], where the dependence of accuracy on the specifics of the data source is considered, where the specifics of the user expression may differ from the classical language.

The second stage involves solving the problem of classifying user texts for real data. The third stage involves assessing the significance of urban functions based on the classification estimates obtained.

## 3.1 The Machine Learning Stage of the Text Classification Component of the Neural Network Language Model

To implement the first stage of the method, the following tasks are performed (Fig. 2).

**Preparation of Texts for Training the Classifier on Urban Functions**
To ensure the representativeness and relevance of the texts for training and evaluating the classifier of publications in social networks by urban functions, the following criteria for selecting texts were used:

1) Publications were selected from the open thematic communities of the social network VKontakte.
2) Publications related to the main city functions were selected. At the same time, one publication could relate to several city functions, that is, the classification categories were not mutually exclusive.
3) The number of publications related to different urban functions remained approximately the same to balance the final data set.

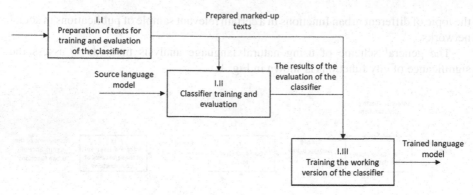

**Fig. 2.** Tasks of the first stage of the method.

The final data set contained 5,000 texts, with 300 to 400 texts related to each of the city functions.

Further, for the implementation of the machine learning method with a teacher, the selected texts were marked up by an expert method for belonging to the topics of the city functions. The results of the markup can be presented in a tabular form (Fig. 3), where for each text, the correspondence (value "1") or discrepancy (value "0") of each of the city functions is indicated.

| Text | Housing | Education | Health | Religion | lic_transporta | Selfcare | Groceries | Finance | nestic_serv | Pets | Sports | iment_and | Work |
|---|---|---|---|---|---|---|---|---|---|---|---|---|---|
| Продам мед. Воронежская обл. Очень высокого качества. 1500 руб. за 3 литра. Показатель качества - наличие | 0 | 0 | 0 | 0 | 0 | 0 | 1 | 0 | 0 | 0 | 0 | 0 | 0 |
| ИЗГОТОВЛЕНИЕ КЛЮЧЕЙ Опытные мастера центра бытовых услуг в присутствии клиентов, оперативно изготовят абсолютно любой ключ. Заказывая изготовление ключей в центре бытовых | 0 | 0 | 0 | 0 | 0 | 0 | 0 | 0 | 1 | 0 | 0 | 0 | 0 |
| После КС месяц назад очень болит спина, прямо отторает между лопатками и шея когда кормлю ребёнка. Ночью просыпаюсь от того, что больно и пытаюсь потянуть лопатки, прямо клинит спину. Более того, стали все косточки хрустеть на | 0 | 0 | 1 | 0 | 0 | 0 | 0 | 0 | 0 | 0 | 0 | 0 | 0 |
| Если вы имеете право на налоговый вычет и хотите получить деньги от государства, не верьте мифам о том, что это долго и | 0 | 0 | 0 | 0 | 0 | 0 | 0 | 1 | 0 | 0 | 0 | 0 | 0 |

**Fig. 3.** Example of data markup in Russian.

Preprocessing of marked-up data to improve the quality of learning, evaluation, and subsequent application of the classifier by normalizing texts and reducing the noise inherent in natural language and, in particular, texts from social networks. Preprocessing included the following basic text transformations:

— adding spaces after punctuation marks to improve the quality of text splitting by the language model into sentences and individual tokens;
— remove hashtags and emojis (emojis);
— remove special characters and numbers;
— removal of Russian-language stop words and tokens in foreign languages;
— removal of tokens related to parts of speech that usually do not carry a semantic load (it was assumed that only nouns, verbs, adjectives and adverbs, as well as proper names, carry a semantic load);
— bringing the remaining tokens to the initial form (lemmatization).

**Training the Model Classifier, Evaluating Its Quality, and Deciding on the Applicability of the Training Parameters for the Task**

At the first step of the task of training and evaluating the classifier, a preliminary assessment of the effectiveness of training the classifier on the prepared data was performed, and a number of experiments were conducted to select the values of the training parameters.

The prepared marked-up data was divided into a training sample of 4000 records and a test sample of 1000 records. The training was carried out according to the recommendations of the spaCy documentation [29] and the initial parameters of the model training were also set according to the recommendations of the documentation for the classification task [30]. The evaluation of the classification efficiency by the trained model was carried out both for individual urban functions and for the classification results as a whole according to machine learning metrics [31], Table 1. Experiments were conducted to determine the operating values of the following classifier training parameters:

- the size of the data packets involved in training the model at each of the iterations (batch size);
- exception percentage (dropout rate);
- the number of iterations of using data from the training sample.

For different laws of changing the size of data packets (batch size) on the same data samples, the following estimates of the classification efficiency were obtained, Table 1.

**Table 1.** Evaluation of the classification efficiency when changing the batch size parameter.

| Batch size | Precision | Recall | F1-score |
|---|---|---|---|
| Compounding (1.0, 64.0, 1.001) | 91.1 | 80.5 | 85.5 |
| **Compounding (1.0, 32.0, 1.001)** | 90.6 | 83.8 | 87.0 |
| Compounding (2.0, 32.0, 1.001) | 90.6 | 81.4 | 85.7 |
| Compounding (4.0, 32.0, 1.001) | 92.3 | 81.2 | 86.4 |
| Compounding (1.0, 16.0, 1.001) | 89.6 | 81.8 | 85.5 |
| Compounding (4.0, 8.0, 1.001) | 90.8 | 83.3 | 86.9 |

As a result, the batch size during training changed according to the compounding law (1.0, 32.0, 1.001).

Then a number of experiments were carried out with the laws of changing the dropout rate parameter, which is responsible for the percentage of random neurons excluded from the model at different iterations of training to reduce overfitting of the model [32] (Table 2).

**Table 2.** Evaluation of the classification efficiency when changing the dropout rate parameter.

| Dropout rate | Precision | Recall | F1-score |
|---|---|---|---|
| **Dropout = 0,2** | 93.7 | 87.9 | 90.7 |
| Dropout = decaying (0.6, 0.2, 1e−4) | 95.6 | 85.0 | 90.0 |
| Dropout = decaying (0.4, 0.2, 1e−4) | 92.4 | 96.8 | 89.5 |

As a result, the dropout rate was assumed to be constant and equal to 20%.

The last series of experiments was conducted with the number of iterations of using the training sample (Table 3).

**Table 3.** Number of iterations of using the training sample.

| Number of iterations | Precision | Recall | F1-score |
|---|---|---|---|
| **I = 10** | 93.7 | 87.9 | 90.7 |
| I = 20 | 92.3 | 86.9 | 89.6 |
| I = 5 | 91.2 | 86.7 | 88.9 |

As a result, the number of iterations was assumed to be 10.

After completing the first step of the task, it could be argued that the classifier is trained with sufficient efficiency on the prepared data.

At the second step of the task of training and evaluating the classifier, in order to eliminate the bias in evaluating the effectiveness of the classifier due to the peculiarities of the random division of data into training and test samples, the model was evaluated by the K-fold cross-validation method, where the value of k was assumed to be 5.

The initial data set was divided into 5 equal parts, then four parts were trained, and the fifth part was used to evaluate the classifier. The procedure was repeated 5 times, each time different parts were used as a test sample according to Table 4.

**Table 4.** Evaluation of the model by cross-validation.

| Experiment | precision | recall | F1-score |
|---|---|---|---|
| Testing on the first part of the data | 93.2 | 85.0 | 88.9 |
| Testing on the second part of the data | 94.8 | 86.3 | 90.3 |
| Testing on the third part of the data | 91.0 | 86.5 | 88.7 |
| Testing on the fourth part of the data | 92.5 | 86.4 | 89.4 |
| Testing on a fifth of the data | 93.3 | 87.3 | 90.2 |

The average value of F1-score: 89.5. As a result of the evaluation, a decision was made on the applicability of the prepared data and the model training parameters for the task.

At the end of the first stage of the method, the classifier was trained on all the prepared marked data using the previously accepted values of the training parameters. The resulting trained language model was saved for future use.

## 3.2   Stage of Text Classification on the Trained Language Model

The implementation of the second stage of the method performs the following tasks, Fig. 4.

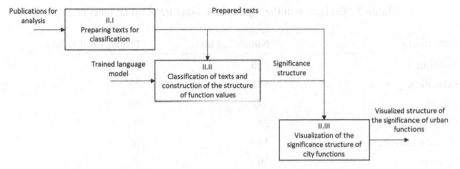

**Fig. 4.** Tasks of the second stage of the method.

## Preparing Texts for Classification

The method assumes that the classifier trained at the first stage will be applied to publications from thematic communities whose participants belong to the population group of interest. During the development process, the method was tested on the publications of the following thematic communities on VKontakte:

- "We live on Vasilyevsky Island" (vk.com/vasilyevskiyostrov)-the community of residents of Vasilievsky Island of St. Petersburg, presumably consists mainly of working citizens from middle to retirement age;
- "Kvadrat Youth Center, St. Petersburg" (vk.com/dm_kvadrat) - a community center for young people from 18 to 30 years of age;
- "Mothers of the Primorsky district" (vk.com/primmama)-the mater-rei community of the Primorsky District of St. Petersburg;
- "Okhta River Embankment Improvement Project Group" (vk.com/proekt_oxta) a group dedicated to the issues of participation of residents in the project of complex improvement of the territory.

3,000 entries were taken from each community.

The data was prepared in accordance with the procedure specified in Sect. 3.1.

**Classification and Construction of the Structure of the Significance of Urban Functions**

After preprocessing, the texts are classified and based on the results of the classification, the structure of the significance of urban functions is constructed. To do this, the number of texts assigned to each of the city functions is calculated, the most represented (most significant) function is determined, and then the proportional values for the other functions are calculated relative to this function. In tabular form, the resulting structure of the values can be presented in Table 5.

**Table 5.** Evaluation of the significance structure of urban functions.

| City function | Number of texts | Proportional values |
|---|---|---|
| Housing | 156 | 59 |
| Education | 141 | 53 |
| Health | 142 | 54 |
| Religion | 23 | 9 |
| Public transportation | 163 | 62 |
| Selfcare | 20 | 8 |
| Groceries | 19 | 7 |
| Finance | 46 | 17 |
| Domestic services | 132 | 50 |
| Pets | 139 | 53 |
| Sports | 53 | 20 |
| **Entertainment and culture** | **264** | **100** |
| Work | 25 | 9 |

Thus, for the three previously selected VKontakte communities for testing the method, the following structures of city function values were obtained and visualized, Fig. 5.

It can be noted that the qualitatively obtained structures of the values of the city functions correspond to the expectations:

– the structure of values for the participants of the community "We live on Vasilievsky Island" (Fig. 5-a) is quite balanced, with the predominance of the importance of the function "Entertainment and culture" and with quite high values of the functions "Housing", "Education", "Health", "Public transport", "Household services" and "Pets", which is quite typical for a diverse group of adult working citizens;

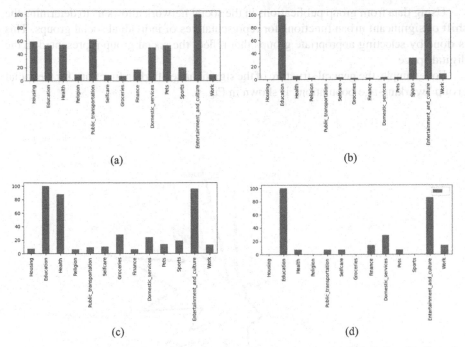

(a)                                    (b)

(c)                                    (d)

**Fig. 5.** Structure of the significance of urban functions for groups: (a) "We live on Vasilyevsky Island"; (a) "Square Center, St. Petersburg"; (c) "Mummies of the Primorsky District"; (d) "Group of the improvement project of the Okhta River embankment".

- in the structure of values for the participants of the community "Youth Center Square" (Fig. 5-b), the values of the functions "Education" and "Entertainment and Culture" are sharply dominated, and the function "Sports" also has some significance, which corresponds to the theme of the youth educational and entertainment club;
- in the structure of values for the participants of the community "Mothers of the Primordial district" (Fig. 5-c), the values of the functions "Education", "Health" and "Entertainment and culture" are sharply dominated, which is typical for the mother community;
- in addition, it can be noted that there is a certain predominance of the importance of the "Entertainment and Culture" function in general, which may be caused by the general entertainment orientation of social networks as a data source.

## 4   Applying Results in Value-Based Management

The application of the results of the assessment of the structure of the significance of urban functions in management is carried out by taking into account the actual values of citizens in the construction of city development programs. Thus, the structure of the significance of urban functions serves as an additional criterion for the focus of urban development policy.

Using data from group publications in the social network allows us to determine the shift of significant urban functions for representatives of individual social groups. This is done by selecting appropriate groups that reflect the social group represented in the digital space.

For example, the general structure of the significance of urban functions for the social group "working-age population" is shown in Fig. 6.

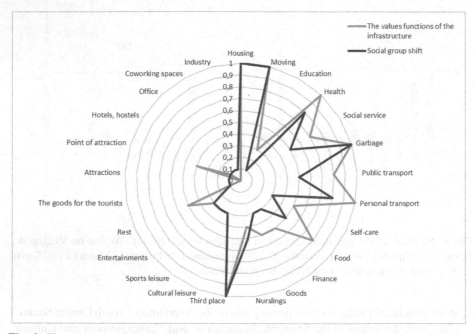

**Fig. 6.** The structure of the significance of urban functions for the social group "Working-age population" with the shift of the social group "Citizens with young children".

Figure 6 shows a comparison of the structure of the significance of urban functions for the basic social group " Working-age population "by taking into account the structure of the significance of urban functions in social network groups corresponding to the social group "Citizens with young children".

Taking into account this bias, which, due to the specifics of the data, is more operational than assessing the values of the base groups, allows us to increase the effectiveness of decisions made in the field of city management. And make city programs more focused on specific population groups.

## 5 Conclusion

The results obtained are generally satisfactory and allow us to conclude that the proposed method is sufficiently effective under the considered conditions of its use.

The advantage of the proposed method for assessing the structure of the significance of city functions based on monitoring user publications in sources that reflect the interests of representatives of individual population groups is efficiency. The use of this method will make it possible to quickly identify the actual needs of the most vulnerable groups of the population and better focus urban development programs.

The obvious disadvantage of the method is the uneven representation of social groups in social networks and in the digital environment in general. The lack of this accounting may lead to some discrimination against certain groups of the population. To avoid this, it is necessary to use this method as a tool for assessing the shift in the needs of citizens of individual social groups from the average value. At the same time, the average value of the significance of urban functions can be determined by traditional methods of monitoring public opinion and sociological research. The combination of the traditional and the proposed approaches can provide mutual compensation for the shortcomings of both.

**Acknowledgements.** This research is financially supported by The Russian Science Foundation, Agreement #20-11-20264.

# References

1. Alawadhi, S., et al.: Building understanding of smart city initiatives. In: Scholl, H.J., Janssen, M., Wimmer, M.A., Moe, C.E., Flak, L.S. (eds.) EGOV 2012. LNCS, vol. 7443, pp. 40–53. Springer, Heidelberg (2012). https://doi.org/10.1007/978-3-642-33489-4_4
2. Kummitha, R.K.R., Crutzen, N.: How do we understand smart cities? An evolutionary perspective? Cities **67**, 43–52 (2017)
3. Mora, L., Deakin, M., Reid, A.: Strategic principles for smart city development: a multiple case study analysis of European best practices. Technol. Forecast. Soc. Change **142**, 1–28 (2018)
4. Kumar, H., Singh, M.K., Gupta, M.P., Madaan, J.: Moving towards smart cities: solutions that lead to the smart city transformation framework. Technol. Forecast. Soc. Change **142**, 1–16 (2018)
5. Husen, S.M.S.: Economic growth and human capital. Int. J. Trend Sci. Res. Dev. **3**(4) (2019). 2456-6470
6. Boulding, K.E.: The economics of knowledge and the knowledge of economics. Jan. Am. Econ. Rev. **56**(2), 1–13 (2019)
7. Klamer, A.: The value-based approach to cultural economics. J. Cult. Econ. **40**(4), 365–373 (2016). https://doi.org/10.1007/s10824-016-9283-8
8. Nussbaum, M.C.: Creating Capabilities. The Human Development Approach. The Belknap Press of Harvard University Press, Cambridge (2011)
9. Baleijusa, S.M.: Sustainable development practice: the central role of the human needs language. Soc. Change **49**(2), 293–309 (2019)
10. Salloum, S.A., Shaalan, K., Al-Emran, M.A.: Survey of text mining in social media: Facebook and Twitter perspectives. Adv. Sci. Technol. Eng. Syst. J. **2**(1), 127–133 (2017)
11. Manning, C.D., Schütze, H.: Foundations of Statistical Natural Language Processing, p. 680. The MIT Press, Cambridge (2000)
12. Jurafsky, D., Martin, J.H.: Speech and Language Processing: An Introduction to Natural Language Processing, Computational Linguistics, and Speech Recognition. Pearson Prentice Hall (2009). 988 p.
13. Derczynski, L.: Complementarity: F-score, and NLP evaluation. In: Proceedings of the International Conference on Language Resources and Evaluation, pp.261–266 (2016)

14. Goldberg, Y.: Neural Network Methods in Natural Language Processing. Morgan & Claypool Publishers (2017). 310 p.

15. Zhang, X., Zhao, J., LeCun, Y.: Character-level convolutional networks for text classification. In: Cortes, C., Lawrence, N., Lee, D., Sugiyama, M., Garnett, R. (eds.) Advances in Neural Information Processing Systems, vol. 28. Curran Associates, Red Hook (2015)

16. Aggarwal, C.C.: Data Classification: Algorithms and Applications, Text Classification. Chapman & Hall (2014). 705 p.

17. Prasanna, P.L., Rao, D.R.: Text classification using artificial neural networks. Int. J. Eng. Technol. **7**(1.1), 603–606 (2018)

18. spaCy 1. (n.d.): About. spacy.io. Accessed 18 Jan 2021

19. spaCy 2. (n.d.): Language Processing Pipelines. spacy.io/usage/processing-pipelines. Accessed 18 Jan 2021

20. Stanford CoreNLP. (n.d.) Stanford CoreNLP – Natural language software. stanfordnlp.github.io/CoreNLP. Accessed 18Jan 2021

21. Cooper, G.: Named Entity Recognition for Twitter, Maxar Blog (2017). https://blog.maxar.com/earth-intelligence/2017/named-entity-recognition-for-twitter. Accessed 24 Jan 2021

22. Liu, X., Zhang, S., Wei, F., Zhou, M.: Recognizing named entities in tweets. In: Proceedings of the 49th Annual Meeting of the Association for Computational Linguistics, pp. 359–367 (2011)

23. How Instagram Started. https://medium.com/@obtaineudaimonia/how-instagram-started-8b907b98a767. Accessed 18 Jan 2021

24. Gillick, D., Brunk, C., Vinyals, O., Subramanya, A.: Multilingual language processing from bytes. arXiv:1512.00103 (2015)

25. Facebook. https://www.ferra.ru/news/techlife/facebook-2-billion-usersmonthly-27-06-2017.htm. Accessed 24 Jan 2021

26. VK Developers. https://vk.com/dev/manuals. Accessed 24 Jan 2021

27. Kuhn, M., Johnson, K.: Applied Predictive Modeling. Springer, New York (2013)

28. Russian language model for the spaCy library. github.com/buriy/spacy-ru. Accessed 24 Jan 2021

29. spaCy. Training spaCy's Statistical Models. spacy.io/usage/training. Accessed 24t Jan 2021

30. spaCy. Optimization tips and advice: URL: spacy.io/usage/training#tips. Accessed 24 Jan 2021

31. Witten, I.H., Frank, E.: Data Mining. Practical Machine Learning Tools and Techniques. 2nd edn. Elsevier (2005)

32. Srivastava, N., Hinton, G., Krizhevsky, A., Sutskever, I., Salakhutdinov, R.: Dropout: a simple way to prevent neural networks from overfitting. J. Mach. Learn. Res. **15**, 1929–1958 (2014)

# Identifying Troubles and Expectations of the Citizens Towards Their Habitat Based on PPGIS Approach

Anastasiia Galaktionova[1] and Aleksandra Nenko[1,2(✉)]

[1] ITMO University, Saint-Petersburg, Russia
`al.nenko@itmo.ru`
[2] Centre for German and European Studies, St. Petersburg State University,
Saint Petersburg, Russia

**Abstract.** Citizens' participation in evaluating the quality of the urban environment has recently gained momentum in urban planning practice. One of the promising approaches to address this task is the participatory mapping approach and one of the most established tools - public participation geoinformation systems (PPGIS). Based on the data coming from the study on the historic local area in St. Petersburg the paper shows the indicators to grasp citizens' subjective perception of the habitat, their troubles, and their expectations. The results session presents the mapping of the items of the habitat which have subjective value - everyday places and routes, favorite and disliked places, places to change and to preserve, spatial analysis of their distribution and its objective environmental characteristics, and correlation analysis of their colocation against each other. Besides the analysis of the typology of the citizens' expressed expectations towards the changes in their habitat is considered and interpreted. The conclusions section sums up the methodological advantages of exploring the subjective quality of the habitat with PPGIS as well as findings on the discovered items of the habitat. The discussion section reflects upon the constraints in using PPGIS toolkit for the studies on the habitat and outlines its further perspectives.

**Keywords:** PPGIS · Participatory mapping · Emotional mapping

## 1 Introduction

It has already become commonplace that during the urban projects' implementation city planners use different quality criteria of the built environment than those of the city dwellers and that to become friendlier to the users the latter has to be created based on the real experience of the citizens. Urban planners and researchers, Jane Jacobs and Kevin Lynch being among them, studied social behavior and environmental perceptions of the city dwellers and presented critical considerations about the professional urban planners' practice, which has not corresponded to the human needs but rather to the rules of the profession [1, 2]. From another side of the coin, urban planning practice was criticised by the social worker and consultant Sherry Arnstein, who presented a

© Springer Nature Switzerland AG 2022
D. A. Alexandrov et al. (Eds.): DTGS 2021, CCIS 1503, pp. 207–221, 2022.
https://doi.org/10.1007/978-3-030-93715-7_15

ladder of citizen participation, advocating real partnership between the citizens and professionals and officials to make decisions in urban development [3]. Participatory planning approach appeared as a solution to the problem of divergence between the disciplinary requirements of urban planning and the real-life expectations of the end-users [4]. Nevertheless, environmental psychologists argue that over 40 years the theory, that could connect the attitudes of people towards their habitat and the physical layout in planners' drawings and schemes, has not been developed [5].

In the paper, we showcase an approach of employing public participation geoinformational systems (PPGIS) to grasp the specific understanding of the habitat structure as well as values and needs of its dwellers during the process of taking urban planning decisions. The case is located in St.Petersburg, the second largest city of Russia, with a population of 5,5 million people [6]. The third part of the city was built in Soviet times in line with the existent planning approach of forming vast microdistricts with all needed social infrastructure inside of them. In 2020 the city authorities, namely the Committee for Urban Planning and Architecture (Committee), decided to launch an urban contest to seek solutions for improving such microdistricts, which have lost quality of their environment in time. This followed with an urban planning contest "Resource of the Periphery" in Spring 2020, which was enframed as an event within the Russian national project "Formation of a Comfortable Urban Environment" [7]. Since about 40% of the city has been developed along with this urban planning approach, the aims of the contest were to extrapolate the solutions received for the other districts, as well as to translate the experience received to other cities in the country.

The research presented here was part of the pre-project phase of the contest and was considered as a sociological survey, from one hand, and as a method for citizen online participation with PPGIS tool, from another. The COVID restrictions of that time shortened the possibilities for participatory modes to digital ones. The goals set for the survey by the Committee were to reveal the points of attraction in the microdistrict, to pinpoint the problematic spots and to collect the geolocated citizens' suggestions for the renovation of the territory. Simultaneously the authors of the paper decided to consider the PPGIS research as a way to conceptualize the structure of an urban habitat.

## 2   The Urban Planning Concepts in Habitat Studies

After the II World War of 1941–1945 the challenge to accommodate the growing number of people coming to the cities with housing demanded from city authorities and urban planners a radical change in designing, planning, and construction. According to the city master plan of 1966, the major part of new residential construction was intended outside the historic center. The growth of construction was achieved through the use of second-generation panel buildings of 9–12 floors. Today the area of the 1980–1990 panel buildings, second generation "Brezhnevkas", in St. Petersburg consists of almost 4000 sq. km.

The planned development of the city territory presupposed its' division into residential, recreational, and industrial zones. The residential territories planned as microdistricts were formed as mass housing blocks built from prefabricated elements [8]. The microdistricts were 'equipped' with schools and nurseries to deliver the basic services at a pedestrian accessibility rate and were not crossed by the ways of public transport. Such an organization of space produced a shift in the traditional view on the layout of the streets, housing and yards, typical for the city center. Soviet urban planners thrived for a clear functional structure. The primary microdistrict with 6–12 thousand inhabitants was considered as a basic unit. A group of microdistricts with a park, a clinic, and leisure amenities formed a planned area [8]. Contrary to that the city center was formed as a configuration of dense and sparse spaces and streets with a variety of environments, whereas microdistricts' development has led to a monotonous environment [9].

The detailed project of "Rzhevka-Porokhovye" planned area was developed in 1974 and approved in 1977. Over the past 40 years, the area has acquired the characteristics of a residential territory (Fig. 1). Today its population is estimated as 196233 residents including 25527 unregistered residents and 5007 temporarily registered residents. The housing is represented mainly by standard soviet projects of 600, 504, 137 series of houses. In total, within the design boundaries, there are 339 apartment buildings built in 1975–2006 [10]. There is no territorial resource for new housing construction.

However, the requirements for the quality of urban life have changed. Residents are in need of living zones as well as comfortable, attractive public spaces, so the local authorities face the challenge to achieve a new quality of the built-up environment. The contest held by the Committee together with the district administration was the first stage to receive conceptual planning ideas for future design changes. The contest ToR drew architects' attention to the problematic local spots - the underused historic cultural object (a summer house which belonged to the aristocratic family "Zhernovka"), uncomfortable banks of the local river Okhta, chaotic parking lots, and wastelands. Besides, the level of comfort and safety had to be improved for the pedestrian and cycling routes linking recreational areas and service facilities, e.g. clinics, shopping centers, and libraries. The sociological study was conducted by the authors to provide the contest participants with the information on the everyday usage of space as well as environmental needs of the residents.

## 3 PPGIS in Identifying Troubles and Expectations of the Residents

The design of the sociological survey was built to cover the actual structure of the habitat: places of everyday usage, places of positive and negative emotions, everyday routes, as well as the expressed public expectations towards change of the area. The survey was conducted in the framework of online participatory mapping with the public participation GIS "Mapsurvey"[1]. PPGIS was used to let the citizens of the project area map their subjective experience of the habitat with direct linkage to space. PPGIS methodology is based on the research of Marketta Kyttä, Gregory Brown, and Jiři Pánek [11, 12].

The term PPGIS came from the meeting of the National Center for Geographic Information and Analysis (NCGIA) in the United States in 1996. The term was used to describe how GIS technology empowers public participation in decision-making on the issues of urban development. Modern PPGISs perform a range of tasks - from involving the public into environmental research to active participation in environmental design.

---

[1] Mapsurvey is PPGIS developed by the authors, more information here: http://www.mapsurvey.ru/.

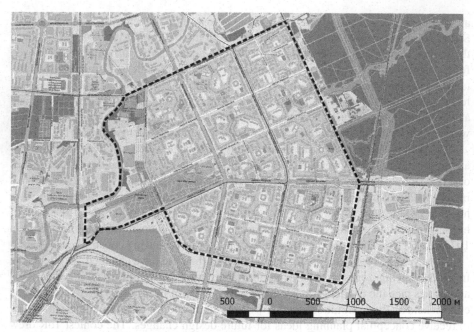

**Fig. 1.** The contest area of 6 sq. km at Rzhevka-Porokhoviye municipality, St. Petersburg

PPGIS' applicability in research consists of collecting data about the urban environment and social attitudes for making up socially grounded spatial analytics. The applicability in environmental design consists in providing residents with an opportunity to mark new demanded functions, environmental features and design elements on the map. Socially engaged PPGIS data can be used for legitimizing the specific design decisions, prioritizing certain functions over others, preserving the state of art in certain areas and taking action in regard to conflict zones [13]. Some PPGIS are created for specific research, for example, the project "Pocitové mapy" - a tool of Czech researchers for mapping the subjective perception of the environment, which allows to map various place markers, but does not pose sociological questions [14]. The sense of place attachment of the residents makes participatory mapping an effective tool in finding the topical and problematic places in the habitat [16, 17].

Despite the wide range of functional and technical possibilities accessible in modern PPGIS tools there are some user experience limitations that should be taken into account by researchers and designers during urban projects. These limitations include difficulties of conducting online mapping within those with low digital literacy (usually underaged and senior people), issue of low comprehensibility of the web interfaces, risk of underrepresentativity of certain social groups, who are not active in electronic participation [18]. Besides, PPGIS data may be politically manipulated if not presented in transparent and accurate format [18]. The eventual quality of participatory mapping with PPGIS depends upon the technical design of the tools and the political context in which it is conducted. Nevertheless, the method is actively developing thanks to its advantages. These are the following (but not limited to): the spatial accuracy of the social data received, the richness of data, the possibility for higher social representation (the digital mapping can be potentially accessed by anyone with the link to the survey).

The sociological mapping questionnaire for "Rzhevka-Porokhoviye" citizens consisted of three blocks: a) daily places and routes, including homeplace, b) emotionally charged places, and c) places of expressed social demand - to preserve or to change the place. The questionnaire was produced in Mapsurvey PPGIS and was disseminated through local online communities in "VKontakte" social network, local mass media, and press releases issued by the local authorities and the Committee. One of the specific social groups involved into the survey were the schoolchildren of 11–17 years old, who were recruited through the administration of the local schools.

The final dataset consists of the following data:

- 230 homeplaces and 523 daily places other than home visited on everyday life basis,
- 1088 emotional places, liked (669) and disliked (399) by citizens,
- 540 suggestions for places to change (301) and places to preserve (238) (Table 1).

All data were analyzed separately for two age groups: 11–17 (adolescents) and 18–70+ (adults), while the junior group makes up a substantial subsample and is different in its socio-spatial behavior.

**Table 1.** Accumulated data for two age groups

| Places | 11–17 age group Markers (markers per person) | 18–70+ age group Markers (markers per person) |
| --- | --- | --- |
| Homes | 101 (1) | 129 (1) |
| Daily | 170 (1.7) | 353 (2.7) |
| Positive | 242 (2.4) | 427 (3.3) |
| Negative | 77 (1.3) | 308 (2.4) |
| To change | 40 (0.4) | 261 (2.0) |
| To preserve | 67 (67) | 171 (1.3) |

The data were processed in a free cross-platform geographic information system QGIS2.16.3 and MS Excel. We have used three methods of data analysis. The first method of spatial analysis was run with the standard QGIS "Heatmap" tool, which reveals the localization of the most popular places where the largest number of different environmental features coincide. The second method was run as name-to-function transformation, based on the names of places provided by residents during mapping. The third method was typifying the environmental features provided by the respondents in the explanatory marks to the liked and disliked places, as well as in the suggestions for changing and preserving urban spots.

## 4   The Habitat's Functional and Emotional Characteristics

The heatmap of daily places shows that the most popular place for the age group of 18–70+ is the only shopping center in the area and the adjacent Malinovka Park. On average adults have marked 3.7 daily places, while adolescents - 2.7 of them, including homeplaces. The most popular places among adolescents are the school and the shopping center (Fig. 2).

The daily places' functions were identified for 309 out of 353 for adults and for 155 out of 170 for adolescents (Fig. 3). The distribution of places used daily shows that streets and recreation spaces, such as parks, are highly used by adults, whereas adolescents rarely use the parks and almost do not mention the streets, while education and leisure spots are more popular within them due to schooling and extracurricular activities.

The positive emotional map shows more matching for the two age groups: positive emotions are evoked in the recreation zones (parks, etc.). However negative places are different: adults despise a local low-cost and overcrowded supermarket, whereas adolescents do not like schools (Fig. 4).

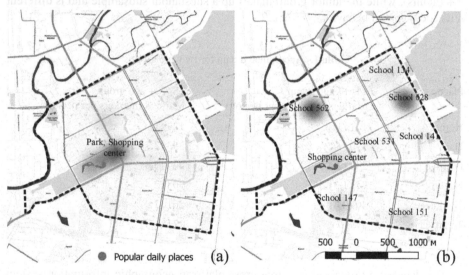

**Fig. 2.** Daily places heatmaps: (a) 18–70+ years old, (b) 11–17 years old

The functional distribution of the positive and negative places shows the leading positive role of the recreation places in the habitat (3 times more mentioned than the second most popular category - commercial places). At the same time there are differences in the negative emotional experience of public space within the different age groups. For adults many negative emotions are connected with the streets, yards, waterfront, and wastelands of their habitat, while for adolescents such places do not seem to "exist" in the structure of their everyday life (Fig. 5, Fig. 6).

Further the reasons for positive and negative emotions towards the habitat were analyzed given by the residents themselves during the mapping procedure. Adults have

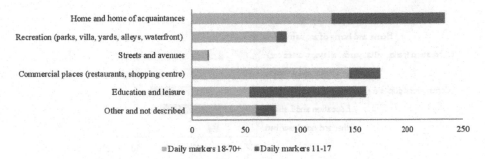

Fig. 3. Functional structure of daily places for two age groups

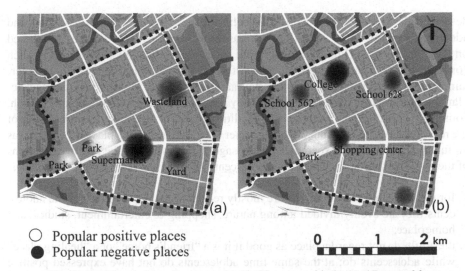

Fig. 4. Emotional places heatmaps: (a) 18–70+ years old, (b) 11–17 years old

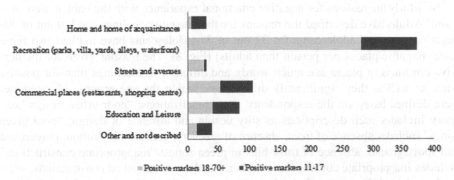

Fig. 5. Functional structure of positive places for two age groups

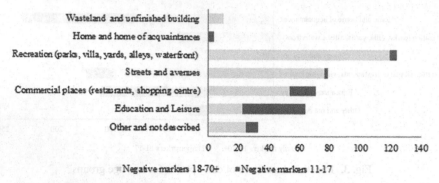

**Fig. 6.** Functional structure of negative places for two age groups

described the reasons for their positive feelings for 237 out of 427 positive spots and adolescents for 116 out of 242. All of the reasons were grouped into 12 categories based on the concepts used (Fig. 7); among those categories "urban greenery" includes such concepts as trees, a park, a riverbank, places for walking and resting in the nature; "entertainment" includes shops, a cinema, restaurants, food places; "education & extracurricular" includes school, nursery, library, hobby center; "other attractions" include church, completed constructions, waste sorting facilities, places of nice memories. A quarter of the reasons therefore is of functional character - the 'goodness' of a place is perceived as its function and positive experience of its usage. The reasons for the positive emotions of the place are similar for adults and adolescents, however there are certain differences:

– for the adults positive emotions are mostly related to nature, whereas for the adolescents they are evenly divided among nature, shopping & entertainment, studies, and homeplace;
– the adults do not regard a place as good if it is a "friend's home" or a "healing place" while adolescents do; at the same time adolescents do not have expressed positive feelings about a new tram, a historic villa, a completed construction, a church, or a waste sorting facility.

Similarly the reasons for negative emotional experience with the habitat were analyzed. Adults have described the reasons for their negative feelings for 210 out of 308 negative spots and adolescents for 32 out of 77 (adolescents have marked two times fewer negative places per person than adults) (Fig. 8). The reasons given for the negative emotions in places are much wordy and different in meanings than for positive ones, as well as they significantly differentiate within the age groups. 14 categories were defined based on the respondents' conceptualizations: "poor urban design" category includes such descriptions as silly design and absence of design; "poor green zones" includes absence of trees, absence of greenery, green zones without playground and sportsground, absence of trash bins in green zones; "inappropriate constructions" includes inappropriate church, supermarket, gated area, unfinished constructions, street market, alcohol shop, power lines; "poor maintenance" includes hogweed, bad drainage,

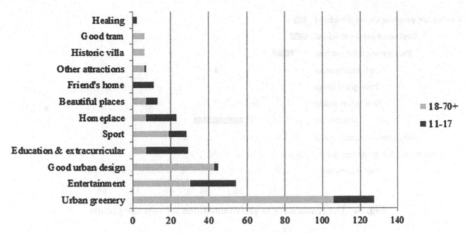

**Fig. 7.** The reasons for positive emotions for two age groups

wasteland, badly maintained buildings, badly maintained pathways; "poor road & trans-portation system" includes traffic jam, parked cars, insecure crossroads, absence of comfortable pathways and road crossings, longevity of traffic signals, absence of com-fortable transportation,; "unpleasant people" includes drunkers, migrants, bad people, hooligans, homeless people, drug addicts; "dull places" includes empty, scary, bad, ugly, unpleasant, sad, not interesting, not liked places and places with bad memories; "poor service infrastructure" includes absence of shops, no services aside of clinic and school; "unpleasant people at school" includes unpleasant teachers, unpleasant schoolmaster, unpleasant schoolmates, unpleasant studies; "unpleasant people in the neighborhood" includes a homeplace of a former friend, a homeplace of an unpleasant person.

- adults find more reasons for negative places in comparison with teenagers (13 categories against 8), with just five categories matching in both age groups;
- adults criticize the quality and maintenance of the built environment and the traffic, while adolescents focus more on the social capital of the place - their feeling of place and the relations with people;
- the reasons adolescents give for their negative emotions in 44% are based on the feelings of "not liking something", unpleasant memories, and fear.

The variety of meanings in the negative feelings of place goes in line with the previous research on the values of place which are more variable than the types of places used in daily life [12]. It is important to mention that the functional focus in the conceptualisations of the negative emotional experience within the adults could be evoked by the contest agenda.

## 5    Identifying Expectations of the Citizens Towards Their Habitat

Another research item in the structure of the study was the allocation of the places which the residents find opt for changing or for preserving in their habitat. The expectation that

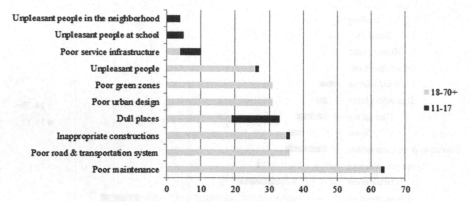

**Fig. 8.** The reasons for negative emotions for two age groups

something should be kept 'as is' reveals the values of place or of its environmental features. On the contrary if a place is mapped and conceptualized as one in need of change it has features that damage the image of the place and contradict the environmental values of the users. Describing such places and their features supports decision making for keeping things as they are on the contrary for investing effort into improving the quality of the environment. In the study participants have mapped these two kinds of places as well as have given specific suggestions for the improvement of those in need of change.

The heatmaps of suggestions for the two age groups are presented at Fig. 9 and again show their match in the positive environmental value - the park, which is considered as a place to be preserved. At the same time there is a variety among the age groups in the overview of the places to be changed. In particular, the adults' suggestions for changing are more spatially distributed and comprise a bigger area considered as habitat than those of the adolescents (Fig. 9).

The diagrams with the types of places to preserve and to change confirms the importance of the natural spots, in particular, the park, as a value to keep, and shows the topicality of the streets as environmental items to be changed (Fig. 10–11). Certain differences become evident across the two age groups in relation to service facilities: the adolescents more often suggest changing the shopping center than yards or waterfront, while the adults insist on improving streets, avenues, waterfront, yards, and parks.

Adults have given reasons for 80 out of 171 places to preserve and adolescents for 22 out of 67. There is quite small number of reasons for preserving places and they are almost identical for both age groups, in particular there is public consensus concerning preserving the park and natural spots (Fig. 12). The difference is that adults pay more attention to the place with symbolic capital as well as to the infrastructure, such as the historic villa and tram line, whereas adolescents value their homeplaces and schools.

As for the places to change, respondents provide many more reasons arguing the need for transformations. However it is more adults than adolescents who are inclined to make such suggestions. Adults gave reasons for 187 out of 261 places suggested for change and adolescents - for 15 out of 40 (five times fewer places per person than adults) (Fig. 13). Again the adults are paying more attention to the environmental changes, while

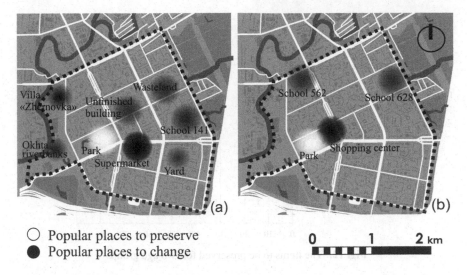

○  Popular places to preserve
●  Popular places to change

**Fig. 9.** Places of the suggestions heatmaps: (a) 18–70+ years old, (b) 11–17 years old

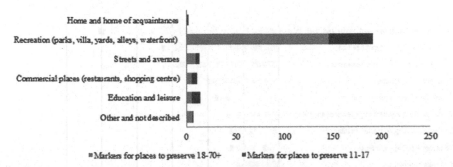

**Fig. 10.** The types of places to preserve for two age groups

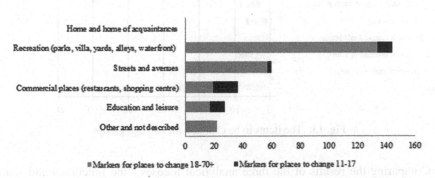

**Fig. 11.** The types of places to change for two age groups

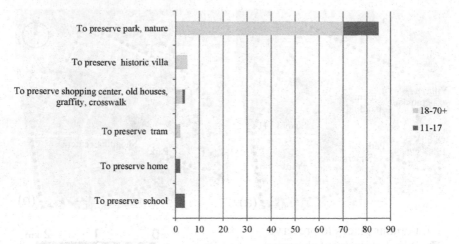

**Fig. 12.** The items to be preserved for two age groups

adolescents are not concerned with urban design, their focus of interest is renovation of the schools and shops.

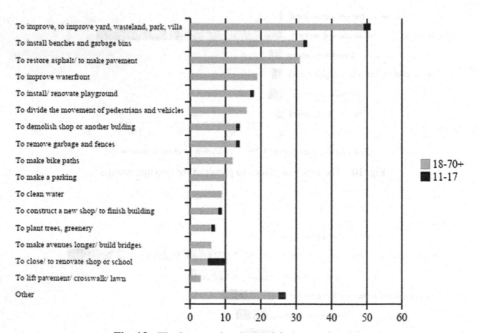

**Fig. 13.** The items to be changed for two age groups

Comparing the results of the three analytical focuses - the functional and spatial structure of the daily places, the emotional places and the places to preserve/to change -

the following conclusions can be made on the habitat's structure of the case under study (Fig. 14):

- Adolescents are marking significantly less daily, emotional and preservation-change places per person than adults.
- In daily and emotional places as well as in suggestions for change adults are paying more attention to the quality of the urban environment, while adolescents are more focused on personal experience of space usage.
- Adolescents are giving much less argumentation for the selection of places they map than adults.
- Streets and their quality are more important for adults than for adolescents.
- Recreational places play a larger role in emotional life than in daily life, especially for adolescents.
- Education and leisure places take a great part of the emotional and daily space, but there are no suggestions for changing them.
- Unfinished building and wasteland are significant in adults suggestions and negative emotions but are not seen in adolescents suggestions and negative emotions
- The functional types of the places for preservation are quite small in number in both age groups and the suggestions are almost identical.
- A greater functional variety of places is proposed for changing in both age groups, especially in adult one, and there are different suggestions for changing.

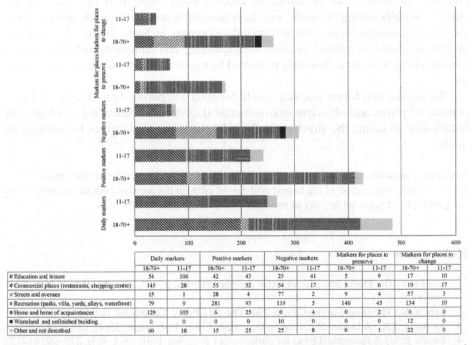

| | Daily markers | | Positive markers | | Negative markers | | Markers for places to preserve | | Markers for places to change | |
|---|---|---|---|---|---|---|---|---|---|---|
| | 18-70+ | 11-17 | 18-70+ | 11-17 | 18-70+ | 11-17 | 18-70+ | 11-17 | 18-70+ | 11-17 |
| ℛ Education and leisure | 54 | 106 | 42 | 43 | 23 | 41 | 5 | 9 | 17 | 10 |
| ℰ Commercial places (restaurants, shopping centre) | 145 | 28 | 55 | 52 | 54 | 17 | 5 | 6 | 19 | 17 |
| ℤ Streets and avenues | 15 | 1 | 28 | 4 | 77 | 2 | 9 | 4 | 57 | 3 |
| ⅊ Recreation (parks, villa, yards, alleys, waterfront) | 79 | 9 | 281 | 93 | 119 | 5 | 146 | 45 | 134 | 10 |
| ▪ Home and home of acquaintances | 129 | 105 | 6 | 25 | 0 | 4 | 0 | 2 | 0 | 0 |
| ▪ Wasteland and unfinished building | 0 | 0 | 0 | 0 | 10 | 0 | 0 | 0 | 12 | 0 |
| ▫ Other and not described | 60 | 18 | 15 | 25 | 25 | 8 | 6 | 1 | 22 | 0 |

**Fig. 14.** Functional character of the daily, emotional and places for preserving/changing mapped by the two age groups

# 6 Conclusions and Discussion

This study shows the analytical approach to study the structure of the habitat using self-reported subjective geolocated data. The research findings are applicable for the urban planning aims. Firstly, the findings show that the planning conception of the soviet urban planners, who placed schools, nurseries, and parks at the heart of the community, proved to be viable in nowadays condition: participatory mapping confirms the significance of parks as neighborhood centers for the age group of adults over 18 years old. This correlates with the claim of the previous studies that the natural settings are important spots of the adult everyday activity [15, 19]. At the same time the findings prove that the importance of natural places is not specific for adolescents as argued in other studies [20]. The findings also confirm the conception of the commercial amenities, such as shops and trade centers, as a necessary element of a community's habitat [21]. The structure of the habitat is age sensitive: while for the adults places with higher symbolic capital and functional usability constitute the everyday space, for the adolescents these are places of immediate personal experience - homeplaces, schools, places to socialize.

The approach illustrated in this paper allows urban planners to identify the structure of the habitat as daily, emotional places and places in need of preservation or change where social life flows, and then create design decisions to enhance everyday scenarios. Such an approach is turning the traditional urban planning process from the top-down perspective to the bottom-up based on real life social needs.

The study results of this study are related to the lifestyle of residents of a five million city and may differ from the results for cities of other sizes. Also, the results of the study, especially among the adults, may have been influenced by the study situation - the architectural contest focused on territorial development. In future studies the sampling procedure should be refined to allow distinguishing and comparing different groups among adults, who are in this study presented by a generalized population over 18 years old.

We suggest that future research should focus on comparing data on subjective perception of places and objective environmental data on their functional typology and localization to define the structure of the habitat and the possibilities for refining its quality.

**Acknowledgements.** This paper was supported by the Russian Science Foundation grant 21-77-10098 "Spatial segregation of the largest post-Soviet cities in the Russian Federation: analysis of the geography of personal activity of residents based on big data" 2021–2024.

# References

1. Jacobs, J.: The Death and Life of Great American Cities, p. 458. Random House, New York (1961)
2. Lynch, K.: The Image of the City, p. 194. The MIT Press, Cambridge (1960)
3. Arnstein, S.R.: A ladder of citizen participation. J. Am. Inst. Plann. **35**(4), 216–224 (1969)
4. Smith, R.W.: A theoretical basis for participatory planning. Policy Sci. **4**(3), 275–295 (1973)
5. Lewicka, M.: Place attachment: how far have we come in the last 40 years? J. Environ. Psychol. **31**(3), 207–230 (2011)

6. Russian Population: City of St Petersburg. Federal State Statistics Service of Russia. https://www.ceicdata.com/en/russia/population-by-region/population-nw-city-of-st-pet ersburg. Accessed 05 July 2021. (in Russian)
7. Russian National Project "Formation of the Comfortable Urban Environment". https://gorods reda.ru/. Accessed 05 July 2021. (in Russian)
8. Zhuravlyev, A., Fyodorov, M.: The microdistrict and new living conditions. Sov. Rev. **2**(4), 37–40 (1961)
9. Trubina, L.K., Tutkusheva, N.A.: Visual environment as a factor of ecological comfort of the population. Regul. Land Property Relat. Russia: Legal Geospat. Support Real Estate Apprais. Ecol. Techn. Solut. **1**, 243–247 (2019). (In Russian)
10. Conditions and program of the competition "Periphery's Resource". https://kgainfo.spb.ru/ wp-content/uploads/2020/11/условия-и-программа-конкурса.pdf. (in Russian)
11. Brown, G., Kyttä, M.: Key issues and research priorities for public participation GIS (PPGIS): a synthesis based on empirical research. Appl. Geogr. **46**, 122–136 (2014)
12. Brown, G., Kyttä, M.: Key issues and priorities in participatory mapping: toward integration or increased specialization? Appl. Geogr. **95**, 1–8 (2018)
13. Kahila-Tani, M., Kytta, M., Geertman, S.: Does mapping improve public participation? Exploring the pros and cons of using public participation GIS in urban planning practices. Landsc. Urban Plan. **186**, 45–55 (2019)
14. Pánek, J.: Emotional maps: participatory crowdsourcing of citizens perceptions of their urban environment. Cartogr. Perspect. **91**, 17–29 (2018)
15. Newell, P.B.: A cross-cultural examination of favorite places. Environ. Behav. **29**(4), 495–514 (1997)
16. Manzo, L.C., Perkins, D.D.: Finding common ground: the importance of place attachment to community participation and planning. J. Plan. Lit. **20**(4), 335–350 (2006)
17. Cilliers, E.J., Timmermans, W.: The importance of creative participatory planning in the public place-making process. Environ. Plann. B. Plann. Des. **41**(3), 413–429 (2014)
18. Brown, G.: Public Participation GIS (PPGIS) for regional and environmental planning: reflections on a decade of empirical research. URISA J. **25**(2), 5–16 (2012)
19. Korpela, K.M., et al.: Restorative experience and self-regulation in favorite places. Environ. Behav. **33**(4), 572–589 (2001)
20. Korpela, K., Kyttä, M., Hartig, T.: Restorative experience, self-regulation, and children's place preferences. J. Environ. Psychol. **22**(4), 387–398 (2002)
21. Brower, S.: Neighbors and Neighborhoods: Elements of Successful Community Design. Routledge, Abingdon (2020)

# Smart Technologies and Their Role in the Modernization of Non-motorized Urban Transport in Russia

Lasse Schneider and Irina A. Shmeleva(⊠) (iD)

ITMO University, St. Petersburg, Russia
{lschneider,i_a_shmeleva}@itmo.ru

**Abstract.** The urban population growth and the negative impacts of the current car focused transport systems imply significant challenges with respect to environmental and social sustainability for governments and planners in cities. At the same time sustainable transport systems in combination with smart technologies could help in solving these challenges. This article is focused on the usage of these smart technologies in sustainable transport modes, such as bike sharing systems and smartphone applications. We discuss the main benefits and disadvantages of non-motorized individual transport i.e., cycling and walking, smart solutions used in cycling and walking and the results of a pilot survey among cyclists in St. Petersburg, Russia. The aim of this article is to present a short overview of existing smart solutions used by cyclist and pedestrians and carry out a short pilot survey about the usage and barriers of these smart solutions. It was found, that not all smart technologies are equally well used.

**Keywords:** Bike-sharing systems · Urban transport systems · Sustainable transport development

## 1 Introduction

Looking on today's situation, many negative impacts of the current car focused transport systems, such as congestion, air- and noise-pollution and obviously as a result the climate change can be noticed [18].

At the same time the development of sustainable transport systems - as was indicated 20 years ago - do not contradict environmental and quality-of-life objectives, rely on non-renewable resources [25], and follow the idea that cities need to adopt sustainable concepts for urban planning and development [5].

These problems will not get smaller in the next years as the United Nations estimated that by 2050 around 68% of the world's population will live in cities [41] and this population growth in cities implies significant challenges with respect to environmental and social sustainability [29]. The concept of sustainable mobility gained rapidly momentum and attention around the world in recent years, as the most and maybe only promising response to the challenges of urban mobility.

D. A. Alexandrov et al. (Eds.): DTGS 2021, CCIS 1503, pp. 222–236, 2022.
https://doi.org/10.1007/978-3-030-93715-7_16

At the same time, we can see a growing number of smart technology solutions, offered in cities around the world. These smart solutions include sharing systems, mapping apps for navigation within the city and applications or "wearables" that monitor and record the activity of the user.

Sustainable modes of transport like cycling and walking have quite some benefits. Both modes do not release any fine particles or polluting gas in contrast to cars and a lesser extend also public transit [26]. Moreover, biking and walking is quite space efficient. One bicycle only requires 10% of the parking space that is needed for an average car [32]. Moreover, cycling and walking are also quite flexible means of transportation because they can be used for individual mobility without any schedule, as most persons have bikes of their own or at least the possibility to rent one while for walking no equipment is needed.

These advantages can be complemented by using the above-mentioned smart technologies. Obviously, a lot of these functions are not new. Printed maps have existed for several centuries, and the first pedometers were developed in the eighteenth century [6]. However, smart technologies make it much easier to use these functions, since everything is combined into one device.

Our aim in this paper is to answer the questions: *How is smart technology used in cycling and walking and what are the main benefits and challenges related to these technologies?*

To answer these questions a questionnaire among cyclists in St. Petersburg, Russia about the usage of cycling apps in this specific community was carried out and the results analysed[1]. The survey includes general questions about the use of the bicycle and specific questions related to the use of cycling apps.

This paper consists of an introduction, literature review, presentation of the research results, discussion, and conclusion. Subsequent paragraphs, however, are indented.

## 2 Literature Review

The enormous concentration of people in small areas leads to huge transportation problems in many cities around the globe: a worsening of the accessibility of city centers due to recurring traffic congestion. Furthermore, the traffic congestion is also negatively impacting the environment and living quality in cities [9]. The EU sees air pollution as the 'biggest environmental risk to public health in Europe and estimates that urban mobility accounts for 40% of all $CO_2$ emissions of road transport and up to 70% of other pollutants from transport" within the EU [15]. Research reveals significant correlation between share of trips made by walking, cycling and public transport and CO2 emissions per capita in different European cities [38].

Moreover, these transport problems in urban areas also lead to economic losses [1, 2]. Christidis. P, Rivas. J, [10] found the reason for congestion in many cities not to lie in the existing capacity of the road infrastructure but instead by a wrong management of demand. So simply building more road infrastructure will not solve the problem of congestion.

The reason for the important role of cycling and walking in sustainable transport systems is, that both modes have a lot of benefits. First since both cycling and walking

---

[1] This questionnaire will act as a pilot survey for research in other European cities.

are physically activities, they can lead to health benefits for the individual user [4]. One may argue that cycling and walking in a huge city with a lot of car traffic could have a negative effect on the health of cyclists and pedestrians due to exposure to air pollution and the risk of accidents. However, a study analysing several bike sharing systems in Europe, taking both health benefits due to increased physical activity and the above-mentioned health risks into account found that overall, the health benefits of cycling outweigh the risks [30].

Another benefit of cycling and walking is the saving of time since bicycle users and pedestrians do not have to deal with congestion [34]. Moreover, in contrast to motorized transport both cycling and walking do not emit any fine particles and polluting gasses [26]. In addition, non-motorized private transport is also much more space efficient than other modes of transport. One parking space can on average accommodate up to 10 bicycles [32]. Moreover, since both cycling and walking can be used without any fixed schedule, they are quite flexible means of transportation.

Next to function as a stand-alone transport mode it can obviously also be combined with other modes of transport. By this non-motorized private transport can provide a solution to the well-known first/last mile problem of public transit.

At the same time a growing number of smart mobility solutions, like bike sharing and smartphone applications appeared worldwide.

Bike – Sharing systems (BSS) saw a rapid expansion worldwide in recent years. There are many reasons for this growth. First BSS can help to establish cycling as an effective solution for the first/last mile problem of public transit by lowering the barrier for using the bike, since there is no need to directly buy a private bike when wanting to start to cycle. Instead, one can buy a much cheaper subscription to a BSS and after some time decide if buying a private bike makes sense.

Moreover, the user of a BSS is not responsible for the maintenance of the bike and need to have less fear about the possibility of the bike getting stolen [31]. Obviously, the user still has a problem if his BSS bike is stolen, since he is unable to bring it back to a station to end the trip in the computer system. However, because of the special design of the bikes they are less likely to get stolen than regular bikes.

Next to this the implementation of a BSS can have positive impacts on all cyclists in a city by increasing the realization of cyclists by other road users [21]. This increased realization can then lead to a greater likelihood of cycling overall and by this a higher level of physical activity of the citizens [19, 35], which will then lead to the above - mentioned health benefits of cycling.

The Brundtland report [42] stresses the quality of life as an important point. By initiating a modal shift from car to bike and cycling more general could be a powerful tool in creating a city that is liveable and effective for the inhabitants [23, 43]. However, now there is no consisted empirical evidence that would suggest that BSS lead to a significant modal shift from individual car to bike. Some cities report a growth in the modal share of bikes after the introduction of a bike sharing system [36]. A study of Melbourne, Washington, D.C., Minnesota/St. Paul, and London even found a reduction in the number of kilometres travelled due to the bike-sharing system in three of the cities [17]. However, the same study also found huge differences in the size of the shifts between the cities. While at the same time finding a strong negative correlation to the size of the area covered by the BSS [17]. This negative correlation can be explained by the fact that in a BSS covering a huge area the redistribution vehicle also needs to cover larger distances. Due to this the number of kilometres travelled by car and with it also the $CO_2$ emissions will increase, reducing the modal shift effect of the BSS.

Moreover, most studies found that modal shift caused by a bike-sharing system is predominantly not from car to bike but mostly from walking, cycling by private bike and public transport [3]. However, these modal shifts could theoretically still lead to a reduction in car usage since BSS can form a solution for the first/last mile problem of public transit. However, there is no empirical evidence for this claim.

If BSS do not lead to a significant modal shift from private car to bicycle this also means that BSS cannot significantly reduce traffic congestion [36].

Smart mobility solutions – as bike – sharing – but also smartphone applications can make using non-motorized private transport more attractive and by this multiply the above-mentioned benefits.

## 3  Smart Cycling Solutions

The most obvious smart solution connected to cycling are cycling apps, that are available for nearly all smartphones. There are different types of cycling apps.

The first type are route recording apps [24]. These smartphone applications record statistics about the ride like average speed, slope of the road, calories burned, and distance travelled by using GPS. Most of this apps offer the possibility to compare the collected data over time either in the app itself or by uploading the data to a website. In addition to these features some apps support ANT+ or Bluetooth LE sensors that can track data like the cyclist's pulse or the pedal speed.

Another related type of apps are fitness apps. These apps not only collect the data but also analyze it, which help the cyclist to see where he has improved. Moreover, most fitness apps are not limited to cycling but instead record and analyze also jogging or a workout at the gym. This enables the cyclist to have all his training statistics within one app.

A third type of cycling smartphone applications are journey planning apps. First also regular navigation apps like Google Maps or Yandex maps offer the possibility to plan a bicycle trip. However, the routes suggested by these apps are often not the safest or most convenient way for a cyclist. For this reason, there are specific cycle journey planners which are a kind of satellite navigation system for cyclists. The user enters his destination, and the application shows him a route based on his preferences (e.g., quickest, simplest, pleasantest, or safest route) [24]. A related type of apps are applications that suggest cyclists with pleasant cycling tours. Most of these journey and tour planners can also be used by pedestrians to find a save and pleasant walking route.

While most route recording, fitness and journey planning apps offer the possibility to indicate which type of bike is used there are also special applications for mountain bike and off-road riders that range from applications that offer route mapping and training features to apps that include a database about mountain bike/off-road trails.

A fourth type of cycling smartphone applications are apps, that supply practical help. These apps cover a very broad range from apps that help cyclist with optimizing the gear ratios on their bicycle to apps that provide instructions for bicycle repair. Moreover, there are smartphone applications that help cyclists to find the ideal bike for them and apps that can help cyclists in case an injury or emergency occurs.

A final type of cycling apps are the smartphone applications of bike-sharing systems. However, these systems itself are at the same time a smart cycling solution.

Further developments in smart technologies could help to make shifting to a BSS or cycling more general more attractive and by this make a real contribution to solving urban mobility problems.

The development of BSS took place in five main generations over the last 50 years. However, the incorporation of smart technologies in the form of smartcards and the use of GPS [12] took only place in the third generation to reduce theft, which was a common problem with the first two generations since the customers were anonym [28]. Many third-generation bike-sharing system use web sites or smartphone applications in addition of the technologies mentioned above to provide users with real time information about the availability of bikes and free racks at docking stations. During the last ten years a trend to incorporate additional technologies to the systems can be observed, which led to the emergence of a fourth generation of BSS [28, 35, 36]. While these fourth-generation systems include all the technological characteristics of the third-generation systems like an electronical kiosk for check-in and checkout of the bikes and smartcards they are in addition integrated with public transport [36]. Moreover, they are part of an integrated traffic management system [7]. Another trend connected with smart technology that already started with the third generation BSS but developed into a fifth generation are BSS with no docking stations at all and the possibility to manage huge amounts of data [7].

These so-called floating bike-share system use a smartphone application for the check-in and checkout of the bikes instead of fixed kiosks. These apps are also used to locate a bike and sometimes even reserve the bike for a short period of time. After the trip the bikes can be left and locked everywhere, and the system automatically recognize where the bike is located by using GPS. This is a huge advantage compared with station-based BSS since by this the bikes are available everywhere in the operation area without the need for any physical infrastructure. This makes it obviously cheaper to operate and more convenient for the user since he does not have to search for a station at the end of the trip [7]. However, for bikes not parked at inconvenient locations like in front of the entrances to metro stations many cities introduced restrictions about where floating bikes can be parked. Some operators included a concept called "Geofencing" in their apps that shows users designated parking areas in a map within the app so that they can leave their bike in an appropriate location [14].

While BSS smartphone applications can obviously not be used when walking outside, most types of the applications mentioned above can also be useful for pedestrians. Pedometer or step counter smartphone applications for pedestrians offer the same functions as the above-mentioned route recording apps. However, some of these functions are mostly interesting for jogging or running on a semi-professional or profession level and not for leisure walkers. Moreover, in contrast to cycling route recording apps newer smartphone and smartwatches have already a step counter integrated ex-factory.

While regular navigation applications like Google Maps or Yandex maps also offer the possibility to plan a walking trip there are no specific navigation applications for pedestrians beside from some local projects like ALIGN ATL for Atlanta, US. Nevertheless, there exist online tools that offer the opportunity to map and measure a walking route and print it out. However, these online services normally do not offer the possibility to choose between the quickest, simplest, pleasantest, or safest route.

## 4 Smart Cycling Solutions Survey

For the smart solutions to influence urban transport it is obviously necessary that cyclists and pedestrians are using the above-mentioned smartphone applications. To research this aspect an online questionnaire among cyclists in St. Petersburg, Russia about the usage of cycling/walking apps is carried out. The questionnaire includes general questions about the use of the bicycle, like "How often do you cycle?" and specific questions related to the use of cycling apps, like "Do you use smartphone applications to plan your trip by bike?". In addition to these two categories of questions, the survey also includes questions about the demographic background of the respondents. The survey was spread by email to members of the cycling movement in St. Petersburg and posted in VK-Groups related to cycling in St. Petersburg. Using these methods, 40 respondents were reached.

### 4.1 Study Area

The city of St. Petersburg, Russia consists of 18 districts covering an area of 1,431 km$^2$ including the suburbs. The city has 5,2 million citizens, which makes St. Petersburg the second biggest city of Russia and the fourth biggest city of Europe [13].

In recent years – driven by a huge cycling community - the city officials started to include cycling in the mobility agenda and a plan to significantly expand the amount of cycling paths from around thirty kilometres in 2000 to 255 kms in 2021 was devised (see Fig. 1). However, in recent years the development of new cycling infrastructure slowed down and only a fraction of the infrastructure planned for 2020/2021 was constructed [22] due to municipal budget cuts [44].

Currently the cycling infrastructure is far from forming a connected network, which in combination with the lack of proper bike parking at public transport stops forms a barrier for both short cycling trips (e.g., to the metro station) and longer trips. Moreover, since a lot of the existing cycling infrastructure are cycling paths marked on the ground without any barrier between the cycling path and the road cyclists possibly do not feel save when cycling on the existing infrastructure.

Currently the city is developing a new concept for the further development of cycling infrastructure under which 300 km of new cycling paths should be constructed by 2030 [22]. By this, an interlinked cycling network would be developed, which could solve the above-mentioned problems with the current infrastructure.

The first bike sharing system in St. Petersburg was opened in 2014 [37] due to the success of a similar system opened in Moscow. While the system was quite successful at the beginning it deteriorated in the following years [39] and eventually closed in 2020

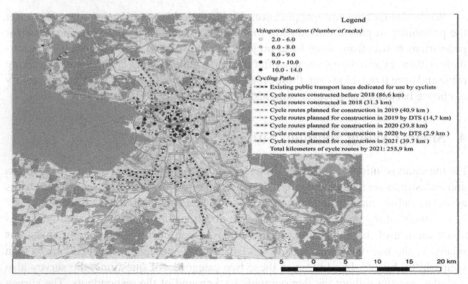

**Fig. 1.** Map of St. Petersburg including the cycling paths and stations of the closed Velogorod system. Source: created by authors of the present paper based on the data collected

due to missing subsidies from the city. However, in the same year a new floating bike sharing system opened in St. Petersburg [44].

At the same time electric scooter sharing services opened in St. Petersburg and by now several different operators are active in the city [27].

## 4.2 Statistics of Survey Participants

Since the survey was distributed to members of the cycling community in St. Petersburg all but 5 respondent lives in St. Petersburg. The survey respondents are in the age group between 20 and 40 years. With respect to the highest completed education all but 3 survey respondents have at least a university degree. Most of the survey participants (26) are employees followed by and students (7), self-employed persons (3), unemployed person (2) and people who cannot work (2). Finally, much more women (26) than men (14) responded to the survey (Fig. 2).

## 4.3 Results

### 4.3.1 Overall Cycling Behavior in St. Petersburg

Of the respondents all but 8 use the bike for trips within the city. This indicates that most respondents use the bike not only for relaxation but also for necessary trips within the city. This is confirmed when looking at the reasons for cycling. A lot of people cycle when meeting with friends and family (14) or use the bike to commute to work or school/university (14). Nevertheless, most cyclists also use to cycle as a hobby (26) or to do sports (11). Since it is much easier to simply walk around in an unknown city than

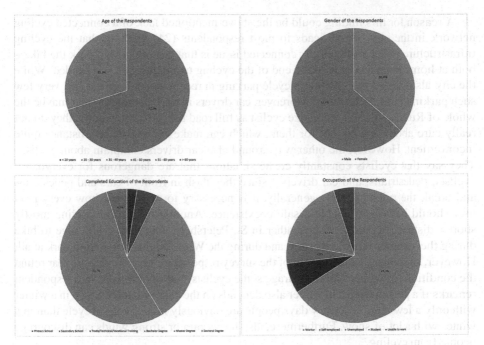

**Fig. 2.** Demographic data of the participants. Source: created by authors of the present paper based on the data collected

renting a bike only a minority (13) cycle when being abroad as a tourist. This finding likely also applies to tourists coming to St. Petersburg.

When looking at the cycling behaviour of the respondents only a minority cycle daily (8). With the biggest single groups (11) cycling several times per week. However, there is also a big share of respondents that cycles only a few times per month or less (18), or do not cycle at all (3). Nevertheless, according to the deputy chairman of the cities transport committee the number of cyclists increased during 2020. However, around half of these new cyclists were bicycle couriers [22] and it needs to be seen if this increase is permanent or only temporary due to the current global pandemic. These mixed findings can be explained by the fact that cycling obviously offers a lot of benefits but that there are also certain barriers for cycling in St. Petersburg. First since St. Petersburg and its surroundings are very flat and due to the typical European development system of the city cycling can be a very convenient transport mode in St. Petersburg [39] in addition to the above-mentioned positive health effects. Furthermore, since it can be quite cold at times in St. Petersburg the physical activity of riding a bike can obviously also warm up the body. Moreover, cycling is obviously a more environmentally friendly way of transport compared to the huge numbers of cars in cities. This huge number of cars to leads congestion [40], which makes cycling often much faster than the car for short distances. The results of the survey seem to confirm that people mostly cycle shorter distances. Most of the respondents cycle one to two hours (14) or less (11). With only a minority cycling more than two hours (12).

A reason for this finding could be the above-mentioned lack of a connected cycling network in the city, which leads to most respondents (24) thinking that the cycling infrastructure is not sufficient. A connected issue is that a safe place to park the bike – both at home but especially at the end of the cycling trip in the city – is needed. While the city also started to construct bicycle parking in recent years there are still very few such parking in St. Petersburg. Moreover, car drivers in St. Petersburg – and maybe the whole of Russia – do not recognize cyclist as full road users. Consequently, they do not really care about or look out for them, which can make cycling longer distance quite inconvenient. However, the other way around also car drivers complain about cyclists. They say that cyclists constantly create situations that are dangerous for everyone – cyclists, pedestrians, and car drivers – since they flash in front of cars and pedestrians and break the rules [20]. So generally, it is necessary to make clear how every road user should behave to enable a safe coexistence. Another reason for cycling mostly shorter distances could be the weather in St. Petersburg. Obviously, it is nice to bike during the summer when it is warm and during the White Nights not getting dark at all. However, as shown by the fact that of the survey respondents only 9 cycle all year round the conditions in winter can discourage some cyclists. Nevertheless, as one respondent remarks if a person cycles in winter also depends on the exact weather. Since in a winter with only a few ice – and snow days people are obviously more likely to cycle than in a winter with a lot of snow. Furthermore, also heavy rain or strong winds can discourage people from cycling.

Finally, St. Petersburg is quite big covering 1439 km², which makes some journeys within the city simply too far, to be done by bike. Moreover, as can be seen in Fig. 1, the new cycling infrastructure is predominantly developed in the city centre. Since there most people can benefit from it but that also means that there is very few cycling infrastructure when commuting from the suburbs. Due to this, people living further away from the centre of the city, are often using the suburban train or metro to commute to work or university. While it would obviously be possible to use the bike as a first/last mile solution for the way from/to the suburban railway or metro station [33] only 12 survey respondents combine cycling with using public transport while the other respondents never combine cycling and public transit. This contrasts with the findings of the transport committee that due to the various bicycle and scooter sharing services it became very popular to use these services in combination with public transport for the first/last mile [22].

This finding could be explained by the fact that most of the respondents (27) use only their private bike. Combining the use of a private bike with public transit is connected with some difficulties. First since the subway is part of the strategic infrastructure of the city, it is prohibited to place external infrastructure or objects on the territory of the metro station. This makes parking a bike at the metro station complicated since it is first officially not allowed and second there are often no bicycle racks. While taking the bike with you is allowed in most kinds of public transit in St. Petersburg it is connected with some effort getting the bike in and out of the transport vehicle.

### 4.3.2 Overall Walking Behavior in St. Petersburg

When looking on walking trips within the city it can be seen that the majority of respondents (36) walk at least on some days per week. Like with cycling most of the respondents walk one to two hours (17) or less (20). A reason for these regular but short walks could be that walking mostly serves as a conveyor to other modes of transport. This also seems to be confirmed by the finding that the majority of respondents (27) combine walking with using the public transport. Again, like cycling the quality of the infrastructure, distance or the weather likely influences the probability of walking. However, all but 3 respondent indicates that in their city pedestrian streets exist, which could have an encouraging effect on the probability of walking.

### 4.3.3 Attitude Towards Smart Technologies

Smart technologies could of course offer a solution for some of the above-mentioned problems. Bike Sharing could offer a solution for the problems related with combining public transit and the private bike since with shared bikes there is both no need for a safe place to park the bike and to take the bike on the transport vehicle. However, only 10 respondents use the local BSS system in their city. The main reason why most people own and use a private bike is likely that a private bike is always available, while with a bike sharing system there obviously needs to be a free bike available at a nearby station or on the street. Moreover, a private bike can obviously also be adapted to the needs of the cyclists which makes it comfortable even for longer rides or intensive sports.

Also, smartphone applications could help in solving some of the above - mentioned problems. For example, smartphone applications can help in finding a convenient route to cycle or help when pursuing cycling as a sport. Among the survey respondents slightly more than half use smartphone applications to plan their walking (24) or cycling trip (21) (Fig. 3).

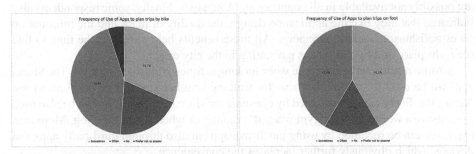

**Fig. 3.** Frequency of Use of Apps for the Planning of trips by bike and on foot. Source: created by authors of the present paper based on the data collected

With respect to the specific type of smartphone applications used, the most popular apps are navigation apps. A majority of the survey respondents indicated that they use Google Maps (24) and Yandex Maps (20) with another 9 respectively 12 knowing the apps but not using them. The second – albeit less popular type of smartphone applications used by the survey respondents are the smartphone applications of sharing systems. Of the survey respondents a minority indicated that they use or least know Smart Bike (12) (bike sharing), Molnia (13) and Whoosh! (14) (electric scooter sharing). These findings can likely be explained by the fact that these two types of smartphone applications are the most useful when cycling or walking within the city while other kinds of smartphone applications are more useful when doing long bike – or hiking tours outside of the city. This is also supported by the finding that Strava is the only fitness/ride tracking app that is popular among the respondents with 16 respondents indicating that they know or use it. The lower number of respondents using the applications of sharing systems could be possibly explained by the fact that Smart Bike and Molnia are sharing services only available in St. Petersburg. So that people from outside of the city are less likely to know or use it.

### 4.3.4 Experience in Using Smart Technologies

Another finding related to the use of the smartphone applications is that the respondents mostly use apps that are not specific for cycling. The bicycle navigation apps (e.g., Bikemap) are only used by individual users. While the most popular navigation apps – Google Maps and Yandex Maps – can be used not only for cycling but also trips by car, public transport, and taxi. An explanation for this finding is the convenience of having one app to plan all trips. Several respondents indicate that they use applications like Yandex Maps because it is convenient that it can be used for navigations with different modes of transport and even routes combining different modes of transport. This obviously also offers the possibility to compare different modes of transport with respect to the time it takes to reach the destination. This convenience is likely also the reason for the fact that none of the respondents used foreign navigation applications like TfL. Since also in this case general navigation apps like Google Maps can be used for planning a trip. Another reason for this finding could be a language barrier. While general apps like Google Maps or Yandex maps are available in a lot of language including Russian, local applications are possibly not available in all countries and languages. Finally, some respondents also indicated that they like the application design, the quality of maps and the information on establishments including reviews. All these benefits help to reduce the time to find the right place and by this makes navigating in the city easier.

Similar results can be observed when looking at fitness/ride tracking apps. The Strava app can be used for cycling but also for walking or other kinds of physical activities. Again, this likely can be explained by convenience since by this the app can be also used to measure a workout in the gym when it's raining or when going for a jog. Moreover, exercises can be recorded by using the Strava app but also through third-party apps and devices, which obviously further increases the convenience.

However, a disadvantage mentioned by 2 of the respondents is that in general navigation applications there is only little information about bike parking and bike infrastructure. Another disadvantage mentioned that holds for all types of apps is that sometimes the apps are slow or do not work properly. Moreover, since some of the apps are free there is advertising in the app that can disturb the user. Another problem can occur if the app loses the connection to the GPS signal and due to this cannot determine the location of the user. Furthermore, it can happen that the app does not work on older smartphones.

A related problem is that to use a certain app a compatible phone or more precisely operating system is needed.

## 5 Conclusion

Based on the findings described in this paper, it can be seen that in an urban community like St. Petersburg not all kinds of smartphone applications are equally successful. Only navigation apps and the smartphone applications of sharing systems and to a much lesser extend fitness or ride tracking apps seem to play a role for cycling within St. Petersburg. Moreover, applications that are not limited to one mode of transport or one kind of sport seem to be more successful than applications specific to cycling. However, it obviously does not have to be a barrier if smartphone applications that are of less use for the mobility behavior in St. Petersburg are consequently less frequently used.

The main barrier for the use of smart technologies in combination with cycling in St. Petersburg seems to be barriers for cycling overall. Whereby a lack of high-quality cycling infrastructure forms the biggest barrier. Moreover, it is quite difficult in St. Petersburg to combine cycling with other modes of transport since there are often no parking facilities for private bikes and not always bike sharing stations at the public transport stops. This makes it complicated to use the bike as a conveyor to public transit.

The problems related to smartphone applications seem to be irritating for the users but not really discouraging them from using the applications.

Concluding it can be said that smart technology in the form of smartphone applications can play an important role in promoting sustainable modes of transport within a city since it makes using sustainable transport options more convenient. However, the findings in St. Petersburg show that next to features of the smartphone applications especially the infrastructure both physical and digital plays a huge role. Since the physical infrastructure for example in the form of bicycle lanes and pedestrian streets need to exist for smartphone application to be successful. Moreover, obviously a smartphone application can only properly work if it is possible to regularly update the application even on older phones.

So, it is important for St. Petersburg to create a good and safe cycling infrastructure including both cycling paths for commuting and recreation but also proper parking for bikes at public transport stops and in residential areas. Only after these conditions are fulfilled – which is not the case now– smartphone applications can unfold their full potential. Furthermore, it is equally important to first provide the information about the (new) cycling infrastructure within the applications and to provide the application for as many smartphones/operating systems as possible.

Obviously, looking on the quite small sample that is in addition also mostly limited to respondents from St. Petersburg it is difficult to draw any conclusions about other Russian cities from it. So additional research is needed to receive results for other Russian/European cities and by this be able to put the results from St. Petersburg into some context. For this the survey obviously would need to be slightly adapted to for example include the smartphone applications of the local bike sharing system. Moreover, additional research is needed in how people use the smartphone applications. This research concentrated on which smartphone applications are used but it is obviously also important to see how these smartphone applications are used.

# References

1. Afrin, T., Yodo, N.: A survey of road traffic congestion measures towards a sustainable and resilient transportation system. Sustainability **12**(11), 46–60 (2020). https://doi.org/10.3390/su12114660
2. Anastasi, G., et al.: Urban and social sensing for sustainable mobility in smart cities. SustainIT **2013**, 1–4 (2013). https://doi.org/10.1109/SustainIT.2013.6685198
3. Bachand-Marleau, J., Larsen, J., El-Geneidy, A.: The much-anticipated marriage of cycling and transit: how will it work? Transp. Res. Rec. **2247**, 109–117 (2011). https://doi.org/10.3141/2247-13
4. Bassett, D.R., Pucher, J., Buehler, R., Tomphon, D.L., Crouter, S.E.: Walking, cycling, and obesity rates in Europe, North America, and Australia. J. Phys. Act. Health. **5**(6), 795–814 (2008). https://doi.org/10.1123/jpah.5.6.795
5. Bulkeley, H., Betsill, M.: Rethinking sustainable cities: multilevel governance and the "urban" politics of climate change. Env. Polit. **14**(1), 42–63 (2005). https://doi.org/10.1080/0964401042000310178
6. Carter, S., Green, J., Speed, E.: Digital technologies and the biomedicalization of everyday activities: the case of walking and cycling. Sociol. Compass. **12**(4), e12572 (2018). https://doi.org/10.1111/soc4.12572
7. Chen, F., Turoń, K., Kłos, M., Czech, P., Pamuła, W., Sierpiński, G.: Fifth-generation bike-sharing systems: examples from Poland and China. Sci. J. Sil. Univ. Technol. Ser. Transp. **99**, 05–13 (2018). https://doi.org/10.20858/sjsutst.2018.99.1
8. Chen, Z., van Lierop, D., Ettema, D.: Dockless bike-sharing systems: what are the implications? Transp. Rev. **40**(3), 333–353 (2020). https://doi.org/10.1080/01441647.2019.1710306
9. Chin, H.C., Rahman, M.H.: An impact evaluation of traffic congestion on ecology. Plan. Stud. Pract. **3**(1), 32–44 (2011)
10. Christidis, P., Rivas, J.N.I.: Measuring Road congestion. Institute for Prospective Technological Studies, Seville (2012). https://doi.org/10.2791/15282
11. Public Bike System Feasibility Study. Quay Communications Inc., Vancouver (2008)
12. DeMaio, P.: Bike-sharing: history, impacts, models of provision, and future. J. Public Trans. **12**(4), 41–56 (2009). https://doi.org/10.5038/2375-0901.12.4.3
13. Demograhia: Demographia World Urban Areas (Edition Nr. 16). Demographia, Belleville (2020)
14. Ellis, J.: https://www.techinasia.com/obike-geofencing-singapore
15. EU Court of Auditors: Air pollution: Our health still insufficiently protected. European Union, Luxembourg City (2018). https://doi.org/10.2865/363524
16. Fishman, E., Brennan, T.: Oil vulnerability in Melbourne. In: 33rd Australasian Transport Research Forum, pp. 1–16. Planning and Transport Research Centre, Crawley (2010)
17. Fishman, E., Washington, S., Haworth, N.L.: Bike share's impact on car use: evidence from the United States, Great Britain, and Australia. Transp. Res. D Transp. Environ. **31**, 13–20 (2014). https://doi.org/10.1016/j.trd.2014.05.013
18. Fishman, E.: Bikeshare: a review of recent literature. Transp. Rev. **36**(1), 92–113 (2016). https://doi.org/10.1080/01441647.2015.1033036
19. Fuller, D., Gauvin, L., Morency, P., Kestens, Y., Drouin, L.: The impact of implementing a public bicycle share program on the likelihood of collisions and near misses in Montreal, Canada. Prev. Med. **57**(6), 920–924 (2013). https://doi.org/10.1016/j.ypmed.2013.05.028
20. Galkina, Y.: Interview with Daria Tabachnikova. https://www.the-village.ru/village/city/city-interview/216605-dasha-tabachnikova

21. Goodman, A., Green, J., Woodcock, J.: The role of bicycle sharing systems in normalising the image of cycling: an observational study of London cyclists. J. Transp. Health **1**(1), 5–8 (2014). https://doi.org/10.1016/j.jth.2013.07.001

22. Kiltsova, D.: Далеко неукатишься: в этом году в городе появится только одна велодорожка [You won't get far: this year only one bike path will be constructed in the city]. dp.ru, 16 April 2021. https://m.dp.ru/a/2021/04/16/Daleko_ne_ukatishsja

23. Kroll, K.: Interview. https://www.the-village.ru/village/city/city-interview/144262-intervyu-mikael-kolvill-andersen-o-razvitii-veloinfrastruktury

24. Lamy, M.: A Guide to smart-phone cycling apps. https://www.cyclinguk.org/cycle/guide-smart-phone-cycling-apps

25. Litman, T.: Exploring the paradigm shift needed to reconcile sustainability and transportation objectives. Transp. Res. Rec. **1670**, 8–12 (1999). https://doi.org/10.3141/1670-02

26. Litman, T.: Quantifying the Benefits of Nonmotorized Transportation for Achieving Mobility Management Objectives. Victoria Transport Policy Institute, Victoria (2010)

27. Lyubina, V.: Кикшеринг наНеве: где в Петербурге взять самокат в аренду [Kick-sharing on the Neva: where to rent a scooter in St. Petersburg]. Peterburg2, 30 April 2021. https://peterburg2.ru/articles/kikshering-na-neve-gde-v-peterburge-vzyat-samokat-v-arendu-72785.html

28. Midgley, P.: Bicycle-Sharing Schemes: Enhancing Sustainable Mobility in Urban Areas. United Nations, New York (2011)

29. OECD: OECD Environmental Outlook to 2050. OECD Publishing, Paris (2012)

30. Otero, I., Nieuwenhuijsen, M.J., Rojas-Rueda, D.: Health impacts of bike sharing systems in Europe. Environ. Int. **115**, 387–394 (2018). https://doi.org/10.1016/j.envint.2018.04.014

31. Parkes, S.D., Marsden, G., Shaheen, S.A., Cohen, A.P.: Understanding the diffusion of public bike sharing systems: evidence from Europe and North America. J. Transp. Geogr. **31**, 94–103 (2013). https://doi.org/10.1016/j.jtrangeo.2013.06.003

32. Presto. https://ec.europa.eu/transport/sites/transport/files/cycling-guidance/14_presto_infrastructure_fact_sheet_on_bicycle_parking_in_the_city_centre.pdf

33. Röthig, M.: Sustainable transport policy with the stronger promotion of cycling infrastructure. In: Röthig, M., Efimenko, D. (eds.) Changing Urban Traffic and the Role of Bicycles – Russian and International Experiences, pp. 09–10. Friedrich Ebert Stiftung, Moscow (2014)

34. Shaheen, S., Cohen, A.P., Martin, E.W.: Public bike sharing in North America: early operator understanding and emerging trends. Transp. Res. Rec. **2387**, 83–92 (2013). https://doi.org/10.3141/2387-10

35. Shaheen, S., Guzman, S., Zhang, H.: Bike sharing in Europe, the Americas, and Asia: past, present, and future. Transp. Res. Rec. **2143**(1), 159–167 (2010). https://doi.org/10.3141/2143-20

36. Shaheen, S., Guzman, S.: Worldwide bike sharing. ACCESS Mag. **1**(39), 22–27 (2011)

37. Shilovskaya, T.: St. Petersburg launches new bike rental network. Russia Beyond the Headlines, 8 July 2014. https://www.rbth.com/society/2014/07/08/st_petersburg_launches_new_bike_rental_network_38025.html

38. Shmelev, S.E., Shmeleva, I.A.: Multidimensional sustainability benchmarking for smart megacities. Cities **92**, 134–163 (2019)

39. Strelka Mag: «Губернатор, сделай для меня велодорожку!» ["Governor, create a bike path for me!"], 15 November 2017. https://strelkamag.com/ru/article/spbike

40. TomTom Traffic Index. https://www.tomtom.com/en_gb/traffic-index/ranking/?country=RU

41. United Nations, Department of Economic and Social Affairs, Population Division: World Urbanization Prospects: The 2018 Revision (ST/ESA/SER.A/420). United Nations, New York (2019)

42. WCED (World Commission on Environment and Development): Our Common Future. Oxford University Press, Oxford (1987)

43. Yumashev, P.N., Tingaev, A.M.: Велосипеды как часть городской. [Bicycles as part of the Urban Enviroment]. Аллея Науки [Alley Sci.] **1**(28), 247–253 (2019). https://alley-science.ru/domains_data/files/76January2019/VELOSIPEDY%20KAK%20ChAST%20GORODSKOY%20SREDY.pdf

44. Zaitseva, D., Afonkin, S.: В Петербурге в условиях пандемии сменились игроки нарынке велопроката [In St. Petersburg, during the pandemic, the players in the bicycle rental market have changed]. dp.ru, 20 May 2020. https://m.dp.ru/a/2020/05/20/Gnat_v elosiped

# Support for RoboCops: Measuring Effects of Attitudes Towards Police and Policing Technologies

Anna Gurinskaya[1,2]([✉]) [iD]

[1] St. Petersburg State University, St. Petersburg, Russia
a.gurinskaya@spbu.ru
[2] Herzen University, St. Petersburg, Russia

**Abstract.** Despite such an intensive spread of digital technologies in policing and law enforcement not too many studies have addressed citizens attitudes towards these shifts. If robots are to be introduced for performing policing function it is not only necessary to test whether they are effective in fulfilling their tasks, but also whether citizens perceive them as safe and capable of providing protection. We use data obtained from a sample of 570 students from the two large universities in the city of St. Petersburg, Russia to explore attitudes towards use of robots in street patrolling. Results show that young people are willing to accept surveillance in public places, but are unsupportive of online surveillance tools and regulations. Our research finds that half of the young citizens of St. Petersburg are supportive of robocops patrolling the streets. These positive attitudes are produced by fear of police and fear of victimization. They are enhanced by acceptance of other surveillance technologies (such as surveillance cameras) and willingness to use other digital innovations (such as accident-reporting apps and unmanned cars). When technology acceptance is not considered gender differences can be observed: compared to females, males have greater support for robots. Perceptions of police legitimacy are not related to attitudes to robots used for patrolling.

**Keywords:** Police technologies · Robots · Digital policing

## 1 Introduction

In 1987 a science fiction film «RoboCop» directed by Paul Verhoeven came out. It told a story of a powerful corporation that launched a war on crime in the city of Detroit employing a cyborg police officer. 30 years after the idea of using complex and powerful technologies to maintain law and order does not seem to be too futuristic. Police officers are equipped with body-worn cameras, closed-circuit television cameras (CCTV) have become a no longer noticeable part of the everyday urban landscape, drones are used for intelligence operations and order maintenance, predictive algorithms are guiding police crime prevention efforts. In 2019 Massachusetts State Police tested a robot dog produced by Boston Dynamics. It was followed by Hawaii and New York Police Departments [1].

© Springer Nature Switzerland AG 2022
D. A. Alexandrov et al. (Eds.): DTGS 2021, CCIS 1503, pp. 237–247, 2022.
https://doi.org/10.1007/978-3-030-93715-7_17

Robot dog of a same kind was used in Singapore to ensure social distancing during the Covid-19 pandemic in 2020 [2].

While robots have a potential of saving officers' lives in dangerous situations their use for policing purposes raises concerns among civil rights activists and politicians. The former are claiming Digidog (that is the name of the canine robot) can be weaponized, evolve from a tool controlled by a human to a fully autonomous decision-maker - and all that can happen without proper public oversight of the implementation process [3]. The latter are worried that while spending for digital tools and solutions in policing is expanding, the extent of digital technologies use for education, healthcare and social services for vulnerable communities remains limited [4]. While in 1987 RoboCop seemed to be a distant dystopia, today we're just one step away from humanoid robot being deployed as a police officer.

Digitalization of public services that has been a staple of governance reforms in Russia in the recent years has had its impact in the different areas of law enforcement. Digital reforms are being introduced by various agencies on the federal and regional levels. Since 2014 «Smart City» program is being implemented in the Russian regions. It introduces a comprehensive information system that provides forecasting, monitoring, prevention, and elimination of possible threats such as crimes and other emergencies, as well as control over the elimination of their consequences. Digital technologies were used by Russian regions during the coronavirus pandemics to monitor citizens' movement and assess health risks. In 2021 Russian Corrections Service (FSIN) has announced an ambitious program of digitalization of its services [5]. Artificial intelligence and robotics are considered to be an important part of the digital economy transformation. Their penetration in the law enforcement system is a matter of time. Russian police had not explicitly declared whether it has intention to use robots in police operations. However, in 2019 a representative of a private robotic company announced that the company is ready to sign a contract with the Ministry of Internal Affairs of Russia to equip traffic police and migration services with company's Promobot by 2030 [6]. This robot is capable of face and speech recognition, communication with people, and independent movement. It also connects to such external system as databases and websites. Given rapid development of robotics we may witness these developments even sooner.

Despite such an intensive spread of digital technologies in policing and law enforcement not too many studies have addressed citizens attitudes towards these shifts. If robots are to be introduced for performing policing function it is not only necessary to test whether they are effective in fulfilling their tasks, but also whether citizens perceive them as safe and capable of providing protection. While perceptions of CCTV cameras [7–9], live facial recognition technology [10], and unmanned aerial drones [11] have been studied, citizens' views about development of robotics did not receive much attention [12]. Personal use and acceptance of technology have been studied through the lens of the unified theory of acceptance and use of technology (UTAUT) [13] and technology acceptance model (TAM2) [14]. However, these two models seem to be more applicable to cases when a user adopts new technology herself rather than comes into interaction (in a passive way – as an object of it's use) with the technology used by governmental authorities. They suggest that person's acceptance of a technology is determined by her voluntary intentions towards it's use. The case of Robocops does not assume that citizens will be active users of the technology. The aim of this study is to assess whether young citizens of Russia have favorable attitudes towards possible use of robots in street patrolling and to predict which factors determine these perceptions. In particular, we are interested in whether attitudes towards police, fear of victimization, and willingness to use new technologies are related to students' assessments of robocops.

## 2 Literature Review: Determinants of Support for New Technologies in Policing

Police legitimacy is a multidimensional concept defined as a "property of authority or institution that leads people to feel that that authority or institution is entitled to be deferred to and obeyed" [15: 514]. Police becomes a legitimate authority in people's eyes if police officers do not trespass the boundaries of their authority, exercise justice both in the process of decision-making as well as in the process of direct interactions with citizens, and act effectively reacting to crime and preventing it [16–19]. Perceptions about police fairness (distributive and procedural) and its effectiveness lead to the sense of being obliged to obey to its decisions and cooperate with police officers. Legitimacy was shown to have an impact not only on direct interactions of citizens with police but also on citizens' perceptions of policing methods and technologies, including unmanned aerial drones [20], live facial recognition technology [10], body-worn [21] and surveillance [9] cameras. The question whether views of police legitimacy will have an impact on support for the use of such a technology as robots has not been explored. However, prior research of the relationship between police legitimacy perceptions and attitudes towards different technologies used for policing purposes suggests that we should expect higher level of support for robotic technology among those who think that police acts in a fair manner and is effective. On the opposite, if people are afraid of police officers they may support substituting them for non-human actors such as robots.

Fear of becoming a victim of crime and terrorism has a strong impact on people's everyday life. It forces them to adopt risk-aversion strategies [22] and erodes trust in the criminal justice institutions [23]. However, fear makes people more supportive of CCTV cameras [24–26]. Citizens believe that security of society is dependent on the use of security technologies, such as cameras, and they allow to prevent more crimes [27]. Therefore, despite the fact that fear of victimization may lead to less confidence in human police, digitalized policing may garner more citizen support.

Another factor that may be related to support for the use of artificial technologies in policing is the general acceptance of technologies, the level of confidence in their potential to deal with complex problems (i.e., reaction to crime and its prevention). Those who express stronger interest in various technological developments (i.e., surveillance cameras, mobile apps that allow to interact with emergency services in case of an accident, unmanned vehicles) should be less apprehensive towards use of technology in different areas of police work. Research shows that citizens of Russia generally have a positive attitude to the introduction of new technologies recognizing their potential for making people's life easier and more convenient [28]. In different parts of the world security-enhancing technologies have swiftly spread without much public debate about their costs and benefits and were often met with support even if they entailed mass surveillance. Hempel and Töpfer [29] describe this situation as a «surveillance consensus». Robots are entering policing at a stage when people have been well prepared to get engaged with this kind of security innovations. In this study we would like to see if those who share more positive attitudes towards non-human intervention in their everyday lives will be more willing to react positively towards a robocop in their neighborhood.

Findings about the role of gender in support for technological innovations in policing have been mixed. Some have found females more accepting of cameras [9], while others came to the opposite conclusion [30]. Gallimore et al. [12] explored gender-based effect on trust of an autonomous robot finding that females report higher trust and perceived trustworthiness of the autonomous guard robot.

Our study looks at students' attitudes towards potential use of robots for policing activities. Given the findings of other studies discussed above, we proceed to test the following assumptions:

*H1: Those who perceive police as a legitimate authority (effective, just, and trustworthy) will grant more support for the use of robotic technology in policing;*
*H2: Fear of human police will result in a greater level of acceptance of robots;*
*H3: Fears related to victimization will lead to higher level of support for the use of robots for street patrolling;*
*H4: Those who have acceptance for such technology as CCTV cameras will be more likely to support the use of robots;*
*H5: Reliance on technology in everyday life (reporting accidents through mobile apps) will result in greater support for robots;*
*H6: Trust in robots in other areas (such as operating a vehicle) will lead to greater trust in police robots;*
*H7: Males will be less likely to support robots in policing.*

## 3   Methods

### 3.1   Sample

Data for the present study was collected while working on the project funded by the Russian Foundation for Basic Research. The survey questionnaire «Technologies in governance and law enforcement» was designed to explore citizens' views about technological developments in law enforcement and public service including their attitudes towards possible encounter with robot policemen.

We administered the survey in 2019 (May and September) in two large public universities in St. Petersburg, Russia. The size of the student population in these universities is above 30 000 and 18 000 respectively. We chose 2–3 departments in each university to administer the survey. Respondents' areas of study ranged from art and design and liberal arts to law, economics, and political science. Thus, only students specializing in humanities and social sciences were included in the sample. We obtained permission from the 3 to 6 professors (total - 18) in each department to administer survey at the beginning/end of their classes or after the final exam. Each class had from 12 to 50 students. In addition, we administered the survey to students during their breaks in the common areas and cafeteria after they confirmed that they have not taken a survey in one of their classes. We distributed a total of 650 surveys. Out of these 597 surveys were filled and returned, yielding a response rate of 92%. 7 surveys were unusable. Thus, final response rate was 88%.

There were more females (321 total - 56.3%) than males (240 total - 42.1%) in the sample. About one third of the students were in their 1st and 2nd years of study (203 - 35.6%), almost one half were in the 3rd and 4th years in the program (268 - 47.0%), and the remaining were MA or PhD students (88 - 15.4%). Half of the respondents (239 - 49.2%) were from families with monthly income above average and 197 (40.5%) reported average income. About 10 percent of respondents came from families with income below average (at the time of survey administration the average monthly salary in St. Petersburg was 59,000 Rubles). Our sampling strategy has limitations that does not allow us to generalize our findings to all young citizens of Russia or even of St. Petersburg as our sample was limited to social sciences and humanities students of large universities.

## 3.2 Measures

In order to evaluate students' perceptions relating to this scenario we asked them to assess on a 7-point Likert scale whether they would agree to the following statement: «I have no objections to the streets being patrolled by robot policemen» (1 denoted «strongly disagree», and 7 denoted «strongly agree»). In order to evaluate which factors may be related to their views about robocops we measured respondents' attitudes towards law and order and their attitudes towards use of technology. In addition, we asked questions relating to socio-demographic characteristics of the respondents.

**Attitudes Towards Law and Order.** Questions relating to citizens' perceptions of police were drawn from literature on police legitimacy and procedural justice [15, 16, 31]. Five questions were used to assess attitudes towards such dimensions of police work as police procedural justice, distributive fairness, and effectiveness. We conducted principal component analysis that revealed that these items load on a single component ($\alpha = .904$; mean of the additive 5-item scale $= 13.16$; standard deviation $= 6.14$). We also asked students a question that taps into their fear of police: «When the police officer approaches me I am afraid he/she will trouble me». Both police legitimacy and fear of police attitudes were measured using a 7-point Likert scale from 1 to 7, where 1 represented «strongly disagree» and 7 represented «strongly agree». In order to measure respondents' fear of becoming a victim of crime (violent and property) and terrorism we asked them to assess the level of their fears on a 7-point Likert scale from 1 to 7, where 1 represented «not afraid at all» and 7 represented «very much afraid». Principal component analysis showed that these items can be used to measure «fear of victimization» construct (loadings $> .761$; $\alpha = .772$; mean of the additive scale $= 14.56$; standard deviation $= 4.86$).

**Attitudes Towards Use of Technology.** Respondents' views about technology were assessed using 3 different measures: attitudes towards surveillance cameras; likelihood of the respondent to report traffic accidents using a mobile app; potential willingness to use unmanned vehicle. We included 3 questions relating to the acceptance of various kinds of video surveillance in public places (cameras on the streets, cameras used by the traffic police, and residential cameras installed during implementation of the 'smart residence' program) ($\alpha = .705$; mean of the additive 3-item scale $= 17.02$; standard deviation $= 3.76$). Responses were measured on a 7-point Likert scale where 1 represented «strongly disapprove» to 7 representing «strongly approve». Questions relating to attitudes towards use of other technologies (online accident reporting, unmanned vehicles) were specifically designed for this study. Students were asked if they agree with the following statements: «When I see a traffic accident or other accident I report it to other people through a mobile app» and «I would not hesitate to use an unmanned vehicle». We used a 7-point Likert scale where a response of 1 represented «strongly disagree» and 7 represented «strongly agree».

## 4    Results

### 4.1    Univariate Analysis

Our analysis shows that respondents are almost equally divided in their attitudes to the potential use of robots for police patrolling. We measured attitudes on a 7-point Likert-type scale where 1 represented "strongly disagree" and 7 – "strongly agree". We have grouped the responses from 1 to 3 into category "Do not support" and from 5 to 7 into "Support" category. The rest were classified as "Neutral." Almost half of the respondents (44%) are not supportive of the robocops patrolling the streets. 17.6% appear to be neutral. The rest (38.4%) have rather positive attitudes towards robots in police patrol function. Robocops find less support among citizens compared to surveillance cameras. Other studies have shown that from 60 to 90% citizens approve use of CCTV [9, 23, 30]. As for other technological innovations, support for drones varies from 47% for their use for crowd monitoring to 94% for their use in search and rescue operation [11]. Descriptive statistics for dependent and independent variables used in the analysis is presented in Table 1.

### 4.2    Multivariate Analysis

We used a series of linear regression analyses that estimate the independent and the net effects of 'law and order' perceptions, attitudes towards use of technology (in the area of policing as well as those meant for personal use), and gender on support for the use of robots for patrolling. Unstandardized regression coefficients, standard errors, and significance levels for each of the coefficients are presented in Table 2.

In Model 1, support for robocops is regressed on police legitimacy, fear of police, and fear of victimization along with gender variables. Fear of police appears to be positively related to robocop support: those who are afraid that their encounters with the police may lead to trouble for them are more likely to support patrolling by robocops (b. $= .121$, p $< .01$). Respondents who are afraid to become victims of crime and terrorism have more positive attitudes towards use of robots in policing (b. $= .045$, p $< .05$). Males appear to

**Table 1.** Descriptive statistics for variables (N = 570).

| Variable | N | %* | Mean | S.D. | Min. | Max. |
|---|---|---|---|---|---|---|
| Support for RoboCops | 563 | | 3.73 | 2.01 | 1 | 7 |
| Police legitimacy (5 item additive index, $\alpha$ = .904) | 546 | | 13.16 | 6.14 | 5 | 35 |
| Fear of police | 559 | | 4.01 | 2.11 | 1 | 7 |
| Fear of victimization (3 item additive index, $\alpha$ = .772) | 560 | | 14.56 | 4.86 | 3 | 21 |
| Approval of cameras (3 item additive index, $\alpha$=.705) | 565 | | 17.02 | 3.76 | 3 | 21 |
| Use of mobile apps to report accidents | 560 | | 2.66 | 1.92 | 1 | 7 |
| Willingness to use unmanned cars | 563 | | 4.04 | 2.03 | 1 | 7 |
| Gender | 561 | | | | | |
| Female | 321 | 56.3 | | | | |
| Male | 240 | 42.1 | | | | |

*May not add up to 100% due to missing cases.

be more supportive of robocops than females (b. = .512, p <. 01). Police legitimacy is negatively related to robocop support, but this relationship is not statistically significant.

Model 2 looks at the influence of variables related to respondents' attitudes towards use of technology in policing (surveillance cameras) as well as for reporting accidents. It also tests whether willingness to use unmanned cars as passengers is related to support for robocops. Approval of cameras is positively related with support, and the effect of this variable is statistically significant (b = .075, p. < .001). Willingness to use unmanned cars appears to be a strong positive predictor of support for robotic police patrol (b = .468, p. < .001). Those who report traffic accidents using mobile apps are more likely to support robots in policing; this relationship is also statistically significant (b = .099, p. < .05). In the presence of variables related to technology use the effect of gender variable becomes not statistically significant.

Model 3 is the most comprehensive model testing the joint effect of both variables related to 'law and order' as well as variables related to technology use. In the presence of the technology group of variables none of the 'law and order' variables appear to be statistically significantly related to support for robocops. However, all three variables related to technology use are predicting support like in Model 2. Willingness to use unmanned cars loses some of its strength compared to Model 2 but its effect is positive and statistically significant (b = .416, p. < .001). In this model the effect of gender is not statistically significant.

## 5  Discussion and Conclusion

Present study was aimed at testing several hypotheses relating to support for robots' use for police patrolling. Our findings suggest that citizens are divided in their views. Half of them do not have any objections for seeing a robocop on the streets, while other half would be disappointed to see regular police being replaced with the new technology.

**Table 2.** OLS regression models of support for RoboCops (N = 570).

|  | Model 1 | | Model 2 | | Model 3 | |
|---|---|---|---|---|---|---|
|  | B | SE | B | SE | B | SE |
| Police legitimacy | −.002 | .014 | – | – | −.014 | .012 |
| Fear of police | .121** | .041 | – | – | .059 | .036 |
| Fear of victimization | .045* | .019 | – | – | .039 | .017 |
| Approval of cameras | – | – | .075*** | .020 | .075*** | .021 |
| Report accidents on app | – | – | .099* | .039 | .096* | .039 |
| Will use unmanned cars | – | – | .468*** | .038 | .416*** | .038 |
| Gender (1 = male) | .512** | .188 | .059 | .155 | .187 | .167 |
| Intercept | 2.395 | .402 | .267 | .392 | .346 | .477 |
| F-test | 5.26*** | | 48.75*** | | 28.97*** | |
| Adj. R² | .031 | | .257 | | .268 | |
| N | 537 | | 552 | | 536 | |

Note: Entries are unstandardized regression coefficients (B) and standard errors (SE).
*p < .05 **p < .01 ***p < .001.

We expected that those who perceive police as a legitimate authority (effective, just, and trustworthy) will grant more support for the use of robotic technology in policing. However, our analysis shows that perceptions of police legitimacy do not predict acceptance of robots in policing. This is a surprising and unexpected finding given a multitude of studies demonstrating a strong positive relationship between perceptions of police fairness and views about innovative police technologies. At the same time, young citizens who are afraid of the police would prefer seeing robots on the streets. Thus, positive attitudes towards police do not necessarily result in positive views about technological innovations in policing while negative views may lead to support for replacing human police officers with the digital analogues. As we have expected fears of becoming a victim of crime leads to support for robocops. People may view them as capable of providing a better sense of safety compared to human policemen.

Exposure to different types of safety technologies makes people more visionary when it comes to other kinds of technologies. Surveillance cameras have long ago become «banal goods» [32]. Our study finds that young citizens who do not object seeing cameras on the streets and other public places would be less likely to object to seeing robots patrolling the streets. Interest in using apps to report traffic accidents and willingness to ride in a car driven by an artificial driver also results in greater acceptance of robots in other areas such as policing.

Our findings relating to gender effect on support for robots are mixed. We have found that males were more supportive to police robots than females in the analysis that looked at the influence of the 'law and order' variables on attitudes towards robocops. However, this finding was not confirmed when other variables were included in the models.

# 6  Conclusion

Our research finds that half of the young citizens in our sample are supportive of robocops patrolling the streets. These positive attitudes are produced by fear of police and fear of victimization. They are enhanced by acceptance of other surveillance technologies (such as surveillance cameras) and willingness to use other digital innovations (such as accident-reporting apps and unmanned cars). When technology acceptance is not considered gender differences can be observed: compared to females, males have greater support for robots. Perceptions of police legitimacy are not related to attitudes to robots used for patrolling.

These findings have policy implications. While policing authorities do not seek citizens' approval when they decide to introduce robots to carry out human tasks or assist human officers. At the same time citizens' acceptance of the new technologies may lead to more efficient interactions between citizens and new policing actors. Therefore, it is necessary to promote this innovation, particularly for those citizens that are skeptical about other digital technologies or are not tech-savvy. Introduction of robots may be accompanied with the assurance of their effectiveness in providing safety and demonstration of their relative advantages compared to human workforce.

Despite these interesting findings, several limitations of this research can be identified. Our study was exploratory in nature. We have asked only one question relating to perception of robots in policing in a function of a patrolling officer. Future studies could look at other areas where robots could be used: in search and rescue missions, counter-terrorist operations, for surveillance purposes, for order maintenance, collection of crime and accident reports and other interactions with citizens. Also, future studies could look at citizens perceptions of animalistic robots (such as dogs, insects) that have entered public imagination through sci-fi films. It would be interesting to see which aspects of robots' use in policing are perceived as beneficial for police performance (i.e., enhancing its effectiveness) and which are related to a dystopian vision of the future of policing (i.e., providing the police with the unlimited surveillance capacity).

A second limitation of our research is that our sample includes only humanities and social sciences students that come from two large universities in the second-largest city of Russia. Our findings cannot be generalized to students from smaller cities or students who are better aware of the developments in robotics due to majoring in other areas of studies (i.e., engineering, computer sciences, etc.). Also, students in our sample reported medium to high levels of income. Therefore, attitudes of other population groups may be quite different from those that we have found in our study. Adults, people with lower income, residents of rural areas may have other perceptions of robocops. Future research should employ a different sampling strategy.

# References

1. Cramer, M., Hauser, C.: Digidog, A Robotic Dog Used by the Police, Stirs Privacy Concerns. The New York Times (2021)
2. Robot dog enforces social distancing in city park. BBC News. https://www.bbc.com/news/av/technology-52619568

3. Robot Police Dogs are Here. Should We be Worried? American Civil Liberties Union. https://www.aclu.org/news/privacy-technology/robot-police-dogs-are-here-should-we-be-worried/
4. Ocasio-Cortez, A.: Please ask yourself: when was the last time you saw next-generation, world class technology for education, healthcare, housing, etc. consistently prioritized for underserved communities like this? https://twitter.com/AOC/status/1365023067769098245
5. Russian corrections to receive 25 billion for digitalization. CNews.ru. https://www.cnews.ru/news/top/2021-01-12_vlasti_odobrili_plan_tsifrovizatsii. (in Russian)
6. By 2030 robots-policemen may serve in the Russian Ministry of Internal Affairs. TASS. https://tass.ru/obschestvo/7032932
7. Bennett, T., Gelsthorpe, L.: Public attitudes towards CCTV in public places. Stud. Crime Crime Prevent. 5(1), 72–90 (1996)
8. Sousa, W.H., Madensen, T.D.: Citizen acceptance of police interventions: an example of CCTV surveillance in Las Vegas, Nevada. Crim. Justice Stud. 29(1), 40–56 (2016)
9. Gurinskaya, A.: Predicting citizens' support for surveillance cameras. Does police legitimacy matter? Int. J. Comp. Appl. Crim. Justice 44(1–2), 63–83 (2020)
10. Bradford, B., Yesberg, J.A., Jackson, J., Dawson, P.: Live facial recognition: trust and legitimacy as predictors of public support for police use of new technology. Br. J. Criminol. 60, 1502–1522 (2020)
11. Sakiyama, M., Miethe, T.D., Lieberman, J.D., Heen, M.S., Tuttle, O.: Big hover or big brother? Public attitudes about drone usage in domestic policing activities. Secur. J. 30(4), 1027–1044 (2017)
12. Gallimore, D., Lyons, J.B., Vo, T., Mahoney, S., Wynne, K.T.: Trusting Robocop: gender-based effects on trust of an autonomous robot. Front. Psychol. 10, 482 (2019)
13. Williams, M.D., Rana, N.P., Dwivedi, Y.K.: The unified theory of acceptance and use of technology (UTAUT): a literature review. J. Enterp. Inf. Manag. 28(3), 443–488 (2015)
14. Yousafzai, S.Y., Foxall, G.R., Pallister, J.G.: Technology acceptance: a meta-analysis of the TAM: part 1. J. Model. Manag. 2(3), 251–280 (2007)
15. Sunshine, J., Tyler, T.R.: The role of procedural justice and legitimacy in shaping public support for policing. Law Soc. Rev. 37(3), 513–548 (2003)
16. Tankebe, J.: Viewing things differently: the dimensions of public perceptions of police legitimacy. Criminology 51(1), 103–135 (2013)
17. Trinkner, R., Tyler, T.R.: Legal socialization: coercion versus consent in an era of mistrust. Ann. Rev. Law Soc. Sci. 12(1), 417–439 (2016)
18. Hamm, J.A., Trinkner, R., Carr, J.D.: Fair process, trust, and cooperation: moving toward an integrated framework of police legitimacy. Crim. Justice Behav. 44(9), 1183–1212 (2017)
19. Pryce, D.K., Johnson, D., Maguire, E.R.: Procedural justice, obligation to obey, and cooperation with police in a sample of Ghanaian immigrants. Crim. Justice Behav. 44(5), 733–755 (2017)
20. Heen, M.S., Lieberman, J.D., Miethe, T.D.: The thin blue line meets the big blue sky: perceptions of police legitimacy and public attitudes towards aerial drones. Crim. Justice Stud. 31(1), 18–37 (2018)
21. Demir, M., Apel, R., Braga, A.A., Brunson, R.K., Ariel, B.: Body worn cameras, procedural justice, and police legitimacy: a controlled experimental evaluation of traffic stops. Justice Q. 37(1), 53–84 (2020)
22. Hale, C.: Fear of crime: a review of the literature. Int. Rev. Victimol. 4(2), 79–150 (1996)
23. Singer, A.J., Chouhy, C., Lehmann, P.S., Walzak, J.N., Gertz, M., Biglin, S.: Victimization, fear of crime, and trust in criminal justice institutions: a cross-national analysis. Crime Delinquency 65(6), 822–844 (2019)
24. Bennett, T., Gelsthorpe, L.: Public attitudes towards CCTV in public places. Stud. Crime Crime Prev. 5(1), 72–90 (1996)

25. Honess, T., Charman, E.: Closed circuit television in public places: its acceptability and perceived effectiveness. Home Office Crime Prevention Unit (1992)
26. Gill, M., Bryan, J., Allen, J.: Public perceptions of CCTV in residential areas: "It is not as good as we thought it would be." Int. Crim. Justice Rev. **17**(4), 304–324 (2007)
27. Gurinskaya, A.: Young citizens attitudes towards CCTV and online surveillance in Russia. In: Alexandrov, D.A., Boukhanovsky, A.V., Chugunov, A.V., Kabanov, Y., Koltsova, O., Musabirov, I. (eds.) DTGS 2020. CCIS, vol. 1242, pp. 61–74. Springer, Cham (2020). https://doi.org/10.1007/978-3-030-65218-0_5
28. Vahshtajn, V., Stepancov, P., Chursina, Y., Bardina, S.: Publichnyj otchet po rezul'tatam sociologicheskogo issledovaniya povedencheskih i institucional'nyh predposylok tekhnologicheskogo razvitiya regionov RF. RVK gosudarstvennyj fond fondov i institut razvitiya venchurnogo rynka Rossijskoj Federacii (2016). (in Russian)
29. Hempel, L., Töpfer, E.: The surveillance consensus: reviewing the politics of CCTV in three European countries. Eur. J. Criminol. **6**(2), 157–177 (2009)
30. Brands, J., van Doorn, J.: Policing nightlife areas: comparing youths' trust in police, door staff and CCTV. Polic. Soc. **30**, 1–17 (2018)
31. Sun, I.Y., Li, L., Wu, Y., Hu, R.: Police legitimacy and citizen cooperation in China: testing an alternative model. Asian J. Criminol. **13**(4), 275–291 (2018)
32. Goold, B., Loader, I., Thumala, A.: The banality of security: "the curious case of surveillance cameras. Br. J. Criminol. **53**(6), 977–996 (2013)

# eHumanities: Digital Education and Research Methods

# Learning Hard or Hardly Learning: Smartphones in the University's Classrooms

Yuliya L. Proekt(✉) (iD), Valeriya V. Khoroshikh(iD), Alexandra N. Kosheleva(iD),
and Violetta F. Lugovaya(iD)

Herzen State Pedagogical University of Russia, Saint-Petersburg, Russian Federation

**Abstract.** Mobile devices are the necessary part of equipment for the busy life of modern people. Recent studies revealed that students use mobile phones in the educational environment more and more often. But there is a gap in empirical works related to the issue of what exactly do Russian students do with their smartphones during the class and how is this smartphone use connected to their academic motivation. In this study authors aimed to examine different aspects of smartphone usage by Russian university students during class in association with academic motivation, satisfaction with education, and indicators of problematic smartphone use. The study involved 437 participants aged between 17 and 34 years, 70,02% female. The findings revealed that students who used smartphones for academic purposes had expressed intrinsic academic motivation and learning achievements. Generally, students had sooner positive intentions towards smartphone use during the class and tended to disclaim distracting forms of smartphone use. Results have shown that students who actively used smartphones while learning, less satisfied with their education. Problematic smartphone use had a strong association with distracting forms of smartphone use during the class.

**Keywords:** Smartphone use during class · Russian students · Learning ·
Involvement · Distraction · Academic motivation · Satisfaction with education ·
Problematic smartphone use · Phubbing

## 1 Introduction

Mobile device use is widely spreading around the world. Recent reports reflected that there had been 258 million SIM cards for about 129 million people in Russia. Moreover, more than 90% of Internet connections were performed using smartphones [26]. Among smartphone users, young people are most sensitive to new opportunities and innovations in ways to change habits of day-to-day life. Modern students have had high expectations for smartphones which are related rather to its features but not the price [16].

Smartphones, as multifunctional devices, implement many computer-related actions, including Internet access. In this case, their functionalities have become the tool tying together virtual and physical reality [14]. In any moment of time, smartphone users are included in remote contexts connected with or distracted from actual activities. Therefore, smartphone usage has changed modern students' learning activity in many ways.

D. A. Alexandrov et al. (Eds.): DTGS 2021, CCIS 1503, pp. 251–265, 2022.
https://doi.org/10.1007/978-3-030-93715-7_18

On the one hand, smartphone usage might improve multitasking [18], increase personal productivity [32], expand opportunities for learning in different situations [1], provide access to M-learning apps and learning management systems (LMSs) at any time whenever a student needs educational support [42]. Researchers have described transformative power of mobile technology for education, expressing its pedagogical advantages to share knowledge, build collaboration, create personalized learning environments [30]. On the other hand, integration of mobile technology in classes has become one of the biggest challenges for faculty. Most of academics doesn't have developed technology integration skills. They are rather so-called "digital immigrants" and have rather negative attitudes towards smartphone use during class (SUDC) by students [40]. Another issue has been identified by researchers who explored disorders connected to smartphone use by young people. They report about the harmful effects of extensive smartphone use, such as the higher level of intolerance of uncertainty [8], depression, and decreasing quality of human interactions [23, 38], declined academic performance [48, 58].

Despite the increasing number of studies on mobile learning, there is a gap in our understanding of internal determination of SUDC by students and its consequences. The following research questions are raised in the paper:

- (RQ1) What exactly do students do with their smartphones during the class?
- (RQ2) How is this smartphone use associated with the students' academic motivation, learning outcomes, and satisfaction with learning?
- (RQ3) Do internet addiction and phubbing behavior connect to different aspects of SUDC?

In the current study, we aimed to examine different aspects of SUDC by Russian university students in association with their academic motivation. Another purpose of the study was to explore connections between SUDC and Internet addiction, phubbing behavior, students' satisfaction with education, academic achievements, and their demographics.

## 2   Review of Related Literature

### 2.1   Smartphones in Higher Education

The broad spreading of digital technologies has changed modern education. The essential feature of mobile technologies using is their ability to provide opportunities for learning anywhere, anyplace, and anytime [11]. Students can use them for accessing academic services, e-mailing, social networking, communicating with the lecturer and classmates, interacting with the course content [18, 55]. Recent studies revealed that students use mobile phones for academic purposes more and more often. The main goals of using smartphones are accessing educational information, reading full-text articles, recording class notes and references, checking course Power-Point slides, and texting about class assignments. [12, 19, 25, 39, 43]. So researchers found that key intentions of students in mobile technology use connected to information exchange, but not active interaction with each other and learning content, sharing ideas or performing of personalized learning tasks. If so, the full functionality of smartphones turns out to be untouched because students use their devices only as a replacement for traditional pens and notebooks. Furthermore, most of the actions with mobile devices for academic purposes occur when students solve learning tasks outside their classes.

At the same time, smartphone use in university classrooms doesn't seem such a suitable thing. Researchers in different countries reported similar findings, which indicated distracting and troubling roles of smartphone usage in university classrooms [2, 6, 9, 57]. So Jacobsen and Forste [27] found that more than 60% of students use their electronic media for non-academic purposes during class or doing homework. Gilroy revealed that every third student in the USA plays video games on the smartphone while in the class [20]. G. R. Jesse found that Thiel College students use smartphones during class at least once a day for texting or going on social media [28]. In summary, the previous research on SUDC has concentrated on its positive or negative forms but it is not enough literature that carefully explores transitions from academic to non-academic purposes of SUDC and vice versa. It is not clear whether these forms of SUDC are immanent in different students or students might reveal them alternately in different situations. Thus we could hypothesize that:

H1 Positive and negative forms of SUDC have associated with different academic motives of students.

## 2.2 Problematic Smartphone Use and Its Impact on Learning Results

Besides some barriers to include mobile devices use in the learning process associated with problematic smartphone use (PSU). An appropriate description of behavioral problems connected to mobile phone overuse has been still discussed in numerous studies. Some authors suppose that it is a type of technological addiction in terms of M.D. Griffiths [22] so far as abuse of phone use often occurs with inattention to usual activities, alterations in mood, personal harm, loss of control and tolerance [24, 29, 34, 36, 51]. Others tend to use the term PSU as a definition of physic and psychological problems caused by smartphone use. They support the opposite point of view, arguing that behavioral problems in smartphone use are consequences of other technological addictions (e.g., Internet addiction, compulsive gambling) [17, 59]. Arguing about youth, Griffiths supposed that PSU could be just an essential feature of "a period of their development with strong needs of social ties rather than a true addiction." [21, p.77].

Cyberloafing is a term that means surfing the Internet for non-work- or non-learning-related purposes during working or learning hours [15]. Usually, cyberloafing is defined as behaviors associated with computer or laptop use but mobile access to the Internet via smartphone gives users more opportunities to cyberloaf at any moment while they are busy with work or learning performance. It is the reason for the growing body of studies on cyberloafing in educational environments [15, 37, 54]. Cyberloafing, as a distracting factor, has led to decreasing interest and attendance of students to the course [5]. It could also be an essential matter for addictive learning behavior and academic procrastination [58]. At the same time, cyberloafing might be considered as a tool that helps an individual to ignore what is happening in the class, lecturer, and classmates. So cyberloafing through mobile phone usage has a strong association with phubbing behavior.

Phubbing behavior is one of the most discussed issues in PSU [10]. Phubbing is a type of behavior when someone ignores others via her or his smartphone. This term describes situations of attention's shift from actual social settings to more comfortable distant or virtual contexts. Most of researchers have been studying phubbing to find out its consequences on health and personal relationship [49]. Researchers suppose that it could be a reason for declining of social interactions' quality and relationship satisfaction [44, 47]. In educational environments, any actions of students through mobile phones use for non-class purposes might be indicated as students' attitudes towards lecturers, academic subjects, and education on the whole. For instance, Naciye Guliz Ugur and Tugba Koc argued that "being busy with mobile phones during courses is an act of phubbing" [56, p. 1024]. At the same time, other researchers suppose that phubbing behavior related to behavioral addictions and personality traits [4, 10, 31], which shifts this issue to the area of individual characteristics of person but not personal attitudes towards actual surroundings. Anyway, previous studies indicated that phubbing and other types of PSU in the educational environment hurt learning performance such as academic procrastination [15, 41], and reducing academic achievements [3, 33, 35, 45, 58]. Therefore, it could be hypothesized that:

H2 SUDC is connected to phubbing behavior, Internet addiction, students' satisfaction with education, and learning outcomes.

## 3 Methods

### 3.1 Participants and Procedure

Students of Russian universities were invited to take part in this study through posts on social media and also mailing lists of students provided by universities-partners. 437 participants were recruited as volunteers without any financial compensation. The study involved 306 women (70,02%) and 131 men (29,98%) aged between 17 and 34 ($x^-$ = 21,66; Me = 21; SD = 3,99). 83,75% of participants were students of metropolitan universities (Moscow, St. Petersburg), and others studied in universities of various regions of Russia (Altai, Yakutia, Volga region, Republic of Bashkortostan, Novgorod, Kursk, Omsk regions, etc.). In terms of education programs, most of the participants were students studying in the field of Humanities (43,48%), Engineering & Technology (17,85%), Social Sciences & Management (17,39%). Others have studied Arts (7,78%), Natural Sciences (7,78%), Life Sciences & Medicine (5,72%). Participants were asked to fill on the online form, which contained a set of questionnaires.

### 3.2 Measures

#### 3.2.1 SUDC Questionnaire

The assessment of positive and negative forms of SUDC was by the questionnaire, which contains 14 items. The questionnaire involves the next statement "I usually use my smartphone…" The five items reflected positive forms of SUDC include suggestions about using the smartphone for educational purposes ("to communicate with classmates about learning tasks", "to search relevant information about course content", "to solve learning tasks", etc.). These statements revealed involvement of students with learning process via mobile phones.

The other nine items were used to reflect negative forms of SUDC such as "to relieve boredom or irritation during class", "to search interesting information about anything other than learning", "to share content on social networks and check my friends' social networking profiles", etc. These items revealed distraction themselves and others from the class via smartphones. A five-pointed Likert scale (1-almost never; 2-rarely; 3-sometimes; 4-often; 5-constantly) was used (see all items in Table 1). Three variables were calculated as means of positive forms of SUDC (Involvement), of negative forms of SUDC (Distraction), and total scores (SUDC total). Cronbach's alpha for the questionnaire scales are given below (See Table 2).

### 3.2.2 Phubbing Questionnaire

This questionnaire is a modified form of the Phubbing Scale developed by Karadağ et al. to measure behavioral tendency to phubbing [31]. The scale contains ten items such as 'My eyes start wandering on my phone when I'm together with others', "My phone is always within my reach", "I feel incomplete without my mobile phone", and so on. A five-pointed Likert scale (1-almost never; 2-rarely; 3-sometimes; 4-often; 5-constantly) was used for evaluation frequency of phubbing behavior demonstration. In our case, we asked participants to evaluate the frequency of phubbing behavior concerning five groups of phubbees (friends, family members, classmates, lecturers, and strangers). The question was "How often do you behave this way when communicating with.../you are in class". The indexes of phubbing for each group were calculated as the sum of points. Cronbach's alpha and split half reliability for the indexes are given below (See Table 2).

### 3.2.3 Excessive Use of the Internet Scale by G.U. Soldatova and E.I. Rasskazova

Internet addiction was assessed using Excessive Use of the Internet Scale [52]. The authors identified three most essential features of Internet addiction, like withdrawal symptoms, loss of control, and escape from reality. The scale consists of 5 items evaluated with a three-point Likert scale (1 – never/almost never; 2 – not very often; 3 – very often/almost always). The common variable was identified as an overall score.

### 3.2.4 Questionnaire for Diagnostics of Students' Academic Motivation by A. Rean and V. Yakunin

This questionnaire is widely used in n Russia for revealing academic motivation among university students [46]. The survey consists of 16 academic motives such as "to become a highly qualified specialist", "to obtain a diploma", "to learn successfully", "to perform pedagogical requirements", "to be praised by the teacher", and so on. Participants were suggested to evaluate a significance of academic motives for themselves. A seven-point Likert scale was used to assess the significance of each motive (1 – absolutely not important; 7 – extremely important).

### 3.2.5  Students' Satisfaction with Education Questionnaire

The questionnaire was developed within the scope of the study. We asked participants to evaluate their satisfaction with various aspects of education and student life such as the choice of profession and university, communication with other students, teachers and academic staff, quality of teaching, learning process organization, social protection, opportunities in future career, etc. along a five-pointed Likert scale (1- completely dissatisfied; 5- completely satisfied). The overall score was calculated as a common variable.

### 3.3  Data Analysis

In this study nonparametric statistical methods were used due to the fact that not all the variables had been normally distributed. As the first step, we conducted a descriptive and comparative analysis to evaluate the frequency of different forms of SUDC and its relation to age and gender of students. The total sample was divided into young (range = 17–21; n = 269) and adult (range = 22–34; n = 168) groups. Comparative analysis was conducted by using Mann Whitney U Test. To explore the connection between different forms of SUDC and the frequency of their manifestation we used the two-way correspondence analysis (CA). CA is a descriptive method that based on Chi-square statistics and allows to conduct principal components analysis without underlying distributional assumptions [13, 50, 53]. As result CA visualizes the relationships between rows and columns of a frequency table. The next step was performed by analyzing a correlational structure of all the study variables via Spearman's rank correlation analysis. All analyses were calculated in Statistica v. 6.1 (StatSoft Inc.).

## 4   Results

The results of revealing characteristics of smartphone use during class according to the gender and age of students are shown in Table 1. Results point out that the most common forms of SUDC are searching relevant in-formation about course content, solving learning tasks, and checking time. Students, regardless of age and gender, tend least likely to admit that they use mobile phones for taking calls, chatting, and browsing social networking sites. They also demonstrated that rarely communicate with classmates about learning tasks via smartphone. In the same time students tend to use smartphones to relieve boredom or irritation during class (mood regulation). Comparative analysis demonstrated that young students significantly more often use their smartphones to regulate their mood during class (U = 19305,5; p < 0,01), to maintain remote contexts (U = 18492,0; p < 0,01), to continue conversation with somebody (U = 18627,0; p < 0,01), and to check time (U = 17957,0; p < 0,01). There are not so many gender differences. Female students, compared with male, significantly more often use smartphones to make notes and take pictures of the lecture points written on the blackboard or screen (U = 17097,0; p < 0,01).

We further carried out two-way CA to test more deeply frequencies of different forms of SUDC (Total $\chi^2$ = 285,79; df = 52; p < 0,0001). The horizontal axis reflects dimension 1, which accounted for the 72,53% proportion of inertia (See Fig. 1). Its extreme

**Table 1.** Means and SD of SUDC characteristics

| SUDC items | Means (standard deviations) | | | | |
|---|---|---|---|---|---|
| | Total sample | GENDER | | AGE | |
| | | Male | Female | Young | Adult |
| INV1: to search relevant information about course content | 3,58 (0,99) | 3,56 (0,97) | 3,59 (1,00) | 3,59 (0,97) | 3,55 (1,03) |
| INV2: to solve learning tasks | 3,39 (0,98) | 3,30 (0,95) | 3,41 (0,99) | 3,61 (1,02) | 3,28 (0,95) |
| INV3: to make notes or to take pictures of the lecture points written on the blackboard or screen | 3,36 (1,07) | 3,15 (1,13) | 3,45 (1,03) | 3,33 (1,10) | 3,40 (1,03) |
| INV4: to note my ideas about course content | 3,18 (1,07) | 2,90 (1,10) | 3,22 (1,07) | 3,26 (1,09) | 3,14 (1,07) |
| INV5: to communicate with classmates about learning tasks | 2,29 (0,86) | 2,24 (0,94) | 2,31 (0,82) | 2,27 (0,82) | 2,31 (0,92) |
| DIS1: to check the time | 3,62 (1,09) | 3,40 (0,97) | 3,65 (1,11) | 3,90 (1,11) | 3,47 (1,06) |
| DIS2: to relieve boredom or irritation during class | 3,20 (1,17) | 3,18 (1,11) | 3,20 (1,20) | 3,32 (1,13) | 3,01 (1,22) |
| DIS3: when I remember that I forgot to do something on the Internet | 3,09 (1,07) | 3,07 (1,00) | 3,10 (1,11) | 3,22 (1,06) | 2,89 (1,07) |
| DIS4: do not interrupt communication with significant others | 3,08 (1,25) | 3,21 (1,12) | 3,02 (1,30) | 3,23 (1,22) | 2,83 (1,27) |
| DIS5: to search interesting information about anything other than learning | 3,07 (1,09) | 3,13 (1,04) | 3,05 (1,11) | 3,13 (1,05) | 2,97 (1,13) |
| DIS6: to take notes about something interesting, but not for learning | 2,90 (1,08) | 2,88 (1,10) | 2,91 (1,08) | 2,88 (1,03) | 2,94 (1,16) |
| DIS7: to share content on social networks and check my friends' social networking profiles | 2,59 (1,25) | 2,70 (1,16) | 2,55 (1,29) | 2,67 (1,25) | 2,47 (1,25) |
| DIS8: to communicate with others | 2,37 (0,88) | 2,50 (0,94) | 2,31 (0,85) | 2,37 (0,87) | 2,37 (0,91) |

(*continued*)

**Table 1.** (*continued*)

| SUDC items | Means (standard deviations) | | | | |
|---|---|---|---|---|---|
| | Total sample | GENDER | | AGE | |
| | | Male | Female | Young | Adult |
| DIS9: to go out to take a call | 1,80 (0,81) | 1,80 (0,79) | 1,80 (0,82) | 1,61 (0,72) | 1,90 (0,85) |

points are represented by going out to take a call, conversations with others regardless to involve with or distract from learning content at the one pole, and checking time, searching relevant information, and solving learning tasks at the other pole. In other words, this dimension depicts extension from communicative activities like conversations with others to individual activities aimed at personal purposes. It is important to note that students tend to disclaim communicative forms of SUDC, while they admit smartphone use to reach the personal purposes.

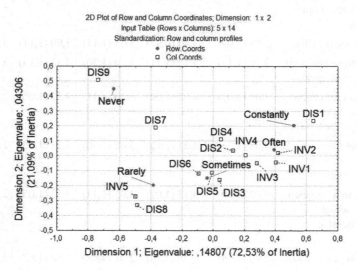

**Fig. 1.** Correspondence analysis of matrix cross-tabulating frequencies of different forms of SUDC

The second dimension accounted for 21,09% proportion of inertia and related to the vertical axis. Its extreme points are associated with the creation or consumption of information. As it is shown on Fig. 1, consumption of information is a more common form of SUDC.

The next step of the analysis was to reveal relationships among indicators of SUDC, phubbing behavior, and Internet addiction (see Table 2).

**Table 2.** Correlation coefficients between indicators of SUDC, groups of phubbees, phubbing behavior, Internet Addiction, means, SD, Cronbach α and Split half reliability (Note: *p < 0.001)

| Variables | 1 | 2 | 3 | 4 | 5 | 6 | 7 | 8 | 9 | 10 |
|---|---|---|---|---|---|---|---|---|---|---|
| 1. Involvement | – | | | | | | | | | |
| 2. Distraction | 0,48* | – | | | | | | | | |
| 3. SUDC total | 0,84* | 0,87* | – | | | | | | | |
| 4. Phubbees-Friends | 0,33* | 0,41* | 0,43* | – | | | | | | |
| 5. Phubbees-Family | 0,36* | 0,49* | 0,50* | 0,73* | – | | | | | |
| 6. Phubbees-Classmates | 0,36* | 0,48* | 0,49* | 0,75* | 0,74* | – | | | | |
| 7. Phubbees-Strangers | 0,23* | 0,40* | 0,37* | 0,50* | 0,56* | 0,74* | – | | | |
| 8. Phubbees-Lecturers | 0,34* | 0,52* | 0,51* | 0,57* | 0,57* | 0,70* | 0,71* | – | | |
| 9. Phubbing total | 0,38* | 0,54* | 0,54* | 0,83* | 0,84* | 0,92* | 0,83* | 0,84* | – | |
| 10. Internet Addiction | 0,04 | 0,29* | 0,20* | 0,26* | 0,35* | 0,30* | 0,33* | 0,26* | 0,35* | – |
| Mean | 3,09 | 2,91 | 2,99 | 12,36 | 12,63 | 12,71 | 11,93 | 13,23 | 62,86 | 8.56 |
| Standard deviation | 0,70 | 0,77 | 1,27 | 3,95 | 4,01 | 3,77 | 3,92 | 4,20 | 16,90 | 2.20 |
| Cronbach α | 0,63 | 0,87 | 0,84 | 0.71 | 0.73 | 0.68 | 0.67 | 0.74 | 0.91 | 0.66 |
| Split half reliability | 0,63 | 0,88 | 0,90 | 0.73 | 0.73 | 0.67 | 0.64 | 0.75 | 0.82 | 0.74 |

The findings of this study revealed a statistically significant correlation among all the indicators of SUDC, phubbing behavior related to different groups of interacting persons and Internet addiction. Furthermore, the most of PSU indicators had high reliability. It is important to note that there wasn't statistically significant connection between Involvement and Internet addiction.

The findings of this study revealed a statistically significant correlation among all the indicators of SUDC, phubbing behavior related to different groups of interacting persons and Internet addiction. Furthermore, the most of PSU indicators had high reliability. It is important to note that there wasn't statistically significant connection between Involvement and Internet addiction.

The results disclose the specifics of association between different forms of SUDC and academic motives. From Table 3, it has been clear, that positive forms of SUDC associated with intrinsic academic motivation. So connections were revealed between involvement and intentions to get intellectual satisfaction ($r = 0,22$; $p < 0,01$), to pursue a successful career in future ($r = 0,17$; $p < 0,01$), to obtain a diploma ($r = 0,17$; $p < 0,01$), and academic grade average ($r = 0,14$; $p < 0,01$). Less strong associations were indicated between involvement and intentions to continue education successfully in subsequent levels ($r = 0,12$; $p < 0,05$), to gain in-depth knowledge ($r = 0,12$; $p < 0,05$), to become a highly qualified specialist ($r = 0,12$; $p < 0,05$).

**Table 3.** Correlation coefficients between indicators of SUDC, academic motives, satisfaction with education, and demographics of students (Note: 1 – involvement; 2 – distraction; 3 – SUDC total; 4 – lecturers as phubbees; *p < 0.05; **p < 0.01)

| Academic motives and other antecedents of SUDC | Indicators of SUDC | | | |
|---|---|---|---|---|
| | 1 | 2 | 3 | 4 |
| To get intellectual satisfaction | **0,22**\*\* | 0,03 | **0,14**\*\* | −0,09 |
| To pursue a successful career in future | **0,17**\*\* | 0,00 | 0,10 | −0,07 |
| To obtain a diploma | **0,17**\*\* | 0,06 | **0,13**\*\* | −0,06 |
| To continue education successfully in subsequent levels | **0,12**\* | 0,03 | 0,09 | −0,06 |
| To gain in-depth knowledge | **0,12**\* | −0,03 | 0,05 | −0,11 |
| To become a highly qualified specialist | **0,12**\* | 0,01 | 0,07 | −0,09 |
| To do not throw studying current courses | 0,10 | −0,04 | 0,03 | **−0,16**\*\* |
| To be praised by the teacher | 0,04 | **−0,11**\* | −0,04 | **−0,18**\*\* |
| To be constantly prepared for next classes | 0,04 | −0,04 | 0,00 | **−0,20**\*\* |
| To learn successfully | 0,04 | −0,03 | 0,00 | **−0,15**\*\* |
| To keep up with classmates | 0,01 | **−0,16**\*\* | −0,09 | **−0,11**\* |
| To perform pedagogical requirements | 0,00 | −0,09 | −0,05 | **−0,16**\*\* |
| To be a good example to classmates | −0,08 | **−0,20**\*\* | **−0,16**\*\* | **−0,12**\* |
| Academic Motivation total | 0,08 | − 0,07 | 0,00 | **− 0,16**\*\* |
| Satisfaction with education | **−0,12**\* | **− 0,21**\*\* | **−0,19**\*\* | **−0,12**\* |
| Academic Grade Average | **0,14**\*\* | 0,01 | 0,08 | −0,01 |
| Age | −0,02 | **−0,21**\*\* | **−0,14**\*\* | **−0,10**\* |

At the same time, other forms of SUDC were negatively correlated with external academic motivation primarily in its social components. Distraction has inversely connected to students' intentions to be a good example to classmates ($r = -0,20$; $p < 0,01$), to keep up with classmates ($r = -0,16$; $p < 0,01$), and to be praised by the teacher ($r = -0,11$; $p < 0,05$). Phubbing the lecturer was negatively correlated with all the academic motives except intrinsic motivation. In addition, negative forms of SUDC were inversely correlated with students' age. All the forms of SUDC have negatively associated with satisfaction with education.

## 5 Discussion

The finding of this study indicates some issues in the modern learning process in higher education. It was assumed that students use their smartphones for different purposes. As the results showed, main forms of SUDC more associated with information consumption and mood regulation than communication with others. We revealed connection between SUDC and academic motivation that was approved the hypothesis 1. Positive forms of SUDC associated with intrinsic academic motivation. Such students have had more expressed intentions to become successful professionals in their field and to enjoy the learning process. Objectively, such students have higher academic performance and study better than others. They tend to rely on their smartphones as personal assistants in learning, which can significantly speed up access to knowledge, help them solve learning tasks effectively. Conceivably, their dissatisfaction with education connected to the digital divide between students and faculty, leading to different perceptions and abilities to use mobile devices during class. It is found in this study that younger students are heavier users of smartphones in the educational environment. S.W. Campbell revealed the similar results [7]. In his study, younger participants, compared with older participants, had more positive attitudes towards using mobile phones in college classrooms and were more tolerant of distracting forms of the technology use.

With regard to the findings of negative forms of SUDC, this study provides support for the reports of other researchers [3, 33, 36, 45, 48, 58]. We revealed many connections between negative forms of SUDC and declined motivation to learn, especially in its social components. Depressed academic motivation and dissatisfaction with the education of students who use their smartphones for non-academic purposes are very significant results that might reflect social exclusion from the educational com-munity and succeeding crisis of professional studying. For such students, SUDC might be a way to avoid mentally the adverse learning situation in which they are present physically [32].

The study approved hypothesis 2 that SUDC is connected to phubbing behavior, Internet addiction, students' satisfaction with education, and learning outcomes. It is important to emphasize that the findings revealed the connection only between positive forms of SUDC and the academic grade average. Previous studies had shown relations between SUDC for non-academic purposes and academic achievements [3, 33, 45, 58]. But in this case, the results didn't reveal the same relationships. It could be associated with specifics of assessment of learning outcomes in Russian universities since the 5-point scale has been used for academic grades. Similarly, A. Yunita et al. didn't reveal any connection between the impact of SUDC on the students' academic performance [60].

All the forms of SUDC positively related both to each other and all the indicators of PSU. This could be evidence of a person's behavioral addiction to a greater extent than his or her intention to use a smartphone during class based on the current situation. Such a statement is well established by the previous studies demonstrated the connections between different forms of PSU, Internet addiction, and personal traits [4, 10, 31]. Additionally, phubbing the lecturers seem to be more appropriate than other people as it occurs in the situation of public communication and might be in-conspicuous.

# 6   Conclusion

Smartphones have rightfully filled most of the personal spaces of modern humans. Its useful features might be drivers for education in an appropriate learning environment. But this requires restructuring of the learning approach by educators who are primarily "digital immigrants". In the present study, we examined connections between different forms of SUDC and its antecedents, such as academic motivation, satisfaction with education, Internet addiction, and PSU indicators. We found that students who used smartphones for academic purposes had expressed intrinsic academic motivation and learning achievements. Generally, students had sooner positive intentions towards SUDC and tended to disclaim distracting forms of SUDC. But in any case, students who actively use smartphones while learning, less satisfied with their education. It is a fact, inspiring to recommend a more active adaptation of mobile technologies in classroom activities.

The study has some limitations. First, only those of students who received the invitation could take part in this study. Although we used the snowball sampling, some students with specific forms of SUDC could be overlooked. Moreover, the first group of participants consisted mainly of women which caused gender distribution of the sample. It could be useful for further research to study male samples with different forms of SUDC. Second, the study was performed by using quantitative data. It would be interesting to gain a pool of students' opinions about SUDC by means of interview or focus groups. Third, the results of this study might not be approval for causal relationships between SUDC and learning activity of students. We only can say that different aspects of SUDC have associated with learning performance, and accompanied by problematic Internet and smartphone use. It is significant for further studies to explore the impact of mobile technology usage in university classrooms on learning performance, motivation, and students' satisfaction with education.

# References

1. Arain, A.A., Hussain, Z., Rizvi, W.H., Vighio, M.S.: An analysis of the influence of a mobile learning application on the learning outcomes of higher education students. Univ. Access Inf. Soc. **17**(2), 325–334 (2018). https://doi.org/10.1007/s10209-017-0551-y
2. Baker, W.M., Lusk, E.J., ve Neuhauser, K.L.: On the use of cell phones and other electronic devices in the classroom: evidence from a survey of faculty and students. J. Educ. Bus. **87**, 275–289 (2012). https://doi.org/10.1080/08832323.2011.622814
3. Bjornsen, C.A., Archer, K.J.: Relations between college students' cell phone use during class and grades. Scholarsh. Teach. Learn. Psychol. **1**(4), 326–336 (2015). https://doi.org/10.1037/stl0000045
4. Błachnio, A., Przepiorka, A.: Be aware! If you start using Facebook problematically you will feel lonely: phubbing, loneliness, self-esteem, and Facebook intrusion. A cross-sectional study. Soc. Sci. Comput. Rev. **37**, 270–278 (2018). https://doi.org/10.1177/0894439318754490
5. Brubaker, A.T.: Faculty perceptions of the impact of student laptop use in a wireless internet environment on the classroom learning environment and teaching information and library science. Master Thesis, University of North Carolina, North Carolina. (2006). https://cdr.lib.unc.edu/concern/masters_papers/kd17cx64h
6. Burns, S.M., Lohenry, K.: Cellular phone use in class: implications for teaching and learning a pilot study. Coll. Stud. J. **44**(3), 805–810 (2010). https://www.questia.com/library/journal/1G1-238474703/cellular-phone-use-in-class-implications-for-teaching
7. Campbell, S.W.: Perceptions of mobile phones in college classrooms: ringing, cheating, and classroom policies. Commun. Educ. **55**(3), 280–294 (2006). https://doi.org/10.1080/03634520600748573

8. Carleton, R.N., Desgagne, G., Krakauer, R., Hong, R.Y.: Increasing intolerance of uncertainty over time: the potential influence of increasing connectivity. Cogn. Behav. Ther. **48**(2), 121–136 (2018). https://doi.org/10.1080/16506073.2018.1476580
9. Chen, Q., Yan, Z.: Does multitasking with mobile phones affect learning? A review. Comput. Hum. Behav. **54**, 34–42 (2016). https://doi.org/10.1016/j.chb.2015.07.047
10. Chotpitayasunondh, V., Douglas, K.M.: How "phubbing" becomes the norm: the antecedents and consequences of snubbing via smartphone. Comput. Hum. Behav. **63**, 9–18 (2016). https://doi.org/10.1016/j.chb.2016.05.018
11. Collis, B.: Tele-Learning in a Digital World: The Future of Distance Learning. International Thomson Computer Press, London (1996)
12. Dahlstrom, E., Bichsel, J.: ECAR study of undergraduate students and information technology. Research report. Louisville, CO: ECAR (2014). https://library.educause.edu/~/media/files/lib rary/2014/10/ers1406.pdf
13. Das, S., Sun, X.: Association knowledge for fatal run-off-road crashes by Multiple Correspondence Analysis. IATSS Res. **39**(2), 146–155 (2016). https://doi.org/10.1016/j.iatssr.2015.07.001
14. de Souza e Silva, A.: From cyber to hybrid: mobile technologies as interfaces of hybrid spaces. Space Cult. **9**(3), 261–278 (2006)
15. Durak, H.Y.: Cyberloafing in learning environments where online social networking sites are used as learning tools: antecedents and consequences. J. Educ. Comput. Res. (2019). https://doi.org/10.1177/0735633119867766
16. Elammari, H.A.B., Cavus, N.: Investigating the factors affecting students' smartphone purchasing behaviors in the context of mobile learning. Int. J. Emerg. Technol. Learn. **14**(22), 111–121 (2019). https://doi.org/10.3991/ijet.v14i22.11748
17. Elhai, J.D., Dvorak, R.D., Levine, J.C., Hall, B.J.: Problematic smartphone use: a conceptual overview and systematic review of relations with anxiety and depression psychopathology. J. Affect. Disord. **207**, 251–259 (2017). https://doi.org/10.1016/j.jad.2016.08.030
18. Firat, M.: Multitasking or continuous partial attention: a critical bottleneck for digital natives. Turk. Online J. Distance Educ. **14**(1), 1302–6488 (2013)
19. Gikas, J., Grant, M.: Mobile computing devices in higher education: student perspectives on learning with cellphones, smartphones & social media. Internet High. Educ. **19**, 18–26 (2013). https://doi.org/10.1016/j.iheduc.2013.06.002
20. Gilroy, M.: Invasion of the classroom cell phones. Educ. Dig. **69**(6), 56–60 (2004)
21. Griffiths, M.D.: Adolescent mobile phone addiction: a cause for concern. Educ. Health **31**(3), 76–78 (2013)
22. Griffiths, M.D.: Technological addictions. Clin. Psychol. Forum **76**, 14–19 (1995)
23. Hawi, N.S., Samaha, M.: To excel or not to excel: strong evidence on the adverse effect of smartphone addiction on academic performance. Comput. Educ. **98**, 81–89 (2016). https://doi.org/10.1016/j.compedu.2016.03.007
24. Hooper, V, Zhou, Y.: Addictive, dependent, compulsive? A study of mobile phone usage. In 20th Bled eConference eMergence: Mergin and Emerging Technologies, Processes and Institutions, 4–6 June, Bled, Slovenia (2007). https://aisel.aisnet.org/bled2007/38
25. Hossain, M.E., Ahmed, S.Z.: Academic use of smartphones by university students: a developing country perspective. Electron. Libr. **34**(4), 651–665 (2016). https://doi.org/10.1108/EL-07-2015-0112
26. Ipsos. (2018) Russia 2019: The time of adjustments. Ipsos editions November 2018. https://www.ipsos.com/sites/default/files/ct/publication/documents/2018-11/flair_rus sia_2019_ipsos.pdf
27. Jacobsen, W., Forste, R.: The wired generation: academic and social outcomes of electronic media use among university student. Cyberpsychol. Behav. Soc. Netw. **14**(5), 275–280 (2011). https://doi.org/10.1089/cyber.2010.0135

28. Jesse, G.: Like, tweet, or pin: college students and their current use of social media. Issues Inf. Syst. **14**(1), 403–414 (2013)
29. Jones, T.: Students' cell phone addiction and their opinions. Elon J. Undergrad. Res. Commun. **5**(1), 74–80 (2014)
30. Kalogiannakis, M., Papadakis, S.: Combining mobile technologies in environmental education: a Greek case study. Int. J. Mobile Learn. Organ. **11**(2), 108–130 (2017)
31. Karadağ, E., et al.: Determinants of phubbing, which is the sum of many virtual addictions: a structural equation model. J. Behav. Addict. **4**(2), 60–74 (2015). https://doi.org/10.1556/2006.4.2015.005
32. Kuznekoff, J.H., Munz, S., Titsworth, S.: Mobile phones in the classroom: examining the effects of texting, Twitter, and message content on student learning. Commun. Educ. **64**(3), 344–365 (2015). https://doi.org/10.1080/03634523.2015.1038727
33. Kuznekoff, J.H., Titsworth, S.: The impact of mobile phone usage on student learning. Commun. Educ. **62**(3), 233–252 (2013). https://doi.org/10.1080/03634523.2013.767917
34. Kwon, M., Lee, J.-Y., Won, W.-Y., Park, J.-W., Min, J.-A., Hahn, C., et al.: Development and validation of a smartphone addiction scale (SAS). PLoS ONE **8**(2), e56936 (2013). https://doi.org/10.1371/journal.pone.0056936
35. Lepp, A., Barkley, J.E., Karpinski, A.C.: The relationship between cell phone use and academic performance in a sample of US college students. SAGE Open **1**, 1–9 (2015). https://doi.org/10.1177/2158244015573169
36. Leung, L.: Leisure, boredom, sensation seeking, self-esteem, addiction symptoms and patterns of cell phone use. In: Konijn, E.A., Tanis, M.A., Utz, S., Linden, A. (eds.) Mediated Interpersonal Communication, pp. 359–381. Lawrence Erlbaum Associates, Mahwah (2007)
37. McCoy, B.R.: Digital distractions in the classroom phase II: student classroom use of digital devices for non-class related purposes. J. Media Educ. **7**(1), 5–32 (2016)
38. Moreno, M.A., Jelenchick, L.A., Breland, D.J.: Exploring depression and problematic internet use among college females: a multisite study. Comput. Hum. Behav. **49**, 601–607 (2015). https://doi.org/10.1016/j.chb.2015.03.033
39. Ng, S.F., Hassan, N.S.I.C., Nor, N.H.M., Malek, N.A.A.: The relationship between smartphone use and academic performance: a case of students in a Malaysian tertiary institution. Malays. Online J. Educ. Technol. **5**(4), 58–70 (2017)
40. O'Bannon, B.W., Thomas, K.: Teacher perceptions of using mobile phones in the classroom: age matters! Comput. Educ. **74**, 15–25 (2014)
41. Odacı, H.: Academic self-efficacy and academic procrastination as predictors of problematic internet use in university students. Comput. Educ. **57**(1), 1109–1113 (2011). https://doi.org/10.1016/j.compedu.2011.01.005
42. Papadakis, S., Kalogiannakis, M., Sifaki, E., Vidakis, N.: Access Moodle using smart mobile phones. A case study in a Greek University. In: Brooks, A.L., Brooks, E., Vidakis, N. (eds.) ArtsIT/DLI -2017. LNICSSITE, vol. 229, pp. 376–385. Springer, Cham (2018). https://doi.org/10.1007/978-3-319-76908-0_36
43. Poll, H.: Pearson student mobile device survey 2015. National report: College students. (2015). https://www.pearsoned.com/wp-content/uploads/2015-Pearson-Student-Mobile-Device-Survey-College.pdf
44. Przybylski, A.K., Weinstein, N.: Can you connect with me now? How the presence of mobile communication technology influences face-to-face conversation quality. J. Soc. Pers. Relat. **30**(3), 237–246 (2013). https://doi.org/10.1177/0265407512453827
45. Ravizza, S.M., Uitvlugt, M.G., Fenn, K.M.: Logged in and zoned out: how laptop internet use relates to classroom learning. Psychol. Sci. **28**(2), 171–180 (2017). https://doi.org/10.1177/0956797616677314
46. Rean, A.A., Yakunin, V.A.: Techniques for diagnostics of educational motivation of pupils and students. Piter, St. Petersburg (2004) (in Russ.)

47. Roberts, J.A., David, M.E.: My life has become a major distraction from my cell phone: partner phubbing and relationship satisfaction among romantic partners. Comput. Hum. Behav. **54**, 134–141 (2016). https://doi.org/10.1016/j.chb.2015.07.058

48. Samaha, M., Hawi, N.S.: Relationships among smartphone addiction, stress, academic performance, and satisfaction with life. Comput. Hum. Behav. **57**, 321–325 (2016). https://doi.org/10.1016/j.chb.2015.12.045

49. Schneider, F.M., Hitzfeld, S.: I ought to put down that phone but I Phub nevertheless: examining the predictors of phubbing behavior. Soc. Sci. Comput. Rev. **39**, 1–14 (2019). https://doi.org/10.1177/0894439319882365

50. Shafir, M.A.: Analiz sootvetstvij: predstavlenie metoda. Sociologiya: metodologiya, metody', matematicheskoe modelirovanie **28**, 29–44 (2009) (in Russ.)

51. Shambare, R., Rugimbana, R., Zhowa, T.: Are mobile phones the 21th century addiction? Afr. J. Bus. Manag. **6**(2), 573–577 (2012). https://doi.org/10.5897/AJBM11.1940

52. Soldatova, G.U., Rasskazova, E.I.: Excessive use of the Internet: factors and signs. Psihologicheskij zhurnal **34**(4), 105–114 (2013) (in Russ.)

53. Sourial, N., et al.: Correspondence analysis is a useful tool to uncover the relationships among categorical variables. J. Clin. Epidemiol. **63**, 638–646 (2010). https://doi.org/10.1016/j.jcl inepi.2009.08.008

54. Taneja, A., Fiore, V., Fischer, B.: Cyber-slacking in the classroom: potential for digital distraction in the new age. Comput. Educ. **82**, 141–151 (2015). https://doi.org/10.1016/j.com pedu.2014.11.009

55. The University of Sheffield. Student Mobile Device Survey 2011. https://www.sheffield.ac.uk/polopoly_fs/1.103665!/file/mobilesurvey2011.pdf

56. Ugur, N.G., Koc, T.: Time for digital detox: misuse of mobile technology and phubbing. Proc.—Soc. Behav. Sci. **195**, 1022–1031 (2015). https://doi.org/10.1016/j.sbspro.2015.06.491

57. Wood, E., Zivcakova, L., Gentile, P., Archer, K., De Pasquale, D., Nosko, A.: Examining the impact of off-task multitasking with technology on real-time classroom learning. Comput. Educ. **58**(1), 365–374 (2012). https://doi.org/10.1016/j.compedu.2011.08.029

58. Wu, J., Mei, W., Ugrin, J.C.: Student cyberloafing in and out of the classroom in China and the relationship with student performance. Cyberpsychol. Behav. Soc. Netw. **21**(3), 199–204 (2018). https://doi.org/10.1089/cyber.2017.0397

59. Yu, S., Sussman, S.: Does smartphone addiction fall on a continuum of addictive behaviours? Int. J. Environ. Res. Public Health **17**, 422 (2020). https://doi.org/10.3390/ijerph17020422

60. Yunita, A., Nursechafia, N., Setiawan, E., Nugroho, H., Ramadhan, H.: The Relationship between mobile phone usage in classroom and academic achievement in college life. IJIM **12**(8), 96–103 (2018). https://doi.org/10.3991/ijim.v12i8.9530

# Designing Educational Trajectories for Generation Z: Identifying Cognitive Factors

Irina Tolstikova[1]([✉]) [iD], Olga Ignatjeva[2] [iD], Konstantin Kondratenko[2] [iD], and Alexander Pletnev[3] [iD]

[1] ITMO University, St. Petersburg, Russia
[2] SPb University, St. Petersburg, Russia
[3] SPb University of Internal Affairs Ministry, St. Petersburg, Russia

**Abstract.** This article is based on the hypothesis that Generation Z's propensity for undivided perception of digital and physical reality (phygital reality) and their fairly easy absorption of new learning formats, in particular blended learning, are interrelated. To prove the existence of this relationship, the authors, based on the methodology of social constructivism and interpretivism, put forward several hypotheses and conduct an empirical study. For a detailed analysis of the research topic the authors conduct three questionnaire polls among university students in St. Petersburg. The first survey is related to identifying the features of socialization of "digital natives", the second - to identify the cognitive inclinations of Generation Z, the third - the choice of type of education (traditional/classroom, blended or distance learning). The results of the study confirm the main hypotheses of the study, which are that the characteristics of Generation Z make them maximally adapted to blended learning and that the propensity to blended learning is due to a number of factors, such as satisfaction with the content of disciplines, propensity for self-development, satisfaction with the organization of the educational process, work in the specialty after graduation, group work in classes and the use of sources recommended by the teacher. Factor and regression analysis conducted during the study confirms the data obtained.

**Keywords:** Generation Z · Forms of education · Phygital reality · Blended learning cognitive closure

## 1 Introduction

The discussion around the phenomenon of generation Z is reminiscent of scientific debates about new technologies, involving "techno-evangelists" and "technopessimists": either generation Z is perceived by the older generation from the position of Socratic arrogance and condemnation, or the liberal view of Chatsky and Bazarov pins greater hopes on it than on the wiser, but inevitably weaker, older generation. A rational approach requires the researcher to free himself from the "generational" prejudices that abound in popular science and mainstream publications. For example, common prejudices about Generation Z are that this generation is obsessed with gadgets and communicates only

D. A. Alexandrov et al. (Eds.): DTGS 2021, CCIS 1503, pp. 266–279, 2022.
https://doi.org/10.1007/978-3-030-93715-7_19

online, that they are lazy, like to wield their rights, think they know everything, are restless and naïve [1]. In fact, the problem often lies in the method of comparison, an engaged search for an answer to the question of which generation is better. In doing so, it is difficult to abandon the comparison itself, as each generation tries to build its own identity, different from previous generations.

Such a comparison, being rather crude and approximate, indicates to the researcher the surprising similarity between Generation Z and the "baby boomers", which is probably explained by the rejection of the values and attitudes of Millennials, who coincide in age with the older siblings of "digital natives", and Generation X, that is, the generation of Gen Z parents. Firstly, the similarity between the baby boomers and Generation Z is expressed in the active mastery of new communication technologies (television and the Internet, respectively), which makes representatives of both generations quite communicative, open and not indifferent to world events. Secondly, in Russia these are the generations of children born after the catastrophic events of World War II and the 1990s, who experienced more care from the older generations and therefore are more narcissistic and infantile than the other generations. The same events determined the trend of both generations towards "living for pleasure". (generation Z more than any other generation is looking for interesting work that brings satisfaction with life) [2], conservatism and rather low indices of tolerance to uncertainty (more about this will be discussed in the article). In the minds of representatives of generations "baby boomers" and Z there are clear and simple life schemes "study-work-family", excluding chaotic scenarios.

At the same time, identifying the features of Generation Z is not a trivial task at all. Interest in this kind of research is shown by marketers, medics, political scientists trying to understand a new type of voter, employee, specialist. In this article we are interested in a new type of student, living simultaneously in digital and physical reality, interested in world events and considering education as a part of professional path. The new requirements of Generation Z representatives to the educational process are likely to change the system of higher education itself.

## 2 Literature Review

The study of the characteristics of generations, specific conditions of their socio-cultural existence, the problems of forming new educational trajectories for each stage of the generational scale has its own history and theoretical foundations. Among them are the theory of cognitive development by Swiss psychologist J. Piaget [3], ways of learning (teaching cultures) in pre-figurative cultures by American anthropologist, cultural scientist, etiologist M. Mead, American Myers-Briggs personality typology, type indicator [4–6]. Russian pedagogy and psychology also had their own scientific approaches (social constructivism of L.S. Vygotsky, studies of psychologist B.G. Ananyev [7] as well as A.N. Leontiev, A.R. Luria, A.V. Zaporozhets, L.I. Bozhovich, P.Y. Halperin, P.I. Zinchenko and others) since the late 19th century.

In the late twentieth century a programmatic work on generational issues was published by American scholars N. Howe and W. Strauss, Generations: A History of America's Future. 1584–2069» [8]. The authors concluded that the system of values was formed not only in the family, but also under the influence of social life and the whole context of the social environment in which a child grows up, i.e. external events. As a result, they created an internationally recognized typology of the generations of the American nation. In the 21st century the generational theme and its specifics, characterizing the inclusion in the socio-cultural horizon of young representatives of Generation Z and even the rising representatives of Generation Alpha, was developed in the works of D. Tapscott [9], M. Prensky [10], M. Bauerlein [11], N. Carr [12, 13], G. Small and G. Vorgan [14], D. Stillman [15] and etc. Canadian scientist D. Tapscott introduced the concept of "network generation" (NET-generation or N-generation), the term "generation Alpha" was coined in 2005 by a scientist from Australia M. McCrindle [16], doing research on the first digital generation of the XXI century. The first digital generation and its trends are also addressed by J. Palfrey and W. Gasser [17]. The well-known statement about the distinctive feature of the new generation, "that the new generation sees no difference at all between the virtual and the real" is due to a new kind of interaction - Phygital as a union of two realities - physical (Physics) and digital (Digital), and Generation Z is called the phygital generation (although the vast synonymy "Generation Z" also reflects other characteristics of Generation Z) [18, 19]. «Among the specific features: non-linearity, the ability to transmit voluminous multidimensional information available at any time in any place, and not only for perception, but also for further transmission of che-verse posts, storis, live broadcasts, etc.» [20]. As Anne Kingston quotes M. McCrindle, "This is the most connected, educated and sophisticated generation in history...They don't just imagine the future, they create it." Back in 2014 McCrindle, declared the leader of Generation Z: "Where Generation Z goes, our world goes." [21].

In the Russian classification proposed by M.R. Miroshkina, generations of the XXI. Have alternative names associated with the specifics of Russian state development: X, Y, Z - generation of perestroika, First non-Soviet generation, Digital generation, "Putin" generation.

Ten years ago Tapscott said that they "spend their time searching, reading, researching, identifying, collaborating, and organizing. The Internet is turning life into a constant mass collaboration, which this generation loves madly. They can't even imagine a life in which citizens don't have the tools to critically reflect, share points of view, clarify, identify or expose deception. If their parents were passive recipients of information, young people are active creators of media content and have a passion for interaction" [22, p. 146]. Accordingly, a flexible educational strategy, adjusting the educational process to each learner, the successful application of blended learning, is caused by these characteristics of Generation Z. In Russian literature these issues are considered by M.R. Miroshkina [23], V.A. Mazilov [24]; factors determining the specifics of Generation Z are defined in the work of N.V. Bogacheva and E.V. Sivak "Myths about Generation Z" [25] and allow agreeing with the conclusions of J.V. Coates "that creation of curricula, which focus on the student's ability to act effectively with the world - the key to success in the XXI century" [26] and M. Kaku's thesis [27] about the important role of motivated self-education in the learning process due to a clearly expressed orientation to "useful" knowledge by Generation Z. As Demetrius Harrison writes: "As #Gen Z reaches adulthood, they're seeking opportunities that will guide them into a better future. Saying this, 82% believe attending university is the most ideal way to get there. However, the global student debt crisis is frightening our youngest generation from putting their great potential to use" [28].

## 3 Theoretical Grounding and Methodology

In 2020, an intercollegiate team of authors continued the research on the social and psychological characteristics of Generation Z, which began in 2019. The results of the first phase of the study were published in the article Generation Z and Its Value Transformations: Digital Reality Vs. Phygital Interaction (DTGS-2020) [18]. The mentioned article contains the analysis of specifics of generation Z and their perceptions by generation Y. The same theoretical paradigm as in the first stage was chosen to construct the research design and interpret the results obtained. It is social constructivism of P. Berger and T. Lukman. Interpretativism was used as an epistemological orientation, which implies inductive data collection followed by theory building.

The purpose of this study was to identify the educational preferences of Generation Z. In order to realize this goal, three questionnaire surveys were conducted among university students in St. Petersburg in the fall of 2020. You can find them here https://vk.com/sociologica?w=wall-4718166_108%2Fall. The first survey was aimed at identifying the features of Z socialization. The sample was 201 respondents (17 years old – 5%, 18 y.o. – 37.8%, 19 y.o. – 36.3%, 20 y.o. – 20.9%). Next, using the questionnaire of the social psychologist A. Kruglanski tested cognitive inclinations of Generation Z representatives. The original sample of 184 people was reduced to 146 people, taking into account the lie criterion. Finally, the third questionnaire consisted of 184 respondents (17 y.o. – 4.3%, 18 y.o. – 38.6%, 19 y.o. – 39.7%, 20 y.o. – 17.4%) and was aimed at identifying the preference of this generation in relation to the choice of the type of education (traditional/academic, mixed or distance). The samples were representative and corresponded to the gender structure of the Russian population between the ages of 15 and 19, i.e. 51% women and 49% men [29].

The forced use of the blended learning model in 2020 as a result of the COVID-19 pandemic showed its effectiveness with regard to generational characteristics. In this regard, two hypotheses have been formulated, the validity of which has been proven in this study.

H1: Generation Z characteristics make it best suited for blended learning.
H2: The propensity for blended learning is due to a number of factors which were to be revealed in the study.

These hypotheses are tested using frequency and factor analysis using SPSS and logistic regression using the R programming language.

## 4 Analysis of the Results of Empirical Research

An important part of the study was to examine the socialization of Generation Z in connection with the influence of educational institutions, namely universities. This means that the study included representatives of half a percent of high school graduates entering universities in 2020. But a considerable part of young people do not plan to get higher education immediately after school. According to the results of the VTsIOM survey in 2020, 54% of graduates declared their desire to receive a higher education immediately after school, 14% of graduates do not intend to enter a university [30].

One of the questionnaires offered to the respondents was aimed at revealing the peculiarities of constructing the life world by representatives of the phygital generation. Another questionnaire was aimed at studying cognitive abilities of Generation Z with the help of a questionnaire developed by American social psychologist A. Kruglanski [31]. And, finally, the third questionnaire was devoted to studying the perception of education by this age group. The empirical data obtained largely do not correspond to the negative image of Generation Z, which can be found in the public discourse and in many scientific publications [25].

The results of the study of students' cognitive closure revealed approximately equal numbers of respondents with high (54%) and low (46%) need for cognitive closure (values obtained by comparing the indicators with the median value of 121). In general, this suggests that half of the students show distinct tendencies to epistemic curiosity - both in terms of interest in knowledge and in terms of deprivation, i.e. through bridging the knowledge gap and implementing the acquired knowledge in practice, in particular, receiving material rewards. The data upon factors were distributed as follows (See Table 1):

**Table 1.** Factors affecting the level of cognitive closure

| Factors | Mean |
|---|---|
| Order | 36,6 |
| Predictability | 29,58 |
| Decisiveness | 26,41 |
| Ambiguity | 33,72 |
| Closeness | 22,6 |

The decisiveness factor was not used in the final processing of the data, because a negative correlation between this factor and other indicators was found. The highest indicators are inclination to order and aversion to ambiguity, which, perhaps, speaks to the specificity of representatives of Generation Z, who do not want to accept the disorderliness of reality. These attitudes at the same time constitute a curious synthesis with a low index of closed consciousness, which indicates a high desire of students to acquire new knowledge in an orderly, understandable for them way. The process of learning is thus perceived by students not as an encounter with new, shocking and surprising experiences, but as an opportunity to satisfy their curiosity and to be rewarded financially in the future.

Generation Z demonstrates an independent position, which leads them to focus on active action in getting an education and building a career. The overwhelming majority of young people (79.3%) consider higher education as the basis on which they should subsequently acquire new professional knowledge. Part of this knowledge is the knowledge of English, which more than half of the respondents (56%) intend to learn on their own or through courses. Another 32% of respondents will improve their level of English in their university curriculum. 7% of respondents are satisfied with their knowledge of English, only 3% do not intend to learn English in the future. Thus, 88% of the respondents will make some efforts to improve their level of English.

Representatives of Generation Z are practical, they value education as the first part of building a career, and they tend to value knowledge that can be directly applied to professional activities. Answering the question about what they expect from studying at university, 38% indicated that they expect to get a profession in demand, and 19% are studying for a state diploma. Sixteen percent of respondents expect to gain research experience in higher education. For 13% of respondents studying at university is primarily an opportunity to make new friends, and for 11% it is a period of bright student life. As a result, 73% of the respondents have pragmatic expectations for their studies and only 23% have hedonistic expectations.

These empirical data refute the negative perceptions, common in everyday discourse and scientific literature, of Generation Z as people with a minimal planning horizon and little interest in learning. University education is presented to Generation Z as a tool for building a career, getting a lucrative and joyful job.

Generation Z demonstrates flexibility, adaptability, the ability to quickly master new technologies and respond to changes in public life. This is reflected in the propensity of this generation to choose blended learning. Blended learning [32] - this term refers to the learning process that uses different event-oriented methods and learning management schemes, such as face-to-face learning, distance learning (asynchronous distance learning) and online learning (synchronous distance learning). Learning is built on the interaction of the student not only with the computer, but also with the teacher in an active form (face-to-face and distance learning), when the studied material is summarized, analyzed and used to solve the tasks [33]. Respondents were asked whether the blended learning model is more effective than the traditional one. Half of the respondents (50.5%) called blended learning more effective, inclined to this opinion 31.5%. 12.5% of respondents are inclined to consider blended education rather ineffective, and only 3.8% consider the blended model ineffective. For Generation Z, virtuality is becoming relevant, which demonstrates the demand to incorporate more elements of digital technology and augmented reality, social media and the inclusion of education in virtual space into the educational process. Therefore, the frequency analysis of questionnaire upon educational preferences confirmed statement in the hypothesis 1.

The next part of research provided testing and confirmation of the hypothesis 2. To identify the latent factors that unite the observed variables, characterizing the conditions of the choice of blended learning, a factor analysis was conducted using the statistical package SPSS[1]. For factor analysis, the variables were transformed into binary variables according to the principle 1 - the quality under study is present and is in the focus of the researcher's attention, 0 - the quality under study is weakly expressed or absent. As

---

[1] Factor analysis using the SPSS statistical package.

noted above, the data obtained from a sociological survey of university students in St. Petersburg in the fall of 2020 was used in conducting the factor analysis.

Preliminary testing of the data has shown that these data can be used for factor analysis. To characterize the data, we use the measure of sample adequacy of Kaiser-Meier-Olkin and Bartlett's sphericity criterion. The first indicator is 0.601, thus approaching to one, which is an indicator of the quality of this criterion. The second criterion has statistical significance at the level of 0.001, which means that correlations in the correlation matrix are statistically significantly different from zero, and the matrix is quite suitable for factor analysis. The results of factor analysis are presented in Table 2.

**Table 2.**  Component matrix after rotation

| | Components | | | | |
|---|---|---|---|---|---|
| | 1 | 2 | 3 | 4 | 5 |
| Satisf_discipline | ,708 | | | | ,306 |
| Self-development | ,636 | | | | |
| Satisf_education | ,583 | ,306 | | ,373 | |
| Work_plan | ,537 | | | | |
| Ind_trajectory | | ,753 | | | |
| Distant2020 | | ,638 | | ,339 | |
| Ed_policy_satif. | | ,625 | | | |
| Employer_policy | | | ,822 | | |
| Ed_for_work | | | ,771 | | |
| Group_work | | | | ,762 | |
| Teacher_books | | | | ,580 | |
| Personal_contats | | | | | ,836 |

The factor analysis revealed five latent factors that determine the choice of blended learning. Each factor included a variable with a factor load greater than 0.4. Each of the five factors included loadings with the same positive sign, which will play an important role in the regression analysis on the selected factors.

The first factor can be designated as "Vocational orientation" because it includes the observed variables "Satisfaction with the content of disciplines", "Self-development tendency", "Satisfaction with the organization of the educational process", "Work in the specialty after graduation".

The next factor can be defined as "Free choice", i.e. the choice conditioned by the internal and external environment of the educational process. It includes such variables as "Choice of individual trajectory", "Satisfaction with pandemic distance learning", "Satisfaction with state educational policy".

The third factor can be defined as "Unity of university and business goals", expressed as interaction of universities and employers, i.e. in education and employment. This factor includes observed variables "Cooperation of universities with employers", "Influence of quality of education on getting a prestigious job".

The fourth factor "Professional communication" is related to the organization of the learning process and includes the variables "Group work in class" and "Use of sources recommended by the teacher".

The fifth factor "Soft Skills" (Emotional Intelligence) consists of one variable "Forming Personal Contacts in the Learning Process".

A preliminary check of the data used in the twelve initial variables shows that there are no outliers in them. The data used in the identified factors ("Vocational orientation", "Free choice", "Unity of university and business goals", "Professional communication" and "Soft skills") are obtained as a result of factor analysis and are standardized values with mean zero and standard deviation one. This point will play an important role in the interpretation of the resulting regression model.

To identify factors (predictors) that are significant for the selection of a blended learning model, we use a logistic regression model based on a binomial distribution. When building a regression model, we use the R programming language, the statistical packages of which allow us to increase the accuracy of regression coefficient estimation and visualize both the diagnostics of the built models and the results of multiple regression analysis more clearly than SPSS.

Our task is to check whether the factors we have identified are significant and how they affect the dependent variable in question. As a result of a series of iterations in R, the logistic regression model converged to the following parameters (coefficient estimates), shown in Table 3.

**Table 3.** Results of logistic regression for binary data

| Predictors | Estimates | Std. error | z value[2] | p-level |
|---|---|---|---|---|
| Intercept | 1.75505 | 0.22879 | 7.671 | 1.71e−14*** |
| Vocational orientation (FAC1_1) | 0.06906 | 0.18857 | 0.366 | 0.71419 |
| Free choice (FAC2_1) | 0.67932 | 0.19715 | 3.446 | 0.00057*** |
| Unity of university and business goals (FAC3_1) | 0.01578 | 0.20304 | 0.078 | 0.93804 |
| Professional communication (FAC4_1) | 0.52901 | 0.21008 | 2.518 | 0.01180* |
| Soft skills (FAC5_1) | −0.21121 | 0.20531 | −1.029 | 0.30358 |

Thus, the results shown in Table 3 show that only 2 factors ("Vocational orientation" and "Professional communication") are statistically significant. Based on these data, we can write down the resulting logistic regression equation:

Efficiency of blended learning~Binomial (n = 1, $\pi$i)

---

[2] Wald's Z-test is an analogue of Student's t-test for testing parameters in linear regression models.

E (Efficiency of blended learning) = πi

The logit link function translates probabilities into logits when interpreting regression coefficients.

$$Ln\left(\frac{\pi i}{1 - \pi i}\right) = \eta i$$

$$\eta i = 1.74 + 0.68 * FAC2\_1 + 0.54 * FAC4\_1 \qquad (1)$$

Checking of the obtained model for compliance with the conditions of applicability according to the residuals graph (Fig. 1) shows that there is no heterogeneity of dispersion, i.e. the ratio of dispersion to mean in this model is approximately equal to one. Checking the model for multicollinearity using the variance inflation factor shows that this factor does not exceed two, so the condition of no collinearity (i.e. no mutual influence) of the predictors is also satisfied. The observations are independent of each other, which is determined by the data collection design. The relationship of the dependent variable with the independent variables is linear, taking into account the linking logit-function.

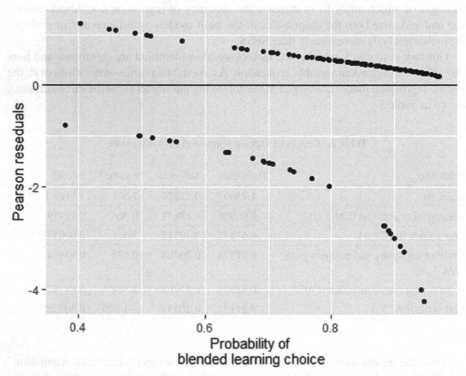

**Fig. 1.** Residuals graph for logistic regression

The model of logistic regression shows that there is a direct relationship between the factors "FAC2_1", "FAC4_1" and the dependent variable "Efficiency of blended learning". At the same time, the factor "FAC2_1" has the greatest influence on the dependent variable, as it has the largest coefficient value. The graphs in Fig. 2 demonstrate the nature of the relationship, represented by the logistic curve, between the probability of blended learning model efficiency and the individual independent variables (factors). The full set of factors (independent variables) is used to visualize the relationship for each graph. However, due to the fact that we are limited to two-dimensional visualization, one independent variable is highlighted on the graph, while the other independent variables are averaged.

As noted above, the factor values for each observation are estimated values and represent standardized data with a mean of zero and standard deviation of one. Figure 2 shows that when the independent variable changes by one standard deviation with a positive sign, the probability of the efficiency of the blended learning model increases in all graphs. However, in the case of the factors "FAC2_1", "FAC4_1" the function saturates between the first and second standard deviation with positive sign, and grows slower. This means that a significant investment in the implementation of this educational model becomes a less effective measure for attracting students at a certain stage. When the values of the independent variable deviate to the negative side, the probability of blended learning model efficiency decreases for all of the identified factors.

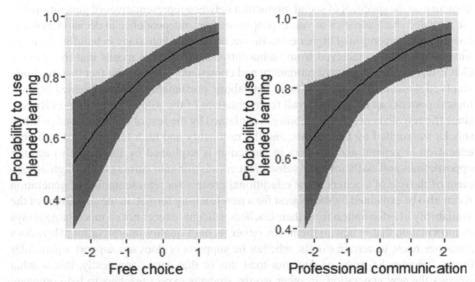

**Fig. 2.** Resulting graphs of the dependence of the probability of effective implementation of the blended learning model from the independent variables (factors)

Interpretation of model coefficients allows us to state that if independent variable "FAC2_1" increases by one unit, the probability of effective implementation of blended learning model increases by 1.96 times, and if independent variable "FAC4_1" increases by one unit, the probability of effective implementation of model increases by 1.71 times. To get corresponding results, we raise Euler's number (2.71) to the power corresponding to the size of the coefficient at the independent variable, for example, 2.71 is raised to the power of 0.68 at "FAC2_1" factor and we get the value 1.96, which means that when this independent increases by one the probability of effective implementation of this educational model increases almost twofold.

Thus, the attractiveness of the blended learning model is due to the freedom to choose the format of learning, as well as the preservation of the possibility of traditional building communication with the student group and the teacher. In addition, professional socialization and career development for representatives of Generation Z is a single process. They are not inclined to consider studying as a period when it is possible to have a good time or to gain knowledge about the world. Learning for them is an opportunity to gain knowledge and skills that can be applied immediately and directly. Generation Z appreciates virtual technology, but it is much more conservative than is commonly believed. For the digital generation, the authority of university professors and serious scientific literature remains of great importance.

## 5   Discussion, Conclusion and Outlook

Based on the study, several important conclusions can be drawn regarding the characteristics of socialization, cognitive inclinations and preferences of representatives of generation Z in relation to the choice of the type of education. Thus, the result of a questionnaire on the specifics of social interaction between representatives of generation Z is the revealed characteristics of young people, such as independence in decision-making, consistency, perception of higher education as an intermediate stage in building a career, trust in information received from authoritative sources. This means that the average Gen Z has a tendency toward rationality and consistency; despite the fact that the study involved students of universities in St. Petersburg, presumably that the obtained psychological portrait can be applied to all representatives of the studied generation in Russia, since the revealed craving for stability is explained by the fear of economic and political shocks transmitted by the parents, and the rationality and high level of trust in higher education in general and teachers in particular is explained by the desire to acquire opportunities and skills for their subsequent conversion into earnings. The high assessment of the role of teachers in the educational process for representatives of generation Z can also be explained by the request for a new teaching format: in the conditions of the availability of information from their teachers, students expect not so much large arrays of information that is new to them, but rather its high-quality interpretation. How does a teacher relate to certain events, whether he supports or does not support a particular theory, whether he trusts or does not trust this or that data - apparently, this is what worries the new generation. In other words, students expect teachers to help organize the multiple streams of information.

Probably, the desire for economic stability and self-development significantly influenced the results of the study of cognitive closure of representatives of generation Z. The percentage of respondents with a high and low need for cognitive closure was approximately the same. At the same time, the factors that have a greater influence on cognitive closeness turned out to be precisely those that are associated with stability and avoidance of uncertainty in the general picture of the world. Gen Z's cognitive attitudes vary, but they are in any case rooted in cognitive schemas that focus on consistency and fear of social change.

A study of the factors that determine the choice of students in a blended learning format showed that the overwhelming majority of students support a blended learning format, while among the factors studied by a team of authors, the most significant were the freedom to choose the learning format and a high level of professional communication. The choice factor had the greatest influence on the dependent variable, since it combined the components of the individuality of learning, as well as satisfaction with the education system in general and the organization of distance education in particular. However, the factor of professional communication also turned out to be significant, since it is this factor that most reflects vertical and horizontal ties in the educational process. Probably, the factors identified are based on trust in the education system and a particular university, as well as the strength of social ties, i.e. social capital, understood in both a narrow and a broad sense, but a detailed study of this topic is the task of future research.

**Acknowledgement.** The study was conducted under support the "Center for Sociological and Internet Research at SPBU Science Park" resource center (the project No. 106-14771). This work was financially supported by the Russian Scientific Foundation, grant No. 19-18-00210 "Political ontology of digitalization: a study of the institutional foundations of digital formats of state governance".

# References

1. Oesch, T.: 5 Myths About Generation Z: Managing and Training the Digital Natives. https://trainingindustry.com/articles/workforce-development/5-myths-about-genera tion-z-managing-and-training-the-digital-natives/. Accessed 29 Jan 2021
2. Ozkan, M., Solmaz, B.: The changing face of the employees – generation Z and their perceptions of work. Proc. Econ. Finance **26**, 476–483 (2015)
3. Piaget, J.: Psikhologiya intellekta [The Psychology of Intelligence]. Piter, Saint Petersburg (2004). (In Russian)
4. Boyle, G.J.: Myers-Briggs Type Indicator (MBTI): some psychometric limitations. Aust. Psyhol. **30**(1), 71–74 (1995). https://doi.org/10.1111/j.1742-9544.1995.tb01750.x
5. Woods, R.A.: Myers Brigg. StatPearls [Internet]. Treasure Island (FL): StatPearls Publishing (2020). https://pubmed.ncbi.nlm.nih.gov/32119483/. Accessed 29 Jan 2021
6. Majers, I., Majers, P.: Opredelenie tipov. U kazhdogo svoj dar [Gifts Differing: Understanding Personality Type]. Business psychology, Moscow (2010)
7. Ananiev, B.G.: Izbranny'e trudy' po psikhologii. V dvukh tomakh. Tom 1–2 [Selected Works on Psychology Volume 1–2]. SPBU, Saint Petersburg (2007). (in Russian)
8. Strauss, W., Howe, N.: Generations: The History of America's Future, 1584 to 2069. Morrow, New York (1991)
9. Tapscott, D.: Grown up Digital: How the Net Generation is Changing Your World. McGraw-Hill, New York (2008)
10. Prensky, M.: Digital Natives, Digital Immigrants. From On the Horizon 9(5), MCB University Press. Bingley (2001). http://www.marcprensky.com/writing/Prensky%20-%20Digital%20N atives,%20Digital%20Immigrants%20-%20Part1.pdf. Accessed 29 Jan 2021
11. Bauerlein, M.: The Dumbest Generation: How the Digital Age Stupefies Young Americans and Jeopardizes Our Future (Or, Don't Trust Anyone Under 30), 1st edn. Tarcher, New York (2009)

12. Carr, N.: Is Google Making Us Stupid? What the Internet is doing to our brains. www.theatl antic.com/magazine/archive/2008/07/is-google-making-us-stupid/306868. Accessed 29 Jan 2021
13. Carr, N.: The Shallows: What the Internet is Doing to Our Brains. W. W. Norton and Co., New York (2010)
14. Small, G., Vorgan, G.: iBrain: Surviving the Technological Alteration of the Modern Mind. HarperCollins Publishers, New York (2008). www.harpercollins.com/browseinside/index. aspx?isbn13=9780061340338. Accessed 29 Jan 2021
15. Stillman, D.: Pokolenie Z na rabote. Kak ego ponyat' i najti s nim obshhij yazy'k [Generation Z at work. How to understand him and find a common language with him]. Mann, Ivanov and Ferber, Moscow (2018). (in Russian)
16. McCrindle, M., Fell, A.: Understanding Generation Alpha. McCrindle Research, Norwest (2020). https://www.researchgate.net/publication/342803353_UNDERSTANDING_G ENERATION_ALPHA. Accessed 29 Jan 2021
17. Palffrey, J., Gasser, U.: Deti cifrovoj e'ry' [Digital age children]. Exmo, Moscow (2011)
18. Tolstikova, I., Ignatjeva, O., Kondratenko, K., Pletnev, A.: Generation Z and its value transformations: digital reality vs. phygital interaction. In: Alexandrov, D.A., Boukhanovsky, A.V., Chugunov, A.V., Kabanov, Y., Koltsova, O., Musabirov, I. (eds.) DTGS 2020. CCIS, vol. 1242, pp. 47–60. Springer, Cham (2020). https://doi.org/10.1007/978-3-030-65218-0_4
19. The Screen Age. https://www.washingtonpost.com/sf/style/2016/05/25/13-right-now-this-is-what-its-like-to-grow-up-in-the-age-of-likes-lols-and-longing/?utm_term=.f7f060c89a1b. Accessed 29 Jan 2021
20. Mamina, R.I., Toistikova, I.I.: Pokolencheskaja problematika v cifrovuju jepohu: filosofskaja proekcija [Generational issues in the digital age: philosophical projection]. Discourse 5(6), 29–41 (2019). https://doi.org/10.32603/2412-8562-2019-5-6-29-41. (in Russian)
21. Kingston, A.: Get ready for Generation Z, July 2014. https://www.macleans.ca/society/life/get-ready-for-generation-z/. Accessed 29 Jan 2021
22. Tapscott, D., Williams, A.D.: Vikinomika. Kak massovoe sotrudnichestvo izmenyaet vse [Wikinomics: How Mass Collaboration Changes Everything]. BestBusinessBooks, Moscow (2009). (in Russian)
23. Miroshkina, M.R.: Interpretaczii teorii pokolenij v kontekste rossijskogo obrazovaniya [Interpretations of generational theory in the context of Russian education]. In: Yaroslavskij pedagogicheskij vestnik [Yaroslavl Pedagogical Bulletin], no. 6, pp. 30–35 (2017). (in Russian)
24. Mazilov, V.A.: Innovaczii v sovremennom obrazovanii: psikhologiya vs pedagogika [Innovations in modern education: psychology vs pedagogy]. In: Yaroslavskij pedagogicheskij vestnik [Yaroslavl Pedagogical Bulletin], no. 1, pp. 8–22 (2018). (in Russian)
25. Bogacheva, N.V., Sivak, E.V.: Mify' o «pokolenii Z» [Myths about the "generation Z"]. In: Sovremennaya analitika obrazovaniya [Modern analytics of education], vol. 22, no. 1, pp. 1–64 (2019). (in Russian)
26. Coats, J.: Pokoleniya i stili obucheniya [Generation and Learning Styles]. MAPDO, Moscow (2011).(in Russian)
27. Kaku, M.: Fizika budushhego [Physics of the future]. Alpina, Moscow (2012).(in Russian)
28. Harrison, D.: Generation Z Is Changing How We Approach University, March 2020. https://www.fenews.co.uk/fevoices/43807-generation-z-is-changing-how-we-approach-university. Accessed 29 Jan 2021
29. Naselenie Rossii po polu i vozrastu: statistika, raspredelenie [Russian population by gender and age: statistics, distribution], http://www.statdata.ru/nasel_pol_vozr. Accessed 09 June 2021. (in Russian)

30. % vy'pusknikov srazu posle shkoly' khotyat pojti rabotat' [14% of graduates immediately after school want to go to work], June 2020. https://russiaedu.ru/news/14-vypusknikov-srazu-posle-shkoly-khotiat-poiti-rabotat. Accessed 29 Jan 2021. (in Russian)
31. Kruglanski, A.W., Webster, D.M.: Motivated closing of the mind: seizing and freezing. Psychol. Rev. **103**(2), 263–283 (1996). https://doi.org/10.1037/0033-295X.103.2.263
32. Dolgova, T.V.: Smeshannoe obuchenie–innovacziya XXI veka [Blended learning-innovation of the XXI century], January 2017. https://interactiv.su/2017/12/31/%D1%81%D0%BC%D0%B5%D1%88%D0%B0%D0%BD%D0%BD%D0%BE%D0%B5-%D0%BE%D0%B1%D1%83%D1%87%D0%B5%D0%BD%D0%B8%D0%B5-%D0%B8%D0%BD%D0%BD%D0%BE%D0%B2%D0%B0%D1%86%D0%B8%D1%8F-xxi-%D0%B2%D0%B5%D0%BA%D0%B0/. Accessed 29 Jan 2021. (in Russian)
33. Tapscott, D.: Educating the net generation. Educ. Leadersh. **56**(5), 6–11 (1999)

# Attitudes Towards Digital Educational Technologies, Academic Motivation and Academic Achievements Among Russian University Students

Irina Novikova(✉) 🆔 and Polina Bychkova 🆔

Peoples' Friendship University of Russia (RUDN University), 6 Miklukho-Maklaya Str., 117198 Moscow, Russia
novikova-ia@rudn.ru

**Abstract.** The purpose of present research is to reveal and compare the relationship of attitudes towards the digital educational technologies (DET) with academic motivation and academic achievements in Russian university students. The sample includes 173 (61% - female) first- and second-year university students of different fields of study (Natural Sciences, Medicine, and Psychology). To determine the motivation of students' educational activity, the "Academic motivation scales" questionnaire by T.O. Gordeeva et al. was used. To diagnose students' attitudes towards DET, the authors' questionnaire was developed. GPA was used to assess the academic achievements of last academic year. The descriptive statistics methods, coefficients Cronbach' α and McDonald's ω, the Spearman's correlation analysis, and factor analysis (Varimax) were used for statistical analysis. Statistical processing was carried out in the R software environment for statistical computing and graphics, version 3.6.1., psych package version 1.9.6. Findings of our research showed that university students with more pronounced intrinsic academic motivation are more involved in the digital space in general and more involved in the use of DET, while more amotivated students, on the contrary, less involved in the digital space and in the use of DET. At the same time, higher performing students tend to be more involved in the digital space in general. However, there is a specificity of these relations in students from different field of study. The obtained data must be taken into account when DET are implemented in the educational programs for students of different fields of study, based on their psychological characteristics.

**Keywords:** Digital educational technologies · University students · Attitudes towards digital educational technologies · Academic motivation · Academic achievements

## 1 Introduction

In recent decades, the problems on development and implementation of the digital educational technologies (DET) constantly have been at the focus of numerous discussions among teachers, psychologists, sociologists, physicians, etc. In this regard, numerous

D. A. Alexandrov et al. (Eds.): DTGS 2021, CCIS 1503, pp. 280–293, 2022.
https://doi.org/10.1007/978-3-030-93715-7_20

studies have been carried out on DET types [2, 12, 22, 36], their particularities [1, 12, 29], opportunities and limitations [4, 7], the impact of DET on the educational process [11, 17] and psychological characteristics of students [31], the use DET during lectures for non-academic purpose [5, 37], etc.

The COVID-19 pandemic simultaneously made DET an essential part of contemporary social life around the world and at all levels of education. This fact has led to both a sharp increase in the number of research on this problem [8, 10, 18, 20, 23, 34, 35, 41], and to intensification of discussions about the "pros" and "cons" of DET, not only in the scientific and pedagogical communities, but also in political and public discourses [19, 25, 30, 32, 40, 42, 44]. First of all, main goals of these investigations and discussions are the issues of teachers' readiness/unreadiness for the transition to DET [25, 42, 44], students and teachers' contentment/discontentment with this process [20, 30, 32, 35], students' acceptance E-Learning [34, 41], impact of remote learning on students' mental health and stress during COVID-19 pandemic [8, 18, 23], students' online learning motivation during COVID-19 [9, 16].

However, both before and during the COVID-19 pandemic, much less attention is paid to the study of the psychological and personality characteristics of students and teachers, which can mediate their attitude towards DET and the effectiveness of its use in teaching and learning. In our opinion, taking into account such psychological factors can help to make optimal the inevitable implementation of DET into educational process for all its participants.

*Digital technologies* in general are a discrete system built on methods of encoding and transferring information, which makes it possible to solve many diverse problems in the shortest possible time intervals [2]. Accordingly, as suggested Anurova [2], *digital educational technologies (DET)* today are a tool for the effective delivery of information and knowledge to students, the development of educational materials, an effective way of teaching, the creation of a new educational environment: developing and technological [2]. We agree that DET can be the effective methods, tools and mechanisms in teaching and learning, but this depends on a large number of social, pedagogical, psychological and other factors.

In recent decades, among the psychological factors associated with DET, the influence of digital technologies and devices on children and students' cognitive processes is primarily investigated [3, 21, 38]. In particular, changes in higher mental functions (memory, attention and thinking) are being studied [38], also the phenomenon of "clip thinking" has been widely discussed [3, 21]. In addition, attempts are being made to investigate social psychological and personality characteristics of students and teachers in the context of DET implementation and use [24, 26]. For example, A. Mustafina [24] studied teachers' attitudes toward digital technology integration at Kazakhstani secondary school [24]. This research revealed that teachers' self-confidence was positively correlated with attitudes toward digital technology integration in education [24]. T.A. Nestik et al. [26] investigated the psychological predictors of the attitudes to new technologies. The results of the study showed that the key factor of adopting new digital technologies is the involvement of the individual in communication with other users. The predictors of 'techno-optimism' are trust in the stakeholders of technological progress, orientation towards the future, beliefs in rewards for efforts, low religiosity and a low level of respect for authorities. At the same time, the individuals' attitude towards scientific and technological progress and their orientation towards the future are less significant predictors of using new technologies than the orientation towards getting pleasure in the present, the attractiveness of digital technology and ease of its use [26].

In our previous research, we studied relations between psychological features and attitude to DET in Russian university students [6, 27, 28]. First of all, we found that there is a specificity of attitude towards DET in Russian university students from different field of study [27]. As was expected, natural sciences students had better attitudes towards DET than medical and psychology students, while medical students had worse attitudes towards DET than students of other fields of study. However, psychological students have the lowest indicator of digital competence [27]. We suppose that this difference is associated with the peculiarities of the learning process and the future professional activities of studied students. It is obvious that natural sciences students most actively interact with DET both in the learning process and in their practical activities. Our further research revealed that the Five Factor Model (FFM) personality traits are associated with attitudes towards DET [28]. Extraversion and openness to experience from FFM personality traits are most closely related to attitudes towards DET in university students, but there is a specificity of these relations in students from different field of study. The attitudes towards DET in the natural sciences and psychological students are more closely related with the FFM personality traits than in medical students [28].

We believe that it is necessary to study other psychological factors that may be associated with attitudes towards DET in university students. The obtained data must be taken into account when DET are included in the educational programs for students of different fields of study, based their psychological and personality characteristics.

One of the most important factors determining the educational activities and academic achievements of students is academic motivation [9, 14–16]. T.O. Gordeeva et al. proposed a comprehensive model of academic motivation, which includes seven types of motivation: three types of intrinsic motivation (intrinsic cognition, achievement, and personal growth), three types of extrinsic motivation (motivation for self-respect, introjected, and external regulation), and an amotivation. T.O. Gordeeva et al. developed "Academic motivation scales" questionnaire for diagnosing these types of academic motivation [13]. Subsequently, the authors showed that different types of academic motivation are predictors of academic performance among high school and university students [15].

However, there are no studies on the relationship between attitudes towards DET, on the one hand, with academic motivation, and on the other hand, with academic achievements in Russian university students. Therefore, *the purpose of present research* is to reveal and compare the relationship of attitudes towards DET with academic motivation and academic achievements among students of different fields of study (Natural Sciences, Medicine, and Psychology).

Based on the literature review, and above all on the previous studies by Gordeeva et al. [14, 15], Nestyk et al.[26], and Novikova et al. [27, 28], we assume that:

1) There are correlations between indicators of attitudes towards DET and scales of academic motivation: university students with more pronounced intrinsic motivation

have more positive attitudes towards DET, and, conversely, students with more pronounced extrinsic motivation and amotivation have more negative attitudes towards DET;

2) There are positive correlations between indicators of attitudes towards DET and academic achievements in university students;

3) There are specific features of the relationship of attitudes towards DET with scales of academic motivation and indicator of academic achievements among students of different fields of study: studied variables are least closely related in the medical students, and most closely related in the natural science students.

## 2 Materials and Methods

*Participants.* A total of 173 (105 female and 67 male) university students, aged 17 to 26 (the mean is 18.67 years) took part in the research. All of them were first- and second-year students of three large Moscow universities (Peoples' Friendship University of Russia (RUDN University), National University of Science and Technology (NUST) MISiS, and Pirogov Russian National Research Medical University (RNIMU University)). The students represent different departments and, accordingly, different field of study, namely:

1) Psychology Sciences – 48 s-year students of RUDN University (39 female and 9 male), aged 18 to 26 (the mean is 20.07 years);

2) Medical Sciences – 62 first-year students of Pirogov RNIMU University (49 female and 13 male), aged 17 to 20 (the mean is 18.23 years);

3) Natural Sciences – 63 first-year students of NUST MISiS (17 female and 45 male), aged 17 to 21 (the mean is 18.00 years).

The research was conducted in February - early March 2020, before the lockdown in Russia due to the coronavirus pandemic. All students participated in the study during classes in psychological disciplines, as one of the additional tasks, for which they received additional points. They were advised that participation would be free and voluntary.

*Techniques.* In accordance with the purpose of the study and research hypotheses, we used three diagnostic tools.

To diagnose students' *attitudes towards DET*, the authors' questionnaire was used. This questionnaire was developed by us based on the analysis of findings of previous research on the use of digital technologies in education [39, 43]. We used Cronbach's alpha and MacDonald's omega coefficients and factor analysis for psychometric verification of the structure and internal consistency of this questionnaire [6]. The final version of *The University Students' Attitudes toward DET Questionnaire* includes 21 questions and 4 indicators (some items can fall on two or three indicators):

1) "General involvement in the use of DET" indicator characterizes the general interest in DET (12 items, raw scores can range from 2 to 39 points);

2) "Involvement in the digital space" indicator reflects the activity of using digital technologies in general, not only for educational purposes (8 items, raw scores can range from 2 to 27 points);
3) "The use of digital technologies in education" indicator more specifically reflects the attitude to digital technologies in the educational process (8 items, raw scores can range from 0 to 24 points);
4) "Digital competence" indicator (4 items, raw scores can range from 0 to 12 points).

To determine the *motivation of students' educational activity*, the "Academic motivation scales" (AMS) questionnaire by T.O. Gordeeva et al. was used [13]. This questionnaire for diagnosing motivation allows to analyze seven qualitatively different types of educational motives of students: three types of intrinsic motivation (intrinsic cognition, achievement, and personal growth), three types of extrinsic motivation (motivation for self-respect, introjected, and external regulation) and an amotivation. This questionnaire consists of 28 direct statements to which the subject expresses the degree of consent on a 5-point Likert scale (from "strongly disagree" to "strongly agree"). Each of the academic motivation scales (Intrinsic cognition motivation, Achievement motivation, Motivation for personal growth, Motivation for self-respect, Introjected motivation, External regulation, Amotivation) contains 4 statements, raw scores can range from 1 to 20 points [13].

To assess the *academic achievements*, we used GPA (grade point average) in all disciplines for the last academic year self-reported by students.

*Statistical Analysis.* The descriptive statistics methods, coefficients Cronbach' α and McDonald's ω, the Spearman's correlation analysis, and factor analysis (Varimax) were used for statistical analysis. Statistical processing was carried out in the R software environment for statistical computing and graphics, version 3.6.1., psych package version 1.9.6 [33].

# 3   Results

The results of the Spearman's correlation analysis between the indicators of attitudes towards DET and the academic motivation in university students are presented in Tables 1, 2, 3 and 4: Table 1 presents results in general sample of all students ($N = 173$), Table 2 presents results in Natural Sciences students ($N = 63$), Table 3 presents results in Medical students ($N = 62$), and Table 4 presents results in Psychology students ($N = 48$).

Table 1 shows that 11 significant correlations were revealed between the peculiarities of the attitudes towards DET and the academic motivation in general sample of university students:

– Two types of intrinsic academic motivation (*intrinsic cognition* and *personal growth*) and one type of extrinsic motivation (*self-respect*) have positive correlations with "General involvement in the use of DET" and "Involvement in the digital space" indicators;

- Two types of extrinsic academic motivation (*introjected motivation* and *external regulation*) have negative correlations with "The use of digital technologies in education" and "Digital competence" indicators;
- *Amotivation* has negative correlations with "General involvement in the use of DET" and "Involvement in the digital space" indicators.

**Table 1.** Spearman's correlations between the indicators of attitudes towards DET and the academic motivation in general sample of university students ($N = 173$)

| Academic motivation scales | Indicators of Attitudes toward DET | | | |
|---|---|---|---|---|
| | General involvement in the use of DET | Involvement in the digital space | The use of digital technologies in education | Digital competence |
| Intrinsic Cognition Motivation | 0.21** | 0.20** | 0.06 | 0.08 |
| Achievement Motivation | *0.14* | *0.13* | 0.11 | *0.12* |
| Motivation for Personal Growth | 0.19* | 0.18* | 0.09 | *0.12* |
| Motivation for Self-Respect | 0.20** | 0.19* | 0.06 | −0.04 |
| Introjected Motivation | 0.01 | 0.01 | −0.20** | −0.20** |
| External Regulation | −0.02 | 0.00 | *−0.15* | −0.18* |
| Amotivation | −0.16* | −0.16* | 0.11 | *−0.12* |

* $- p \leq 0.05$; ** $- p \leq 0.01$; *in italic* $- p \leq 0.1$

Consequently, university students of all three fields of study with more pronounced intrinsic academic motivation are more involved in the digital space in general and more involved in the use of DET, while more amotivated students, on the contrary, less involved in the digital space and in the use of DET. It is interesting that different types of extrinsic motivation have opposite correlations with DET attitudes indicators: students with more pronounced motivation for self-respect are more involved in the digital space in general and more involved in the use of DET, but students with more pronounced introjected motivation and external regulation as rule have less digital competence and more negative attitudes to use of digital technologies in education.

Table 2 shows that 5 significant correlations were revealed between the indicators of the attitudes towards DET and the academic motivation in natural sciences students:

- Only one types of intrinsic academic motivation (*intrinsic cognition*) has positive correlations with "General involvement in the use of DET" and "Involvement in the digital space" indicators;

- Two types of extrinsic academic motivation (**introjected motivation** and **external regulation**) have negative correlations with "The use of digital technologies in education" and "Digital competence" indicators, respectively;
- **Amotivation** has negative correlation with "General involvement in the use of DET" indicator.

**Table 2.** Spearman's correlations between the indicators of attitudes towards DET and the academic motivation in natural sciences students (N = 63)

| Academic motivation scales | Indicators of Attitudes toward DET | | | |
|---|---|---|---|---|
| | General involvement in the use of DET | Involvement in the digital space | The use of digital technologies in education | Digital competence |
| Intrinsic Cognition Motivation | 0.25* | 0.27* | 0.00 | 0.02 |
| Achievement Motivation | 0.07 | 0.11 | −0.09 | 0.16 |
| Motivation for Personal Growth | 0.15 | 0.16 | 0.08 | 0.06 |
| Motivation for Self-Respect | 0.19 | 0.20 | 0.10 | −0.02 |
| Introjected Motivation | −0.01 | −0.03 | −0.16 | −0.29* |
| External Regulation | −0.19 | −0.16 | −0.29* | −0.23 |
| Amotivation | −0.27* | −0.21 | −0.10 | 0.02 |

$^* - p \leq 0.05$; $^{**} - p \leq 0.01$; in italic $- p \leq 0.1$

In this case, natural sciences students with more pronounced intrinsic cognition motivation are more involved in the digital space in general and more involved in the use of DET, while more amotivated students, on the contrary, less involved in the digital space. At the same time, natural sciences students with more pronounced introjected motivation as rule have less digital competence, and students prone to external regulation have more negative attitudes to use of digital technologies in education. In general, the correlations in this group of students correspond to the nature of the correlations in the general sample (the smaller number of significant correlations is explained by the smaller sample size).

Table 3 shows that only one significant correlation was revealed between the indicators of the attitudes towards DET and the academic motivation in medical students: intrinsic motivation for **personal growth** positive correlates with "The use of digital technologies in education" indicator. Consequently, medical students with higher self-development motivation tend to have better attitudes to use of digital technologies in education. It should be noted that there are several insignificant correlations ($p \leq 0.1$) in the medical students' sample, the nature of which is close to the correlations in the general sample.

**Table 3.** Spearman's correlations between the indicators of attitudes towards DET and the academic motivation in medical students ($N = 62$)

| Academic motivation scales | Indicators of Attitudes toward DET | | | |
|---|---|---|---|---|
| | General involvement in the use of DET | Involvement in the digital space | The use of digital technologies in education | Digital competence |
| Intrinsic Cognition Motivation | *0.22* | 0.15 | 0.11 | −0.02 |
| Achievement Motivation | 0.18 | 0.14 | 0.16 | −0.03 |
| Motivation for Personal Growth | 0.18 | 0.15 | 0.26* | 0.03 |
| Motivation for Self-Respect | 0.17 | 0.13 | 0.19 | −0.16 |
| Introjected Motivation | −0.07 | −0.09 | −0.12 | *−0.25* |
| External Regulation | 0.08 | 0.06 | −0.05 | *−0.21* |
| Amotivation | *−0.21* | *−0.24* | 0.08 | −0.11 |

\* − $p \leq 0.05$; \*\* − $p \leq 0.01$; *in italic* − $p \leq 0.1$

Table 4 shows that 4 significant positive correlations were revealed between the indicators of the attitudes towards DET and the academic motivation in psychology students:

- All three types of intrinsic academic motivation (*intrinsic cognition, achievement,* and *personal growth*) have positive correlations with "The use of digital technologies in education" indicator;
- Intrinsic motivation for *personal growth* also has positive correlations with "General involvement in the use of DET" indicator.

Consequently, psychology students with a higher intrinsic academic motivation tend to have better attitudes to use of digital technologies in education, in addition, they tend to have a greater overall involvement in the use of DET (with taking into account correlations at $p \leq 0.1$). It is interesting to note that there are practically no negative correlations (even insignificant) in this group of students.

**Table 4.** Spearman's correlations between the indicators of attitudes towards DET and the academic motivation in psychology students (N = 48)

| AMS scales | Indicators of Attitudes toward DET | | | |
|---|---|---|---|---|
| | General involvement in the use of DET | Involvement in the digital space | The use of digital technologies in education | Digital competence |
| Intrinsic Cognition Motivation | 0.25 | 0.19 | 0.36* | 0.15 |
| Achievement Motivation | 0.22 | 0.16 | 0.42** | 0.25 |
| Motivation for Personal Growth | 0.29* | 0.24 | 0.34* | 0.20 |
| Motivation for Self-Respect | 0.22 | 0.13 | 0.28 | 0.11 |
| Introjected Motivation | 0.18 | 0.19 | −0.20 | −0.01 |
| External Regulation | −0.01 | 0.06 | −0.14 | −0.05 |
| Amotivation | −0.09 | −0.05 | −0.03 | −0.15 |

$^{*} - p \leq 0.05$; $^{**} - p \leq 0.01$; *in italic* $- p \leq 0.1$

Finally, the results of the Spearman's correlation analysis between the indicators of attitudes towards DET and the *academic achievements* in university students of different fields of study are presented in Table 5.

**Table 5.** Spearman's correlation between the indicators of attitudes towards DET and the academic achievements in university students of different fields of study

| Indicators of Attitudes toward DET | Academic achievements (GPA) | | | |
|---|---|---|---|---|
| | General Sample (N = 170) | NSS (N = 60) | MS (N = 62) | PS (N = 48) |
| General involvement in the use of DET | 0.15 | 0.11 | 0.09 | 0.27 |
| Involvement in the digital space | 0.23** | 0.21 | 0.15 | 0.35* |
| The use of digital technologies in education | −0.00 | 0.09 | −0.04 | 0.05 |
| Digital competence | 0.08 | 0.13 | −0.13 | 0.14 |

$^{*} - p \leq 0.05$; $^{**} - p \leq 0.01$; *in italic* $- p \leq 0.1$
NSS – natural science students, MS – medical students, PS – psychology students.

Table 5 shows that the *academic achievements* positive correlate with "Involvement in the digital space" in the general students' sample ($p \leq 0.01$), in psychology students' sample ($p \leq 0.05$), and in natural students' sample ($p \leq 0.1$). Consequently, higher-performing students tend to have more engagement in the digital space in general not only in educational goals.

## 4 Discussion and Conclusions

The purpose of present research is to reveal and compare the relationship of attitudes towards DET with academic motivation and academic achievements among Russian University students of different fields of study. Summarizing the results of the study, we can conclude that our hypotheses were mainly confirmed.

In accordance with the first hypothesis, there are positive correlations between such indicators of attitudes towards DET as "General involvement in the use of digital educational technologies", "Involvement in the digital space", "Use of digital technologies in education" with three scales of intrinsic academic motivation (intrinsic cognition motivation, achievement motivation, motivation for personal growth). In general, students with higher indicators of these motivational characteristics are more involved in the digital space in general and have a better attitude towards digital educational technologies.

Also, as expected, there are negative correlations between indicators of attitudes towards DET with amotivation. However, different types of extrinsic motivation have opposite correlations with DET attitudes indicators: students with more pronounced motivation for self-respect are more involved in the digital space in general and more involved in the use of DET, but students with more pronounced introjected motivation and external regulation as rule have less digital competence and more negative attitudes to use of digital technologies in education.

It should be noted that there are no completely matching correlations between the studied variables in three groups of students of different fields of study. Only one matching correlation was found in medical and psychological students: students of these fields of study with more pronounced motivation for personal growth tend to have a better attitude towards DET. We believe that this coincidence can be explained by the fact that medicine and psychology belong to the professions "human-to-human", for which reflection and personal self-development are of great importance.

But, in general, the attitudes towards DET are more closely related with the academic motivation in the natural sciences and psychological students than in medical students. This fact partially confirms our third hypothesis and corresponds to the data of our previous research [28] that psychological characteristics (i.e. personality traits) are most closely related in the natural sciences and psychological students.

Our second hypothesis assumed positive correlations between the attitudes towards DET indicators and academic achievements (GAP) in university students. However, only one significant correlation was revealed between "involvement in the digital space" indicator and GAP in general sample and in psychology students: higher performing students tend to be more involved in the digital space. Perhaps this result is due to the fact that we used only one GAP indicator self-reported by students.

Thus, we can conclude that there are specific features of the relationship of attitudes towards DET with scales of academic motivation and indicator of academic achievements among students of different fields of study: studied variables are least closely related in the medical students, which is almost in line with our third hypothesis. We believe that this fact is explained by the peculiarities of professional training of future physicians, which to a lesser extent includes interaction with digital technologies than training specialists in the field of natural sciences.

The findings of our research contribute to the scientific and practical search for psychological factors associated with the inclusion, implementation and effective use of the digital technologies in modern university education. The obtained data will be useful in the development of the psychological support programs for the students of different field of study in the educational process using DET.

Summing up all the findings and limitations of our research, we can determine its future prospects: (1) samples expansion and its balancing by the female-to-male ratio; (2) studying other factors related with attitude toward DET (personality traits, intellectual abilities, creativity, etc.); (3) investigation psychological predictors of attitudes towards DET among university students of another fields of study; (4) research on psychological predictors of teachers' attitudes toward DET; and (5) use of additional measurement methods for attitudes toward DET, as well as other methods of statistical analysis.

# References

1. Andryukhina, L., Sadovnikova, N., Utkina, S., Mirzaahmedov, A.: Digitalisation of professional education: prospects and invisible barriers. Educ. Sci. J. **22**, 116–147 (2020). https://doi.org/10.17853/1994-5639-2020-3-116-147
2. Anourova, N.I.: Digital technologies in education. In: Ershova, R.V. (ed.) Digital Society as a Cultural and Historical Context of Human Development: Sat. scientific Articles, pp. 29–32. State Social-Humanitarian University Publ., Kolomna (2018). (in Russian)
3. Avdulova, T.P.: Psychology of Adolescence. "Yurayt" Publishing House, Moscow (2018). (in Russian)
4. Burganova, L.A., Yurieva, O.V.: Attitude of higher educational teachers to the usage of digital technologies: sociological analysis. Rev. Econ. Law Sociol. **1**, 105–108 (2020). (in Russian)
5. Butler, M.J.: Limiting off-task behavior on laptops in classrooms increases student engagement: use it, or they will abuse it. In: Alexandrov, D.A., Boukhanovsky, A.V., Chugunov, A.V., Kabanov, Y., Koltsova, O., Musabirov, I. (eds.) DTGS 2020. CCIS, vol. 1242, pp. 447–459. Springer, Cham (2020). https://doi.org/10.1007/978-3-030-65218-0_33
6. Bychkova, P.A.: Psychological characteristics of students and their attitude to digital educational technologies: MA. Psychology thesis. RUDN University, Moscow (2020). (in Russian)
7. Ceci, J.-F.: Learning by and with digital technology: educating the young for a balanced use. Digit. Technol. Life Soc. (6) (2019). hal-02310807
8. Chaturvedi, K., Vishwakarma, D.K., Singh, N.: COVID-19 and its impact on education, social life and mental health of students: a survey. Child Youth Serv. Rev. **121**, 105866 (2021). https://doi.org/10.1016/j.childyouth.2020.105866
9. Chiu, T.K.F., Lin, T.-J., Lonka, K.: Motivating online learning: the challenges of COVID-19 and beyond. Asia Pac. Educ. Res. **30**(3), 187–190 (2021). https://doi.org/10.1007/s40299-021-00566-w
10. Clark-Wilson, A., Robutti, O., Thomas, M.: Teaching with digital technology. ZDM Math. Educ. **52**(7), 1223–1242 (2020). https://doi.org/10.1007/s11858-020-01196-0

11. De Martino, M., Gushchina, Y.S., Boyko, Z.V., Magnanini, A., Sandor, I., Guerrero Perez, B.A., Isidori, E.: Self-organisation in lifelong learning: theory, practice and implementation experience involving social networks and a remote format. RUDN J. Psychol. Pedagogics **17**(3), 373–389 (2020). https://doi.org/10.22363/2313-1683-2020-17-3-373-389

12. Fedorenko, E.H., Velychko, V.Y., Stopkin, A.V., Chorna, A.V., Soloviev, V.N.: Informatization of education as a pledge of the existence and development of a modern higher education. Educ. Dimens. **1**(52), 5–21 (2019)

13. Gordeeva, T., Sychev, O., Osin, E.: "Academic motivation scales" questionnaire. Psikhologicheskii Zhurnal **35**(4), 96–107 (2014). (in Russian)

14. Gordeeva, T.O., Sychev, O.A., Pshenichnuk, D.V., Sidneva, A.N.: Academic motivation of elementary school children in two educational approaches—innovative and traditional. Psychol. Russia: State Art **11**(4), 19–36 (2018). https://doi.org/10.11621/pir.2018.0402

15. Gordeeva, T.O., Sychev, O.A.: Motivational profiles as predictors of students' self-regulation and academic achievement. Moscow Univ. Psychol. Bull. Ser 14. Psychol. (1), 67–87 (2017). https://doi.org/10.11621/vsp.2017.01.69 (in Russian)

16. Gustiani, S.: Student's motivation in online learning during Covid-19 pandemic era: a case study. Holist. J. **12**(2), 23–40 (2020)

17. Halonen, N., Hietajarvi, L., Lonka, K., Salmela-Aro, K.: Sixth graders' use of technologies in learning, technology attitudes and school well-being. Eur. J. Soc. Behav. Sci. **18**(1), 2307–2324 (2017). https://doi.org/10.15405/ejsbs.205

18. Hasan, N., Bao, Y.: Impact of "e-Learning Crack-up" perception on psychological distress among college students during covid-19 pandemic: a mediating role of "Fear of Academic Year Loss." Child Youth Serv. Rev. **118**, 105355 (2020). https://doi.org/10.1016/j.childyouth.2020.105355

19. Iivari, N., Sharma, S., Venta-Olkkonen, L.: Digital transformation of everyday life - how COVID-19 pandemic transformed the basic education of the young generation and why information management research should care? Int. J. Inf. Manag. **55**, 102183 (2020). https://doi.org/10.1016/j.ijinfomgt.2020.102183

20. Irawan, A., Dwisona, D., Lestari, M.: Psychological impacts of students on online learning during the pandemic COVID-19. KONSELI: Jurnal Bimbingan dan Konseling (E-J.) **7**(1), 53–60 (2020). https://doi.org/10.24042/kons.v7i1.6389

21. Kerdellan, K., Grezillon, G.: Processor children: how the Internet and video games shape tomorrow's adults. "U-Factoria" Publishing House, Yekaterinburg (2006). (in Russian)

22. Koroleva, D.: Always online: Using mobile technology and social media at home and at school by modern teenagers. Educ. Stud. (1), 205–224 (2016). https://doi.org/10.17323/1814-9545-2016-1-205-224. (in Russian)

23. Lischer, S., Safi, N., Dickson, C.: Remote learning and students' mental health during the Covid-19 pandemic: a mixed-method enquiry. Prospects, 1–11 (2021, Advance online publication). https://doi.org/10.1007/s11125-020-09530-w

24. Mustafina, A.: Teachers' attitudes toward technology integration in a Kazakhstani secondary school. Int. J. Res. Educ. Sci. **2**(2), 322–332 (2016). https://doi.org/10.21890/ijres.67928

25. Narbut, N.P., Aleshkovski, I.A., Gasparishvili, A.T., Krukhmaleva, O.V.: Forced shift to distance learning as an impetus to technological changes in the Russian higher education. RUDN J. Sociol. **20**(3), 61–62 (2020). https://doi.org/10.22363/2313-2272-2020-20-3-611-621. (in Russian)

26. Nestik, T.A., Patrakov, E.V., Samekin, A.S.: The psychology of person's attitudes toward new technologies: current state and further research directions. In: Zhuravlev, A.L., Koltsova, V.A. (eds.) Fundamental and Applied Research of Modern Psychology: Results and Development Prospects, pp. 2041–2050. RAS Publ., Moscow (2017). (in Russian)

27. Novikova, I.A., Bychkova, P.A.: Attitude towards digital educational technologies among students of different field of study. In: Kudinov, S.I., Mikhailova, O.B. (eds.) Personality in the Modern World: Education, Development, Self-Realization, pp. 469–476. RUDN University Publ., Moscow (2020). (in Russian)
28. Novikova, I., Bychkova, P., Zamaldinova, G.: Personality traits and attitude towards digital educational technologies in Russian university students. In: INTED2021 Proceedings, pp. 9999–10005. IATED, Valencia (2021). https://doi.org/10.21125/inted.2021.2087
29. Petrova, P., Jotsov, V., Dimitrov, G.: A new approach to digitalisation in education for the development of young talents. In: EDULEARN20 Proceedings, pp. 5637–5643. IATED, Palma (2020). https://doi.org/10.21125/edulearn.2020.1479
30. Poluekhtova, I.A., Vikhrova, O.Yu., Vartanova, E.L.: Effectiveness of online education for the professional training of journalists: students' distance learning during the COVID-19 pandemic. Psychol. Russia: State Art **13**(4), 26–37 (2020). https://doi.org/10.11621/pir.2020.0402
31. Poshekhonova, V.A.: The humanities educational technology of the digital age. Pedagog. Educ. Russ. **5**, 13–20 (2018). (in Russian)
32. Radu, M.C., Schnakovszky, C., Herghelegiu, E., Ciubotariu, V.A., Cristea, I.: The impact of the COVID-19 pandemic on the quality of educational process: a student survey. Int. J. Environ. Res. Public Health **17**(21), 7770 (2020). https://doi.org/10.3390/ijerph17217770
33. Revelle, W.: Psych: Procedures for Psychological, Psychometric, and Personality Research (R package) (2019). https://cran.r-project.org/package=psych
34. Rizun, M., Strzelecki, A.: Students' acceptance of the COVID-19 impact on shifting higher education to distance learning in Poland. Int. J. Environ. Res. Public Health **17**(18), 6468 (2020). https://doi.org/10.3390/ijerph17186468
35. Sawarkar, G., Sawarkar, P., Kuchewar, V.: Ayurveda students' perception toward online learning during the COVID-19 pandemic. J. Educ. Health Promot. **9**, 342 (2020). https://doi.org/10.4103/jehp.jehp_558_20
36. Shamatonova, G.L., Zaytseva, M.A.: Electronic educational materials in learning. In: Ershova, R.V. (ed.) Digital Society as a Cultural and Historical Context of Human Development: Sat. Scientific Articles, pp. 427–431. State Social-Humanitarian University Publ., Kolomna (2018). (in Russian)
37. Simanjuntak, E., Nawangsari, N.A.F., Ardi, R.: Do students really use internet access for learning in the classroom?: Exploring students' cyberslacking in an Indonesian University. Behav. Sci. **9**(12), 123 (2019). https://doi.org/10.3390/bs9120123
38. Soldatova, G., Zotova, E., Lebesheva, M., Shlyapnikov, V.: Internet: opportunities, competencies, security. Toolkit for employees of the general education system. Lectures. Part 1. Center for Book Culture "Gutenberg", Moscow (2013). (in Russian)
39. Soldatova, G.U., Rasskazova, E.I.: Brief and screening versions of the Digital Competence Index: verification and application possibilities. Natl. Psychol. J. **3**(31) 47–56 (2018). https://doi.org/10.11621/npj.2018.0305. (in Russian)
40. Tomasik, M.J., Helbling, L.A., Moser, U.: Educational gains of in-person vs. distance learning in primary and secondary schools: a natural experiment during the COVID-19 pandemic school closures in Switzerland. Int. J. Psychol.: J. Int. de Psychologie (2020, Advance online publication). https://doi.org/10.1002/ijop.12728
41. Vladova, G., Ullrich, A., Bender, B., Gronau, N.: Students' acceptance of technology-mediated teaching - how it was influenced during the COVID-19 pandemic in 2020: a study from Germany. Front. Psychol. **12**, 636086 (2021). https://doi.org/10.3389/fpsyg.2021.636086
42. Watermeyer, R., Crick, T., Knight, C., Goodall, J.: COVID-19 and digital disruption in UK universities: afflictions and affordances of emergency online migration. High. Educ. **81**(3), 623–641 (2020). https://doi.org/10.1007/s10734-020-00561-y

43. Yuzefovich, T.S.: Relation between activity of using digital technologies and educational motivation and academic achievement in students of different areas of study. MA. Psychology thesis. RUDN University, Moscow (2018). (in Russian)
44. Zawacki-Richter, O.: The current state and impact of Covid-19 on digital higher education in Germany. Hum. Behav. Emerg. Technol. **3**, 218–226 (2020). https://doi.org/10.1002/hbe 2.238

# The Role of Values in Academic Cheating at University Online

Anastasiia Vlasenko[1] and Anna Shirokanova[2]

[1] HSE University, St. Petersburg, Russian Federation
[2] Laboratory for Comparative Social Research, HSE University, Moscow, Russian Federation
a.shirokanova@hse.ru

**Abstract.** This study investigated the role of basic human values in explaining academic dishonesty among undergraduate students in Russia (N = 471) during the emergency online learning in 2020. It was hypothesized that higher levels of self-enhancement would be associated with higher levels of dishonest behavior and that values would partially explain the differences by field of study, controlling for gender, age, grade-point-average, and perceived severity of penalty. Descriptive analysis revealed high levels of two types of online academic dishonesty: using unauthorized sources at exams and allowing others to copy exam answers. Majors differed by how much they reported plagiarism and contract cheating. Students' basic values were also different from the representative national sample. Regression analysis revealed that the effects of majors are not compensated fully by basic human values. Achievement and power values had an average predictive value for the types of dishonesty making up 24% of the explained variance. The results are discussed in terms of consistency and further use of results for curbing online academic dishonesty at university.

**Keywords:** Online learning · Academic dishonesty · Plagiarism · Cheating · Academic integrity · Human values

## 1 Introduction

To start off a discussion about a sensitive topic such as academic dishonesty, clarifications should be made as well as references as to why it is important to study. One of the many things that make academic dishonesty a valuable source for discussion is the fact that a large share of students tends to engage in it [1–4]. The number of students who engage in academic dishonesty has been constantly increasing since the second half of the 20th century, thus, posing a threat to educational standards [5]. It was found that more than two thirds of undergraduate US students self-reported academic dishonesty in the past six months, with increasing rates of Internet plagiarism and collaborative cheating, while plagiarizing from books was decreasing [6]. Along with that, new forms of dishonest academic behaviors have appeared that either revolve around new technologies or involve them [7]. They include international essay mills, copying test answers from dedicated websites, or hiring a company to fully complete an online course.

© Springer Nature Switzerland AG 2022
D. A. Alexandrov et al. (Eds.): DTGS 2021, CCIS 1503, pp. 294–307, 2022.
https://doi.org/10.1007/978-3-030-93715-7_21

Academic dishonesty is defined as the 'forms of cheating and plagiarism that involve students giving or receiving unauthorized assistance in an academic exercise or receiving credit for work that is not their own' [8]. It can also be defined as 'the use or provision of any unauthorized materials or assistance in academic work and/or activities that compromise the assessment process' [9]. There are many different types and scales of academic dishonesty acts varying be perceived seriousness and whether they are applied to exams, papers, etc. [10] Overall, the researchers seem to point out mostly the same thing—the use of unauthorized materials or sources. Another similarity is profiting off of dishonest behavior. Thus, we will be treating academic dishonesty as the use of unauthorized materials or help by a student to get credit for work they have not done or have not done fully.

The dangers of academic dishonesty lie deeper than it first might seem. Not only the scholars are under attack of profanity, the workplaces that invite individuals who engaged in academic dishonesty risk to employ disqualified specialists who also tend to engage in dishonest behaviors at work [11]. It was also found that repeating cheaters normalize dishonest behavior and justify it to fit their needs [12].

The pandemic emergency online teaching in 2020 meant a shift from online distance education as a perspective area engaging a small share of college students (e.g., 15% in the US [13]) to a necessity for all university students. Previous studies of cheating in online classes provided mixed results [14] where some reports indicated higher rates of on-campus cheating due to collaborative behaviors and unplanned, 'panic' cheating. The problem, however, has been the popular belief that it is easier to cheat online. Common reasons named in support of this belief include tech-savvy students exploiting electronic tests, more distance and lack of relationship between the students and instructors which causes less guilt for cheating, and higher barriers at identifying the cheaters even when the fact of cheating is known [14].

The goal of this paper is to explain online academic dishonesty through the framework of basic human values in addition to the more traditional explanation with field of study. Basic human values have been studied as potential social causes of cheating [15, 16]. They can help to reveal individual predispositions to act in particular ways that are independent of institutional measures. The study is based on a new survey about academic cheating during emergency online teaching in 2020. This work will try to bring awareness to the reasons behind academic dishonesty online that could be used by policy-makers and education practitioners.

## 2  Background

### 2.1  Russia in the Values Context

In this study, we collected and analyzed the data from Russia. A socio-psychological study that was carried out in 49 countries to describe the 'average person' from each country found out that Russians fall within the same levels of average along with European nations on various traits; however, the Russian participants had a higher level of 'achievement striving' [17]. According to the World Values Survey results, Russia scored low on self-expression and quality of life; both contribute to a greater emphasis on economic and physical security [18], which could result in higher pressure to succeed and, thus, to cheat.

Academic dishonesty is wide spread among students in Russia [19], and Russian students are very tolerant towards dishonest academic behaviors. The share of students partaking in academic dishonesty continues to grow, and the frequency with which it happens increases after finishing high school and starting university [20]. Moreover, the rates of dishonest academic attitudes rise even among high-achieving Russian students [21].

In one international study, Russia (compared to the US, Israel and the Netherlands) had the highest tolerance towards academic dishonesty in academia [22]. In another study, Russian students' self-reported high collaborative cheating scores were positively related to high corruption perception index [23]. This is consistent with the data on the Eastern Europe region, which is close to Russia geographically, that reported the highest probability to cheat in another study [24]. Russian students, along with Lithuanians and Ukrainians, also reported the highest probability of observing others cheat but only an average probability of getting caught [25].

Compared to other countries which also report high rates of academic cheating, Russia shows lower tolerance of the 'informers', i.e., students who inform the faculty on the fact of cheating [22]. Many other cultures value competition among students and encourage it, meaning that dishonest academic behaviors condemn 'healthy' interactions and take away from the mutual learning experience. Other current of the Russian education system also contribute to high tolerance towards academic cheating, such as the policy of publishing students' grades (vs. sharing them privately), which increases public pressure on the student to have high grades.

## 2.2  Basic Human Values

We add to previous research on academic cheating by gathering information on students' basic human values, i.e., their ultimate preferences for acting in life situations [26]. Students were offered questions on how they associated themselves with various portraits of their own gender. Previous studies have shown in multiple ways how individual values moderate human action both for individuals and on societal level across cultures.

Schwartz basic values include 10 values: 1) self-direction, 2) stimulation, 3) hedonism, 4) achievement, 5) power, 6) security, 7) conformity, 8) tradition, 9) benevolence, and 10) universalism. These are 'first-order values' that can be further united into four 'second-order values':

- Openness to Change (self-direction, stimulation, hedonism),
- Self-Enhancement (hedonism, achievement, power),
- Conservation (security, conformity, tradition),
- Self-Transcendence (universalism, benevolence) [26].

In a study based on the European Social Survey data, Russia was ranked at the top of Europe on self-enhancement and at the very bottom of the list by self-transcendence, a value of universal care [27]. It means that 'the average Russian' values power, tradition, security, conformity and achievement, while being less committed to self-direction, stimulation, hedonism, universalism and benevolence. In previous research, the importance of self-enhancement values tended to boost the search for social approval and, then, cheating [15]. On the other hand, the normativity inherent in conservation values could nurture a drive against cheating. Consequently, conservation and self-enhancement are the two second-order values we will be focusing on and including in the analysis.

## 2.3 Field of Study in Academic Cheating

Some differences in academic cheating can be expected between the students of different years and majors. In one large-scale survey, graduate business students were found to cheat more than non-business graduates [28]. Other studies found the same result, proposing several explanations like the effect of business curriculum that may give the students an impression that success is impossible without unethical behavior [29]. Therefore, we also expect business students to report more cheating. Additionally, humanities students reported much fewer acts of academic dishonesty, while business majors self-reported more serious forms of academic dishonesty, e.g. paying someone else to write a paper [30].

Different forms of academic dishonesty are also prevalent in different study years [30, 31]. Selwyn [30] notes that seniors are more prone to copying a whole assignment or paying someone to do it, while junior students are more likely to do it only partly. A study conducted in Russia concluded that the last-year undergraduate students were more ready to comply with corrupt practices; on average, they had more positive attitudes towards dishonest practices [32].

Other individual factors include gender, and grade-point-average (GPA). Various studies find out that males tend to cheat more often [33], while it has also been demonstrated that gender differences are very small within the same major [3].

Student's GPA is another important factor of engagement in dishonest practices. Higher GPA is associated with reporting less academic dishonesty behavior [34]. However, if students focus on keeping their grades as high as possible for any reason, they tend to engage in dishonest academic behavior more often [35]. In other words, GPA is negatively associated with the level of academic dishonesty, but top students could engage in dishonest behaviors because of their desire to stay on top [6]. A meta-analysis of relationships between cognitive abilities and academic cheating concluded that even more able students has recently started to cheat more frequently [36].

Severity of punishment is a contextual factor that does not depend on purely individual student's characteristics [20]. However, if anti-cheating sanctions are not applied on time, this induces the feeling of injustice among other students and instigates more cheating [37]. According to Jendrek [38], of 60% of the faculty who observed cheating, one-third met with the student or took any other serious measures, thus sending a message to others that cheating was acceptable. A factor contributing to such reluctance to report a cheating student could be the lack of flexibility in university's policy on cheating [10]. Taking all this into account, we will control for the year of study, gender, GPA, and perceived strictness of real punishment for academic cheating.

## 3 Data and Materials

### 3.1 Sampling and Data Collection

We used a cross-sectional survey design aiming to cover the undergraduate population of social sciences and humanities students at a Russian university. The advantage of focusing on one university was the similarity of institutional conditions shared by all the students. This was an important feature, given the goal of the study to evaluate the role of basic values compared to the field of study. Collecting data on one particular university ensured that students were placed in similar institutional conditions and were acting in the same organizational environment. The rules and sanctions of the institution also applied to each student, which is important for comparing groups.

The population consisted of all undergraduate students of the social sciences and humanities of a medium-sized state university. Graduate student were excluded as they are a heterogeneous group that tends to be more academically motivated [22]. We used quota sampling to gather data on all the majors. The survey was conducted among non-international students in Russian, students' native language, in December 2020.

Taking into account the emergency online teaching at universities, the survey was distributed online via three dozens of opinion leaders who were contacted personally and presented with the goals of the study. These opinion leaders were heads of student organizations who have a large network of acquaintances among other students.

The form was filled out by 471 students representing all the targeted majors, including 140 students of Business and Finance, 119 students of Humanities, 58, Law, and 154, Social Sciences. All the students answered questions on conservation and self-enhancement values which were part of our hypotheses; every tenth student filled out a full, 21-item Schwartz values battery on basic values (n = 44). This was done in order to reduce the cognitive load on the majority of respondents and to shorten the time to complete the survey and keep as many respondents as possible.

During the survey, the procedure of anonymization doubted by some respondents, which resulted in missing data on personally identifiable data such as GPA. Whenever possible, such cases were addressed personally to explain the anonymity of the survey. When opening the questionnaire, the participants were asked consent to partake in the survey. Additionally, they were informed that the data would be used only in its aggregated form and would not be used against them in any sense. Finally, the participants were ensured that their university was not initiating the research and, thus, would not have any access to the data.

### 3.2 Measurements

Basic human values were measured with the short Schwartz questionnaire adopted from the European Social Survey, for comparative reasons. Security, conformity, power and achievement were measured on inverted, 6-point, labelled scales adjusted to gender for each individual, then averaged across majors and compared to the average for the Russian national sample.

Majors were registered along with demographic variables such as gender, year of study (1–4), paying for tuition (yes/no), GPA, and perceived severity of punishment for cheating (1–5 scale). Online academic dishonesty was measured with five indicators, which matches the tradition in the literature. These indicators were adapted from Maloshonok and Shmeleva [19]. The students were asked how often in the six months preceding the survey they committed plagiarism, paraphrased someone else's ideas without footnoting, paid someone to write a paper in their name ('contract cheating'), allowed other students to copy their exam answers, or copied exam answers themselves. The 4-point answer scale for each question ranged from 'never' to '5 or more times'.

## 4   Results and Discussion

### 4.1   Descriptive Results

There were 83% females and 17% males in the sample; the mean age of respondents was 19.5 (SD = 1.38) years, which corresponds to the typical undergraduate student in Russia. The obtained sample is generally representative of the shares of students by field of study in this university. One notable exception is Business students of all years (1/4 short of their actual share in the university population)—despite several reminders, students of all years in this field were less likely to fill out the survey than in other fields. Junior Law students were also underrepresented in the sample.

There were 29% freshmen, 24% sophomores, 19%, juniors, and 28% seniors; 52% had a state scholarship, while 48% paid for tuition. About 26% of students preferred not to share their GPA (more so among Law students) for the fear of revealing their identity. They were added to the models as a separate group. The prevalence of online cheating behavior is shown in Table 1.

**Table 1.**  Prevalence of online academic dishonesty, by popularity.

| Type of academic dishonesty (online) | Never | 1–2 times | 3–4 times | 5 or more times |
|---|---|---|---|---|
| Used crib sheets, devices, or other students' help during exam | 23% | 38% | 23% | 16% |
| Allowed somebody to copy answers during an exam | 42% | 35% | 14% | 9% |
| Paraphrased ideas of others without giving reference | 49% | 36% | 9% | 6% |
| Plagiarized | 68% | 23% | 5% | 4% |
| Turned in a paper written by someone else for pay | 93% | 5% | 1% | 1% |

The shares differed by majors. The median levels of using crib sheets at exams was 1–2 times for all four fields of study; in allowing others to copy answers, the median was 1–2 times for Business, Humanities, and Social Science students, and 0 times for Law students. For paraphrasing, the median was 1–2 times for Business, Law, and Social Sciences, but 0 for Humanities. For plagiarism and contract cheating, the median was

0 across all fields of study. To sum up, Law students were less likely to allow other students to copy their exams and to plagiarize, while Humanities students were less likely to paraphrase. In addition, the share of students who bought a paper at least once was larger among Business students (15% vs. 3–4% in other fields). For frequencies of cheating by major, see Fig. 1.

In human values, we compared the sample of students who answered the full 21-item battery on ten values with the reported levels in a representative sample of Russians described in the literature [27] and the publicly available European Social Survey data for Russia of 2016. The values were ipsatized and centered. No Business majors were found in this subset. The three other majors did not differ across all values but Power, where Humanities students scored lower (Dunn test, p = .02).

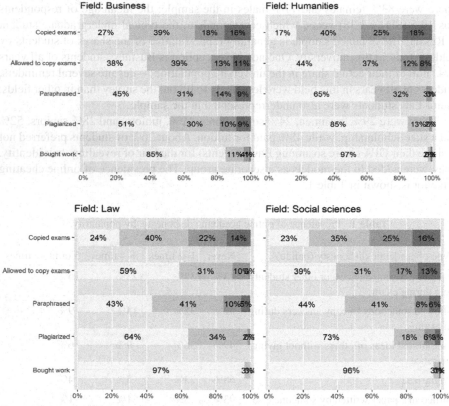

**Fig. 1.** Prevalence of academic dishonesty by four majors (never, 1–2 times, 3–4 times, 5+ times), percent by type of dishonesty, panes by major.

The researchers [27] placed Russia very high on Power and Achievement with a mean score of approximately −0.15, while students have reported a mean score of 0.28 on these values, which is even higher. Security was also very important for Russian people, as they scored 0.7 on it, while the students have reported only a score of 0.21. For both Conformity and Tradition, which are of high importance for Russians, the average score for the country was around 0.15, while students reported a mean score of −1.33. On the other hand, Russia scores low on Benevolence and Universalism with a mean score of 0.4, and students have reported a mean of 0.34, i.e., they have similar values with regard to concern about other people and their surroundings. This was not true for Stimulation, Self-Direction and Hedonism: Russians reported scores of −0.9, 0.15 and −0.6, respectively, while students had −0.03, 0.57, and 0.46. Overall, only such values as Benevolence and Universalism are presented in the student sample at the same rate and the rest of the values are varying. A further comparison of student data with the youth subsample (17–21 years) and the representative Russian sample yields similar results: students scored much lower on Conformity and Traditionalism, and much higher on Achievement and Self-Direction than the youth or the average citizen of Russia.

The rest of student sample (n = 427) had almost no missing data on human values, with the exception of the second security indicator ('Important that government is strong and ensures safety'), with 7% missing.

## 4.2 Modeling Results

To test the hypothesis about the role of values, we estimated three models with a summary index of online academic dishonesty types (Cronbach's alpha = .63) as the outcome. The first model regressed cheating on majors only. The second model added human values believed to be related to cheating, that is, the importance of being admired, successful, rich, risky, on the one hand, and safe, behaving right, and doing what is told, on the other. The third model added controls. All continuous variables start at 0 which means the lowest possible values. After deleting the missing values, the sample shrank by 5% (n = 446). Modeling results are presented in Table 2.

Table 2 shows that majors were significantly related to online academic cheating, similar to some human values. In the full model, Business students reported highest rates of online cheating, on par with Social Science students, while Humanities and Law students reported significantly less cheating. Students with higher value of being rich (Power) and admired (Achievement) reported higher rates of online cheating.

In the full model, gender, study year, or paying a tuition fee were not significantly related to academic cheating. However, the perceived severity of sanctions for academic dishonesty had a significant negative relationship with reported cheating. Additionally, this model shows that students who did not disclose their GPA tend to cheat significantly less. Given the overall negative relationship between GPA and cheating, we conclude that students with higher GPA were more likely to hide their data for the fear of revealing their personality as their score on cheating for this group was lower than among other groups but was also higher than zero.

Each larger model was statistically better than the smaller one by R-squared and AIC. Human values added about 2.2% of explained variance, out of 9.2% overall, which makes about 24% of all the explained variance. Notably, none of the majors' relationships with cheating turned non-significant when values were in, which means that they are rather the result of institutional factors and not students' self-selection.

**Table 2.** Majors and human values as predictors of online academic dishonesty (unstandardized coefficients).

| DV: Online academic dishonesty (0–15) | Model 1 | Model 2 | Model 3 |
|---|---|---|---|
| Humanities (reference = Business) | −1.16*** | −1.11** | −0.92** |
| Law | −1.17** | −1.17** | −0.84* |
| Social Sciences | −0.42 | −0.38 | −0.40 |
| Achievement (be admired) | | 0.22 | 0.32* |
| Achievement (be successful) | | −0.07 | −0.11 |
| Power (be rich) | | 0.22* | 0.24* |
| Stimulation (to risk) | | −0.09 | −0.06 |
| Security (be safe) | | −0.17 | −0.16 |
| Conformity (do what is told) | | −0.17 | −0.16 |
| Conformity (to behave right) | | −0.09 | −0.09 |
| Perceived severity of sanctions | | | −0.38** |
| Male (reference = Female) | | | 0.29 |
| Study year | | | 0.07 |
| Pays tuition fee (reference = No) | | | −0.03 |
| GPA quartile 2 (reference = Q1, lowest) | | | −0.53 |
| GPA quartile 3 | | | −0.54 |
| GPA quartile 4 | | | −0.71 |
| GPA missing data | | | −1.19** |
| Constant | 4.08*** | 4.20*** | 5.39*** |
| Adjusted R-squared | 2.8% | 5.0% | 9.2% |
| AIC | 2116.9 | 2113.7 | 2101.4 |

### 4.3 Discussion

The goal of this study was to explore and analyze the role of basic human values in predicting self-reported cheating at university during emergency teaching in 2020. We surveyed undergraduate students from a state Russian university and asked them to report on various types of cheating in the past six months. We expected to find out high rates of cheating and significant differences by major, as predicted by the literature. The contribution of this study was in exploring how the indicators of basic human values could improve the explanatory model of cheating by adding long-term life orientations to it.

The results add to the literature in several ways. First, they show that it is not only self-selection of students into particular majors but also institutional environments shape cheating habits. We have seen that, for instance, higher cheating among Business majors is not explained away by their relative rates of importance to be rich or be admired, although these factors are significant. Second, we have clearly seen how the values of students as a distinct social group compare to society. Students are extremely high on Self-Enhancement, low on Conservation, and just like everyone else on Self-Transcendence values. These results could be taken further to study which values prevent students from cheating [15]. Third, we have explored the prevalence of online cheating across majors. Our results provide a benchmark for monitoring the patterns and frequency of cheating as the pandemic continues and online teaching persists.

As predicted, we discovered that a majority of 60–70% undergraduate were involved in at least some types of academic dishonesty behavior, most probably used crib notes during an exam or shared their answers with other students. In a major US study [3], students who had one or more instances of copying or using unauthorized crib notes, deemed 'serious test cheaters', were estimated at 63%; 66% reported repeated plagiarism, paraphrasing, or contract cheating. A survey in Sweden, however, showed an opposite pattern, with a minority of 9% reporting using crib notes and a majority of 61%, plagiarism. Therefore, the patterns vary much across educational systems. According to our data, there are much fewer serious written work cheaters among Russian students, ranging from 7% (buying someone's work) to 51% (paraphrasing).

One reason for this rather optimistic result, despite the overall bad history of academic dishonesty found in Russian universities [19–21], might be the online mode of learning, where students' written submissions were regularly monitored for plagiarism. Another explanation for smaller rates of serious cheating could be a clearer understanding of the university sanctions applied for cheating at written work.

Our study also confirmed the literature-based observation that Business students—even those few who agreed to take part in our survey—were more likely to report academic dishonesty. Business students were less willing to participate in general, which resulted in a smaller share of them in the sample. Even so, they reported the highest rates of serious cheating on written work (Fig. 1, Table 2).

The results on human values showed that, of all the tested items of Self-Enhancement and Conservation values, the most important predictors of cheating were Achievement and Power questions about the importance of being rich and admired—the 'neoliberal values' [15] that encourage contextual, not universal, ethics and urge the pursuit of social approval. These values improved the model above and beyond majors.

The combination of high Self-Enhancement and search for approval could hit some high-performance students hardest. Some literature points at the increasing rates of cheating among high-achieving students in Russia [21]. Thus, the popular conclusion that GPA is negatively related to cheating might need to be clarified. However, we found no evidence for this conditioning in our data, and this should be the focus of further research.

Numerous surveys report that a majority of students and staff believe that to cheat online is either easier or as difficult as in on-campus learning [2, 14, 39–42]. The discussed reasons for the perceived ease of online cheating are the anonymity and distance that remove guilt [42] and the different motivation in online learning as compared to face-to-face learning [43]. A competitive reason is the ease of identity fraud and development of new cheating methodologies [14]. After a full year of online teaching, one could add to the list students' fatigue and discomfort of communicating online for several hours a day, which simultaneously exhausts and requires greater self-organization. The perspective of a few more year of regular online learning at university will offer more incentives for the personalized online teaching and learning.

An obvious recommendation would be to organize online teaching in smaller groups so as to enhance the feeling of community. Some literature recommendations to prevent online cheating include regular updating of all testing materials (as the answers leak to the Internet); reworking exam problems for open-book exams; and challenging students with alternative types of work where 'traditional cheating' would not be an option [14]. In addition, all borderline, ambiguous cases of cheating should be explained to the staff and students and clarifying the rules before studies begin [10]. This could be valuable as a way to mitigate student anxiety [44] which also rose during the pandemic.

More sophisticated options are also available. In particular, basic human value profiles of students could be studied and used within majors to develop personalized control tasks matching their predispositions and geared to prevent cheating. This might be particularly relevant for Business students who tend to cheat more, but it could also make online cheating a more enjoyable experience for all students. Other applications include personalized recommendations on types of homework tasks which could match personal value profiles and tap into students' motivations to study.

Is there anything positive about the high prevalence of cheating among students? From students' perspective, definitely so. As one of our respondents commented, 'coopcration is a useful soft skill', and this is hard to confront as networked collaboration is part and parcel of many jobs. On the other hand, online cheating is putting an end to creating personal crib notes which could allegedly help students revise the material. When most of the answers are available online, there is no need to write such cribs by hand; information literacy and tech savviness come to the foreground as key factors of success at online cheating.

We believe the results of our study are moderately reliable. The survey was conducted in a non-hierarchical way and relied on personal authority in spreading the questionnaire. However, personal questions raised additional concerns as to the safety of participation and disclosing any sensitive information, which resulted in refusals and substantial missing rates for personally identifiable data. We recommend that, in further research, the procedures be explained to the students in small detail about how the data would be stored and used as some students found it hard to match the anonymity of the survey results with collecting their personal information.

A limitation of the study is that survey data tend to underestimate real rates of socially undesirable behavior, which could make the results overly optimistic. Another limitation is that perceived peer dishonesty was left out of the focus. Peer influence and perceived prevalence of cheating in the group are important contextual factors of cheating [4, 45]. A recent survey has showed that peer influence is even more important than perceived sanctions for cheating [45], therefore, questions about peer behavior should be part of such surveys.

Although widely practiced, academic dishonesty continues to haunt not only instructors and administrators but also the partaking students. The topic has to be discussed by interest groups with a view to updating teaching and learning practices for current online teaching, i.e., implementing learning skill courses everywhere, informing students about the long-term implications of cheating behavior, and mixing students of various majors in intergroup projects. Further research should compare student profiles of basic values across majors and universities, match them with various patterns of cheating and non-cheating, and develop personalized recommendations on the types of control tasks and cheating-preventing measures.

**Acknowledgements.** The paper was prepared within the framework of the HSE University Basic Research Program.

# References

1. Davis, S.F., Grover, C.A., Becker, A.H., McGregor, L.N.: Academic dishonesty: prevalence, determinants, techniques, and punishments. Teach. Psychol. **19**(1), 16–20 (1992). https://doi.org/10.1207/s15328023top1901_3
2. Kennedy, K., Nowak, S., Raghuraman, R., Thomas, J., Davis, S.F.: Academic dishonesty and distance learning: student and faculty views. Coll. Stud. J. **34**(2), 309–314 (2000)
3. McCabe, D.L., Treviño, L.K., Butterfield, K.D.: Cheating in academic institutions: a decade of research. Ethics Behav. **11**(3), 219–232 (2001). https://doi.org/10.1207/S15327019EB1103_2
4. Malesky, A., Grist, C., Poovey, K., Dennis, N.: The effects of peer influence, honor codes, and personality traits on cheating behavior in a university setting. Ethics Behav. (2021). https://doi.org/10.1080/10508422.2020.1869006
5. Murdock, T.B., Anderman, E.M.: Motivational perspectives on student cheating: toward an integrated model of academic dishonesty. Educ. Psychol. **41**(3), 129–145 (2006). https://doi.org/10.1207/s15326985ep4103_1
6. McCabe, D.L., Butterfield, K.D., Trevino, L.K.: Cheating in College: Why Students Do it and What Educators Can Do About it. JHU Press, Baltimore (2012)
7. Sileo, J.M., Sileo, T.W.: Academic dishonesty and online classes: a rural education perspective. Rural Spec. Educ. Q. **27**(1–2), 55–60 (2008). https://doi.org/10.1177/8756870508027001-209
8. Ercegovac, Z., Richardson, J.: Academic dishonesty, plagiarism included, in the digital age: a literature review. Col. Res. Libr. **65**(4), 301–318 (2004). https://doi.org/10.5860/crl.65.4.301
9. Grijalva, T.C., Nowell, C., Kerkvliet, J.: Academic honesty and online courses. Coll. Stud. J. **40**(1), 180–185 (2006)
10. Pincus, H.S., Schmelkin, L.P.: Faculty perceptions of academic dishonesty: a multidimensional scaling analysis. J. High. Educ. **74**(2), 196–209 (2003). https://doi.org/10.1080/00221546.2003.11777196
11. Wowra, S.A.: Academic dishonesty. Ethics Behav. **17**(3), 211–214 (2007). https://doi.org/10.1080/10508420701519122
12. Fida, R., Tramontano, C., Paciello, M., Ghezzi, V., Barbaranelli, C.: Understanding the interplay among regulatory self-efficacy, moral disengagement, and academic cheating behaviour during vocational education: a three-wave study. J. Bus. Ethics **153**(3), 725–740 (2016). https://doi.org/10.1007/s10551-016-3373-6
13. Seaman, J.E., Allen, I.E., Seaman, J.: Grade Increase: Tracking Distance Education in the United States. Babson Survey Research Group (2018)
14. Peterson, J.: An analysis of academic dishonesty in online classes. Mid-West. Educ. Res. **31**, 24–36 (2019)

15. Pulfrey, C., Butera, F.: Why neoliberal values of self-enhancement lead to cheating in higher education: a motivational account. Psychol. Sci. **24**(11), 2153–2162 (2013). https://doi.org/10.1177/0956797613487221

16. Pulfrey, C., Durussel, K., Butera, F.: The good cheat: benevolence and the justification of collective cheating. J. Educ. Psychol. **110**(6), 764–784 (2018). https://doi.org/10.1037/edu0000247

17. Allik, J., et al.: Personality profiles and the "Russian Soul": literary and scholarly views evaluated. J. Cross-Cult. Psychol. **42**(3), 372–389 (2011). https://doi.org/10.1177/0022022110362751

18. Inglehart, R., Basáñez, M., Díez-Medrano, J., Halman, L.C.J.M., Luijkx, R. (eds.): Human Beliefs and Values: A Cross-Cultural Sourcebook Based on the 1999–2002 Value Surveys. Siglo XXI, Mexico City (2004)

19. Maloshonok, N., Shmeleva, E.: Factors influencing academic dishonesty among undergraduate students at Russian universities. J. Acad. Ethics **17**(3), 313–329 (2019). https://doi.org/10.1007/s10805-019-9324-y

20. Shmeleva, E.: Academic dishonesty in modern universities: a review of theoretical approaches and empirical findings. J. Econ. Sociol. **16**(2), 55–79 (2015)

21. Chirikov, I., Shmeleva, E., Loyalka, P.: The role of faculty in reducing academic dishonesty among engineering students. Stud. High. Educ. **45**(12), 2464–2480 (2020). https://doi.org/10.1080/03075079.2019.1616169

22. Magnus, J.R., Polterovich, V.M., Danilov, D.L., Savvateev, A.V.: Tolerance of cheating: an analysis across countries. J. Econ. Educ. **33**(2), 125–135 (2002). https://doi.org/10.1080/00220480209596462

23. Orosz, G., et al.: Linking cheating in school and corruption. Eur. Rev. Appl. Psychol. **68**(2), 89–97 (2018). https://doi.org/10.1016/j.erap.2018.02.001

24. Teixeira, A.A.C., Rocha, M.F.: Cheating by economics and business undergraduate students: an exploratory international assessment. High. Educ. **59**(6), 663–701 (2010). https://doi.org/10.1007/s10734-009-9274-1

25. Grimes, P.: Dishonesty in academics and business: a cross-cultural evaluation of student attitudes. J. Bus. Ethics **49**, 273–290 (2004). https://doi.org/10.1023/B:BUSI.0000017969.29461.30

26. Schwartz, S.: An overview of the Schwartz theory of basic values. Online Read. Psychol. Cult. **2**, 1–20 (2012). https://doi.org/10.9707/2307-0919.1116

27. Magun, V., Rudnev, M.: Basic human values of the Russians. In: Harrison, L., Yasin, E. (eds.) Culture Matters in Russia—and Everywhere: Backdrop for the Russia-Ukraine Conflict, pp. 431–450. Lexington Books, Lanham, MD (2015)

28. McCabe, D.L., Butterfield, K.D., Trevino, L.K.: Academic dishonesty in graduate business programs: prevalence, causes, and proposed action. Acad. Manag. Learn. Educ. **5**(3), 294–305 (2006). https://doi.org/10.5465/amle.2006.22697018)

29. Kumar, K., Borycki, C., Nonis, S.A., Yauger, C.: The strategic decision framework: effect on students' business ethics. J. Educ. Bus. **67**(2), 74–79 (1991). https://doi.org/10.1080/08832323.1991.10117520

30. Selwyn, N.: 'Not necessarily a bad thing …': a study of online plagiarism amongst undergraduate students. Assess. Eval. High. Educ. **33**(5), 465–479 (2008). https://doi.org/10.1080/02602930701563104

31. Yu, H., Glanzer, P.L., Johnson, B.R.: Why students cheat: a conceptual framework of personal, contextual, and situational factors. In: Velliaris, D.M. (ed.) Handbook of Research on Academic Misconduct in Higher Education, pp. 35–59. IGI Global, Hershey (2017)

32. Denisova-Schmidt, E.: Academic dishonesty or corrupt values: the case of Russia. In: Torsello, D. (ed.) Corruption in Public Administration, pp. 105–137. Edward Elgar Publishing, Cheltenham (2016). https://doi.org/10.4337/9781785362590.00012

33. Chala, W.D.: Perceived seriousness of academic cheating behaviors among undergraduate students: an Ethiopian experience. Int. J. Educ. Integr. **17**(1), 1–15 (2021). https://doi.org/10.1007/s40979-020-00069-z
34. McCabe, D.L., Trevino, L.K.: Individual and contextual influences on academic dishonesty: a multicampus investigation. Res. High. Educ. **38**, 379–396 (1997). https://doi.org/10.1023/A:1024954224675
35. Aaron, L.S., Roche, C.M.: Stemming the tide of academic dishonesty in higher education: it takes a village. J. Educ. Technol. Syst. **42**, 161–196 (2013). https://doi.org/10.2190/ET.42.2.h
36. Paulhus, D.L., Dubois, P.J.: The link between cognitive ability and scholastic cheating: a meta-analysis. Rev. Gen. Psychol. **19**(2), 183–190 (2015). https://doi.org/10.1037/gpr0000040
37. Ramos, R., Gonçalves, J., Gonçalves, S.P.: The unbearable lightness of academic fraud: Portuguese higher education students' perceptions. Educ. Sci. **10**(12), 351 (2020). https://doi.org/10.3390/educsci10120351
38. Jendrek, M.P.: Faculty reactions to academic dishonesty. J. Coll. Stud. Dev. **30**(5), 401–406 (1989)
39. King, C.G., Guyette, R.W., Jr., Piotrowski, C.: Online exams and cheating: an empirical analysis of business students' views. J. Educ. Online **6**(1), 1–11 (2009)
40. Miller, A., Shoptaugh, C., Wooldridge, J.: Reasons not to cheat, academic-integrity responsibility, and frequency of cheating. J. Exp. Educ. **79**(2), 169–184 (2011). https://doi.org/10.1080/00220970903567830
41. Watson, G., Sottile, J.: Cheating in the digital age: do students cheat more in online courses? Online J. Distance Learn. Adm. **13**(1) (2010). http://www.westga.edu/~distance/ojdla/spring131/watson131.html
42. Adzima, K.: Examining online cheating in higher education using traditional classroom cheating as a guide. Electron. J. e-Learn. **18**(6), 476–493 (2020). https://doi.org/10.34190/JEL.18.6.002
43. Peled, Y., Eshet, Y., Barczyk, C., Grinautski, K.: predictors of academic dishonesty among undergraduate students in online and face-to-face courses. Comput. Educ. **131**, 49–59 (2019). https://doi.org/10.1016/j.compedu.2018.05.012
44. Trost, K.: Psst, have you ever cheated? A study of academic dishonesty in Sweden. Assess. Eval. High. Educ. **34**, 367–376 (2009). https://doi.org/10.1080/02602930801956067
45. Hendy, N.T., Montargot, N., Papadimitriou, A.: Cultural differences in academic dishonesty: a social learning perspective. J. Acad. Ethics **19**(1), 49–70 (2021). https://doi.org/10.1007/s10805-021-09391-8

# Designing Workflow for Improving Literature Review Process Based on Co-citation Networks

Anastasiya Kuznetsova(✉)

National Research University Higher School of Economics in St. Petersburg,
Saint Petersburg, Russia

**Abstract.** Literature reviews are essential parts of every academic paper, and there are many tools, which are trying to suggest relevant articles and make the process of working with citations easier. Many of them offer to focus on just specific recommended papers or provide a general picture of the area without explanations or hints on how particular papers can help. Co-citation networks serve as a foundation of multiple useful methods for citation recommendations, enabling the analysis of the structure of the scientific field. However, existing instruments using them have a steep learning curve. In this paper, we present the workflow prototype to elicit and evaluate a set of heuristics employing co-citation network analysis in the literature review process. We performed a step-by-step analysis, including analysis of bibliographic data visualization service VOSviewer patterns of use, which allowed us to synthesize Job Stories for the specification of possible user needs for citation recommendation. We produced a set of heuristics for the analysis of co-citation networks based on Job Stories. The heuristics are then evaluated on the set of papers from two Human-Computer Interaction conferences to reflect on their applicability and usability. Our results can be used to inform more straightforward navigation through co-citation networks, possible design improvements of services for literature management and bibliographic data visualization, as well as a foundation for learning designs for enhancing academic writing skills.

**Keywords:** Co-citation networks · Bibliometrics · Literature search · Human-computer interaction

## 1 Introduction and Related Work

The skill of writing a good and useful literature review is an essential one for all academic writers, from junior students to professors. Previous writing experience or lack of thereof informs the way of literature review writing [11] and can put especially entry-level researchers at a disadvantage. The traditional process

© Springer Nature Switzerland AG 2022
D. A. Alexandrov et al. (Eds.): DTGS 2021, CCIS 1503, pp. 308–318, 2022.
https://doi.org/10.1007/978-3-030-93715-7_22

of teaching how to write them is usually pretty standardized – most of the knowledge can be obtained from academic writing lessons if they exist nearby. Scientific advisors could facilitate this process and help navigate through the scientific field by recommending references, but not all of them do that or keep up with the state of modern research on specific topics themselves.

Today, there are different instruments, which could help to understand a scientific field of interest and facilitate the choice of "Whom and what to cite?" [10].

Among methods to support these tasks are a variety of combinations of collaborative filtering [9], ranking [6], social network analysis methods (co-citation) [7,12,15], text analysis methods [2,4]. Recent works for example apply supervised learning methods to existing literature surveys to derive predictive models [8] for future citation recommendations [1]. The key assumption beyond such an approach is that the model implicitly learns the way authors of the surveys approach mapping of the field.

Unfortunately, many of these systems, due to their inherent 'black box' nature, do not provide necessary affordances to improve researcher skills, focusing on specific recommendation tasks or overall representation of the field, and failing to provide and communicate hints and instruments to figure out how the proposed papers can help and why.

In contrast, network methods of analyzing citations (e.g., co-citation networks) are quite distinct in their ability to simplify the complexity and unfold the scientific field's structural organization. They serve as a foundation of some widely-used citation recommendation methods [3,9], based on whether articles were cited together or not. However, applying traditional social network analysis tools for performing such an analysis has a steep learning curve and can scare people, driving them to the traditional method of web search or relying on 'black box' recommendations without an understanding of underlying logic.

In this paper, we present a prototype of a workflow to elicit and evaluate a preliminary set of heuristics employing co-citation network analysis in the literature review process.

We elicit a preliminary list of heuristics that can be used for navigation through the scientific field, responding to the requirements of different users with different research and writing backgrounds and help them to find papers for citation. This paper reports on the results of the first iterations of the Design Science approach [5], focused on the preliminary set of heuristics with their evaluation on a sample of HCI papers. The results can be used to inform User and Learning Experience (LX) design elements for existing services for bibliographic data visualization and literature management systems and enhance EdTech support of academic writing courses.

## 2 Design Approach

Following user-centred design practices, we looked at how users with different levels of research and academic skills expertise can use co-citation networks for their literature reviews (Fig. 1).

Firstly we examined literature about citation patterns and citation typologies to understand motivation and usage behind citations. We also analyzed the most popular citation recommendation ways to understand which bibliographic network would be better to use.

As we mostly focus on co-citation networks for finding literature, we took VOSviewer[1] - one of the best-known tools creating bibliographic networks [14] for the analysis of how bibliographic network analysis could help in writing a literature review. The empirical part includes an analysis of VOSviewer usage in published papers, especially how authors use VOSviewer for conducting their research. Based on the literature review and VOSviewer analysis, we developed job stories associated with different levels of proficiency in academic writing. Such job stories helped to understand the possible needs and fears of users while working with co-citation networks.

As a result, a heuristics set for co-citation networks was developed. This set helps to navigate through co-citation networks for finding needed papers for citation as well as helps to understand the structural complexity of the scientific field. This set was also evaluated on the sample of published papers in the area of Human-computer interaction. More specifically, for each paper, we re-established a possible Scopus query that can be used for making a co-citation network for their research. After that, heuristics were applied to the received papers, and we checked whether the authors cited articles that were proposed by heuristics.

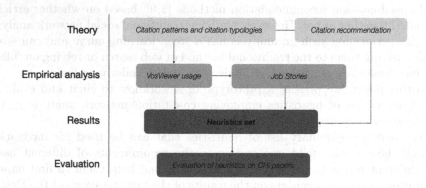

**Fig. 1.** Design description

# 3   Analysis and Results

## 3.1   VOSviewer Analysis and Job Stories Development

VOSviewer was made as software for visualization of bibliographical data in the format of maps [14]. The authors mention two main applications of VOSviewer:

---

[1] https://www.VOSviewer.com.

maps creation and data visualization, as it is even possible not only to use bibliographic data but any other kind of network data. The main algorithm for mapping is a visualization of similarities (VOS) - it locates objects in the network based on their similarity to each other [13].

We took 20 papers from the list of applications[2] taking into account each 25th publication. Several purposes of VOSviewer usage were distinguished: description of the field and sub-field; analysis of collaboration networks of a journal or organization; data visualization and use of unique VOSviewer methods.

The first type of analysis in VOSviewer used in the sample is term maps. It allows us to understand the general content of the field and the scientific discussion within it. Often, when using this type of representation, researchers additionally enrich the analysis by mentioning authors who belong to thematic clusters. At the moment, VOSviewer does not allow directly find authors associated with the regions of the term map. In co-citation, citation and bib-coupling maps, researchers often look not only at the network as a whole but also focus on the key works of each cluster. Often, the network structure itself is practically not described, but the top nodes within each cluster are presented in the form of a table. Many authors approach to describe clusters in the citation, co-citation, co-authorship, bib coupling networks thematically. Moreover, users often focus separately on the target cluster and look for central papers inside it.

| # | Situation | Motivation | Outcome |
|---|---|---|---|
| JS1 - beginner  | The first acquaintance with the scientific field. Lack of research skills. | Understand how my scientific field is organized and what papers are worth reading. | Understanding of the structure of the field, main articles for the literature review. |
| JS2 - middle  | Review of a scientific field with an initial acquaintance with it. Some existing research skills. | Evaluate the scientific field from above and understand interaction of researchers inside it works. | Specific works for the main topic and future research. |
| JS3 - advanced  | Interactive research of existing gaps in the whole scientific field. Existing research skills. | Find a scientific gap in an area where I could add something from my own research. | Existing opportunities for further development of research. |

**Fig. 2.** Job stories

Also, the service is used differently in works with a high number of citations in comparison to the low-cited works: in highly cited papers, there was more complex social network analysis, focus on bridge authors in different subfields, evaluations of the field's development. The same reasons limiting citation behaviour may limit interaction with the VOSviewer or any other instrument for bibliographic analysis. Users with a low level of expertise in academic writing

---

[2] https://www.vosviewer.com/publications.

won't use all features of the service and will follow basic paths from the manual. Thus, the meagre use of the service at work and the lack of a comprehensive analysis can be correlated with a low number of citations and reflect the quality of the work as a whole. Inspired by the idea of Job Stories (Klement 2016), we captured JS related to academic users with different levels of research skills (JS, Fig. 2). Here we focus on just some of the Job Stories extracted from research where VOSviewer was used and literature analysis; however, we expect to find more of them with a wider user study.

### 3.2 Eliciting Heuristics for Citation Recommendation

Based on the existing literature and empirical part of the analysis, several stages of the citation recommendation process can be distinguished. The development of the set of heuristics was based on VOSviewer usage and literature analysis. The heuristics are targeted to support more straightforward navigation through co-citation networks so that beginners would understand where to start and how to organize their literature review. Also, some possible usage examples of discovered papers are written (Table 1).

These heuristics set could be used as an entry point for the analysis of co-citation networks or be an internal flow for paper recommendations. Further, these heuristics will be applied to existing works to verify their real applicability. In full compliance with the rules: if the papers that would be offered for citation are chosen by a user for a citation, then this indicates that the heuristic assists the user in navigating the set and choosing works for citation. For a better understating of heuristics application, they can be seen in Fig. 3 on the basis of the co-citation network.

Moreover, all these heuristics are important for Job Stories presented before. For **JS2** it would be very important to follow the heuristics **H2** for they probably already have some general idea of their scientific field and need more specific papers. **H3** and **H4** would help users from **JS3** to find structurally important papers and find possible gaps for further research development. H1 would be extremely important for beginners with the lack of academic writing skills from **JS1**, as it will give the main authors to read and cite. However, to structure a systematic and qualitative literature review, all these heuristics should be used.

### 3.3 Evaluating Heuristics Based on the Sample of Papers from Human-Computer Interaction Field

To reflect on the feasibility of the heuristics, we take two contrasting enough cases of articles from two different conferences with A* and B ranks[3]: CHI 2019 Best Papers[4] and OZCHI'19: Proceedings of the 31st Australian Conference on Human-Computer-Interaction 2019[5]. This made it possible to contrast adherence

---

[3] https://www.core.edu.au/conference-portal.

[4] https://chi2019.acm.org/2019/03/15/chi-2019-best-papers-honourable-mentions/.

[5] http://ozchi2019.visemex.org/wp/accepted-papers/.

**Table 1.** Heuristics

| Heuristics for co-citation network | How does this help a literary review | Rationale | Operationalization |
|---|---|---|---|
| **H1** - General view: at least one paper from each cluster should be mentioned | Shows that the entire scope of the field is analyzed. It helps to get familiar with the whole field | These works can be used in the introduction or in the description of the background and related works | Clustered co-citation network with a counted degree for each node. Focus on nodes with the highest degree within each cluster (especially for clusters with 10+ papers inside) |
| **H2** - Detailed analysis of articles in the cluster that describes your subfield in detail | Help to show the focus of the study and the whole set of other works in it | Such papers can be used through all the text for justifying words or showing interesting examples of papers in this field | Top-5 papers for each cluster based on their degree |
| **H3** - Search for structurally important papers (connecting some sub-filed): based on betweenness centrality | To show the relationship between scientific subfields. It should be applied only if it connects at least one cluster, which is the main one for the work | It shows the scientific field development or links parts of the literature review | Arranged list of articles with the highest betweenness centrality |
| **H4** - Search for isolated items is taken into account if they relate to the main subfield | It is an optional part, but there could be situations when isolated works/nodes could also be important and useful. They should be checked | Optionally, it could be connected to the field but be isolated from the network | List of articles that are not connected to the main component |

to the heuristics on the case of the papers of community process-certified quality on the major conference in the field, and on the conference within the same field but with slightly lower status.

For each paper in both sets, we tried to recreate possible source Scopus datasets (mostly based on keywords), make a co-citation network and apply heuristics to them to find whether needed articles were cited or not (Table 2).

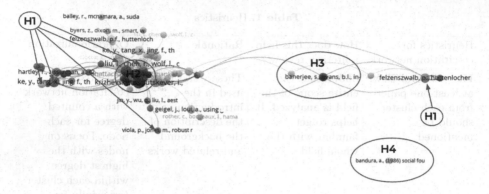

**Fig. 3.** Heuristics shown on co-citation network

At this stage, we present mostly illustrative qualitative evaluation, showing the face plausibility of the heuristics.

For each article, we made a Scopus query, computed a co-citation network and applied heuristics set on them. Results are presented in the table below with specification of Scopus query and results of heuristics application to them as well as the score for compliance with heuristics from 1 to 6 (2 points if one of the heuristics is fully followed, 1 – if it has some limitations, 0 with no citations from heuristics, Table 2).

As a result, 1st articles from the A*-rank conference showed full compliance with heuristics (all suggested papers were cited), another one cited almost all papers, but a couple of small clusters were not described. In the 1st article from the B rank conference H1, H2 failed, and only 2/7 clusters presented on the co-citation network were described. In the 2nd one, H3 failed - no structurally important papers were mentioned. We explicitly formulated a number of heuristics useful for co-citation network analysis and demonstrated their feasibility by analysing the best papers from HCI and showing that their authors intrinsically rely on them. The heuristics that we proposed to search for articles for citation on the basis of bibliographic networks of co-citation can be used by those who first come across a citation network and do not know where to start. Experts in the scientific field (authors of CHI'19 Best Papers) almost fully follow them, authors of articles from the conference with lower rank follow them just partly, showing possible room for improvements.

**Table 2.** Heuristics analysis on CHI papers

| Conf | Paper | Scopus query | Heuristics analysis |
|---|---|---|---|
| A* - CHI 2019 Best Papers | *"PicMe: Interactive Visual Guidance for Taking Requested Photo Composition"* | Photography Assistance (296 results), Interactive Visual Guidance (385 results), Photo Composition (limited to Computer Science, 869 results) | H1 - there are no articles from the one cluster, but as it is too small, therefore, we can consider this rule to be fully satisfied; H2 - they mostly focused on the two big clusters and took many works from it, so this one if completed too; H3 - bridge author work is analyzed. Score: $(2 + 2 + 2 = 6)$ |
| A* - CHI 2019 Best Papers | *"Voice User Interfaces in Schools: Co-designing for Inclusion With Visually-Impaired and Sighted Pupils"* | Voice User interfaces + Education (212 results), Voice User interfaces + Inclusion (18 results), Visual Impairment + Education (limited to Computer Science, 272 results), Visual Impairment + Inclusion (Excluded Medicine, 367 results), Co-design + Inclusion (106 results), Co-design + Education (527 results) | H1 - there are no articles from some clusters which could be mentioned in the literature review; H2 - authors fully described one cluster which is important for them; H3 - they managed to describe some connections between papers. Score: $(1 + 2 + 2) = 5$ |
| B - OZCHI'19 | *"Towards Surgical Robots: Understanding Interaction Challenges in Knee Surgery"* | There were pretty general keywords, so we made our own query: "TITLE-ABS-KEY (human AND computer AND interaction) AND TITLE-ABS-KEY (medical OR assist* OR surge*) AND TITLE-ABS-KEY (robot*)" with limited to Computer Science, which gave us 1812 results | H1 - works from only two among 7 clusters were mentioned; H2 - no full cluster description; H3 - mention the bridge author. Score: $(1 + 1 + 0) = 2$ |
| B - OZCHI'19 | *"Challenges and Opportunities in Using Augmentative and Alternative Communication (AAC) Technologies: Design Considerations for Adults with Severe Disabilities"* | Augmentative Alternative Technologies (705 papers); Adults with Severe Disabilities (limited to Computer Science, 66 papers); We also added Augmentative technologies (905 papers) | H1 - works from all main clusters were referenced, but the top one was missed; H2 - mostly focused on papers from blue and purple clusters; H3 - no description of structurally important bridge authors. Score: $(1 + 2 + 0) = 3$ |

# 4  Conclusion

In this paper, using the Design Science approach [5], we report the workflow prototype to derive the set of heuristics that employ co-citation network analysis in the literature review process.

A step-by-step analysis was carried out with the ultimate goal of creating a set of heuristics for citation recommendation based on a bibliographic network. The first step was to analyze the works in which the repository VOSviewer used to understand its actual use. This allowed us to understand the communication of users with this instrument and understand user needs for this type of instrument. This helped to single out some job stories: **JS1** - about getting familiar with the new field with the lack of skills on academic writing, **JS2** - about acquaintance with the almost unfamiliar field but with the previous experience of writing academic papers and **JS3** - about the search of existing gaps in the literature for finding new interesting sub-filed and gaps for the research.

After that, a heuristics set allowing the use of co-citation networks to search for citations was elicited. They consist of several parts: **H1** - analysis of the top papers in each cluster of co-citation networks, **H2** - focus on the most important clusters for finding more literature, **H3** - special focus on structurally important articles, and **H4** - optional look at the isolates on the network. These rules also correspond to the usage of citation typologies. For example, analysis of structurally important papers (like articles with the highest betweenness) will help to establish links between sources, enriching literature review.

For working evaluation of these heuristics, we took papers from conferences in the Human-computer interaction field with different levels of quality (best papers in A*-rank conference and B-rank conference papers). As a result, these heuristics were fully followed by papers from the A*-rank conference, suggesting that the set of heuristics reflects what experts in the field do. For B-rank conference papers, there was some room for possible improvements in citation practices. These results suggest that the workflow based on the heuristics can serve as a prototype to inform the navigation through a co-citation network.

Presented results combine many important points regarding the analysis of user interaction with services for bibliographic visualization, as well as an attempt to link citation typologies with bibliographic networks. The work is at the crossroads of research on citation recommendations and citation behaviour. It can be a step to developing the use of a more comprehensive analysis of papers for citation, improvements for services that help navigation through literature and bibliographic data analysis and help newcomers to academic writing. The results can be used to inform the design of the workflow and Learning Experience (LX) elements.

Despite the entire scope of work, some limitations of the work can be distinguished: the VOSviewer users' study was performed only in the case of existing papers of its usage, and a complete picture could be obtained by analyzing the interaction of users with the service in real-time. Moreover, the test and evaluation case selection should be expanded from only HCI papers for comparison of more and less technical fields. Another promising future approach is to combine a co-citation network-based approach with applications of Interpretable Machine Learning methods to contemporary ML-based recommendation tools.

**Acknowledgements.** I am grateful to Ilya Musabirov for his help and support in this research. The article was prepared within the framework of the Academic Fund Program at HSE University in 2020–2021 (grant No. 20-04-024).

# References

1. Belter, C.W.: Citation analysis as a literature search method for systematic reviews. J. Am. Soc. Inf. Sci. **67**(11), 2766–2777 (2016)
2. Gupta, S., Varma, V.: Scientific article recommendation by using distributed representations of text and graph. In: Proceedings of the 26th International Conference on World Wide Web Companion, pp. 1267–1268 (2017)
3. Habib, R., Afzal, M.T.: Paper recommendation using citation proximity in bibliographic coupling. Turk. J. Electr. Eng. Comput. Sci. **25**(4), 2708–2718 (2017)
4. He, Q., Pei, J., Kifer, D., Mitra, P., Giles, L.: Context-aware citation recommendation. In: Proceedings of the 19th International Conference on World Wide Web, pp. 421–430 (2010)
5. Hevner, A., Chatterjee, S.: Design science research in information systems. In: Hevner, A., Chatterjee, S. (eds.) Design Research in Information Systems. ISIS, vol. 22, pp. 9–22. Springer, Boston (2010). https://doi.org/10.1007/978-1-4419-5653-8_2
6. Huynh, T., Hoang, K., Do, L., Tran, H., Luong, H., Gauch, S.: Scientific publication recommendations based on collaborative citation networks. In: 2012 International Conference on Collaboration Technologies and Systems (CTS), pp. 316–321. IEEE (2012)
7. Küçüktunç, O., Saule, E., Kaya, K., Çatalyürek, Ü.V.: Recommendation on academic networks using direction aware citation analysis. arXiv preprint arXiv:1205.1143 (2012)
8. Marshall, I.J., Wallace, B.C.: Toward systematic review automation: a practical guide to using machine learning tools in research synthesis. Syst. Rev. **8**(1), 1–10 (2019). https://doi.org/10.1186/s13643-019-1074-9
9. McNee, S.M., et al.: On the recommending of citations for research papers. In: Proceedings of the 2002 ACM Conference on Computer Supported Cooperative Work, pp. 116–125 (2002)
10. Portenoy, J., West, J.D.: Constructing and evaluating automated literature review systems. Scientometrics **125**(3), 3233–3251 (2020). https://doi.org/10.1007/s11192-020-03490-w
11. Schembri, N.: Citation practices: insights from interviews with six undergraduate students at the University of Malta. University of Reading Language Studies Working Papers, vol. 1, pp. 16–24 (2009)
12. Tantanasiriwong, S., Guha, S., Janecek, P., Haruechaiyasak, C., Azzopardi, L.: Cross-domain citation recommendation based on hybrid topic model and co-citation selection. Int. J. Data Min. Model. Manag. **9**(3), 220–236 (2017)
13. van Eck, N.J., Waltman, L.: VOS: a new method for visualizing similarities between objects. In: Decker, R., Lenz, H.-J. (eds.) Advances in Data Analysis. SCDAKO, pp. 299–306. Springer, Heidelberg (2007). https://doi.org/10.1007/978-3-540-70981-7_34

14. Van Eck, N.J., Waltman, L.: Software survey: VOSviewer, a computer program for bibliometric mapping. Scientometrics **84**(2), 523–538 (2010). https://doi.org/10.1007/s11192-009-0146-3

15. White, H.D.: Bag of works retrieval: TF* IDF weighting of co-cited works. In: BIR@ ECIR, pp. 63–72. Citeseer (2016)

# Interpretable Machine Learning in Social Sciences: Use Cases and Limitations

Alena Suvorova[✉]

HSE University, St. Petersburg, Russia
asuvorova@hse.ru

**Abstract.** The increasing use of intelligent technologies, the development and implementation of machine learning systems in various spheres of life require explaining machine learning-based decisions in such systems. This need for interpretation leads to the increasing development of new methods for interpreting machine learning models and their more intense use in real systems. The paper reviews existing studies with applications of the interpretable machine learning (IML) methods in social sciences and summarizes results using bibliometric analysis. In total, seven research topics were described based on 210 papers. Moreover, the paper discusses the opportunities, limitations, and challenges of the interpretable machine learning approach in social science research.

**Keywords:** Explainable AI · Machine learning · Research design · Social sciences

## 1 Introduction

Machine learning (ML) methods are increasingly spreading in various fields, affecting many areas of life, including social and economic spheres. They are used for decision making and as a result, they raise many questions from both society and researchers about ethics, non-discrimination, etc. [2,11]. Such extensive use both in research and practice focused the attention on the explainability and interpretability issues, on the questions like "what influence that prediction", "what changes if...", "how I can change the prediction", etc. [34]. For the last several years the topic of interpretable machine learning is actively discussed at various conferences (including CHI, NeurIPS, ICML, IJCAI, KDD), every day a large number of new articles related to the issues of explainability, fairness, unbiasedness, transparency of machine learning models is published in journals and proceedings and uploaded as preprints. Most papers are about algorithms, systems and their evaluation, the large proportion of papers are applications in medicine and health, but social science applications are almost invisible.

The purpose of this paper is to review the state of research on interpretable machine learning in social sciences and summarize the current research agenda. The paper is organized as follows: the next section gives an overview of the

© Springer Nature Switzerland AG 2022
D. A. Alexandrov et al. (Eds.): DTGS 2021, CCIS 1503, pp. 319–331, 2022.
https://doi.org/10.1007/978-3-030-93715-7_23

key concepts (what is machine learning, what is black-box models, what are the examples of machine learning applications in social sciences, what is interpretable machine learning), then we describe the procedure for paper selection and analysis, summarize the results and finally in discussion give a critical review of the approach, including both the limitations of interpretable machine learning methods and promising application areas and use cases, for example, for model-related communication between experts from different domains.

## 2     Background

### 2.1   Machine Learning

There is no strict "ideal" or even "accepted by everyone" definition for machine learning (ML). For example, Tom Mitchell [39] (and Wikipedia page about Machine Learning that cited him) defined machine learning as "the study of computer algorithms that improve automatically through experience". Grimmer, Roberts and Stewart [20] mentioned that "machine learning is as much a culture defined by a distinct set of values and tools as it is a set of algorithms". Since terminology issue is not the purpose of this paper, the following concept will be used: consider as machine learning methods the ones that allow defining rules (or patterns) automatically from data. Assume that a researcher has a collection of product reviews and wants to know if the review is positive or negative. The rule can be defined manually, for example, if a review includes particular words it is considered as positive – this approach is based on data, it can be really effective but it is not a machine learning method since the rule is known in advance. On the other hand, if data has labels, i.e. for each previous review it is known if it is positive or negative, a researcher can use one of the algorithms to construct the rule, i.e. build the model that can predict if the review is positive or negative for each new review. So machine learning model "learns", i.e. automatically builds this rule using existing data. A variety of machine learning algorithms is explained by a variety of procedures for "rules" construction and/or constraints on results. For example, a well-known linear regression model describes relationships between variables in linear form, decision tree model can be presented as a set of if-else rules.

The recent paper in the "Annual Review of Political Science" [20] discusses the potential of machine learning for social sciences. The authors mentioned that traditionally research in social science is deductive, the researchers must have a clear theory before viewing any data [57]. Data collection, variable selection, model building fully depend on the initial theory. In the terms used above, this means that the researcher already knows the "rule" and with data just checks if it is satisfied. All of that does not mean that machine learning is useless in social science research, it can be used in a slightly different way. The authors of review [20] propose an interesting approach that suggests using machine learning in earlier stages for generating ideas and discovering patterns in data. The important part of this approach is that the results of machine learning modeling are not regarded as ground truth or real-world phenomena (since results can change significantly with another algorithm or another set of parameters) but only as the first step for further exploration and validation. The authors called this approach agnostic since they did not assume by default that the ML model reveals real relationships in data, they described it as "we doubt our models but trust our validations" [20].

One of machine learning application extensively used in political science is Natural Language Processing: researchers used ML-algorithms to classify press releases [21], measure the tone of news [6], estimate ideological placement [43]. Machine learning is used to predict personality from social media [5], academic performance from smartphone use [52], etc.

Note that machine learning is not limited to prediction tasks. There is a whole class of machine learning algorithms that deal with data without previously known labels (unsupervised learning). These algorithms are aimed at solving tasks in data analysis such as defining groups of similar or close objects (clustering), dimensionality reduction, anomaly detection [26]. Grimmer, Roberts and Stewart [20] describing their agnostic approach mentioned these algorithms as tools for solving discovery task when grouping similar observations or features together makes large datasets more clear and easier to examine and analyze.

## 2.2 Interpretable Machine Learning

The "rule" (or pattern) that was constructed by the machine learning algorithm can be too complex and not be presented in closed form as a set of relationships between domain concepts. Such types of models are called "black box models" illustrating the process of model usage: we apply the model on input data (our new data we want to make a prediction for) and get the answer but have no idea how we get this result and what data properties were used. The main goal of prediction models is to have more accurate prediction (fewer errors or smaller variation between real and predicted values) and more complex models such as ensembles, neural networks usually show better results [18] and in most cases, they are black boxes.

In many ways, the difficulties of application ML in social sciences are caused by the fact that many methods of machine learning are black boxes by design and do not allow the interpretation of the model. The researcher can evaluate a kind of quality metric, i.e. it can be measured that the first model gives a more accurate prediction than the second one, but it is almost impossible to say why it happens and what are the variables that explain this difference. Moreover, different metrics might select different best models, and the researcher makes the final decision based on previous experience adopted by the practitioner [9]. The desire to obtain more accurate estimates leads to the creation of increasingly sophisticated models [18].

As a result, more and more researchers are focusing on the influence of algorithms on society, and interactions with algorithms (Algorithmic Experience) [2], algorithmic biases in models and ways to overcome them [11]. One of the research directions is the development of methods for constructing interpretable structures of black box models [23,31], and the other is to study the interaction between the user and the model in cases where the user needs to make a decision based on the results of the models (e.g. which model will be trusted more, how the choice is made, which factors are more important) [10,58]. The last direction also includes issues related to the need to interpret and understand complex models not to make a decision or any conclusions based on it, but to ensure the possibility of giving informed consent, privacy protection, and compliance with the General Data Protection Regulation (GDPR).

In recent years, the number of studies on the problem of interpretable machine learning has increased rapidly, and in general, there are four main types of studies. The first type is the application of interpretability algorithms in various domains: medicine, political sciences, etc. The second type is the development of new or modification of existing algorithms for interpretability; this area also includes the development of complex software systems that combine several methods and algorithms [40,53]. The third type of studies is the general discussion of the methodological problems of interpretability of models, most often these are reviews [35,60], criticism of approaches [30], terminology issues [36] and open questions, for example, what is meant by "interpretability" [14,45]. Finally, the fourth type includes user studies investigating user perception of interpretations [27,32,34], their preferences and expectations [33] and influence of interpretation on decision making [13].

To date, there are a lot of algorithms for explaining machine learning models [35]. Some of them have limitations on the scope or type of model (for example, algorithms that interpret deep learning models (see [4,46,59])), others can be applied to any model (model-agnostic methods); some algorithms are aimed at interpretation of individual local examples (for example, LIME [44]), others characterize the behavior of the model as a whole (features importance, partial dependence plots (PDP [17]), individual conditional expectations (ICE [19], global surrogate models [55]), some algorithms can be used for both local and global interpretation (SHAP, see examples in [40]). Algorithms differ in the type of input data (images, texts, tabular data), the result (model, schedule, ranked list, rule, list of counter-examples, feature set, etc.), the task to be solved [34] (explain why the result is exactly like this, find the factors influence the decision, explore possible biases, etc.). Different taxonomies of interpretation (or explanation) approaches are presented in several thorough review papers [35,60] but a detailed description is out of the scope of the current paper.

The general idea of all methods for explaining machine learning models is to provide the user (researcher, developer, client) with a way to recover, reconstruct, at least approximately, the relationship between data features, values of input variables and the result obtained in the model. Among the most widely used methods are various techniques for assessment of feature importance, surrogate models, and example-based explanations. Feature importance measures how useful each feature for prediction and what are the most influential features, locally or globally influential, depending on the method used [40]. The idea of surrogate models (e.g. LIME, SHAP, Anchors) is to approximate the initial complex model with simpler one that is interpretable by design ("white box") [35] like linear regression or decision tree. Example-based explanation methods select particular data points or instances of the dataset to explain the behavior of the machine learning model or to illustrate the prediction results [40], e.g. typical instances or prototypes, influential instances, instances with wrong predictions, instances with the similar predictions but completely different in properties, instances with the opposite predictions but with the same or similar properties (counterfactual and contrastive explanations).

## 3    Procedure and Methods

To summarize the current state of research, literature searches for studies on interpretable machine learning methods in social sciences were performed in the Scopus database.

The search query was constructed iteratively. The first query was aimed to searching studies mentioning [explainable artificial intelligence] or [interpretable machine learning] combining with social science mentions ([social science*] or [political science] or [sociology] or [psychology] or [media studies] or [communication] or [psychological] or [economical]). This query retrieved 1139 papers but most of them explored algorithms (providing descriptions of new ones or experiments with existing ones) and social sciences were mentioned in the introduction section only to explain the importance of interpretability and possible application areas. Limitation of social science mentions to the title, abstract and keywords significantly reduced the list of papers to 120 studies but that strategy did not change the thematic structure, most papers were still about algorithms. To focus the search on studies about the application of interpretable machine learning methods in social sciences, the initial query was restricted to Social Science subject area in Scopus. Additionally to exclude studies with main topic related to medicine and health the final search was restricted to papers without mentioning [medicine] and [health] in title, abstract or keywords (simplified query: ([explainable artificial intelligence] or [interpretable machine learning]) and ([social science*] or [political science] or [sociology] or [psychology] or [media studies] or [psychological] or [economical]) and not TITLE-ABS-KEY [medical] and not TITLE-ABS-KEY[health] and (LIMIT-TO (SUBJAREA, "SOCI"))). Titles and abstracts were additionally screened for relevance.

The first part of the analysis included bibliometric analysis with VOSViewer software, version 1.6.16 (www.vosviewer.com) [49]. Key publications were extracted from the citation network. Approximate topics discussed in the selected papers were described on the basis of cluster analysis of the term co-occurrence. To cover topics outside author-specified keywords [37], we use keywords extracted from titles and abstracts with VOSViewer software.

## 4    Results

The initial query retrieved 1139 papers, limitation to Social Science subject area resulted in 210 papers. Figure 1 shows the distribution of papers per year, where both initial query (light grey) and restricted to social sciences area (dark grey) present a rapid increase in a number of studies during recent years.

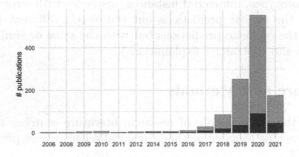

**Fig. 1.** Number of papers per year

Two of the five most cited papers [24, 25] were not about black-box models, the authors discussed the problem of interaction terms interpretation in the classical regression model and examples from political science journals. These studies are examples of interpretable models by design and they are often cited in papers about the uncertainty [54] and bias detection [8]. The other two considered machine learning algorithms and interpretable ML methods as the research object, they did not use these algorithms as tools but explore such systems from ethnography [48], philosophy and social psychology [38] points of view.

The last one from the five most cited papers is a large review of the application of artificial intelligence (AI) from multidisciplinary perspectives [15]. The authors discussed major AI themes and described multiple perspectives on various aspects of AI: technological perspective, business and management perspective, arts, humanities and law perspective, science and technology perspective, government and public sector perspective. Explainable AI was highlighted as a promising topic from a technological perspective, but its importance was mentioned in other sections too. For example, describing government and public sector perspective of AI the authors proposed the TAM-DEF (Transparency audit, Accountability Legal issues, Misuse protection, Ethics, Fairness Equity, Digital Divide Data Deficit) framework, that is intended to use by policy practitioners in assessing the safety and social desirability of any AI system. Stakeholders' attitudes towards AI, ethics and trust were mentioned as open research topics in Digital Marketing.

Moreover, the authors listed types of common AI challenges (social, ethical, economic, organizational and managerial, technological, political and legal challenges) and gave examples for each type. Note that the need for interpretation and explanation in research and practice is always motivated by one or several types of these challenges recommendations for future research.

## 4.1   Topics Description

To summarize themes discussed in the retrieved papers the term co-occurrence network was constructed using VOSViewer software. The network was built on terms that occurred at least 7 times in papers' titles or abstracts, then the vertices (terms) were clustered. As a result, seven topics were highlighted (Fig. 2). The Fig. 2 shows the most frequent terms, the cluster descriptions below were based on the whole list of terms available in the VOSViewer software.

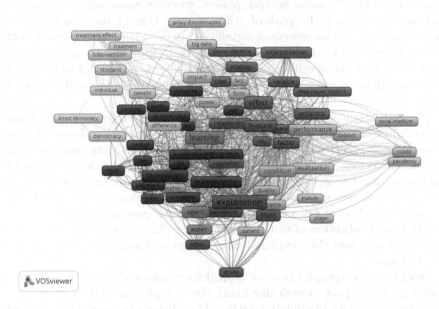

**Fig. 2.** Clusters (topics) of key terms (Color figure online)

The first topic (red) discusses general and future-oriented concepts, opportunities and perspectives (automation, principle, technology, direction, extent, society, world, humanity, opportunity, future, explainable AI) and ethics-related questions (ethics, right, respect, transparency, law) that are often highlighted in reviews about artificial intelligence and explainability.

The second topic (green) illustrates the discussion of the technical, algorithm-related items (input, variable, feature, effect, accuracy, variety, algorithms – random forest and deep neural network).

The next topic (dark blue) is about a different aspect of evaluation (quality, evidence, importance, effectiveness), including types of users (customer, author, patient, teacher, player) and information evaluation (misinformation, information, social media, of course, including the "hot" topic of covid-related evaluations). For example, Dominik Schraff evaluated the concept of trust to political institutions during the COVID-19 pandemic [47], Nenad Petrovic [42] provided the information system that estimates the level of conspiracy of user-formulated hypothesis on the basis of texts from online information sources (PubMed and other web-pages, not specified in the paper). The authors of both papers explored concepts of trust and misinformation and they both use modeling methods that are interpretable by design: linear models with interaction term in the first paper and fuzzy logic rules in the second one.

Topic of evaluation is discussed from different angles: several papers are focused on technical aspects (e.g. how to compare explanation and ground truth [22]), others – on methodological issues [33] or user studies and experiments [16,28,50]. Finally, several papers describe cases when interpretable machine learning was the part of study design. One of the examples is the study about bullying awareness in serious games [1], where authors used feature extraction methods to derive game learning analytics variables (e.g. number of interactions with the specific character) from an existing model to explore the variables with great influence on changes in bullying awareness and improve the model.

The fourth topic (yellow) is focused on political science research (governance, legislator, responsibility, accountability, stakeholder, expert) and several general technical terms, mostly about texts (text, book, deep learning, chatbot, collection, classification), that can be explained by the fact that machine learning in political science research is very often used for automatic text processing. An example of such research is described in "The impression of influence: Legislator communication, representation, and democratic accountability" [21], where authors used a collection of Congressional texts, classify press releases as credit claiming or not, and then explored how legislators form their public image in press releases.

The fifth topic (purple) is more typical for economics-related research (risk, conflict, power, impact, complexity, firm). For example, one of the papers reviews ethical considerations of applying Artificial Intelligence in auditing [41], describing both algorithmic and human ways to make ethical decisions and reconsidering professional standards.

The sixth topic (blue) is a regression-oriented topic that related to classical algorithms with effect estimates and terminology inherited from clinical studies (treatment effect, treatment, difference, student, nature), term "democracy" in this cluster can be explained by the fact that regression model with interaction terms is one of most popular method in political sciences.

Finally, the last topic (orange) focuses on reinforcement learning applications and self-driving cars (trust, participant, perception, driver, effort, action), raising questions about legal and ethical issues and trust in socio-technical systems. Andras et al. [3] discussed levels of trust and position explainable AI as a tool for establishing trust between a user and a new intelligent machine at the stage of technology adaption.

## 4.2   Applications of iML in Social Sciences

To sum up the literature review, it is worth mentioning that the search for interpretable machine learning applications in social sciences retrieves a lot of studies that discuss challenges of explainability and model interpretation and usually the solution is just not to use black-box model but classical regression or rule-based model. This is a feasible solution, but to show the complete structure of the domain, here are some explicit examples of the application of interpreted machine learning. Kleinerman et al. implemented the system for social matching, i.e. it recommended user to other user [29]. The system included an explanation module describing why the user was recommended to increase the probability of positive responses. Xu et al. [56] explored the factors of ridesharing adoption by using a random forest model for prediction and feature importance evaluation for further explanations. Wang et al. [51] implement the technique in the opposite way: to predict phishing websites they at the first step build simple interpretable rules and then combine them in a more complex model preserving explainability.

## 5   Discussion: Limitations of iML

With all the promising opportunities of interpretable machine learning (IML) methods, it is important not to forget the limitations and assumptions. IML is not a "magic" that provides great accurate explanations for complex models with high performance, it is just a tool, that can be misused [27]. The first and the most important point is that any iML method explains the model, not the reality. If the researcher has a poor model or poor data, an explanation will not make it better, in the best scenario, it will help to reveal that it is something wrong with the model or data. For example, feature importance will show the most important features for the model, not for the underlying process. Another model built on the same dataset can show other important features comparing with the first model. A good strategy is to use insights from models to generate ideas and then evaluate these ideas on new data [20].

Another limitation of iML is an approximation. Any explanation approximates the complex structure of the model or data. It is not critical but this is what the researcher needs to keep in mind. If there are two models with close performance and one of them is a black box, it is better to choose another one. Any model is an approximation and a single approximation is better than an approximation of approximation [45].

## 6   Conclusion

Black box nature of popular machine learning algorithms, inability to detect relationships limits their usage in social sciences. Even agnostic approach [20], described in the Background section, in many cases rely on human validation and estimation testing. Interpretable machine learning can make these processes feasible for complex black-box models.

Taking into account the limitations described above, interpretable machine learning seems to be a good tool both for individual researchers, expanding the list of possible solutions, and for a group of researchers, providing a way of interaction and communication between experts from different domains about the meaningful aspects of the constructed models, not the technical details [7]. Moreover, expert knowledge can be used to develop a better explanation system [12].

**Acknowledgments.** The work is supported by the Russian Science Foundation grant (project No. 19-71-00064).

# References

1. Alonso-Fernández, C., Calvo-Morata, A., Freire, M., Martínez-Ortiz, I., Fernández-Manjón, B.: Evidence-based evaluation of a serious game to increase bullying awareness. Interact. Learn. Environ. 1–11 (2020). https://doi.org/10.1080/10494820.2020.1799031
2. Alvarado, O., Waern, A.: Towards algorithmic experience: initial efforts for social media contexts. In: Proceedings of the 2018 CHI Conference on Human Factors in Computing Systems, pp. 1–12 (2018). https://doi.org/10.1145/3173574.3173860
3. Andras, P., et al.: Trusting intelligent machines: deepening trust within sociotechnical systems. IEEE Technol. Soc. Mag. **37**(4), 76–83 (2018). https://doi.org/10.1109/MTS.2018.2876107
4. Angelov, P., Soares, E.: Towards explainable deep neural networks (xDNN). Neural Netw. **130**, 185–194 (2020). https://doi.org/10.1016/j.neunet.2020.07.010
5. Arnoux, P.H., Xu, A., Boyette, N., Mahmud, J., Akkiraju, R., Sinha, V.: 25 tweets to know you: a new model to predict personality with social media. In: Proceedings of the International AAAI Conference on Web and Social Media, vol. 11 (2017)
6. Barbera, P., Boydstun, A.E., Linn, S., McMahon, R., Nagler, J.: Automated text classification of news articles: a practical guide. Polit. Anal. **29**(1), 19–42 (2021). https://doi.org/10.1017/pan.2020.8
7. Biran, O., Cotton, C.: Explanation and justification in machine learning: a survey. In: IJCAI-2017 Workshop on Explainable AI (XAI), vol. 8, pp. 8–13 (2017)
8. Blackwell, M., Olson, M.: Reducing model misspecification and bias in the estimation of interactions, pp. 1–35. Working paper (2020)
9. Brundage, M., et al.: The malicious use of artificial intelligence: forecasting, prevention, and mitigation. arXiv preprint arXiv:1802.07228 (2018)
10. Burrell, J.: How the machine 'thinks': understanding opacity in machine learning algorithms. Big Data Soc. **3**(1) (2016). https://doi.org/10.1177/2053951715622512
11. Caliskan, A., Bryson, J.J., Narayanan, A.: Semantics derived automatically from language corpora contain human-like biases. Science **356**(6334), 183–186 (2017). https://doi.org/10.1126/science.aal4230
12. Clewley, N., Dodd, L., Smy, V., Witheridge, A., Louvieris, P.: Eliciting expert knowledge to inform training design. In: Proceedings of the 31st European Conference on Cognitive Ergonomics, pp. 138–143 (2019). https://doi.org/10.1145/3335082.3335091
13. Dodge, J., Liao, Q.V., Zhang, Y., Bellamy, R.K., Dugan, C.: Explaining models: an empirical study of how explanations impact fairness judgment. In: Proceedings of the 24th International Conference on Intelligent User Interfaces, pp. 275–285 (2019). https://doi.org/10.1145/3301275.3302310
14. Du, M., Liu, N., Hu, X.: Techniques for interpretable machine learning. Commun. ACM **63**(1), 68–77 (2019). https://doi.org/10.1145/3359786

15. Dwivedi, Y.K., et al.: Artificial intelligence (AI): multidisciplinary perspectives on emerging challenges, opportunities, and agenda for research, practice and policy. Int. J. Inf. Manag. **57**, 101994 (2019). https://doi.org/10.1016/j.ijinfomgt.2019.08. 002

16. Feng, S., Boyd-Graber, J.: What can AI do for me? Evaluating machine learning interpretations in cooperative play. In: Proceedings of the 24th International Conference on Intelligent User Interfaces, pp. 229–239 (2019). https://doi.org/10. 1145/3301275.3302265

17. Friedman, J.H.: Greedy function approximation: a gradient boosting machine. Ann. Stat. **29**(5), 1189–1232 (2001)

18. Gaudl, S.E., Bryson, J.J.: The extended ramp model: a biomimetic model of behaviour arbitration for lightweight cognitive architectures. Cogn. Syst. Res. **50**, 1–9 (2018). https://doi.org/10.1016/j.cogsys.2018.02.001

19. Goldstein, A., Kapelner, A., Bleich, J., Pitkin, E.: Peeking inside the black box: visualizing statistical learning with plots of individual conditional expectation. J. Comput. Graph. Stat. **24**(1), 44–65 (2015). https://doi.org/10.1080/10618600. 2014.907095

20. Grimmer, J., Roberts, M.E., Stewart, B.M.: Machine learning for social science: an agnostic approach. Ann. Rev. Polit. Sci. **24**, 395–419 (2021). https://doi.org/ 10.1146/annurev-polisci-053119-015921

21. Grimmer, J., Westwood, S.J., Messing, S.: The Impression of Influence: Legislator Communication, Representation, and Democratic Accountability. Princeton University Press, Princeton (2014)

22. Guidotti, R.: Evaluating local explanation methods on ground truth. Artif. Intell. **291**, 103428 (2021). https://doi.org/10.1016/j.artint.2020.103428

23. Gunning, D.: Explainable artificial intelligence (XAI). Defense Advanced Research Projects Agency (DARPA), nd Web **2**(2) (2017)

24. Hainmueller, J., Hazlett, C.: Kernel regularized least squares: reducing misspecification bias with a flexible and interpretable machine learning approach. Polit. Anal. **22**(2), 143–168 (2014). https://doi.org/10.1093/pan/mpt019

25. Hainmueller, J., Mummolo, J., Xu, Y.: How much should we trust estimates from multiplicative interaction models? Simple tools to improve empirical practice. Polit. Anal. **27**(2), 163–192 (2019). https://doi.org/10.1017/pan.2018.46

26. James, G., Witten, D., Hastie, T., Tibshirani, R.: An Introduction to Statistical Learning, vol. 103. Springer, New York (2013). https://doi.org/10.1007/978-1-4614-7138-7

27. Kaur, H., Nori, H., Jenkins, S., Caruana, R., Wallach, H., Vaughan, J.W.: Interpreting interpretability: understanding data scientists' use of interpretability tools for machine learning. Technical report, Working paper (2019)

28. Kenny, E.M., Ford, C., Quinn, M., Keane, M.T.: Explaining black-box classifiers using post-hoc explanations-by-example: the effect of explanations and error-rates in XAI user studies. Artif. Intell. **294**, 103459 (2021). https://doi.org/10.1016/j. artint.2021.103459

29. Kleinerman, A., Rosenfeld, A., Ricci, F., Kraus, S.: Supporting users in finding successful matches in reciprocal recommender systems. User Model. User-Adap. Inter. **31**(3), 541–589 (2020). https://doi.org/10.1007/s11257-020-09279-z

30. Krishnan, M.: Against interpretability: a critical examination of the interpretability problem in machine learning. Philos. Technol. **33**(3), 487–502 (2019). https://doi. org/10.1007/s13347-019-00372-9

31. Lakkaraju, H., Arsov, N., Bastani, O.: Robust and stable black box explanations. In: International Conference on Machine Learning, pp. 5628–5638. PMLR (2020)

32. Lakkaraju, H., Bastani, O.: "How do i fool you?" Manipulating user trust via misleading black box explanations. In: Proceedings of the AAAI/ACM Conference on AI, Ethics, and Society, pp. 79–85 (2020). https://doi.org/10.1145/3375627.3375833

33. Langer, M., et al.: What do we want from explainable artificial intelligence (XAI)?- A stakeholder perspective on XAI and a conceptual model guiding interdisciplinary XAI research. Artif. Intell. **296**, 103473 (2021). https://doi.org/10.1016/j.artint.2021.103473

34. Liao, Q.V., Gruen, D., Miller, S.: Questioning the AI: informing design practices for explainable AI user experiences. In: Proceedings of the 2020 CHI Conference on Human Factors in Computing Systems, pp. 1–15 (2020). https://doi.org/10.1145/3313831.3376590

35. Linardatos, P., Papastefanopoulos, V., Kotsiantis, S.: Explainable AI: a review of machine learning interpretability methods. Entropy **23**(1), 18 (2021). https://doi.org/10.3390/e23010018

36. Lipton, Z.C.: The mythos of model interpretability. Queue **16**(3), 30:31–30:57 (2018). https://doi.org/10.1145/3236386.3241340. http://arxiv.org/abs/1606.03490

37. Maltseva, D., Batagelj, V.: Towards a systematic description of the field using keywords analysis: main topics in social networks. Scientometrics **123**(1), 357–382 (2020). https://doi.org/10.1007/s11192-020-03365-0

38. Miller, T.: Explanation in artificial intelligence: insights from the social sciences. Artif. Intell. **267**, 1–38 (2019). https://doi.org/10.1016/j.artint.2018.07.007

39. Mitchell, T.M., et al.: Machine Learning (1997)

40. Molnar, C.: Interpretable Machine Learning. Lulu.com (2020)

41. Munoko, I., Brown-Liburd, H.L., Vasarhelyi, M.: The ethical implications of using artificial intelligence in auditing. J. Bus. Ethics **167**(2), 209–234 (2020). https://doi.org/10.1007/s10551-019-04407-1

42. Petrović, N.: Tackling the COVID-19 conspiracies: the data-driven approach. In: 2020 55th International Scientific Conference on Information, Communication and Energy Systems and Technologies (ICEST), pp. 27–30. IEEE (2020). https://doi.org/10.1109/ICEST49890.2020.9232760

43. Rheault, L., Cochrane, C.: Word embeddings for the analysis of ideological placement in parliamentary corpora. Polit. Anal. **28**(1), 112–133 (2020). https://doi.org/10.1017/pan.2019.26

44. Ribeiro, M.T., Singh, S., Guestrin, C.: Why should i trust you?. In: Proceedings of the 22nd ACM SIGKDD International Conference on Knowledge Discovery and Data Mining - KDD 2016, pp. 1135–1144. ACM Press, New York (2016). https://doi.org/10.1145/2939672.2939778. http://dl.acm.org/citation.cfm?doid=2939672.2939778

45. Rudin, C.: Stop explaining black box machine learning models for high stakes decisions and use interpretable models instead. Nat. Mach. Intell. **1**(5), 206–215 (2019). https://doi.org/10.1038/s42256-019-0048-x

46. Samek, W., Wiegand, T., Müller, K.R.: Explainable artificial intelligence: understanding, visualizing and interpreting deep learning models. arXiv preprint arXiv:1708.08296 (2017)

47. Schraff, D.: Political trust during the COVID-19 pandemic: rally around the flag or lockdown effects? Eur J Polit Res **60**(4), 1007–1017 (2020). https://doi.org/10.1111/1475-6765.12425

48. Seaver, N.: Algorithms as culture: some tactics for the ethnography of algorithmic systems. Big Data Soc. **4**(2) (2017). https://doi.org/10.1177/2053951717738104

49. Van Eck, N.J., Waltman, L.: Software survey: VOSviewer, a computer program for bibliometric mapping. Scientometrics **84**(2), 523–538 (2010). https://doi.org/10.1007/s11192-009-0146-3

50. van der Waa, J., Nieuwburg, E., Cremers, A., Neerincx, M.: Evaluating XAI: a comparison of rule-based and example-based explanations. Artif. Intell. **291**, 103404 (2021). https://doi.org/10.1016/j.artint.2020.103404

51. Wang, C., Hu, Z., Chiong, R., Bao, Y., Wu, J.: Identification of phishing websites through hyperlink analysis and rule extraction. The Electronic Library (2020)

52. Wang, R., Harari, G., Hao, P., Zhou, X., Campbell, A.T.: SmartGPA: how smartphones can assess and predict academic performance of college students. In: Proceedings of the 2015 ACM International Joint Conference on Pervasive and Ubiquitous Computing, pp. 295–306 (2015). https://doi.org/10.1145/2750858.2804251

53. Wexler, J., Pushkarna, M., Bolukbasi, T., Wattenberg, M., Viégas, F., Wilson, J.: The what-if tool: interactive probing of machine learning models. IEEE Trans. Vis. Comput. Graph. **26**(1), 56–65 (2019)

54. Wiemann, T.T., Lumsdaine, R.L.: The effect of health care policy uncertainty on households' consumption and portfolio choice. SSRN 3418411 (2020). https://doi.org/10.2139/ssrn.3418411

55. Xu, K., Park, D.H., Yi, C., Sutton, C.: Interpreting deep classifier by visual distillation of dark knowledge. arXiv preprint arXiv:1803.04042 (2018)

56. Xu, Y., Yan, X., Liu, X., Zhao, X.: Identifying key factors associated with ridesplitting adoption rate and modeling their nonlinear relationships. Transp. Res. Part A Policy Pract. **144**, 170–188 (2021)

57. Yarkoni, T., Westfall, J.: Choosing prediction over explanation in psychology: lessons from machine learning. Perspect. Psychol. Sci. **12**(6), 1100–1122 (2017). https://doi.org/10.1177/1745691617693393

58. Yu, K., Berkovsky, S., Conway, D., Taib, R., Zhou, J., Chen, F.: Do i trust a machine? Differences in user trust based on system performance. In: Zhou, J., Chen, F. (eds.) Human and Machine Learning. HIS, pp. 245–264. Springer, Cham (2018). https://doi.org/10.1007/978-3-319-90403-0_12

59. Zhang, X., Yin, Z., Feng, Y., Shi, Q., Liu, J., Chen, Z.: NeuralVis: visualizing and interpreting deep learning models. In: 2019 34th IEEE/ACM International Conference on Automated Software Engineering (ASE), pp. 1106–1109. IEEE (2019). https://doi.org/10.1109/ASE.2019.00113

60. Zhou, J., Gandomi, A.H., Chen, F., Holzinger, A.: Evaluating the quality of machine learning explanations: a survey on methods and metrics. Electronics **10**(5), 593 (2021). https://doi.org/10.3390/electronics10050593

# Normalization Issues in Digital Literary Studies: Spelling, Literary Themes and Biographical Description of Writers

Tatiana Sherstinova[1,2]([envelope]) [ORCID] and Margarita Kirina[1] [ORCID]

[1] National Research University Higher School of Economics,
123 Griboyedova emb., St. Petersburg 190068, Russia
tsherstinova@hse.ru, makirina_1@edu.hse.ru

[2] Saint Petersburg State University, 7/9 Universitetskaya emb., St. Petersburg 199034, Russia

**Abstract.** Digital literary studies are a branch of digital humanities, which deals with national or world literatures. In this paper, we discuss normalization issues which are crucial for compiling eCulture resources, designed for cultural analytics, social and literary studies, as well as various aspects of digital humanities. One of such resources is the Corpus of Russian short stories of 1900–1930s with the detailed information about Russian writers of the epoch in concern intended for stylometric, linguistic and literary studies of Russian prose. We see our task to create a literary resource based on a system approach to the literature of a certain time period, which implies inclusion into consideration literary texts of the maximum number of writers, who created their works in the given period, both well-known and peripheral. The paper concerns the problem of data normalization, which is a necessary requirement for statistical processing of data of any kind. We describe how we deal with the problem of different spelling, how we normalize manual annotation of literary themes made by an expert and how we tackle the problem of standardization of biographical descriptions of authors. The obtained normalized data can be used for various kinds of research in the field of literary studies, digital humanities, computational linguistics, and cultural heritage studies.

**Keywords:** Cultural heritage · Digital humanities · Russian literature · Literary corpus · Literature studies · Normalization · Spelling · Thematic annotation · Biographical descriptions of writers

## 1 Introduction

Digital literary studies are a branch of digital humanities which deals with national or world literatures. In this paper, we discuss normalization issues which are crucial for compiling eCulture [29] resources, designed for cultural analytics [20], social and literary studies [4, 5, 25, 26], as well as various aspects of digital humanities [6, 7, 11, 15, 21, 47]. The importance of data normalization is justified by the fact that it is a necessary requirement for statistical processing of data of any kind [27].

© Springer Nature Switzerland AG 2022
D. A. Alexandrov et al. (Eds.): DTGS 2021, CCIS 1503, pp. 332–346, 2022.
https://doi.org/10.1007/978-3-030-93715-7_24

We consider normalization issues from the point of view of a literary digital resource – the Corpus of Russian short stories of 1900–1930s with the detailed information about Russian writers of the epoch in concern, which is intended for stylometric, linguistic and literary studies of Russian prose in the first third of the 20th century [24]. This digital resource is currently being developed in St. Petersburg State University in cooperation with National Research University Higher School of Economics, St. Petersburg. Its design is based on the notion of a literary system proposed about 90 years ago by an outstanding representative of the Russian formal school Yury N. Tynyanov [44]. Tynyanov's ideas, proposed many years ago, have much in common with the modern approach in literary studies known as *distant reading* [26].

The annotated part of the corpus includes texts of 300 writers (one story by each writer, randomly selected) and contains more than 1 million words [23]. It was lemmatized and annotated on morphological and selectively on syntactic and rhythmic levels; all texts were segmented into fragments of narrator's speech, narrator's remarks and characters' speech. Literary annotation includes type of narrative, themes, and some structural features of texts [38, 39].

The results of automatic text processing were subjected to manual correction (removal of homonymy, segmentation tagging, syntactic annotation). Three types of frequency lists — for words, lemmas, parts of speech — have been compiled for each short story, for each of the three historical periods, and for the annotated subcorpus as a whole; statistical parameterization of these frequency lists has been carried out, and the keywords for each of the periods have been statistically calculated [33]; the variation of syntactic complexity was measured [36], and automatic thematic modeling via non-negative matrix factorization was carried out [45].

The corpus becomes the base for stylometric text analysis of Russian prose and cultural studies on Russian writers, both famous and forgotten writers. However, in order to expand its capabilities we plan to enrich it with new texts and new description parameters. Some of these data require normalization, which should allow to prepare literary data for processing by quantitative methods. On the other hand, the suggested transformations, especially for thematic and biographical annotations, present a necessary step for the digital text analysis of corpus data and better human-machine interaction. In this paper, we consider three aspects which require normalization: text spelling, annotation of literary themes and biographical descriptions of writers.

## 2 Normalization of Spelling

The need to normalize spelling is determined by two reasons: 1) the use of old (pre-revolutionary) spelling in Russian texts published earlier than 1918, 2) the deliberate use of non-standard spelling by writers with the aim to provide texts with certain stylistic features — dialectal, vernacular, outdated, etc. The problem of different word spellings requires a solution, since the variety of spelling prevents efficient data parsing, which use standard dictionaries.

## 2.1 Modern Spelling vs. the Post-revolutionary One

The last reform of Russian spelling was carried out in 1917–1918, just in the midst of revolutionary events. Despite the fact that the reform was developed long before the revolution by professional linguists headed by Aleksey Shakhmatov and had no political goals, because of the fact that its practical implementation took place recently after the October revolution, the reform has been long associated with the Bolsheviks' rule. In general, this reform was considered to be successful, partially because it was linked to a political turning point, so that the new writing system became associated with the new order [6].

The aim of the reform was to simplify Russian spelling in general and to unify several inflections and prefixes [1]. In particular, the four letters Ѣ, Ѳ, I and Ѵ were excluded from the alphabet; instead of them the letters Е, Ф, and И were prescribed to be used; the hard sign (Ъ) should no more be used in the end of words and parts of compound words, but it was remained as a dividing mark inside words, etc.

The example of the old and new spelling is presented below. This is a piece of the short story by Arkadij Averchenko *Zheltaya Prostynya* (*The Yellow Sheet*) in old (left) and modern (right) spelling:

| | |
|---|---|
| *Настоящій купальный сезонъ еще не начинался, но, несмотря на это, весь пляжъ, окруженный съ трехъ сторонъ кабинками, былъ усѣянъ лѣнивыми, полузасыпанными пескомъ, фигурами, которыя, какъ ящерицы на солнцѣ, замерли въ каменной неподвижности.* | *Настоящий купальный сезон еще не начинался, но, несмотря на это, весь пляж, окруженный с трех сторон кабинками, был усеян ленивыми, полузасыпанными песком, фигурами, которые, как ящерицы на солнце, замерли в каменной неподвижности.* |

In the Corpus of Russian short stories, it was decided to keep all texts in modern spelling and to convert the old spelling into a new one when necessary. The need for conversion arises primarily for those texts that were not published in modern spelling and were digitized specifically for the corpus. In addition, a number of digitized texts available in open Internet sources are presented in the old spelling.

Due to the fact that the list of spelling changes introduced as a result of the reform of Russian orthography of 1917–1918 is closed, one can use automatic replacements to translate texts in the old spelling into the new one. First of all they are the following:

1) to remove all Ъ at the end of words,
2) to replace Ѣ with Е,
3) to replace Ѳ with Ф,
4) to replace both I and Ѵ with И,
5) to make selective replacements in flexions: *-ыя → -ые, -аго → -ого/-его, -ея → -ее, -ия → -ие, -яго → -его*, etc.
6) to replace particular words: e.g., *оне* (they) → *они*,
7) to remove hyphens before particles *-бы, -ли*,
8) to insert hyphens in the words *что-то, что-либо* and similar,

9)  to change the combinations *-зс* with *-сс, -зп* → *-сп, -зк* → *-ск, -зч* → *-сч*, etc.

However, this procedure cannot currently be performed fully automatically and requires editorial revision.

While spelling procedures are relatively well formalized, the same cannot be said for the use of punctuation marks. Traditionally, the number of punctuation marks is considered to be an indicator of the complexity of syntactic structures, so the rules for placing punctuation marks should also be standardized. However, in the pre-revolutionary prose there is a big variety in this aspect, as different writers might use punctuation in quite different ways — therefore, when texts are brought to a modern punctuation rules, some of the author's marks may be lost. At the moment, the question: *How should the use of punctuation marks be normalized in the transition from the old spelling to the modern one?* — still remains open.

## 2.2   The Deliberate Use of Non-standard Spelling

Another difficulty arises when writers deliberately use non-standard spelling of words in order to provide texts with certain stylistic features. Most often it happens in text fragments referring to spoken speech of characters, reflecting its dialectal or vernacular character. However, many publications concerning peculiarities of the language in the revolutionary historical period note its numerous lexical features: 1) abbreviations, 2) toponymic changes, 3) neologisms, 4) bureaucratese, formulaicity, and phraseology, 5) vulgar tongue, popular speech and slang words [3, 14, 28, 31]. The last means that popular speech became widespread, moreover, it is also used in literary works, especially by the new writers of young Soviet Russia, many of whom did not have the appropriate education [22]. A quantitative confirmation of this fact is, for example, the appearance of the colloquial spelling of the conjunction *что?* (*what?*) as *шо?* in the list of keywords of post-revolutionary era.

According to [41], the following vernacular variants frequently occur in the annotated part of the corpus: *щас* (a colloquial form of the adverb *сейчас* "*now*", which coincides with its real sounding), *пожалста* (a shortened form of the word *пожалуйста* "*please*"), *туды* (a vernacular variant of pronoun *туда* "*there*" / "*thereto*") and *длиньше* (a grammatically incorrect form of the adverb *длиннее* "*longer*"). Moreover, if the first two examples are relatively standard forms which reflect real phonetic sounding of the corresponding words, then the last two examples are grammatically incorrect variants that are not acceptable in speech of educated people, therefore they are markers revealing the character's low social origin.

The presence of words with incorrect spelling in literary texts complicates their processing, as usually they are not included in the dictionaries on the basis of which lemmatization, POS and grammatical parsing is carried out. This problem can be solved in two ways. First of all, it may be proposed to expand the customized dictionaries used by morphological parsers. Another option is to translate copies of texts into normalized forms for their subsequent automatic processing. It seems that the second option is more preferable in those cases when it is supposed to use different software.

# 3  Normalization of Literary Themes Annotation

## 3.1  Expert Literary Themes Annotation

In last two decades, one may observe an increase of studies of fiction language by formal, corpus and statistical methods [2, 12, 19, 47]. Besides, this research area takes advantage of ideas, tools and practices being developed within digital humanities [7, 8, 11, 37]. However, a common drawback of the existing resources is a poor representation of literary annotation. The reasons for this lag are understandable: at present, there are no automation procedures for literary annotation.

The need for thematic annotation is determined by a number of factors. First, it is necessary for correct interpretation of frequency word lists of different writers, as well as for clusters of writers, built on the basis of the proximity of these dictionaries [33]. It is obvious that the vocabulary of some particular literary work is largely determined by its themes, not only by stylistic preferences of its author. Therefore, when creating the corpus, it seemed advisable to introduce into the corpus database such a description field as the "main themes" of the story.

When creating a list of themes, it was decided to abandon the use of standard thematic sets like "100 common thematic topics", which 1) from our point of view, are not always suitable for describing the genre of short prose like short story, and 2) do not take into account the historical specifics of the period under review, in the center of which are the revolutionary years, which radically changed the face of Russia and could not but affect literary creativity.

When forming the list of topics, it was decided that they should be based on literary data, that is, to follow the empirical path. The initial list of topics was suggested by Tatiana Skrebtsova and described in [39]. Here, it should be noted that the creation of a theme mark-up for the corpus which consists of literary texts only is a quite challenging objective. The explanation lies in the controversial position of theme in literary tradition. Even the term itself has various definitions, not to mention the ambiguity of its representation in the story. Due to the difficulties that theme-naming procedure reveals, the scholars are often reluctant to consider the theme as a valuable source of information about the text [10]. However, a different view on theme as a combination of semantic components of text is also present, declaring its relevance to literary analysis [43, 46].

As a result, the list of 89 themes was suggested, which covers a diverse range of themes occurred in Russian short stories. The initial theme mark-up was done manually by an expert. The chosen approach is "the identification of all semantic components that contribute to the plot, determine the protagonist's motives and actions and directly bear on the conflict and its resolution" [35]. The number of detected themes per story is not fixed: one story can be described via several themes at the same time. This scheme was proven to be quite descriptive and effective for the comparison of corpus entities [ibid.].

## 3.2  Normalization of Expert Literary Themes Annotation Scheme

However, the list of 89 themes turned out to be rather complex to work with and, what is more important, it had too many detailed thematic elements lying on the random levels of explicitness. Because of that, it was decided to carry out data normalization for this list of themes.

The aim of this procedure was to reduce the number of thematic tags, combining several similar tags into the generalized one. For example, three different tags *Civil war*; *Russo-Japanese war*; *World War I* can be generalized by the common tag WAR. The procedure reminds the labeling with the limited number of categories, or in our case — tags. Each tag has been given a unique code. As a result, the list of themes has been reduced from 89 to 30. The normalized theme annotation scheme includes the following tags: FUTURE, MODE OF LIFE, RELATIONS, WAR, CITY LIFE, MONEY, CHILDREN, VIRTUE, LEISURE TIME, ART, BEAUTY, LOVE, DREAM, YOUNG PEOPLE, VIOLENCE, POLITICAL STRUGGLE, VICE, NATURE, PROGRESS, MENTAL STATE, REVOLUTION, RELIGION, FREEDOM, FAMILY, DEATH, SLEEP, SOCIAL GROUPS, SOCIAL PROCESSES, LABOR, and FANTASY. The correspondence between the initial scheme and the normalized one can be found in Table 1.

The undertaken movement from the detailed thematic elements to the more abstract ones is reflected in the main approach to tagging that underlines a metaphoric nature of theme as a radial linguistic category [17]. Evidentially, one certain theme, acting as a semantic invariant of the text, can cover several meanings that are being expressed by various authors. Besides, it is possible for one theme to include a number of semantic features which are not necessarily related in an obvious way.

In the light of this, the reader's figure becomes crucial. During the reading, the reader participates in the decoding of fiction reality, otherwise the interpretation of text would be impossible. This procedure as well as categorization is cognitive by nature [42]. The interpretation which leads to the identification of the story's theme is possible due to imagination — the understanding of text via conceptual metaphors. Thus, the theme of text is not being embedded entirely by author. The theme's formulation mainly depends on the reader, his/her ability to read through the text. With regard to this specificity of the theme's nature, it is needed to conduct the theme annotation for a certain group of readers.

According to [46], it is recommended to distinguish themes, having an average reader in mind. This kind of reader demands the combination of abstract and explicit themes together. These themes have to be understandable, expressed by the wide-known terms. In other words, any sophistications or, on the other hand, overgeneralizations are unwanted. For example, the tag LOVE connects such subthemes as *romantic love, unrequited love, mutual love, passion, sexual affection,* and etc. At the same time, it was decided to put the thematic element *parent's love* into a different category — FAMILY, uniting it with such themes as *fathers and sons, marriage, unfaithfulness,* and etc. This is the evidence of the annotation on two levels of explication, induced by the aim to not only unite the texts by one theme but also to strike the differences between them.

In the ongoing study the thematic annotation seems to be crucial because of the historical specificity of the corpus. The stories have been written during important social, political, and ideological changes in Russia: for instance, World War I, the February and October Revolutions, and the Civil war. This kind of meta-information in the corpus database allows to learn about the literary text "as a part, expression of something more

**Table 1.** The list of theme tags matched with themes in expert annotation.

| Normalized tags | Related themes in expert annotation |
| --- | --- |
| ART | Art, creative activity |
| BEAUTY | Ideal vs. reality |
| CHILDREN | Children |
| CITY LIFE | City vs. nature; country vs. city life |
| DEATH | Death from gunshot wounds; death from natural causes; execution; sudden and accidental death; suicide; murder (not at war) |
| DREAM | Dreams vs. reality; frustrated hopes, disillusionment |
| FAMILY | Fathers and sons; marriage; parental love; unfaithfulness |
| FANTASY | Doppelgänger theme; mysticism, hallucinations, presentiments |
| FREEDOM | Feeling of freedom |
| FUTURE | Bright future |
| LABOR | Non–peasant work |
| LEISURE TIME | Christmas; Christmas tree; New Year's Eve |
| LOVE | Body life; mutual sexual love of man and woman; prostitution; romantic love; unrequited love |
| MENTAL STATE | Insanity; loneliness; passion for life; remorse; shame |
| MODE OF LIFE | Boredom; monotonous life |
| MONEY | Bribery; money; poverty, hunger, hardships; the rich vs. the poor |
| NATURE | Country life; land as property; pets and animals; hunting |
| POLITICAL STRUGGLE | Punishments for political crimes (prison, hard labor, deportation); revolutionary movement |
| PROGRESS | Explorations and inventions; industrial advance; new lands development |
| RELATIONS | Deceit; fraternity, solidarity; friendship; jealousy; mentorship; revenge; rivalry; treachery |
| RELIGION | Christian God; religion as a social institution |
| REVOLUTION | October revolution |
| SINS | Alcoholism; envy; greed; pretense; platitude; outer self vs. inner self |
| SLEEP | Disturbed sleep; sleep vs. reality |
| SOCIAL GROUPS | Cossacks; peasant life; relations and conflicts between different nations; the Jewish question; working class |
| SOCIAL PROCESSES | Emigration; mass education; new social order; the old vs. the new; pre–revolutionary unrest; women's emancipation |
| VIOLENCE | Rape; cruelty; blood |
| VIRTUE | Nobility of character, magnanimity, self–sacrifice; readiness to forgive; spiritual rebirth; willingness to help, be of use, philanthropy |
| WAR | Civil war; Russo–Japanese war; World War I |
| YOUNG PEOPLE | Young people |

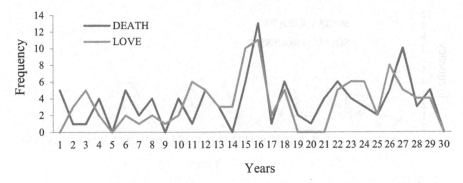

**Fig. 1.** Frequency distribution of tags DEATH and LOVE.

meaningful than the text itself: the poet's personality, psychological moment or social situation" [18]. For the same reason the annotation tends to be balanced and includes not only "popular" themes (*love, friendship, death*, etc.) but history-related ones (*political struggle, revolution, war*, etc.) as well.

It has to be mentioned, though, that even the "popular" (or common) themes can be used to characterize a certain period. The diachronic comparison of tags shows that they are not evenly distributed. Figure 1 illustrates the increase in the number of stories labeled with tags DEATH and LOVE between the years 1914 and 1917. After the revolution, the decline in the usage of the theme LOVE can be noticed. At this time the frequency of the tag DEATH remains to be stable until the next significant growth in the years of the Civil war in Russia and the period after marked by the years from 1925 to 1928. This sort of tendency has been expected for history-related themes, however, not for the common ones.

With regard to social and political themes, a strong revival of interest also correlates with the year of text's creation. Moreover, it is vividly seen during the time of historical changes. There is a clear expansion in the number of stories labeled with tags SOCIAL_GROUPS and SOCIAL_PROCESSES after the revolution (Fig. 2). The tag SOCIAL PROCESSES shares such themes of expert annotation as *pre-revolutionary unrest, new social order, emigration* and so on. The tag SOCIAL GROUPS includes the following thematic elements: *Cossacks, peasant life, working class, relations and conflicts between different nations,* and *the Jewish question*. It explains the popularity of these tags in the named period.

The advantage of this list of tags is that it can easily be changed. On the whole, the idea of annotation echoes the main principles of thematic implication and explication [46]. With respect to these principles, it should be possible to convert any proposed theme from one level of explicitness to another. The tags in the present list allow this kind of both-sided transformation. So, the tags that do not help to distinguish the texts from each other can be removed and replaced with the detailed versions of them. The tags that are, on the contrary, too specific can be joined with the ones they were originally separated from.

All things considered, the interpretation of this tagging system proves to be effective, however, requires an additional commentary on the contents of each tag. For the named

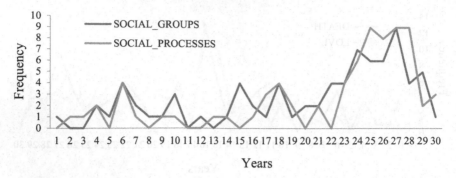

**Fig. 2.** Frequency distribution of tags SOCIAL_GROUPS and SOCIAL PROCESSES.

reason, the subthematic mark-up is planned to be provided in order to ease the search in the corpus for users. The inner level of the theme annotation demands a rereading of the stories by several different experts and another normalization procedure – individually approaching the certain thematic groups, but yet abstractedly corresponding them with each other.

## 4 Normalization of Biographical Information About Writers

The task of including in the corpus texts by the maximum number of Russian writers whose creative work falls into the period under study is closely related with another important task, namely, the preservation and popularization of Russian literary heritage, a significant part of which during the Soviet period and until recently was practically erased from the memory of the people. As already noted, to date, a list of writers that has been formed exceeds 2800 names. Of these, the average reader is relatively familiar with 100 names at best, whereas the overwhelming majority of writers is little-known even for literary critics or completely forgotten. Therefore, unlike well-known biographical systems that are developed on the basis of already existing biographical databases [9, 13, 15, 16], in our case we cannot use any ready-made biographical resource but must develop that of our own. This contributes to the humanitarian value of our project.

The biographical module is designed of as one of the parts of the Corpus of Russian short stories. Thus, for building a formal model of a literary system, as well as for studying individual author's styles and artistic trends, it seems appropriate to take into account certain sociological characteristics and biography features of writers. Apparently, social environment, education and profession of the writer make a significant contribution in the formation of his/her stylistic skills and ideological preferences. Taking these factors into account for the quantitative analysis of literary texts will make it possible to determine whether a relationship between social characteristics of an author (and some important features of his/her biography) and the personality of his language and style really exists, and what is its real measure.

## 4.1  Biographical Database

The first version of the biographical database contains three main modules: 1) the list of authors, 2) biographical data, 3) sources of biographical data. The detailed description of the database fields can be found in [32]. The task was to collect biographical information in order to accumulate material and assess the prospects for its optimal normalization, therefore, at this stage there were no strict requirements for filling these fields.

As a result, from the list of 300 prose writers whose texts were included into the annotated corpus, biographical data of varying degrees of detail were found for 284 out of 300 writers; the biographical data found for 7 little-known writers is minimal, and for 9 authors (P. Uryupinsky, Anton Gorelov, Alexander Tyukhanov and others) we did not find any reliable information, even the years of their lives.

## 4.2  Normalization of Biographical Information

The next important task of creating the biographical database of Russian writers is the normalization of information presented in description fields, which should allow automatic search and filtering of data by appropriate parameters. Combining biographical information with corpus annotation of literary works will make it possible to look at literary texts, language and style features from a new angle – from the point of view of individual sociological characteristics of authors and specific features of their life path. We think that such an interdisciplinary approach could be very promising.

Taking into account the enormous amount of unsorted data, it was attempted to normalize the information that has already been collected, starting with those authors whose texts are presented in the annotated subcorpus. The first step includes dealing with numerous aliases that authors used while publishing their works. To begin with, each author in the database has a unique code. For example, *A041* is a code for *Budishchev Aleksej Nikolaevich* (1867–1916). Information about pseudonyms mainly obtained from [40] is presented in a special table which is linked with the main one by the writer's code. Thus, for Budishchev we have the following pseudonyms: *A. B., Aljosha Chudilovich, Alikber*, and etc. [ibid.]. The indication of this category is inevitable due to the cases of the reoccurring pseudonyms among different authors.

The next procedure was aimed to standardize the dates. Here, the problem lies in the complexity of the output: in Russia, before the revolution, the Julian calendar was used; it was switched to the Gregorian one only after 1918. In the considering timespan a majority of dates is shown in both systems. The years of birth and death were removed from the dates given in the "day-month" formatting style to a separate column. By the year, the modern days and months of birth and death were calculated. According to [30], for the years from 1st March 1800 to 29th February 1900 the added to the "old-fashioned" date number of days should be equal to 12, for the next years, until 2100, the number of days is 13.

Moreover, the causes of death have been proposed to be included too. They were classified in the following way: *death from old age, disease, suicide, unnatural death*. A more detailed version of the list implies naming the specifics of death, mentioning its circumstances (if it is possible). For instance, the *disease phthisis* could be induced by such circumstances as *banishment, accident, age*, and so on.

With regard to the places of birth, death, and living, the situation is similar. A lot of cities and towns that are found in the sample do not have the same names today. For instance, *Saint Petersburg* was renamed at the beginning of the World War I as *Petrograd* and then, after Lenin's death, as *Leningrad*. So, some of the authors were born in *Saint Petersburg* but died in *Petrograd* or even in *Leningrad*. This kind of transformation seems to be relevant for the visualization which is to be conducted afterwards. Besides, it is also planned to add information about the commemorative places of these writers later.

To derive the social background the authors come from, the information about their parents needs to be sorted. The suggested fields are *mother's name, father's name, mother's nationality, father's nationality, mother's descent,* and *father's descent*. In this way the nationality and descent of the authors themselves can be identified.

Logically, another piece of information related to the author's background is the type of education. The peculiarity here is connected with the tendency to homeschooling in the 19th century when the majority of authors presented in the corpus were born. So, the education was divided into two categories: *secondary education* and *higher education*. The statuses for each level of education are *yes, no, unfinished*. A more detailed version includes the name of university (*Saint Petersburg State University, Sorbonne, Kazan University, Kiev University,* and etc.), its location (*Moscow, Saint Petersburg, Paris, Kazan, Kiev,* and etc.), and the year of graduation.

Another biographical feature that prompts interest is the professions of Russian writers. However, we mean to consider not the profession they acquired at the university but only that kind of professional activity in which they were actually involved. For instance, *writer, playwright, journalist, doctor, official (chinovnik)*, and so on. For that matter, the places where the writers worked also become crucial.

From the previous point emerges the systematization of the publishing activity. Though the main focus of the corpus is short stories, it is worth mentioning the other genres these authors are usually associated with, too, alongside with the main literary movements to which their works belong. The list of other genres includes *short story, essay (ocherk), novel, poetry,* etc. With regards to literary movements, the frequent ones are *symbolism, realism, social realism,* etc.

A huge part of Russian pre-revolutionary writers finished their lives in emigration. It is intended to learn how many of the authors emigrated from Russia and, on the contrary — how many stayed. So, the main part of the database presents the common information: *yes* (emigrated) or *no* (did not emigrate). For those authors who did emigrate the table will include data about the place where they lived during the time of emigration and when it started and ended.

The suggested ways of biographical data normalization are aimed to lay a solid ground for the further work towards the creation of a fully-fledged annotated database of Russian short stories. As there is no unified resource that contains information about all of these writers, it makes the intended objectives even more challenging.

## 5  Conclusion

The paper concerns the problem of data normalization, which is a necessary requirement for quantitative processing of any data. We described our approaches to normalization of spelling, literary themes and biographical descriptions of authors. Normalization provides new opportunities for further quantitative studies. For example, basing on normalized literary themes distribution, an experiment aimed at comparison of results of topic modelling via non-negative matrix factorization (NMF) with that of manual theme annotation performed by an expert was carried out [34]. The obtained normalized data can be used for various kinds of research in the fields of eCulture, literary studies, digital humanities, computational linguistics, and cultural heritage studies.

Obviously, the proposed normalization approaches have certain drawbacks, therefore they cannot be considered to be final, but at the moment they are quite effective. Another difficulty is that the described procedures cannot be fully automatized. For example, for normalization of spelling, even if some scripts are used, additional verification is still needed; with regards to normalization of themes, it can only be conducted by a human since it often requires referring to the text in concern and its close analysis. In future, the latter may be improved by implementing the training of models on the results of expert thematic annotation.

Further, it should be noted that the number of levels of data annotation that may also require normalization is increasing. In particular, an experiment is now being conducted on the parallel literary annotation of the corpus by three independent experts, which, on the one hand, will allow assessing the level of agreement in the interpretation of literary texts by different experts, and on the other hand, will give a new array of datasets, which will obviously require further normalization techniques.

All these measures should allow to enhance the quality of normalization of the different types of annotation that are suggested for the literary texts and, what is more important, to make it more user-oriented. This study suggests that the literary corpus data can be used for various purposes and by a wide range of cultural institutions. Normalization thus is aimed to present the information in question not only as detailed and comprehensive but also applicable in different fields that are undergoing digital transformation at the moment, first of all – education (universities, schools, museums, libraries, etc.), to what extent it is possible.

**Acknowledgements.** The research is supported by the Russian Foundation for Basic Research, project # 17-29-09173 "The Russian language on the edge of radical historical changes: the study of language and style in prerevolutionary, revolutionary and post-revolutionary artistic prose by the methods of mathematical and computer linguistics (a corpus-based research on Russian short stories)".

# References

1. Abramenko, F.: Novoe russkoe pravopisanie [New Russian orthography], Vol. 1 of Polnyj sbornik pravil pravopisanija s uprazhnenijami i kratkimi svedenijami o znakah prepinanija [The compilation of orthographic rules with exercises], Moscow (1918)
2. Balossi, G.: Corpus Linguistic Approach to Literary Language and Characterization: Virginia Woolf's The Waves. John Benjamins Publishing Company, Amsterdam (2014)
3. Barannikov, A.: Iz nablyudenij nad razvitiem russkogo yazyka v poslednie gody [From observations of the development of the Russian language in recent years] (1921)

4. Bordoni, C.: Introduzione alla sociologia della letteratura. Pacini, Pisa (1974)
5. Bourdieu, P.: Rules of Art: Genesis and Structure of the Literary Field. Stanford University Press, Palo Alto (1996)
6. Bunčić, D.: Factors influencing the success and failure of writing reforms. Studi Slavistici **14**(1), 21–46 (2017)
7. Cameron, F., Kenderdine, S.: Theorizing Digital Cultural Heritage: A Critical Discourse. MIT Press, Cambridge (2007)
8. Carter, B. (ed.): Digital Humanities: Current Perspective, Practices, and Research. Emerald Publishing Limited, Bingley (2013)
9. Dutch Biography Portal. http://www.biografischportaal.nl/en/. Accessed 20 June 2021
10. Esin, A.: Prinzipi i Priyemi Analyza Litaraturnogo Proizvedeniya [The Principles and Techniques of Analysis of Literary Text]. Flinta, Nauka [Science], Moscow (2000)
11. Fischer, F., Trilcke, P., Kittel, C., Milling, C., Skorinkin, D.: To catch a protagonist: quantitative dominance relations in German language drama (1730–1930). In: Digital Humanities 2018: Book of Abstracts [Libro de resúmenes], pp. 193–201. Red de Humanidades Digitales A. C., Mexico (2018)
12. Fischer-Starcke, B.: Corpus Linguistics in Literary Analysis: Jane Austen and Her Contemporaries. Continuum, London (2010)
13. Fokkens, A., ter Braake, S., et al.: BiographyNet: extracting relations between people and events. In: ICT.OPEN 2016. Amersfoort, Netherlands (2016)
14. Granovskaya, L.: Russkij literaturnyj yazyk v konce XIX i XX veke [Russian Literary Language at the End of the 19th and 20th Centuries]. Elpis, Moscow (2005)
15. Gruber, C., Wandl-Vogt, E.: Austrian Biographical Dictionary 1815–1950 (ÖBL), Wien (2017)
16. Hyvönen, E., et al.: BiographySampo – publishing and enriching biographies on the semantic web for digital humanities research. In: Hitzler, P., et al. (eds.) ESWC 2019. LNCS, vol. 11503, pp. 574–589. Springer, Cham (2019). https://doi.org/10.1007/978-3-030-21348-0_37
17. Lakoff, G.: Women, Fire, and Dangerous Things: What Categories Reveal About the Mind? University of Chicago, Chicago (1987)
18. Lotman, Y.: O poetakh i poezii [About Poets and Poetry]. Iskusstvo, St. Petersburg (1996)
19. Mahlberg, M., Stockwell, P., et al.: CLiC Dickens: novel uses of concordances for the integration of corpus stylistics and cognitive poetics. Corpora **11**(3), 433–463 (2016)
20. Manovich, L.: Cultural Analytics. The MIT Press, Cambridge (2020)
21. Martynenko, G.: Metody matematicheskoj lingvistiki v stilisticheskikh issledovanijakh [Methods of Mathematical Linguistics in Stylistic Studies]. Nestor-Istoriya, St. Petersburg (2019)
22. Martynenko, G.: Stilizovannyye sintaksicheskiye triady v russkom rasskaze pervoy treti XX veka [Stylized syntactic triads in Russian short story of the first third of the 20th century]. In: Proceedings of the Int. Conference on 'Corpus Linguistics – 2019', pp. 395–404. St. Petersburg State University, St. Petersburg (2019)
23. Sherstinova, T., Martynenko, G.: Linguistic and stylistic parameters for the study of literary language in the corpus of Russian short stories of the first third of the 20th century. In: R. Piotrowski's Readings in Language Engineering and Applied Linguistics, Proceedings of the III International Conference on Language Engineering and Applied Linguistics (PRLEAL-2019), St. Petersburg, Russia, CEUR Workshop Proceedings, vol. 2552, pp. 105–120 (2020)
24. Martynenko, G.Y., Sherstinova, T.Y., Popova, T.I., Melnik, A.G., Zamirajlova, E.V.: O printsipakh sozdaniya korpusa russkogo rasskaza pervoy treti XX veka. In: Proceedings of the XV International Conference on Computer and Cognitive Linguistics "TEL 2018", pp. 180–197. Kazan Federal University, Kazan (2018)
25. Milner, A.: Literature, Culture and Society. Routledge, London (2005)

26. Moretti, F.: Distant Reading. Verso, London (2013)
27. Oppel, A.: Data Modeling: A Beginner's Guide, McGraw-Hill Education, New York (2010)
28. Polivanov, E.: Revolyuciya i literaturnye yazyki soyuza SSR [The revolution and the literary languages of the USSR]. Polivanov E. Za marksistskoye yazykoznaniye. Federatsiya, pp. 73–94. Moscow (1931)
29. Ronchi, A.M.: eCulture. Cultural Content in the Digital Age, Springer, Heidelberg (2009). https://doi.org/10.1007/978-3-540-75276-9
30. Seleshnikov, S.I.: Istoriya kalendarya i khronologiya [History of the Calendar and Chronology]. Nauka, Moscow (1970)
31. Selishchev, A.: Yazyk revolyutsionnoy epokhi: Iz nablyudeniy nad russkim yazykom poslednikh let (1917–1926) [The Language of the Revolutionary Era: From Observations of the Russian Language of Recent Years (1917–1926)]. Rabotnik prosveshcheniya, Moscow (1928)
32. Sherstinova, T.: Bibliographic database of Russian writers: towards creation of the Russian short stories corpus of the 20th century. In: Proceedings of the International Conference "Corpus Linguistics-2019", pp. 439–447. Publishing House of St. Petersburg University, St. Petersburg (2019)
33. Sherstinova, T., et al.: Frequency word lists and their variability (the case of Russian fiction in 1900–1930). In: 27th Conference of Open Innovations Association FRUCT, pp. 366–373. University of Trento, Italy (2020)
34. Sherstinova, T., Mitrofanova, O., Skrebtsova, T., Zamiraylova, E., Kirina, M.: Topic modelling with NMF vs. expert topic annotation: the case study of Russian fiction. In: Martínez-Villaseñor, L., Herrera-Alcántara, O., Ponce, H., Castro-Espinoza, F.A. (eds.) MICAI 2020. LNCS (LNAI), vol. 12469, pp. 134–151. Springer, Cham (2020). https://doi.org/10.1007/978-3-030-60887-3_13
35. Sherstinova, T., Skrebtsova, T.: Russian literature around the October revolution: a quantitative exploratory study of literary themes and narrative structure in Russian short stories of 1900–1930. In: Proceedings of the International Conference "Internet and Modern Society" IMS-2020. CEUR Workshop Proceedings, vol. 2813, pp. 117–128 (2021)
36. Sherstinova, T., Ushakova, E., Melnik, A.: Measures of syntactic complexity and their change over time (the case of Russian). In: Proceedings of the 27th Conference of Open Innovations Association FRUCT, pp. 221–229. University of Trento, Italy (2020)
37. Skorinkin, D.: Extracting character networks to explore literary plot dynamics. In: Komp'juternaja lingvistika i intellektual'nye tehnologii: po materialam ezhegodnoj mezhdunarodnoj konferencii "Dialog" [Proceedings of the International Conference on "Dialog", 1.16 (23), pp. 257–270. Pub. [Izd-vo] RGGU, Moscow (2017)
38. Skrebtsova, T.: Struktura narrativa v russkom rasskaze nachala XX veka [Narrative structure of the Russian short story in the early XX century]. In: Proceedings of the International Conference on Corpus Linguistics-2019, pp. 426–431. St. Petersburg (2019)
39. Skrebtsova, T.G.: Thematic Tagging of literary fiction: the case of early 20th century Russian short stories. In: Proceedings of the International Conference "Internet and Modern Society" IMS-2020, CEUR Workshop Proceedings, vol. 2813, pp. 265–276 (2021)
40. Slovar' psevdonimov [Dictionary of pseudonyms]. http://feb-web.ru/feb/masanov/. Accessed 20 June 2021
41. Sokolova, A.: Dialect, Colloquial and Phonetic Features in Literary Texts: Approaches to Corpus Linguistics Analysis, bachelor coursework. National Research University Higher School of Economics, Saint Petersburg (2020)
42. Stockwell, P.: Cognitive Poetics: An Introduction. Routledge, London (2002)
43. Tomashevsky, B.: Teoriya literatury [The Theory of Literature], pp. 176–192. Aspekt Press [Aspect Press, London] (1996)
44. Tynyanov, Y.: Arkhaisty i novatory [Archaists and Innovators]. Priboi Publ., Leningrad (1929)

45. Zamiraylova, E., Mitrofanova, O.: Dynamic topic modelling of Russian fiction prose of the first third of the XXth century by means of non-negative matrix factorization. In: R. Piotrowski's Readings in Language Engineering and Applied Linguistics, Proceedings of the III International Conference on Language Engineering and Applied Linguistics (PRLEAL-2019), CEUR Workshop Proceedings, vol. 2552, pp. 321–339 (2020)

46. Zholkovsky, A., Shcheglov, Yu.: K Ponyatiyam 'Tema' i 'Poeticheskiy Mir' [About the concepts "theme" and "poetic world"]. In: Shcheglov, Y.K. (ed.) Izbrannye Trudy, pp. 37–78. Izdatelsky zentr Rossiyskogo gosudarstvennogo gumanitarnogo universiteta (2013)

47. Zyngier, S.: Macbeth through the computer: literary evaluation and pedagogical implications. In: The Quality of Literature: Linguistic Studies in Literary Evaluation, Linguistic Approaches to Literature, vol. 4, pp. 169–190 (2008)

# Prototyping of a Client for Board Games Automated Testing and Analysis

Vlada Krainikova[✉] [iD]

Higher School of Economics, Saint-Petersburg, Russia
vakraynikova@edu.hse.ru

**Abstract.** The process of tabletop game design is a complex iterative process that involves many tasks. Given the development of the industry, Computer Aided and even Mixed Initiative Design (MID) practices appear more and more often. Moreover, the academic field produces a variety of tools relevant for game designer's assistance. However, the question arises: to what extent these tools meet the needs of modern tabletop game designers and do they fit into the current structure of the board game development process. This work aims to identify tabletop game designers needs and based on them prototype tabletop game design assistant (TGDA). We conducted in-depth semi structured interviews with tabletop game designers and described needs with a Job Story framework. Then, we partially implemented and prototyped them within a Jumanji Game test case for reliable interactive system assessment (Wizard of Oz). Findings demonstrate that game designers do not use any specialized or academic tools, even though the tabletop game development requires computer assistance. We indicate several reasons for that and propose principles of close-to-end-user production approach for convenient and reliable development. We also provide list of uncovered tabletop game designers needs for future implementation together with overall TGDA system requirements and areas of potential academic interest regarding tabletop game design.

**Keywords:** Game design · Tabletop games · Mixed initiative design · User research · Prototyping

## 1 Introduction

In recent decades the tabletop game design industry has undergone significant development: each year a plenty of both new games and sequels are released, the number of players and authors is growing[1]. However, development is accompanied by new challenges, additionally, the pandemic has hit the industry significantly, given that social interaction as one of the main features of non-solitaire board games [1] was partially restricted. Nevertheless, this has served as an incentive for the creation, development,

---

[1] https://boardgamegeek.com/.

© Springer Nature Switzerland AG 2022
D. A. Alexandrov et al. (Eds.): DTGS 2021, CCIS 1503, pp. 347–361, 2022.
https://doi.org/10.1007/978-3-030-93715-7_25

or more active usage of digital tools such as Tabletopia[2], Tabletop Simulator[3], Yucata[4] and others that allow distant game playtests to be conducted, etc.

All this evidence the tabletop game design process diving deeper into Computer Aided Design (CAD) practices, whose main idea is assisting a person with computer initiative to create certain artifacts. It remains unclear how far the use of CAD practices goes and whether it achieved Mixed initiative design (MID) or co-creation (MI-CC) level, which suggest to drive decision not only by human, but by a machine as well, which results in a synergy of initiatives of both (not necessarily equal) [2]. In the academic field, they are found separate examples of practices [3–5], as well as autonomous app solutions [6–8], with a different, sometimes even polar, ratio of Human initiative (HI) and Computer initiative (CI).

They mention various advantages computer computational capabilities, machine learning (ML), artificial intelligence (AI), or the MID method may have while testing and analyzing board games, especially, comparing to conventional classical playtests. Thus, Borovikov et al. concludes that player-assisted playtesting is an expensive and not always efficient practice, while AIs can handle same sessions faster while exploring a larger play area with a greater number of tests [9]. Large exploration area, according to Mahlmann et al., allows one to perfectly cope with the task of identifying unbalanced elements or combinations [5], while Guhe and Lascarides use the same advantage to balance entire game strategies [10]. Despite the AI excellence, Beyer et al. question how much playtests can and should be automated and conclude the most effective approach to playtesting, in terms of the results obtained, is a combination of manual and computer test [3]. De Mesentier Silva et al. also agree upon MID being best practice, especially in the early stages of design, as it allows to evaluate the fundamentals of a game, identify exploits not covered by the rules, determine the dominant strategies or elements and, together with the game designer (GD), come to the optimal game set, from a mathematical and experiential sides [4].

Notwithstanding advantages and disadvantages described the question remains: do these solutions meet the needs of modern tabletop GDs and do they fit into the current structure of the board game development process?

The paper goal is to answer this question by identifying the needs of GDs and prototyping an appropriate assistant client. The prior scope of this research is devoted to board games testing and analysis, as this area represents the iterative nature of game design process and takes a major part of it [11].

We conducted 7 in-depth semi-structured interviews with experienced tabletop GDs. Based on obtained data, client concept was developed: from user scenarios and functionality to integration requirements. Interactive prototype was used to test the concept in the second round of interviews with same participants.

---

[2] https://tabletopia.com/.

[3] https://www.tabletopsimulator.com/.

[4] https://www.yucata.de/en/.

# 2 Related Research

## 2.1 Game Design as Business Process

Game design is a complicated process of game or play creation [11], where the game is a formal interactive dynamic system, which parts relate to each other in a certain manner [12]. The structure of game design process as of any design is not strictly determined. Thus, Cardona-Rivera [13] relies upon the situated artifact-centric Function–Behavior–Structure model of the design activity in general [14], while Duke considers game design precisely indicating 9 core steps [15]. However, both points out the iterative nature of design process, in which trial-and-error part is crucial for the progress. Schell claims the same comparing the game design process to software development, where iteration or each loop drives development [16]. Feichin proposes a higher level paradigm with only three prior levels: idea conceptualization, design detailing and implementation with creativity flowing through out all of them [17].

O'Donnell summarizes expands process structure: game design tasks get accompanied by business operations [18]. Baba and Tschang also considered structure of process and described several schemes evolutionarily replaced by each other: a linear model from requirements analysis to testing; a waterfall model adding overlapping and iterations; and a spiral model which made this sequence repeat itself over and over [19]. Salen discussed a different game design conceptual framework based on Rules, Play and Culture schemas, where Rules are responsible for a game formal logic or its mathematical structure, Play focuses on experiential part of player's interaction and Culture captures the cultural surrounding or a game context [11].

The above-mentioned game design process description allows to conclude several game design process features settling framework for a computer assistant development. Firstly, game design is an iterative process, and the major loops are related to the artifact creation itself. It makes trial-and-error stage, on one hand, the core activity of game design, but, on the other hand, its bottleneck majorly lacking for computer assistance. Then, game design is also a business process with several adjacent tasks beyond game creation that should not be eliminated when speaking of assistant functionality. Finally, the game is a synthesis of formal rules, allowing automatization, and experiential play, bringing in a strong necessity for a human to be involved in testing and development together with the computer assistant.

## 2.2 Existing Tabletop Game Test Services

Academic environment does not provide many articles dedicated to development of full-fledged clients associated with the tabletop game design. Such studies predominantly observe service for the play testing and game analysis that can be divided into two fundamentally different groups.

First group use digital capabilities to conduct games remotely and practically do not differ from real game sessions in terms of the information obtained. For example, Tabletopia, a digital platform where real players from all over the world can remotely test the game or its prototype, however, it does not provide any statistics or analysis of the game features. Tabletop Simulator is like Tabletopia but has additional features:

VR support, players team voice or text chat, administration over game session (to avoid bulling or griefing). Services provide interface for interacting and constructor alike game creation system, however, lack for computer opponents.

Second group use the computer computational capabilities to test game AI rather than a game. Therefore, received game insights are by-product. Tabletop Framework (TAG) is one of the examples [6, 20]. TAG allows user to prototype a game and test it through AI-facilitated analysis or a human-computer game via GUI. Currently, TAG unites 7 modern games (can be customized) to cover various mechanics and characteristics, and several AI agents exploiting different strategies. The reasoning behind TAG development is that modern board games are very complex and receive little academic attention, as researchers mostly focus on traditional board games (Go, Chess, etc.) or limited general game playing frameworks (GGP, Open Spiel, Ludii).

Indeed, latter frameworks also fall into the second group because of a substantial AI-orientation. For example, OpenSpiel is a collection of algorithms and frameworks for research on reinforcement learning and game AI development, even though some of its analysis tools might be used for game design analysis (e.g. the game tree) [7].

The described division is not strict, and transitions are possible between groups. JSettlers provide an example of service moved from the first to the second group. JSettlers designed as a digital desktop version of the Settlers of Catan for remote playing (first group) [8] is now used by GDs and researchers for game analysis or development of game AI (second group) [10]. However, examples alike latter are limited which indicates a gap of a tabletop game design computer assistant focused on tabletop GDs' tasks possible to facilitate with computer capabilities.

### 2.3 Game Design Assistant Services

Some articles examine computer game design assistance beyond testing. One of the main areas receiving scholar attention is the area of Procedure Content Generation (PCG): creation of game objects, maps, etc. For instance, Google Stadia project "Chimera" uses generatively adversarial networks to generate same-type content (game cards). However, Stadia R&D head Erin Hoffman-John notes[5] that the human-free Chimera generation lead to the "*nightmare fuel*", the creation of artifacts completely unacceptable by humans, invoking discussion over HI and CI relation.

Yannakakis mentions several game design assistants with different HI and CI ratio: Tanagara, Sentient Sketchbook, Unreal Development kit, Garden of Eden Creation Kit, Oblige, etc. [2]. The focus of the tools is level design assistance (PCG). Tanagara allows to automatically design 2D platformer levels based on GDs input of level constraints (rule-based generation) ensure playability [21]. Sentient Sketchbook[6] automatically constructs low-resolution 2D map sketches that can be edited by GD in real time. Service also suggests further map modifications (via genetic search) regarding the structure and the map characteristics (balance, playability, etc.). Garden of Eden Creation Kit (G.E.C.K.)[7]

---

[5] https://www.gamesindustry.biz/articles/2020-03-16-how-can-machine-learning-be-applied-to-game-development.

[6] http://www.sentientsketchbook.com/.

[7] https://www.wired.com/2008/12/fallout-3-creat/.

allows user to create Fallout maps, characters, weapon, storylines, etc. Unreal Development Kit (UDK) had the same capabilities but for a wider range of games, unfortunately, it is no longer supported[8]. Finally, Oblige is a computer driven tool for random Doom game levels generation [22].

While UDK and G.E.C.K. are fully driven by GD's decision, Oblige limits GD opportunity to interfere level creation causing backlash [2]. In contrast, Tanagara and Sentient Sketchbook follow MID, where a human and a computer both take part in creation process resulting in "more creative" outputs [23]. The MID framework and the GUI usage for communication between the system and the designer can be used as relevant practices for tabletop game design assistant development.

## 2.4 Automated Game Analysis Approaches

This section contains separate scholar examples of automated approaches to tabletop games testing and analyzing not packaged as standalone scalable clients. Such approaches usually rely on one of the following testing schemas: large-scale game simulation, search for the "ideal game", approbation of individual elements.

The large-scale game simulation, due to computing power, allows GD to cover a huge pool of possible game scenarios and determine areas not covered by rules. An example is provided by De Mesentier Silva et al., who tested the Ticket to Ride game versions with AI-based playtesting to identify imbalanced game elements. Game sessions were automated to test different strategies and AI behaviors, GD had an ability to change rules depending on the results. Such approach allowed authors to identify scenarios uncovered by the rules: Wild Loops, cities lack for attention, and "winning" routes, and to conclude that suitability and winning of a strategy depends upon the map and the number of players [4].

Search for the "ideal game" enables the optimization of various elements of game rules, sets of cards and other game elements, often with genetic algorithms. For example, Mahlmann et al. tried to achieve balanced (optimal) card deck for Dominion card game with help of genetic algorithm and game AIs of different skill level. The authors identified cards that were "too strong" or had "hidden power" for more experienced players, undermining game balance [5]. Another example is work of Hom and Marks, who aimed at defining the "ideal" game rules – when winning is equally difficult for any player, and number of draws is minimized. Genetic algorithm with random inheritance varied game rule components, received rule set was tested by AI and analyzed using the balance and diversity. Unfortunately, the algorithm called the rule set played in 5 moves perfectly balanced, while the other chosen rule sets also turned out to be not particularly interesting from the players perspective [24]. Evolutionary algorithms were also applied by Beyer et al., who suggested the mixed initiative model of rules balancing. Unlikely previous, authors tested video game and changed only those rules features indicated by players as requiring rebalance. As authors claim, automatic playtest allowed to save time significantly, and provided extraordinary solutions (which would be rejected by experts otherwise). However, such tests are expensive to carry out in terms of technical transcription and computing power, while obtained results still has to be tested with

---

[8] https://www.unrealengine.com/en-US/previous-versions.

real players [3]. The common problem of the discrepancy of the "ideal game" concept between machine and real players, was deeply examined by Browne, who highlighted that completion, balance, advantage, and duration were the most significant criteria for players, while the criteria strongest correlation with human experience were uncertainty, killer moves, constancy, change of leader, completeness, duration [25]. These game quality criteria should be considered while developing tabletop game analysis tool as they are alternative to real player system interference.

Approbation of individual elements in the context of the game through the abusive exploitation of these elements or, vice versa, restriction on their use for some players was used by Jaffe et al., who designed a balancing tool based the restricted-play framework. The main idea of the framework is to assess balance in terms of fairness of starting conditions via players win rates: one agent has a feature being assessed, while another one does not (the restriction), and compare the win rates. This allows to evaluate any potential changes the author wants to make by create an "early warning system" and thus, balance the game along the development way [26].

Discussed balancing approaches can be integrated into tabletop game design assistant as core automatic testing schemas. However, one should consider the moment of its application. For instance, large scale simulation and ideal-game search approaches are preferable for early stages as they test the basics of the game mechanics, while the latter approach is more convenient when the game core is fixed, and auxiliary mechanics/elements are evaluated. Nevertheless, there is still a necessity for human participation (GD or real player) in testing as the best games, according to the computer, can be unplayable or perceived as boring by players, while fun is heart of the game [16, 18], bringing us back to MID.

## 3   Methodology

Considering this paper focuses on development of user-oriented client, which means needs of GDs drive the development, an iterative study design with the use of a deep semi-structured interview was chosen as the methodology core. As supportive methods, inductive context analysis, prototyping with subsequent Wizard of Oz simulation based on Jumanji case were applied.

### 3.1   Interview

We conducted in-depth semi-structured interviews with 7 participants who had experience in tabletop game design: predominantly, respondents are professional Russian tabletop game developers, but 2 non-professionals we also included, as first interviews showed game design origin to be a hobby. The interview guide included questions regarding the current design of the game development process, testing/balancing, and automation.

Data obtained during interview sessions was encoded in several iterations using bottom-up approach to identify all relevant aspects without strict binding to the semantic blocks. Then, for context analysis we used affinity diagrams or affinity walls method: meaningful segments taken from interview transcription were hierarchically grouped into larger themes and topics [27]. This allowed to capture insights and GDs' needs on such blocks as GDs' tasks and responsibilities, current tool pool, game development process, game testing, game analysis and balancing, additional desires, and pains relevant for automation features, and real players role within development. Some of segments were turned into Job stories (JS) – an approach to user needs description, which takes into account the context that forms the situation when a need arises, and also takes into account the general goal set by the user [28].

The extracted insights served as the basis for creating future system requirements: another iteration of hierarchically grouping was done to form system functionality blocks. Each block was supplemented with JS corresponding to it to reflect situation for automatization and prototyping.

### 3.2 Case Study

The system assessment must be conducted in conditions close to real testing or game evaluation. To recreate these conditions, we took Jumanji (game of one of the respondents), designed by a non-commercial project (testing resources are limited) and being under the development stage. Jumanji is a competitive game for maximum 4 players with fixed turn order and cards and dice as major elements. These game features are widely spread among modern tabletop games (see Footnote 1) making Jumanji a relevant example. The game covers most of obtained JS and has little dependence on a player, allowing GDs to immerse themselves in the process, check system performance in real use focusing on game elements and mechanics not player's perception.

Though several functionality blocks were identified during interview, the realization and prototyping scope was reduced back to game testing and concomitant analysis. The game automation and the JS implementation was carried out using the Python language. The code is publicly available in a devoted GitHub repository[9].

### 3.3 Prototyping and Wizard of Oz Assessment

To evaluate the system's concept (Tabletop Game Designer Assistant – TGDA), the results obtained during technical implementation and Jumanji analysis were presented in a user-friendly form and tested by GD.

For TGDA assessment we choose Wizard of Oz method. The Wizard of Oz approach allows to simulate system performance using the human "wizard" that acts instead of a system itself during user interaction with service via real interface [29]. In our case, the approach benefited in avoiding creating time consuming connections between the Python programming code with the results, subsequent interactive Tableau[10] visualization and the interface. Using Figma[11] we created high-level prototype with result of the system's performance to simulate interaction with the TGDA. GDs could interact with prototype, while interviewer guided them through system and its functionality making notes on any relevant moments. During the observation, special attention was paid to how the results

---

[9] https://github.com/vladakray/Jumanji.
[10] https://www.tableau.com/.
[11] https://www.figma.com/.

correspond to the expectations of GDs, what conclusions those results allow to draw, what is missing or, on the contrary, superfluous, what actions they would like to do next. The insights gained from the assessment led to the prototype renewal and were added to the "What's next" screens section to distinguish them from initial prototype design.

# 4   Results

This block successively reviews the results obtained with all the methods described above. We start with the information obtained via the interviews: from discussing the current structure of the tabletop game development process and identifying GDs' needs to the conceptual framework and system requirements. Then, we present the results of prototyping and implementation of system fragments and move to the assessment done by experts through Wizard of Oz testing.

## 4.1   Interview Insights

**Tabletop Game Development.** Based on the respondents' description of the current state of the tabletop game development process, its stages, inputs and outputs, the Fig. 1 illustrating the process scheme was created.

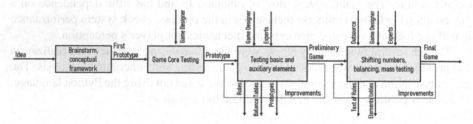

**Fig. 1.** Design process as a business process according to O'Donnell [18]

For convenience, the process is presented relatively linearly, however, as noted by Baba and Tschang [19], it is more like a spiral: each block is a new turn of the spiral, it uses the results of the previous block and attract new resources with new outputs are branched off. This confirms that the development process in the tabletop game industry is highly iterative, and each iteration has its own purpose, requiring its own type of resources. Iteration is characteristic also of parts of process. The GDs noted that often during one testing session, several iterations of various game settings can be carried out, which also leads to resource consumption growth. A high level of iterations presents the main bottleneck, as each iteration requires resources, some of which can be problematic to acquire. As an example, in addition to the obvious time resource, another challenge is the search for suitable players (by type: gaming experience, temperament, etc.) in a suitable amount (mass testing).

Since testing is a major part of tabletop game development (confirmed by interviewees), automation of some parts of the process could reduce time costs as well as overall resource load. Interestingly, respondents claim the opposite: an automation is "*an expensive and complex process with limited opportunities"*. The latter, indeed, presents a serious problem, as we found: the abundance of game mechanics prevents the creation of a scalable system. Respondents also associate limitation with restriction of creativity, which is an integral part of development process. One of the GDs has mentioned the idea of co-creativity [2], saying that *"an automatic analysis should help designer get into the creative stream"*. This reinforces the need to align MID framework and integrate a GD in a system.

Nevertheless, player is another "human" to be considered while development as players opinion is of critical value for the game authors, as the game success fully depends on it. The latter statement reveals an associated concept of subjective balance - how the balance in the game is perceived by the players. For the GDs, subjective balance is more important than mathematical: *"Mostly, balance is driven by the perception of players: calculations in this regard can only set the basis"*. And its components can hardly be mathematized: interest and engagement, tasks complexity, etc., can be only assessed by players directly. Moreover, GDs claim that some games do not have balance and there is no necessity for it to be (e.g. Party games). Trying to create a mathematical model of human assessments may be an interesting area for academic research [25], but GDs are not interested in automating such aspects or mistrust such solutions. Such focus on human assessment makes replacement of classic manual testing with automated testing impossible.

Beside testing being the game development core, the functionality of a GD also includes management and business development responsibilities, creative process tasks, visual design duties and text editing. The toolkit GDs use to cover these tasks is listed in Table 1. Interestingly, beside testing platforms, GDs do not have any specialized game development tools. Prototype making tools were named the least satisfying.

**System Requirements.** The above insights lead us to the design of multifunctional system as either one large-scale system or a microservice system covering testing, creation, management system, text editing. Whichever option to be chosen, the system should follow MID framework and general user requirements. Below we briefly describe the system requirements and illustrate it with JS examples.

*Testing.* This block covers the functions to facilitate various aspects of game testing and analysis and includes information about game indicators to record (players parameters, elements characteristics, session parameters, balance) testing approaches (crash tests, mass testing, different player type testing, element testing) and gave variability (enumeration of game situation, game element combinations, game decisions).

Following JS dedicated to game core testing through exploit (element) testing illustrates one of approaches to be implemented within TGDA:

**When** *I have defined basic game mechanics,*

**I want to** *test different primitive patterns of player behavior,*

**So that I can** *see what happens to the game and check for a game break down*

*Creation.* A block combines functions for creating elements and artifacts corresponding to them covering creative process and design tasks. We deliberately combined them into one as output of one (game elements obtained during the Creation Process) are the direct input of the other (game elements acquire visual form in Design).

**Table 1.** Current game design tools and associated tasks.

| Tasks | Tools |
|---|---|
| Calculation of game and game elements balance, elements preparation for design and illustration | Microsoft Office Excel tables, Google Spreadsheets |
| Creation of a prototype (both digital and printed) | Power Point, Google Presentation, Corel Draw, Quark Express, Microsoft Publisher, Photoshop |
| Remote testing game sessions | Tabletopia, Tabletop Simulator |
| Communication with testers, colleagues before, during and after testing | Vkontakte, Discord, Telegram |
| Collecting statistics and feedback on testing sessions, subsequent analysis | Google Forms and Google tables |
| Editing of game texts | Glavred (Chief-Editor) by Maksim Ilyakhov |
| Manufacturing physical prototypes | Color printer and scissors/cutter |

Given the iterative nature of the game design, experts have repeatedly spoken about routine tasks that are considered as creative but do not require much creativity. Generating same type game elements was noted as such a task in following JS:

*When I need to create many elements of the same type,*
*I want to auto generate them according to a template with the ability to modify,*
*So that I can spend less time and creativity coming up with them.*

*Management System.* The block covers management and business development tasks for the development process supervision. When creating a unified system, this would serve as node through which one can monitor the state of processes in other blocks or track the progress of participants, for example:

*When I have a list of permanent testers,*
*I want to track their gaming experience, previous reviews, test scores,*
*So that I could quickly select specific testers for special testing purposes and easier report it to reward testers afterwards.*

*Text Editing.* Working with game texts and solving related tasks are often outsourced (as well as visual design), but outside experts are not familiar with the game/gaming industry at the proper level, which leads to misinterpretation and misunderstandings. This establishes the need for an editor focused on game texts and specifics as below:

*When I have text rules of the game or text information on cards,*
*I want to check if text is unambiguous and ensure same terms address same things,*
*So that I can be sure that the game is perceived / played the way I intended it.*

**Testing and Analysis: Implementation and Prototyping.** Though we focus on game testing and analysis, the approach described below can be used for implementation and assessment of other blocks (with relevant modifications).

First, we divided the Testing and Analysis JS into semantic blocks based on similarity of operations required to perform. We acquired following groups:

1. Testing overall game sets by collecting mass statistics:

   - Game statistics: win rates, score, cycles, etc., for different game sets.
   - Element Strength Analysis: mass testing to summarize element behavior.
   - Session Analysis: indicating sessions outstanding average session rates.

2. Element testing: assessment of specific game elements/mechanics within the game.
3. Enumeration: assessment of possible game situations and element combinations that are difficult to cover with classic manual testing.
4. Decision Tree: assessment of rational choices a player has in different game states.

Then, we assessed the stories if the scenario can or cannot be implemented within the Jumanji game. "Passed" stories were adapted, executed in Python, and the (real) results were demonstrated in TGDA prototype[12]. "Failed" JS, e.g., Element testing, were conceptually visualized (if possible) based on the related studies considered. This approach allowed us to evaluate most of the JS.

*Testing Overall Game Sets by Collecting Mass Statistics* assumes an automatic game session run with record of various parameters for further. The game rules system set out through if-else branches and python classes were taken as automation basis. All players' moves are recorded, which enables further game analysis: win rates and score of each player, average game score, average number of cycles. Any game session can be viewed in detail and is highlighted as outlying if possesses too high or low average score or number of moves. Considering that the record of the move includes the elements used per turn, this serves as basis for further Element Strength Analysis by average win rates (number of wins with this card / number of uses) and contribution to victory (percentage contribution to the goal achievement).

*Element Testing* could not be tested in Jumanji as elements are assigned to the player randomly and cannot be deliberately exploited. Nevertheless, we invited the authors to imagine presence of such an element and, similarly to how it was done by Jaffe et al. [26], demonstrated the possible results of using the restricted-play framework.

*Enumeration* is dedicated to sorting out various combinations of game elements. Considering that the Jumanji main game elements are cards, we named this block Deck Analysis to underline that this block can be scaled to any card games with a proper modification. Inside GDs had 4 relevant options:

1. Outliers' identification that can be fulfilled with Element Strength Analysis.
2. Combination Enumeration. In Jumanji the elements are played one at a time, thus, we conceptually presented function results, if 2–3 cards were drawn at a time.

---

[12] https://www.figma.com/file/6VLAM9tN089ofAZRSY0rUA/Game-Test-Service.

3. Deck optimization uses genetic algorithm with random element mutation for an optimal game element set selection (deck with a lowest difference in the win rates).
4. Generation of additional elements feature was not implemented or prototyped, as it refers to Creation (PCG), however, it was added as Gds claimed, "*it is logical to offer help with element generation when we speak about elements*".

*Decision Tree* is the block devoted to the players' decision or opportunities analysis. Jumanji does not imply a rational choice, thus, there was no way to change the mechanics or offer a modification that allowed saving the game core but introduce the choice and implement JS.

**Testing and Analysis: Assessment.** During Wizard of Oz testing, GDs noted mass testing, which "allowed to look at the full picture, instead of scattered data", as well as "save time (and nerves), perhaps even money" on testing "where human factor is not that important". However, they said that mass testing often includes players' perceptions and general game feedback the TGDA lacks. The session analysis was also popular as many designers initially expressed the desire to run session step by step. They noted: "the ability to watch a mechanical iteration of different game moves allows you to test some basic concepts before prototyping and testing them on humans." This is especially crucial for games with a choice, as it allows to check various game branches, bringing back the relevance of the game decision tree.

Regarding Element testing via exploitation, many mentioned it as "*interesting, but unnecessary, replaceable with home test or 1–2 games*", but more cases needed as "*some players really play in such a way, and it is important to check such things*".

Deck optimization caused an ambiguous reaction. GDs considered it "*incomprehensible*". Despite the explanation of the underlying algorithm, the automatic generation was claimed "*difficult to verify*" and has caused mistrust. However, the idea of element generation by similar value enumeration made better impression as it is same to manual sorting through the values, and designers can easily check what "*the machine has spawned*", while with deck "*you have to take its word for it.*"

For the rest, GDs noted that TGDA would significantly reduce the time, due to higher computational speed and opportunity to test elements without "*permanent prototypes cutting*". The ability to interact with elements, information transparency, absence of "complex code" and system conclusion prompts (result interpretation) were noted as TGDA advantages. The overloaded design and the overall "complexity" ("*everything is familiar, but you still get lost*") were noted as minor flaws, that can be avoided by breaking all-in-one tool into mentioned microservice system.

## 5 Discussion and Design Implication

Currently GDs do not use any specialized tools: they mostly employ non-specialized programs (e.g., Microsoft Office) except for remote testing applications. This indicates that the existing academic solutions are not used by tabletop GDs, though the process of developing a tabletop game requires optimization and improvement, which can be carried out with computer capabilities. There might be several reason for ignoring existing solutions: excessive focus on researching AI not game analysis, programming skills required (tabletop game design, in contrast to video game industry, does not imply programming), creativity restriction with high CI level, ambition to substitute current solutions instead of assistance, high costs for system integration and mismatch between the need and proposed solution (in our case, deck optimization similar to the solution of Mahlmann et al. [5] caused distrust).

All this emphasizes the need to use a user-needs-driven framework when developing a system as it allows to specify relevant user tasks and current solutions, determine the context, and obtain a list of functional scenarios. Such close-to-end-user development also provide an opportunity to test the designed concepts at any time.

Another important development framework to consider is MID. This is reinforced by the high importance of the human factor in the game development process assumed by the authors' creativity and the perception of this creativity by the players. According to GDs, an automated client can help with routine or vast tasks, as well as facilitate creativity (mates with opinion in related studies [2]), thus acting as an assistant rather than just a tool.

The most significant point of the paper is that there is a need for such an assistant: during our user research, we identified a large pool of tasks, that went even beyond testing and balancing, requiring developing of suitable solutions. By the example of the testing and balance block, we checked the applied value of such solutions: the automation of at least part of the tasks can reduce the resource load and the number of iterations, which are the main problem areas of the development process. In addition, game session automation can be used as the basis for the future digital presentation and implementation of the game (not only within the framework of remote testing).

Summing up, designers are ready to transfer many of these tasks to a computer, however, as related studies and interviews show, full outsourcing is impossible, as the result of game design is a very human-centered product. In this regard, the participation of a human is necessary, which makes the above-described user-need orientation, MID and assistant role frameworks obligatory for developing tabletop game service.

## 5.1 Future Research

During our research, we have identified various specific game design tasks for automation. For example, the creation of a management system possesses potential, especially considering possible collaboration with existing services (e.g., Boardgamesgeek.com knowledge base). Considering creative processes, elaboration on PCG and subsequent design and visualization for element prototyping is crucial.

Beyond suitable software toolkit the industry also seeks for an appropriate hardware. Thus, physical prototype creation was claimed to be the most exhausting process due to plenty of iterations and absence of convenient tools. Development of such a tool presents an important practical task (reduce load) and an interesting research challenge as game elements vary from game to game and have its own specifics.

We also encountered two serious difficulties that impede the development of scalable tabletop game design systems: the operationalization of mechanics and the simulation of players (human) estimates of the game. The first deals with the large number and variability of game mechanics, their systematization with an emphasis on subsequent automation would solve the problem of single-game solutions. Simulation of human assessment, in turn, would allow to introduce human factor into the system which is crucial for tabletop game design industry. Moreover, this may also help reduce resource consumption and iteration like how this work describes.

# References

1. Browne, C.: Connection Games: Variations on a Theme. CRC Press, Boca Raton (2018)
2. Yannakakis, G.N., Liapis, A., Alexopoulos, C.: Mixed-initiative co-creativity, vol. 8 (2014)
3. Beyer, M., et al.: An integrated process for game balancing. In: 2016 IEEE Conference on Computational Intelligence and Games (CIG), pp. 1–8 (2016)
4. de Mesentier Silva, F., Lee, S., Togelius, J., Nealen, A.: AI-based playtesting of contemporary board games. In: Proceedings of the 12th International Conference on the Foundations of Digital Games, pp. 1–10. Association for Computing Machinery, New York (2017)
5. Mahlmann, T., Togelius, J., Yannakakis, G.N.: Evolving card sets towards balancing dominion. In: 2012 IEEE Congress on Evolutionary Computation, pp. 1–8 (2012)
6. Gaina, R.D., Balla, M., Dockhorn, A.: TAG: A Tabletop Games Framework, vol. 7 (2020)
7. Lanctot, M., et al.: OpenSpiel: a framework for reinforcement learning in games. arXiv:1908.09453 [cs] (2020)
8. Monin, J.: JSettlers2 (2021)
9. Borovikov, I., et al.: Winning Isn't Everything: Training Agents to Playtest Modern Games, vol. 9 (2019)
10. Guhe, M., Lascarides, A.: Game strategies for the settlers of Catan. In: 2014 IEEE Conference on Computational Intelligence and Games, pp. 1–8. IEEE, Dortmund (2014)
11. Salen, K., Tekinbaş, K.S., Zimmerman, E.: Rules of Play: Game Design Fundamentals. MIT Press, Cambridge(2004)
12. Crawford, C.: The Art of Computer Game Design, vol. 89 (1982)
13. Cardona-Rivera, R.: Foundations of a computational science of game design: abstractions and tradeoffs. AIIDE 16, 167–174 (2020)
14. Gero, J.S., Kannengiesser, U.: The situated function–behaviour–structure framework. Des. Stud. 25, 373–391 (2004). https://doi.org/10.1016/j.destud.2003.10.010
15. Duke, R.D.: A paradigm for game design. S&G 11, 364–377 (1980). https://doi.org/10.1177/104687818001100308
16. Schell, J.: The Art of Game Design: A Book of Lenses. CRC Press, Cambridge (2008)
17. Feichin, T.T.: When Does an Idea Become an Innovation? The Role of Individual and Group Creativity in Videogame Design, vol. 28 (2003)
18. O'Donnell, C.: Developer's Dilemma: The Secret World of Videogame Creators. MIT Press, Cambridge (2014)
19. Baba, Y., Tschang, T.: Product development in Japanese TV game software: the case of an innovative game. Int. J. Innov. Manag. 05, 487–515 (2001). https://doi.org/10.1142/S13639 19601000464
20. Gaina, R.D., Balla, M., Dockhorn, A., Montoliu, R., Perez-Liebana, D.: Design and implementation of TAG: a tabletop games framework. arXiv:2009.12065 [cs] (2020)
21. Tanagra | Proceedings of the Fifth International Conference on the Foundations of Digital Games. https://dl.acm.org/doi/abs/10.1145/1822348.1822376
22. Trenholme, S.: Oblige Random Map Generator (2020)
23. Liapis, A., Yannakakis, G.N., Togelius, J.: Sentient sketchbook: computer-assisted game level authoring, vol. 8 (2013)

24. Hom, V., Marks, J.: Automatic Design of Balanced Board Games, vol. 6 (2007)
25. Browne, C.: Automatic Generation and Evaluation of Recombination Games (2008). https://www.medra.org/servlet/aliasResolver?alias=iospress&doi=10.3233/ICG-2010-33405
26. Jaffe, A., Miller, A., Andersen, E., Liu, Y.-E., Karlin, A., Popovic, Z.: Evaluating competitive game balance with restricted play. AIIDE **8** (2012)
27. Lazar, J., Feng, J.H., Hochheiser, H.: Research Methods in Human-Computer Interaction. Morgan Kaufmann, Burlington (2017)
28. Klement, A.: When Coffee and Kale Compete: Become Great at Making Products People will Buy. NYC Press, New York (2018)
29. Maulsby, D., Greenberg, S., Mander, R.: Prototyping an intelligent agent through Wizard of Oz. In: Proceedings of the INTERACT 1993 and CHI 1993 Conference on Human Factors in Computing Systems, pp. 277–284. Association for Computing Machinery, New York (1993)

# eCommunication: Online Discources and Attitudes

# Automated Classification of Potentially Insulting Speech Acts on Social Network Sites

Liliya Komalova[1,2](✉) ⓘ, Anna Glazkova[3] ⓘ, Dmitry Morozov[4] ⓘ,
Rostislav Epifanov[4], Leonid Motovskikh[2], and Ekaterina Mayorova[1]

[1] Institute of Scientific Information for Social Sciences of the Russian Academy of Sciences,
51/21 Nakhimovsky Prospect, Moscow 117418, Russia
komalova@inion.ru

[2] Moscow State Linguistic University, 38 Ostozhenka Str., Moscow 119034, Russia

[3] University of Tyumen, 6 Volodarskogo Str., Tyumen 625003, Russia

[4] Novosibirsk State University, 1 Pirogova Str., Novosibirsk 630090, Russia

**Abstract.** Insulting speech acts have become the subject of public discussion in the media, social media, the basis for speculation in political communication, and a working concept in the legal environment. The present research article explores insulting speech acts on the social network site "VKontaktc" aiming to develop an algorithm for automatic classification of text data. We conducted semantic analysis of the text of "Article 5.61" of the Code of Administrative Offenses of the Russian Federation, which made it possible to formulate inclusion criteria for formal classification. We used three common word embeddings models (BERT, ELMo, and fastText) on the original Russian language dataset consisting of 4596 annotated messages perceived as insulting speech acts. General findings argue that even in a specialized dataset the share of messages that meet criteria of inclusion is negligible. This indicates a low probability of going to court on the fact of an administrative offense under Article 5.61 based on speech communication on social network sites, even though such communication is public in nature and is automatically recorded in writing. Machine learning text classifier based on BERT model showed best performance.

**Keywords:** Automated classification · Vector word embedding · Annotated dataset · Forensic linguistics · Corpus linguistics · Linguistic expertise · Insulting speech act · Internet language · Social network site

## 1 Introduction

Speech acts of insult in modern society are discussed far beyond the professional community of linguists. Currently, this type of speech acts has become the subject of public discussion in the media, social media, the basis for speculation in political communication, and a working concept in the legal environment.

Taking into account the requirement to establish the fact of violation of human rights and the subjective or multiple nature of the interpretation of an insulting act, law enforcement officers are forced to address linguistic professional community to expertise

© Springer Nature Switzerland AG 2022
D. A. Alexandrov et al. (Eds.): DTGS 2021, CCIS 1503, pp. 365–374, 2022.
https://doi.org/10.1007/978-3-030-93715-7_26

controversial speech acts. Currently, the number of cases based on materials posted on social network sites, Internet blogs, forums and other public digital communication platforms on the Internet is growing.

As an electronic, global and interactive environment, the Internet has greatly influenced the language of its users (see [22, 36]). The language of the Internet is not homogeneous, and its characteristics largely depend on the communication situation. The language of the Internet is not codified, which is confirmed by its variability and dynamism with which it develops. Representatives of Internet linguistics tend to consider net-speak as a specific hybrid form of speech (see [7, pp. 56–76]), and Internet communication as communicative interaction in the global computer network of Internet users with different cultural and educational levels [2, p. 13].

Working with speech products of Internet users requires from a linguist not only mastery of the methods and means of studying the language system and its elements, taking into account the specifics of Internet communication, but also the skills of handling large arrays of text data that make up the communicative situation in which the studied speech product is explored. That means immersion into the individually specific context of the generation of the studied speech act [11, p. 111].

Special attention should be paid to features of communication realized through social network sites. It is generally accepted that scales of personal values besides self-esteem evaluation also include assessment of people's social environment. A person is in a constant search for social approval and wants to become an expert in assessing the achievements of as many representatives of his/her community as possible. From this perspective, social network sites become a space for socialization [13, 23] and self-identification (the formation of self-esteem and self-image) [10, pp. 50, 70]. We have a basic biological imperative: to communicate with other people. This directly affects the release of dopamine into the mesolimbic tract: this system is based on millions of years of evolution, so we come together and live as a community, find partners, reproduce as a species. So there is no doubt that an environment such as a social network that optimizes connections between people will have the potential for addiction [21].

Insulting as a speech act of a conflict type (see more details in [15, 16]) "is performed by expressing speaker's negative opinion of the addressee in a disrespectful way, with the intention to humiliate and hurt him/her" [34, p. 143].

Within linguistic expertise the content of the notion "insulting act" could be described through the concept of "communicative perversion" and implies the realization of the following basic strategies of speech behavior: 1) defamation – public dissemination of information discrediting someone; 2) verbal discrimination – expression in one's speech superiority for racial, ethnic, economic or other reasons; 3) verbal discrediting – undermining authority, belittling the importance of someone, undermining trust; 4) verbal insinuation – prerequisites creation for a negative perception of someone's social image [19, pp. 52–53]. The following components of communication situation show themselves in the structure of insulting speech act: 1) external institutional component (publicity, official setting, etc.); 2) participants in the situation and the ratio of their social roles; 3) the author's intention (illocutionary force); 4) perlocutionary component that correlates the statement with the impact it has on the addressee [32, p. 269].

While dealing with insulting speech acts on the Internet, a linguist faces certain difficulties. On the one hand, the research focus on the insulted people's subjective perception leads to the fact that speech acts marked as offensive (insulting) by a naive user cannot be considered as facts subject to legal regulation. On the other hand, the focus on the mandatory establishment of all diagnostic features of insulting act (see more [12, pp. 44–45]) while expertise leads to excessive liberty among Internet users who disregard the norms of civilized speech behavior.

A way to resolve the situation could be an intermediate institution of public self-regulation on a concrete social network site, based on the processing of large data arrays by a linguistic processor, as well as with a built-in mechanism for Internet users to contact the holders of the social network site. On the territory of the Russian Federation, the first steps in this direction are being taken by large technology companies and research centers (see, for example, [1, 26]).

## 2 Methodology

The present research article explores verbalized insulting acts on the social network site "VKontakte". The notion of *insulting speech* describes a perceptual construct that represents the emotional-psychological state of a person experiencing negative emotions as a result of attribution of insulting intention to someone's actions, behavior, and speech. The use of this term turns our attention to a sender (see for example [35]) and a recipient, widening the traditional research scope to analysis of a communicative situation as a whole instead of focusing only on a speech product. Within these boundaries insulting speech applies to cases of hate speech (see for example [27]), hard criticism, verbal abuse, offensive language, hate crime language [8], verbal crime (see for example [6]) and so on as they could be perceived as insulting.

The purpose of the research project was to develop an algorithm for automatic classification of text data in order to identify insulting speech acts on the Internet social network site "VKontakte" in Russian language dataset.

We hypothized that, within the framework of social network communication on the Internet, the share of messages classified as insulting speech acts, using the legislative description of such speech acts, is extremely small, even if the diagnostic criteria are not strictly met. We call the applied approach "quasi-legal", since it implies reliance on the legislative description of insulting act, however, the diagnostic features do not seem to be as discrete as is customary when conducting linguistic expertise in the framework of legal procedure (see, for example, [17, pp. 233–235, 12, pp. 34–45]).

At the first research step we conducted semantic analysis of the text of "Article 5.61" of the Code of Administrative Offenses of the Russian Federation (hereinafter – Article 5.61) [3], which made it possible to formulate the following inclusion criteria for formal classification:

(1)  the presence of an indecent form in the message perceived as insulting speech acts (in Russian language an indecent form of expression is assigned to abusive, obscene vocabulary);
(2)  the presence of lexical markers that fix the orientation of the statement towards Internet users – interlocutor (posts with direct appeal using nicknames or pronouns);

(3) the presence of vocabulary that represents the immoral and publicly condemned qualities of a person's character and behavior. (This criterion has caused a lot of discussion between annotators, since it was not possible to formalize it. However, a convention was adopted in which annotators relied on their linguistic flair and theoretical material on the topic "Philosophical foundations of morality and ethics".)

A VKontakte post (text message) was classified as insulting speech act if it met the three criteria outlined above. To indicate compliance or non-compliance with the criterion, labels were used while annotating: decent – obscene, person – impersonal, moral – immoral.

A message (post) of an Internet user to one of the entries on an open thematic community (public) in Russian language was taken as a unit to analysis.

Due to the fact that we found no appropriate dataset among the existing datasets of aggressive communication (see for example [31]), the second research step was to collect data. The social network site "VKontakte" was chosen as a source of text information extraction. The reasons for choosing this site were:

– openness of data in general access terms;
– popularity of "VKontakte" on the Russian-speaking Internet: according to the network itself, the portal's monthly audience accounts 73.4 million unique users [37], most of them communicate in Russian language [4];
– a large number of examples of speech production of communicants available for analysis in the studied conditions;
– no moderation within some communities.

To select publics, we turned to the VK API tool of VKontakte interface, which allowed us to collect in an aggregated form a sufficient number of messages with publicly available information about their authors (given names, surnames and genders). We selected 13 large VK-communities in which potentially toxic topics were discussed (foreign policy, feminism, rap, etc.) and there was no obscene lexemes moderation in the comments. For each of them, we automatically collected comments to the last (at the time of collection) 50 posts (each post could consist of more than two utterances/messages). The collection was held in July 2020. As a result, 4610 messages were selected, 14 of them were excluded as they did not consist any text information.

At the third research step, the resulting data array of 4596 messages was annotated by a group of annotators (n = 5) using *ipywidgets* based interface. Five annotators were trained bachelors. Then two specialists (authors of this paper) validated their annotation and after that an expert in forensic linguistics examined the selected data.

At the fourth step, the obtained dataset was divided into two sub-corpuses: the training sample and the target sample in a ratio of 80:20 of the total volume of the dataset. In absolute terms, the samples consisted of 3227 and 1383 messages, respectively.

For the purpose of text classification, we used three common word embeddings models: BERT, ELMo, and fastText. Word embeddings are fixed-size numeric vectors that describe word features in a form suitable for computer processing.

FastText [5] is based on the distributive hypothesis that semantically close words occur in similar contexts. This principle was previously used in the Word2Vec model [24], representing words in a vector form, based on their joint occurrence in text collections. Unlike Word2Vec, fastText generates vector representations not for words of the training sample directly, but for N-grams of symbols. Therefore, this model could be used for new words that were not encountered during the learning process.

ELMo [30] and BERT [9] present representations that consider the context of a word. This result was achieved since the architecture of ELMo and BERT is based on neural networks trained on text fragments, such as recurrent networks in the case of ELMo and transformer neural networks regarding BERT. Currently, models using contextualized word representation techniques show state-of-the-art results for many natural language processing tasks.

Based on the presented models, we built three machine learning text classifiers.

1. A classifier based on RuBERT, which is a BERT model for Russian, trained on the Russian-language texts of Wikipedia and news portals [18]. The classifier was finetuned using corpus data for three training epochs.
2. A feedforward neural network trained on ELMo embeddings for the Russian language [20]. The network includes two hidden layers of 512 and 256 neurons, respectively. The text is fed into the model in the form of averaged word embeddings.
3. A feedforward neural network trained on the fastText embeddings for the Russian language [ibid.]. The architecture is similar to that described in the previous paragraph.

The classifiers were implemented using Python 3.6 and open-source libraries for machine learning, such as Transformers [38], PyTorch [28], and Scikit-Learn [29]. The source code of the models is available in the repository at [25].

## 3 Results

Table 1 provides a description of research dataset collected [14]. It shows that even in a specialized corpus of messages perceived as insulting speech acts, the share of messages that meet three criteria of inclusion (in accordance with "Article 5.61" of the Code of Administrative Offenses of the Russian Federation) is negligible (1.1%). This indicates a low probability of going to court on the fact of an administrative offense under Article 5.61 based on speech communication on social network sites, even though such communication is public in nature and is automatically recorded in writing.

Messages in the research dataset are characterized by:

- short length (the average message length was 14 word forms, the most frequent were messages up to 10 word forms – semantic analysis was performed using https://istio.com, stop words were included),
- zoosemantisms in the invective notion (for example: *bitch, perch, cock, rat, goat, sheep*),
- the presence of references to the ethnical identity of people being insulted (for example: *Armenian, Azer – Azerbaijani, Ukrainian, Jew*).

**Table 1.** Dataset description.

| Corpus description | Number of messages | |
|---|---|---|
| | In absolute terms | In % |
| *Corpus of messages extracted out of the social network site "VKontakte" and perceived as insulting speech acts Of these (sub-corpuses overlap):* | 4 596 | 100 |
| *1) sub-corpus of messages with "you" directed vocabulary in real contexts of use;* | 630 | 13,7 |
| *2) sub-corpus of messages with obscene vocabulary in real contexts of use;* | 572 | 12,5 |
| *3) sub-corpus of messages with vocabulary carrying the semantics of immorality and censure in real contexts of use;* | 446 | 9,7 |
| *4) sub-corpus of messages near to legal criterion of insult in terms of Article 5.61 of the Administrative Code of the Russian Federation (these messages represent three vocabulary groups listed above)* | **51** | **1,1** |

The dataset analysis revealed that most frequently used for insulting purposes obscene lexemes (we excluded the use of abusive vocabulary in interjection function) were variations with the root "fuck" ("ebalo" in Russian) (probably due to their applicability to any gender). Frequently used lexemes that carry the semantics of immorality and censure include variations of the word "pederast" (*pedoras, fagot, fag, pedrilo, pedrilio*) and a group of words synonymous with the word "prostitute" (*whore, prostitute, dalbanka*). Messages, as a rule, were built according to the scheme "pronoun + verb + noun" (*you are that*), in which verb could be omitted, and the pronoun could be replaced with the nickname of a user who was an object of an insulting speech act.

Table 2 presents performance results of three vector words representation models (BERT, ELMo, fastText) aimed at solving natural language classification task in relation to the collected dataset.

We used the standard F-measure for two classes. It is calculated as follows:

$$F1-score = 2 * (Precision * Recall)/(Precision + Recall),$$
$$Precision = TP/(TP + FP),$$
$$Recall = TP/(TP + FN),$$

where $TP$ is the number of true positive results, $FP$ is the number of false positive results, and $FN$ is the number of false negative results.

According to the data obtained, the most productive is the BERT model. Of the three models used, it more accurately classified the inclusion criteria entities ("you" directed vocabulary, obscene vocabulary, vocabulary carrying the semantics of immorality and censure). At the same time, classification of the third criterion (immorality, blame) occurs with a probability of 1:2, which is logical, since it was not possible to apply formalized classification rules to this category, and the training of the model proceeded only on the basis of the annotated dataset.

**Table 2.** Results of vector models approbation.

| Metrics | Models | F1-score (in %) | | |
|---|---|---|---|---|
| | | "You" directed vocabulary | Obscene vocabulary | Vocabulary with semantics of immorality and censure |
| *F1* | **BERT** | **73,77%** | **89,46%** | **50,21%** |
| | ELMo | 66,04% | 61,95% | 39,63% |
| | fastText | 46,25% | 56,94% | 34,83% |
| *Precision* | **BERT** | **77,59%** | **90,32%** | **49,19%** |
| | ELMo | 72,41% | 64,79% | 46,24% |
| | fastText | 50,68% | 63,49% | 45,45% |
| *Recall* | **BERT** | **70,31%** | **88,61%** | **51,26%** |
| | ELMo | 60,69% | 59,35% | 34,68% |
| | fastText | 42,53% | 51,61% | 28,23% |

## 4 Discussion and Conclusion

The problem of low formalization of automatic processing of large arrays of specific information identified on the Internet social network sites was solved using the example of one legal case – administratively punishable insulting speech acts described as in "Article 5.61" of the Code of Administrative Offenses of the Russian Federation. Such quasi-legal approach was based on three criteria: (1) speech delivered in indecent form (using obscene lexemes); (2) personal orientation of insulting speech acts towards other people (using "you" directed vocabulary and nicknames to address interlocutors); (3) and presence of a semantic reference to the immorality and censure of people's behavior and actions.

Present research did not explore the establishment of the subjective side of the administrative offense "insulting speech act": the intention of the insult and the assessment of the awareness of the act, as well as the degree of impact on the people insulted, were not marked in any way. In our opinion, the establishment of the subjective corpus delicti is the exclusive prerogative of the court.

The dataset collected is of practical interest for further research in the field of linguistic expertise of social network site "VKontakte" users' speech products, as well as for teaching methods of analyzing controversial speech products based on Internet-mediated quasi-spontaneous communication.

Implementation of the elaborated classifiers in real practice does not mean that an insulting speech act has been established in legal terms. The strength of the algorithm is that its application allows to identify and exclude text messages, which in the ordinary sense are perceived as insults, but in the legal field of "Article 5.61" are not an administrative offense. Thus, the developed algorithm, on the one hand, allows naive native speakers and linguists-experts to classify potentially insulting speech acts within the framework of "Article 5.61"; on the other hand, the classification algorithm is an effective tool in linguistic expertise, in particular, its use could reduce the burden of formal expertise and increase productivity in relation to qualitative expertise of a controversial speech acts.

Among tested vector of words models BERT showed best results of performance in *F1*, *precision* and *recall* metrics. The most difficult criterion to classify was "vocabulary with semantics of immorality and censure": all models showed low performance. It could be explained by the fact that moral categories of "honor" and "dignity" still have no codified legal meaning.

In the future, we plan to evaluate the quality of other pretrained language models on the presented dataset (including the conversational RuBERT, trained on the texts of social network sites[1], and the RuBERT model, trained on the posts of VKontakte[2] [33]). As far as we know, at the time of the project realization (June 2020) these models did not exist yet.

In our opinion, the formalization of insulting speech acts has a general humanitarian value, since this speech genre is considered within the framework of psychological violence. Based on the trends in the practice of forensic linguistics, it should be predicted that the language of Internet social network sites, instant messengers, e-mails, chats, Internet-blogs as an autonomous form of speech activity will become the main object of research of forensic linguistics in the near future.

**Funding.** The research done for this work has been supported by the 1st Workshop at the Mathematical Center in Akademgorodok (project No 26 "Mathematical support for linguistic expertise", 13 July–14 August, 2020) http://mca.nsu.ru/workshopen/. The authors express their sincere gratitude to the students of the Engineering School of Novosibirsk State University, especially to M.V. Fedorova and E.V. Timofeeva, as well as a student of the Higher School of Economics M.O. Maslova, who made an invaluable contribution to the collection of the dataset and acted as annotators.

# References

1. Ahrenova, N.A.: Internet-lingvistika: Novaja paradigma v opisanii jazyka Interneta. Vestnik Moskovskogo gosudarstvennogo oblastnogo socialno-gumanitarnogo instituta **3**, 8–14 (2016)
2. AI from Siberia will find covert forbidden texts on the Web (2019) . https://roskomsvoboda. org/53920/
3. Article 5.61 of the Code of Administrative Offenses of the Russian Federation. https://www. consultant.ru/document/cons_doc_LAW_34661/d40cbd099d17057d9697b15ee8368e499 53416ae/
4. Audience's features of "VKontakte". https://www.demis.ru/articles/celevaya-auditoria-vko ntakte/
5. Bojanowski, P., et al.: Enriching word vectors with subword information. Trans. Assoc. Comput. Linguist. **5**, 135–146 (2017)
6. Brusenskaya, L.A., Arsenieva, V.A., Suryanto, T.: Verbal crime: the problem of insult in the media text. Media Educ. (Mediaobrazovanie) **58**(3), 12–23 (2018). https://doi.org/10.13187/ me.2018.3.12

---

[1] https://huggingface.co/DeepPavlov/rubert-base-cased-conversational.

[2] https://huggingface.co/sismetanin/rubert_conversational-ru-sentiment-rusentiment.

7. Crystal, D.: The Language Revolution. Polity Press Ltd., Cambridge (2008)
8. Culpeper, J., Iganski, P., Sweiry, A.: Linguistic impoliteness and religiously aggravated hate crime in England and Wales. J. Lang. Aggr. Confl. **5**(1), 1–29 (2017). https://doi.org/10.1075/jlac.5.1.01cul
9. Devlin, J., et al.: Bert: pre-training of deep bidirectional transformers for language understanding. arXiv preprint arXiv:1810.04805 (2018)
10. Durán Sánchez, C.A.: Aspectos interventores en la participación política y electoral de jóvenes. Una reflexión sobre la información, interacción y difusión de contenidos en redes sociales para futuras investigaciones en Santander. Desafíos **27**(1), 47–81 (2015). https://doi.org/10.12804/desafios27.01.2015.02
11. Galyashina, E.: The distinction between the forensic linguistic and scientific activity of linguist analyst: competencies, methods and technologies. Acta Linguistica Petropolitana **1**(15), 104–129 (2019). https://doi.org/10.30842/alp2306573715105
12. Jaroshhuk, I.A., Zhukova, N.A., Dolzhenko, N.I.: Linguistic expertise. BelGU, Belgorod (2020)
13. Kennedy, J.: Rhetorics of sharing: data, imagination, and desire. In: Lovink, G., Rasch, M. (eds.) Unlike Us Reader: Social Media Monopolies and Their Alternatives, pp. 127–136. Institute of Network Cultures, Amsterdam (2013)
14. Komalova, L., Goloshchapova, T., Motovskikh, L., Epifanov, R., Morozov, D., Glazkova, A.: MCA Workshop – Toxic Comments (2021). https://doi.org/10.17632/fktgy52645.1, https://data.mendeley.com/datasets/fktgy52645/1
15. Komalova, L.R.: Agressogen Discourse: The Multilingual Aggression Verbalization Typology. Publishing House «Sputnik +», Moscow (2020)
16. Komalova, L.R.: Repertory of verbal realization of reciprocal aggression in situation of status-role asimmetry. Vestnik of Moscow State Linguistic University. Humanities **9**(695), 103–111 (2014)
17. Kukushkina, O.V., Safonova, J., Sekerazh, T.N.: Theoretical and Methodological Foundations for Psycho-linguistic Text Expertise on Extremism Cases. RFCSJe pri Minjuste Rossii, Moscow (2011)
18. Kuratov, Y., Arkhipov, M.: Adaptation of deep bidirectional multilingual transformers for Russian language. Comput. Linguist. Intellect. Technol. **18**, 333–339 (2019)
19. Kusov, G.V.: Kommunikativnaja perversija kak sposob diagnostiki iskazhcnij pri oskorblcnijah. Jurislingvistika **6**, 43–55 (2005)
20. Kutuzov, A., et al.: Word vectors, reuse, and replicability: towards a community repository of large-text resources. In: Proceedings of the 58th Conference on Simulation and Modelling, pp. 271–276. Linköping University Electronic Press (2017)
21. Lambke, A.: The social dilemma. In: Netflix, Documentary Films (2020). https://www.netflix.com/ru-en/title/81254224
22. McCulloch, M.: Because Internet: Understanding the New Rules of Language. Riverhead Book, New York (2019)
23. Miconi, A.: Under the skin of the networks: how concentration affects social practices in web 2.0 environments. In: Lovink, G., Rasch, M. (eds.) Unlike Us Reader: Social Media Monopolies and Their Alternatives, pp. 89–102. Institute of Network Cultures, Amsterdam (2013)
24. Mikolov, T., et al.: Distributed representations of words and phrases and their compositionality. In: Advances in Neural Information Processing Systems, pp. 3111–3119 (2013). https://proceedings.neurips.cc/paper/2013/file/9aa42b31882ec039965f3c4923ce901b-Paper.pdf
25. MSA-Workshop (2020). https://gitlab.com/rostepifanov/mca-workshop
26. News for the Press (2020). https://vk.com/press/no-hate-speech

27. Paasch-Colberg, S., Strippel, C., Trebbe, J., Emmer, M.: From insult to hate speech: mapping offensive language in German user comments on immigration. Media Commun. **9**(1), 171–180 (2021). https://doi.org/10.17645/mac.v9i1.3399
28. Paszke, A., et al.: Pytorch: an imperative style, high-performance deep learning library. In: Advances in Neural Information Processing Systems, pp. 8026–8037 (2019). https://procee dings.neurips.cc/paper/2019/file/bdbca288fee7f92f2bfa9f7012727740-Paper.pdf
29. Pedregosa, F., et al.: Scikit-learn: machine learning in Python. J. Mach. Learn. Res. **12**, 2825–2830 (2011)
30. Peters, M.E., et al.: Deep contextualized word representations. arXiv:1802.05365 (2018)
31. Russian language toxic comments. https://www.kaggle.com/blackmoon/russian-language-toxic-comments
32. Shahmatova, T.S.: Oskorblenie kak instrument jazykovogo nasilija v rechevyh situacijah institucionalnogo obshhenija. Uchenye zapiski Kazanskogo universiteta. Serija. Gumanitarnye nauki **155**(5), 267–278 (2013)
33. Smetanin, S., Komarov, M.: Deep transfer learning baselines for sentiment analysis in Russian. Inf. Process. Manag. **3**(58), 102484 (2021). https://doi.org/10.1016/j.ipm.2020.102484
34. Špago, D., Maslo, A., Špago-Ćumurija, E.: Insults speak louder than words: Donald Trump's tweets through the lens of the speech act of insulting. Folia Linguistica et Litteraria **27**, 139–159 (2019)
35. Sponholz, L., Christofoletti, R.: From preachers to comedians: Ideal types of hate speakers in Brazil. Glob. Media Commun. **15**(1), 67–84 (2019). https://doi.org/10.1177/174276651881 8870
36. The Multilingual Internet: Language, Culture, and Communication Online. Oxford University Press, Oxford (2007)
37. VKontakte told about increase of more than 22% to 73 million in Russian audience. https://vk.com/press/q1-2020-results
38. Wolf, T., et al.: Transformers: state-of-the-art natural language processing. arXiv:1910.03771 (2019)

# Following the Lead When Nothing is Certain? Exploring the Image of Russia in Kazakhstani and Ukrainian Digital News Media

Anastasia Prytkova[1,2], Sergei Pashakhin[1(✉)] ⓘ, and Sergei Koltcov[1,2] ⓘ

[1] National Research University Higher School of Economics, St. Petersburg, Russia
aaprytkova@edu.hse.ru, spashahin@hse.ru
[2] Laboratory for Social and Cognitive Informatics, HSE University, St. Petersburg, Russia

**Abstract.** International news plays an important role in shaping public opinion about the foreign policy and leadership of a country. Yet research shows that the bias in favor of the current political leadership is prevalent in foreign news coverage. In this study, we explore whether these assumptions hold in the case of digital news outlets in media systems outside of established democracies. We examine the representations of Russia in digital news streams of Kazakhstan and Ukraine based on a collection of news published by about 30 top news websites in each of the countries during 2018 (n = 2,339,583 news items). To study the coverage of Russia, we follow an approach combining topic modeling for extraction of news agendas and qualitative analysis of news framing. Then, we compare Kazakhstani and Ukrainian news agendas and their framing. The results suggest that digital news media in the selected cases follow expectations based on the research of offline media despite the transformations that happened in news production with the advance of the Internet.

**Keywords:** Digital news media · Topic modeling · The image of Russia · Ukrainian crisis · Agenda-building · Framing

## 1 Introduction

Public support of foreign policy depends on information input from news media more than support for any other policy [1, 2]. People often lack the knowledge and direct experience related to foreign countries and rely solely on news outlets when they form opinions about cross-national relations and socio-political situations beyond the borders of their home countries [3]. Research shows that news media are limited in their ability to provide impartial coverage of international relations [4]. Too often, news outlets rely on the voices from the governments when they select topics and their interpretations [5]. The further lies the country under coverage, the heavier the media's reliance on these voices and the weaker their impartiality [6, 7]. However, the cases when countries are closely situated, possess large cross-border social networks, and long histories of close relationships are still understudied.

© Springer Nature Switzerland AG 2022
D. A. Alexandrov et al. (Eds.): DTGS 2021, CCIS 1503, pp. 375–388, 2022.
https://doi.org/10.1007/978-3-030-93715-7_27

The Internet has transformed both media systems and journalism practices across the globe. Thus, the digital space has made the boundaries between media systems more transparent, leaving the language and access to the Internet as the only barriers between them [8]. Journalists assembled in vast cross-border online networks expanding access to informational resources for news making. Furthermore, the Internet made the process of making and publishing international news cheaper than ever, allowing news outlets to keep providing international news while not having any foreign offices or staff in the covered countries. For the societies with political regimes that exertight media control, this new space became a venue where independent news coverage could be published and accessed by local and international audiences [9, 10]. These changes allow us to assume that the production of international news in digital conditions could be less reliant on the voices of the political establishment. Nevertheless, beyond established democracies, the cases of closely connected countries and their digital news about their neighbors remain understudied [11].

Specifically, ex-Soviet countries have received less attention than Western countries in the literature on media systems and international news [12]. Kazakhstan, Russia, and Ukraine are three ex-Soviet neighboring countries with strong ties in both social and political contexts [13, 14]. Moreover, all three countries are bounded by the strong presence of the Russian language and, thus, overlapping media-systems. However, the current cross-national relations of Kazakhstan and Ukraine with Russia could not be more different. While Russia and Kazakhstan are considered political and economic partners, Russia and Ukraine are experiencing a lasting and complex conflict with both political and economic dimensions. Kazakhstan has explicitly proclaimed neutrality in the conflict and proposed to become a mediating party between Russian and Ukraine backed by the EU and the US. This role requires acknowledging Ukraine's claims while not subverting the relationships with Russia. Given Kazakhstan and Ukraine's geographical proximity and shared language with Russia, will their digital news media draw a similar to Ukraine's picture of their neighbor? Or will Kazakhstan media balance their coverage of Russia to support their proclaimed neutrality in the conflict between Ukraine and Russia?

In this paper, we explore the images of Russia constructed by digital news media of Kazakhstan and Ukraine. To compare these two images, we select about 30 most popular digital news outlets from Ukraine and Kazakhstan and select all the relevant news items for the period of one year. We follow a mixed-method approach combining computational analysis of large text data with qualitative analysis of news framing to explore images of Russia in the respective news streams.

## 2 Literature Review

News coverage of foreign countries and international relations differs from domestic reporting in several aspects [4]. Traditionally, news organizations were heavily dependent on their foreign offices and international news agencies providing information from abroad. Considering the limited—relatively to the domestic coverage—demand for international news, in such arrangements, only news outlets able to afford pools of reporters abroad could enter the market of international news. These limitations, on the one hand, mean that international news is served for a specific segment of the audience with broader interests in socio-political and economic matters and, on the other hand, an audience with limited knowledge and experiences of foreign contexts. Hence, as a product, to fulfill the journalistic duty of keeping the citizenry informed, international news requires 'domestication' to make apparent to the audience the relevancy of the covered events and suggest interpretations of international relations unavailable to the average news consumer [15]. These production constraints make an explicit impact on the impartiality of international news by limiting access to the full spectrum of perspectives needed for balanced and neutral reporting. However, beyond these explicit factors, foreign news is subject to implicit factors originating in the home country of media organizations.

There are two major models describing the relationships between foreign policy, public opinion, and international news: the propaganda model and the indexing theory [5, 16]. Both of them stress the lack of perspectives on issues of foreign policy and international relations that are critical of the political establishment of the home country. While the propaganda model focuses on the structure of media ownership and interests of business and political establishment, the indexing theory focuses on the journalistic practices that introduce bias in the coverage. These models are not entirely contradictory, and some recent works aim to synthesize both of them into a new model [17, 18]. Nevertheless, the empirical basis of these theoretical initiatives remains largely based on Western countries, leaving out the question to what extent they are applicable to cases outside the established democracies and to ex-Soviet countries particularly.

Research on media systems outside Western countries exposes other types of arrangements between the political establishment of a country and media organizations. Most of this research is concerned with the question of how a political regime can use media to secure public support and avoid damaging image discourses in the public sphere [19–21]. The most frequent finding of this strain of research is that political regimes are more concerned with controlling television with nation-wide broadcasting than digital news channels. This often implies that in some countries, the Internet serves as the only medium between audience and establishment-independent news coverage. Although the independence of digital outlets is frequently in focus such this research, the specificity of international coverage is rarely considered. Furthermore, as far as we know, there are no studies aiming to compare news coverage of a country by their close neighbors outside cases of established democracies when one neighbor has an open conflict with the covered country, and the other has to keep partner-relationships with both of them. Considering the typical restraints of international coverage combined with factors restraining journalistic freedoms in non-democratic regimes, are digital news outlets still open to critical perspectives on the neighboring country?

The dependence of public opinion on news in matters of international relations makes it important what image of a foreign country is constructed by news streams for the audience [1, 2]. A negative image can undermine international partnership and support for the current leadership driving the foreign policy, while a positive image has little to no impact [22–24]. An image of a country is a product of news agenda and framing [25]. On the one hand, by selecting topics for coverage, news media highlight certain aspects of a country that may contribute to either positive or negative impressions in the audience, depending on the topic. This agenda building could be viewed as a ranking process where news outlets assign importance to some topics at the expense of others [26]. For instance, a negative image might be constructed by focusing on the military aggression of a neighboring country at the expense of economic benefits the home country will have from recent trade agreements with the aggressor. On the other hand, the choice of a topic alone is not enough to establish whether the image is negative or positive. Thus, military aggression might be framed in news items as a peacekeeping operation aiming to secure the common geopolitical space that, in the long run, will benefit both the home country and the partner covered in the news. News framing is achieved by selecting certain aspects of events and making them more salient than others to promote either positive or negative interpretations of the events [27–29]. Unlike agenda-building focusing on the selection of topics and events, framing operates on the level of individual news items dedicated to a topic. Thus, to capture what image news media construct, it is necessary to study both the news agenda and framing of each agenda item.

Hence, research elucidates that international news tends to align with the political establishment of the home country in the selection of topics and their framing. Such bias is common in media systems of established democracies and could be expected in systems of other political regimes with fewer freedoms. However, in the case of the latter, the Internet often becomes a space for more independent and critical views. Moreover, the digitalization of news media allows producing international news with fewer resources than ever which suggests that in digital space, news outlets in non-democratic regimes are able to bring critical to the establishment agendas and framing while avoiding reliance on biased sources inside the home country. In this work, we aim to explore these assumptions in the case of ex-Soviet states that remain understudied. As the remaining significant barriers between flows of news online are language and access to the Internet, the cases for such exploration should be neighboring countries with the presence of shared language and foreign policies regarding a common international problem to identify the stances of the political establishment and their critical counterparts.

Ex-Soviet countries and recent international developments provide such cases of strained relations between countries with non-democratic regimes bounded together by geographical proximity, long shared history, and a strong presence of a common language. Russia, Ukraine, and Kazakhstan are such states that recently entered a phase when their relations became complicated by an international conflict. The Ukrainian crisis of 2014 had united the international community against the threat to Ukrainian independence and Russian actions in Crimea. While Russian-Ukrainian relations escalated, Kazakhstan became pressured to pick a side. Instead of siding with either of the conflicting parties, Kazakhstan chose to openly declare itself a neutral body and suggested becoming a mediator [30, 31]. This international conflict has clear definitions of opposing stances: Ukraine and the EU accuse Russia of breaking Ukrainian and international laws, while Russia denies all accusations. At the heart of these accusations is the status of the Crimean Peninsula. To claim a side in this conflict is to accept or deny its current status in favor of one side. Additionally, we choose these cases because the Kazakhstani digital media remain even more understudied than Russian and Ukrainian media. Thus, we aim to contribute to the understanding of international news produced by digital media beyond established democracies. In this paper, we aim to compare images of Russia emerging in news items published by online outlets from Kazakhstan and Ukraine. We formulate the following research questions:

- What are the agendas of Ukrainian and Kazakhstan digital media regarding Russia: what topics are discussed, and which ones are omitted?
- How the news about Russia is framed in Ukrainian and Kazakhstan digital media? Is there any difference between these two countries?

## 3  Data and Methods

Answering our research questions requires sampling digital news outlets from Ukraine and Kazakhstan that are popular and provide foreign news with attention to neighboring countries. To explore the image of Russia constructed by them, we choose a one-year period to account for seasonal dynamics in news coverage. We choose to focus on the news produced during the entire 2018 year as it had several events that were relevant for the region highly discussed: presidential elections in Russia (as well as Ukraine and Kazakhstan), FIFA championship, opening a bridge across the Kerch Strait, and other. As the presidential election year in all three countries, this period is likely to exhibit all perspectives on the role of the Russian leadership in the Ukrainian crisis, given that Vladimir Putin was aiming for reelection. At the same time, in Kazakhstan, Nursultan Nazarbayev was arranging himself a retirement as the president, having spent in the office 29 years. With such radical change in the leadership, we expect to find increased attention to foreign policy in Kazakhstan.

We selected Ukrainian and Kazakhstani online news media using commercial social media aggregator Medialogiya [32, 33]. The service claims to monitor all Russian-language social and news media, including news media from neighboring countries such as Kazakhstan and Ukraine. To identify news outlets covering public affairs, and international events in particular, we used keywords with the names of the two winning candidates for the presidential post of Ukraine and Kazakhstan: 'Zelenskyi' and 'Tokayev,' respectively. Thus, our sampling strategy is based on the assumption that if Ukrainian media cover elections in Kazakhstan, they are more likely to cover events from other parts of the CIS region and vice versa. This would filter out Ukrainian outlets focusing exclusively on the conflicting relations of the Ukrainian government with Russia. The resulting sample consists of 30 Russian-language Ukrainian news websites and 31 outlets from Kazakhstan (see Table 1). Then, we collected all news items posted on the sampled websites during 2018. The resulting dataset is comprised of 2,339,583 news items with metadata. Further, to sample news items mentioning Russia, we filtered the collected texts using keywords: 'Russia,' 'RF,' 'Russian Federation.' After filtering, 293,531 news items remained: 20,795 texts from the Kazakhstani media and 272,736 items from the Ukrainian media. At this stage, the sample of Kazakhstani media lost four sources as they did not return items matching our keywords.

News agendas and framing of particular issues have been traditionally studied with content analysis [34] sometimes coupled with other methods. However, the main limitation of the traditional approach is its labor intensiveness as it relies on manual reading and coding of news items by humans [35]. Given the size of our corpus (n = 272,736), the best approach is computational. We adopted the framework able to handle such volumes based on topic modeling [36, 37]. Topic modeling is an agile clustering method for text data that estimates N latent variables (topics) using joint distributions of words

**Table 1.** Sampled websites and number of their news mentioning Russia during 2018.

| Ukrainian media | | | | Kazakhstani media | |
|---|---|---|---|---|---|
| Rank | Website | N-relevant items | | Website | N-relevant items |
| 1 | segodnya.ua | 48,076 | 1 | sputniknews.kz | 3,005 |
| 2 | obozrevatel.com | 18,771 | 2 | datnews.kz | 2,898 |
| 3 | newsfront.info | 17,262 | 3 | zakon.kz | 2,789 |
| 4 | gordon.ua | 16,111 | 4 | forbes.kz | 1,742 |
| 5 | dsnews.ua | 16,098 | 5 | informburo.kz | 1,511 |
| 6 | nv.ua | 15,361 | 6 | kaztag.kz | 1,385 |
| 7 | liga.net | 13,934 | 7 | tengrinews.kz | 1,378 |
| 8 | dialogua.ru | 13,682 | 8 | 365info.kz | 1,361 |
| 9 | politeka.net | 11,575 | 9 | newtimes.kz | 706 |
| 10 | ukrinform.ua | 10,274 | 10 | kt.kz | 700 |
| 11 | 24tv.ua/ru | 9,750 | 11 | total.kz | 633 |
| 12 | tsn.ua | 9,049 | 12 | caravan.kz | 609 |
| 13 | apostrophe.ua/ru | 8,215 | 13 | kazpravda.kz | 442 |
| 14 | novorosinform.org | 7,991 | 14 | azattyq.org | 413 |
| 15 | glavred.info | 7,598 | 15 | vlast.kz | 311 |
| 16 | korrespondent.net | 7,307 | 16 | holanews.kz | 220 |
| 17 | zik.ua | 6,051 | 17 | camonitor.kz | 198 |
| 18 | inforesist.org | 5,889 | 18 | ng.kz | 142 |
| 19 | strana.ua | 5,461 | 19 | nur.kz | 76 |
| 20 | unian.net | 4,574 | 20 | 24.kz/ru | 64 |
| 21 | lb.ua | 4,560 | 21 | webinfo.kz | 61 |
| 22 | kp.ua | 2,914 | 22 | novgaz.com | 60 |
| 23 | sharij.net | 2,805 | 23 | village.kz | 51 |
| 24 | ukr.com | 2,768 | 24 | baribar.kz | 24 |
| 25 | gazeta.ua | 2,586 | 25 | 7sunews.kz | 10 |
| 26 | elise.com.ua | 1,814 | 26 | today.kz | 4 |
| 27 | fraza.ua | 1,225 | 27 | kt.kz | 2 |
| 28 | epravda.com.ua | 718 | 28 | village.kz | 0 |
| 29 | 5ua.ru | 304 | 29 | vlast.kz | 0 |
| 30 | espreso.tv | 13 | 30 | webinfo.kz | 0 |
| | | | 31 | zakon.kz | 0 |
| | Total | 272,736 | | | 20,795 |

and documents [38]. Currently, Latent Dirichlet Allocation (LDA) is the most tried and established algorithm used for the extraction of news agendas [37, 39]. It requires a user to manually set the number of topics as a parameter. Following the recommendations of algorithm developers, we set the number of topics to 100 [40]. To handle the stochasticity of the algorithm, we followed the pipeline for extraction and labeling of the stable topics proposed in [37]. The resulting LDA solution contained 45 stable topics. However, only 38 topics were used in the analysis, as the rest turned out uninterpretable after the labeling procedure (see Figs. 1 and 2 for the assigned labels) by three independent coders (Krippendorff's alpha = 0.71). We used these 38 topics to calculate the salience of agenda items as the sums of topic probabilities aggregated by country. Provided that our corpus is unbalanced, topic salience was weighted by the number of documents of both countries. In this analysis, we aim to identify country-specific agendas and agenda items common for both countries. We used the shared agenda items in the qualitative part of our analysis to identify the differences in news framing.

To analyze the framing of extracted news agendas, we used qualitative reading. We followed the standard definition of news frame and its components proposed in [27]. For each country and topic, 40 documents were selected; thus, the sample of the texts used in qualitative analysis contained 800 documents. The texts were read in consistence with theoretical sampling [41], discovering the frames until the saturation is reached. We identified one topic containing news based predominantly on the citations from the news from Russian media and excluded it from qualitative analysis as it was out of the scope of this study.

## 4 Results

Figure 1 that contains topic salience distribution between the media of the two countries, clearly shows that some topics are covered predominantly by the Kazakhstani media, while others are typical almost exclusively for the Ukrinian media Among the latter, a significant proportion can be treated as connected to the Ukrainian crisis and current state of relationships with Russia – particularly, the news about the conflict between Russia and Ukraine, peacekeepers initiative in the Donbas region, Crimea as a part of Russian territory, aggression towards Russians, news on imprisonment of ukrainian filmmaker Oleg Sentsov and the incident in the Kerch Strait involving Ukrainian and Russian military. Another large group of topics is related to the events that took place in Russia or connected to it. For instance, they cover the poisoning of the former Russian spy Skripal in Britain, international sanctions against Russia, street protests in Russia, gas supplies from Russia to Europe, and the conflict between the Russian Orthodox Church and the Istanbul Synod. Kazakhstani media, in their turn, have a different focus of attention. For example, they cover more sport and cultural events in Russia. Apart from this, there is a rather salient coverage of economic and government news – problems cross-border trade, international relations involving Russia, and the changes in the Russian legislation.

Figure 2 demonstrates the difference between the countries in topic salience. For the Ukrainian media, topics related to the conflict between Ukraine and Russia (stated above) can be treated as country-specific, while for Kazakhstani media, these are economic news about Kazakhstan in cooperation with other countries including Russia, such as news on export and import.

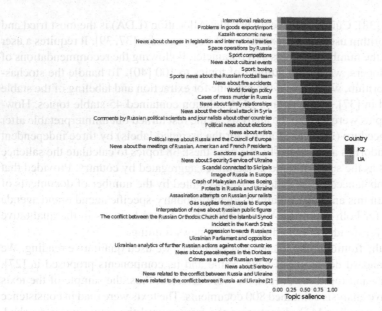

**Fig. 1.** Relative topic salience by channel.

**Fig. 2.** Differences in weighted topic salience by country. The color shows country-specific topics.

Thus, based on the analysis of topics salience, we can answer the first research question. Overall, we observe a difference in news agendas between the two countries. On the one hand, Ukrainian media cover events connected to Russia more often than Kazakhstani media. Moreover, the content of agendas varies a lot: Ukrainian media focus predominantly on the news connected to the Ukrainian-Russian conflict, related incidents, protests, and sanctions. On the other hand, Kazakhstani media cover these topics to a smaller extent while paying a higher attention to more peaceful and less politicized topics, such as the economy, sport, cultural events, and space operations.

However, there are topics whose salience is almost equal between the studied countries. Such topics include "Political news about Russia and the Council of Europe," "News about celebreties," "Political news about Armenia," "Comments by Russian political scientists and journalists about Ukraine," "News about meetings of Russian, American and French Presidents," "News about the chemical attack in Syria," "News about family relationships," "Cases of mass murder in Russia," "World foreign policy," "News about fire accidents." However, among these topics and the topics that are more specific to the media of each country, framing of issues connected to Russia varies: the framing of news about events that took place on the territory of Russia is different from the news which covers the role of Russia in international events.

Table 2 provides a summary of the key features of such framing. Overall, the two countries differ in tonality when they cover events connected to the Russian political establishment. Ukrainian news outlets emphasize every possible connection of the covered events with the Russian-Ukrainian conflict always stressing the aggressiveness of the Russian actions. Moreover, when the covered events relate to Russian domestic politics, Ukrainian media seek and stress the angle that undermines the Russian political

**Table 2.** Summary of the key framing features in agenda items shared by Kazakhstan and Ukraine.

| Topics | Ukraine | Kazakhstan |
| --- | --- | --- |
| *News about events that took place in Russia* | | |
| Political news about elections | Connection to the Ukrainian crisis, underlining public discontent with the ruling political regime | Neutral tone, reporting of facts and figures |
| Cases of mass murder in Russia | Kerch as an occupied town | Kerch as a Crimean town |
| News about fire accidents | Negative framing when events in any way connected to Russian political forces or the Russia-Ukraine conflict | Overall neutral tone, factual reporting |
| *News about foreign events in which Russia played specific role* | | |
| Political news about Russia and the Council of Europe | Well-pronounced defense of the Ukrainian interest | Neutral and factual reporting |
| News about meetings of Russian, American and French Presidents | Negative portrayal of the Russian president | Positive portrayal of the Russian president, use of Russian sources |
| News about the chemical attack in Syria | Emotional reporting, blaming Russians for the chemical attack | Neutral, factual reporting. Search for a guilty party without blaming |

establishment. Ukrainian media are less restrained than typical Kazakhstani media in the choice of wording when events involve actors connected to the conflict. Kazakhstani media provide more neutral and balanced coverage. However, when the events involve Russian foreign affairs, Kazakhstani news outlets carefully avoid sharp angles that may put the image of Russia in a negative light.

More interesting results are provided by the topics with quotes of Russian public figures and political actors about Ukraine and Russia. First of all, the selection of the voices and quotes follows the general principle: Ukraine seeks offensive sayings, while Kazakhstan tries to stress the stability of the Russia-Kazakhstan partnership. Moreover, Ukrainian outlets almost always attempt to provide evaluations and answers to the selected statements made by the Russian officials, stressing their overall inadequacy. At the same time, Kazakhstani media nearly never comment or evaluate the selected statements.

## 5 Conclusions

In this paper, we aimed to explore whether digital media follow some of the important agenda-setting and framing trends discovered earlier in the research on offline media. We chose the case of the two ex-Soviet countries where one country is in active conflict with the country under coverage, while the second has to remain neutral. We assumed that the digital news outlets in these regimes are less likely to follow the agenda and framing of the political establishment than the traditional media, such as television because of presumably smaller control over them, especially in Ukraine. Our primary interest, in this case, was Kazakhstani media since, as far as we know, there are no studies of international news produced by digital media of the country. Moreover, we expected more critical news coverage of Russia in the case of Kazakhstan, given that during the sampled period, Nursultan Nazarbayev planned to retire from the office after 29 years of tenure. Furthermore, 2018 was a presidential election year for Russia and Ukraine too. Given the presence of political events of such magnitude, we expected that digital media would become less aligned with the perspective of the current political establishment in respective countries on Russia. As our aim was to explore the representations of Russia in Ukrainian and Kazakhstani digital news streams, in this paper, we formulated the following questions.

1. What are the agendas of Ukrainian and Kazakh media regarding Russia – what topics are discussed, and which ones are omitted?
2. How the news about Russia is framed in the Ukrainian and Kazakh media? Is there any difference between these two countries?

Already at the level of agenda-building, we find the difference between Ukrainian and Kazakhstani media consistent with the positions of the governments of both countries on Russia. Ukrainian media select more events with a connection to the Ukrainian crisis and respective international relations with Russia: news about the conflict between Russia and Ukraine, peacekeepers in the Donbas, Crimea as a part of Russian territory, aggression towards Russians, news about Sentsov, and incident in the Kerch Strait.

Another part of the Ukrainian digital news agenda is related to the events that took place in Russia or connected to it: the poisoning of Skripals', international sanctions against Russia, protests, gas supplies from Russia to Europe, the conflict between the Russian Orthodox Church and the Istanbul Synod. Such agenda selection appears to focus on the topics that are able to present Russia as either an aggressor or a loser on the international arena.Kazakhstani digital media have visibly more peaceful and neutral news agendas. For instance, they select more sport and cultural events. Another part of the Kazakhstani agenda is coverage of economic and government news: problems in export/import, international relations, or the changes in the Russian legislation.

While we have not found topics completely omitted in the media of either country, there were topics e that were salient in the media of just one country, and such topics can be treated as partly omitted by the media of the other country. For Kazakhstani media, these agenda items are "News related to the conflict between Russia and Ukraine," "News about Sentsov," "Crimea as a part of Russian territory"; for Ukrainian ones, such topics are "KZ International relations," "KZ problems in goods export/import," "KZ economic news" covering mostly Russia as a partner in the Eurasian Economic Union. Obviously, while typical Ukrainian topics underline conflict, Kazakhstani topics focus on cooperation.

Regarding the second research question, we find that even though there are similarities in the framing of some events in Ukrainian and Kazakhstani digital media, news about Russia is predominantly framed differently. It is especially noticeable in the framing of the events that are somehow connected to the Russian domestic politics or the Ukrainian crisis. In such cases, the framing of news in Ukrainian media becomes negative: the conflicting tone is maintained through media, repeatedly stressing the unlawfulness of Russia's actions in Crimea. Kazakh media adhere to a positive/neutral framing and avoid judgemental phrases. Despite that the current status of the relationships between Russia and Kazakhstan is questioned by some public figures in Russia, the prevalent number of such news is framed in a way that Russia remains an ally, partner who cares about the stability of cross-national relationships.

Thus, we find that the representations of Russia constructed by the digital news media of Ukraine and Kazakhstan are closely aligned to the interests of the political establishments of the respective countries. The causes for this alignment, however, might be different. In Ukraine, the political media landscape is relatively diverse, in consistency with the fractured political landscape. Therefore, here we may observe the "rally around the flag" effect - an effect of mobilization around the national government and its agenda in the situation of a sharp international conflict, when the lack of support of the government by certain media on other issues is fading in comparison to the desire to support it in a struggle for the national sovereignty. This effect is often observed even in the established democracies, and the Ukrainian case looks consistent with them. In Kazakhstan, where no "rally-around-the-flag" effect can be expected due to the lack of a conflict with Russia, we are most probably dealing with the dominance of the government media online.

Thus, our assumption that the presidential elections in the two studied countries would promote a critical perspective in digital media that are likely to be less dependent on the agenda and framing of the establishment than national-broadcasting television was not confirmed. This points out an avenue for further research. In particular, our exploratory design could be improved by mapping the political stances of the sampled media and rebalancing, if needed, the sample so as to capture both voices of dissent and support. Such mapping is particularly required for Kazakhstan, as there is a lack of research on news media in this country. Based on a richer sample of media, the exploratory design could be extended with a confirmatory analysis by estimating the strength of associations between media stance, agenda items, and keywords suggesting certain framing. It could also shed light on the prevalence of the pro-government point of view in the media of the two countries, thus giving an idea on how dominant the governments are in their media systems, as compared to a neighboring country.

**Acknowledgments.** The research was implemented in the framework of the Russian Scientific Fund Grant №19-18-00206 at the National Research University Higher School of Economics (HSE) in 2021.

# References

1. Brewer, P.R.: National interest frames and public opinion about world Affairs. Harvard Int. J. Press/Polit. **11**, 89–102 (2006). https://doi.org/10.1177/1081180X06293725
2. Bloch-Elkon, Y.: Studying the media, public opinion, and foreign policy in international crises: the united states and the Bosnian crisis, 1992–1995. Harvard Int. J. Press/Polit. **12**, 20–51 (2007). https://doi.org/10.1177/1081180X07307184
3. Evans, M.: Framing international conflicts: media coverage of fighting in the Middle East. Int. J. Media Cult. Polit. **6**, 209–233 (2010). https://doi.org/10.1386/mcp.6.2.209_1
4. Novais, R.A.: National influences in foreign news: British and Portuguese press coverage of the Dili Massacre in East Timor. Int. Commun. Gaz. **69**, 553–573 (2007). https://doi.org/10.1177/1748048507082842
5. Bennett, W.L., Lawrence, R.G., Livingston, S.: When the Press Fails: Political Power and the News Media from Iraq to Katrina. University of Chicago Press, Chicago (2007)
6. Nossek, H.: Our News and their news: the role of national identity in the coverage of foreign news. Journalism **5**, 343–368 (2004). https://doi.org/10.1177/1464884904044941
7. Van Belle, D.A.: New York Times and Network TV news coverage of foreign disasters: the significance of the insignificant variables. Journal. Mass Commun. Q. **77**, 50–70 (2016). https://doi.org/10.1177/107769900007700105
8. Chadwick, A.: The Hybrid Media System: Politics and Power. Oxford University Press, New York (2017)
9. Bodrunova, S.S., Litvinenko, AA: New media and political protest: the formation of a public Counter-Sphere in Russia, 2008-12. In: Russia's Changing Economic and Political Regimes: The Putin Years and Afterwards, pp. 29–65 (2013). https://doi.org/10.4324/9780203730669
10. Oates, S.: Revolution Stalled: The Political Limits of the Internet in the Post-Soviet Sphere. Oxford University Press, Oxford (2013)
11. Stoycheff, E., Liu, J., Wibowo, K.A., Nanni, D.P.: What have we learned about social media by studying Facebook? A decade in review. New Media Soc. **19**, 968–980 (2017). https://doi.org/10.1177/1461444817695745
12. Hallin, D.C., Mancini, P. (eds.): Comparing Media Systems Beyond the Western World. Cambridge University Press, New York (2012)
13. Zabortseva, Y.: Russia's Relations with Kazakhstan: Rethinking Post-communist Transitions in the Emerging World System. Routledge, New York (2016)

14. Yekelchyk, S.: The Conflict in Ukraine: What Everyone Needs to Know. Oxford University Press, Oxford (2015)
15. Alasuutari, P., Qadir, A., Creutz, K.: The domestication of foreign news: news stories related to the 2011 Egyptian revolution in British, Finnish and Pakistani newspapers. Media Cult. Soc. **35**, 692–707 (2013)
16. Herman, E., Chomsky, N.: Manufacturing Consent: The Political Economy of the Mass Media. Pantheon Books, New York (1988)
17. Kennis, A.: Synthesizing the indexing and propaganda models: an evaluation of US news coverage of the uprising in Ecuador, January 2000. Commun. Crit./Cult. Stud. **6**, 386–409 (2009). https://doi.org/10.1080/14791420903335127
18. Kennis, A.: An unworthy social movement? An evaluation of the media dependence model and the news media performance of the *New York Times* on Vieques: An Evaluation of the MDM on NYT coverage of vieques. Commun. Cult. Critiq. **9**, 438–457 (2016). https://doi.org/10.1111/cccr.12112
19. Oates, S.: Television, Democracy and Elections in Russia. Routledge, Abingdon (2006)
20. Baysha, O.: Miscommunicating Social Change: Lessons from Russia and Ukraine. Lexington Books, Lanham (2018)
21. Oates, S.: Russian media in the digital age: propaganda rewired. Russ. Polit. **1**, 398–417 (2016). https://doi.org/10.1163/2451-8921-00104004
22. Wanta, W., Golan, G., Lee, C.: Agenda setting and international news: media influence on public perceptions of foreign nations. Journal. Mass Commun. Q. **81**, 364–377 (2004). https://doi.org/10.1177/107769900408100209
23. Wanta, W., Hu, Y.-W.: The agenda-setting effects of international news coverage: an examination of differing news frames. Int. J. Publ. Opin. Res. **5**, 250–264 (1993)
24. Zhang, C.: International coverage, foreign policy, and national image: exploring the complexities of media coverage, public opinion, and presidential agenda, **18** (2012)
25. Wanta, W., Mikusova, S.: The agenda-setting process in international news. Central Eur. J. Commun. **3**, 221–235 (2010)
26. McCombs, M.: Setting the Agenda: Mass Media and Public Opinion. Wiley, New York (2014)
27. Entman, R.M.: Framing: toward clarification of a fractured paradigm. J. Commun. **43**, 51–58 (1993)
28. Muddiman, A., Stroud, N.J., McCombs, M.: Media fragmentation, attribute agenda setting, and political opinions about Iraq. J. Broadcast. Electron. Media **58**, 215–233 (2014). https://doi.org/10.1080/08838151.2014.906433
29. Entman, R.M.: Framing bias: media in the distribution of power. J. Commun. **57**, 163–173 (2007). https://doi.org/10.1111/j.1460-2466.2006.00336.x
30. Nurbekov, A.: Kazakhstan urges peaceful resolution to ukraine conflict, reiterates minsk agreements. https://astanatimes.com/2015/01/kazakhstan-urges-peaceful-resolution-ukraine-conflict-reiterates-minsk-agreements/. Accessed 24 Feb 2021
31. Abdulova, Z.: Nazarbayev offers to mediate in Ukraine, stresses Kazakhstan's economic resilience. https://astanatimes.com/2014/12/nazarbayev-offers-mediate-ukraine-stresses-kazakhstans-economic-resilience/. Accessed 24 Feb 2021
32. Medialogiya - monitoring and analysis of media and social networks (Medialogiya - monitoring i analiz SMI i sotssetey). https://www.mlg.ru/. Accessed 08 May 2020
33. Media citation index [Indeks tsitiruyemosti SMI]. https://www.mlg.ru/about/technologies/#mediaindex. Accessed 08 May 2020
34. Krippendorff, K.: Content Analysis: An Introduction to Its Methodology. Sage, Thousand Oaks (2004)
35. DiMaggio, P., Nag, M., Blei, D.: Exploiting affinities between topic modeling and the sociological perspective on culture: application to newspaper coverage of US government arts funding. Poetics **41**, 570–606 (2013). https://doi.org/10.1016/j.poetic.2013.08.004

36. Grimmer, J., Stewart, B.M.: Text as data: the promise and pitfalls of automatic content analysis methods for political texts. Polit. Anal. **21**, 267–297 (2013). https://doi.org/10.1093/pan/mps028

37. Koltsov, S., Pashakhin, S., Dokuka, S.: A full-cycle methodology for news topic modeling and user feedback research. In: Staab, S., Koltsova, O., Ignatov, D.I. (eds.) SocInfo 2018. LNCS, vol. 11185, pp. 308–321. Springer, Cham (2018). https://doi.org/10.1007/978-3-030-01129-1_19

38. Griffiths, T.L., Steyvers, M.: Finding scientific topics. Proc. Natl. Acad. Sci. **101**, 5228–5235 (2004). https://doi.org/10.1073/pnas.0307752101

39. Daud, A., Li, J., Zhou, L., Muhammad, F.: Knowledge discovery through directed probabilistic topic models: a survey. Front. Comput. Sci. China **4**, 280–301 (2010). https://doi.org/10.1007/s11704-009-0062-y

40. Blei D.M., Lafferty J.D.: Topic models. In: Text Mining: Classification, Clustering, and Applications. pp. 71–94. CRC Press, Boca Raton (2009)

41. Charmaz, K.: Constructing Grounded Theory. Sage Publications, London (2006)

# Participation of Transnational Migrants in the Formation of the Host Country Image Through Mass Self-communication

Anna Smoliarova(✉) ⓘ, Yuliya Taranovaⓘ, and Marianna Vagaitceva

St. Petersburg State University, Universitetskaya nab. 7/9, 199034 St. Petersburg, Russia
a.smolyarova@spbu.ru

**Abstract.** This exploratory study focuses on the role of transnational migrants as stakeholders in the process of shaping the image of a place, in particular, the host country. We studied the content created by 10 Russian-speaking Instagram bloggers with migration background residing on different continents. Through the content-analysis of 441 posts published in 2018, we have found that Russian-speaking Instagram bloggers addressing global Russophone audiences paid a significant amount of attention to the dissemination of information about the host country. They covered several aspects of host country image, including climate and geography, history and culture, security and stability, representatives of the host society, and general quality of life in the host country. While the three first categories received almost exclusively positive evaluations, the last ones, rooted in the personal daily experience represent a more diverse and complex picture. Both the bloggers and their audiences form a story about the host countries, which, in turn, forms the mediated image of the countries in the minds of the audience.

**Keywords:** Mass self-communication · Social media · Place marketing · Branding and image-making · Stakeholders · Transnational migrants · Russophone bloggers

## 1 Introduction

In place marketing residents are considered as brand ambassadors of places [1]. As stakeholders, they have a significant impact on the process of territory branding [2]. Scholars distinguish between three roles played by the residents: "as an integral part of the place brand through their characteristics and behavior; as ambassadors for their place brand who grant credibility to any communicated message; and as citizens and voters who are vital for the political legitimization of place branding" [2]. The role of stakeholders in the creation, development and ultimately ownership of place brands "goes well beyond that of customers/consumers as they are citizens who legitimize place brands and heavily influence their meaning" [3].

The increasing role of stakeholders in place marketing, branding, and image-making has been extensively researched. This tendency can be explained by several reasons [3]. Firstly, territorial branding is a public activity of management, and such activity

D. A. Alexandrov et al. (Eds.): DTGS 2021, CCIS 1503, pp. 389–402, 2022.
https://doi.org/10.1007/978-3-030-93715-7_28

needs to be supported by society. Secondly, the popularity of the concept of co-branding is increasing in general. The branding process is presented as a process of dialogue between stakeholder groups on brand formation. Finally, the third reason is related to the development of digital and online technologies and, accordingly, to the formation of online communities dedicated to territories and their brands [3].

The involvement of residents as stakeholders is largely facilitated by the development of digital technology and online communication [3]. Affordances of online platforms led to the creation of networked publics [4] where people come together in online communities, discuss issues of interest to them, and share experiences or useful information. Contrary to the audiences, networked publics involve meaningful interaction between participants [e.g. 5]. In the modern networked environment, place brands are created and managed by multiple participants who fill them with meaning.

Among other participants, transnational migrants as individuals that establish multiple and regularly reproduced transnational connections [6] can play an important role in place marketing. One might presuppose that the heterogeneous character of transnational migrants' social ties including the latent ties [7] formed through mass self-communication [8] defines the diverse nature of the audience that can be exposed to the content about the host countries created by transnational migrants. Whether they unite in interest groups through online platforms or broadcast private experiences through their personal blogs, the role of transnational migrants as stakeholders in the process of shaping the image of a place remains understudied. In this exploratory study, we contribute to filling this gap by focusing on the content created by Russian-speaking Instagram bloggers with migration background residing on different continents.

## 2 Theoretical Framework

### 2.1 Digitalization of Migrant Public Communication

From letters through expensive international calls to FaceTime, communication technologies connecting individuals across large geographical distances have historically been essential for mobility, integration into the host society, as well as for relationships within the diaspora and between transnational migrants and home society [9]. Digitalization has profoundly influenced the personal and mass communication of transnational migrants [6, 10]. Contrary to print or even TV media created by migrant communities in host countries, migrant media online are easily accessible worldwide [10]. Mass self-communication has even more intensified cross-border flows of information and added new layers to the multi-layered networks of communication comprising a global public sphere [11].

'Relationships of identity, territorial or geographical belonging and (global) political engagement' [12] are deeply mediatized [13]. Social media help transnational migrants "to continuously renew their bond with their home environment" and to establish contacts within the host country [6]. Most research on discursive spaces formed by transnational migrants via social media has focused on arenas that provide opportunities to share useful information [10] or to discuss political issues [14]. These arenas, for example, a Facebook group, are selected by potential participants on a territorial basis, local or national, and the decision to join is connected to the unique identity as transnational migrants in a particular place [15].

Social media also "serve as a tool to preserve and to convert transnational migrants' cultural capital that is not recognized automatically by the host country" [16]. This potential is especially important for transnational migrants who started blogs to share migration experiences and information about the host country. According to our previous findings, the Russophone Instagram blogosphere flourishes worldwide [17]. A significant share of Russian-speaking Instagram bloggers with migration background can be perceived as social media influencers (at least, micro-influencers). The number of their followers differs from several to hundreds of thousands, making their audience fully comparable with those of migrant news media. The everyday experience of living in and personal attitudes towards the host countries become publicly accessible in a networked environment where the boundaries between the private and the public are blurring [18].

Followers of Instagram bloggers are motivated by encouragement, curiosity, and amusement [19]. In the case of blogs about life in foreign country access to stories about daily life with all mundane aspects commands the attention of potential audiences driven by the interest in a particular country. We might assume that migrant blogs can attract a very broad audience, contrary to the migrant news media and migrant groups on social media. For others, exposure to transnational communication on social media may serve as a new source of social ties and information for prospective transnational migrants [7]. The authors found that "the use of online media to communicate with transnational migrants in Western Europe is explained by the non-migrants migration propensity, indicating that online communication in migration networks is supporting migration aspirations and decision-making" [7].

Thus, the digitalization of migrant public communication has led to their involvement in the formation of the host country's image. Previous research has shown that transnational migrants are perceived as ambassadors of their home countries [20, 21], while their influence on the image of the host country remains significantly understudied [22, 23]. Moreover, the researchers focused mostly on the institutionalized diasporic actors [24]. In this paper, we will explore whether Russian-speaking Instagram bloggers with migration background are involved in the formation of the host country image.

## 2.2 Transnational Migrants as Publics and Audiences of Image Communication of Places

In the context of place marketing, transnational migrants can be seen as a target group of communication [25]. In this case, scholars and practitioners consider migrants as individuals the territory is interested in, for example, students, specialists of occupation in demand in the country, professionals capable of creating innovation and high added value, representatives of the creative class, and others [26]. Immigrant attraction through place branding is well studied [27, 28, 29]. Communication with target audiences is aimed at potential transnational migrants - to attract talents/professionals/specialists/students needed by the territory, etc.

At the same time, migrants represent a group that participates in the formation of the image of the territory and potentially influences the image of the territory as a destination for migration or tourism. In this case, transnational migrants turn to act as influencers, ambassadors, mediators, who have the ability to build bridges between cultures, due to their knowledge of the cultural codes of both cultures of the host and home countries.

Firstly, they can be considered as stakeholders that are involved in shaping the image of the home country, for example, as an attractive destination for tourism [30, 31]. "Citizens who go abroad for work, are also likely to contribute to the branding and marketing of their home destinations. Migrant workers, in fact, potentially assist residents in gaining knowledge of tourism attributes and positive feelings towards their countries of origin and hence, influence the related tourist destination images" [32].

Secondly, once in the country of residence, transnational migrants become part of the internal community and their communication is explored as part of the communication of the place's residents. Exploring the role of transnational migrants (and their involvement) in the process of place marketing in five South African municipalities, Mapitsa [33] demonstrated that "local government officials are assuming a population that is sedentary and geographically bounded, while migration is actively shaping communities. This mobility provides an opportunity for management practices to become more inclusive and effective" [33].

At the same time, transnational migrants form publics endowed with a special quality. A complex combination of knowledge, experience, and belonging to the culture of the home country with the immersion in the culture and long direct experience with the culture of the host country provides grounds for the formation of trust in the source for the audiences communicating with them. Their trustworthiness should even increase in the digital environment where users are exposed to personalities with migration background through social networks, blogs, and other digital communication channels.

The content created by bloggers with migration background is close and understandable to the audiences that request different information about the country of interest. Their motivation might be pragmatical if they search for useful information to meet a decision about migration or to organize a vacation abroad. However, these audiences might be driven by the general interest in the country that has been formed before the social media users exposed to the account of a blogger or a community of bloggers writing about their experience of living in this country. The desire to perform a certain action concerning this country - i.e. the transition to the 4th stage according to the classical model of consumer behavior AIDA (Attention, Interest, Desire, Action) or - in the context of image communication of the territory - to the upper level according to the pyramid of the image of the territory suggested by Gavra [26] - from implicit evaluative image to conative one - hypothetically depends also on the success of communication about the country through the information transmitted in social networks and blogs.

We assume that transnational migrants are able to influence the media image of the host country. To our best knowledge, their involvement in the formation of the host country's image through mass self-communication remains significantly under-researched. This paper aims to contribute to filling this gap with research on mass self-communication of Russian-speaking emigrants on Instagram.

# 3  Sample and Methodology

## 3.1  Sample

In our previous research [34] we have identified a global networked public consisting of Russian-speaking female Instagram users with migration background. This public coalesces through the posts of a specific type where bloggers suggest their followers learn more about the same issue in different countries. The bloggers provide direct links to the bloggers contributing to this issue (@bloggerA – country A) and create a unique hashtag accordingly to the issue (#страховка_в, #работа_в, etc.). The posts were created to reach global Russian-speaking audiences through the follower/followee networks of different bloggers participating in the hashtagging activity.

We collected a dataset of 1,887 posts published under an umbrella hashtag #international girl from January 24, 2018, to December 20, 2018, by 466 users that resided in 81 countries and covered their migration experience in a blog on Instagram. From this dataset, we selected 10 bloggers who published more than 40 posts with the umbrella hashtag and acted as a quasi-editorial team initiating activities of other bloggers. They represent France, Mexico, the Republic of Cyprus, Serbia, Spain, Sri Lanka, Sweden, Turkey, United Arab Emirates, United States. Thus, the final sample comprised 441 posts.

## 3.2  Research Questions

In this paper, we examine the content created by Russian-speaking Instagram bloggers for the global Russophone audiences from the point of view of the following research questions:

RQ1: Through which topics the host country image is constructed?
RQ2: Which aspects of life in the host country bloggers evaluated positively?
RQ3: Which aspects of life in the host country bloggers evaluated negatively?

## 3.3  Content Analysis

The codebook used for this study has been elaborated from previous research on territorial branding in social networks [35].

It included the following categories:

I.  Is the information about the following issues present in the post (absent/mentioned/main topic of the post)?
   1) climate and geography
   2) history and culture
      a.  tourist places (nature, architectural, cultural attractions including restaurants and local dishes and drinks)
      b.  customs (language, legends, traditional arts and crafts)
      c.  personalities (historical and contemporary)

     d.  achievements (in sport, for ex.)
3) representatives of the host society (social norms, practices, attitude towards foreigners, knowledge of languages)
4) security and stability (from pilfering to terrorist attacks)
5) the general quality of life (professional perspectives; availability of quality products, housing, good jobs, education, healthcare; environmental issues).
II.  Does the coverage of the issue from the list above contain evaluative statements? (yes/no). If yes, is it positive or negative?

The second and third authors both coded 41 (10%) of the posts. For this exploratory study, we evaluated only the percent agreement that reached 0.91. They later each coded half of the remaining 440 posts.

# 4   Findings

**RQ 1. Through which topics the host country image is constructed?**
Among 441 posts, 86.6% of publications (382) contained statements related to at least one of the following categories: 1) climate and geography of the host country, 2) its history and culture, 3) representatives of the host society 4) security and stability 5) general quality of life. More than half of all posts (245 out of 441) were fully devoted to the host country and the life there.

Most often bloggers covered the history and culture of the host country, including customs (26.3%) and tourist places (21.1%) as well as achievements (8.2%) and famous personalities (6.1%) that were significantly less popular. Representatives of the host society were mentioned in every third post (32.7%). The general quality of life was slightly less popular and was covered in 28.1% of posts, followed by the climate and geography of the host country (17, 5%). The smallest number of mentions was received by security and stability (7.2%). In each category of posts, we can reveal repetitive topics and issues mentioned by bloggers.

Describing the climate and geography of the host country bloggers often mentioned such aspects as climate, the closeness of the sea, beaches, and mountains, the number of sunny days and the comfortable temperatures, weather in winter and summer as well as the beauty of landscapes. As bloggers with migration background, they tend to compare the climate in their home countries or, more detailed, home cities, and the climate in the country where they now live.

Speaking about tourist places, the authors of publications paid special attention to natural objects and architectural structures. They recommended various locations and activities that they think the tourist should enjoy. Districts of the city or the island and their features are other topics that are often mentioned in this category. The posts also provide recommendations about food, shopping, and photo spots.

Covering customs of the host society, bloggers write about traditional food and alcohol, national clothing, national languages (differences and similarities with Russian), national and religious holidays, religious traditions, superstitions, wedding customs, and customs in relationships and family life. They also compared how New Year is celebrated in post-Soviet tradition and the host society, as well as customs of party gathering. Calm and lifestyle without hurry were mentioned by bloggers from different countries.

Several posts were fully dedicated to the famous writers (Margaret Mitchell, Astrid Lindgren, Françoise Sagan, and others). In other posts, bloggers mentioned musicians, filmmakers, religious and historical prominent persons. Among achievements bloggers repeatedly covered records, local cuisine, wine, fashion, famous brands, and cutting-edge technologies. Besides stories about the greatest pie made in a village and included in the Guinness Book of World Records, bloggers also wrote about events known throughout the world (for example, the Tour de France) and locations of famous movies that were filmed in their host countries.

Representatives of the host society hold a prominent place in the posts targeting global Russian-speaking audiences. Their behavior, habits, and manner of communication is an acute topic, regardless of the country, the blogger resides in. In the publications of various authors, phrases slip through that the locals smile a lot and are generally friendly and welcoming, that they are unhurried and not obligatory, they know how to live beautifully and well. Among other issues, the posts often touch upon the topic of gender equality and family budgeting.

In posts devoted to the general quality of life, the topic of the cost of living most often comes up: the cost of electricity, food, the Internet, real estate, medicine, and, accordingly, the level of salaries and taxes. Bloggers also provide information about job opportunities, possibilities to travel, attitudes towards Russians, and the absence or presence of environmental issues.

According to our findings, while publishing posts for the global audience, bloggers almost do not cover issues of security and stability. The only exception when the bloggers specially focused on the questions of safety was the topic of the deception of tourists that have been marked with a special thematic hashtag. In other posts, bloggers also mentioned the absence of wars, safety of women and children, or general political (in)stability.

**RQ 2. Which aspects of life in the host country bloggers evaluated positively?**
The climate and geography of the host country are mainly described as an advantage of the host country (62% of posts). The mild climate, sea, sun, absence of winter, and beautiful nature were mentioned in different contexts. Bloggers tell about their first impressions even before they moved into the country they currently reside in:

*Indescribable beauty! I saw how tea grows for the first time. Mountains, waterfalls, valleys, endless beaches with turquoise waters, and much more. Even then I thought about how great it is to live here.*

They also describe the reasons why they selected this country or why they enjoy living there:

*There is a sea, mountains, and so much sun! Isn't that enough?*

*At the beginning of January, it's +15 degrees, and walking in summer shoes inspired me.*

Climate and geography belong to the significant aspects of the quality of life:

*Now I don't have to go on vacation to the sea. I have more than enough of it!*

*Warm climate, the abundance of fresh fruits and vegetables all year round, beautiful beaches.*

Touristic places are mentioned positively in the majority of the posts. Some of the publications are fully devoted to recommendations of locations and activities that a tourist might like:

*If you drive 6 hours from La to Mammoth lake, you can enjoy real snowy landscapes and great slopes.*

They also talk about shopping, food, and places for photos with a positive connotation:

*This photo was taken from the best site in Stockholm, where there are few people and a lot of beautiful nature! In general, everything is how I like it!*

Bloggers give recommendations and share their own impressions with full confidence: "I would *definitely* go to enjoy Serbian nature in one of the national parks"; "Brooklyn bridge is an *indescribable* might".

Customs are covered mostly in neutral (42%) or positive (40%) tone. Traditional food occupies a special place, and in almost all cases it is mentioned as an advantage:

*You should definitely try the kaymak, but it's better to buy it at the market. This is a creamy-creamy foam with a curd consistency, a very tasty Balkan product.*

The national alcohol is described in the same way. These posts often include recommendations not only on what to eat and drink but also what to buy as a souvenir. Thus, they seem to be targeting first of all tourists as the core audience, or even add judgments made by tourists:

*Tourists are very fond of sangria (guys, this is sangría), and the locals choose tinto de verano - a drink based on red wine mixed with soda.*

Several posts were fully dedicated to the famous writers (Margaret Mitchell, Astrid Lindgren, Françoise Sagan, and others). In other posts, bloggers mentioned musicians, filmmakers, religious and historical prominent persons. Famous people are mostly mentioned in a neutral context. Bloggers shared encyclopaedical knowledge about writers or prominent persons. If the positive evaluation was present, it was added through the lenses of the personal experience:

*Margaret Mitchell's 'Gone with the Wind.' My handbook. I'd read it avidly several times.*

*I finally fell in love with "Manel" last year when Estrella Damm gave their free concert on the beach. It was perfect.*

Among achievements bloggers repeatedly covered records, local cuisine, wine, fashion, famous brands, and cutting-edge technologies. Besides stories about the greatest pie made in a village and included in the Guinness Book of World Records, bloggers also wrote about events known throughout the world (for example, the Tour de France) and locations of famous movies that were filmed in their host countries.

The coverage of achievements of the host country is closely related to positive reporting. Bloggers also tended to report positively about the development of the host country:

*A very worthy fashion week and Turkish designers are becoming more and more famous outside the country.*

The attitudes toward citizens of the host country, their habits, behavior, and way of life expressed by bloggers are the most diverse. Posts fully dedicated to the residents usually include simultaneously neutral, positive, and negative statements. In the publications of various authors three characteristics are repeated, regardless of the country the blogger resides in:

1)  the locals smile a lot and are generally friendly and welcoming.
    *Neighbors in Serbia ... mostly friendly and very talkative people.*
2)  the locals know how and love to live beautifully and well.
    *Although the French people are constantly complaining, they know how to live beautifully and enjoy every moment.*

The posts contained references to the high level of medicine, salaries, the availability of quality products, a commitment to a healthy lifestyle:
*Almost all apartments have a free gym and swimming pool*
*Medicine is at the highest level, interest on loans is low, and on an average salary you can live, if not like a prince, then not like a beggar, definitely!*
Bloggers also appreciated feminism, equality, and support for minorities:
*They definitely support all the minorities. Well, where would I be without my feminist appeals?*
In 53% of publications that covered security and stability, the host country is presented positively. Bloggers compare the safety of women and children in the home and the host countries and describe it as a great advantage of a new country:
*By the way, when I lived in Moldova, I always took an electric shock with me. Fortunately, in the Emirates the need for this miracle device disappeared.*
*Safety. This is the most important point for me. A girl can walk alone down the street at 3 o'clock in the morning and no one will touch her.*
In the case of European states, they appreciated protection of civil rights and democracy: "democracy reigns", "a secular country with normal laws".
*I like living in a country where you are not condemned for orientation, religion, age, gender, etc.*

**RQ 3. Which aspects of life in the host country bloggers evaluated negatively?**
Among difficulties with adaptation after moving to the new country, unfamiliar climate conditions were mentioned:
*Lack of loved ones, friends, climate change, fresh air - it snowballs and then pours out into depression.*
While sharing personal experience, the bloggers also complained about disadvantages of the climate:
*In the summer (and it lasts for six months) it is unbearably hot during the day and in the evening. And the water in the bay is so hot that you can "cook".*
In two cases bloggers also mentioned natural disasters: the tsunami in Sri Lanka, the earthquake in Mexico.
Only twice bloggers criticized or complained about touristic places, and in both cases, they shared a mismatch of expectations and reality:
*The Walk of Fame is the city's biggest disappointment.*
*On the way, I saw all the "charms" of LA - poor neighborhoods, bad roads, and homeless people.*

In several posts bloggers not just cover the local customs, but explicitly share judgments based on their values and attitudes:

*A rebel lives inside me who hates prohibitions. And Ramadan for me personally is the month of "CAN'T's.*

The post-Soviet background that is common for the bloggers in our sample influences, first of all, the attitudes towards the traditions related to the celebration of the New Year:

*There was no champagne! At that moment, I thought about what kind of people they are and how do they live if they don't open champagne for the New Year.*

*New Year in Dubai infuriates me. The festive mood is not just "Zero", it's below zero.*

The achievements and the records were in general positively covered, with one exception:

*The UAE is mentioned 190 times in the Guinness Book of Records. There are so many delusional achievements, there is something to laugh at.*

Bloggers from different countries complain that the residents are sluggish and irresponsible.

*I was stressed by work, fellow Cypriots, their eternal "tomorrow", slowness and unwillingness to take responsibility ... you still will not become "yours" for the Cypriots.*

Bloggers negatively evaluate the lack of a culture of visiting. They compare the hospitality of the residents with their own experience in the home country:

*Well, I still can't get used to the fact that they are not hospitable people like us.. firstly, you will not come to visit unexpectedly (you must agree in advance, call and agree on the date and time), and secondly, you will not get anything but crackers, chips and some other snacks.*

The strength of the negative attitudes might be explained by the social isolation newcomers face in the host country:

*They celebrate all events except Glory outside the home but in some institutions. Personally, for the first year after the move, I missed little get-togethers with my friends.*

Bloggers criticize the obtrusiveness, bad manners, and arrogance of representatives of the residents. They mentioned some unpleasant situations as part of a personal narrative. In several posts, they even generalized their experience to the whole population:

*I don't want to offend anyone, but this nation is very noisy, especially for children.*

*Perhaps the reason is the low level of culture and education, they are not interested in the heritage that is the same as what Italy or France gave to the world.*

Bloggers also complained about the permissiveness of children and animals:

*Parents have no time for children, no one watches them, no one scolds them, but they rush about inches from you almost over their heads.*

*Animals are loved to madness, they are allowed to do everything, and that is a minus.*

Bloggers criticize the high cost of living, or rather high property prices, prices in restaurants, prices for medical services, and high taxes:

*The prices are sky-high in the Emirates.*

*The student insurance that I had at that time, a student, would not even cover a visit to a doctor.*

The complexity of employment and work, in general, might be mentioned with a negative connotation:

*Your competitors in your job search are not only Cypriots but all citizens of the European Union (including, for example, Russian-speaking Balts), for which employers do not need to make efforts to find a job.*

In some cases, bloggers complain about the complex bureaucracy system, the negative attitudes towards Russian women, and the unavailability of shops on Sundays.

The following characteristics of countries had a negative connotation: deception of tourists, theft, lack of freedom of speech, longitudinal crisis (in the case of Turkey).

## 5  Discussion and Conclusion

This paper aims to investigate the participation of transnational migrants in shaping the image of the country of residence through mass self-communication on social media. Our findings suggest that Russian-speaking Instagram bloggers with migration background focus attention on the host countries in the posts targeting global audiences. Almost 90% of all posts that were published n 2018 by the quasi-editorial team of bloggers with the hashtag #international_gir1 included some information about the host countries. Stories about the host country and people that reside in it or practical information about living in this country were in the focus of every second post in our dataset.

The bloggers covered several aspects of the host country's image, including climate and geography, history and culture, security and stability, representatives of the host society, and general quality of life in the host country. While the three first categories received almost exclusively positive evaluations, the last ones, rooted in the personal daily experience represent a more diverse and complex picture.

Contrary to the migrant news media with their specific agenda-setting and to the migrant groups, these blogs share personal and mundane experiences, and their credibility is based on the fact that they reside in the country they report about. A blogger's immediate 'personal' experience brought into the public realm is perceived as theirs (albeit mediated) experienced by those who are exposed to the bloggers and communicate with them in one way or another - by subscribing, liking, commenting, saving posts (regarded as especially significant for the person who saved them), reactions in posts, reactions to the engagement techniques used in the blog (polls, participation in competitions, IGTV viewings and others).

The content published by bloggers directly or indirectly influences the formation of the image of the country. Datafication of communication on social media provides access to the reactions of the interested audiences who took part in the communication with the bloggers with the migration background. Digital traces might include approval (through likes and relevant emoji), additional interest (questions in the comments), sharing their experience in the comments, etc.

Thus, both the bloggers and their audiences form a story about the host countries, which, in turn, forms the mediated media (new media) image of the countries in the minds of the audience.

The audiences targeted by the Russian-speaking Instagram bloggers with migration background are heterogeneous. They include individuals planning the migration, Russophone emigrants residing in the same country and worldwide, residents of the home countries of bloggers that are interested in international storytelling or in a particular country, etc. A mixed method of studying content and digital traces of the audiences should be deployed to investigate this variety.

Further research is needed to explore the difference between the cases when the host country image is constructed through explicit positive evaluations (*"French wine is an unshakable standard of quality"*) and through mentioning of the records and achievements (*"Barcelona is a smart city"*, *"Mexican Cuisine is the UNESCO Heritage of Humanity"*).

Another question that remained outside the scope of this study is the credibility of bloggers with migration background. According to our observations, bloggers in our sample very rarely quote any sources of information, thus, performing as original sources for their followers. Among other stakeholders, this practice distinguishes them from news media. Still, the perception of the trustworthiness of bloggers with migration background as primary sources of information is a subject of further research. Audiences might also react differently to bloggers with migration background and travel bloggers.

As we observed while studying the dataset, in the majority of posts the residents of the host countries are named by nationality, thus, represent an "Other". Still, in several cases, the bloggers described themselves as belonging to the "imagined community". The construction of "We" and "Other" in the posts targeting global Russophone audiences might provide interesting insights into the understanding of mediated identities of transnational migrants.

In our previous research, we have shown that arenas created through global communication of Russian-speaking bloggers with migration background form a parallel realm to the political communication of the home and host societies [34]. Developing this argument, we may conclude, that the practices of mass self-communication studied in the paper on hand possess the potential of "counter-power" [8:90]. Participation of transnational migrants in the formation of the host country image possesses the potential of challenging the power relations institutionalized in society.

**Acknowledgments.** The research has been supported in full by Russian Presidential Grant for Young PhD Scientists, research grant MK-1448.2020.6.

# References

1. Wassler, P.: Residents and destination brands: understanding residents' destination brand ambassador behavior and its antecedents (Diss.). The Hong Kong Polytechnic University, Hong Kong SAR, China (2015)
2. Braun, E., Kavaratzis, M., Zenker, S.: My city – my brand: the different roles of residents in place branding. J. Place Manag. Dev. **6**(1), 18–28 (2013)
3. Kavaratzis, M.: From "necessary evil" to necessity: stakeholders' involvement in place branding. J. Place Manag. Dev. **5**(1), 7–19 (2012)
4. Tiidenberg, K., Siibak, A.: Affordances, affect and audiences-making sense of networked publics, introduction to AoIR 2017 special issue on networked publics. Stud. Transit. States Soc. **10**(2), 1–9 (2018)

5. Couldry, N., Livingstone, S., Markham, T.: Media Consumption and Public Engagement: Beyond the Presumption of Attention. Springer, Heidelberg (2016). https://doi.org/10.1057/9780230800823
6. Diminescu, D.: The connected migrant: an epistemological manifesto. Soc. Sci. Inf. **47**(4), 565–579 (2008)
7. Dekker, R., Engbersen, G., Faber, M.: The use of online media in migration networks. Popul. Space Place **22**(6), 539–551 (2016)
8. Castells, M.: Communication power: mass communication, mass self-communication, and power relationships in the network society. Media Soc. **25**(5), 3–17 (2010)
9. Leurs, K., Smets, K.: Five questions for digital migration studies: learning from digital connectivity and forced migration in (to) Europe. Soc. Media Soc. **4**(1), 1–16 (2018). https://doi.org/10.1177/2056305118764425
10. Marino, S.: Making space, making place: digital togetherness and the redefinition of migrant identities online. Soc. Media Soc. **1**(2), 1–9 (2015). https://doi.org/10.1177/2056305115562 2479
11. Volkmer, I.: The global network society and the global public sphere. Development **46**(1), 9–16 (2003)
12. Kok, S., Rogers, R.: Rethinking migration in the digital age: transglocalization and the Somali diaspora. Global Netw. **17**(1), 23–46 (2017)
13. Hepp, A., Bozdag, C., Suna, L.: Mediatized migrants: media cultures and communicative networking in the diaspora. Migr. Diaspora Inf. Technol. Glob. Soc. 172–188 (2012)
14. Ajder, T.: Romanian diasporic Facebook groups as public spheres. Open Cult. Stud. **2**(1), 723–734 (2018)
15. Vihalemm, T., Juzefovičs, J., Leppik, M.: Identity and media-use strategies of the Estonian and Latvian Russian-speaking populations amid political crisis. Eur. Asia Stud. **71**(1), 48–70 (2019)
16. Morgunova, O.: National living on-line: some aspects of the Russophone digital diaspora. In: Diminescu, D. (ed.) Exploration and Cartography of Diasporas on Digital Networks. Editions de la Maison des Sciences de l'Homme, Paris (2012)
17. Smoliarova, A., Platonov, K., Sharkova, E., Gromova, T.: Defining network borders on Instagram: the case of Russian-speaking bloggers with migration background. In: Meiselwitz, G. (ed.) HCII 2020. LNCS, vol. 12194, pp. 647–657. Springer, Cham (2020). https://doi.org/10.1007/978-3-030-49570-1_46
18. Boyd, D.: Social network sites as networked publics: affordances, dynamics, and implications. In: Papacharissi, Z. (ed.), A Networked Self: Identity, Community and Culture on Social Network Sites, pp. 39–58. Routledge, New York (2010)
19. Tukachinsky, R., Stever, G.: Theorizing development of parasocial engagement. Commun. Theory **29**(3), 297–318 (2019)
20. Dickinson, J.: Visualising the foreign and the domestic in diaspora diplomacy: images and the online politics of recognition in# givingtoindia. Camb. Rev. Int. Aff. **33**(5), 752–777 (2020)
21. Birka, I., Kļaviņš, D.: Diaspora diplomacy: nordic and baltic perspective. Diaspora Stud. **13**(2), 115–132 (2020)
22. Brinkerhoff, J.M.: Diasporas and public diplomacy: distinctions and future prospects. Hague J. Dipl. **14**(1–2), 51–64 (2019)
23. Choi, S.H., Tam, L., Ayhan, K.J., Lee, D.M.: Why and how do sojourners talk about Macao? Effects of perceived risk and expected benefit. Asian Int. Stud. Rev. **20**(2), 29–51 (2019)
24. Uysal, N.: The rise of diasporas as adversarial non-state actors in public diplomacy: the Turkish case. Hague J. Dipl. **14**(3), 272–292 (2019)
25. Kotler, P., Asplund, C., Rein, I., Haider, D.: Marketing places Europe: how to attract investments, industries, residents and visitors to cities, communities, regions, and nations in Europe. Financial Times (1999)

26. Gavra, D.P., Taranova, U.V.: The image of territorial subjects in the modern information space: textbook, St. Petersburg (2013). (in Russian)
27. Cassel, S.: Trying to be attractive: image building and identity formation in small industrial municipalities in Sweden. Place Brand. Publ. Dipl. **4**, 102–114 (2008)
28. Nadeau, J., Olafsen, A.H.: Country image evaluations and migration intentions. Place Brand. Publ. Dipl. **11**(4), 293–308 (2015)
29. Cleave, E., Arku, G.: Immigrant attraction through place branding? Evidence of city-level effectiveness from Canada's London. Cities **97**, 102502 (2020)
30. Mathijsen, A.: Home, sweet home? Understanding diasporic medical tourism behaviour. Exploratory research of Polish immigrants in Belgium. Tour. Manag. **72**, 373–385 (2019)
31. Huang, W.J., Ramshaw, G., Norman, W.C.: Homecoming or tourism? Diaspora tourism experience of second-generation immigrants. Tour. Geogr. **18**(1), 59–79 (2016)
32. Nguyen, T.H.H.: The role of migrant workers in forming tourist destination image of their home country. In: Proceedings of the 2nd Conference of the International Place Branding Association, pp. 80–81. IPBA, Swansea University (2018)
33. Mapitsa, C.B.: Migration governance as place making: South African experiences. J. Place Manag. Dev. **12**(3), 391–407 (2019)
34. Smoliarova, A.S., Bodrunova, S.S.: InstaMigrants: global ties and mundane publics of Russian-speaking bloggers with migration background. Soc. Media Soc. **7**(3) (2021). https://doi.org/10.1177/20563051211033809
35. Taranova, Y.V.: Formation of the image of the territory in the news media and social media. Res. Methodol. Success. Mod. Sci. **1**(3), 129–133 (2016)

# Exploring the Parliamentary Discourse of the Russian Federation Using Topic Modeling Approach

Anna V. Chizhik[1]([envelope]) [iD] and Dmitry A. Sergeyev[2]([envelope]) [iD]

[1] Saint Petersburg State University, 10th line of Vasilievsky Island,
49, 199178 St.-Petersburg, Russia
a.chizhik@spbu.ru
[2] Oura Health Oy, Elektroniikkatie 10, 90590 Oulu, Finland

**Abstract.** The parliamentary discourse is the important component of the socio-political basis of modern society. The study of its characteristics can explain many social dynamics processes, for example, the activity and apathy of society at elections, as well as the features of civil society. Qualitative studies, based on sociological methodology and discourse analysis, can benefit greatly from automated topic mining provided by topic models such as latent Dirichlet allocation (LDA). In this paper we present the results of analysis the speeches of deputies of the State Duma of the Russian Federation (seven parliamentary sessions). The aim of our work was to find relation between the behavior of parties during parliamentary sessions and the public skepticism about the idea of a multiparty system as a basis of democracy.

**Keywords:** Natural language processing · Topic modelling · Cauterization · Open data · Parliamentary discourse · Multiparty political system

## 1 Introduction

A multiparty political system is a powerful incentive to develop democracy, civil society and the rule of law. In Russia, this concept of domestic political system is laid down by the Constitution, adopted in 1993 (the current version dates from July 2020). In the same year, the first parliamentary elections were held. Obviously, the relationships between society and government form the core of the domestic political system, and success of this communication impacts on the emerging general socio-economic and political strategies at all levels. Thus, this communication initiates the whole government sector process management. The actual communication instrument in this dialogue is parliamentary parties. They synthesize impulses of society and transmit them to the government structure through participation in the formation of the authorities and the socio-political decision-making at parliamentary sessions. All parliamentary deliberations are recorded in the transcripts; therefore these texts are available over time for research interests. The parliamentary system of modern Russia is 28 years old (7 convocations), this time period is significant enough to attempt the analysis of party system

© Springer Nature Switzerland AG 2022
D. A. Alexandrov et al. (Eds.): DTGS 2021, CCIS 1503, pp. 403–416, 2022.
https://doi.org/10.1007/978-3-030-93715-7_29

dynamics by comparing the socio-political contexts that has varied over the years in the speeches of the deputies.

## 2  Distinctive Features of Parliamentary Discourse

As a mediator between social forces, ideologies and official government institutions, parliamentary parties are active and important participants of domestic political decisions. Therefore, parliament can be considered as an information model of society. This implies that the communicative goals of parliamentary discourse are information, persuasion, and motivation for action [1]. These types of intentions imply the following types of speaker activity: demonstration of disagreement with an opponent approach, a request for mending laws, and any actions for shaping public opinion [2]. Parliamentary speeches are divided into functional-semantic types of speech, which could be categorized into informational, analytical (with argument system) and imperative ones. Two core functions can be distinguished for the parliament discourse: 1) nominative (a word represents the world of reality into sign system); 2) axiological (a word forms a system of public and political opinion). Thus, a word becomes the basic discourse unit.

The tendency to narrative development of a topic prevails in an information type speech [3]. Opening remarks of a chairman for starting session, usual ritual speeches (taking the oath, congratulations), and etc. could be considered as examples of this kind of speech. In our research, this type of parliamentary speeches was related to noise, because it does not carry special information about social and political dynamics of the discourse. Analytical type of statements is characterized by textual constructions enriched with reflections. There are a clearly logical-semantic organization of a text, including inferences, arguments and proofs [4]. Subsequently this helps to highlight semantic core of a speech and detect an ideological vector of a deputy. Our data collection was assembled from samples of this type. The dataset included both mono-speeches from the parliamentary rostrum (report, presentation of bills, substantiation of a request, etc.) and discussions (commentaries on the rostrum, i.e. excluding from research questions and comments from the floor).

The desire to effectively and persistently influence on an audience is observed in the imperative type of speeches. For this, evaluative adjectives, emotional exclamations, imperative forms of the verb, expressive assessments, intensives, hyperboles are used. This type is characterized by categorical and emotional judgments, but in general, it is representative texts for analysis of social and political orientations of speaker in a particular time period.

The parliamentary discourse is characterized by usage of three main genres. A political report is a monologue speech, the structure of which has common features with a scientific report: presentation of the topic (introduction), statement of problems, description of possible ways to solve them, argumentation of ways for solving problems (or attitude to the problem), a list of conditions for carrying out certain actions. A discussion speech is the next prevalent example of monologue speech [5], but it contains elements of polemics (each following speaker complements the topic, but a direct answer is not required). An aim of discussion is finding a definitive and acceptable solution, because the model of co-operative governance is set in a parliament as the basis of democratic political system. The structure of this genre is similar to a directed graph, where each vertex is a complete semantic segment that can be taken as the analyzed unit. The one-liners (in meaning refutation, answer, objection) are a short objections or remarks that complement speaker report (pronounced without going to parliamentary rostrum). The main motivations in this case are cooperation, conflict, solidarity.

## 3 Historical Context of the Development of Parliamentary System in Russia

The formation of the Russian party system dates back to constitutional and electoral reforms of 1993. The constituent (first) and post-founding (second) parliamentary elections were held in 1993 and 1995. During these elections, half of members of the State Duma of the Federal Assembly of the Russian Federation were elected by the party-list system. It was the historic moment when the modern multi-party democracy began to take shape in the country.

In the transition from the single party rule (USSR) to the multiparty system (modern Russia), the first elections performed three functions: 1) institutional (the political institutional structure was outlined, within which it was supposed to develop electoral competition); 2) behavioral (the spectrum of preferences and voting patterns were formed, the shape of the new party system was determined); 3) transformational (the stable basis for the legitimacy of the new political regime was created).

Party discourse of modern Russia has gone through several distinct phases during its formation. Each of them reflected the social and historical context, together with the dynamics of the party system (as the key component of access to representative democracy institutions).

Therefore, parliamentary elections could be considered as indicator of tipping points in intra-party trends, which recorded the results of interaction with society during a parliamentary cycle (direct impact on voter turnout) and the success of collaborations with neighboring parties (latent coordination between parties for a successful passing of an electoral threshold) (Table 1).

A large number of parties took part in the elections to the Duma during seven electoral periods. The Communist Party of the Russian Federation (KPRF) and the Liberal Democratic Party of Russia (LDPR) stand out from other parties, because they were able to pass all elections and form their party factions in the State Duma during all parliamentary sessions. "A Just Russia" and "United Russia" (the former party "Unity") had emerged more recently in the new political space. They also became permanent participants in the parliamentary process. It is necessary to mention the Russian United Democratic Party "Yabloko" as the fifth significant party that was active participant of political governance until 1999, and then it fought for power in the period 2011–2016.

Voter turnout amounted to 60% on average until 2011 (6 election seasons), and fell down to 46% in 2016. This indicates a decline in interest to expression of the will as the legitimate source of society. This leads to disorientation of society and destruction of the complex system of linkages between civil society and the government. This means that parliamentary political parties are in functional recession. While maintaining a high degree of party identification and electoral activity, Russians are very skeptical

**Table 1.** The results of elections to the State Duma (1993–2016). The parties that have achieved to overcome the electoral threshold are presented [6].

| Political parties | Received votes, % | | | | | | |
|---|---|---|---|---|---|---|---|
| | 1993 | 1995 | 1999 | 2003 | 2007 | 2011 | 2016 |
| «United Russia» | - | - | - | 37,57 | 64,30 | 49,32 | 76,22 |
| Communist Party of the Russian Federation (CPRF) | 12,40 | 22,30 | 24,29 | 12,61 | 11,57 | 19,19 | 9,33 |
| Liberal Democratic Party of Russia (LDPR) | 22,92 | 11,80 | 5,98 | 11,45 | 8,14 | 11,67 | 8,67 |
| A Just Russia | - | - | - | - | 7,74 | 13,24 | 5,11 |
| The Russian United Democratic Party "Yabloko" | 7,86 | 6,89 | 5,93 | - | - | 3,43 | - |
| Russia's Choice | 15,51 | - | - | - | - | - | - |
| Women of Russia | 8,13 | - | - | - | - | - | - |
| Agrarian Party of Russia (APR) | 7,99 | - | - | - | - | - | - |
| Party of Russian Unity and Accord (PRES) | 6,73 | - | - | - | - | - | - |
| Democratic Party of Russia (DPR) | 5,52 | - | - | - | - | - | - |
| Our Home – Russia (NDR) | - | 10,13 | - | - | - | - | - |
| Unity | - | - | 23,32 | - | - | - | - |
| Fatherland – All Russia (OVR) | - | - | 13,33 | - | - | - | - |
| The Union of Right Forces (SPS) | - | - | 8,52 | - | - | - | - |
| Rodina | - | - | - | 9,1 | - | - | 0,22 |

about the idea of a multi-party system. That is confirmed by both the election results and public opinion polls. This brings into question the capability of parties to be the central factor in political decision-making. In this research we attempt to analyze what leads to the devaluation of political parties as the backbone of domestic political system in the mindsets of Russian voters. The parliamentary discourse with its sociopolitical conditioning in deputies' speeches with connections to the retrospective review became the object of the analysis.

## 4   Materials and Methods

The State Duma has an open data portal with a public API [7]. We use this service to collect the transcripts of all the deputies' speeches, starting from the first convocation. In total, we gather 359077 transcripts from 2021 unique deputies. During the text data preprocessing, we remove all punctuation and common stop-words. Additionally, we delete all speeches containing less than 30 words to reduce the noise in the data. Finally, we lemmatize the remaining words to transform them into dictionary forms.

We used topic modelling, specifically Latent Dirichlet Allocation (LDA) [8], to extract meaningful information from the collected speeches. A topic model's goal is to find a limited set of common themes that arise in a text's body. It does that by estimating the frequencies of words co-occurrences within texts and grouping the texts in which co-occurrences are more frequent. The number of groups, or topics, is the main hyperparameter of the model and is selected either manually or by optimizing quality metrics. Our research uses a coherence score that measures semantic similarity between the most frequent words within a topic. By maximizing the coherence score, we found 30 topics to be optimal. Next, we manually interpreted the topics based on the most frequent words in each. Finally, we predict the topic distribution for every speech transcript in our dataset, which gives us vectors of probabilities for every speech. To obtain topic profiles for the parties or years, we average the probability vectors of deputies' speeches from these parties or years. As a result, we have a single vector for every party and year that we can use for clustering or visualizations.

Additionally, we utilize Uniform Manifold Approximation and Projection (UMAP) [9] to compress 30-dimensional topic vectors into 2-dimensional representations to make it easier to plot the discourse maps. The UMAP transformation is a dimension reduction technique that preserves the original scales of distances between the objects. That allows us to interpret the distances between parties or years, even though the new 2-dimensional representations are uninterpretable.

## 5   Experiments and Results

The first elections to the State Duma were held three months after the events of October 1993, when the Supreme Soviet was abolished and the history of modern Russia has begun. Eight parties broke the five-percent threshold, and this record still stands after all next election. The largest number of votes on party lists was won by the LDPR party, which seemed to be a radical opposition at that time. The important feature of this parliamentary session was that none of the political forces had the stable majority: the left opposition (CPRF party and the Agrarian Party) was balanced by the democrats (DPR party and the Party "Yabloko"). LDPR, "Women of Russia" and the Party of Russian Unity and Accord (PRES) actively cooperated with the party of power ("Russia's Choice"). The Democratic Party of Russia (DPR) received 15 parliamentary seats, but it did not actively participate in the discussions. In 1994 the Duma faction of this party split into two groups, which completely removed it from presence within the common discourse. All these trends are visible on the discourse map of the parties (Fig. 1).

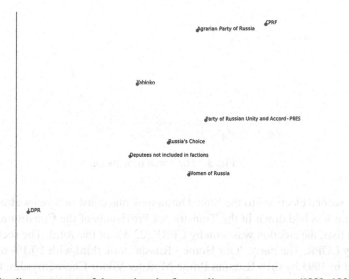

**Fig. 1.** The discourse map of the parties, the first parliamentary season (1993–1994)

One of the first decisions of this parliamentary season was the political amnesty, according to which members of SCSE and participants of the October 1993 events were released from prison. The permanent theme of all party speeches was the political system that was being created at that moment (including the fixation of basic concepts regarding the party system and elections). The full thematic profile of the period is shown in Fig. 2 below.

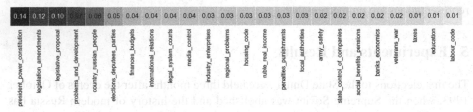

**Fig. 2.** Topic profile of the first parliamentary season

The first convocation of the State Duma was the era of the birth of faith in democracy and human rights, and at the same time it was the difficult economic and political phase. The thematic profile of this parliamentary season demonstrates these trends clearly.

Referring to the peaks in the graph (Fig. 3), which shows the social benefits topic, is actual to illustrate the dynamic of the parliamentary discourse of that period. In 1994–95 raising this theme was motivated by the humanitarian views of politicians, while all next peaks of this topic relate to the economic recovery in the country.

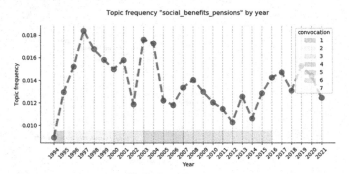

**Fig. 3.** The social benefits topic

The second elections to the State Duma took place just two years after the first: this procedure was laid down in the Transitional Provisions of the Constitution. According to party lists, the election was won by CPRF (22.3% of the vote). The second place was taken by LDPR. The party "Our Home - Russia" took third with 10.1% of votes. It was founded in 1995 by then Russian Prime Minister Viktor Chernomyrdin, thus this party represented the interests of the current government. In the legislative elections in 1995, Agrarian Party of Russia did not make it over the 5% threshold, obtaining only 3.78% of the votes. But the "Agrarian Group" was created with the assistance of KPRF. Thus, almost 50% of the seats in parliament were controlled by the left opposition, represented by the communists and agrarians. The blue dots in Fig. 4 demonstrate the closest allies and political opponents of this parliamentary season, the brown ones correspond to the first convocation (this comparison helps to assess the ideological shifts of the parties that participated in the political life of both parliamentary periods).

**Fig. 4.** The discourse map of the second parliamentary session (blue dots) compared with the discourse of the first convocation (brown dots) (Color figure online)

It strikes the attention that the impeachment of Boris Yeltsin almost took place during this parliamentary session. In 1998, the State Duma twice rejected Viktor Chernomyrdin's candidacy proposed by the president, and Yevgeny Primakov, with support from the communists, became prime minister.

The third elections to the State Duma were formally won by the communists (24.3%), ahead of the party "Unity" by 1% (the government's pre-election bloc). The main rival of "Unity" at that time was the party "Fatherland-All Russia" (OVR) headed by the potential presidential candidate Yevgeny Primakov; they received 13.3% in the elections. After the elections, "Unity", having agreed with the KPRF, brought down OVR, "Yabloko" and "Union of Right Forces" in the distribution of the Duma posts. Two years later, "Unity" consumed OVR, the once rival factions had united, and new party "United Russia" began to control the majority of votes. The communists have become unnecessary (therefore there are two points of bifurcation of the communist discourse in one parliamentary season). At the same time, it should be noted that this was the last convocation, when at the initial stage of the work of the chamber, all political forces represented in the Duma were forced to reckon with the opinions of their opponents and look for allies for making decisions, because none of the factions had controlling block of votes, and the issues raised were resolved in the format of discussions.

This moment in the political development of the country became the turning point (Fig. 5). The powerful party arose, and around it the political space was strengthened. Major bills developed by the deputy corps were not adopted. Despite objections of opposition, in particular, "Unity"/"United Russia" approved the pension and electricity reforms. The comprehensive consideration of the State budget in Parliament was ended

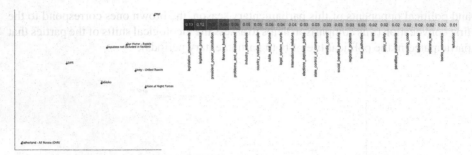

**Fig. 5.** The discourse map of the second parliamentary session and its common topic profile

(this trend began in the second parliamentary session and reached the critical point in the third one), thus the State Duma's control over the budget was lost (and the Fig. 6 illustrates this).

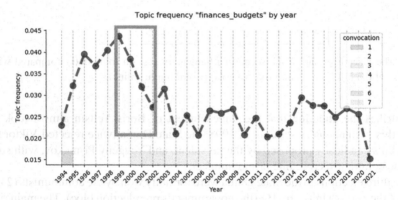

**Fig. 6.** The dynamic of budget topic

In the fourth elections to the State Duma, "United Russia" not only won the majority of votes on party lists (37.6%), but also won a constitutional majority by recruiting single-mandate deputies (more than 300 out of 450 seats). It was the first time when the party, which represented the interests of the current government, gained total influence in the Parliament. This gave the government opportunity to put through Parliament any laws (including constitutional ones with requiring 2/3 of deputies' votes) without complementary discussion with opposition, and to adopt amendments to the Constitution. All leading posts, which determined through the Parliament, were occupied by members of this party. General parliamentary discourse shifts from the deliberative context to the narrative one. Party apathy is illustrated by comparing the ideological closeness of parties at the beginning and end of the season (Fig. 7).

The monopoly of United Russia is being established during this period. The Direct Payments scheme and the Housing Code of Russia were adopted in this convocation (Fig. 8), and, since then, these topics have since become permanent subjects of discussion.

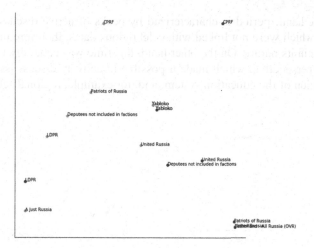

**Fig. 7.** The discourse map of the 4th convocation throw the start positions in 2003 (blue dots) and the final ones in 2007 (brown dots) (Color figure online)

**Fig. 8.** Dynamics of the Housing Code topic

Legislative drafting capacity of deputies is permanently withdrawn from use; especially the opposition was particularly affected. The narrative of speeches delivered from the rostrum increasingly came into contact with the categories used in modeling the propaganda space (Fig. 9).

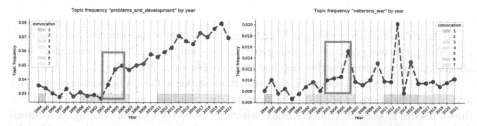

**Fig. 9.** The two topics that show the processes of degradation of the parliamentary discourse

On the one hand, period is characterized by peaks of active discussion about the war veterans, which were not linked with celebrations dates, therefore they are clearly propagandistic in its nature. On the other hand, this time was generally favorable from the economic perspective, which made it possible to actively discuss issues related to the reorganization of the education system, and, for example, regional self-government (Fig. 10).

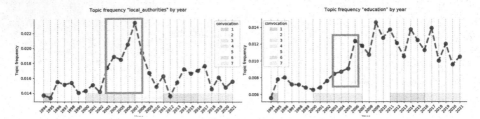

**Fig. 10.** Indicators of positive trends in the domestic political life of Russia

In this and the next parliamentary sessions, mass-media and public figures played increasingly active role in the political system; this is well illustrated by the number of their requests for information and complaints. The graph shows that the parties appealed to mass-media and were guided by public opinion, which was completely formed through the media as the only channel for receiving information (Fig. 11).

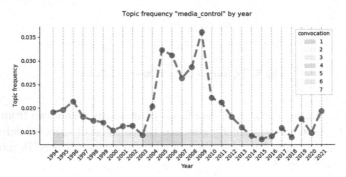

**Fig. 11.** The Media control topic

Before the fifth elections to the State Duma, the system of its formation was changed: all 450 deputies were elected according to party lists, single-mandate constituencies were abolished (preparations for this step had been visible since 2002, Fig. 12).

Only 11 parties took part in the elections, this was due to the strengthening of electoral and party legislation. In addition, the electoral threshold was increased from 5% to 7%, thus 4 parties crossed it. United Russia, which received 64% of the vote, again received more than 300 mandates and therefore the right to amend the Constitution. But if in the Duma of the fifth season they did not use this right, then in this convocation the Basic Law of the country was changed for the first time since 1993, thereby parliamentary session

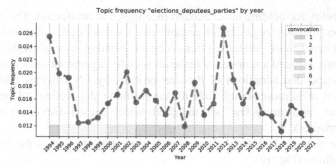

**Fig. 12.** The relevance of preparations for the elections in dynamical view

extended from 4 to 5 years, and the term of the President was increased to 6 years. These tendencies during the parliamentary session were quite noticeable in speeches, which were recited from the rostrum. This could be demonstrated, for example, through the frequency of the new draft legislations topic, and the same tendency is visible in the heat topics map (Fig. 13).

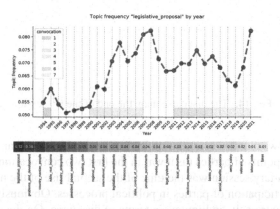

**Fig. 13.** Legislative proposal topic

This time is characterized by the impossibility of influencing the adopted bills through the parliamentary rostrum, at the same moment the convergence of Just Russia and United Russia in their ideological vectors, and this dynamic process that gone hand-in-hand with the attempt to gain attention through appealing to the categories of patriotism in their speeches. CPRF and LDPR demonstrated the stable thematic profiles, which suggest the ideological removal of these parties from active participants in the debate.

Seven parties took part in the sixth elections to the State Duma. United Russia significantly worsened its previous result: according to official data, 49.3% voted for it. During this parliamentary session, the amendments were amended to the electoral and party legislation, mitigating the requirements for parties' participation in elections, and also the system of the heads of regions elections was restored partially. At the same time, the responsibility for holding unsanctioned meetings was reinforced. The amendments to the Law on Nonprofit organization complicated the work of non-business entity (this especially affected those collectives that received subsidies from abroad). In addition, the State Duma adopted a number of resonant socially significant laws that introduced new bans (suspended adoptions of Russian orphans by US citizens, prohibitions of the promotion of homosexuality, liability for insulting the feelings of believers was introduced, an "anti-piracy law" was adopted, which caused discontent among large Internet companies).

Thus, the map of ideological changes was formed by the end of the parliamentary session as follows (Fig. 14).

**Fig. 14.** The discourse map, the end of the 6<sup>th</sup> session

The figure shows that this convocation is characterized by the clear division between the different viewpoints of parties (as it was in the first two convocations). This suggests that this parliamentary session was the time of the second rise of the multiparty system and the active participation of parties in political processes. Obviously, the parliamentary session was extremely ambiguous in terms of discourse. On the one hand, United Russia ideologically moved away from everyone. On the other hand, this time period is characterized by the absence of the constitutional majority on the side of United Russia. This situation modeled positive prerequisites for changing its attitude both to lawmaking and to initiatives that come from the opposition. However, in the second half of this political period the opposition had acquired a tendency to marginalization due to forward shocking bills (for the resonance effect in the media). Thus, the struggle for the communicative space is seen again, but it is quite destructive in its essence.

It is rather difficult to analyze the current, 7th, parliamentary session as the accomplished political period. Moreover, the parliamentary system seriously affected by the global crisis of the last year (coronavirus), that broke the planned agenda of country's life. Thus, the number of discussions on the future of Russia (business support, measures to protect the population from the virus, etc.) is observed on Fig. 15 with the graph of the relevant topic.

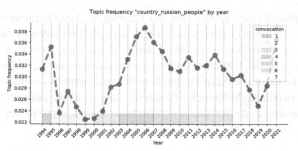

**Fig. 15.** The main topic of 7$^{\text{th}}$ parliamentary session

# 6   Concluding Remarks

The studied data clearly shows that all parties react to foreign policy events, economic crises and economic recovery, as well as to the current balance of power between the executive and parliamentary authorities; and at the same time they have not a motivation to aggregate the interests of society to parties' vectors of work. This leads to the fact that parliamentary discourse is divorced from the real interests of society, leads to stagnation in the formation of the institution of civil society. The common feature of all old-timers of parliament is the prevalence of ideological statements as the main element of speeches. Specific processes in the party system are illustrated through the general map of parliamentary discourse for seven parliamentary sessions with the ideological ratio of all parties relative to each other (Fig. 16).

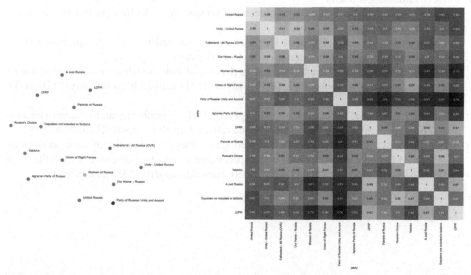

**Fig. 16.** Comparison of the parties in their ideological manifestation through its discourse for seven parliament convocations (the reflection points on the plane is shown on the left, the detection convergence by cosine similarity is on the right)

The map explains voter apathy that has become the key characteristic of the latest election race. This indirectly affects the structures of civil society and the entire political system as a whole, therefore the circle of actors in the legislative process is gradually narrowing. Moreover, this tendency is motivated as the dynamical process both from vertical influence (the natural fight of United Russia to maintain its exclusive influence) and horizontal borders (through the lack of citizens' interest in the parliamentary process).

The programming code and datasets have been shared in public repository[1].

# References

1. Curato, N.: A sequential analysis of democratic deliberation. Acta Politica **47**(4), 423–442 (2012). https://doi.org/10.1057/ap.2012.15
2. Chambers, S.: Rhetoric and the public sphere: has deliberative democracy abandoned mass democracy? Polit. Theory **37**(3), 323–350 (2009). https://doi.org/10.1177/0090591709332336
3. Bächtiger, A., Niemeyer, S., Neblo, M., Steenbergen, M., Steiner, J.: Disentangling diversity in deliberative democracy. J. Polit. Philos. **18**, 32–63 (2010). https://doi.org/10.1111/j.1467-9760.2009.00342.x
4. Bächtiger, A., Spörndli, M., Steenbergen, M., Steiner, J.: Deliberation in legislatures: antecedents and outcomes. In: Rosenberg, S. (ed.) Deliberation, Participation and Democracy: Can the People Govern?, pp. 82-100. Palgrave, New York (2007). https://doi.org/10.1057/9780230591080
5. Zima, E., Brône, G., Feyaerts, K.: Patterns of interaction in Austrian parliamentary debates: the pragmasemantics of interruptive comments. In: Ilie, C. (ed.) European Parliaments Under Scrutiny: Discourse Strategies and Interaction Practices, pp. 135–164 (2010). https://doi.org/10.1075/dapsac.38.08zim
6. The open data source of The Central Election Commission of the Russian Federation. http://www.cikrf.ru/opendata/
7. The open data source of The State Duma of the Russian Federation. http://api.duma.gov.ru/pages/dokumentatsiya/stenogrammi-vistupleniy-deputata
8. Jelodar, H., et al.: Latent Dirichlet allocation (LDA) and topic modeling: models, applications, a survey. Multimedia Tools Appl. **78**(11), 15169–15211 (2018). https://doi.org/10.1007/s11042-018-6894-4
9. McInnes, L., Healy, J., Saul, N., Grossberger, L.: UMAP: uniform manifold approximation and projection. J. Open Source Softw. **3**, 861 (2018). https://doi.org/10.21105/joss.00861
10. Liu, D., Lei, L.: Discourse, context and media, the appeal to political sentiment: an analysis of Donald Trump's and Hillary Clinton's speech themes and discourse strategies in the 2016 US presidential election, **25**, 143–152 (2018). https://doi.org/10.5539/ijel.v9n3p13

---

[1] https://github.com/DmitrySerg/open-data/tree/master/russian-parlament-2021.

# The Other Side of Deplatforming: Right-Wing Telegram in the Wake of Trump's Twitter Ouster

Kirill Bryanov[✉], Dina Vasina, Yulia Pankova, and Victor Pakholkov

National Research University Higher School of Economics, St. Petersburg, Russia
kbryanov@hse.ru

**Abstract.** Is banning political figures who propagate controversial political speech from mainstream social platforms an effective way to improve the health of the public debate? Looking at the most conspicuous case of an anti-mainstream politician's deplatforming – Donald Trump's ban from several major social media platforms in January 2021 – we explore the less immediate effects that such measures can have on a wider information ecosystem. Specifically, we analyze the right-wing segment of social platform Telegram that has reportedly seen an influx of politically conservative users as a result of Trump's expulsion from the mainstream social media. We demonstrate that the largest right-wing communities on Telegram has seen a multifold increase in user base during the period of observation. Furthermore, we employ network analysis and topic modelling to uncover familiar structures, agendas, and media repertoires characteristic to right-wing ecosystems that exist on mainstream social media platforms. These findings suggest that deplatforming should not be seen as the ultimate solution to the problem of toxic speech, and that further research into fringe political communities emerging on alternative social media in response to perceived free speech suppression is needed.

**Keywords:** Telegram · Deplatforming · Online communities · Extreme speech · Alternative social media · Network analysis · Topic modelling

## 1 The Double-Edged Sword of Deplatforming

Recent years have seen mounting pressure on major social media companies such as Facebook, Twitter, and Instagram to proactively limit the spread of harmful political speech that has been gaining visibility on their platforms [9, 11]. Among the harshest measures available to these firms in combating extremist, hateful, or otherwise harmful expression is deplatforming, i.e. suspending or outright banning controversial individuals or communities from their websites. While harmful speech is not exclusively limited to the political right, the prevalence of conservative voices among those expelled from major social media platforms in recent years has sparked rhetoric of the Big Tech's liberal bias and "tech censorship" [6]. Ideological quarrels aside, the debate on whether deplatforming is an effective means of constraining harmful online speech is far from settled. At least one study produced empirical evidence suggesting that banning groups

© Springer Nature Switzerland AG 2022
D. A. Alexandrov et al. (Eds.): DTGS 2021, CCIS 1503, pp. 417–428, 2022.
https://doi.org/10.1007/978-3-030-93715-7_30

found to be in violation of the community anti-harassment policies from Reddit resulted in some extreme users leaving the platform for good and the overall discussion becoming less toxic [5]. Others, however, focused on the question of what happens after mainstream social media ban the alleged extremists, and where do the expelled go after they are silenced. A growing body of literature traces both deplatformed influencers [16] and their followers [22] to the "dark corners of the Internet," such as the so-called alt-tech platforms Gab and Parler, as well as user privacy and anonymity-focused messaging service Telegram.

In practical terms, the central question in this dispute is whether severing extreme opinions from mainstream social networking spaces can produce negative externalities that outweigh the auspicious effects of deplatforming. One concern is that, once the spreaders of extremist speech are expelled from mainstream platforms, they can find refuge in alternative social media spaces where the audiences form even more ideologically isolated bubbles and extreme views are further amplified. In other words, while the amount of toxic speech visible to the general public decreases following bans, there is a possibility that the problem only gets swept under the rug, as fringe communication infrastructures migrate to secluded online spaces serving further radicalization of the speech and its consumers. However, robust empirical evidence supporting either of the views on the effectiveness of deplatforming remains scarce. We seek to address this gap by investigating the ultimate case of deplatforming: The permanent ban of then-United States President Donald Trump from Twitter and its effects on the U.S. right-wing community on Telegram.

## 2    Telegram and the U.S. Right

One of the online communication platforms frequently labelled as part of the alternative social media universe is Telegram, a cloud-based messaging service that was one of the first to provide comprehensive end-to-end encryption and is explicitly focused on security of communications. Telegram allows for both peer-to-peer communication (messaging) and anonymously broadcasting content to a wide audience via its public channel functionality. According to some scholars, this combination of features solves the so-called 'online extremist's dilemma' by enabling a combination of public outreach and anonymity [16].

Previous research documented Telegram's increasing popularity with English-speaking (primarily U.S. and U.K.-based) right-wing online personalities and their followers, noting how the number and population of alt-right, nativist, anti-mainstream, and conspiracy-promoting groups grew since at least mid-2019.

Importantly, the spikes in such communities' following have been found to coincide with waves of extreme right influencers' bans on mainstream social media platforms [22]. The same study found that the global right-wing Telegram network has been centered around Trump-supporting channels.

Throughout his presidential tenure, Donald Trump used his personal Twitter account as a means to circumvent the mainstream media and address his supporters directly, often with controversial or outright provocative messages. Many studies noted the outsized role that this tool played in Trump's communication strategy [15]. As Twitter moved to ban Trump's account permanently in the aftermath of the Capitol riot on January 7, 2021, calls to abandon Twitter for alternative social media platforms, most notably Telegram, emerged among Trump's supporters. In the following days, U.S. mainstream media documented a significant number of Trump followers joining the ranks of Telegram users [19].

We regard these events as a near-perfect scenario to test the effects of a major mainstream social media site deplatforming a controversial, politically right-wing figure with a massive online following on a segment of alternative social media where many of his supporters were directed to go.

It must be noted that we do not consider any and all Trump supporters or U.S. conservatives as extremists or potential spreaders of harmful speech. Yet, prior research suggests that Donald Trump has normalized political speech previously considered extreme, and online communities populated by his supporter have consistently been among the prime venues where toxic expression proliferated [14].

In this exploratory study, we set out to take a snapshot of Telegram's English-language, politically right-wing segment in January 2021, and answer the following broad research questions designed to generate empirical evidence relevant for the debate around the effectiveness of deplatforming:

RQ1: How did the population of the right-wing Telegram change in the wake of Trump's Twitter ban?
RQ2: What was the structure of the right-wing segment of Telegram in January 2021?
RQ3: What topics dominated the conversation in this segment amid the above events?
RQ4: What ties did the right-wing segment of Telegram maintain with the mainstream media and social media platforms?

## 3    Methods

As a starting point in our investigation, we relied on the data from a proprietary web service, Tgstat [17], which specializes in Telegram analytics. We extracted a list of top-100 English-language political channels as defined by Tgstat based on two criteria: Number of subscribers and the reach of each post, giving us a list of top communities with an active user base. We further filtered out channels that 1) were not in the English language (a few German-language ones were erroneously included in the ranking by Tgstat); 2) were labeled as scam by Telegram itself, and 3) had more than 6 missing values in the data on daily subscriber numbers. We ended up with 68 most populated English-language channels dedicated to political topics for which detailed subscriber statistics were available.

Next, based on consensus coding by all four authors, we assigned each of these channels into one of two categories: 1) U.S. right-wing and 2) Other political. The first category included all channels in which the majority of posts covered United States politics from conservative, pro-Trump, or anti-mainstream positions, or those dedicated to right-leaning political causes, organizations, and personalities. The second category included all political channels dedicated to non-U.S. politics, as well as U.S. political channels that were not right-wing/conservative. As a result, we arrived at N = 56 of U.S.

right-wing and N = 12 other channels, suggesting that the type of communities that we were interested in dominated the English-language political landscape of Telegram.

To address RQ1, we calculated the average daily number of subscribers in both segments, using non-U.S. political segment as a quasi-control group against which we compared the dynamics of U.S. right-wing numbers. We used Tgstat data to capture the number of subscribers per date for each channel. The period of observation was from January 7 to January 31.

We employed network analysis to answer RQ2. To define the relations be- tween right-wing communities, we worked with mentions and their directions. In our networks, nodes are the channels and directed links between them are directed mentions. Notice that both Telegram and Twitter use the "@" sign to state the name of the channels. In our data, we observed many forwarded tweets containing these signs. Such messages are also followed with the weblinks to these tweets. In order to reduce the amount of noise in the results, we disregarded the posts containing both the "@" mention and "twitter.com/... " weblink. Thus, our network mostly has mentions of Telegram channels specifically. We started with the 56 right-wing channels that we identified originally, then used a walktrap community detection algorithm to define communities inside this network. In visualizations, the size of the node and label correspond to its degree, the thick- ness of the arrow shows the number of links, the color of the node and the color of the arrow indicate the cluster they belong to.

In addressing RQ 3, we relied on topic modelling. We defined 20 topics inside the texts that the communities of our interest posted throughout the period of observation using the LDA algorithm [3]. Seventeen out of twenty topics emerged as meaningful and comprehensive.

## 4 Results

### 4.1 User Dynamics

Our first question was informed by the idea that, starting from the day of Donald Trump's ouster from Twitter and the calls for his supporters to join Telegram, the English-language political segment of this social platform should have experienced a visible influx of new users. Tgstat data on these communities' subscriber data supports this expectation, as visible in Fig. 1.

Throughout January, the average number of subscribers of the top right-wing com- munities skyrocketed from 7425 to 118984, a 16-fold increase. The average number of users subscribed to non-U.S. right-wing channels only rose from 13055 to 15095 over the same period. Although it is not a conceptually and statistically clean test, this differ- ence can at least serve as an indirect evidence that it was not all political Telegram, but exclusively the U.S. right-wing segment that experienced explosive growth in January.

Interestingly, the spikes in new subscriber numbers tend to correlate to news about "Big Tech censorship" and other social platforms-related political developments (e.g., Trump's ban, Parler's removal from AppStore and Google Play), corrected for a small lag.

At the same time, the dynamics of posting intensity (Fig. 2.) appear to be more sen- sitive to major political events (e.g., Trump impeachment trial Joe Biden's inauguration

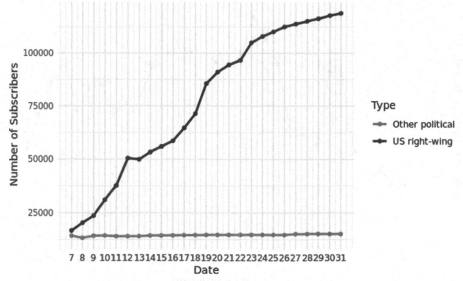

**Fig. 1.** The average number of subscribers in U.S. right-wing vs. other political Telegram channels, January 7 to 31, 2021.

on January 20). In the first figure, a steady growth is observed starting from January 7 (escalated on 9th of January), when the de- platforming campaign against Trump and his supporters began (7th of January – Trump was blocked on Facebook and Instagram, 8th of January – Trump was permanently suspended from Twitter). After a brief plateau, another spike in the number of subscribers can be observed. It may be attributed to the lagging effect of Apple, Google, and Amazons' campaigns against Parler, a Twitter alternative popular in the right circles. The number of messages shows greater correlation with major political events and processes in the US. Several distinguishable peaks of activity can be clearly seen in the second figure. The huge peak on January 5-7 can be attributed to the Capitol Hill Riot and subsequent events, like Trump's speeches and the beginning of deplatforming. Another peak from 10th to 13th January could be attributed to hearings in the House of Representatives of the United States Congress on the matter of Trump's impeachment. One of the highest peaks on 20th of January correlates to Biden's inauguration day. The January 24–26 peak could be attributed to the Senate hearings on the impeachment trial. These dynamics paint the picture of an information ecosys tem deeply responsive to the political agenda relevant for the U.S. political right during the period of observation [10].

## 4.2  Network Analysis

Our network analysis confirms the findings of Urman and Katz (2020) regarding the centrality of Trump-related channels to the right-wing political ecosystem of Telegram.

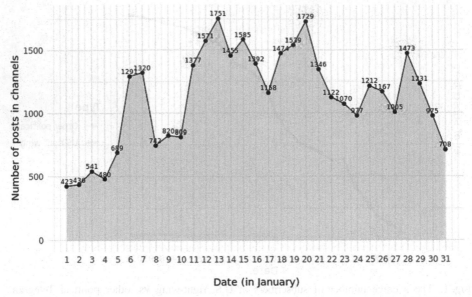

**Fig. 2.** The aggregate number of posts in U.S. right-wing channels, January 7 to 31, 2021.

Channels @trumpchannel and @real_donaldjtrump had the highest network degree metric (83 and 69, respectively), indicating their deep integration into the right-wing ecosystem. The same two channels also lead in terms of betweenness (308 and 232), which suggests the high degree of their centrality to the network.

As Fig. 3 illustrates, the communities of the right-wing Telegram network have sorted themselves into two distinct clusters: The ones that represent official accounts of various conservative personalities and media outlets and can be regarded as more mainstream (colored in yellow), and those that can be considered more fringe. The latter category is centered around the usvoterfraud channel and encompasses conspiracy theories-related channels, as well as those explicitly dedicated to trolling and riddled with hate speech.

### 4.3 Topic Modeling

Out of 20 topics identified by the LDA algorithm in the corpus of posts that the right-wing channels generated in January 2021, 17 were meaningful and interpretable. Most of them corresponded to the ongoing U.S. conservative political agenda and represented the way of framing political issues characteristic to the American right: the grievances of mainstream media's anti-conservative bias, Big Tech "censorship," Trump impeachment, the White House handover to Biden, the Capitol riot, and the critical Senate runoff election in Georgia, allegedly rigged by the Democrats.

Interestingly yet hardly surprisingly, the most heavily loaded topics were related to mainstream "fake news" (news post media dominion times icle ca sidney cnn fake) and the alleged suppression of free speech at the hands of technology firms (twitter telegram media facebook account tech censorship social please chat).

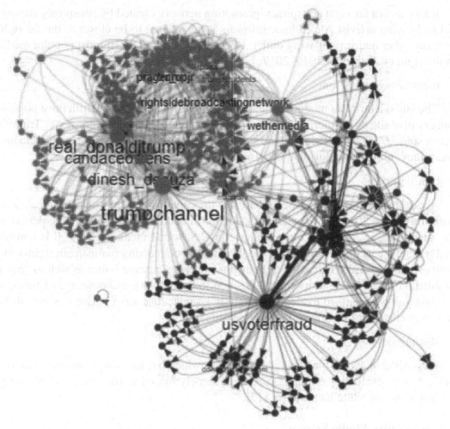

**Fig. 3.** The right-wing network based on mentions. (Color figure online)

### 4.4   External Links

Finally, addressing RQ4, a look at the links leading back to news media and the more mainstream social media ecosystem can give us an idea of what content has been shared within the right-wing Telegram ecosystem during the period of observation. We have identified 14 most frequently occurring news media and social media sources, of which most belong to the core of the U.S. right-wing media space.

**Mass Media**
welovetrump.com

This site has some social media features (like posts can be created by visitors) and acts like a blog aggregator but has very strict moderation and approval rules governing authors' political views and editorial content. The site has the title obviously referring us to Trump's supporters and the "about us" section includes a direct plea to "support Trump" [1].

infowars.com

Infowars is a far-right conspiracy-promoting network created by conspiracy theorist and right-wing activist Alex Jones. Infowars is considered to be closer to the far right than any other major right-wing outlet. It was listed 8th out of 10 most popular media on the right on Twitter in 2015–2017. [2, 10]

thegetawaypudint.com

The site is a far-right media publication. It was estimated to be the fifth most popular conservative site on Twitter in 2016 and labeled as one of the cornerstones of "Trump's media sphere" [7, 10]. Researchers stated that it supplied readers with xenophobic and conspiracy information during the 2016 presidential election [7].

breitbart.com

According to many reports, Breitbart was the center of the right-leaning media network during the 2016 US presidential election. In addition, during that time period, it was one of the most shared news sources on U.S. social media at large. It is considered a crucial part of the right-wing media network, connecting mainstream right-wing media sources and alternative alt-right media, covering extreme issues as well as "more established topics". Due to its central position in the network and coverage of far-right discussion it was claimed to "legitimize an illegitimate discourse". Also it is one of the two most cited sources among Trump supporters [2, 7].

summit.news

According to Media bias/Factcheck Review, which has its own proprietary methodology of bias evaluation, summit.news is extremely biased to the right, and promotes conspiracies and white nationalism [13].

**A Conservative Media Source**
nypost.com

New York Post can be regarded as a reliably right-leaning newspaper that has been in circulation for more than two centuries. It openly supported Trump during the 2016 presidential election, casting his opponents in a negative light. It was also named one of the top ten most popular media sources on the right both for Twitter and Facebook users during the election [7].

**Social Media**
twitter.com and t.co

Most of top tweets in our sample were deleted at the time of our analysis or were produced by suspended accounts, though available through web archives. The most popular reference is suspended tweet by Alexander Sangmoore (ASang- moore), which urges right-wing Twitter users to proceed to his Telegram channels. [12] Other highly-referred-to tweets are devoted to the Capitol riot. [20, 21] Several referred tweets including the deleted ones are from Disclose.tv, which was referred as "conspiracy-pseudoscience" "that is low in factual reporting due to numerous failed fact checks and a lack of transparency" by Media Bias/Fact Check aggregator [12]. In addition, top links contain several tweets from Trump, which are unavailable due to his permanent ban.

t.me

The most referred links to Telegram website usually contain public channel links for pro-Trump organizations (as TrumpTeam News, US voter fraud or Patriot Alerts) or invitations to pro-Trump chats (e.g., WeLoveTrump).

youtube.com

Similar to Twitter links, roughly half of the most-shared links lead to deleted videos on YouTube. Other prominent referred videos are Trump speeches [26, 27] and the Congress session approving Biden's victory [25], all streamed by the Right Side Broadcasting Network (RSBN), which is prominent for its pro-Trump position and covering all of his speeches and rallies [4].

rumble.com

Rumble is a Canadian-based video hosting platform that is supposed to be an alternative for YouTube with less strict content moderation. It is popular among conservatives for less moderation and stronger right-wing community formed within. The most popular links shared relate to conspiracy theories, especially prominent is x22 report channel [8].

gab.com

Gab was created in 2016 as an alternative to Twitter. It claims to be championing free speech and welcoming deplatformed users from mainstream social networks. As researchers pointed out, Gab is widely used for discussion of news and politics, with especially strong reactions on issues connected with Trump and white nationalists. Hate speech was also mentioned as an important char acteristic of the platform [28].

bitchute.com

Researchers refer to Bitchute as a "low content moderation platform" with a focus on video content. The most popular content on the platform relates to far-right conspiracy theories and hate speech. Also, there were frequent calls for violence and white nationalist recruitment [18].

archive.is

Archive.is is neither a media resource nor a social platform. Rather, it is a web archive saving copies of internet pages to allow access after the original versions are banned or modified. We suggest it appeared among the top referred external links because of providing a fast way to access deleted content from mainstream social media, like Trump's tweets or deleted YouTube videos. Based on this overview, we can conclude that the external sources shared via links on selected right-wing Telegram channels belong to the conservative "bubble" and constitute a homogeneous right-wing to far-right communication infrastructure with the channels themselves.

## 5   Discussion

In a bid to investigate the effects of Donald Trump's expulsion from major mainstream social media platforms on the alternative social media ecosystem, we undertook a multi-method analysis of the right-wing segment of Telegram. Our data suggested that, in line with the reports of U.S. mainstream publications, in January 2021 the platform has seen a significant inflow of users into communities associated with U.S. right-wing and alt-right politics. The spikes in user growth roughly coincided with the newsworthy developments of the deplatforming campaign against Trump, suggesting that the influx of new Telegram users could be associated with it. Throughout January 2021, the right-wing segment of the platform grew explosively against the background of other large political channels' audiences growing at much slower rates.

Consistent with existing scholarship, the exploration of networked structures of the Telegram's right-wing ecosystem suggested that the communities of Donald Trump's supporters were at the very center of the graph. However, we lack data from before Trump's deplatforming to tell whether these events resulted in pro-Trump communities strengthening their central position. We also uncovered two large clusters of communities: The group of the more "official" channels mainly associated with conservative political figures, commentators and organizations, and a cluster of fringe communities focused on trolling and conspiracies where toxic speech was rampant. These two mark distinct groups in Trump's online coalition that have been described before [7].

Our topic modelling analysis demonstrated that some of the major themes that were conspicuous within the right-wing Telegram ecosystem were the key events of the U.S. politics that were unfolding throughout the tumultuous month of January 2021. Furthermore, topics ostensibly informed by the resentment towards the mainstream media and social media platforms were especially prominent. The analysis of external links shared within the right-wing segment suggested that the outside websites and social media platforms and channels represented an expected repertoire of right-wing to alt-right sources.

Taken together, these findings suggest that the mass migration of right-wing audiences to Telegram in January did occur, and there are good reasons to believe that it has been at least partly driven by the resentment toward mainstream social media ecosystem that Donald Trump's deplatforming sparked. The on-line space that has thus emerged ostensibly retained many of the trappings of the conservative "bubbles" that existed on mainstream social media platforms. The structure of community clusters, issue agendas and main talking points, as well as the range of sources invoked in the channels' messaging all resembled respective features of right-wing online communities that researchers have already documented in other contexts. In the grand scheme of things, this lends further credence to the idea that deplatforming should not be seen as the ultimate solution to the problem of the proliferation of extreme political speech, and such radical measures should be taken with due consideration of the possible system-wide consequences. Granted, our study did not incorporate any tools to measure whether the Telegram-based right-wing ecosystem has become more extreme compared to those that existed around Donald Trump's accounts on the social networks from where he got banned or suspended. In this context, we can only speculate about such possibility.

Among other limitations of our study is the fact that we only looked at the time period in the immediate aftermath of the deplatforming campaign. We have no data on the state of the Telegram right-wing ecosystem prior to the said events, rendering it impossible to draw robust comparisons between before and after and make any causal inferences. We also cannot be certain about how persistent the hypothesized effects are:

It is possible that heightened user activity and explosive growth would subside after a few weeks from the initial shock of the ex-president's deplatforming. Subsequent studies should incorporate a longitudinal lens to investigate the dynamics of right-wing political communities on alternative social platforms over time.

**Acknowledgements.** Authors received funding from the Basic Research Program at the National Research University Higher School of Economics (HSE) to support their work on this project.

# References

1. About Us—We Love Trump. https://welovetrump.com/about-us/
2. Benkler, Y., Faris, R., Roberts, H.: Network Propaganda: Manipulation, Disinformation, and Radicalization in American Politics. Oxford University Press, Oxford (2018)
3. Blei, D.M., Ng, A.Y., Jordan, M.I.: Latent Dirichlet allocation. J Mach Learn Res. **3**. (2003). https://doi.org/10.5555/944919.944937
4. Business Insider. https://www.businessinsider.com/what-is-right-side-broadcasting-2016-9
5. Chandrasekharan, E., Pavalanathan, U., Srinivasan, A., Glynn, A., Eisenstein, J., Gilbert, E.: You can't stay here: the efficacy of Reddit's 2015 ban examined through hate speech. In: ACM Hum.-Comput. Interact. (2017). https://doi.org/10.1145/3134666
6. Ellinas, A.A.: Media and the radical right. In: Rydgren, J. (ed.) The Oxford Handbook of the Radical Right, pp. 1–14. Oxford University Press, Oxford (2018)
7. Faris, R., Roberts, H., Etling, B., Bourassa, N., Zuckerman, E., Benkler, Y.: Partisanship, propaganda, and disinformation: online media and the 2016 U.S. presidential election. Berkman Klein Center for Internet Society Research Paper (2017)
8. Fortune.      https://fortune.com/2020/11/30/rumble-video-service-youtube-rival-popular-among-conservatives
9. Gillespie, T.: Regulation of and by platforms. In: Burgess, J., Marwick, A , Poell, T. (eds.) The SAGE Handbook of Social Media, pp. 254–278. SAGE Publications Ltd., Thousand Oaks (2018). https://doi.org/10.4135/9781473984066.n15
10. Kaiser, J., Rauchfleisch, A., Bourassa, N.: Connecting the (far-)right dots: a topic modeling and hyperlink analysis of (far-)right media coverage during the US elections 2016. Digit. J. **8**, 422–441 (2019)
11. Kreiss, D., Mcgregor, S.C.: The "arbiters of what our voters see": Facebook and Google's struggle with policy, process, and enforcement around political advertising. Polit Commun. **36**, 499–522 (2019). https://doi.org/10.1080/10584609.2019.1619639
12. Media Bias Fact Check—Disclose TV. https://mediabiasfactcheck.com/disclose-tv/
13. Media Bias Fact Check—Summit News. https://mediabiasfactcheck.com/summit-news/
14. Mudde, C.: The Far Right Today. Cambridge University Press, Cambridge (2019)
15. Ott, B.L.: The age of Twitter: Donald J. Trump and the politics of debasement. Crit. Stud. Media Commun. **34**, 59–68 (2016). https://doi.org/10.1080/15295036.2016.1266686
16. Rogers, R.: Deplatforming: following extreme Internet celebrities to Telegram and alternative social media. Eur. J. Commun. **35**, 213–229 (2020). https://doi.org/10.1177/0267323120922066
17. Tgstat. https://tgstat.ru/
18. Trujillo, M., Gruppi, M., Buntain, C., Horne, B.D.: What is BitChute? Characterizing the" Free Speech" Alternative to YouTube (2020)
19. Trump's mob is on Telegram and they're already getting organized. https://www.wired.co.uk/article/trump-telegram

20. Twitter—Allegedlyzo Status. https://twitter.com/allegedlyzo/status/1350833322428145672?s=20
21. Twitter—Bennyjohnson Status. https://twitter.com/bennyjohnson/status/135241192239051 5714?s=21
22. Urman, A., Katz, S.: What they do in the shadows: examining the far-right networks on Telegram. Inf. Commun. Soc. 1–20 (2020). https://doi.org/10.1080/1369118X.2020.1803946
23. Van den Bulck, H., Hyzen, A.: Of lizards and ideological entrepreneurs: Alex Jones and Infowars in the relationship between populist nationalism and the post-global media ecology. Int Commun Gaz. **82**, 42–59 (2020)
24. Wells, C., Shah, D., Lukito, J., Pelled, A., Pevehouse, J.C.V., Yang, J.H.: Trump, Twitter, and news media responsiveness: a media systems approach. New Media Soc. **22**, 659–682 (2020). https://doi.org/10.1177/1461444819893987
25. YouTube Joint Session of Congress Resumes Electoral College Count After Capitol Lockdown. https://www.youtube.com/watch?v=b7coLmNP41o
26. YouTube President Trump farewell to address the nation. https://www.youtube.com/watch?v=oIbLtumN_U
27. YouTube President Trump Speaks at Sendoff Ceremony at Joint Base Andrews. https://www.youtube.com/watch?v=jebuWS871IQ
28. Zannettou, S., et al.: What is gab: a bastion of free speech or an alt-right echo chamber. In: WWW 2018: Companion Proceedings of the Web Conference 2018, Geneva, pp. 1007–1014 (2018). https://doi.org/10.1145/3184558.3191531

# eEconomy: Challenges of the COVID-19 Pandemic

# COVID-19 Pandemic Impact on Customer Loyalty Factors in Russian E-Commerce Market

Vera Rebiazina[✉] and Mehran Haddadi

HSE University, Moscow, Russia
rebiazina@hse.ru

**Abstract.** The main objective of this paper is to explore the impact of the COVID-19 pandemic on customer loyalty factors in the Russian e-commerce market. The pandemic has dramatically changed consumer behavior in e-commerce. Russia's e-commerce has grown significantly since 2020 due to the COVID-19 pandemic. The new customers entering the online market and an increase in online shopping frequency due to the quarantine are among the reasons for the growth in the financial value of Russia's e-commerce. There was a 44% growth of the industry in 2020 compared to 2019. To explore the possible impact of the COVID-19 pandemic on customer loyalty factors, quantitative empirical data was gathered in 2019 and 2020, with 836 and 926 accurate observations respectively. Methods of exploratory factor analysis, confirmatory factor analysis, and the t-test were used to analyze the data along with the validity and reliability indices. After confirming the CFA model, nine constructs affecting consumer loyalty in 2019 and 2020 were examined to investigate possible changes in the mean values of their indicators. The results showed that factors Consumer satisfaction, Ease of making online purchases, e-WOM, and Number of reviews have a statistically significant difference in the mean value of the indicators between Pre- and the COVID-19 era. These findings can help Russian online business managers to adapt to changes in consumer behavior. To enhance e-WOM, having a platform to get customer feedback and understand their perception about the service and product is recommended.

**Keywords:** COVID-19 · Customer loyalty · E-commerce · Russia

## 1 Introduction

In December 2019, news of the COVID-19 outbreak first detected in Wuhan, China, became global [1]. The virus then rapidly spread to other parts of the world, and the World Health Organization announced it as a pandemic on 11 March 2020 [2]. Since the pandemic, many countries have adopted strict rules to combat the spread of the virus, including nationwide quarantines, closing land and air borders, and shutting down crowded public places such as parks, museums, subways, and restaurants.

Despite governments' actions to contain the spread of the virus during 2020, the COVID-19 pandemic has had profound consequences not only in China, which has been the origin of the virus, but all over the world. These effects are not only limited to

D. A. Alexandrov et al. (Eds.): DTGS 2021, CCIS 1503, pp. 431–445, 2022.
https://doi.org/10.1007/978-3-030-93715-7_31

the shrinking of the global economy and the loss of many jobs, but they also have led to new business paradigms aimed at diminishing human contact and preventing further spread of the virus. Consequently, various businesses have enhanced their e-commerce platforms to respond more quickly and effectively to their customers' needs.

On the other hand, different businesses' consumers, who comply with government rules during the quarantine, are inevitably more interested in satisfying their needs through e-commerce platforms instead of going out and risking getting infected. In a situation of pandemic, e-commerce has played a more significant role than ever for global and regional business owners. Kim [3], in a paper on the impact of the COVID-19 pandemic on consumer behavior, states that e-commerce has become popular due to consumers' need to make online purchases and financial transactions. In line with this research, paying close attention to the factors affecting customer loyalty during the pandemic can provide a way to retain customers.

Due to Russia's size, large population, emerging economy, e-commerce growth rate, and the global ranking of confirmed cases of COVID-19, the Russian Federation can be considered as a case study to analyze the effects of the pandemic on customer loyalty factors in e-commerce. Russian health authorities declared Russia's first two cases of COVID-19 on Friday, January 31, 2020 [4]. According to the World Health Organization data, on 18 Feb 2021 Russia ranks fourth worldwide in the number of confirmed cases of COVID-19 and has the first place among European countries [5].

The outbreak during 2020, as well as its impacts on the global economy, has also had a profound impact on the Russian economy and its various industries. Several Russian industries got into financial troubles due to restrictions imposed by the Russian government during the quarantine to control the spread of the virus. Consumers also chose to minimize out-of-home visits to avoid the contagion. However, according to the Statista, the e-commerce industry has been able to take advantage of the circumstances created by the epidemic [6]. The Statista also notes that the Russian e-commerce market is one of the largest emerging commerce markets in the global marketplace, which has been growing steadily since 2010, and the current pandemic is anticipated to drive further growth in the industry. In this context, a study about the state of consumer payments under the influence of the COVID-19 pandemic and digitization has revealed that Russian consumers are more accustomed to non-cash payment methods from various e-commerce platforms [7].

The Data Insight estimates that the Russian e-commerce market grew 44% in 2020 compared to 2019, and its monetary value increased from 1.7 trillion rubles to 2.5 trillion rubles in 2020. Further, it also estimates the growth of Russian e-commerce market for 2021 and 2022 at 34% and 32%, respectively [8].

The other projections made by Data Insight [8] reported that the COVID-19 crisis in 2020 will additionally increase the growth of Russian e-commerce by another 1.6 trillion rubles up to 2024, and the total monetary value of the Russian e-commerce industry will reach 7.2 trillion rubles. Factors influencing the increase in the size of the Russian e-commerce market due to the pandemic include new online customers, home quarantine, an increase in online shopping frequency even after isolation, remote work, and Growth of online sales of fast moving consumer goods (FMCG) [8].

The COVID-19 pandemic has led to a rapid increase in e-commerce growth in Russia, followed by the Russian customers' greater desire to purchase online. Thus, there is a need to examine possible changes in the factors influencing the loyalty of customers in online shopping. In this paper, the research question is formulated as follows.

- Does the COVID-19 pandemic impact customer loyalty factors?

To explore the subject of this paper and investigate any possible changes in customer loyalty factors, the survey data collected in 2019 and 2020 were analyzed by methods EFA, CFA, and independent samples t-test.

This paper consists of five sections: Sect. 1 is introduction, Sect. 2 discusses the literature related to definitions of customer loyalty in e-commerce, customer loyalty factors, and the impact of COVID-19 on e-commerce and customer loyalty factors. The Sect. 3 explains the data and methods of analysis. The authors report the results of the paper in the Sect. 4. The Sect. 5 summarizes the conclusion of this paper.

# 2 Theoretical Framework

## 2.1 COVID-19 Impact on E-commerce

The COVID-19 pandemic has drastically changed consumer behavior regarding health and economic issues such as resource scarcity and panic buying [9]. The SARS epidemic between 2002 and 2004 also hit the affected countries in a similar way to the COVID-19 pandemic. Forster and Tang [10] found that online shopping grew due to fears of catching the virus. Kim [3] was one of the first to explore the impact of the COVID-19 pandemic on e-commerce. He believes these changes have a long-term impact on e-commerce and consumer behavior. In his view, the pandemic has boosted the e-commerce industry, and a large percentage of consumers who did not previously shop online are now joining online shoppers. In line with Kim's findings, Ghandour and Woodford [11], using the regression method in their research by analyzing e-commerce data of the United Arab Emirates, reached a similar conclusion that the pandemic has a positive effect on the consumer tendency to shop online. Another study has mentioned the positive and significant impact of the epidemic on e-commerce, along with the increased supply of goods by producers over the Internet [12].

A study by Hasanat et al. [13] about the effects of the COVID-19 on e-commerce in Malaysia points at challenges for online retailers such as delivery times, shipping problems, and quarantines. Contrary to Kim's view [3], they [13] conclude that due to restrictions on exports and imports from China, many online businesses that used to source their goods from China, are in serious trouble now. Another study about the effects of the epidemic found a significant positive relationship between online shopping before and after the outbreak [14]. The majority of other studies also believe that COVID-19 pandemic changes consumer behavior and stimulates them to make online purchases to meet their needs during the quarantine [15, 16].

According to the World Health Organization, Russia has the fourth highest number of people infected with the COVID-19 in the world [5]. However, the pandemic has sparked growth in Russian e-commerce. Data Insight [8] projected that the growth of e-commerce in Russia would increase even more because of the COVID-19. In their view, while the epidemic has caused limitations and problems for the everyday life of Russians, there are also positive aspects in its e-commerce adaptation. They consider factors such as new online shoppers, isolation at home, online shopping frequency, remote work, and growth of online sales of fast moving consumer goods (FMCG) effective in enhancing the e-commerce growth during the crisis.

One of the first reasons for the growth of Russian e-commerce during the pandemic is the increase in the number of new customers, who during the quarantine period prefer to stay at home in order to preserve their health, and shift to online shopping to satisfy their needs. Data Insight [8] estimates that these new Russian customers are likely to continue their purchases after the quarantine period. The cause of the rising number of new customers due to the new epidemic in 2020 is consistent with research conducted by a group of Russian researchers about the factors that influence the Russian consumers' switch to e-commerce. The researchers [17] state that the ease and benefits of shopping online can influence the decision of Russian customers to adopt e-commerce. Hence, the ease of shopping online and its benefits, such as saving time and money, as well as the necessity to stay away from a contagious virus, have increased the number of customers in Russian ecommerce during the pandemic. According to Data Insight [8], the second driver of the increased financial value of Russian e-commerce is home quarantine. Home isolation limits the consumer to shopping online. The third reason that increases the size of the online shopping market is due to the increase in the frequency of online purchases by consumers even after the quarantine period. According to another estimate by the same company, approximately 5–7 million Russian employees have worked remotely in 2020 due to a shift in companies' policies. This source considers this as the fourth reason for the growth in the use of e-commerce in Russia. The surge in online sales of fast moving consumer goods (FMCG) could be another factor that leads to the overall growth of Russian e-commerce in 2020 [8].

## 2.2 Consumer Loyalty in E-commerce

The previous section outlined the influence of the COVID-19 pandemic on e-commerce worldwide and in Russia. In this section, the authors discuss different definitions and approaches to the concept of customer loyalty based on previous researches. In the past, scholars had different perspectives on customer loyalty, and they studied customer loyalty using different approaches. One of the first views on customer loyalty was the behavioral loyalty approach. Cunningham [18] was one of the first scholars to study the behavioral aspects of customer loyalty. He expresses customer loyalty as being driven by consumer behaviors or actions, such as making a repeat purchase or the number of times they do shopping. Jacoby and Chestnut [19] argue that the behavioral attitude of the consumer alone does not properly distinguish genuine consumer loyalty from spurious loyalty, which may result from a lack of other alternatives for the consumer. The common belief among these researchers is that the behavioral perspective of consumer loyalty does not consider the emotional and psychological aspects of consumer behavior.

On the other hand, several researchers have expressed a second perspective on the definition of consumer loyalty, which stems from the perceptions and attitudes of consumers, and called it the attitudinal loyalty approach. Day and Baldinger [20, 21] believe that perceived loyalty can be the result of a customer's true emotional evaluation of a product, service, or company. Thus, attitudinal loyalty creates a kind of commitment between the consumer and the company that can prevent the consumer from tending to alternatives that differ slightly from the current product or service of choice. Perceptual loyalty goes even further. It makes consumers resist competitors' offers, pay a premium price for the current product or service, and recommend it to others. Oliver [22] explains that attitudinal loyalty is a kind of psychological approach that includes emotional, perceptual, and cognitive elements. He also defined loyalty as "a deeply held commitment to rebuy or repatronize a preferred product or service consistently in the future, despite situational influences and marketing efforts having the potential to cause switching behavior".

The fundamental discrepancy between the two perspectives on customer loyalty is that behavioral loyalty concentrates more on consumer behavior and describes their actions, but attitudinal loyalty focuses on consumer feelings and perceptions about a product or a firm. Despite having a sufficient explanation of the two approaches, Jacoby and Chestnut [19] believe that studying consumer loyalty based on attitudinal or behavioral loyalty perspectives can't provide an appropriate understanding of the concept of consumer loyalty. Therefore, Jacoby and Kyner [23] were among the first researchers to come up with the idea of combining these two approaches to consumer loyalty. They considered the link between consumers' actions and their perceptions to develop a more accurate and complete conceptualization about loyalty. Day [20] was, perhaps, the very first scholar to realize and utter the necessity of integrating both approaches after them. In 1994, Dick and Basu [24] supported the idea of combining two approaches to having a common framework of behavior and perception, and they grouped loyalty into four categories, namely loyalty, spurious loyalty, latent loyalty, and no loyalty based on repeated patronage and relative attitude.

In this paper, the authors also conceptualize consumer loyalty in e-commerce by incorporating behavioral and attitudinal approaches. In addition, customers' feelings and perceptions, as well as their behavior, such as the frequency of online purchases and recent online shopping, are considered to measure consumer loyalty in the ecommerce market.

### 2.3   Consumer Loyalty Factors

The authors of this paper have revealed the following constructs that influence consumer loyalty in e-commerce based on the previous studies.

**Consumer Experience.** This factor can be defined as the customer experience of buying from an online store and the continuation of his/her relationship with the company. Companies try to attract new customers by creating a better shopping experience to retain customers. Reducing operating costs is beneficial for both the company and the customers [25]. Another group considers the customer experience as a psychological feeling in the customer's mind. These researchers believe that customer experience influences behavioral and attitudinal loyalty [26].

**Online Store Reputation.** Besides creating intense competition, the presence of numerous firms in e-commerce, also leads to a large amount of information. In this situation, customers tend to well-known brands to simplify their decision-making process and consider their reputation as a sign of a good product [27].

**Consumer Satisfaction.** A number of scholars have accepted that satisfaction is a prerequisite of attitudinal loyalty. Others have supported the relationship between customer satisfaction and attitudinal customer loyalty as a desire to recommend [28]. Anderson and Srinivasan [27] have investigated the impact of customer satisfaction on customer loyalty in the e-commerce environment, and they have found that higher customer satisfaction leads to higher customer loyalty. Supporting Anderson and Srinivasan [27], Eid [29] has achieved similar results in Saudi Arabian e-commerce, finding that customer satisfaction profoundly affects customer loyalty. In another study, the author considers the impact of customer satisfaction on loyalty in the online environment more than in the offline one [30].

**Electronic Word of Mouth (e-WOM).** Studies have proven that the velocity and outreach of electronic Word-of-Mouth is much higher and greater than of the traditional one [31]. Numerous online retailers try to motivate their consumers to create electronic WOM, and they think that their words are more trusted by new potential consumers [32].

**Trust (vs. Risks).** In online shopping, trust is a major player in retaining consumer loyalty. This even extended to the Technology Acceptance Model (TAM) theory that trust positively influences consumers' intentions to switch to e-commerce [33].

## 3 Methodology

The research methodology includes three parts: data collection, operationalization, and data analysis process.

### 3.1 Data Collection

This paper data was collected to examine possible changes in Russian consumers' perceptions about loyalty factors in Russian e-commerce. To gather the required data, the response of Russian participants in 2019 was used as the period Pre-COVID-19 and in 2020 as the COVID-19 era. All of the respondents were enrolled in an online marketing course. The selection criteria for survey respondents was their online shopping experience, and these individuals have responded to questions through an online questionnaire on the Russian National Education Platform "Open Education'. The data collection has been conducted during the years 2019 and 2020. The survey was voluntary, anonymous, and without any remuneration for participants with a convenience sampling technique. The proportion of women among online shoppers in Russia ranges from 55% to 64% [34].

Out of 1025 respondents who filled out the questionnaire in 2019, 80 only bought at retail and 27 did not buy online. Taking into account these individuals and the presence of 82 cases of missing data, a total of 836 observations were used, which is 82% of the total data collected. Similarly, out of the 1,056 people who responded to the survey in 2020, 41 bought only at retail, and 12 bought nothing online at all. Excluding 77 incomplete observations, only 926 observations were studied, equivalent to 88% of all data collected. General characteristics of participants, including gender, age, and level of income, are shown in Table 1 for the both periods the pre- and COVID-19 era.

**Table 1.** Description of the sample of the empirical research

| Measure | Item | Frequency | |
| --- | --- | --- | --- |
| | | Pre-COVID-19 | The COVID-19 era |
| Sex | Men | 178 | 160 |
| | Women | 658 | 766 |
| Age | Before 18 | 10 | 16 |
| | 18–25 | 651 | 670 |
| | Above 25 | 175 | 240 |
| Income level | Low | 20 | 28 |
| | Middle | 615 | 691 |
| | High | 201 | 207 |

## 3.2 Operationalization

Conceptualizing and measuring customer loyalty has always been a conundrum for researchers, and there has always been much debate about measurement constructs. The research questionnaire was designed on the basis of thematic literature in the field of customer loyalty and its determinants, as well as Russian e-commerce. Respondents who have filled out the questionnaire gave their opinion concerning 45 statements made of the seven points Likert scales, including number 1, which means completely disagree and number 7, which means completely agree.

In the process of conceptualizing customer loyalty and measuring it, a number of indicators were eliminated from analysis because they explain the small variance and have very low values in rotated component matrix. Kaiser-Meyer-Olkin and Bartlett's Test was one of the methods used to validate the applicability of factor analysis. In addition, Cronbach's alpha has been used for reliability of the questionnaire and convergent and discriminant validity tests have been performed to assess the validity of the constructs [28].

### 3.3 Analysis Methods and Process

This paper uses Methods exploratory factor analysis (EFA), confirmatory factor analysis (CFA) and independent samples t-test to investigate the impact of the COVID-19 epidemic on factors affecting customer loyalty in Russian e-commerce. In the first step, the researchers examined the observable indices by EFA method in IBM SPSS Statistics software to be able to categorize them based on correlations between them for plausible latent variables to measure customer loyalty. In this phase, the researchers used Principal Component Analysis (PCA) and Varimax rotation to perform an exploratory factor analysis. Later on, the authors have chosen between the various proposed number of factors based on their eigenvalues and they have decided to put manifest indicators into the factors which they have the highest possible rotated factor loadings accordingly.

In the second stage, the latent variables identified as a result of the initial factor exploration are modeled with CFA method and analyzed with IBM SPSS AMOS 24. Certain metrics including standardized estimate, estimate p-value, and model fit indices assist the researchers at this stage in evaluating the proposed EFA factors and confirming them. The researchers have also performed convergent and discriminant validity check in this phase to ensure the results obtained [35].

Following the previous two steps of analysis and understanding the consistency of the manifest factors regarding customer loyalty for both years, the final part of the data analysis needs to be performed in order to answer the research question. In the final step, the data from the two times before and during the pandemic are analyzed using independent t-test method to examine the difference between the respondents' mean values for each of the indicators by using software IBM SPSS Statistics.

## 4   Results of an Empirical Research

In this part of the paper, the results of data analysis using methods EFA, CFA and t-test for both periods before and during the pandemic are described.

### 4.1   Exploratory Factor Analysis

At the initial stage of reviewing the 45 indicators, eight of them were excluded from the analysis because they had extracted common variance less than 50% in the communality table and also a low factor loadings. Thus, the exploratory factor analysis was performed on 37 items that have a common extracted variance greater than 50%. According to EFA, nine factors are obtained for both periods, with considering eigenvalue larger or closer to one.

In 2019, the nine factors explain about 73% of the total variance, and that number is the same in 2020. The first factor, which authors refer to as customer satisfaction based on the subject literature and its indicators, explains the maximum variance at about 32% in both years with a slight difference. This factor applies to all statements that indicate consumer satisfaction with online shopping. The second factor, which is called the online store's reputation, is related to concerns such as customer respect, no price fluctuations, and trust. The third factor is called the risk factor and is related to safety issues at the time of online purchase. The fourth factor relates to consumer shopping experiences. In the fifth factor, ease of shopping online is important to the consumer. Factors sixth and seventh relate to issues regarding customer orientation and competitive advantage of stores respectively. The eighth factor describes an electronic word of mouth, and the ninth factor explains the volume of online reviews.

The KMO in both years is approximately 0.92, and this number is higher than the value of 0.5 and indicates that the data is suitable for a factor analysis. In addition, the significant value of Bartlett's Test of Sphericity in both periods is further evidence of the adequacy of the data. Furthermore, Cronbach's Alpha is larger than the accepted threshold for all factors.

## 4.2 Confirmatory Factor Analysis

After obtaining the exploratory results of factor analysis in order to verify them, it is essential to conduct a modeling using CFA method. All standardized estimates are significant, and the average variance extracted (AVE) for all latent variables is greater than 0.5, which confirms the convergent validity of the CFA model in 2019. In addition, the model fit indices for the CFA model in 2019 are close to or exceed the accepted thresholds. (Chi-Sq/df = 3.515, RMR = 0.069, GFI = 0.874, TLI = 0.916, CFI = 0.925, RMSEA = 0.055).

In the CFA model for pre-COVID-19, discriminant validity is achieved when the Square root of AVE is larger than its corresponding rows and columns. Note that the Square root of AVE in the Table 2 is larger than its rows and columns, and is shown with a bold and underlined font.

**Table 2.** Discriminant validity for Pre-COVID-19 CFA model

| ID | Factor | F1 | F2 | F3 | F4 | F5 | F6 | F7 | F8 | F9 |
|----|--------|----|----|----|----|----|----|----|----|----|
| F1 | Consumer satisfaction | **0.76** | | | | | | | | |
| F2 | Online store reputation | 0.59 | **0.75** | | | | | | | |
| F3 | Risks | −0.12 | −0.15 | **0.80** | | | | | | |
| F4 | Consumer experience | 0.54 | 0.54 | −0.02 | **0.84** | | | | | |
| F5 | Ease of making online purchases | 0.74 | 0.57 | −0.10 | 0.48 | **0.84** | | | | |
| F6 | Customer orientation | 0.47 | 0.74 | −0.07 | 0.46 | 0.46 | **0.82** | | | |
| F7 | Online store competence | 0.54 | 0.58 | −0.06 | 0.36 | 0.49 | 0.63 | **0.75** | | |
| F8 | e-WOM | 0.33 | 0.29 | 0.10 | 0.42 | 0.37 | 0.26 | 0.24 | **0.85** | |
| F9 | Number of reviews | 0.10 | 0.06 | 0.00 | 0.04 | 0.06 | 0.09 | 0.09 | 0.15 | **0.92** |

In CFA model for the COVID-19 era, AVE is larger than 0.5 for all nine latent variables and can confirm convergent validity. All standardized estimates are significant.

Furthermore, there are accepted value for the COVID-19 era CFA model fit indices. (Chi-Sq/df = 3.801, RMR = 0.059, GFI = 0.874, TLI = 0.916, CFI = 0.925, RMSEA = 0.055).

Similar to the Table 2, the discriminant validity for The COVID-19 era CFA model meets the condition that square root of AVE is larger than the corresponding rows and columns and obtains the necessary validity.

## 4.3  Independent t-test

This section presents the results of the t-test for independent samples. All manifest indicators based on the CFA models have a significant impact on the latent variable and the difference between their mean values before and the COVID-19 era can show a change in consumer's attitude towards e-commerce. Since groups of indicators affect the latent variables, these changes can also be seen in the overall view of those factors. The following table shows the results of the t test for all of the manifest indicators that had significant changes in their mean value before and the COVID-19 era.

**Table 3.** Independent samples t test for Pre- and The COVID-19 era

| Factor name | Indicator (item) | Variance | F | Sig. | Sig. (2-tailed) |
|---|---|---|---|---|---|
| Consumer satisfaction | If I need something, I will buy it on the Internet | Equal | 9.95 | .002 | .000 |
| | | Not equal | | | .000 |
| | I'm glad I started buying on the Internet | Equal | .23 | .635 | .000 |
| | | Not equal | | | .000 |
| | I will continue to buy online | Equal | 7.71 | .006 | .002 |
| | | Not equal | | | .002 |
| | My online shopping experience meets my expectations | Equal | 1.50 | .221 | .000 |
| | | Not equal | | | .000 |
| | Decision to start buying online was the right decision | Equal | 3.30 | .070 | .000 |
| | | Not equal | | | .000 |
| | I am happy with my online shopping | Equal | .45 | .503 | .000 |
| | | Not equal | | | .000 |
| | In general, I am satisfied with the quality of goods/services offered by online stores | Equal | 1.11 | .292 | .000 |
| | | Not equal | | | .000 |

*(continued)*

**Table 3.** (*continued*)

| Factor name | Indicator (item) | Variance | F | Sig. | Sig. (2-tailed) |
|---|---|---|---|---|---|
| Ease of making online purchases | In general, shopping online is easy | Equal | 12.4 | .000 | .001 |
| | | Not equal | | | .001 |
| | It is easy for me to shop online | Equal | 3.01 | .083 | .032 |
| | | Not equal | | | .033 |
| | It's easy for me to interact with an online store while making a purchase | Equal | .000 | .993 | .027 |
| | | Not equal | | | .027 |
| | It is easy for me to perform any operations during the purchase in the online store | Equal | 5.74 | .017 | .002 |
| | | Not equal | | | .002 |
| Online store reputation | In general, online shopping can be trusted | Equal | 1.35 | .246 | .032 |
| | | Not equal | | | .032 |
| Consumer experience | I will make the next purchase in the online store, where I have already bought before | Equal | .15 | .696 | .022 |
| | | Not equal | | | .022 |
| | I will make a purchase in the online store where I already bought before during the next year | Equal | .61 | .436 | .000 |
| | | Not equal | | | .000 |
| Number of reviews | I pay attention to the number of reviews when choosing a product and/or store | Equal | 7.72 | .006 | .039 |
| | | Not equal | | | .040 |
| | The more reviews, the higher the likelihood that I will choose a product and/or store to buy | Equal | 2.34 | .126 | .027 |
| | | Not equal | | | .028 |
| e-WOM | Over the past year I have been posting reviews online more often | Equal | 1.31 | .252 | .001 |
| | | Not equal | | | .001 |
| | I write long reviews (more than 1–2 sentences) | Equal | .02 | .898 | .028 |
| | | Not equal | | | .028 |

Table 3 does not show the other indicators that their mean has not changed significantly between the two samples. As shown in Table 3, all the manifest indicators that form the four latent variables consumer satisfaction, Ease of making online purchases, e-WOM, and Number of reviews in the two periods before and the COVID-19 era have significant differences in mean values. In the same way, one indicator that has a significant influence on online store reputation, as well as two indicators that significantly influence Consumer experience, have meaningful different mean values from the perspective of the Russian consumer.

Thus, to answer the research question of this study about the impact of the COVID-19 pandemic on customer loyalty factors, Authors use the findings to confirm this impact because of the significant change in the mean value of all items in the four factors. Hence, COVID-19 impact has been significantly approved in factors related to consumer satisfaction, Ease of making online purchases, e-WOM, and Number of reviews.

## 5   Discussion and Conclusion

This paper reviewed the literature on the impact of COVID-19 on e-commerce to reveal possible changes in consumer perceptions concerning loyalty factors in the Russian e-commerce market. Based on the exploratory factor analysis, nine factors were obtained for the pre- and COVID-19 era periods, which are in line with Rebiazina et al. [36] findings on Russian e-commerce. Naming latent variables is also based on the same research. Later, the researchers confirmed the existence of nine constructs for each period by CFA modeling based on exploratory factor analysis findings. Finally, the researchers compared the mean values of all 37 indicators of latent variables in two periods using the t test and found that the indices of four latent variables have a statistically significant difference in the mean value. These latent customer loyalty variables include Consumer satisfaction, Ease of making online purchases, e-WOM, and Number of reviews. Among them, consumer satisfaction is particularly important in terms of subsequently explaining the amount of variance. In EFA, this factor explains 32% of the 73% of the total variance of nine factors, which shows its importance in relation to consumer satisfaction when shopping online. On the other hand, we can see a noticeable difference in the values of average variance extracted (AVE) for these four factors in the pre- and COVID-19 era periods. There is a noticeable difference in the values of AVE for these four factors between the pre- and COVID-19 era periods. For instance, the average variance extracted by e-WOM and the number of reviews have significantly varied between the two periods from 0.72 and 0.84 for pre-COVID-19 CFA models to 0.65 and 0.96 for the COVID-19 era, respectively. Indeed, these variations may confirm changes in consumers' perceptions of the mentioned four factors during these periods.

The results of this paper on the importance of customer satisfaction and ease of making online purchases for consumers to switch to e-commerce in the Russian market are consistent with Rebiazina et al. [17] findings about the ecommerce adaptation factors in Russia. Kursan [37] likewise has discovered that customers who are satisfied with their online purchases are more likely to return to the same retailer and re-purchase during the pandemic and this can make them loyal customers. Moreover, e-WOM's impact on purchase decisions during a pandemic was significantly noticed in another research that may somehow confirm the importance of this factor during this era [38]. Praptiningsih [39] has also emphasized that understanding e-WOM is very important during a pandemic, especially for activities such as shopping.

The findings of this paper may pave the way for online business executives to pay more attention to finding solutions for an enhancement in customer satisfaction, especially for new customers. In addition, companies' managers can provide customers with more appropriate and convenient platforms to search for a product or service and include safe and user-friendly payment options. Finally, the marketing and customer service departments' managers must provide appropriate platforms for customers to submit their feedback and have better control over the e-WOM.

This study has some limitations that may be addressed in further research. The main limitation of this study is related to the evidence focused specifically on Russia. Therefore, it is very vital to conduct further studies involving other countries in order to understand the impact of COVID-19 on customer loyalty factors in the various e-commerce market across countries. In this way, online business owners may become familiar with the factors in their geographic regions and pay more attention to enhance them. The second limitation concerns the participants in this study, which is necessary to consider a more robust sampling technique in order to improve the generalization of the findings.

**Acknowledgment.** This research has been conducted within the applied research project "Development of Multifactor Model to Improve Innovative Companies Com-petitiveness in the Digital Transformation Age" as a part of the HSE Graduate School of Business Research Program (protocol No.5, 19.06.2020) in 2020–2021.

# References

1. WHO. Pneumonia of unknown cause – China. http://www.who.int/csr/don/05-january-2020-pneumonia-of-unkown-cause-china/en/
2. WHO. Director-General's opening remarks at the media briefing on COVID-19 - 11 March 2020. https://www.who.int/director-general/speeches/detail/who-director-general-s-opening-remarks-at-the-media-briefing-on-covid-19---11-march-2020
3. Kim, R.Y.: The impact of COVID-19 on consumers: preparing for digital sales. IEEE Eng. Manag. Rev. **48**(3), 212–218 (2020)
4. Russia Confirms First Two Cases of Coronavirus, Two Chinese Nationals Quarantined. https://www.rferl.org/a/russia-confirms-coronavirus-first-cases-chinese-nationals-quarantined/30410166.html
5. WHO. Coronavirus Disease (COVID-19) Dashboard.https://covid19.who.int
6. Russia: forecasted e-commerce market value 2025. https://www.statista.com/statistics/1016094/russia-e-commerce-market-value/
7. Korobeynikova, O., Burkaltseva, D., Dugina, T., Kozenko, Z., Shaldokhina, S.: The state of the Russian payment market: digitalization and the impact of COVID-19. In: E3S Web of Conferences, p. 06003. EDP Sciences (2020)
8. DataInsight. Ecommerce 2020–2024. https://datainsight.ru/DI_eCommerce2020_2024
9. Prentice, C., Quach, S., Thaichon, P.: Antecedents and consequences of panic buying: the case of COVID-19. Int. J. Consum. Stud. (2020)

10. Forster, P.W., Tang, Y.: The role of online shopping and fulfillment in the Hong Kong SARS crisis. In: Proceedings of the 38th Annual Hawaii International Conference on System Sciences, p. 271a. IEEE (2005)
11. Ghandour, A., Woodford, B.J.: COVID-19 impact on e-commerce in UAE. In: 2020 21st International Arab Conference on Information Technology (ACIT), pp. 1–8. IEEE (2020)
12. Bhatti, A., Akram, H., Basit, H.M., Khan, A.U., Raza, S.M., Naqvi, M.B.: E-commerce trends during COVID-19 Pandemic. Int. J. Future Gener. Commun. Netw. 13(2), 1449–1452 (2020)
13. Hasanat, M.W., Hoque, A., Shikha, F.A., Anwar, M., Hamid, A.B.A., Tat, H.H.: The impact of coronavirus (COVID-19) on e-business in Malaysia. Asian J. Multidisc. Stud. 3(1), 85–90 (2020)
14. Ivanović, Đ, Antonijević, M.: The role of online shopping in the Republic of Serbia during COVID-19. Econ. Anal. 53(1), 28–41 (2020)
15. Salem, M.A., Nor, K.M.: The effect of COVID-19 on consumer behaviour in Saudi Arabia: switching from brick and mortar stores to e-commerce. Int. J. Sci. Technol. Res. 9(07), 15–28 (2020)
16. Hashem, T.N.: Examining the influence of COVID 19 pandemic in changing customers' orientation towards e-shopping. Mod. Appl. Sci. 14(8) (2020)
17. Rebiazina, V.A., Smirnova, M.M., Daviy, A.O.: E-commerce adoption in Russia: market- and store-level perspectives. РЖМ. 18(1), 5–28 (2020). https://doi.org/10.21638/spbu18.2020.101
18. Cunningham, R.M.: Brand loyalty-what, where, how much. Harv. Bus. Rev. 34(1), 116–128 (1956)
19. Jacoby, J., Chestnut, R.W.: Brand loyalty: measurement and management (1978)
20. Day, G.S.: A two-dimensional concept of brand loyalty. In: Funke, U.H. (ed.) Mathematical Models in Marketing. LNEMS, vol. 132, p. 89. Springer, Heidelberg (1976). https://doi.org/10.1007/978-3-642-51565-1_26
21. Baldinger, A.L., Rubinson, J.: Brand loyalty: the link between attitude and behavior. J. Advert. Res. 36(6), 22–34 (1996)
22. Oliver, R.L.: Satisfaction: A Behavioral Perspective on the Consumer. Routledge, Abingdon (2014)
23. Jacoby, J., Kyner, D.B.: Brand loyalty vs. repeat purchasing behavior. J. Mark. Res. 10(1), 1–9 (1973)
24. Dick, A.S., Basu, K.: Customer loyalty: toward an integrated conceptual framework. J. Acad. Mark. Sci. 22(2), 99–113 (1994). https://doi.org/10.1177/0092070394222001
25. Reichheld, F.F., Teal, T., Smith, D.K.: The Loyalty Effect, vol. 1, no. 3, pp. 78–84 (1996)
26. Srivastava, M., Kaul, D.: Exploring the link between customer experience–loyalty–consumer spend. J. Retail. Consum. Serv. 31, 277–286 (2016). https://doi.org/10.1016/j.jretconser.2016.04.009
27. Srinivasan, S.S., Anderson, R., Ponnavolu, K.: Customer loyalty in e-commerce: an exploration of its antecedents and consequences. J. Retail. 78(1), 41–50 (2002)
28. Lam, S.Y., Shankar, V., Erramilli, M.K., Murthy, B.: Customer value, satisfaction, loyalty, and switching costs: an illustration from a business-to-business service context. J. Acad. Mark. Sci. 32(3), 293–311 (2004)
29. Eid, M.I.: Determinants of e-commerce customer satisfaction, trust, and loyalty in Saudi Arabia. J. Electron. Commer. Res. 12(1), 78 (2011)
30. Shankar, V., Smith, A.K., Rangaswamy, A.: Customer satisfaction and loyalty in online and offline environments. Int. J. Res. Mark. 20(2), 153–175 (2003)
31. Yoo, C.W., Sanders, G.L., Moon, J.: Exploring the effect of e-WOM participation on e-Loyalty in e-commerce. Decis. Support Syst. 55(3), 669–678 (2013)
32. Gauri, D.K., Bhatnagar, A., Rao, R.: Role of word of mouth in online store loyalty. Commun. ACM 51(3), 89–91 (2008)

33. Qiu, L., Li, D.: Applying TAM in B2C E-commerce research: an extended model. Tsinghua Sci. Technol. **13**(3), 265–272 (2008)
34. Давий, А.О., Ребязина, В.А., Смирнова, М.М.: Барьеры и драйверы при совершении интернет-покупок в России: результаты эмпирического исследования. Вестник Санкт-Петербургского университета. Менеджмент. (1) (2018)
35. Fornell, C., Larcker, D.F.: Evaluating structural equation models with unobservable variables and measurement error. J. Mark. Res. **18**(1), 39–50 (1981)
36. Rebiazina, V., Stamalieva, A., Smirnova, M.: Consumer loyalty factors in the Russian e-commerce market. In: Alexandrov, D.A., Boukhanovsky, A.V., Chugunov, A.V., Kabanov, Y., Koltsova, O., Musabirov, I. (eds.) DTGS 2019. CCIS, vol. 1038, pp. 268–280. Springer, Cham (2019). https://doi.org/10.1007/978-3-030-37858-5_22
37. Kursan Milaković, I.: Purchase experience during the COVID-19 pandemic and social cognitive theory: the relevance of consumer vulnerability, resilience, and adaptability for purchase satisfaction and repurchase. Int. J. Consum. Stud. (2021)
38. Suciati, D., Rosandi, A., Trijanuar, D., Amalia, F., Kurniawan, R.: The influence of electronic word of mouth and discount on purchase decisions at Traveloka app during Covid-19 (survey on Traveloka user in Bandung 2020). Psychol. Educ. J. **58**(3), 699–705 (2021)
39. Praptiningsih, N.A.: Electronic word of mouth during adaptation pandemic Covid-19 towards the new normal: cases in Indonesia. In: 2nd International Conference on Business and Management of Technology (ICBMT 2020), pp. 180–183. Atlantis Press (2021)

# Management and COVID-19: Digital Shift to Remote Work and Remote Management

Araksya Mirakyan[1](✉) ⓘ and Svetlana Berezka[2] ⓘ

[1] Lomonosov Moscow State University, 1-46, Leninskiye gory, Moscow 119991, Russia
[2] HSE University, 26, Shabolovka str, Moscow 119049, Russia

**Abstract.** The study is devoted to the digital shift in management, forced by the precautions during the COVID-19 pandemic. The purpose of this paper is to provide an understanding of remote management, its challenges and opportunities faced in remote working by digital natives, young undergraduate students. The bibliometric analysis with VOSviewer revealed five research avenues on remote management in 2018–2021, that are digital transformation, technologies and supply chain; consumer behaviour, ICT and small business; business innovations and COVID-19 challenges; Industry 4.0 and manufacturing; sustainability. The paper includes an exploratory study of the opinion of undergraduate students regarding modern management practices. Based on the results of the qualitative research, the authors identify key benefits and challenges of remote management for the employees, employers and organisations. The respondents consider that remote work format is a driver of positive and negative organisational change that impact different organisational aspects – decision making, communication, conflict, organisational culture, leadership and motivation. The paper discusses the results and raises new questions that further research needs to answer.

**Keywords:** Digital management · Remote management · Management · Bibliometric analysis · COVID-19

## 1 Introduction

The novel coronavirus pandemic, declared in Spring 2020, by the WHO became the impetus of many changes in business and management [2]. Even though digital transformation had started several years ago, it was forced dramatically during measures taken by governments all over the world [3, 8]. Businesses had to adjust their business models and management approaches. Nationwide lockdowns that were introduced in many countries made remote management the only available option to maintain business processes. That brings close attention of practitioners and academics to the different aspects of remote management and its impact on the organisations and major organisational processes.

The purpose of this study is to provide an understanding of the challenges and opportunities associated with remote management in remote working, forced by the precautions during the COVID-19 pandemic. The respondents are young undergraduate students who represent "digital natives" [9, 10]. Thus, this study taps into the perception

D. A. Alexandrov et al. (Eds.): DTGS 2021, CCIS 1503, pp. 446–460, 2022.
https://doi.org/10.1007/978-3-030-93715-7_32

of the challenges and other specifics of remote work by the generation who has grown up under the influence of information technologies and online communications, in other words, in an environment that is natural (native) to them.

The paper structure is as follows. Firstly, the authors provide a bibliometric analysis of academic literature on remote management and digital shift in management with VOSviewer and highlight the differences in research "before" and "during" the pandemic. Secondly, they present findings from a qualitative study of students' understanding of remote management and remote manager, opportunities and challenges of remote management in remote work, and the impact of distance work on managerial aspects. The digital shift of management approaches and prospects for remote management are discussed, and further avenues for research are highlighted.

## 2   Bibliometric Analysis on Digital Shift in Management

We use a bibliometric analysis of papers to provide an overview of the recent research (since 2018) on remote management and the digital shift in management.

Publications indexed in the Scopus (scopus.com) global citation database were selected for the analysis using the following criteria: (1) Subject areas: Economics, Business and Management; (2) An occurrence of at least one of the terms "digital management"; "remote management"; "online management"; "digital transformation" in the title, abstract or keywords, or the combination of terms "digital shift" or "digitalisation" with "management"; (3) Published between 1st January 2018 and 28th February 2021.

The database obtained from Scopus contains 1,841 papers. Table 1 shows that the number of publications on this topic increased from 250 in 2018 to 905 in 2020. Moreover, 210 publications have been indexed in the Scopus database in 2021 (up until the end of February). 22 of these publications deal with the COVID-19 pandemic.

**Table 1.** The number of publications on digital shift in management, by year, 2018–2021.

| № | Year | Number of papers |
|---|---|---|
| 1 | 2021 (January and February) | 210 |
| 2 | 2020 | 904 |
| 4 | 2019 | 477 |
| 5 | 2018 | 250 |

Source: Retrieved from Scopus (https://www.scopus.com/) at 28.02.2021

VOSviewer Software (http://www.vosviewer.com) was used to analyse keywords co-occurrence. The main sample contains 7,743 author keywords. Following the standard procedure, a special thesaurus was developed to combine keywords in different forms or similar meanings. At the next step, keywords that indicate the methods of the study or type of the article (such as *design, methodology, structural equation modeling, literature review, surveys*) were excluded. Figure 1. presents the overview of the bibliometric study.

During the co-occurrence analysis, 40 different author keywords were identified at least 25 times. Table 2 shows five thematic clusters that were recorded with VOSviewer

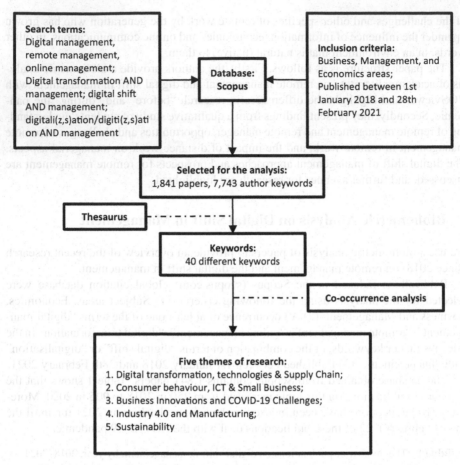

**Fig. 1.** Research design for the bibliometric study. Source: Developed by authors.

default parameters of keyword analysis (attraction $= 2$, repulsion $= 0$, and normalisation as an association method).

Figure 2 illustrates the distribution of themes from 2018 to 2021. The keywords that were intensively used in the first part of the period are coloured with violet, and the keywords of the recent trend are yellow. Following Fig. 2, different issues of technology adoption, big data, and information systems (these words mainly belong to thematic clusters 1 and 2) while industrial revolution, forced by the COVID-19 pandemic, is a fast-emerging trend. High attention in recent papers is given to changes in consumer behaviour, challenges for supply chain management, and small and medium-sized enterprises (SMEs) during the COVID-19 pandemic.

Connor M., Conboya K., and Dennehya D. (2020), studied the temporal complexity of remote working [7] within information systems development (ISD). They identified four challenges faced by remote ISD workers, such as (1) "failure to incorporate or adapt co-located social construction of time" [7, p. 10], (2) "mismanagement of types of time and social constructions of time" [7, p. 13], (3) "failure to capture changing frequencies

**Table 2.** Keywords of publications on digital shift in management indexed in Scopus, 2018–2021.

| № | Keyword | Number of occurrences |
|---|---|---|
| **Cluster 1: Digital transformation, technologies and Supply Chain** | | |
| 1 | Digital transformation | 194 |
| 2 | Big data | 58 |
| 3 | Supply chain management | 53 |
| 4 | Supply chains | 48 |
| 5 | Blockchain | 43 |
| 6 | IoT | 40 |
| 7 | Knowledge management | 36 |
| 8 | Information systems | 35 |
| 9 | Competition | 34 |
| 10 | Technology | 32 |
| 11 | Digital platforms | 28 |
| 12 | Information technology | 27 |
| **Cluster 2: Consumer behaviour, ICT and small business** | | |
| 13 | Social media | 60 |
| 14 | Decision making | 54 |
| 15 | ICT | 50 |
| 16 | SMEs | 49 |
| 17 | E-commerce | 46 |
| 18 | Technology adoption | 42 |
| 19 | Consumer behaviuor | 30 |
| 20 | Social networking (online) | 29 |
| 21 | Sales | 28 |
| 22 | Information management | 26 |
| 23 | Internet | 25 |
| **Cluster 3: Business innovations and COVID-19 challenges** | | |
| 24 | Digitalisation | 155 |
| 25 | Innovation | 86 |
| 26 | Digital technologies | 61 |
| 27 | Artificial intelligence | 50 |
| 28 | Business models | 39 |
| 29 | COVID-19 | 32 |
| 30 | Entrepreneurship | 30 |
| 31 | Open innovation | 30 |
| 32 | Co-creation | 29 |
| 33 | Technological development | 28 |
| **Cluster 4: Industry 4.0 and manufacturing** | | |
| 34 | Industry 4.0 | 151 |
| 35 | Manufacture | 35 |
| 36 | Industrial revolutions | 34 |
| 37 | Industrial research | 33 |
| 38 | Manufacturing | 25 |
| **Cluster 5: Sustainability** | | |
| 39 | Sustainable development | 59 |
| 40 | Sustainability | 52 |

Source: Authors' analysis with VOSviewer (http://www.vosviewer.com), 1841 publications

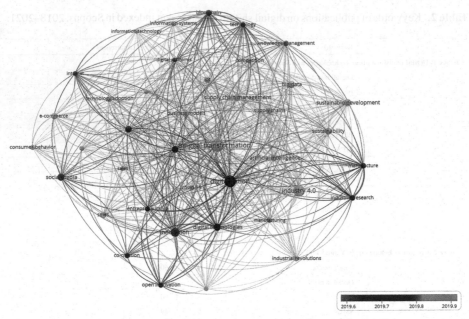

**Fig. 2.** Co-occurrence map of keywords in articles publications on digital shift in management indexed in Scopus, 2018–2021. Source: Authors' analysis with VOSviewer (http://www.vosviewer.com)

of events" [7, p. 14], (4) "mismanagement of various speeds of ISD communicational tools" [7, p. 15], (5) "mismanagement of entertainment of events" [7, p. 17], (6) "lack of awareness of changes in temporal personality" [7, p. 19].

Some researchers focused on the response of SMEs to the challenges of the COVID-19 pandemic [6, 11] and described the main approaches to cope with the crisis. They are associated with the digital transformation: adopting open innovation practices, digitalising sales, finding digital partners to reach the market, and overall accelerating transition toward a more digitalised firm [11], managers had to focus on new IT solutions [6]. Besides, some attention was paid to outcomes for global supply chains [4], vital changes in healthcare ecosystems [1, 5, 13], and to *servitisation* of manufacturing firms [12].

The COVID-19 pandemic accelerated the digitalisation of firms and led to dramatic changes in different aspects related to leadership and management [2]. Today, most of the articles are focused on the challenges of digital shift for "digital immigrants", who were used to in-person communications [9, 10]. It takes them time and effort to change the general way of thinking and working routine and adapt to digital context reinforcing remote management practices. The study of the opinion of digital natives, regarding modern management practices, could reveal new aspects which could be commonly overlooked.

# 3   An Empirical Study and Findings

## 3.1   Research Methodology and Sample

The exploratory qualitative online-research was conducted from April to June 2020 to study the perception of remote management specifics by digital natives, undergraduate students. The survey consisted primarily of open-ended questions in a semi-structured format to discover the general understanding of remote management, opportunities and threats, and its impact on the organisations and organisational processes.

The sample size was 189 people (age range 18–23 years old, 41% male and 59% female). To ensure the quality of the answers, only responses provided by undergraduate economics and management students were accepted for further analysis (127 participants, 18–22 years old, 36% male and 64% female). Table 3 presents the general information of respondents.

**Table 3.**   Empirical sample description.

|  | Gender | | Education specialisation: economics and management | | Work experience | |
|---|---|---|---|---|---|---|
|  | *Male* | *Female* | *Yes* | *No* | *Yes* | *No* |
| *Initial sample size N = 189, 18–23* | 78 | 111 | 127 | 62 | 70 | 119 |
|  | 41.3% | 58.7% | 67.2% | 32.8% | 37% | 63% |
| *Final sample size N = 127, 18–22* | 46 | 81 | 127 | 0 | 56 | 71 |
|  | 36.2% | 63.8% | 100% | 0% | 44% | 56% |

Source: Empirical study

The study clarified the general attitude of undergraduate students towards remote management, showed how they perceive its nature, key problems and challenges, and its impact on the company's various organisational characteristics, processes (communication, conflict, decision making, leadership, etc.). Study results empathised future research avenues (either repeated study based on the same sample or new comparative study to analyse how the perception has been changed during 1 or 2-year period; qualitative studies on "best" and "worst" remote management practices, etc.).

The next part of the paper provides findings on the key research questions:

(1)   What is remote management?
(2)   What are the challenges and opportunities of remote management?
(3)   Which aspects and processes of the organisation are mainly influenced by remote work?

**Table 4.** Remote management is... (examples of definitions).

| | Definition | Respondent |
|---|---|---|
| 1 | "a company management system, where physical contact of two employees is not necessary for effective interaction... their communication is established through remote channels (online calls, messengers, online services) and applications/tools (for goal setting and reporting)." | Male, 22 years old, has work experience |
| 2 | "management without real contacts...in current realities, this is art, and, to a significant extent, luck." | Male, 20 years old, has work experience |
| 3 | "team building and team management at any distance, where the goal of the manager is to build conditions, where every employee can perform his task and still connected with the rest of the team." | Female, 19 years old, no work experience |
| 4 | "a new type of management... like a traditional management, it has an inherent management structure, includes organisation, goals and people, but there is one specific feature – management occurs remotely, all interactions are carried out remotely – usually via digital technology that works as a communication tool." | Female, 20, no work experience |

Source: Empirical study

## 3.2  Results and Discussion

In this section, findings are organised around central questions with descriptions, quotes, and examples depicting them.

**Remote Management.** In a broad sense, respondents understand it as organisation management, including employees, activities, organisational processes, methods, systems, while the manager and team are located remotely. The employees interact using modern innovative technologies. Remote management is a set of managerial relations built in a virtual format. Table 4 presents examples of the answers provided by the undergraduate students.

To summarise, remote management is an *"art to combine various forms, methods and means of management for the effective work of various departments of the company at a limited physical presence... the distant manager plans and organises tasks and work processes, selects and uses methods suitable specifically for remote control, coordinates employees' virtual interactions to achieve the company's goals and results..."*. In short, it is the art of managing people, teams, processes, systems via digital tools without face-to-face contact.

According to the economics and management undergraduate students, the components of remote management include trust, independence and honesty of employees, an individual approach to each worker and team, self-management, IT components and software (technology, network, hardware), a coherent remote work system and scheme, remote communication channels, specific leadership qualities and management style. Part of them describes the requirements for managers, the second – for employees, the third – for organisations as a complex system.

**Challenges and Opportunities.** Remote management carries many *challenges*. They are grouped into several areas, such as managerial, technical, legal, psychological, mental, social and cultural.

The majority of respondents mentioned the following obstacles: limited working conditions (e.g., limited space, software), deterioration of interpersonal relationships (e.g., less engagement, understanding, moral support, development), reduction of work quality, increase of technical investments, emotional pressures (e.g., uncertainty about the future, limited socialisation, fear of a job loss, fear of a freedom loss), technological illiteracy, work-home conflict.

The most common challenges of remote management are listed below:

- how to perform managerial functions – remote planning and goal setting, remote organisation, remote motivation, remote control, etc.;
- how to shift business processes to remote format;
- how to maintain the involvement of the employees, teams, and departments;
- how to control and delegate;
- how to interact proficiently in a remote format;
- how to maintain remote employees' wellbeing and performance;
- how to organise paperwork;
- how to organise working space (either "in" or "out" the office);
- how to support privacy, etc.

Interestingly, some respondents underlined that remote management problems are interrelated:

*...In fact, all the obstacles* [respondent mentioned the problem of self-management, psychological issues, lack of community spirit] *revolve around one topic – the lack of the ability to "control" employees (both in a positive and in a negative sense).*

(female, 20 years old, no work experience)

*...Problems are lined up in a certain order – each problem subsequently originates from another. Communication barriers lead to a slowdown in business and decision-making processes. They form time lag – it becomes challenging to involve most of the employees in specific activities. This distorts the sense of involvement and leads to demotivation.*

(female, 22 years old, has work experience)

**Table 5.** Remote work (benefits).

| | Descriptions | Respondent |
|---|---|---|
| 1 | "It provides opportunities for employees – distribution of working hours as you wish, equal opportunities for people with disabilities, comfortable work conditions, as well as opportunities for employers – no rent for office space and work equipment, attraction of qualified employees from other regions, flexibility in setting the work schedule." | Male, 20 years old, has work experience |
| 2 | "Remote format makes it possible to work literally from any corner of the planet where there is an Internet connection, that means a person can explore the world, choose the most suitable place of residence (live outside the city without spending time and money on transportation). Many people have an individual biological clock (the remote format makes it possible to perform assigned tasks when you are most active). Working remotely helps to maintain a job and a constant income, which is challenging during the pandemic" | Female, 20, has work experience |

Source: Empirical study

Overall, remote management creates various complications for employees, managers, and organisations. One challenge could be daunting for a particular department or company and less for another, it depends on the preparedness for remote practice.

In response to a question about the ***opportunities*** connected with remote management, students underlined general benefits for employees, managers, and companies (see Table 5).

The most common benefits for the employees are "reduced expenses on traveling", "flexible work schedule and opportunity to achieve work-life balance (spend more time with the family)", "global interactions", "ability to find or keep a job in difficult situations", "sense of freedom and responsibility", "feeling of trust", "opportunity to mix several jobs or professions".

While, for the manager, remote practice allows them to "organise high levels of close monitoring and control", "opportunity to find employees globally", "transformation of the organisational processes", "ability to develop flat organisation structure based on networks".

The remote working practice provides numerous advantages for the organisation, such as "reduced office expenses", "access to cheap labour", "low staff turnover", "automation of organisation management processes", "development of electronic document management", "equal job rights for people with disabilities", "opportunity to create organisations of a continuous cycle", "opportunity going international, creating new markets or branches".

The results show numerous advantages and disadvantages of the remote working practice.

**Remote Work and Its Impact on the Company and Organisational Processes.** The shift to distant working models, mainly caused by the measures imposed to contain the COVID-19 pandemic, initiated various changes in companies. These truly affect the structure and characteristics of the job, business and intra-organisational processes, and many other components and elements of the organisations. In this part, the general aspects will be described.

*Changes.* Remote work format is a driver of positive and negative organisational changes:

> ..."*remote*" *and "change" are almost synonyms – everything changes constantly, unpredictably and rapidly. The transition to distant working resulted in adaptation to various changes, work and interactions adjustment, changes in the ways to deliver tasks to employees, etc.*

(female, 19 years old, has work experience)

> ...*most of the changes were negative... communication has become more compli-cated, organisational culture has suffered, leadership, employee motivation and development, decision-making – all these aspects of management have experienced some kind of "pain" during the shift to remote format.*

(male, 19 years old, has work experience)

> ...*significant changes occurred in many areas of the organisation, such as organi-sational structure, culture, control system, etc. Remote management required con-stant corrections, changes to maintain work efficiency. For example, my company established new rules and structures.*

(female, 19 years old, has work experience)

> ...*remote form of work had a positive influence, it was a kind of innovation...- work processes were digitised, the concept of managing an organisation was reconsidered.*

(male, 19 years old, no work experience)

Respondents with work experience put more emphasis on the negative aspects of the changes, while undergraduate students without experience – on the positive.

*Communication.* Remote work transforms data communication channels and forms of communications. Channels are narrowing, some verbal and emotional parts are miss-ing, communication becomes more formal, and feedback is limited. All in all, it leads to "communicational absenteeism". From the positive perspective, new channels and instruments are developing, transparency is rising, the boundaries of subordination are reducing. It can be concluded that remote managers might control and maintain information workflow to solve communication problems, one of their major tasks is to develop communicative strategies.

*Decision-Making.* On the one hand, it has become easier to make decisions, since it is not difficult to bring the whole team together in a virtual place. On the other hand, it is challenging to manage high uncertainty ("it is extremely difficult to make any decisions in the new digital reality") which affects both communication and decision-making processes:

> *...The level of uncertainty in the external environment increases, communication between employees becomes more complicated, it influences the process of decision-making.*

> (female, 19 years old, no work experience)

It can be added that remote working increases the autonomy of the employees, which escalates independent individual decision-making processes.

*Conflict.* Individuals expressed a controversial opinion about the conflict. Undergraduate management students believe that interpersonal conflicts in remote working are defused, though role and goal conflicts will occur more often. One of the common sources of the conflict might be a misconception. Moreover, there might be a shift towards a latent type of conflict. A remote manager has to develop appropriate distant conflict-solving strategies.

*Organisational Culture.* There is a high risk of culture diminution. How to sustain a company's culture when people work remotely becomes one of the challenging issues:

> *...management has to maintain the collective spirit and atmosphere, corporate identity, its uniqueness and integrity, positive psychological climate. Leaders have to establish new rules, traditions, values applicable for remote work.*

> (female, 22 years old, has work experience)

Leaders and managers need to take actions to support culture, they are driving forces influencing remote culture development. Cohesive remote culture might be based on specific values (e.g., equality, transparency, trust, mutual respect). It includes new social remote work rituals (virtual coffee and tea breaks, high five greetings, check-in in the virtual group chats etc.), digital etiquette. Overall, new manifestations of virtual culture will appear.

*Leadership.* The role of the leaders is significant. A remote leader is someone who has full access to information, who integrates, encourages, supports the employees and leads by example.

*...Leaders are important! They unite, support, help and make us believe that we are still appreciated. During the lockdown, our top manager made his best to clarify the situation, communicated informally via Zoom. It was a great support and motivation.*

(female, 22 years old, has work experience)

Remote leaders might practice participative leadership to impact employees' work engagement, psychological empowerment, job satisfaction, commitment. He empowers the team and makes the working process comfortable.

*Motivation.* The remote format opens up questions regarding the changes in the motivational aspect. Among new trends is a shift to autonomous and intrinsic motivation, focus on results, not working hours. Remote working has both positive and negative impact on motivation, respondents often used negative points:

*...level of motivation will decrease, because at work we usually satisfy different needs, such as the need for recognition, self-realization, and social needs. We need other people to stay in the "flow".*

(male, 20 years old, has work experience)

*...motivation weakens. Firstly, competition between employees disappears, it stimulated them to be productive. Secondly, there is no working atmosphere at home. Third, the problem of procrastination. Forth, the lack of direct control – you relax, you reduce the quality of your work. Finally, no one knows about your "everyday victories" and professional achievements, you lose the urge to self-development.*

(female, 20 years old, has work experience)

Since personal involvement decreases, remote managers have to be sensitive to the needs of employees, provide feedback, praise for small achievements, organise individual and group meetings, create a positive climate, etc.

In this study, we found how undergraduate economics and management students understand the general issues of remote management in remote working. It is worth noting that the results revealed controversial attitudes. By and large, the development of remote work has a strong impact on the processes of communication, organisational change, conflict, adaptation and development, leadership, etc., it can negatively affect various components (functions, processes, elements) of the organisation (e.g., organisational culture, motivation).

Communication as the most important intra-organisational process was mentioned when discussing opportunities as well as the key problems in the distant management format. Poor organisation of remote working creates misunderstandings, loss of valuable information, disruptions in the decision-making process and implementation of changes. It is important to prepare and provide high-quality, convenient and reliable technology for all employees, think over formal and informal ways of interaction between managers and team members. Remote work provides positive outcomes when it is designed well, when managers and employees are educated and prepared, when autonomy is high. Otherwise, a manager will practice ineffective micromanagement that will result in managerial mistrust.

Thus, in the era of digital transformations, effective interaction between a remote manager and remote employees requires the correct organisation of the work, as well as the use of innovative methods, tools, and technologies. These are essential elements to ensure the organisational resilience. To increase the competitiveness of a modern company, it is also necessary to develop human capital capable of providing high-quality remote management. It creates the necessity for the development and implementation of new educational practices.

Coronavirus disease accelerated the attention to issues concerned with remote management. Future studies might address current tendencies in the field of remote management. It would be interesting to conduct a repeated study based on the same sample or a new comparative study to analyse how the perception has been changed during a 1 or 2-year period.

The study raises new questions, that further research needs to answer. Since remote management is becoming ever more common practice, it is necessary to examine how remote management is perceived by managers and employees; how requirements for various positions (e.g., managerial, operational) have transformed before and after the COVID-19 pandemic; how companies manage interactions with external stakeholders during remote format; what digital technologies organisations use to support administrative and operational work; how various organisations implement remote practices and which challenges they face.

Although issues of digital transformation and business adaptation, as well as remote working, have shown particular importance in 2020–2021, it is worth emphasizing that many companies used the virtual interaction format long before. Further research comparing the experience of companies "born in" and "adapting to" the new reality can be useful to identify successful practices of virtual management, the culture of remote work, as well as to determine the specifics of the work of a remote manager and leader and the necessary competencies to organise business processes.

## 4    Conclusion and Future Research

The present study of digital natives represented by undergraduate economics and management students revealed an overall understanding of remote management, opportunities and challenges created by remote working format, as well as the impact that last has on the company and its organisational processes.

In general, students express controversial opinions about the positive and negative influence of distance working on remote management aspects. To make remote practices positive it is necessary to conduct deeper research on specific characteristics of the organisation, analysing specific business cases. It is important to pay attention to challenging points. Ignoring certain aspects of remote management, could raise problems and risks which can undermine the competitiveness and sustainability of the company in the digital economy age.

The study provides valuable insights into research questions and indicates further research avenues. More research is needed on current tendencies in the field of remote management in Russia and other countries. To get a better and more comprehensive understanding of the specifics of remote management, it is recommended to study the following issues:

- Remote management perception in a 2020–2021 period and onwards;
- Perception of remote management and remote work by managers and employees (both "digital natives" and "digital immigrants");
- New requirements for various positions (e.g., managerial, operational);
- Specifics of remote management with internal and external stakeholders;
- Digital tools and software used by the companies to maintain the working processes;
- Remote management implementation experience by big, medium, and small companies and/or by companies working in different spheres;
- Comparative analysis of managerial practices in companies, practicing "total remote" and "partial remote" (hybrid) working format;
- Comparative analysis of managerial practices in companies "born in" and "adapting to" the new digital reality;
- Factors, influencing the quality of work and management in remote format.

Remote management will undoubtedly continue to be a significant part of contemporary economics and business environment. It is required to conduct new qualitative and quantitative research investigating the appropriate remote management practices in the digital age.

**Acknowledgements.** The theoretical part of the research has been conducted within the fundamental research project "Digitalization as a driving force of open innovation and co-creation: Implications for value creation and value capture" as a part of the HSE Graduate School of Business Research Program in 2021–2023 (Protocol No. 23 dd 22.06.2021 of the HSE GSB Research Committee).

# References

1. Bahl, S., et al.: Telemedicine technologies for confronting covid-19 pandemic: a review. J. Ind. Integr. Manag. **5**(4), 547–561 (2020). https://doi.org/10.1142/S2424862220300057
2. Donthu, N., Gustafsson, A.: Effects of COVID-19 on business and research. J. Bus. Res. **117**(June), 284–289 (2020). https://doi.org/10.1016/j.jbusres.2020.06.008
3. Fetzer, T., et al.: Global behaviors and perceptions at the onset of the COVID-19 pandemic. Natl. Bur. Econ. Res. (2020). https://doi.org/10.31234/osf.io/3kfmh
4. Fonseca, L.M., Azevedo, A.L.: COVID-19: outcomes for global supply chains. Manag. Mark. Challenges Knowl. Soc. **15**(s1), 424–438 (2020). https://doi.org/10.2478/mmcks-2020-0025
5. Haleem, A., Javaid, M.: Medical 4.0 and its role in healthcare during COVID-19 pandemic: a review. J. Ind. Integr. Manag. **05**(04), 531–545 (2020). https://doi.org/10.1142/S24248622 20300045
6. Kukanja, M., et al.: Crisis management practices in tourism SMEs during the Covid-19 pandemic. Organizacija. **53**(4), 346–361 (2020). https://doi.org/10.2478/orga-2020-0023

7. Connor, M.O., et al.: COVID-19 affected remote workers: a temporal analysis of information system development during the pandemic. J. Decis. Syst. 1–27 (2021). https://doi.org/10.1080/12460125.2020.1861772
8. Petherick, A., et al.: Variation in government responses to COVID-19—Blavatnik School of Government (2020)
9. Prensky, M.: Digital natives, digital immigrants part 1. Horiz. 9(5), 1–6 (2001). https://doi.org/10.1108/10748120110424816
10. Prensky, M.: Digital natives, digital immigrants part 2: do they really think differently? Horiz. 9(6), 1–6 (2001). https://doi.org/10.1108/10748120110424843
11. Priyono, A., et al.: Identifying digital transformation paths in the business model of SMEs during the COVID-19 pandemic. J. Open Innov. Technol. Mark. Complex. 6(4), 104 (2020). https://doi.org/10.3390/joitmc6040104
12. Rapaccini, M., et al.: Navigating disruptive crises through service-led growth: the impact of COVID-19 on Italian manufacturing firms. Ind. Mark. Manag. 88, 225–237 (2020). https://doi.org/10.1016/j.indmarman.2020.05.017
13. Secundo, G., et al.: Digital technologies and collective intelligence for healthcare ecosystem: optimizing internet of things adoption for pandemic management. J. Bus. Res. (2021). https://doi.org/10.1016/j.jbusres.2021.01.034

# Labor Demand and Supply Adaptation to the Pandemic-Induced Shock
## Analysis of Online Recruitment Data in Novosibirsk region of Russia

Irina Sizova[1] ⓘ, Maxim Bakaev[2](✉) ⓘ, and Vladimir Khvorostov[2]

[1] Saint Petersburg State University, St. Petersburg, Russia
i.sizova@spbu.ru
[2] Novosibirsk State Technical University, Novosibirsk, Russia
{bakaev,xvorostov}@corp.nstu.ru

**Abstract.** In our paper we explore the development of labor market in Novosibirsk, a region of Russia's Siberian Federal Okrug, during the unprecedented events of 2020. In this, we rely on digital representation of the market, collecting the data from several online sources. These are the three popular Russian online job-related portals that publish vacancy and resume ads: HeadHunter, ZarplataRu and TrudVsem. We devise the joint taxonomy for the three somehow discordant portals to better cover the regional specifics and reveal the balance between workforce demand and supply in various industries in 2017–2020. The results of our analysis suggest while the supply, as manifested in resume ads, had short-term flexibility, no remarkable changes were noted in the demand. However, vacancies better reflect the situation in the labor market, even though the wages they propose were only 77.1% of the official wages for the region. The discovered lack of correlation between the numbers of the ads and the wages in the ads suggests that online recruitment is not competitive. Also, at least in the considered region, the recruitment through job-related portals largely involves straightforward and immediate hiring for less qualified and lower paid positions.

**Keywords:** Employment · Online data · Wages · Human resources · Industries

## 1 Introduction

The development of Internet and the Information and Communication Technologies (ICT) unavoidably affects the labor market [1]. This is reflected in the growing impact of various online job-related platforms where employers and employees can find each other. In 2019, surveys reported that job seekers named online job ads as the second most popular channel after informal enquiries with their acquaintances [2]. Meanwhile, in the current COVID-19 pandemic crisis these online platforms have further gained in significance: although the volume of the ads might have dropped in some countries, finding new occupations instead of the ones affected by the restrictive measures became crucial for many people [3].

© Springer Nature Switzerland AG 2022
D. A. Alexandrov et al. (Eds.): DTGS 2021, CCIS 1503, pp. 461–476, 2022.
https://doi.org/10.1007/978-3-030-93715-7_33

In our research we analyze labor market or a Russian region through online data – resume and vacancy ads placed on specialized online platforms. Three major platforms that currently operate in Russia are HeadHunter, ZarplataRu and TrudVsem. They generally report steady growth in the numbers of visitors and ads: e.g. HeadHunter has boasted a 26% increase in the number of published vacancies and 14% increase in the number of resumes in 2019. In the next year, despite the alleged hit that the employment took from the pandemic crisis, the vacancies grew already by about 37%, while the volume of resume ads was nearly unchanged[1].

The Russian Statistical Committee reported that the unemployment rate in Russia at the end of 2020 was 5.9%, a notable increase from 4.6% a year before. Some regions were especially severely hit by the pandemic and saw the unemployment exceeding 10%: Republic of Altai, Buryatia, Tomsk region, Tuva, etc. Novosibirsk region, which is the focus of our research, had unemployment rate of about 7% at the end of 2020, which is a rather low value for the Siberian Federal Okrug, but is higher than the Russian average. Due to different effects of the restrictive measures on various businesses, the number of people who change their jobs has grown, and information on current standings and prospects of various industries became particularly valuable. More than half of the temporary unemployed job-seekers in Russia never register with the state Employment Service and increasingly rely on specialized online services.

Naturally, both remote work and remote establishment of labor relations (which we shall call *online recruitment* in our study) became more common during the pandemic. While workers are rapidly losing their primary or traditional social ability, remote employment requires advancement in ICT proficiency, as well as in skills related to the new formats of work. The changes of the work formats and the communication norms in the job environment are likely going to affect the attraction of the workforce too. It is quite probably that even peripheral enterprises and workers, previously unaffected by the digital labor-related channels, will finally get involved and become the clients of the online platforms that we mentioned above. Accompanying these trends in the labor markets, the concept of "smart employment" is being formed within smart cities. It implies development of social humanitarian technologies that radically change the traditional understanding of industries and professions [4]. It also entails decision-making by a worker on his or her optimal career development based on the current and expected condition of the labor market, as reflected in the corresponding online data and trends in online environment. In fact, in the modern digitizing economy that is based on knowledge and ICT, the entire human labor activity undergoes transformation [5], and this is largely relevant for the labor market. As during any transition, innovations require conceptual understanding and practical decision-making. Decreasing the social tension is another important consideration in labor market analysis aimed towards understanding how its status and trends contribute to the country's welfare, how they stimulate economic development and support self-sufficiency of citizens and families. Implementation of a Russian national project scheduled for 2018–2024, "Work Productivity", requires promoting employment, studying trends in the digitizing labor market and developing effective mechanisms for investing into the country's social and working sphere.

---

[1] Data from https://stats.hh.ru, 18 March 2021.

The purpose of this study is to identify and investigate the changes in the Novosibirsk region labor market as it was affected by the unprecedented events of 2020, with its COVID-19 pandemic and the restrictive measures imposed by the government. We do so through the analysis of labor demand and supply as represented by the data available on online job-related platforms. We believe that better understanding of the gaining online recruitment can contribute to the overall reduction of forced frictional and structural unemployment, as well as provide better employment conditions for the young people who just start their careers. In Sect. 2 of the paper, we review some related work and detail our approach with respect to data collection and structuring. In Sect. 3, we present the results of the online data analysis and make some comparisons to the official statistics on wages. In the final section, we discuss the results and provide conclusions.

## 2 Methods and Related Work

### 2.1 Labor Market Research with Online Data

The usage of computing and modeling tools to extend the traditional employment statistics with online data is already widely established in research. Actually, the online environment in the context of labor studies is largely associated with *online employment* – i.e. the workers performing minor tasks over the Internet, basically in freelance mode. However, traditional employment still has greater scale, and the new field of *HR Mining* that is dedicated to extraction of data on employment and labor markets in various industries is being shaped. One of the cornerstone works is probably [6], which considered feasibility and effectiveness of web mining as a method for innovative research in the field. The authors reviewed strengths and weaknesses of the online data with respect to accuracy, completeness, timeliness, scale, flexibility and availability. In one of our own previous works on the topic [7], we have outlined and applied the following principles for assessing feasibility of online data collection: value for the customer, existence of "online footprint", legal and social acceptability, representativeness and stability of data sources, etc.

Among more recent practical applications in the field, we'd like to note the work [8], in which the data related to demographics, unemployment, etc. were collected for municipalities of Spain using web scraping, and then analyzed in R environment. It was demonstrated that creating such a database is useful to gain knowledge on economic activity both for the cities of Spain, and for individual citizens. Indeed, it is increasingly believed that timely and rational decisions today can only be made based on significant volumes of data. In a relatively recent large-scale research of labor market in the USA [9], they processed about 2 million vacancy ads to analyze the demand for IT skills. Thus they obtained a hierarchy of the skills and linked them to 30 professions of various complexities. In [10] the authors extracted qualification requirements towards researchers, engineers and other innovative specialists in Turkey from a large dataset. In the initial stage of this project, they performed automated classification of online vacancy ads based on classification methods. Another remarkable example of a sophisticated classification is [11], where the authors used ontologies (KNOWMAK) to match the results of their analysis and the decisions made by politicians.

Among the works of Russian authors we would like to note [12] that studied supply and demand in labor market using online data of July 2018, without considering the dynamics. An analysis of both Russia-wide and Ural Federal Okrug labor markets with HeadHunter's data was done in [13], but only for a single industry, Human Resources. We believe that accurate and multi-aspect datasets are the key concern, and discuss this in the subsequent chapter.

## 2.2 Data Sources and Data Collection

Currently, HeadHunter is clearly ahead of the other competing online platforms in scale, with its 60 million users. A few years ago, they started to provide analytical insights on the labor market-related data accumulated in their database, particularly through the novel *HH Index*[2] service. It focuses on the changes in the numbers of vacancy and resume ads per regions of Russia and per "professional fields", as well as tracks the "portrait of a job-seeker". The free service, however, does not allow analyzing data that is older than 1 year, and is reluctant to disclose absolute numbers (for the average wages, there is actually a good reason for that, which we will note later). Also, although HeadHunter is clearly the leader on the Russia-wide scale, in some smaller or remote Russian regions it does have strong competitors, such as ZarplataRu in Novosibirsk, whose data it does not cover entirely.

Correspondingly, in our research work we rely on labor market monitoring system[3] that we developed and launched in 2011 (see technical description in [7]). Currently it collects data for Novosibirsk region and some other regions of the Siberian Federal Okrug from several online platforms: HeadHunter, ZarplataRu and TrudVsem. Initially, all the collection was performed via web scrapping, but several years ago job-related online platforms, including HeadHunter, started providing API access, which gradually became the main collection method for our system. The system employs smart mechanism based on hash-code for detecting duplicate ads within and across the platforms, which are removed from the analysis (see [14] for details). After about 10 years of operation, the database of the systems contains over 10 million unique records with vacancy and resume ads collected from the platforms. The main labor market monitored parameters are numbers of ads per professions and industries, as well as proposed and requested wages extracted from vacancy and resume ads respectively. The calculation of average wages is not straightforward, since most of the platforms allow the users to specify the range (from M to N) in vacancy and resume ads, both ends of which are optional. So, in our system we have introduced the following empirical rules [14]:

- If N is not specified (the ad says "wages from M"), we accept the range as [M; M + 0.66M];
- If M is not specified (the ad says "wages up to N"), we accept the range as [0.66 N; N].

Correspondingly, the absolute values for the wages reported by the system and presented in the current paper **should not be considered the real ones**. Indeed, in one of

---

[2] https://stats.hh.ru/.

[3] http://sai.vgroup.su/ (in Russian).

our previous works [14] we note their disparities with the ones from the official employment statistics. However, comparisons between periods, industries, and ads types do make sense, so in our analysis we shall be mostly relying on relative values and change indexes. The data were aggregated by 6-month periods, which we denote as I-year and II-year, and the analysis runs from II-2017 (July, 1 to Dec, 31 of 2017) to II-2020 (July, 1 to Dec, 31 of 2020).

Some additional limitations in the current analysis are due to incompleteness of the data in certain periods, when the data collection encountered breaks due to technical problems with the monitoring system or with the online platforms. So, the shares of each data source in the analyzed datasets might vary across the periods, and the absolute numbers of ads are not entirely reliable. Another cause for bias in the research is disparities in categories employed for vacancy and resume ads by different platforms – for a handful of cases, direct matching could not be performed. In the following chapter we outline our approach to create the universal taxonomy of industries that we use in our study.

## 2.3   The Industries in Online Labor Market

First we consider the industries identified in the online platforms, with which it is possible to study labor demand and supply in Novosibirsk region in 2017–2020. Since the online platforms independently form the breakdown by industries for the labor market, the outcomes are notably different. Roughly, in the three platforms we identified about 62 industries for vacancies and about 50 industries for resumes.

Our assessment of the general structure of demand and supply in the labor market suggests very significant disparities. They concern not just the total number of structural elements in the set of resumes and vacancies, but also their content. To illustrate this, we present some notable examples in Table 1. We should also note that there are certain work activities that do not fit into the industrial breakdown of the labor market, such as *Start of career, students* or *Work for the youth*.

**Table 1.**  An example of different names of the industries for vacancy and resume ads

| In vacancy ads | In resume ads |
| --- | --- |
| *Banks, investment, leasing* | *Accounting, finance, banks* |
| *Accounting, management accounting, enterprise finance* | |
| *Purchases* | *Logistics, warehouse, procurement* |
| | *Sales, purchases, supply, trade* |
| *Arts, entertainment, mass media* | *Printing, publishing, mass media* |
| *Sports clubs, fitness, beauty salons* | *Sports, beauty, health* |
| *Personnel management, trainings* | n/a |

Since different online platforms present different breakdowns for the same labor market, it appears useful to make certain generalizations. In our opinion, the rather classical four-sector structure would be the most appropriate:

1. Sector 1 includes industries related to agriculture (land cultivation, husbandry).
2. Sector 2 incorporates the production and mining industries.
3. Sector 3 covers the provision of various services (finance, trade, etc.).
4. Sector 4 represents the modernized and new digital areas of the economy (IT, telecom, Internet, etc.).

Following this structure, we can summarize the industries identified in the different online platforms in the following model of the labor market (Table 2). When calculating the numbers of industries for the two last columns, we did not consider the names of the same industries on different online platforms; gaps in industries for certain periods were not taken into account; non-industry designations were excluded; generalized designations, such as *Service sector* or *Industry* were removed; some industries were linked to more than one sector, in which case they were counted several times; the result reflects data for the entire observation period. The difference between the numbers for

**Table 2.** The four-sector classification of the industries for vacancy and resume ads

| Sector | Industries | # in vacancy ads | # in resume ads |
|---|---|---|---|
| 1. Agricultural | *Forestry, agriculture, ecology, veterinary* | 2 | 2 |
| 2. Industrial | *Mining, equipment maintenance, woodworking, pulp and paper industry, logistics, warehouse, mechanical engineering, pharmaceuticals, metallurgy, food industry, printing, publishing, construction, transport, energy, chemical, fuel* | 15 | 11 |
| 3. Services | *Administrative work, auto business, finance, banks, housing and communal services, investments, leasing, security, guards, accounting, management, civil service, non-profit organizations, design, culture, education, science, healthcare, real estate, social security, mass media, repair, service, personnel services, consulting, marketing, advertising, personnel for home and office, trade, catering, beauty and sports, insurance, tourism, hotels, jurisprudence* | 34 | 29 |
| 4. Digital | *Telecommunications, IT, Internet, computer support* | 3 | 3 |

the vacancies and the resumes is due to the different industries that the online platforms use for these two types of ads.

As the data presented in Table 2 suggest, the most detailed classification is utilized is the one for the Services sector. It includes more than twice as many industries as the second largest sector, Industrial, while the other sectors include even fewer of them: the Agricultural sector that is presumably shrinking nowadays, and the new Digital one. So, the online recruitment appears to be mostly about various services. Our subsequent analysis is mostly not going to consider the industries belonging to the Digital sector, as internal (i.e. not characterizing the labor market) changes in IT-related professions taxonomy are too significant during the considered 3-year period.

## 3 The Analysis Results

### 3.1 The Dynamics of the Demand

There is a long-term growing trend for the numbers of ads in online job-related platforms, which is reflected by the data in Table 3, which shows dynamics for the numbers of vacancy ads (denoted by #) for the popular industries (that have at least 1000 vacancy ads in II-2020). The rightmost column shows the change of the industry's vacancies share in the considered set of industries during the period (II-2017 to II-2020), in percentage points.

As the data presented in Table 3 suggest, the greatest number of vacancy ads is published for the Service sector. The industries that constitute it are commonly recognized as widely popular and growing in Russia: trade, catering, finance, IT, etc. The aggregated Industry category (includes most of the industries from the Industrial sector except for the *Food industry*) has the greatest number of vacancy ads, but the sum of the numbers in the detailed industries related to the Service sector is far greater.

The analysis of the dynamics suggests that during the three years the set of the most popular industries did not change much. Only one industry has joined the list of the ones having over 1000 vacancies in the second half of 2020: *Work for the youth*. With a few exceptions, the shares of the industries did not change much either, as Table 3 demonstrates. The shares of vacancies have notably decreased for *Accounting, finance, banking, Office support staff* and *Sports, beauty, social welfare*. At the same time, the Industry sector saw the highest relative growth, as represented by *Production* and *Industrial personnel*. The three industries that had great losses that can be easily explained by the pandemic shock are *Marketing, advertisement and PR* (-55.6%), *Design, art and entertainment* (-50.6%), and *Tourism and hotels* (-41.9%). At the same time, the long-term workforce demand demonstrated remarkable growth for most of the industries – at least 36 of them, although it is hard to calculate for sure, due to their shifting names. Let us see how this was reflected in the wages proposed by companies in the vacancy ads.

### 3.2 The Dynamics of the Proposed Wages

Further we consider the wages proposed in the vacancy ads, in the assumption that they better reflect the situation in the labor market than the resume ads. The general trend

**Table 3.** Changes in the numbers of vacancy ads for the selected industries (2017–2020)

| # | Industry | # of vacancy ads in II-2017 | # of vacancy ads in II-2020 | Change of the share, pp. |
|---|----------|----------------------------|----------------------------|--------------------------|
| 1 | Production | 6483 | 9662 | +2.9 |
| 2 | Sales, trade, wholesale, marketing | 3826 | 6074 | +2.4 |
| 3 | Retail trade | 3822 | 4445 | -0.6 |
| 4 | Restaurants, cafes, catering | 3419 | 4233 | -0.1 |
| 5 | Transport, auto business | 3329 | 3797 | -0.7 |
| 6 | Information technology, internet, telecom | 2344 | 3445 | +1.0 |
| 7 | Logistics, warehouse, procurement | 2855 | 3436 | -0.2 |
| 8 | Industrial personnel | 1892 | 3313 | +1.8 |
| 9 | Construction, real estate | 2277 | 2626 | -0.4 |
| 10 | Education, science | 1782 | 2169 | -0.1 |
| 11 | Medicine and Pharmacy | 1536 | 2044 | +0.2 |
| 12 | Sports, beauty, welfare | 1700 | 1592 | -1.0 |
| 13 | Accounting, finance, banking | 2428 | 1539 | -2.8 |
| 14 | Office support staff | 1844 | 1479 | -1.5 |
| 15 | Consulting, strategic development, management | 1427 | 1455 | -0.6 |
| 16 | Food industry | 1280 | 1365 | -0.4 |
| 17 | Work for the youth | 767 | 1113 | +0.3 |
| | # in the entire set | 43,011 | 53,787 | +25.1% |

here is the overall wages increase in Novosibirsk region, which according to the Russian Committee on Statistics was 27.4% in 2017–2020 (an average of +8.4% per year). So, in majority of the industries there was absolute growth of the wages proposed in the vacancy ads, and in Table 4 we only present the industries for which the growth of the wages from II-2017 to II-2020 was higher or equal to the baseline of 27%.

The somehow arbitrary classification of vacancy ads by the online platforms makes it rather problematic to precisely calculate the growth in wages in specific professional groups. For instance, the category *Others* is pretty impressive in terms of increase in the number of vacancies and the proposed wages, but is understandably hard to detail. We can note from the Table 4 though that in certain industries (e.g. *Agriculture*) the wages regress to the labor market-average value, while in some others (*Government service, Construction*) the growth is relatively moderate, but they keep getting away from it.

Now let us compare the average proposed (in vacancy ads) and required (in resume ads) wages, to better understand the balance in the labor market (Table 5). We also include the official data from the Russian Statistical Committee for Novosibirsk region and for entire Russia, to set up the context for the online wages. The online wages are non-weighted averages for the considered industries.

Although the absolute values and the growth of the proposed wages were lower than the official statistics, the correlation[4] between these two types of wages were very high: $r_4 = 0.988$. Due to the sharp drop in 2020 (-10.53%), the requested wages had negative correlations with both the proposed wages ($r_4 = -0.704$) and the official wages ($r_4 = -0.588$). Thus, we can conclude that the resume ads represent the labor market situation differently and deserve separate analysis.

**Table 4.** Changes in the wages in vacancy ads for the selected industries (2017–2020)

| Industry | Proposed wages in II-2017, rub | Proposed wages in II-2020, rub | Growth |
|---|---|---|---|
| Mining | 23,994 | 42,871 | 78.7% |
| Government service, non-profit organizations | 28,000 | 44,918 | 60.4% |
| Agriculture, ecology, veterinary medicine | 13,831 | 21,526 | 55.6% |
| Career start, students | 19,931 | 30,352 | 52.3% |
| Arts, culture and entertainment | 13,127 | 19,985 | 52.2% |
| Forestry, woodworking, pulp & paper industry | 15,503 | 23,149 | 49.3% |
| Health care, sports, beauty, social security | 21,203 | 31,477 | 48.5% |
| Others | 21,495 | 30,940 | 43.9% |
| Home personnel | 22,133 | 31,459 | 42.1% |
| Construction, real estate | 32,565 | 45,834 | 40.7% |
| Installation and service | 27,277 | 38,082 | 39.6% |
| Design, art, entertainment | 23,332 | 31,977 | 37.1% |
| Chemical, petrochemical, fuel industry | 17,186 | 23,206 | 35.0% |
| Metallurgy, metalworking | 24,803 | 33,143 | 33.6% |
| Jurisprudence | 17,937 | 23,648 | 31.8% |
| Industrial personnel | 23,960 | 31,474 | 31.4% |
| Medicine, pharmaceuticals | 25,598 | 33,431 | 30.6% |
| Light industry | 15,885 | 20,439 | 28.7% |
| Work for the youth | 21,840 | 27,759 | 27.1% |

---

[4] We use Pearson correlation coefficients in the paper.

**Table 5.** Detailed dynamics of the online and official wages (2017–2020)

| | 2017 | 2018 | 2019 | 2020* | 2017-2020 |
|---|---|---|---|---|---|
| **Proposed wages** | 23,583 | 25,287 | 27,450 | 29,637 | +6504 |
| **(in vacancy ads), rub.** | | +7.23% | +8.55% | +7.96% | +25.67% |
| **Requested wages** | 21,678 | 22,052 | 22,068 | 19,745 | -1933 |
| **(in resume ads), rub.** | | +1.72% | +0.08% | -10.53% | -8.92% |
| **Official wages** | 32,287 | 35,686 | 39,076 | 41,120 | +8833 |
| **(Novosibirsk), rub.** | | +10.53% | +9.50% | +5.23% | +27.36% |
| **Official wages** | 39,167 | 43,724 | 47,867 | 51,083 | +11,916 |
| **(Russia), rub.** | | +11.63% | +9.48% | +6.72% | +30.42% |

\* The official data for 2020 is preliminary

## 3.3 The Dynamics of the Manifest Supply

The next important question concerns how the demand for workforce corresponds to its supply. We shall consider the resume ads in the online platforms placed during the same period of 2017–2020. First of all, we should note that it appears appropriate to use the same set of industries for resume ads as we did for the vacancy ads, as the data presented in Table 2 suggest that their numbers for each type of ads are roughly similar. The minor differences, i.e. the less detailed classification for the resumes, are rather imposed by the online platforms, which seem to have vacancies as the primary focus. In Table 6 we demonstrate the changes in the number of resumes per the periods of analysis (we only consider industries with over 1000 resumes in II-2020). The rightmost column has color coding for the cases when the differences between the industry's popularity in vacancy and in resume ads is greater than 1. Red color indicates prevalence of supply in the industry, green color indicates prevalence of demand.

The data presented in Table 6 suggest high oversupply of workforce in certain industries, particularly *Office support staff* and *Accounting, finance, banking*. The latter industry is also the leader in the shrinkage of the share, followed by *Top managers, directors* and *Construction, real estate*. On the contrary, *Retail trade* and *Restaurants, cafes, catering* saw considerable increases in the workforce supply, which is easily explained by the pandemic-related restrictive measures that hit these businesses the most. The total number of resume ads for the selected industries (54,227) has nearly matched the number of vacancy ads (53,787) in II-2020. So, the labor market tension coefficient that essentially corresponds to the *HH Index* went from 1.24 in II-2017 to 1.01 in II-2020, meaning that the competition for jobs has decreased. This is somehow puzzling, particularly in combination with the sharp drop in the requested wages in 2020 (see Table 5).

## 3.4 The Dynamics of the Requested Wages

Despite the general drop in the requested wages, for some industries they did increase, as we demonstrate in Table 7.

The data presented in Table 7 demonstrates changes during the whole considered period of 2017 to 2020, but there were also fluctuations within the period. The overall

**Table 6.** Changes in the numbers of resume ads for the selected industries (2017–2020)

| No. | Industry | # of resume ads in II-2017 | # of resume ads in II-2020 | Change of the share, pp. | No. in vacancy ads |
|---|---|---|---|---|---|
| 1 | Retail trade | 5162 | 7367 | +3.96% | 3 |
| 2 | Office support staff | 6230 | 6414 | +0.21% | 14 |
| 3 | Logistics, warehouse, proc. | 4653 | 4701 | -0.01% | 7 |
| 4 | Restaurants, cafes, catering | 2720 | 4586 | +3.38% | 4 |
| 5 | Transport, auto business | 4749 | 4517 | -0.53% | 5 |
| 6 | Production | 4120 | 4071 | -0.18% | 1 |
| 7 | Accounting, finance, banking | 6151 | 3663 | -4.72% | 13 |
| 8 | Industrial personnel | 1532 | 2632 | +2.00% | 8 |
| 9 | Medicine and pharmacy | 1167 | 2267 | +2.00% | 11 |
| 10 | Construction, real estate | 3653 | 2252 | -2.66% | 9 |
| 11 | Work for the youth | 1927 | 2246 | +0.55% | 17 |
| 12 | Education, science, lang. | 1152 | 1700 | +0.99% | 10 |
| 13 | Sports, beauty, health | 1160 | 1481 | +0.57% | 12 |
| 14 | IT and Internet | 2175 | 1428 | -1.42% | 6 |
| 15 | Top management, directors | 3006 | 1342 | -3.13% | n/a |
| 16 | Design, art, entertainment | 1481 | 1309 | -0.35% | n/a |
| 17 | Security and guards | 1502 | 1126 | -0.73% | n/a |
| 18 | Marketing, advertising, PR | 1066 | 1125 | +0.09% | n/a |
| | **# in the entire set** | **53,606** | **54,227** | **+1.16%** | |

**Table 7.** The growth of the requested wages for some of the industries (2017–2020)

| Industry | Requested wages in II-2017, rub | Requested wages in II-2020, rub | Growth |
|---|---|---|---|
| Industrial personnel | 15,532 | 34,086 | 119.5% |
| Design, art, entertainment | 12,240 | 18,611 | 52.1% |
| Security and guards | 15,623 | 21,233 | 35.9% |
| Home personnel | 8,074 | 9,821 | 21.6% |
| Construction, real estate | 19,688 | 23,835 | 21.1% |
| Education, science, languages | 10,260 | 12,282 | 19.7% |
| Office support staff | 15,451 | 18,057 | 16.9% |
| Retail trade | 16,514 | 18,180 | 10.1% |
| Work for the youth | 12,104 | 12,668 | 4.7% |
| Others | 15,634 | 16,329 | 4.4% |

dynamics of the requested wages generally corresponds to the dynamics of resume and vacancy ads in online platforms, thus reflecting unstable development of the labor market. Among the 30 industries for the resumes, only 10 had seen a growth in requested wages. The largest their increase in resumes was observed in the *Industrial personnel* industry, while for all the others growth was quite modest, at 1000–6000 rubles for the entire period.

Also, the data is indicative of the transformation of the job-seekers' requirements in each industry. For instance, in II-2017 the highest requested wages were in the *Top management, directors* category, with the average value of 27,023 rubles. The minimal requested wages were observed for such low-qualification industries as *Home personnel* and *Work for the youth*, but also, unexpectedly, for *Education and science*. Three years later, in II-2020, certain changes are clearly visible. First, the requested wages have increased for the *Industrial personnel*, achieving 34,086 rubles, which corresponds to the overwhelming 120% growth. Second, the set of industries with the highest and the lowest wages has changed too. Although the previous leaders had mostly lost their top positions, they remained as runner-ups: management, logistics, purchases, trade. At the bottom of the rating there are *Occupational safety and Human resources* (-64.2%) and *Agriculture* (-55.3%). *Tourism and hotels* and *Restaurants, cafes, catering* were understandably affected by the restrictive measures and saw decreases of 26.3% and 21.5% respectively. So, the general structure of the wages required by the job-seekers did not change much, but **has shifted towards the most and the least paid jobs**. The available online data suggest the growing divergency in the requested wages: on the one hand, low pay for a greater number of industries compared to 2017, but on the other hand rapid growth in certain industries and categories.

Then we calculated correlation between the numbers of resume ads and the requested wages in II-2020 for the 30 popular industries, which turned out not to be significant ($r_{30} = -0.032$). Further, despite the certain differences in the set of industries for vacancy and resume ads in the online platforms, we managed to match some of them by names. Another requirement for a data record to enter the sub-set was that an industry had at least 500 resume and at least 300 vacancy ads in II-2020. The total number of industries selected this way turned out to be 20, which is roughly equivalent to the size of the samples in our previous analyses. In Table 8 we present the comparison data, with the industries sorted by the tension coefficients (i.e. the ones with the highest competition for job-seekers' come on top), and also including the wages balance – the ration between the proposed and the requested wages.

The correlation between the numbers of vacancy and resumes ads per the industries turned out to be highly significant: $r_{20} = 0.725$ ($p < 0.001$). The correlation between the proposed and the requested wages was lower, but still significant: $r_{20} = 0.525$ ($p = 0.017$). The correlations between the number and wages were not significant in this sub-set, just like in the whole set of industries, neither for resume ($r_{20} = -0.073$) nor for vacancy ($r_{20} = 0.034$) ads. The correlation between the industries' tension coefficient and the wages balance turned out not to be significant ($r_{20} = -0.098$), in certain violation of the classical laws of economics.

**Table 8.** Numbers and average wages for vacancy and resume ads in II-2020

| Industry | Vacancy ads | | Resume ads | | Tension coef. | Wages balance |
|---|---|---|---|---|---|---|
| | # | Wages | # | Wages | | |
| Office support staff | 1479 | 24,385 | 6414 | 13,932 | 4.34 | 175% |
| Sports, beauty, health | 456 | 29,088 | 1481 | 11,861 | 3.25 | 245% |
| Top management, managers | 537 | 39,930 | 1342 | 34,086 | 2.50 | 117% |
| Accounting, finance, banks | 1539 | 28,665 | 3663 | 18,835 | 2.38 | 152% |
| Government services, NGOs | 346 | 36,955 | 731 | 14,072 | 2.11 | 263% |
| Work for the youth | 1113 | 27,759 | 2246 | 6,711 | 2.02 | 414% |
| IT and Internet | 729 | 33,932 | 1428 | 16,766 | 1.96 | 202% |
| Retail trade | 4445 | 23,607 | 7367 | 12,246 | 1.66 | 193% |
| Occupation safety, HR | 456 | 26,812 | 699 | 18,611 | 1.53 | 144% |
| Marketing, advertising, PR | 753 | 33,006 | 1125 | 12,282 | 1.49 | 269% |
| Logistics, warehouse, proc | 3436 | 31,708 | 4701 | 16,329 | 1.37 | 194% |
| Security and guards | 825 | 23,367 | 1126 | 12,668 | 1.36 | 184% |
| Transport, auto business | 3797 | 45,624 | 4517 | 17,315 | 1.19 | 263% |
| Medicine and Pharmacy | 2044 | 34,008 | 2267 | 9,821 | 1.11 | 346% |
| Restaurants, cafes, catering | 4233 | 22,564 | 4586 | 12,701 | 1.08 | 178% |
| Sales, trade, wholesale, marketing | 3279 | 33,958 | 3519 | 22,136 | 1.07 | 153% |
| Production | 4746 | 33,374 | 4071 | 18,880 | 0.86 | 177% |
| Construction, real estate | 2626 | 45,834 | 2252 | 21,233 | 0.86 | 216% |
| Industrial personnel | 3313 | 33,300 | 2632 | 12,302 | 0.79 | 271% |
| Education, science | 2169 | 19,711 | 1700 | 10,195 | 0.78 | 193% |

# 4 Discussion and Conclusions

In our work, we sought to analyze the changes in the labor market as it adapts to the unprecedented situation caused by the pandemic in 2020 and the imposed restriction measures – an urgent topic in today's sociology and economics [15]. For this end, we analyzed the data collected by our monitoring system from several online job-related platforms, not just the currently prevalent HeadHunter. The data were aggregated and averaged for the analysis, and given the possible biases in them we mostly relied on relative values and inter-period cross-industries comparisons. The main parameters were numbers of vacancy and resume ads and the wages specified in them, while the period of analysis was from July 2017 to Dec 2020. We believe our key findings are:

- the labor demand, as reflected by the number of vacancy ads and the proposed wages, was not affected by the 2020 pandemic much;
- the requested wages that were slower to grow even before the pandemic period, have diminished considerably during it;
- the wages proposed and requested in online ads are notably lower than the average wages in the region reported by the official statistics, so an average job seeker might be better off using other channels for employment;
- abundance or scarcity of human resources (job-seekers) in an industry does not affect the ratio between the proposed and the requested wages.

A well-known advantage of online data is that it allows capturing short-living phenomena. The reflection of the pandemic shock in the online job-related ads demonstrates that **online supply in the labor market has short-term flexibility, whereas online demand does not**. A quick and sharp drop in the requested wages took place in 2020 (Table 5), likely caused by the restrictive measure and the closing of businesses. At the same time, companies were seemingly reluctant or slow to change their online recruitment habits and did not cut on the proposed wages.

Overall, the online labor market implies a sort of **"double downshifting"** for a job-seeker (Table 5): 1) the wages proposed in online vacancy ads are just 71.1% of the official wages in the region, plus 2) the requested wages, at least given their drop in 2020, are just 77.5% of the average proposed wages. These phenomena however can be to some extend explained by the incompleteness of the information that companies and job-seekers disclose, as both sides have certain incentive to lower the wage level or hide one end of its range.

As expected, we found significant correlations between the proposed and requested wages ($r_{20} = 0.525$), as well as between the numbers of ads ($r_{20} = 0.725$) per the industries that we managed to match. This supports the validity of our approach and the collected data, and also suggests that wages is a more subjective parameter, while **numbers better reflect the balance in the labor market**. Somehow surprisingly from the perspective of economics, there was no significant correlation between the abundance or scarcity of job-seekers with respect to the offered vacancies (as represented by the tension coefficient) and the ratio between the proposed and requested wages (see in Table 8). Furthermore, the numbers and the wages did not correlate in neither type of the ads, which might suggest that **online recruitment involves no direct competition in neither demand nor in supply in the labor market**.

Our analysis of online data for the vacancy and resume ads placed in online platforms suggests that the open labor market is being formed. It is hardly unique compared to other ways to find jobs and employees; rather we should make the conclusion about the development of the online recruitment infrastructure in Russia. The geographic and socio-cultural context matters here, since in many nations government regulation of labor markets affects the online recruitment as well. In Russia, however, the absolute freedom and commercial interest of the online platforms lead to certain distinctive effects. One of them is structuring of the labor market by the industries, which are remarkably different from the official government classification. The overall direction of this process is shaped by the consumers – companies and citizens who use the platforms – who basically render their own vision of the names for the professions. As the result, a new taxonomy of professions and industries emerge, which, one could argue, better reflects economic reality. At the same time, the high dynamics of this structure, with the shrinking, emerging and partially duplicating industries, makes a formal analysis of the online recruitment much harder, if possible at all.

As the above considerations suggest unfinished and ever-transforming process, it can be indeed termed online recruitment, not just the labor market reflected in online platforms. As such, online recruitment does have certain specific features. First of all, currently it incorporates mostly facile and affordable labor, with trade and certain other mass services for the population as the most popular industries. The professions that involve more sophisticated economic relations are only fragmentary represented. One could assume that the economy in the region only requires simple jobs, but this is hardly likely. Rather we can conclude that the labor market is divergent, in the sense that job-seeking is done via corporate and other non-transparent channels, particularly for substantial positions. However, as further development will be shaped by the intensifying technological as social processes, it could take an overturning direction. The labor markets in online platforms can become analogues to gig-markets of the Western developed countries, with more and more work assignments being placed online (i.e. moving to the actual online employment). Another possibility is that the increasing freedom and equability of the online platforms, improvement of their services, would lead to the universal competitive labor market.

The limitations of our study include certain incompleteness of the data, for which we attempted to compensate by mostly analyzing relative, not absolute values. Also, we did not consider ICT industries from the Digital sector, since the related categories in online platforms are too unsteady and do not allow hard analysis. Actually, some features suggest that this sector is moving to other recruitment channels – ironically, IT doesn't hire online. Another possible explanation is that this industry uses other specialized online platforms that were not covered by the authors. All in all, we believe that the results we obtained for the Novosibirsk region labor market in the times of the unprecedented pandemic are of certain usefulness to both employment researchers and to policy-makers.

**Acknowledgment.** The reported study was funded by RFBR and BRFBR, project number 20-511-00011.

# References

1. Sizova, I.L., Grigorieva, I.A.: Fragility of labor and employment in the modern world. Sociol. J. **25**(1), 48–71 (2019). https://doi.org/10.19181/socjour.2018.25.1.6279-inRussian
2. Labor and Employment in Russia. 2019: Statistical Data Book, vol. 78, p. 44. Rosstat (2019). (in Russian)
3. Hensvik, L., Le Barbanchon, T., Rathelot, R.: Job search during the COVID-19 crisis. J. Publ. Econ. **194**, 104349 (2021)
4. Kaczorowski, W.: Die smarte Stadt-Den digitalen Wandel intelligent gestalten: Handlungs-felder Herausforderungen Strategien. Richard Boorberg Verlag (2014)
5. Carstensen, T.: Digitalisierung als eigensinnige soziale Praxis: Empirische Ergebnisse zur Social-Media-Nutzung in Unternehmen. Arbeit **26**(1), 87–110 (2017)
6. Gök, A., Waterworth, A., Shapira, P.: Use of web mining in studying innovation. Scientometrics **102**(1), 653–671 (2014). https://doi.org/10.1007/s11192-014-1434-0
7. Bakaev, M., Avdeenko, T.: Intelligent information system to support decision-making based on unstructured web data. ICIC Expr. Lett. **9**(4), 1017–1023 (2015)
8. Vallone, A., Chasco, C., Sánchez, B.: Strategies to access web-enabled urban spatial data for socioeconomic research using R functions. J. Geogr. Syst. **22**(2), 217–239 (2019). https://doi.org/10.1007/s10109-019-00309-y
9. Beblavý, M., Fabo, B., Lenearts, K.: Demand for digital skills in the US labour market: the IT skills pyramid. CEPS Special Report No. 154/December 2016. Demand for Digital Skills in the US Labour Market: The IT Skills Pyramid (2016)
10. Ozcan, S., Sakar, C.O., Suloglu, M.: Human resources mining for examination of R&D progress and requirements. IEEE Trans. Eng. Manag. (2020)
11. Maynard, D., Lepori, B., Petrak, J., Song, X., Laredo, P.: Using ontologies to map between research data and policymakers' presumptions: the experience of the KNOWMAK project. Scientometrics **125**(2), 1275–1290 (2020). https://doi.org/10.1007/s11192-020-03664-6
12. Maltseva, A.V., et al.: Features and trends in Russian labor market development with respect to workforce demand and supply. Soc. Labor Res. **4**(41). (2020). (in Russian)
13. Dolzhenko, R.A., Nazarov, A.V.: Demand and supply for HR specialists in labor markets of Russian and Ural Federal Okrug, as reflected in HeadHunter data. Bull. South Ural State Univ.: Econ. Manag. **13**(1) (2019). (in Russian)
14. Aletdinova, A., Bakaev, M.: Intelligent data analysis and predictive models for regional labor markets. In: Alexandrov, D.A., Boukhanovsky, A.V., Chugunov, A.V., Kabanov, Y., Koltsova, O., Musabirov, I. (eds.) DTGS 2019. CCIS, vol. 1038, pp. 351–363. Springer, Cham (2019). https://doi.org/10.1007/978-3-030-37858-5_29
15. Khamis, M., et al.: The early labor market impacts of COVID-19 in developing countries: evidence from high-frequency phone surveys. In: Jobs Working Paper, No. 58. World Bank, Washington, DC (2021)

# How has the COVID-19 Pandemic Transformed the E-Commerce Market on the Firm Level: Qualitative Insights from the Russian Market

Megi Gogua[1]([✉]) [iD], Vera Rebiazina[2] [iD], and Maria Smirnova[1] [iD]

[1] Graduate School of Management, St Petersburg State University, St. Petersburg, Russia
{m.gogua,smirnova}@gsom.spbu.ru
[2] HSE University, Moscow, Russia
rebiazina@hse.ru

**Abstract.** Due to markets' digitalization, both consumers and businesses are increasingly involved in e-commerce activities throughout the globe. Current study aims to investigate what drives and what limits firms' integration into e-commerce activities with the focus on comparison of pre-, during and post-pandemic foci by the firms in Russian emerging market. The study is based on insights from qualitative interviews of firms' representatives, collected in 2016 and 2021. Based on comparison of interview's insights and content analysis, we identified the influencing factors from the firms' perspective, further we also introduced potential consequences of the pandemic based on the respondents' replies. One contribution of this study is to identify the limiting and the driving factors that are specific for the Russian e-commerce market. Besides, we discover some factors that can supplement the current frameworks for structuring the limiting and the driving factors of the e-commerce market. In addition to that, based on the theoretical and empirical research conducted, we can state that the factors influencing e-commerce five years ago and now are evolving rapidly and may lead to more prominent changes.

**Keywords:** E-commerce · E-commerce potential · Emerging markets · Russia · The COVID-19 pandemic

## 1 Introduction

When e-commerce entered the realm of business, it redefined the structure of the market, affected consumer behavior patterns, and required that both firms and consumers develop new skills and abilities. This type of commerce has become one of the factors of the active digital transformation of the economy and society, and its effects can be classed as positive, negative, and ambiguous. The COVID-19 pandemic had caused a significant impact on the e-commerce development and offered a potential for the extensive research.

Current study seeks to compare the factors that drove or limited the development of Russian B2C e-commerce market in 2016 (during the crisis) with those that were obtained in 2021. Because of the exploratory nature of the study we conducted qualitative research, interviewing the representatives of Russian internet businesses; doing this allowed us to

D. A. Alexandrov et al. (Eds.): DTGS 2021, CCIS 1503, pp. 477–490, 2022.
https://doi.org/10.1007/978-3-030-93715-7_34

ensure a preliminary validation of the results. The comparison is based on the theoretical model developed through our literature review.

The choice of the market and the timing of comparison is of particular interest. Before 2014–2015 Russian e-commerce market was booming, demonstrating impressive growth rates, and involving more and more consumers. However, Russian Federation went through drastic changes in 2014–2015 (which include, for example, the introduction of a new legislative framework, an economic and a political crisis, an increase of number of mobile devices in use, as well as dramatic decrease in consumers' real incomes). Further data gathering in 2021 is explained by the COVID-19 pandemic strong impact on the market and consequent changes of the perspectives of the business practitioners in terms of the necessity of moving online to keep the customers during the social distancing, engagement in the extensive online promotion to survive among competitors, and redefine existing communication with customers. Finally, based on the experience of the pandemic period further development of e-commerce is due to the changed behavioral pattern of the consumers and their rapid integration in the online platforms.

The aimed contribution of the study is twofold: firstly, we develop the theoretical perspectives on e-commerce market development through the lens of the specifics of emerging markets on the example of Russia. The topic of the influence of COVID-2019 pandemic in particular countries is developing [28, 29] and current paper adds to this trend. Secondly, this paper's empirical analysis of the driving and limiting factors of e-commerce market development helps create a profile of factors that are relevant when viewed from the perspective of theoretical investigation, managerial effort, and consumer perception. Finally, we investigate the changes in perception of what drives firm's behavior and choices before and due to pandemic effects.

## 2 Theoretical Framework

### 2.1 What Influences E-commerce in Developed and Emerging Markets?

Whenever we talk about e-commerce, we need to properly define the term, explaining why we chose to use this term specifically. According to research, there are several other terms that are similar to "e-commerce" or are even synonymous to it. These terms are "e-shopping", "online shopping", "online purchasing", "e-trade", "e-purchasing". Even though all of them relate to the transactions on the Internet, they differ by the purpose and the object they refer to. E-trade can be regarded as the broadest field of the electronic mechanisms that use technology and the Internet; it does not only cover commercial transactions between economic agents but also includes the consumers' (e.g. investors') processing of stocks (graphical financial information), relates to the financial products and services, public and governmental policies, and consumer welfare [9], banking and lending systems [10]. E-shopping (or internet shopping) is considered as a way of shopping and is related to the understanding of the consumer behavior patterns, with their specific traits and characteristics, such as gender [1], the desired consumer experience [3], and digital engagement and sentiment [8]. A similar approach is described by the term "online shopping" [7]; however, it adds specificity to the means by which the purchase is made [4]. Also, whenever we talk about buyers' involvement in "online shopping", we must keep in mind that these individuals are subject to the influence of online recommendation and review systems and agents [2, 7], with the reference to the established online shopping paradigm [5], implying the influence of prior experience on the further purchase intentions of the consumers, as well as information availability and the disclosure of information to manipulate alternative choice selection [6].

We can note that the topics associated with the aforementioned terms reflect the attitudes of consumers towards their purchases (represent consumer perspective) and marginally cover firms' perspectives. In this research, e-commerce is defined as any type of purchasing or selling goods and services by large and small firms via the Internet [19]. Analysis of extant literature indicates that the factors – incentives and barriers to e-commerce market development – are rather inconsistent in terms of naming, grouping, and content [14]. Figure 1 presents the scheme of the existing influencing factors: a general classification by external, internal, and dualistic [11, 12] factors was further redefined as environmental, organizational-/store-related, and product-/service-related [11–18, 20, 21].

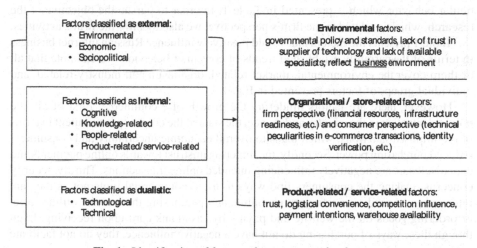

**Fig. 1.** Identification of factors of e-commerce development

The relevance of the Fig. 1 is ensured at the stage of data collection: the questions of the semi-structured interviews employed the refined factors' set to touch upon for further investigation. Additionally, the factors listed in the Fig. 1 set the boundaries for the Russian market analysis in the following subchapter.

### 2.2 The Limiting and Driving Factors of E-commerce on the Russian Market

The Russian market has been turbulent in the recent years due to Russia's economic difficulties and uncertain political situation, which led to the changes in the business environment after 2014–2015. However, even though certain stagnation became evident, a slow but positive growth in e-commerce and in the number of consumers is apparent. According to statistics [22], the share of online consumers was as high as 42% of the whole population in 2019. In addition to the growth of e-commerce consumers, the distribution of the means used for making purchases has also changed – the number of purchases made on smartphones increased from 10% in 2016 to 30% in 2019, which can be explained by the fact that firms have been getting more involved into providing consumers with more secure and convenient tools for shopping and are hence getting more proficient in this type of commerce. There are evident changes in terms of what payment methods are in use on the Russian market. According to Statista, the most commonly used means of payment is still cash on delivery; however, this situation may change in the coming years because of developments in the bank transfer system. However, lack of trust towards internet business is declining – this trend can be seen from statistics, which indicate a clear increase in the share of orders that are paid for before delivery takes place, rather than when the shopper receives the order [22].

Consumer profiles also show that buyers are becoming increasingly competent when making purchases and are able to use technological advancements that businesses provide, making more economically advantageous decisions. Using a 2019 study conducted by Google, Ipsos and Kantar TNS, the average Russian online consumer shows a particular behavior, which is presented in Table 1. In order to pursue the objective of the research, which is related to the firm's perspective, we also identify the firm's activities.

Table 1 presents the factors that would positively influence Russian internet business in terms of the currently established trends of consumer behavior. We can note that all of them cover the environmental, market-related, organizational, industry-related, and individual groups of factors presented in Fig. 1.

However, there are factors hindering the growth of e-commerce. First of all, the political situation in the country and, hence, the state of the economy is turbulent in terms of the imposed sanctions, which leads to overall economic uncertainty and consumers' reduced purchasing power. Secondly, the lingering mistrust towards online payments and data disclosure are negatively influencing intended online transactions. Thirdly, security concerns, making the consumers find ways to use e-commercial tools not as they are intended to be used – selecting goods online and purchasing them at the offline store, or ordering goods on the website and paying by cash/bank card upon receiving. Even though these ways of purchasing do not have a negative influence, they do not facilitate e-commerce either.

## 3  Research Design and Methodology

The study is explorative with the objective of revealing the limiting and driving factors of e-commerce market development in Russia from the firm perspective. To identify limiting and driving factors of e-commerce market development in Russia, 60 in-depth interviews with representatives of Russian internet businesses to consider firms' view of the driving and limiting factors were conducted. Firms contain more expertise and knowledge about current market situations, that's why the in-depth interviews are chosen as the most relevant method of gathering information. Also, companies comprising the sample represent different industries, and vary in size and location. That's why they have a better picture of the real factors that drive and limit e-commerce market development in Russia. Next step was to conduct the interviews in 2021 to reflect the changes that evidently arose after the COVID-19 pandemic. For these purposes additional 10 interviews took place in February 2021, also including the suggestions of the respondents

**Table 1.** Russian consumer traits are required activities of the firms to support such behavior

| Consumer behavior patterns | Firm's (brand's) corresponding activities (The driving factors of e-commerce market in Russia) |
|---|---|
| Regularly compare prices and the conditions of delivery, they rarely make purchase in the first online shop; Require immediate information about the price | Clear web-site of the online shop with stated options of delivery and payment Unique products and correct pricing policies |
| Appreciate clear navigation at the web-site and logical structure | Reliable servers to support online operations Clear web-site design Clear marketing strategy with consumers' needs identification |
| Usually look up products and information on Google, Yandex, and AliExpress, YouTube and Google Maps | Careful e-word-of-mouth control; Understanding of the consumers' needs and preferences at particular geographical locations (even within one country); Strong social network presence |
| Require accurate and clear information about the products, require section with the feedback of people who have already purchased the selected item | Automatic updates on the web-sites – utilization of new technological tools for consumers' better experience, and for internal faster proceeding of the information and orders |
| Appreciate loyalty programs and free delivery | Inclusion of gamification in the marketing activities; understanding of the needs of the consumers in relation to the gifts they would like to obtain and hence creating the intention to participate |
| Appreciate the section "Favorite" at the web-sites to safe the items they liked | Use of the personalization tools and recommendation systems for fast and convenient consumer experience Careful control regarding the personal information and security issues to keep the consumers with high perception of risk |
| Require fast delivery, hence prefer delivery with the tracking, or picking up from the offline shop to avoid waiting for the delivery; require fast and simple way of payment; Prefer high variety of selection: of products and categories, options of delivery and payment; Claim that the privacy of the payment is the most important criterion of the website/online shop selection | Expansion of the geographical presence for faster delivery, or engagement with delivery organizations for specific types of delivery (and quality, for example, for medical goods); Cooperation with banks and implementation of their payment systems, and payment services (Yandex.Pay, Qiwi, etc.); Legal support in terms of financial transactions |

Source: Consumer behavior patterns – Google, Ipsos and Kantar TNS, 2019; Firm's (brand's) corresponding activities – developed by the authors

regarding the possible development of e-commerce after the COVID-19 pandemic. The further sequence of 10 interviews enriches prior findings with respect to the emerging issues of caused by the ongoing pandemic.

*Sampling.* In-depth interviews contributed to identifying e-commerce limiting and driving factors from the firm perspective. The respondents were the managers, representing strategic decision makers and/or responsible or related to the e-commerce activities in a firm, were selected and interviewed. Purposive selection was used, following accepted qualitative interview criteria. Respondents varied in age, gender and position in the company – from the marketing specialist or digital manager to the head of the project, CEO or the owner of the firm.

The firms that composed the sample are different in size (SME and large firms) and industry, segment (product or service) and location of the headquarters (Moscow and St. Petersburg where 51.6% of e-commerce market sales proceeds are generated). The operations sectors of the firms were diverse, as they covered educational, retail and consulting agencies. The diversity of the sample guaranteed variety in the set of opinions, identifying the variety of different e-commerce market barriers and drivers.

Sixty in-depth interviews were conducted from February 2016 to November 2016; additional ten in-depth interviews were conducted in February 2021. The questions for the semi-structure interviews covered the factors identified in the Fig. 1 and allowed for further elaboration based on the nature of the companies.

*Interview Procedure.* All interviews with the respondents were conducted personally or by Skype. The duration of interviews ranged from 30 to 60 min. The in-depth interviews were conducted in Russian. The respondents were asked to give the interviewer their permission to record the conversation and use some statements for citation purposes in future. The guide for the in-depth interview was semi-structured and included questions about the firm's profile, its marketing activities, and the specifics of e-commerce development in Russia, including driving and limiting factors. If the respondents did not answer the question in full, the interviewer suggested clarifying or additional questions. The obtained data was analyzed using content analysis [23] for the data collected in 2016 and the preliminary results of the data collected in 2021.

# 4  Results of the Empirical Research

Based on the content analysis of the interviews in 2016, 87 semantic items describing obstacles of the e-commerce market development in Russia were identified and grouped into 13 limiting factors, while analyzing of the first wave of collected data revealed 62 semantic items and 13 limiting factors. In 2021 the preliminary results focused on the transition to the online environment, the difficulties associated with this transition and potential further development.

Barriers connected with the customers, their perception of the online shopping in general and online shops in particular are among factors that can adversely affect the e-commerce market. For example, 20.9% of respondents in 2016 mention trust as the core barrier. Respondents noted that the quality of the products, cashless payment and other issues are jeopardizing consumer trust. The central role of trust is in line with existing research [24–26]. Another core barrier is related to the overall economic situation in Russia that has worsened over the year 2019, mainly due to a sharp weakening of the ruble and accelerated inflation which has led to reduced demand in the consumer market. The same topics were identified in the interviews conducted in 2021, as with the increased penetration of new customers to the online segment, the issue of trust and appropriate infrastructure became of high significance.

In general, the results of interviews provide overlaps with theoretically derived limiting factors, e.g. inadequate logistics, weak legal and regulatory frameworks, problems with data protection. On the other hand, previous research does not reveal barriers directly related to the company's activities like marketing activity or problems inside the company.

Interestingly, a small number of respondents in 2016 indicated that they did not see any barriers. The construct "no barriers" was named with the frequency of 3.9%. As one interviewee said, *"We have difficulties, but not problems"*. This view was echoed by another respondent who stated that *"there is no problem, there is a task. You simply need to up and do something. Often the barriers are only in your head. Nothing prevents the creation of online business; you just need to work"*. Also, respondents pointed out that they faced problems in the past, but now their interactions with partners, suppliers and clients are completely adjusted. The same approach was in 2021, as the respondent said that there are *"no barriers, just nuances, specificities"*.

Overall, these results indicate that the pressure of the market environment, especially from the consumer behavior, and the economic and market situation were the most striking constraints of e-commerce market development in Russia. Infrastructural and institutional challenges were also pointed out as the important barriers. They reduce the overall motivation for this type of business, and also weaken the competitive position of small companies compared to large contractors (suppliers and major competitors). The COVID-19 pandemic influenced the Russian market even further, since it moved the customers to the online environment within the introduced social distancing. The infrastructural and institutional challenges remained; however, their impact was mitigated due to the increased motivation of the firms to keep their customers through the online channels (*"we learn how to address the customers through online channels"*). These challenges were also addressed by the governmental facilities through certain financial waivers and financial support.

Among the most frequently mentioned driving factors in 2016 were those that relate to the overall market development. More than 30% of respondents said that despite the fact that the year of 2015 was difficult, they are optimistic due to significant growth of the market during the following years. The increase in the number of buyers in conjunction with changes in the internal activities of online stores (e.g., expansions of the range of goods, the pricing policy review, the promotion effectiveness), and the increase in the share of the regional sales creates favorable conditions for the e-commerce growth. Moreover, every eighth respondent pointed out that firms are not using their potential in a full measure and see a lot of opportunities to develop their business by making changes in operating activities. This process was indeed fueled by the market changes in 2020 due to the COVID-19 pandemic as the firms begun to engage in more complex customer communication and goods promotion (through the personalization tools, targeted and contextual marketing, marketplaces, and viral marketing through the social media).

The second most popular driver is consumer behavior. Interviewees commented that despite the economic crisis and reduced consumers' willingness to pay, they do not stop buying online, realizing the benefits of the online shopping. Still, consumers are become more demanding, requiring better service and higher professionalism, this creates opportunities for more customer-oriented strategies. This trend was also recognized during the COVID-19 pandemic, because even though the customers were forced to buy online due to the social distancing, they were attentive to the quality of the products, the variety of which was expanded due to the increased number of sellers. The penetration of unscrupulous sellers to the online market and the limited digital literacy of new customers in the e-commerce for quick recognition of untrustworthy deals led to the need for more information to the customer about the sources of the products, characteristics and the secure payment. The need for quick and careful delivery and return was also identified based on the respondents' replies.

The most significant growth opportunities in the respondents' opinion are associated with the development of technology and infrastructure. Moreover, offering innovative and more customized products and services is considered as the important driver for the e-commerce market in Russia.

## 5    Discussion and Managerial Implications

This study provides a theoretical analysis of driving and limiting e-commerce market factors and identify limiting and driving factors of the e-commerce market development in Russia particularly from the firm perspective. In reviewing a literature, we identify different approaches to structuring the limiting and driving factors. We summarize the proposed frameworks into such groups of factors as environmental, organizational/store-related and product-related/service-related factors. Empirical investigation of the Russian e-commerce market contributes to the suggested framework by adding the market-specific findings. Also, we found that issues concerning consumers, trust and security are the sources of e-commerce market development. In terms of comparison of the pre-COVID-19 pandemic state of e-commerce, current state and the possible future developments, it is possible to notice that the factors remained the same, however, the approach and the extent of their development have changed.

One of the main features that differ emerging markets from developed ones is inadequate infrastructure [27]. Infrastructure includes some elements, among which a complex logistics system for the distribution of goods; transport systems that provide customers with easy access to point of sales; universal telecommunications services; financial services, etc. [27]. While it creates the basic conditions for doing business, Russian firms consider the infrastructure as one of the most significant barriers for the Russian e-commerce market. Market participants even suppose that overcoming barriers related to the infrastructure is the key to win the competition.

While it creates the basic conditions for doing business, Russian firms consider the infrastructure as one of the most significant barriers for the Russian e-commerce market. What is important, consumers also stress the importance of this factor, emphasizing the delivery conditions as the driver for online purchasing.

Trust is one of the limiting factors for the Russian e-commerce markets from firm perspective. At the same time trust is driving factor from the consumer perspective and associated with the store-related group of factors – perceived transparency and trustworthiness. Thus, it seems that revealed structuring of e-commerce market factors are quite relevant to the emerging context because it can capture the specifics of the market, can show its controversial nature and underdevelopment status.

This study also supports the proposition that content of the factors depends on the perspective chosen for factors' investigation. Results presented in the Table 2 detect the evidence for this claim: factors content depends significantly on the investigated perspective. Moreover, some factors have an ambiguous nature because in dependence of the perspective they can be either external factors or internal ones. Organizational factor exemplifies this idea. Firms consider organizational factor as internal and mention here firm's potential, financial capabilities or problems inside the firm, in contrast – for consumers firms are the part of their external surrounding. In Table 2 the most commonly mentioned factors are highlighted though the bold letters.

According to the Table 2, the indicated factors are evolving according to the customer behavior and their needs, as well as the economic profitability and efficiency. The section on the tentative predictions on the COVID-19 pandemic consequences based on the Russian business representatives' responses allows to indicate that the e-commerce has a strong potential and the customers will continue to engage in the online environment.

**Table 2.** Results of perspective study on the e-commerce market development in Russia through the firm focus

| Before the COVID-19 pandemic | | |
|---|---|---|
| Environmental | **– Average growth of e-commerce**<br>– Availability of warehouses in the regions and offline shops is beneficial<br>**– Infrastructural fragmentation for delivery and customer support** | |
| Organizational | Firm perspective | – High costs and limitations of delivery to the regions<br>– High financial spending for online payment systems' utilization |
| | Consumer perspective | **– Lack of trust to the online procurement**<br>– Unwillingness to pay online and concerns about payments' security |
| Product-/service-related | – Inclination to e-commerce for cheaper products compared with offline prices<br>– Willingness to buy online good quality goods | |
| During the COVID-19 pandemic | | |
| Environmental | **– Difficulties in keeping up with the trends of e-commerce due to the rapid changes caused by emergence on new products and services (medicines, online education, online entertainment, online babysitters, etc.)**<br>– Sharp and rapid growth of e-commerce due to the inclusion new players and stakeholders<br>– Limitations of foreign payment systems' availability in Russia (& high commissions for using the existing ones)<br>– Lack of infrastructure in the Russian regions became the core issue<br>– High prices for the e-commerce infrastructure development<br>– Price war between online and offline and the limitations of access to the latter<br>– Need for the investments due to better recognition of technological and logistical needs (warehouses management and delivery control) | |

(*continued*)

**Table 2.** (*continued*)

| Before the COVID-19 pandemic | | |
|---|---|---|
| Organizational | Firm perspective | **– Lack of control in delivery process and its duration**<br>– Increased attention at the average check to avoid free delivery of cheap goods and, hence, unworthy expenses<br>– High prices for online promotion (including IT and software for data allocation and processing)<br>– Expensive warehouse keeping (due to the turbulence and, hence, difficulty of product orders planning)<br>– Customer "banner blindness" during promotion due to the increased intentions of firms to promote themselves |
| | Consumer perspective | **– Lack of competences for online purchases due to the lack of experience and knowledge about online purchase process**<br>– Inability to see the product before purchase and test the quality and characteristics<br>– Unwillingness to learn new type of purchase (online)<br>– Unwillingness to pay for delivery<br>– Unwillingness to use outdated formats of internet-shops without filters and sorting options |
| Product-/service-related | **– Mistrust to the quality of goods due to the increased rate of penetration of low-quality and counterfeit**<br>**– Lack of information available for the customer about the product, the seller and the online purchase process**<br>– Mistrust to confidentiality regulations and payment security<br>– Less quality communication with customers due to increased sales and lack of employees | |
| After the COVID-19 pandemic | | |

(*continued*)

**Table 2.** (*continued*)

| Before the COVID-19 pandemic | | |
|---|---|---|
| Environmental | – **Modification of business models to the necessity of inclusion of online features**<br>– Increase in importance of infrastructure for the growth during pandemic<br>– Increased perception of lacking infrastructure by market participants<br>– Increased potential for further investments due to the increased awareness of the firms regarding e-commerce potential and increased number of firms with online presence<br>– Redefined education towards the online platforms | |
| Organizational | Firm perspective | – **Engagement in the online promotion to have enough competitiveness among other firms**<br>– Extensive implementation of distance work to further avoid meeting other people in case of sickness |
| | Consumer perspective | – **Customer' changed attitudes to the online purchases and increased of the levels of participation in online activities**<br>– Strong online presence both as a customer and within the social media<br>– Increased digital literacy and capabilities due to the forced relocation to the online environment |
| Product-/service-related | – **Rise of online consulting, education and services**<br>– Opportunities for everyone who decides to engage in e-commerce due to the better understanding for the e-commerce potential<br>– Increased speed of development of online promotion services, such as personalisation tools, targeted and contextual marketing and all other data-driven marketing tools<br>– Habitual online procurement of regular goods (food, medicines, goods for pets) due to the recognised convenience and well-functioning system<br>– Offline purchases as the entertainment rather than necessity due to the unwillingness of the customers to stay at home | |

# 6    Conclusion and Future Research

The findings from the in-depth interviews with respondents representing a firm perspective contribute to the deeper understanding of factors that have a negative and positive impact on the development of the e-commerce market in Russia. The findings obtained during the study are grounded on the evidence and opinions of real market participants, who have the necessary experience and skills for objectively assessing the Russian e-commerce market in today's realities.

It was found that firms pay a lot of attention to such external factors as environmental, organizational and product-/service-related. In the e-commerce that was strongly influences by the COVID-19 pandemic, the main factors remain the same from 2015, however, their evolution and acceptance is evident.

Dependence of these factors on the external forces determine their dualistic nature: all of them can be both barriers and drivers for firms. For example, firms notice the government support, increase in the number of consumers, development of payment system as driving e-commerce market factors, at the same time they point out weak legislation regulation, low purchasing capacity or consumers' unwillingness to pay by card and pay for the product before getting it. The controversial content of these factors corresponds with the initial stage of development of Russian e-commerce market that was mentioned in the market analysis. It also reflects the emerging market context.

**Funding.** This research has been conducted within the fundamental research project "Digitalization as a driving force of open innovation and co-creation: Implications for value creation and value capture" as a part of the HSE Graduate School of Business Research Program in 2021–2023 (Protocol No. 23 dd 22.06.2021 of the HSE GSB Research Committee).

# References

1. Dholakia, R.R., Chiang, K.P.: Shoppers in cyberspace: are they from Venus or Mars and does it matter? J. Consum. Psychol. **13**(1–2), 171–176 (2003)
2. Ariely, D., Lynch, J.G., Jr., Aparicio, M., IV.: Learning by collaborative and individual-based recommendation agents. J. Consum. Psychol. **14**(1–2), 81–95 (2004)
3. Bleier, A., Harmeling, C.M., Palmatier, R.W.: Creating effective online customer experiences. J. Mark. **83**(2), 98–119 (2019)
4. De Haan, E., Kannan, P.K., Verhoef, P.C., Wiesel, T.: Device switching in online purchasing: examining the strategic contingencies. J. Mark. **82**(5), 1–19 (2018)
5. Fernandes, D., Puntoni, S., van Osselaer, S.M.J., Cowley, E.: When and why we forget to buy. J. Consum. Psychol. **26**(3), 363–380 (2016)
6. Ge, X., Häubl, G., Elrod, T.: What to say when: influencing consumer choice by delaying the presentation of favorable information. J. Consum. Res. **38**(6), 1004–1021 (2012)
7. Goodman, J.K., Broniarczyk, S.M., Griffin, J.G., McAlister, L.: Help or hinder? When recommendation signage expands consideration sets and heightens decision difficulty. J. Consum. Psychol. **23**(2), 165–174 (2013)
8. Meire, M., Hewett, K., Ballings, M., Kumar, V., Van den Poel, D.: The role of marketer-generated content in customer engagement marketing. J. Mark. **83**(6), 21–42 (2019)
9. Priya, R., Das, S.R.: The long and short of it: why are stocks with shorter runs preferred? J. Consum. Res. **36**(6), 964–982 (2010)

10. Semenyuta, O.G., Andreeva, A.V., Sichev, R.A., Filippov, Y.: Digital technologies in lending small and medium-size enterprises in Russia. Int. J. Econ. Bus. Adm. **7**, 40–52 (2019)
11. Abou-Shouk, M., Megicks, P., Lim, W.M.: Perceived benefits and e-commerce adoption by SME travel agents in developing countries: evidence from Egypt. J. Hosp. Tour. Res. **37**(4), 490–515 (2013)
12. Abualrob, A.A., Kang, J.: The barriers that hinder the adoption of e-commerce by small businesses: unique hindrance in Palestine. Inf. Dev. **32**(5), 1528–1544 (2016)
13. Valmohammadi, C., Dashti, S.: Using interpretive structural modeling and fuzzy analytical process to identify and prioritize the interactive barriers of e-commerce implementation. Inf. Manag. **53**(2), 157–168 (2016)
14. Wymer, S.A., Regan, E.A.: Factors influencing e-commerce adoption and use by small and medium businesses. Electron. Mark. **15**(4), 438–453 (2005)
15. Kshetri, N.: The adoption of e-business by organizations in China: an institutional perspective. Electron. Mark. **17**(2), 113–125 (2007)
16. Rodriguez-Ardura, I., Meseguer-Artola, A.: Toward a longitudinal model of ecommerce: environmental, technological, and organizational drivers of B2C adoption. Inf. Soc. **26**(3), 209–227 (2010)
17. Lin, S.W., Fu, H.P.: Uncovering critical success factors for business-to-customer electronic commerce in travel agencies. J. Travel Tour. Mark. **29**(6), 566–584 (2012)
18. Zhang, M., Huang, G.Q., Xu, S.X., Zhao, Z.: Optimization based transportation service trading in B2B e-commerce logistics. J. Intell. Manuf. **30**(7), 2603–2619 (2016). https://doi.org/10.1007/s10845-016-1287-x
19. Solaymani, S., Sohaili, K., Yazdinejad, E.A.: Adoption and use of e-commerce in SMEs. Electron. Commer. Res. **12**(3), 249–263 (2012)
20. Ho, S.C., Kauffman, R.J., Liang, T.P.: A growth theory perspective on B2C e-commerce growth in Europe: an exploratory study. Electron. Commer. Res. Appl. **6**(3), 237–259 (2007)
21. Oreku, G.S., Mtenzi, F.J., Ali, A.D.: A viewpoint of Tanzania e-commerce and implementation barriers. Comput. Sci. Inf. Syst. **10**(1), 263–281 (2013)
22. Development of E-commerce in Russia, Yandex.Market and GFK (2019). https://yandex.ru/company/researches/2019/market-gfk. Accessed 19 Jan 2020
23. Krippendorff, K.: Content Analysis: An Introduction to Its Methodology. Sage Publications, Thousand Oaks (2018)
24. Aljifri, H.A., Pons, A., Collins, D.: Global e-commerce: a framework for understanding and overcoming the trust barrier. Inf. Manag. Comput. Secur. (2003)
25. Corbitt, B.J., Thanasankit, T., Yi, H.: Trust and e-commerce: a study of consumer perceptions. Electron. Commer. Res. Appl. **2**(3), 203–215 (2003)
26. Metzger, M.J.: Privacy, trust, and disclosure: exploring barriers to electronic commerce. J. Comput. Mediat. Commun. **9**(4), JCMC942 (2004)
27. Sheth, J.N.: Impact of emerging markets on marketing: rethinking existing perspectives and practices. J. Mark. **75**(4), 166–182 (2011)
28. Gao, X., Shi, X., Guo, H., Liu, Y.: To buy or not buy food online: the impact of the COVID-19 epidemic on the adoption of e-commerce in China. PloS ONE **15**(8), e0237900 (2020)
29. Salem, M.A., Nor, K.M.: The effect of COVID-19 on consumer behaviour in Saudi Arabia: switching from brick and mortar stores to e-commerce. Int. J. Sci. Technol. Res. **9**(7), 15–28 (2020)

# eEconomy: E-Commerce Research

# Fast-Growing eCommerce and Omnichannel Concept Development: Empirical Evidence from Russian Retail

Oksana Piskunova[✉]

HSE University, Moscow, Russia

**Abstract.** The omnichannel business model is becoming increasingly popular nowadays. The COVID-19 crisis has strongly influenced consumer behavior, with the role of e-commerce becoming ever more important. The "new normal" requires that retailers adapt quickly in order to, on the one hand, satisfy consumer needs in the most appropriate way and, on the other, maintain their competitive advantage in the market. This study aims to identify and analyze the omnichannel activities of retailers in order to provide a concept of the development of a short-term omnichannel business model under pressure of the crisis. The research found that the COVID-19 crisis has boosted the development of the omnichannel model in retail. The research suggests the following step-by-step measures for implementation of the omnichannel approach have been adopted: introduction and expansion of online shops and delivery services; immediate response to customers' needs and purchase barriers; establishment of an automatization process inside the company; alignment of company strategies with omnichannel model development; further development of omnichannel strategy via collaboration mechanisms; and improvement of category management & consumer-oriented factors. The study provides retailers' reflections on the new ways of operating, and suggests how the omnichannel development concept may be driven by external factors, as well as proposing opportunities for further research in the development of the omnichannel concept: detailed analysis of omnichannel strategies, or further steps in medium-term omnichannel development after the pandemic period. This research offers practical guidance to managers in retail companies, such as the step-by-step omnichannel business model implementation approach.

**Keywords:** Omnichannel concept · Retail · COVID-19 · e-Commerce

## 1 Introduction

The COVID-19 pandemic has brought unexpected changes to the world that have had a considerable impact on people's everyday lives. People, businesses and economies have faced many uncertainties and have had to be ready to confront them. Retailers were among the first types of businesses to be faced with a new reality in the wake of the pandemic. Populations have been under lockdown, shops have been closed; consumer traffic has therefore decreased rapidly. New ways of living have changed consumer

D. A. Alexandrov et al. (Eds.): DTGS 2021, CCIS 1503, pp. 493–505, 2022.
https://doi.org/10.1007/978-3-030-93715-7_35

behavior. The FMCG sector has had to deal with the consequences of the pandemic and has had to adapt to the new reality as quickly as possible. The purpose of this study is to determine how Russian retailers have utilized the mechanisms of the omnichannel business model in order to adapt to the COVID-19 crisis.

## 2   Literature Review

### 2.1   Omnichannel Strategy and Consumer Behavior

The retail industry has developed in a step-by-step fashion over the last several decades: from mono- to multi- to the omnichannel approach to doing business [20]. Since the first study of the omnichannel retail concept was conducted by Rigby, more than 100 papers, research documents & business reports have been compiled explaining the idea [17]. Omnichannel is the business concept whereby retailers offer goods & services to consumers for purchase seamlessly, via several channels[9]. The omnichannel model is the embodiment of the key message from consumers: convenience is king, that is, goods should be able to be purchased anytime, anywhere and from any device [6].

In terms of category management, omnichannel development involves creating and managing categories in the right direction with consideration given to new "digitalized" consumer behavior. Furthermore, it affords new opportunities for collaboration between retailers and brands. Omnichannel seeks to create a holistic shopping experience by merging various touchpoints, allowing customers to use whichever channel is best for them at whatever stage of the customer journey they are in.

Figure 1 (left part) illustrates the key ideas of the omnichannel concept: the seamless connection is experienced by the customer whichever touch point is used. On the other hand, omnichannel strategy does not only involve the synergy of channels. Figure 1 (right part) shows that there are also various marketing tools in the "marketing mix" and barriers that must be re-evaluated in terms of seamless consumer behavior, both online & offline.

The omnichannel strategy is based on two tactical principles: showrooming and webrooming. Showrooming is a way of product purchasing whereby consumers are familiar with goods from viewing them in retail stores and then switch to e-commerce to buy them. With the showrooming approach, the consumer tends to receive a favorable price: before making a purchase, he or she wants to be aware about all the features of a product [3]. On the other hand, webrooming is a kind of consumer journey, where he or she searches for information about products online and then goes to the offline store to make a purchase, armed with knowledge about features, prices, responses & ratings [2]. Webrooming allows consumers to make a well-informed choice via comparative analysis of the websites, taking into consideration prices and the reviews of other purchasers. Smart shoppers tend to be those consumers who seek to minimize time, money and energy costs while enjoying a pleasant and worthwhile shopping experience [3]. Using the webrooming strategy, consumers consider themselves as smart shoppers more when they behave as a showroomer. [6]. When they use an omnichannel approach, consumers make a selection from a number of retailers, comparing them in both online and offline stores [8]. In order maximize omnichannel strategy efficiency, so that borders between online & offline become smooth, it is very important to consistently implement and follow the 4P marketing mix concept [8].

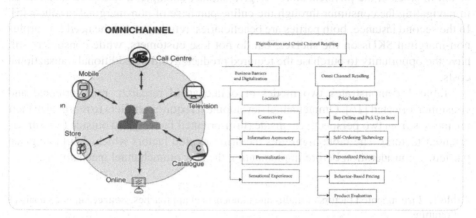

**Fig. 1.** Omnichannel retailing, overview of digitalization and omnichannel retailing. Source: [4].

## 2.2 Omnichannel Tactical and Factors for Concept Development

E-commerce demonstrates the highest growth rate among all channels due to the greater opportunities presented for retailers and consumers to make the customer journey more efficient [1]. Realizing consumer omnichannel behavior gives retailers an advantage over others in terms of satisfying consumers' needs in the most appropriate way and building up their loyalty [23]. Webrooming is the fastest-growing behavioral strategy among online users. Nearly half of all offline sales are influenced by web searches [11]. This finding provides valuable insights to retailers into the importance of online searches, in terms of not only purchasing goals but also convenience goals. It means retailers must ensure that their web-based platforms provide all of the essential information for users. Do their websites feature in the top search results? Does the retailer give full consideration to 4P, make continuous improvements in these areas and actively respond to consumers' challenges?

For instance, a good product cart with high-quality, detailed images and descriptions gives a comprehensive overview of the product but does not give a true understanding of the product "in reality".

Another very important element of 4P considerations is the reviews of current users: positive reviews greatly increase the probability of a consumer making a purchase [20]. Online recommendations are a tool for making purchases, and consumers who follow the showrooming approach usually make use of this tool.

Nearly 82% (Google research) of users make use of smartphones to make purchases or to learn about the features of a product. To make the consumer journey more efficient, retailers must consider this fact and facilitate the process for consumers, for example by offering free WI-FI in shops. Besides this, the omnichannel approach requires that retailers be more efficient with in-store merchandising.

There are various mechanisms for connecting e-commerce & offline sales. For example, a sales assistant may help people to go online and buy products that are unavailable or not in stock in the physical store. To give another example, a salesperson can assist in navigating the consumer through the online purchase of non-marginal products [5]. In the second instance, both parties are beneficiaries; retailers avoid the need for surplus non-marginal SKUs on the shelves, but do not lose customers, while consumers still have the opportunity to purchase the required product, avoiding additional transactional costs.

Table 1 demonstrates two modes of omnichannel research: retail-oriented and consumer-oriented [16]. Omnichannel development requires retailers to reorganize their businesses from two perspectives: inside (firm-oriented factors) and outside (consumer-oriented factors). The table highlights the firm-oriented factors which should be given particular consideration before implementing the new omnichannel mechanisms.

**Table 1.** Firm-oriented factors of multi- and omnichannel approaches. **Source**: author's analysis of literature

| Firm-oriented factors | Multichannel | Omnichannel |
|---|---|---|
| Logistics & distribution [2] | Separate logistics units for offline & online stores, responsibilities, separate return & deliveries | Flexible & demand allocation, common producers stock zone [10], i.e. picking processes, inventory holding, IT systems |
| Supply chain | Each seller may sell different number of SKUs, not aligned with inventories | Highly similar across all channels |
| Management | Managed independently | Single executive (mix of people) |

Two distinct approaches can be taken in the formulation of an omnichannel model:

- focusing on the primary role of retail and the subsequent reciprocal consumer fractions, or
- considering how changes in consumer behavior determine the behavior of retail in the market [22].

In the wake of COVID-19, buyers' behavior has changed due to quarantine measures being introduced in almost all countries of the world. Some retailers have changed their strategies in response to the emergence of new players in the market; for example, Marks and Spencer in India has adjusted its supply chain, while Ford has shifted its production from automobiles to highly proprietary ventilators and hospital beds by collaborating with local manufacturers [7]. The luxury industry has adapted to new emotions, employment, and expectations (EEE) by providing the same customer experience online as offline [13].

## 2.3  Research Questions

The research literature describes the general changes that have taken place in the industry in response to COVID-19 but does not consider which tactical and strategic steps have been required by retailers to modify or introduce elements in order to adapt to the new reality. A systematic review approach was implemented to analyze the literature for outlining tools that retailers can use to overcome some issues in devising an omnichannel approach.

This research proposes that:

- A shift in consumer behavior caused by COVID-19 has driven omnichannel development in Russian retail since the onset of the pandemic and the subsequent introduction of quarantine measures.
- Those retailers who developed delivery services, improved processes, and effectively implemented collaborations in their businesses benefited from the new reality by shifting to e-commerce in order to adapt to the customer journey.

## 3  Research Design: Method, Data, Methodology

The research is designed to identify how retailers in Russia have adapted their businesses to a COVID-19 framework. Moreover, the paper demonstrates the step-by-step development of, and adaptation to, the omnichannel concept in different kinds of shopping outlets: hypermarkets, supermarkets & convenience stores.

There is no doubt that the COVID-19 pandemic and the subsequent lockdown measures have forced consumers and retailers to rethink & re-evaluate the purchasing process. To maintain their competitive advantage and not lose customers, retailers have had to work quickly and effectively in order to adapt to the new purchasing patterns. In the quarantine scenario, e-commerce has become very popular. This is one of the reasons why there has been rapid implementation of the omnichannel concept. In order to highlight changes that have been made in retail, the research is based on a case study approach. This method was chosen within a framework of critical realism. Cluster analysis and quantitative methods have also been applied.

Business cases have been analyzed. From May 2020 onwards, when the first responses from retailers were recorded, news from mass media & from ECR meetings was gathered and was analyzed using quantitative methods. The cases selected for analysis were news pieces and other articles describing innovations & modifications in business structures among a chosen selection of retailers; Lenta represents hypermarkets, Perekrestok was chosen for supermarkets, and Pyaterochka & Magnit for convenience stores. The cases have been taken from business papers, magazines, and online business & news resources, for example Kommersant, Vedomosti, Rbc.ru and Retail.ru, among others.

The case study approach is the most appropriate method for this research, for the following reasons:

- The object of analysis (i.e., FMCG retail) is very dynamic and, for assessment to be effective, it is very important to examine real cases in order to analyze changes that have had to be made due to the COVID-19 crisis.

- The subject of analysis (i.e., the tactical steps of retailers) is also reflected in real cases that can be selected accordingly.
- Real cases allow for the accumulation of practical tools for building knowledge that could be applied to further research in FMCG retail.

The case study method comprises three stages: providing a description, generating a theory, and testing that theory [25].

To identify how retailers have adapted to the new reality, and to construct a theory of omnichannel development in FMCG retail under crisis conditions, analysis of retailers' tactical steps was conducted and, based on this analysis, a timeline was drawn up. Retailers' initiatives were analyzed from two different perspectives: retailers' self-positioning (retailers' self-reflections, cases being derived from ECR meetings throughout 2020) and their input in omnichannel development; and media reflections on initiatives of retailers (with cases being derived from mass-media).

The first step was to analyze cases of retailer initiatives in ECR meetings. 57 separate cases of retailers' and manufacturers' initiatives to improve the consumer journey in terms of omnichannel development were examined. The cases mostly involve e-commerce & cross-channel projects but also include some purely offline schemes.

The following methodology was used. All cases were analyzed and categorized into several groups according to the answers to the following research questions:

- Who was the prime mover of the initiative implementation? Was it the producer or the retailer who was more prepared to promote a new way of doing business and offer the best experience to the consumer?
- Which tools were more useful for retailers, and which were more useful for producers? (This helps to recognize opportunities for further development.)
- What are the current trends of the retail & manufacturing industries? (This is useful in making assumptions for future trends.)
- Are manufacturers more focused on consumer retail factors?

The next step was to gather news articles in which retailers have been highlighted. There was a total of 148 news articles under analysis. The following methodology was applied:

1. Four of the largest retailers—representing different market formats—were chosen: Lenta (hypermarkets); Perekrestok (supermarkets); Pyaterochka and Magnit (convenience stores).
2. Trading and marketing news items from May to December 2020—gathered from the internet and from business mass-media—which mentioned retailers were analyzed.
3. In the next step, the articles were synthesized into different groups based on their main idea: omnichannel development, online development or offline development. In the case of omnichannel development, news was clustered into the following subgroups: offline, online, or both.
4. The articles were further categorized based on context; each item was put into a relevant category (e.g., automatization, distribution extension, collaborations, delivery extensions, etc.).

5. In the building of this hierarchy, two principles were applied: news directly belonging to a group (due to name, words from article, mentions of created category and article wording), and context analysis based on critical estimation.

## 4 Research Results of Omnichannel Concept Development in Russian Retail Under Covid-19 Framework

Case analysis reveals that in 2020, nearly 70% of all initiatives were developed solely by retailers, manufacturers or agencies, while just 30% of e-commerce & omnichannel initiatives were driven by collaborations between the above. The data can be observed in Fig. 2. However, it is very important to note that, by the end of 2020, the quantity of collaboration initiatives had increased.

Furthermore, manufacturers and retailers, along with marketplaces, built up their ecommerce initiatives in equal proportion. This answers the question about which sector was more interested in building a new type of business strategy. It could be interpreted that retailers & manufacturers have prepared the ground (improving processes, eliminating unnecessary processes) for cross-industry correlation. As proof of this, closer collaboration was observed at the end of 2020.

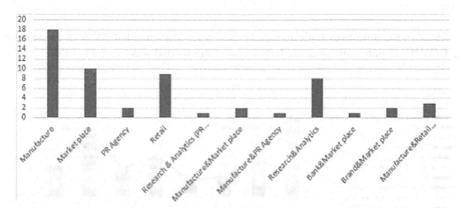

**Fig. 2.** Cases of initiatives in e-commerce & omnichannel concept development clustered by initiator. Source: author's analysis

The following motivational factors can be assumed: an omnichannel synergy of retailers & brands started to be actively developed immediately after manufacturers and retailers adjusted their processes. The paper's suggestion that manufacturers will be more focused on consumer retail factors driven by the coronavirus was partially approved.

Manufacturers have mostly started to work with analytic data, building supply chain and distribution processes: the main goal of analytics is to gain a deeper understanding of consumer behavior. Firm-driven factors allow manufacturers to cut unnecessary costs and improve processes.

On the other hand, retailers & marketplaces have been more concerned with consumer-oriented factors since the start of COVID-19. It was crucially important to build up high-quality content regarding the product in online platforms (products cart, reviews, quality of pictures, ratings & responses, rearrangement of price and promo).

The second tool to be implemented by retailers has been online delivery. Retailers have addressed various consumer barriers and devised ways to overcome them as quickly as possible, for example, expansion of the express-delivery service to save time for consumers.

News research analysis yielded the following results. 54% of all news was related to omnichannel tactical steps, while 46% merely highlighted changes made offline or online. Furthermore, due to the development of the omnichannel concept, the emphasis has been on mechanisms and strategies concerned mostly with online channels, or those related to both online & offline. In terms of development, offline channels have seen four times as many changes as online ones. Omnichannel detailed analysis reveals that the top 5 steps that have been made by retailers in the period under analysis are:

- process automatization
- express-delivery concept development
- online delivery expansion
- consumer satisfaction tools (e.g. promos, specials clubs, personalized discounts, etc.)
- collaborations with manufacturers, other retailers, restaurants, delivery companies, etc.

Most of the initiatives (approximately 2/3) were implemented either at the start of the COVID-19 pandemic or at the beginning of the second wave (see Fig. 3).

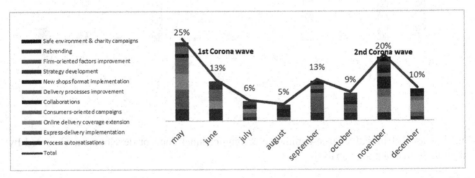

**Fig. 3.** Cases of initiatives in e-commerce & omnichannel concept development clustered by initiators. Source: author's analysis

Figure 4 illustrates which tactics were most often implemented by retailers. The research reveals that both hypermarkets and convenience stores mostly introduced, improved and extended delivery services in response to the crisis, while supermarkets focused—in equal proportion—on delivery extension, process automatization, and consumer-oriented and collaborative schemes. These results may be explained by the following factors:

- Hypermarkets addressed consumers' fears around visiting crowded places, and in order to satisfy consumer needs, while at the same time handling huge costs & capacities, retailers had to devise and develop new methods of selling products as quickly as possible.
- Convenience stores usually sell goods at a price lower than the market price. Due to the coronavirus, a significant proportion of people either lost their jobs or suffered salary cuts. Retailers mostly concentrated on overcoming the disposable income barrier. This is why they not only developed their delivery services, but also implemented many promotional campaigns and social initiatives; for example, Payterochka & Magnit extended the range of goods for sale without premium during the first wave of the pandemic.
- Supermarkets were balanced in their range of initiatives and, in general, tended to improve their processes, perhaps highlighting that the crisis helped them to realize their disadvantages. They actively participated in collaborative activities; for example, Perekrestok sells restaurant dishes in their outlets. Through such initiatives, retailers could, on the one hand, enable consumers to eat restaurant-quality food and, on the other hand, help restaurants by supporting their businesses.

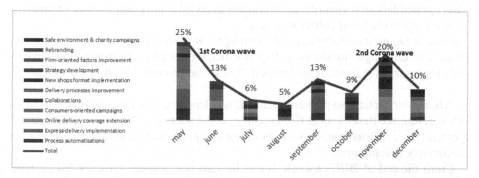

**Fig. 4.** News clustered into relevant groups, by month. Source: author's analysis

# 5   Conclusions and Discussions

Based on case analysis up to the end of 2020, it can be concluded that the retail and manufacturing industries have shifted from reorganizing their processes separately to collaborating with one another.

The direction of collaboration between industries is more consumer-oriented. The main goal of this is to satisfy consumers' needs via the following tools & mechanisms:

- collaboration in consumer analytics based on data and exchange of insights.
- building effective promotional strategies (personalized promo, cross-channel promo—for example, if a product is not available in the shop, the consumer may order it online).

- category management both online & offline, strong relationship with partners.

In addition, the COVID crisis revealed certain disadvantages or limitations in the retail industry and caused businesses to address these issues. The research has also demonstrated that the crisis forced retailers to develop an omnichannel strategy, with many of them working effectively to satisfy consumers' needs, introducing express-delivery services and lower prices, for example. The FMCG sector realized that customers' journeys tended towards omnichannel behavior.

Considering all of this, and as shown by the research, the implementation and development of omnichannel strategies in Russia was based on the following stages:

- reactively responding to consumers' needs, online channel development, introduction and extension of delivery services (due to lockdown constraints).
- maintaining prices in terms of disposable revenue (quick reduction, boosting new purchasing channels with prices lower than, or equivalent to, offline), introducing promotional offers for some purchases where delivery has been specified
- considering the needs of consumers and working with them effectively: introduction of express delivery, implementation of no-contact delivery services.
- automatization of processes and optimization of capacities (for example, Payterochka has opened dark stores in order to optimize delivery time and to have sufficient capacity for increased click and collect services).
- effective promo introduction: price campaigns, or cross-channel activation (with the seamless campaign introduced by Payterochka, for example, the consumer receives a sticker in the store, goes online, uploads a video and receives a gift in the store).

After these tactical steps were realized, retailers changed their strategies to fit in with e-commerce development (for example, at the start of 2020, Payterochka wanted to extend their distribution network, but their resources were rearranged to prioritize e-commerce development).

From the end of 2020 onwards, it can be seen that retailers have tended to work mostly with quality: launching seamless online & offline campaigns, collaborating with manufacturers & agencies to improve e-commerce services (for example, improving content, launching promotional strategies, and managing assortments and categories both online and offline).

Thus, the research has supported the proposition that retailers' behavior has tended toward the development of omnichannel strategies; indeed, they have made huge steps in these developments. From the accumulation of data presented, the research proves that the COVID crisis, or indeed other crises, can actually be advantageous for development, but in order for a business to preserve a good position in the market, a swift response to consumers' needs—even without a set of strategies—is fundamentally important. As an extension of the research, Fig. 5 presents a series of omnichannel developmental steps (from a short-term perspective) that could be used in further research as a model of omnichannel development for businesses in the face of crises such as COVID-19.

This scheme of development will be useful for retail managers whose companies are suitable for the development of omnichannel strategies in the frame of crisis-factors. The model could also be useful in helping managers to realize which stage they are at now and what their next steps should be in the short term. This step-by-step omnichannel development concept could be especially practical for countries in which a common multichannel business approach is already in use in the FMCG market.

In addition to this research, the following steps for further analysis and proposition testing are suggested:

- continuing to follow up retailers' behavior in the post-COVID period in order to develop and improve the theories.
- conducting deeper research into which tools and drivers could help retailers to follow the consumer-centric approach (researching the characteristics of showrooming & webrooming behavior, realizing what consumers want).
- researching category management tools—both online and offline—that help make the purchase journey seamless for the consumer and evaluating the roles of manufacturers and retailers in the collaborative development of an omnichannel business model).

**Fig. 5.** Timeline of omnichannel concept implementation in retail from a short-term perspective. Source: author's analysis

# References

1. Alsheyadi, A.: Collaborative e-business efforts and firm performance. Int. J. Prod. Perform. Manag. **70**(4) (2020). https://www.researchgate.net/publication/346842176_Collabora tive_e-business_efforts_and_firm_performance
2. Arora, S., Parida, R.R., Sahney, S.: Understanding consumers' showrooming behavior: a stimulus–organism–response (S-O-R) perspective. Int. J. Retail Distrib. Manag. **48**(11), 1157–1176 (2020)
3. Atkins, K., Youn-Kyung, K.: Smart shopping: conceptualization and measurement. J. Int. J. Retail Distrib. Manag. **40**, 360–375 (2012). https://doi.org/10.1108/09590551211222349
4. Aw, E.C.-X.: Understanding the webrooming phenomenon: shopping motivation, channel-related benefits and costs. Int. J. Retail Distrib. Manag. **47**(10), 1074–1092 (2019). https://doi.org/10.1108/IJRDM-01-2019-0026
5. Berman, B., Thelen, S.: Planning and implementing an effective omnichannel marketing program. Int. J. Retail Distrib. Manag. **46**(7), 598–614 (2019)
6. Carlos, F., Raquel, G., Orús, C.: Combining channels to make smart purchases: the role of webrooming and showrooming. J. Retail. Consum. Serv. **52** (2020). http://www.sciencedi rect.com/science/article/pii/S0969698919300992

7. Ivanov, D.: Lean resilience: AURA (Active Usage of Resilience Assets) framework for post-COVID-19 supply chain management. Int. J. Logistics Manag. **1** (2021). https://doi.org/10.1108/IJLM-11-2020-0448

8. Gültekin, B., Erdem, S.: Managing Customer Experiences in an Omnichannel World: Melody of Online and Offline Environments in the Customer Journey. Emerald Ink Publishing, London (2021)

9. Flores J., Sun J.: Online versus in-store: price differentiation for multi-channel retailers. J. Inf. Syst. **7**(4) (2014), https://scholar.google.ru/citations?view_op=view_citation&hl=sv&user=KTPzxIQAAAAJ&citation_for_view=KTPzxIQAAAAJ:zYLM7Y9cAGgC

10. Hübner, A., Wollenburg, J.: Retail logistics in the transition from multi-channel to omni-channel. Int. J. Phys. Distrib. Logist. Manag. **46**(6/7), 562–583 (2016)

11. James, W.: Omni-channel research framework in the context of personal selling and sales management. J. Res. Interact. Mark. **10**, 2–16 (2016)

12. Darrell, K.: The future of shopping. J. Harward Business Review, The Future of Shopping. (hbr.org)

13. Klaus, P., Manthiou, A.: Applying the EEE customer mindset in luxury: reevaluating customer experience research and practice during and after Corona. J. Serv. Manag. **31**(6), 1175–1183 (2020)

14. Савчук, К.: Шоуруминг и вебруминг: революция в торговле. Все про еком-шоппинг. https://elnews.com.ua/ru/shou-rumyng-y-veb-rumyng-revolyuczyya-v-torgovle/

15. Lim, S.F.W.T., Srai, J.S.: Examining the anatomy of last-mile distribution in e-commerce omnichannel retailing: a supply network configuration approach. Int. J. Oper. Prod. Manag. **38**(9), 1735–1764 (2018)

16. Mishra, R.: An analysis of factors influencing omnichannel retailing adoption using ISM-DEMATEL approach: an Indian perspective. Int. J. Retail Distrib. Manag. **49**, 550–576 (2020). https://doi.org/10.1108/IJRDM-03-2020-0108

17. Mosquera, A., Pascual, C.O., Ayensa, E.J.: Understanding the customer experience in the age of omni-channel shopping. J. Revista Icono **14**, 235–255 (2017). https://doi.org/10.7195/ri14.v15i2.1070

18. Murali, K.: Category management and captains. J. Bus. Res. **77**, 14–22 (2017). https://doi.org/10.4337/9781786430281.0003

19. Mercier, P., David, W.: Omnichannel retail, it's still about detail Guillaume Crétenot. https://www.bcg.com/publications/2014/supply-chain-management-sourcing-procurement-omnichannel-retail-still-about-detail

20. Orús, C., Gurrea, R., Ibáñez-Sánchez, S.: The impact of consumers' positive online recommendations on the omnichannel webrooming experience. Span. J. Mark. **23**(3), 397–414 (2019)

21. Karacali, J., Gultekin, S.: Managing Customer Experiences in an Omnichannel World: Melody of Online and Offline Environments in the Customer Journey. Emerald Ink Publishing, London (2019)

22. Oktay, B.: Consumer Behavior in Omnichannel Retailing. Managing Customer Experiences in an Omnichannel World: Melody of Online and Offline Environments in the Customer Journey. Emerald Publishing Limited, 75–95 (2020)

23. Deimantė, V.: Popular 30 Ecommerce Trends for 2021. https://searchnode.com/blog/ecommerce-trends/

24. Rana, A., Shankar, R.: Crisis or opportunity: Marks and Spencer's tryst with Indian retail. CASE J. **16**(6), 671–690 (2020)

25. Ridder, H.G., Hoon, C., McCandless, A.: The theoretical contribution of case study research to the field of strategy and management. Res. Methodol. Strat. Manag. **4**, 137–175 (2009)

26. Truong, T.H.H.: The drivers of omni-channel shopping intention: a case study for fashion retailing sector in Danang, Vietnam. J. Asian Bus. Econ. Stud. **28**(2) (2021)
27. Xi, L., Huazhong, Z.: Digitalization and Omnichannel Retailing. The Oxford Handbook of Supply Chain Management. Wagner (2019)

# Using Triple Exponential Smoothing and Autoregressive Models to Mining Equipment Details Sales Forecast

Kirill Kashtanov[1]([⊠]), Alexey Kashevnik[2], and Nikolay Shilov[2]

[1] ITMO University, Saint-Petersburg, Russia
[2] SPC RAS, Saint-Petersburg, Russia
{alexey.kashevnik,nick}@iias.spb.su

**Abstract.** Stock planning is an essential part of supply management. Mistaken planning can lead to high costs and expenses. So, the correct plans are required, which should satisfy sales demand at any time. Forecasting is one of the planning techniques. This paper aims to present the sales forecasting models for the mining equipment details based on the historical sales data for two years. To this end, the triple exponential smoothing (Holt-Winters) and integrated autoregressive moving average (ARIMA) methods are used. To create periodic time-series for each detail the original data set is grouped by month. Defined time series are segregated into training and test data sets. Models for each detail are built using automated parameters selection in a such way to make absolute percentage error (APE) of the model minimized. Each model is followed by visualized plot graphs, which simplify the model and original data comparison. Achieved results demonstrate high average performance (95% for Holt-Winters, 93% for ARIMA). Built algorithms can be used in practical conditions for equipment forecasting.

**Keywords:** Triple exponential smoothing · Holt-winters · ARIMA · Forecasting

## 1 Introduction

Management of large enterprises is a very complex process that can include an enormous number of subprocesses, each of which is aimed to optimize and maximize the efficiency of the enterprise. One of the most important parts of them is supply management. This is not surprising since competent inventory management can result in maximization of economic efficiency due to minimization of costs, related to inventory support and maintenance [1].

However, the bigger is enterprise, the more nonreactive its processes become, including supply planning. Made approved plans are very difficult to change on the run, which can result in high costs and expenses. This is why every enterprise requires proper plans that could satisfy sales demand at any time.

Supply and inventory forecast is one of the planning approaches. Based on the historical data future predictions can be made. Modern tendencies of digital transformation

© Springer Nature Switzerland AG 2022
D. A. Alexandrov et al. (Eds.): DTGS 2021, CCIS 1503, pp. 506–521, 2022.
https://doi.org/10.1007/978-3-030-93715-7_36

require methods and technologies that would support the automatization of forecast modeling, which is applicable in a wide variety of human activity including business.

The purpose of this paper is to build forecasting models for supplies of the mining and metallurgical inventory, basing on historical data of sales. In order to achieve the described goal, the following tasks have been set:

- review of the related work;
- examination of used forecasting methods;
- analysis and pre-processing of the historical data;
- building forecasting models;
- review and analysis of the achieved results.

## 2 Related Work

There are several commercial solutions that provide agile forecasting functionality. They provide diverse functionality for demand and supply forecasting with many criteria, which allows creating the most accurate forecasts, according to solutions distributors. However, those solutions are expensive and provide excessive functionality, regarding mining and metallurgical equipment – as an example, it is an uncommon situation for such equipment to have an expiration date, special transportation, or maintaining conditions. The following table collects information about such solutions (Table 1).

Considering the above, it was decided to implement basic forecasting functionality, that would consider information about previous sales only.

Generally, the problem of supply forecasting basing on historical data is the problem of time series forecasting. So it was decided to review several research papers related to time series forecasting to find the best applicable forecasting method considering mining and metallurgical equipment (Table 2).

The triple exponential smoothing method (TES, Holt-Winters method) is one of the most used forecasting models, which has been studied and applied in many areas. This method is considered one of the most effective models due to its low operating costs and simplicity [7]. For example, it can be used for transportation dynamics forecasting [8]. Jiang and others apply improved TES by using the fruit fly optimization algorithm, which allowed finding the best possible parameters for the Holt-Winters model regarding electricity consumption [9].

Different variations of autoregressive models are also widely used. For example, the autoregressive moving average (ARMA) model can be applied for forecasting stationary time series such as taxi demand [10]. Sahai with co-authors states that the autoregressive integrated moving average model (ARIMA) can be used both for stationary and non-stationary time series, such as detecting and forecasting outbreaks of infectious diseases [11]. Moreover, ARIMA models can be used for demand and sales predictions by forecasting trend movement and seasonal fluctuations [12].

On the other hand, Dissanayake with co-authors states that ARIMA models are weak and inefficient in terms of forecasting non-stationary time series.

In their work authors examine other prediction models such as ARIMAX, vector autoregressive model (VAR), and long short-term memory model (LSTM) in order to

**Table 1.** Commercial solutions

| Name | Subscription price (rub, thousands/month)/Box (rub, thousands) | Forecasting criteria |
|------|------|------|
| Forecast now! [2] | 55-225/950-4950 | · Dates<br>· Expiration date<br>· Seasonality<br>· Cannibalization |
| Net stock [3] | 18/- | · Actual demand<br>· Demand changes<br>· Seasonality<br>· Product alternativity<br>· Actual budget |
| GoodForecast [4] | - | · Promotions and holidays<br>· Noise filtering<br>· Supply schedules |
| Inventor [5] | - | · Warehouse bandwidth<br>· Suppliers ratings<br>· Credit and debit |
| Stock-m [6] | 80/- | · Transportation conditions<br>· Seasonality<br>· Sales & promotions<br>· Multi-currency<br>· Product alternativity |

**Table 2.** Research papers

| Paper | Method(s) | Applying area | Results |
|------|------|------|------|
| [7] | Triple exponential smoothing (TES), ANNs | Weather forecast (wind) | up to 81% accuracy |
| [8] | TES | Transportation planning | 94.41% accuracy |
| [9] | TES with fruit fly optimization algorithm | Electricity consumption | 96.42% accuracy |
| [10] | ARMA | Taxi demand | - |
| [11] | ARIMA | Decease spreading | 96–99% accuracy |
| [12] | ARIMA | Retail sales | - |
| [13] | ARIMAX, VAR, LSTM | Traffic | 91.46% accurate for VAR model |
| [14] | ANNs | Power consumption | 92–98% accurate model |
| [15] | Croston method | Equipment inventory | - |
| [16] | Bayesian Network | Demand for spare parts | - |

build traffic forecasts [13]. Using mentioned models allowed to consider the correlation between traffic and snow volumes. As the result, they achieved a forecast model with 91.46% accuracy.

Runge and others apply artificial neural networks to develop a multi-step-ahead short-term forecasting model, which predicts power consumption of supply fans in industrial buildings [14]. They propose a solution to the automated search of the ANN architecture based on exploring all possible combinations for the number of input neurons and selecting the minimized RMSE. The results of their study show that such an approach allows building forecasts with 92.7–98.2% accuracy.

Moreover, probabilistic approaches can be used in terms of time series forecasting. For example, the Croston method can be applied for forecasting intermittent demands [15]. Also, according to Boutselis and McNaught, Bayesian Networks can be very efficient in terms of manipulating probability distributions [16].

## 3   Historical Data Description

Historical data of sales have been provided by the company, which specializes in the trading of mining and metallurgical equipment details. Originally, data has been given as a table sheet (see Fig. 1), which contains data about done equipment sales structured by Deal ID, purchased detail (Element ID) per deal, the number of purchased details within the deal, and date of the deal. The table includes data of deals within the period from November 2018 till October 2020.

Within this paper, only the following columns have been included for the analysis: 'Element ID', 'Q-ty', 'Created'. Additionally, each of the details sales have been taken not by the exact dates but grouped by months. This is done in order to create periodical time series with a length of 12 months. So, only 24 periods have been provided by the company, i.e. two complete seasons (two years).

| | A | B | C | D | E | F | G | H | I | J |
|---|---|---|---|---|---|---|---|---|---|---|
| 1 | Deal ID | Type | Stage | Company | Source | Assumed close date | Created | Element ID | Q-ty | UOM |
| 2 | 7028 Goods | Negotiations | 746 - | | 30.11.2020 | 02.11.2020 11:28 | 7010000356 | 1 | PCE |
| 3 | 7028 Goods | Negotiations | 746 - | | 30.11.2020 | 02.11.2020 11:28 | 1010001114 | 4 | PCE |
| 4 | 7028 Goods | Negotiations | 746 - | | 30.11.2020 | 02.11.2020 11:28 | 7060000050 | 4 | PCE |
| 5 | 7027 Goods | Quote preparation | 42 - | | 09.11.2020 | 02.11.2020 9:40 | 1010004443 | 5 | PCE |
| 6 | 7027 Goods | Quote preparation | 42 - | | 09.11.2020 | 02.11.2020 9:40 | 1010004444 | 1 | PCE |
| 7 | 7027 Goods | Quote preparation | 42 - | | 09.11.2020 | 02.11.2020 9:40 | 1010003155 | 1 | PCE |
| 8 | 7027 Goods | Quote preparation | 42 - | | 09.11.2020 | 02.11.2020 9:40 | 1010004486 | 2 | PCE |
| 9 | 7027 Goods | Quote preparation | 42 - | | 09.11.2020 | 02.11.2020 9:40 | 1010004472 | 1 | PCE |
| 10 | 7027 Goods | Quote preparation | 42 - | | 09.11.2020 | 02.11.2020 9:40 | 1010004471 | 1 | PCE |
| 11 | 7027 Goods | Quote preparation | 42 - | | 09.11.2020 | 02.11.2020 9:40 | 1010003156 | 1 | PCE |
| 12 | 7027 Goods | Quote preparation | 42 - | | 09.11.2020 | 02.11.2020 9:40 | 1010004481 | 1 | PCE |
| 13 | 7026 Goods | Quote preparation | 4198 E-parts | | | 30.10.2020 18:05 | 1010000065 | 1 | PCE |
| 14 | 7025 Goods | Quote preparation | 4198 E-parts | | | 30.10.2020 18:04 | 1010000478 | 1 | PCE |

**Fig. 1.** Historical data sample

## 4   Methodology

Since the historical data of equipment sales include time series of a wide variety (seasonal/non-seasonal, stationary/non-stationary), it was decided to build forecasting models based on the triple exponential smoothing (Holt-Winters model) and ARIMA model, due to its expected simplicity and applicability for a wide variety of time series.

## 4.1 Triple Exponential Smoothing Model

Single exponential smoothing is a useful tool, which allows to reduce the noise of the series and forecast future values using a weighted average of all previous values of the time series. However, simple exponential smoothing (SES) uses values itself, without any additional information about the nature and behavior of the original time series. It does not allow to consider the impact of other time series parameters such as trend and seasonality.

Holt-Winters method is the improvement of the original SES method and it allows to build forecasts taking into account seasonality and trend components of the original time series. This can result in more accurate future predictions [7].

There are two possible variations for triple exponential smoothing, which differ by the behavior of the seasonality component [17]:

- Multiplicative seasonality – when amplitude of the seasonal oscillations is likely to change in time,
- Additive seasonality – when amplitude of the seasonal oscillations does not tend to change in time.

**Holt-Winters Multiplicative Model.** The multiplicative form of the triple exponential smoothing is defined by the following Eqs. (1–4):

$$L_i = \frac{\alpha \cdot Y_i}{S_{i-s}} + (1 - \alpha) \cdot (L_{i-1} + T_{i-1}) \tag{1}$$

$$T_i = \beta \cdot (L_i - L_{i-1}) + (1 - \beta) \cdot T_{i-1} \tag{2}$$

$$S_i = \frac{\gamma \cdot Y_i}{L_{i-1} + T_{i-1}} + (1 - \gamma)S_{i-s} \tag{3}$$

$$F_{i+m} = (Y_i + T_i \cdot m) \cdot S_{i+m-s} \tag{4}$$

where

- $Y_i$ – actual value of the time series in period $i$,
- $L_i$ – overall (level) smoothing for the period $i$ (for the initial period $L_1 = Y_1$),
- $L_{i-1}$ – overall (level) smoothing for the previous period,
- $T_i$ – trend exponential smoothing for the period $i$,
- $T_{i-1}$ – trend exponential smoothing for the previous period,
- $S_i$ – seasonal exponential smoothing for the period $i$,
- $S_{i-s}$ – seasonal exponential smoothing for the previous period,
- $F_{i+m}$ – forecast value for $m$ periods ahead regarding last actual value,
- $S_{i+m-s}$ – seasonal exponential smoothing for the last the forecasting period in the last actual season,
- $\alpha$ – level smoothing factor,

– $\beta$ – trend smoothing factor,
– $\gamma$ – seasonal smoothing factor.

In fact, $\alpha, \beta, \gamma$ determines how much weight is given to the past values of the smoothed arrays. These factors can be defined as memory decay rate – the bigger the factor is, the more forecast depends on the recent data.

**Holt-Winters Additive Model.** The component form for the additive triple exponential smoothing method is the following (5–8):

$$L_i = \alpha \cdot (Y_i - S_{i-s}) + (1 - \alpha) \cdot (L_{i-1} + T_{i-1}) \tag{5}$$

$$T_i = \beta \cdot (L_i - L_{i-1}) + (1 - \beta) \cdot T_{i-1} \tag{6}$$

$$S_i = \gamma \cdot (Y_i - L_{i-1} - B_{i-1}) + (1 - \gamma)S_{i-s} \tag{7}$$

$$F_{i+m} = Y_i + T_i \cdot m + S_{i+m-s} \tag{8}$$

**Computing Initial Trend Values.** In order to increase the accuracy of the forecast, it is necessary to compute the initial value for the trend. It can be computed for the time series with one complete season using the following formula (9):

$$T_1 = \frac{1}{L} \cdot \sum_{i=1}^{L} \frac{Y_{L+i} - Y_i}{L} \tag{9}$$

where

– $L$ – number of periods in the season (season length),
– $Y_{L+i}$ – time series value for a similar period in the next season.

**Computing Initial Seasonality Values.** To compute the initial values for the seasonal components, it is required to find the average value for each period through all observed seasons, considering each season average. Firstly, the season average should be found for each season (10), after which the average value of identical periods through all seasons is taken for each initial period (11):

$$A_s = \frac{\sum_{i=1}^{L} Y_{i+(s-1) \cdot L}}{L} \tag{10}$$

$$I_i = \frac{1}{L} \cdot \sum_{s=1}^{k} \frac{Y_{i+(s-1) \cdot L}}{A_s} \tag{11}$$

## 4.2 Integrated Autoregressive Moving Average Model

Auto-Regressive Integrated Moving Average (ARIMA) is a class of models that combines a list of components, which are the following:

- Autoregression (AR) refers to a model that shows a changing variable that regresses on its own lagged, or prior, values,
- Integrated (I) represents the differencing of raw observations to allow for the time series to become stationary, i.e., data values are replaced by the difference between the data values and the previous values,
- Moving average (MA) incorporates the dependency between an observation and a residual error from a moving average model applied to lagged observations.

ARIMA model can be characterized by 3 terms, each of which represents each ARIMA model component described above. These parameters are the following:

- p – the number of lag observations in the model,
- d – the number of times that the raw observations are differenced,
- q – the size of the moving average window.

The ARIMA (p, d, q) can be presented in the following form (12):

$$\Delta^d Y_i = c + \sum_{j=1}^{p} a_j \cdot \Delta^d Y_{i-j} + \sum_{j=1}^{q} b_j \cdot \varepsilon_{i-j} + \varepsilon_i \qquad (12)$$

where

- $\Delta^d Y_i$ – value of observation in the period $i$ differenced $d$ times,
- $c$ – constant,
- $a_i$ – autoregressive parameter for the period $i$,
- $\varepsilon_i$ – white noise in the period $i$,
- $b_i$ – moving average coefficients for the period i.

Within this paper ARIMA method has been implemented using python library 'statsmodels.tsa.arima_model', which automatically computes forecasting values based on given time series based on model parameters (p, d, q).

## 4.3 Modeling and Evaluation Methods

Time series of the historical data have been divided into training and test data sets in the ratio of 75% to 25% (first 18 periods for model training, last 6 periods for testing). However, within this paper, it was decided to use 100% of the historical data set for computing of initial trend and seasonality for the triple exponential smoothing models. It has been done to use a larger number of periods for the initial analysis since the historical time series is already short (there are only two complete seasons).

Parameters for each model ($\alpha$, $\beta$, $\gamma$, and additivity/multiplicativity – for Holt-Winters models; p, d, q – for ARIMA models) have been computed so that the error would be minimum. Since the historical data may contain 0 values, the mean absolute error cannot be used. So it has been decided to evaluate model performance by the average percentage error (APE) for the whole testing period (13):

$$APE = \frac{\sum_{i=start}^{end} (Y_i - F_i)}{\sum_{i=start}^{end} Y_i} \cdot 100\% \tag{13}$$

where

- *start* – period number when the testing period starts (19th period),
- *end* – period number when the testing period ends (24th period).

Also, to evaluate the deviation of the model the mean square error (MSE) can be used. Such metric allows giving weight to differences depending on their value. MSE can be presented in the following form (14):

$$MSE = \frac{1}{n} \cdot \sum_{i=start}^{end} (Y_i - F_i)^2 \tag{14}$$

However, MSE by itself is difficult to use for comparison of forecasting models performance for different details since the scale of sales can be different. For comparison, percentage values are more applicable. So it was decided to use rooted MSE, divided by the average number of actual time series values, which allows computing model percentage deviation (RMSPE) (15):

$$RMSPE = \frac{\sqrt{MSE}}{\frac{1}{n} \cdot \sum_{i=start}^{end} Y_i} \cdot 100\% \tag{15}$$

For the Holt-Winters models, each of $\alpha$, $\beta$, and $\gamma$ has been iterated from 0,1 to 0,9 with step 0,1. For each set of these factors both additive and multiplicative models have been built.

For ARIMA models, parameters p and q have been iterated from 0 to 4 with step 1. For parameter d, the following values have been taken: 0, 1, 2.

## 5   Results

Analysis and predictions have been performed for the ten most tradable details (within this paper each detail has been given an identification label from 'A' to 'J'). Figures below capture line graphs of built models for every detail (Figs. 2, 3, 4, 5, 6, 7, 8, 9, 10, 11, 12, 13, 14, 15, 16, 17, 18, 19, 20 and 21) according to the calculated parameters (see Table 3). The vertical axis defines quantity of sold/forecasted elements; the horizontal axis defines a period number in the format 'year.month' (e.g., '18.11' – November of 2018). Red line graph represents actual time series; green – modeled training part of the data set; blue – built forecast based on modeled training part. The built forecast includes 6 periods of testing part and additional 4 periods, which exceed the original number of periods. It is done to visualize the overall future behavior of the model (additional 4 periods are not used for performance evaluation).

The following table collects information about parameters for Holt-Winters and ARIMA models for each detail, where 'a' stands for 'additivity' model, and 'm' stands for 'multiplicity' model (Table 3).

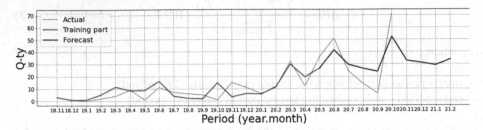

**Fig. 2.** Detail 'A' plots: Holt-Winters model.

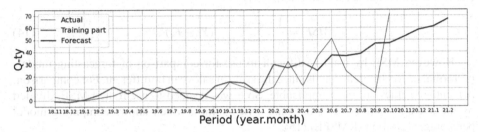

**Fig. 3.** Detail 'A' plots: ARIMA model.

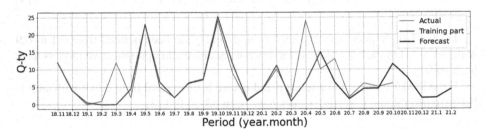

**Fig. 4.** Detail 'B' plots: Holt-Winters model.

## 6 Analysis

As can be observed from the graphs above, Holt-Winters models build forecasts with a more precise reproduction of the nature and patterns of the original data than ARIMA models. For example, for detail with id 'A' (see Figs. 2, 3) TES model repeats the original peaks and drops at periods 20.6, 20.9, 20.10, while the ARIMA model reproduces increasing trend only. Additionally, Holt-Winters models reproduce the training part of the data set with more accuracy, as it is for details 'B' (see Fig. 4), 'C' (see Fig. 6), 'D' (see Fig. 8), 'F' (see Fig. 12).

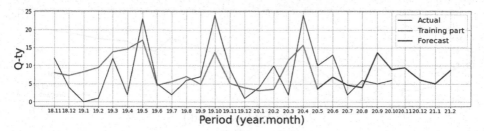

**Fig. 5.** Detail 'B' plots: ARIMA model.

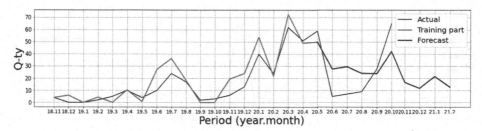

**Fig. 6.** Detail 'C' plots: Holt-Winters model.

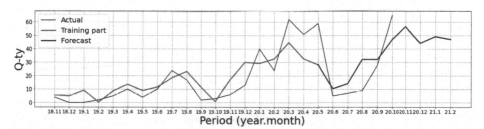

**Fig. 7.** Detail 'C' plots: ARIMA model.

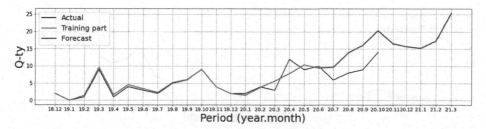

**Fig. 8.** Detail 'D' plots: Holt-Winters model.

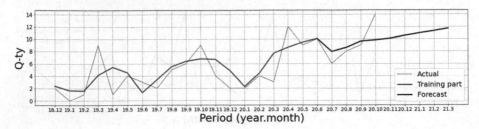

**Fig. 9.** Detail 'D' plots: ARIMA model.

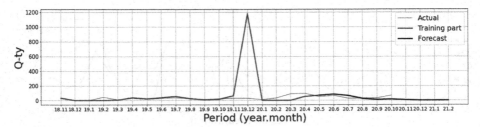

**Fig. 10.** Detail 'E' plots: Holt-Winters model.

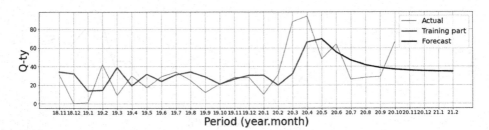

**Fig. 11.** Detail 'E' plots: ARIMA model.

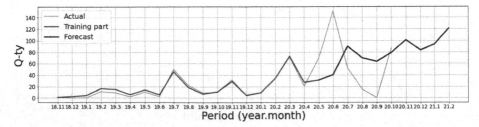

**Fig. 12.** Detail 'F' plots: Holt-Winters model.

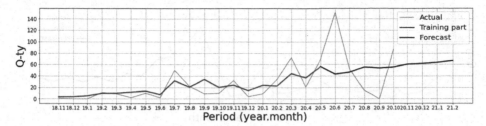

**Fig. 13.** Detail 'F' plots: ARIMA model.

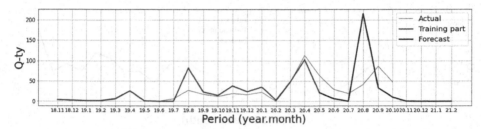

**Fig. 14.** Detail 'G' plots: Holt-Winters model.

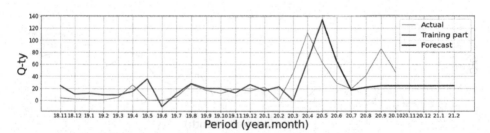

**Fig. 15.** Detail 'G' plots: ARIMA model.

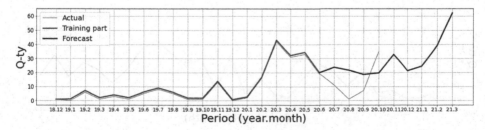

**Fig. 16.** Detail 'H' plots: Holt-Winters model.

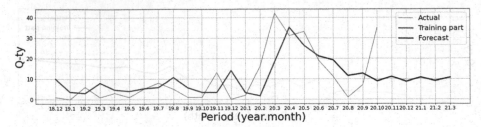

**Fig. 17.** Detail 'H' plots: ARIMA model.

**Fig. 18.** Detail 'I' plots: Holt-Winters model.

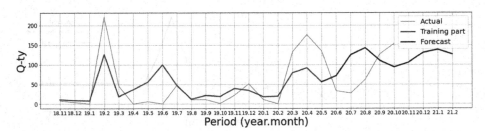

**Fig. 19.** Detail 'I' plots: ARIMA model.

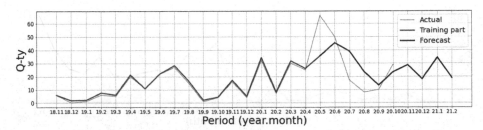

**Fig. 20.** Detail 'J' plots: Holt-Winters model.

**Fig. 21.** Detail 'J' plots: ARIMA model.

**Table 3.** Models' parameters

| Detail | Holt-Winters parameters | APE | MSE | RMSPE | ARIMA parameters | APE | MSE | RMSPE |
|---|---|---|---|---|---|---|---|---|
| A | $\alpha = 0.5; \beta = 0.3; \gamma = 0.1;$ (a) | 0.01% | 171.5 | 38% | $p = 2; d = 2; q = 0;$ | 14.1% | 533 | 69.84% |
| B | $\alpha = 0.6; \beta = 0.4; \gamma = 0.1;$ (m) | 2.6% | 17.1 | 59% | $p = 4; d = 0; q = 0;$ | 0.16% | 28.65 | 76.46% |
| C | $\alpha = 0.7; \beta = 0.4; \gamma = 0.1;$ (m) | 0.15% | 920.9 | 105% | $p = 4; d = 1; q = 4;$ | 5.03% | 316.4 | 61.68% |
| D | $\alpha = 0.2; \beta = 0.3; \gamma = 0.2;$ (a) | 0.11% | 3.9 | 21% | $p = 2; d = 1; q = 4;$ | 2.1% | 4.42 | 22.37% |
| E | $\alpha = 0.7; \beta = 0.9; \gamma = 0.9;$ (m) | 0.12% | 859.4 | 67% | $p = 1; d = 0; q = 0;$ | 10.5% | 350.9 | 43.06% |
| F | $\alpha = 0.1; \beta = 0.7; \gamma = 0.8;$ (a) | 0.01% | 3682 | 97% | $p = 2; d = 1; q = 0;$ | 16.9% | 2859 | 86.32% |
| G | $\alpha = 0.4; \beta = 0.9; \gamma = 0.6;$ (m) | 0.04% | 6192 | 165% | $p = 0; d = 0; q = 4;$ | 0.69% | 1835 | 90.2% |
| H | $\alpha = 0.1; \beta = 0.1; \gamma = 0.9;$ (a) | 42.2% | 191 | 94% | $p = 3; d = 0; q = 1;$ | 0.11% | 179.8 | 91.86% |
| I | $\alpha = 0.3; \beta = 0.1; \gamma = 0.1;$ (a) | 0.52% | 990 | 35% | $p = 4; d = 1; q = 0;$ | 11.4% | 4584 | 75.79% |
| J | $\alpha = 0.6; \beta = 0.3; \gamma = 0.4;$ (a) | 0.02% | 285 | 56% | $p = 0; d = 1; q = 0;$ | 0.1% | 520.4 | 76.045 |
| **Average** | | 4.6% | 1331 | 74% | | 6.12% | 1127 | 69.4% |

As can be seen from the table, the average APE for Holt-Winters models is lesser than the average APE for the ARIMA model. Additionally, after a direct comparison of both APEs for every detail, it can be stated that Holt-Winters models are much more accurate than the ARIMA models (except for details with ids 'B', 'H').

But on the other hand, Holt-Winters models perform worse in terms of MSE and RMSPE in comparison with ARIMA models. It indicates that TES models forecast with greater dispersion of values.

The higher accuracy of the Holt-Winters models in terms of seasons and trends replication can be explained by the fact that the whole data set has been used for computing the initial trend and seasonality. But for the ARIMA model only the training data set has been used as input data. So ARIMA builds models with information about a lesser number of periods, which could impact the accuracy of the models. So, the hypothesis made in the 'Analysis and Modelling Approach' section has been confirmed.

## 7 Conclusion

In conclusion, in the course of this work time series forecasting has been examined. Two forecasting methods have been reviewed and applied for forecasting supply inventory of the mining and the metallurgical equipment based on the historical data – triple exponential smoothing (Holt-Winters) and ARIMA. Mentioned methods have been successfully implemented using python.

Considering the small number of periods of historical data, APE for the whole testing period is small for the most of Holt-Winters model. Which would mean, that triple exponential smoothing is more applicable for short-term forecasting of the mining and metallurgical supplies time series.

However, the limitation should be noted. Analyzed time series are extremely short since the historical data includes only 24 periods (i.e. 2 complete seasons). So, time series have been divided into ratio 18 training periods and 6(+4) forecasting periods, which is the most optimal solution – moving forecasting range to the left to the start of data (increasing testing periods by decreasing the training set), will worsen the forecast accuracy (lesser the training – lesser the accuracy); moving forecasting range to the right, out of the original data ending (decreasing testing set), will worsen the performance evaluation since a lesser number of forecasted and original values could be compared.

The built forecasting algorithms are ready to be used and applied for metallurgical-mining inventory predictions in practical conditions.

As a continuation of this paper, a solution will be built to enhance the usage of additional forecasting methods. They would allow strategy and plan control by considering additional factors and parameters, which can affect the overall forecast model. For future work the following methods can be studied: Bayesian network, neural network, and machine learning.

## References

1. Tejesh, S.S.B., Neeraja, S.: Warehouse inventory management system using IoT and opensource framework. Alexandria Eng. J. **57**(4), 3817–3823 (2018)

2. Forecast NOW! https://fnow.ru. Accessed 26 Feb 2021
3. Net-stock. https://digital-company.ru/net-stock/?gclid=Cj0KCQiAwMP9BRCzARIsA PWTJ_GECrm6aZqYw6N39NhuEh8O-TAh6uyI0iQNQhSP8VDKqKFVGX0nw64aAo dGEALw_wcB. Accessed 26 Feb 2021
4. GoodsForecast. https://goodsforecast.ru/. Accessed 26 Feb 2021
5. Inventor Soft. https://inventorsoft.ru/. Accessed 26 Feb 2021
6. Stock-M Consulting. https://stockm.ru/. Accessed 26 Feb 2021
7. Ferreira, M., Santos, A., Lucio, P.: Short-term forecast of wind speed through mathematical models. Energy Rep. **5**, 1172–1184 (2019)
8. Karami, Z., Kashef, R.: Smart transportation planning: data, models, and algorithms. Transp. Eng. **2**, 100013 (2020)
9. Jiang, W., Wu, X., Gong, Y., Yu, W., Zhong, X.: Holt–Winters smoothing enhanced by fruit fly optimization algorithm to forecast monthly electricity consumption. Energy **193**, 116779 (2020)
10. Faghih, S., Shah, A., Wang, Z., Safikhani, A.: Kamga, C: Taxi and mobility: modeling taxi demand using ARMA and linear regression. Procedia Comput. Sci. **177**, 186–195 (2020)
11. Sahai, A.K., Rath, N., Sood, V., Singh, M.P.: ARIMA modelling & forecasting of COVID-19 in top five affected countries. Diab. Metab. Synd.: Clin. Res. Rev. **14**(5), 1419–1427 (2020)
12. Ramos, P., Santos, N., Rebelo, R.: Performance of state space and ARIMA models for consumer retail sales forecasting. Robot. Comput.-Integr. Manuf. **34**, 151–163 (2015)
13. Bhanuka, D., Osanda, H., Nuwan, L., Dilantha, H., Adeesha, W.: A comparison of ARIMAX, VAR and LSTM on multivariate short-term traffic volume forecasting. In: Conference of Open Innovations Association, FRUCT, vol. 5, pp. 564–570 (2021)
14. Runge, J., Zmeureanu, R., Le Cam, M.: Hybrid short-term forecasting of the electric demand of supply fans using machine learning. J. Build. Eng. **29**, 101144 (2020)
15. Prestwich, S.D. Tarim, S.A., Rossi, R.: Intermittency and obsolescence: a Croston method with linear decay. Int. J. Forecast. **37**(2), 708–715 (2021)
16. Boutselis, P., McNaught, K.: Using Bayesian Networks to forecast spares demand from equipment failures in a changing service logistics context. Int. J. Prod. Econ. **209**, 325–333 (2019)
17. Hyndman, R.J., Athanasopoulos, G.: Forecasting: Principles and Practice, 2nd edn. OTexts, Melbourne (2013). OTexts.com/fpp2

# Facilitating Adoption of B2B e-Commerce Platforms

Anastasiia Berezina, Ekaterina Buzulukova[⊠], and Olga Tretyak

Higher School of Economics, Myasnitskaya 20, 101000 Moscow, Russian Federation
{aoberezina,ebuzulukova,otretyak}@hse.ru

**Abstract.** Currently there is a lot of research that stresses the importance of customer relationship management based on the development of e-commerce platforms. However, when we make the transition to the b2b market we are faced with problems of customer adoption of such systems. Even though we live in a digital era with the recent pandemic forcing the shift to online processes, many companies still prefer to deal with real people and company representatives. The aim of the present research is to reveal and analyze factors that contribute to adoption of e-commerce systems in b2b markets and give recommendations on how to engage partners in it without losing revenues and clients. The methodology includes an analysis of answers of 329 respondents who have used the e-commerce b2b platform in the last 6 months. Data analysis was done with structural modeling that helped to understand the main drivers of e-commerce system adoption.

**Keywords:** e-Commerce platform · B2B · Factors of adoption

## 1 Introduction

Global B2B e-commerce volume has been showing an almost threefold growth over the past decade [10]. The Russian e-commerce market is significantly behind the world, growing at a rate of 23%, behind the market leaders USA and China. However, this accounts for less than 1% of the global e-commerce investment market [9]. The reasons for the rapid growth of B2B e-commerce are changes in customer behavior, the recent pandemic and the fact that B2B e-commerce platforms are becoming a crucial marketing channel for many businesses. According to the recent research implementation of e-commerce platforms can significantly reduce costs, increase competitive advantage, improve customer experience [14] and become a factor of business growth [8]. Many Russian companies (Severstal, Sberbank, Yandex) are making significant investments in b2b e-commerce platforms. In the current research we will focus on the experience of Heineken platform that was launched in 2018. Despite the fact that introducing e-commerce platforms is the current trend, many companies are still facing problems in engaging their partners in it: low level of platform use, negative feedback from the users, and unwillingness of customers to switch from the traditional channels of dealing with company representatives. Therefore, understanding the factors that facilitate the adoption of e-commerce platforms is of crucial importance for companies. More precisely it

D. A. Alexandrov et al. (Eds.): DTGS 2021, CCIS 1503, pp. 522–535, 2022.
https://doi.org/10.1007/978-3-030-93715-7_37

can help increase return on investments in the development, improve customer engagement, and optimize costs for managing company representatives. The aim of the present study is to reveal factors that contribute to adoption of e-commerce systems in b2b markets and give recommendations on how to engage partners with the platforms without losing revenues and clients. The research is based on data obtained from the partner engagement in b2b e-commerce platform of the leading beer company in the Russian market. The 329 respondents are the representatives of retail outlets, which used the e-commerce platform to order goods over the past 6 months. The main tool for conducting the study was an online questionnaire that is widely used in e-commerce adoption studies [26]. The study was conducted between January and April 2020. Data analysis was performed using structural equation modeling that helped reduce the number of factors under consideration and identified latent and dependent variables in the research.

## 2 Literature Review

### 2.1 Review of Technology Adoption Models

In the present paper, we examine theoretical models for the adoption of information technologies, which can be defined as the use of computer equipment, programs, and applications to support business operations [25]. Researchers use several theoretical models to explain factors influencing innovation adoption. including e-commerce. We consider some of them, that are more appropriate for the research goal, summarize all the mentioned determinants and develop research model that will test in the quantitative research.

In the technology organizational-environmental model [26] there are mentioned technological, organizational, and environmental factors. Technological factors include internal ones (existing technologies within the company) and external (the pool of available technologies in the market). Organizational factors include the size of the company; scope of application; centralization; formalization and complexity of the management structure; quality of human resources (staff qualifications); the number of available resources. External factors are the firm's industry, competitive environment, access to resources and relations with the government.

Rogers' theory of innovation diffusion (DOI) [22] is based on the fact that innovation adoption occurs in several stages, including understanding, persuasion, decision-making, implementation, and confirmation. Also, he mentioned the influence of technological characteristics (innovative attributes) that can affect the level of acceptance and dissemination of innovations: relative advantage, compatibility, complexity, suitability for testing, observability of innovation [22]. This theory of innovation diffusion is one of the popular theoretical models in researches of B2B e-commerce adoption [1, 2].

1. The relative advantage is the degree to which innovation is perceived better than the one that preceded it.
2. Compatibility is the degree to which innovation is perceived as relevant (not contradicting) existing values, needs, and past experiences of potential receivers.
3. Complexity is the degree to which innovation is perceived as complex to use.
4. Test suitability is the degree to which innovation can be tested before use.

5.  The observability of innovation is the degree to which the results of an innovation are visible to the company.

Another widely used concept is the Technology Acceptance Model, which was proposed by Davis [7]. The model takes into account perceived attributes such as "perceived utility" and "perceived ease of use," which affect the adoption of information technologies. The study model is shown in Fig. 1.

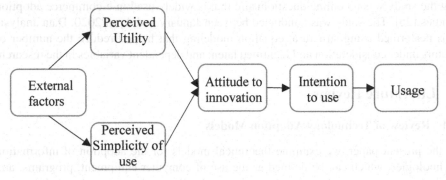

**Fig. 1.** Technology adoption model [7].

Perceived utility is interpreted as the degree to which a person "believes that using a certain system can increase its performance," and perceived ease of use is "the degree to which a person believes that using a system will not require much effort." All this affects the potential user's attitude to the use of a new system, which is directly related to the intention to use new technology within that system.

The remaining studies mention factors related to internal organization, software costs, complexity, and cost of software and also highlight a set of attributes, like network security [8] launch costs [28], the cost of software aimed at integrating e-commerce.

## 2.2  The Research Model

During the literature review it became clear that the adoption of innovations in the B2B market is influenced by a range of factors related to both the innovation itself and the characteristics of the organization and decision-making agents, as well as external factors, such as the competitor pressure and the level of technological progress [16].

**Innovation Characteristics**

The factors related to the characteristics of the innovation itself most often include the perceived benefits that a company receives from operating an e-commerce platform and the perceived costs that a company will incur if it decides to use the innovation. Such costs include additional expertise and the need to train the staff, and therefore the time it will take to adapt to a new way of interacting with a partner [14]. Perceived benefits refer to the company's important benefits that it could gain only through the use of an online store [28]. Benefits mean the likelihood that using the platform will increase performance in the organizational context [7]. In other words, if an organization does not realize or see the benefits of the new technology, it will be less predisposed to use it.

Another important characteristic of innovation that either promotes or impedes its adoption is the perceived complexity of its use [21]. Obviously, less complex innovations are more likely to be adopted than those that seem too complex and difficult to understand. That is the degree to which a potential user expects that using the platform will not require additional effort.

**Decision-Maker Characteristics**

A study by Mirchandani and Motwani [19] found that a number of decision-maker characteristics determine the likelihood of using e-commerce platforms. Other researchers argued that technical skills of the user, experience of using e-commerce for personal purposes, and their attitudes to online purchases that affect the success of information technology adoption [17]. In other words, small companies, which include traditional trade enterprises, the circle of decision-makers is limited to a small number of people, and their experience with online stores in everyday life. The decision-makers in this case, are worried about leaks of information, lost data about their orders, etc., or if they had some negative online shopping experience, they are definitely less inclined to use e-commerce platforms for business purposes. In addition, Internet skills, as well as the level of competence with electronic devices, can either foster or hinder the adaptation of e-commerce platforms [20].

**External Factors**

External factors in the literature most often include pressure from buyers, suppliers, and competitors, as well as the level of support from the integrator (organization introducing a new platform) [21]. In the context of B2B e-commerce, many scholars have identified competitive pressures as an important factor in platform adoption [23, 29] if companies see such adoption as a competitive edge that will help them get better positions in the market.

In the present study, by external factors, we mean the degree of awareness by traditional commercial companies of the use of e-commerce platforms to replenish the stock of goods by other outlets, as well as the influence of the integrator's sales representative on the facilitation of the use of the online store. According to research, the success of e-commerce implementation depends on the pressure of trading partners to use for business [16].

The integrators' sales representatives can provide training to the staff of outlets to operate the new platform, as well as talk about the benefits of its use. At the same time, the study suggests that the commercial enterprise staff are usually not interested in promoting innovation, as they understand that one of the goals it is reducing the cost of their labor. Because the communication of sales representatives with customers is not under the company's supervision, the only way to verify the validity of our assumption is by including questions regarding the work of sales agents in a survey for a field study.

Based on the literature review we identify hypotheses for further research:

Hypothesis 1: There is a negative correlation between perceived complexity and level of B2B e-commerce adoption.

Hypothesis 2: There is a negative correlation between technical flaws and level of B2B e-commerce adoption.

Hypothesis 3: There is a positive correlation between perceived benefits and level of B2B e-commerce adoption.

Hypothesis 4: There is a negative correlation between perceived costs and level of B2B e-commerce adoption.

Hypothesis 5: There is a positive correlation between the technical skills of decision-makers and the adoption level of B2B e-commerce.

Hypothesis 6: There is a negative correlation between the past online shopping experience and level of B2B e-commerce adoption.

Hypothesis 7: There is a positive correlation between sales representatives' impact on enterprise and level of B2B e-commerce adoption.

Hypothesis 8: There is a positive correlation between competitor's pressure and level of B2B e-commerce adoption.

Thus, the research model is illustrated in Fig. 2.

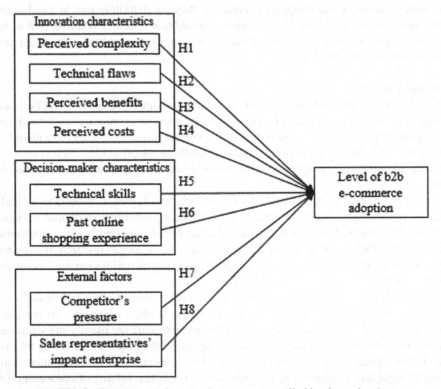

**Fig. 2.** The research framework ( source: compiled by the authors).

# 3  Methodology

Data were obtained from answers of corporate users of e-commerce b2b platform of leading beer producer in the Russian market that have ordered products over the past six months. The study was conducted between January and April 2020. There are 329 responses have been received from online questionnaire and analyzed by structural equation modeling (SEM). The general population is 40,000 retail outlets who have access to the b2b e-commerce platform. SEM is the main method of analysis which is widely used in the academic environment to study the implementation of electronic technologies, their acceptance, and the conditions under which they can be achieved [18].

## 3.1  Respondent Profile

The respondents are the representatives of traditional retail outlets. Their profile can be found in the Table 1.

**Table 1.**  The respondents profile.

| Var. | Average | Median | Mode | St.dev |
|------|---------|--------|------|--------|
| Number of orders per month | 4 | 4 | 4 | 2 |
| Monthly beer turnover, rub | 259 958 | 198 725 | 192 301 | 271 000 |
| Number of purchased SKU | 66 | 62 | 60 | 37 |
| Weekly purchase volume, boxes | 39 | 30 | 20 | 37 |
| N | **329** | **329** | **329** | **329** |

The average age of respondents is 38 (st.dev. = 8.81), they live mainly in Ulan Ude (29%), Ekaterinburg (25%), Vladivostok (13%), St. Petersburg (12%). 84% of respondents had the online purchase experience. Most respondents mentioned that platform helped them save time on placing orders (Fig. 3).

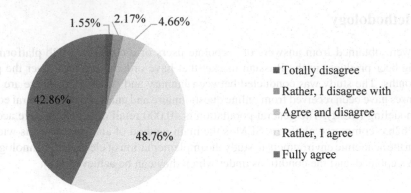

Fig. 3. Using e-commerce platform allows faster to place an order

## 3.2 Data Analysis

Initially, indicator questions were compiled based on the study of the theoretical part to identify latent variables affecting the level of innovation adoption (Table 2).

As part of the preparatory phase, the KMO (Kaisera- Mayera- Olken) -0.849 and Bartlett's Test of Sphericity were performed, where the significance was Sig = 0.000, which showed that the data could be used for the principal component method. Five latent variables were constructed using a metric analysis of the main components with the Varimax rotation method, relating to the experience of respondents interacting with e-commerce platforms. According to the Kaiser criterion, latent variables explain 60.5% of the total variance, the remaining 17 variables have eigen numbers less than one.

According to the matrix of factor loadings, the general structure turned out to be similar to the original theoretical model. Indicators such as Online Shopping Experience and Technical skills have been categorized as well as Perceived expenses and Perceived Benefits. The main reason why latent variables are grouped is the relationship in the eyes of the company's customers, and the method of the main components cannot build correlating factors. The total number of factors turned out to be less than in the theoretical model.

The variables related to online shopping experience were merged with technical skills of the user into one. This is possible due to the close value in the eyes of respondents since they relate to the decision-maker characteristics. Also, the variables "Perceived costs" and "Perceived Benefits" related to the characteristics of innovation have become one factor, as they are of close importance in terms of complexity, time costs, and platform convenience. The structure of factors was hence to build a measuring and structural model. The hypotheses will be adjusted according to the structural model.

**Table 2.** Variables that reflect the experience of using B2B e-commerce platform.

| Constructs | Variable indicators | Indicators |
|---|---|---|
| Past online shopping experience | I like to shop online | Ex_1 |
| | I shop online regularly | Ex_2 |
| | Overall, I can describe my online shopping experience as positive | Ex_3 |
| Technical skills | I always use the Internet for personal purposes, including to communicate with friends and family | Techusage_1 |
| | I am good with various technical devices (computer, phone and tablet) | Techusage_2 |
| | I regularly use the internet to get up-to-date information | Techusage_3 |
| Perceived costs | Ordering through planform seems to be more time-consuming than ordering through a sales representative | Cost_1 |
| | To use the platform, I need to purchase some extra technical equipment | Cost_2 |
| | Learning to use the platform was difficult for me | Cost_3 |
| Perceived benefits | Using the platform allows me to place an order at a convenient time for me | Benefit_1 |
| | Using the platform saves me time | Benefit_2 |
| | With the use of SS, it became easier for me to get the necessary information about the goods and their prices | Benefit_3 |
| Environmental | I am sure that rival stores are already using SS to order Heineken goods | External_1 |
| | Sales representatives motivate me to use the platform | External_2 |
| | I am aware of the need to use the platform to stay competitive with other stores | External_3 |
| | Sales representatives explain to me in detail the benefits of using the platform | External_4 |
| Technical flaws | When placing an order through the platform, errors often occur in the assembly of orders (wrong number of articles, errors in the invoice, etc.) | Problems_2 |

*(continued)*

**Table 2.** (*continued*)

| Constructs | Variable indicators | Indicators |
|---|---|---|
| | The platform often contains non-descriptive information about goods or their prices | Problems_3 |
| Intention to use | How likely is it that you will use the platform for placing orders in the future? | Intention |
| Preferences | Would prefer to use the platform to order an item instead of an order through a sales representative? | Preference |

Structural model parameters are evaluated on the same sample of 329 respondents. The quality of approximation of the correlation matrix according to the chi-square criterion ($\frac{1}{4}$ 2) $= 442.197$, two absolute approximation quality indices, GFI $= 0.9$ and CFI $= 0.93$, exceeding the required threshold values, also indicate the acceptability of the model. Absolute index RMSEA $= 0.057$. SRMR $= 0.053$ which does not exceed the limit for validity. The indicators are within acceptable limits for validity, which allows us to move on to the model interpretation (Table 3).

**Table 3.** Structural model quality indices

| Index | Model data | Standard value |
|---|---|---|
| GFI | 0.90 | 1 |
| AGFI | 0.86 | 1 |
| SRMR | 0.053 | $\leq 0.09$ |
| RMSEA | 0.057 | $\leq 0.08$ |
| NFI | 0.87 | $\geq 0.9$ |
| NNFI | 0.91 | $\geq 0.9$ |
| CFI | 0.93 | $\geq 0.9$ |
| TLI | 0.914 | 1 |
| PGFI | 0.691 | 1 |
| PNFI | 0.733 | 1 |

The final model is performed in the Fig. 4.

So, almost all correlations between model constructs are statistically significant, except for Perceived Complexity, which has a weak negative effect on the adoption of B2B e-commerce. Although the impact of this variable is small, it is negative and can play a role in the customer's decision to shift to the platform. Here you need to pay attention to web platform navigation and its functionality. As for variable expenses which reflect potential benefits from use, it has a weak positive influence on B2B e-commerce. The

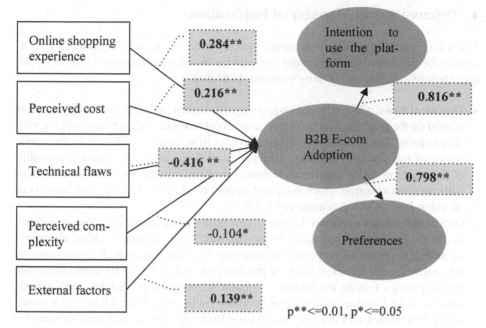

**Fig. 4.** The final structural model of B2B e-commerce adoption

variable of B2B e-commerce Adoption itself is formed from the potential Intention to use and Preferences to this platform by respondents who, in general, as far as they say about how much customers are ready to try a new way to interact with the company and place an order on the site.

According to the results of the analysis, the following hypotheses were confirmed:

H1 was supported: there is a negative correlation between perceived complexity and level of B2B e-commerce adoption in traditional trade.

H2 was supported: there is a negative correlation between technical flaws and level of B2B e-commerce adoption in traditional trade.

H4 was rejected, because the model proved a positive correlation between perceived costs and level of B2B e-commerce adoption in traditional trade.

H6 was supported: there is a positive correlation between the online shopping experience and level of B2B e-commerce adoption in traditional trade.

The variables mentioned in hypothesis 7 (sales representative impact) and 8 (competitors pressure) were combined in a single factor – the external factors, that has a positive correlation with the level of B2B e-commerce adoption. Variables from the hypothesis 3 (perceived benefits) and 5 (technical skills) didn't show the significant influence to e-commerce adoption factor.

## 4   Discussion and Managerial Implications

According to the final research model special attention in development of b2b e-commerce platforms should be paid to variables that have the greatest impact on the transition of customers to B2B e-commerce platform:

- **Technical flaws**, which have the largest negative impact, reflect the reliability of information on the platform and the presence of any errors with orders when working with the platform. There are indeed negative reviews from customers. Based on the significance of this variable, company managers should pay more attention to the quality of the platform and eliminate all technical problems on the site. This is consistent with previous research which indicated impact of platform features and benefits to adoption level of b2b e-commerce [3, 22].
- **Online shopping experience** has the largest positive impact and expresses the ability to use the Internet and technical devices, as well as the attitude to online shopping, including for personal purposes. In particular, the adoption of B2B e-commerce is influenced by the technical skills of the decision-maker. The main components are the frequency of using the Internet to obtain information, proficiency with various devices, and a positive attitude to purchases on the Internet. This in line with research which find influence IT experience and knowledge on b2b e-commerce adoption [12, 27].
- **External factors** have the second-largest positive influence and refers to pressure from competitors and sales representatives of the company. It reflects an awareness of the need for transition and the benefits of using the platform. The main factor here is the influence of the sales representative and the awareness of the need to use the platform to maintain the competitiveness of the company. This fact supported by earlier research which agreed that competitive pressure a significant factor of B2B e-commerce adoption. The findings of this study support earlier investigations [13, 14].

The conducted research allowed us to formulate the following recommendations:

Firstly, it is worth paying attention to Technical flaws of the platform, since it has been identified as one of the factors with the greatest negative impact. Therefore, to increase customer satisfaction with the platform interaction experience, it is recommended to create test groups of stores and outlets that will be used to identify all technical problems before introducing innovations. Particular attention should be paid to errors in putting together the orders, setting KPIs to the employees of the logistics department on the number of correctly assembled orders. This is consistent with many negative reviews on the experience of ordering goods through the platform.

Secondly, it is worth revising the goals of the sales team and developing a new approach aimed at connecting new outlets that are not permanently covered and previously did not have experience in interacting with the company. This could be one of the key elements of the strategy aimed at increasing the share of e-commerce in the company's sales. You can expect an increase in the positive impact of the 'external factors' on the intention to use the system leading to the adoption of e-commerce if you join forces with other FMCG companies. Follow the concept of open innovation by concluding partnership agreements, increasing the influence of an external factor - pressure from a trading partner. This will help to take the first step towards additional profit from the platform, as well as provide an opportunity to reduce the cost of developing technology by dividing them among all partners. Expanding the range with the products of other companies will increase the attractiveness of the platform, as it potentially carries time savings for communication with various sales representatives. As practice has shown, customers do not hurry to switch to the e-commerce platform, so it is necessary to make the transition of existing customers smoother, leaving them the opportunity to interact with sales representatives through additional communication channels (online chat), without the physical presence of sales representatives at the outlet. This will give them more time to explore the platform and understand the benefits of its use. This is an unconditional benefit for the company too, as it will have a large reserve to improve new processes of interaction with customers through the platform and adapt to the new business model.

Thirdly, pay attention of the experience of online purchases of customers, as this can become the main indicator when deciding on the transfer of the client to the platform and calculating the required investments in their training and motivation. Customers with more experience in buying through e-commerce platforms, and proficient with various technical devices, require less investment.

It is also worth reducing the expenses of using the platform with the help of exclusive promotions, personalized offers, and unique types of services, to differentiate the b2b e-commerce channel from the standard experience of purchasing products through a sales representative. Increase the perceived benefits of this factor by creating training materials that explain the functionality of the platform and demonstrate interactive "tutorials" on the site, which will help to guide newcomers around the site and make an order faster. Consider providing free technical equipment to retail outlets to provide access to the site. Also, pay special attention to the perceived complexity of the platform. It is worth considering the possibility of developing a simplified registration mechanism for customers without interacting with a sales representative (self-registration). For example, create a mobile application that provides simplified access to the site through a mobile phone and does not require special technical equipment. But all this does not need to replace personal interaction, which can convey the benefits of use and increase the speed of training. Therefore, the company could provide training materials and faster customer service to provide a positive impression on the interaction with the digital channel and the company as a whole in the future.

## 5   Limitations

The respondents of the research were corporate representatives of only one e-commerce b2b platform, so the significance of the identified factors may differ if we add the experience of working in other b2b e-commerce platforms. Additionally, it is the possible influence cultural characteristics and level of country development on the adoption of the platforms mentioned earlier [1], in the current research we have investigated only Russian users' experience of current customers who were already using the platform. This is consistent with previous research of b2b e-commerce adoption [5, 11]. Also noteworthy fact is the positive correlation between perceived costs (cost_1, cost_2, cost_3 indicator) and level of b2b platform adoption, probably that is because the spending more time on learning the more positive I perceived the platform, but this fact requires additional interviews with the respondents.

# References

1. Al-Qirim, N.: The adoption of eCommerce communications and applications technologies in small businesses in New Zealand. Electron. Comm. Res. Appl. **6**(4), 462–470 (2007)
2. Alsaad, A., Mohamad, R., Ismail, N.A.: The moderating role of power exercise in B2B E-commerce adoption decision. Procedia – Soc. Behav. Sci. **130**, 5–523 (2014)
3. Alsaad, A., Mohamad, R., Ismail, N.A.: The moderating role of trust in business to business electronic commerce (B2B EC) adoption. Comput. Hum. Behav/ **68**, 157–169 (2017)
4. Bajwa, D.S., Lewis, L.F., Pervan, G., Lai, V.S.: The adoption and use of collaboration information technologies: international comparisons. J. Inf. Technol. **20**, 130–140 (2005)
5. Chakravarty, A., Kumar, A., Grewal, R.: Customer orientation structure for internet-based business-to-business platform firms. J. Mark. **78**(5), 1–23 (2014)
6. Crook, C.W., Kumar, R.L.: Electronic data interchange: a multi-industry investigation using grounded theory. Inf. Manag. **34**, 75–89 (1998)
7. Davis, F.D.: Perceived usefulness, perceived ease of use, and user acceptance of information technology. MIS Q. **13**(3), 319–340 (1989)
8. Doherty, N.F., Fulford, H.: Aligning the information security policy with strategic information systems plan. Comput. Secur. **25**(1), 55–63 (2006)
9. E-commerce in Russia part 1: Market trends and players 'strategies. https://ecommerce.ewdn.com/
10. E-commerce worldwide, Statistics and Facts Published. https://www.statista.com/topics/871/online-shopping/
11. Grewal, R., Chakravarty, A., Saini, A.: Governance mechanisms in business-to business electronic markets. J. Mark. **74**(4), 45–62 (2010)
12. Ghobakhloo, M., Tang, S.H.: The role of owner/manager in adoption of electronic commerce in small businesses: the case of developing countries. J. Small Bus. Enterp. Dev. **20**(4), 754–787 (2013)
13. Ghobakhloo, M., Arias-Aranda, D., Benitez-Amado, J.: Adoption of e-commerce applications in SMEs. Ind. Manag. Data Syst. **111**(8), 1238–1269 (2011)
14. Hamad, H., Elbeltagi, I., El-Gohary, H.: An empirical investigation of business-to-business e-commerce adoption and its impact on SMEs competitive advantage: the case of Egyptian manufacturing SMEs. Strateg. Change **27**(3), 209–229 (2018)
15. Hong, W., Zhu, K.: Migrating to internet-based e-commerce: factors affecting e-commerce adoption and migration at the firm level. Inf. Manag. **43**(1), 204–221 (2006)
16. Ifinedo, P.: An empirical analysis of factors influencing internet/e-business technologies adoption by SMEs in Canada. Int. J. Inf. Technol. Decis. Mak. **10**(4), 731–766 (2011)
17. Kuan, K.K., Chau, P.Y.: A perception-based model for EDI adoption in small business using a technology-organizational-environment framework. Inf. Manag. **38**, 517–521 (2001)
18. Malhotra, A., Gosain, S., El Sawy, O.A.: Leveraging standard electronic busines interfaces to enable adaptive supply chain partnerships. Inf. Syst. Res. **18**(3), 260–279 (2007)
19. Mirchandani, D.A., Motwani, J.: Understanding small business electronic commerce adoption: an empirical analysis. J. Comput. Inf. Syst. **41**(3), 70–73 (2001)
20. Morteza, G., Daniel, A., Jose, A.: Adoption of e-commerce applications in SMEs. Ind. Manag. Data Syst. **111**(8), 1238–1269 (2011)

21. Premkumar, G., Roberts, M.: Adoption of new information technologies in rural small businesses. Int. J. Manag. Sci. **27**(4), 467–484 (1999)
22. Rogers, E.M.: Diffusion of Innovations, p. 512, 5th edn. Free Press, New York (2003)
23. Sila, I.: Factors affecting the adoption of B2B E-commerce technologies. Electron. Comm. Res. **13**, 199–236 (2013)
24. Son, J., Benbasat, I.: Organizational buyers' adoption and use of B2B electronic marketplaces: efficiency- and legitimacy-oriented perspectives. J. Manag. Inf. Syst. **24**(1), 55–99 (2007)
25. Taylor, S., Todd, P.: Decomposition and crossover effects in the theory of planned behavior: a study of consumer adoption intentions. Int. J. Res. Mark. **12**, 137–155 (1995)
26. Thong, J., Yap, C.: CEO characteristics, organizational characteristics and information technology adoption in small businesses. Omega **23**, 429–442 (1995)
27. Thi, L.S., Lim, H.E.: Estimating the determinants of B2B e-commerce adoption among small land medium enterprises. Int. J. Bus. Soc. **12**(1), 142–150 (2011)
28. Venkatesh, V.: User acceptance of information technology: towards a unified view. MIS Q. **27**(3), 425–447 (2003)
29. Wirtz, J., Wong, P.K.: An empirical study on Internet-based business-to-business ecommerce in Singapore. Singapore Manag. Rev. **23**(1), 87–112 (2001)

# Worker's Motivation and Planning Strategies on Crowdsourcing Platforms. The Case of Yandex Toloka

Elizaveta Danilova(✉)

National Research University Higher School of Economics, St. Petersburg, Russia
emdanilova_1@edu.hse.ru

**Abstract.** The analysis of the crowdsourcing platform Yandex Toloka started from the investigation text reviews about the work on the platform. Ed text reviews were analysed using the Structural Topic Modelling approach and Biterm Topic Modelling. Performed text analysis of negative and positive reviews revealed that microworkers deliver their attention to the underpayment problem, to the problems connected with not enough working experience, lacking the skills or personal characteristics such as lacking the patience or assiduity.

**Keywords:** Crowdsourcing platforms · Topic modelling · Reviews

## 1 Introduction

For the past 10 years, the opportunities for the distant work via Internet increased dramatically. That have happened due to the several reasons. One of the reasons is developing of the new technologies in the sphere of machine learning, that are now widely used for market research and advertisement and require large amounts of manual classification work to train models on and verify their quality. Such development lead to the emergence of crowdsourcing platforms for online work that use human resources for the improving artificially based algorithms. Workers on such platforms perform various tasks after the quick guide and training. The tasks itself presents searching for actual information about the organization, sorting of the images, copywriting, analyzing search results, moderating comments, and publications. Such category of workers on online platforms are called microworkers. The basic problem of such platforms is that the level of rewards for the tasks that demand enough time and effort for their performance can be very low [6], and may create and reinforce poverty traps for some social groups, instead of alleviating them. The increasing interest of user's participation in the crowdsourced project has heightened the amount of studies that explore the workers behavior on such platforms that presents new types of online work service. Most works in this sphere of scientific research are based on the exploration of the American based platforms, Amazon Mechanical Turk, which is spread across USA and India; other platforms like Clickworker, Onespace are less common to be stated in the scientific articles. One of the common interests among researchers is investigating the behavioral patterns of the

© Springer Nature Switzerland AG 2022
D. A. Alexandrov et al. (Eds.): DTGS 2021, CCIS 1503, pp. 536–544, 2022.
https://doi.org/10.1007/978-3-030-93715-7_38

microworkers, their motivations for engagement, planning strategies, task preferences and coping with existing problems in the new niche of the work via the Internet.

The latest works about the big crowd labor platforms consider that "crowdsourcing represents an early manifestation of fluid fair, on laisser-demand workforce" [8]. In that way, authors speaking about the crowdsources in a gig economy, assume microworkers as a part of contingent workforce that have no contract for the long-term employment. Whereas, the survey of the AMT workers proves the statement about the income inconsistency in crowdsourcing, that is a part of the precarious employment. The limited practical regulation, low paid work with unstable conditions lead to the changes in workers behaviour and psychology, that makes difficult long-term employment on the various crowdsourcing platforms.

In platform economy, design of the particular platform, local market of work suppliers and task performers can dramatically influence worker financial outcomes and work experience. That is why building on the previous research on crowdsourcing the goal of this paper is to understand: *how workers evaluate and interpret their subjective experiences with the platform*.

In this paper the focus would be on the research question studied through performing a text analysis of the reviews:

- how socio-economic structure of worker's population on Russian crowdsourcing platform Yandex.Toloka is organized

## 2   Literature Review

What we know about the working experience on the crowdsourcing platforms is largely based upon empirical studies that investigate how the microworkers perform on the platforms and cope with existing problems and specificities. However, there is lack of information about the place of the microworker in the gig economy and theoretical interpretation. The possible explanation of the worker-requester relationships on the crowdsourcing platforms could be taken from the case of freelance workers.

The sphere of crowdsourcing earning systems is close to the freelance industry, where the employer and employee do not participate in standard relationship of hiring. Apart from the communication that is held through the online informational technologies like in freelance, the overall communication is totally anonymized in crowdsourcing [8]. According to that specificity, the employee may have difficulties in communication about the working conditions, but the platform administration partly takes control over that issues. From the side of the employee, the control measures over the task put the worker into the strict limits. In the crowdsourcing, it is common, that instead of the solving working problems with the one employee, the employer can distribute the task to others that constantly put pressure on the initial worker.

The crowdsourced work on the online platforms as and freelance can be described by the process of employment destandartization. From the one side, new types of employment gives freedom in the time and work distribution, planning strategies and opportunity of self-realization in various spheres. The other side of that flexible employment brings several problems, including lack of self-organization and self-management. As stated by Castell the so-called "self-programmed" labour present not only opportunities, but also many risks connected to unstable employments conditions [3].

Basically, empirical research field is concentrated on the use of behavioral data from crowdsourcing platforms about the users completed tasks on the platform and the requesters of the tasks. Researcher pay enough attention in their studies on the evaluation of the monetary reward and the problem of underpayment or minimizing the non-paid activities on the platform [2, 6], that is directly connected to the spent effort and time, that in proved by the rational decisions of microworkers [5]. Speaking about the motivation, some attempts were made by Liu and Sundar in 2018. In their study, they apply the concept of cognitive dissonance for the understanding the difference in the perception between effort on task performing and low paid monetary reward [10]. They stated that when the subjective perception of the user about the completed tasks is positive and the level of engagement in the activity is high, then the actual low payment for completing the work, demanding enough concentration would present an inconsistent perception or cognitive dissonance [10]. The other researchers also were conducting experiments about the quality of crowdsourcing work performed by user. For example, Kittur demonstrates that the crowdsource workers can complete the quite difficult tasks such as writing the rating of the Wikipedia articles very professional, in comparison with the local company experts [9]. Therefore, to perform on the platforms successfully a microworker should have some specific skills and qualities.

The classification of factors that can influence the user's motivation on the American crowdsourcing platforms can be found in the article written by Ye and Kankanhalli. Authors explore that such factors as monetary reward, skill enhancement and work autonomy do have an impact of the user's performance [11]. More than that, the factor of enjoinment is also valuable, because some microworkers stated that engaging in the platform for them is a good and fruitful spending of a time [4, 11].

During the analysis of text reviews, the main point is to focus on the subjective perception of the worker's experience in task performance, estimation of the faced problems and the factors that are important to overcome them.

## 3    Data and Methods

### 3.1    Data

For the estimation of how workers evaluate and interpret their subjective experiences about the work on the platform the detailed text reviews from the cite Irecommend (https://irecommend.ru/content/sait-yandeks-toloka) were collected with the use of the R Studio special packages (rvest, html, tidyr) for parsing(gathering) the data from html web pages. In total 404 full text reviews were collected in the spring of 2019 and 44 more reviews for the period of March-April 2020, including the metadata about the date of the publication and the rating of the review (scaled from 1 to 5).

### 3.2    Text Analysis of the Reviews

The aim of the reviews analyses was to investigate to what extend the microworkers experience common problems existing on the platform, connected to the low payment, task rejection and other problems, influencing the users' motivation of future engagement in the platform. The structural topic modelling text analysis approach was implemented in the study to analyze the reviews of the microworkers. According to previous studies using STM method, this method is appropriate to use for the topic identification of the detailed reviews of workers. The methods of topic modelling such as LDA (Latent Dirichlet Allocation), LSA (Latent Semantic Analysis) and STM was highly used in identifying topics of the reviews and comments in the sphere of tourism, especially hotel industry, such articles reveal the benefits of using these methods [1]. LDA and STM are Bayesian generative topic models, which assume that each topic is a distribution over words and each document is a mixture of corpus-wide topics. The benefits of STM over LDA in the that the document-level structure information is introduced to influence topical prevalence and topic content, thereby emphasizing the suitability of investigating how covariates affect text content [7],. The previous studies, which estimates the topics of the hotel reviews, mostly concentrate their STM analysis on the distinguishing between the negative and positive comments, using this variable as the main covariate [7]. This approach provides the better results interpretation due to the valuable comparison the document structure. In this case, it is essential to have a possibility to explore the difference in topics according to covariates, such as negative and positive rating of the review. That method would help to identify the content of topics and significance of used words that is essential for identifying issues connected to motivation.

Apart from the STM, the Biterm Topic Modelling method for short texts, which finds topics by explicitly modelling word-word co-occurrences, was used to explore the reviews collected in March-April 2020.

## 4 Analysis and Results

### 4.1 Perceived Microworkers Experience and Faced Problems Through the Analysis of Text Reviews (Structural Topic Modelling)

**Topic Summary and Validation**
One of basic topics that can be mentioned through almost all topics is the set of words connected to the type of task and its evaluation. The trend there is the description of popular type of tasks that does not require the special skills and the whole instruction and training are not so difficult. These are tasks with picture filtering and classification, sometimes including the material with "forbidden" content, copywriting and translating tasks and "field" tasks, aimed to gather the relevant information about the building, shops and organization. The last task requires using the smartphone with camera and gps system to put the geolocation on photos, that are the only tasks that are performed outside, that is why the payment for that type of task is higher. There is the entire amount of topics mentioning using smartphone and mobile app; in addition, the word "geo" collocates with these words.

From the reviews about the work of system of Yandex Toloka, let move to some social characteristics that can be recognized in the selected words from the topic. They are "maternity decree, children, husband". That characteristics shows that the platform is used by the mothers on the maternity vacation, the topics that include such word are highly correlated.

One of the topics reveal the word that shows the identification of the workers of Yandex Toloka, the word "толокер" states for all the workers of the platform, exactly like the "turkers" in Amazon Mechanical Turk.

## Problems Experienced by Users of Yandex Toloka

The topic of payment to the users, which also mentioned in many documents, includes not only the type of used payment system (PayPal, Yandex Wallet) but also some difficulties connected with it, delays of getting money and other problems. In addition, the word money in other topics are expressed as different currencies, it happened because all values for tasks are in dollars; however, the Russian microworkers are used to the national currency (rubles). A curious finding is that the word "kopek" is often identified in topics with relatively high frequency (51 reviews include this word), this can be explained either because of the small payment sums, lower than the ruble or that the Russian often use such expression as "work for kopeks", which states that for the low paid work. Looking for the collocations (bigrams) with the word "kopek" it that this word is mostly used in a negative sense with such descriptive words as: "existing", "excess", "first", "spend», that prove the not serious and negative worker relationship to the platform. This can be proved by the citation from one of the negative reviews: "Toloka is a resource that pays literally a kopek for work from which your eyes literally go blind and there is not a single intellectual task.". There user complains not only for the low payment condition, but also to the content of tasks and the sufficient time spent on them.

Themes of task rejection, moderation and banning of the user or rating reducing also presents in the corpus. The word "mistake" always appears with the word about rejection and moderation or the word "ban". The reviews with such topic are more detailed and the users can be defined as more experienced.

In contrast to the topic of mistakes and rejection, some defined topics are quite positive and demonstrates the good evaluation of the work on the platform. Some write about the beneficial opportunity for part time job and use the word "recommend", "affordable earnings", "flexible schedule", that can be seen in the reviews: "Let's start with the pros: payment in dollars, convenient withdrawal of funds, no work experience, no special skills, free work schedule". These words demonstrate the low barriers of engaging in the platform.

## Positive and Negative Evaluation of User's Experience

The estimate effect of STM model with the prevalence of covariate "star", that states for the rating of the review and split the data on negative and positive reviews, STM reveal more descriptive words that express some emotionality.

From the negative side of the comments, the most frequent words were: "regret", "long", "small", "little", "difficult", that shows the some complains of the users that are dissatisfied. However, from the other side, the positive word also presented among the highly frequent word: "favorite", "interesting", "fast", which represents some interest of the microworkers in the task performing and having some favorite tasks.

According to the covariate with positive and negative comments, the topics are divided into two categories that make the comparison possible. Some of the negative or positive topics cannot be truly distinguished, whereas others are clearly defined. The positive topics mostly present the similar words distribution and topic coherence. They raise the topics of easy and fast online earning, favorite tasks and some issues connected with banks and the money withdrawal. From the other side the negative comments consist of more different topics. The topics relate to the direct problems that users face such as blocking of the user or task reputation (39th topic) and some user complains about the low rewards (29th topic), monotonous task performing process and inappropriate content in the tasks. The reviews of users-beginners sometimes suppose that the problems of underpayment and value of tasks depends on their lack of skills of lack of luck, that is why they work with the significant time breaks trying to get fully engaged into the platform activity: "Yes, I sat almost every day for an hour a day, despite the meager pennies, because I'm not used to giving up right away", "Sometimes, of course, Toloka pisses me off, but I still come back to it.". The examples of the negative and positive topics comparison are presented in the graphs below.

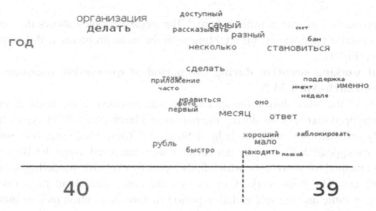

**Fig. 1.** Comparison of negative and positive topics content (Topic 40 and 39)

Speaking about the problem's interpretation, in comparison with foreign-based platforms, the users describe not only issues connected to the low payment and task submitting, but also the issues connected with the aim of the tasks and the personal interest. Many people are concerned in some degree about their interest in task managing and the content of the task. The possible reason of such situation is that most Yandex Toloka users that wrote a post see the platform as a part-time job or even some kind of the spending free time usefully, that is why their perception about value of labour on the platform can be specific.

Looking at the distribution of positive and negative topic words within one topic, there can be mentioned that in the topics with the higher positive covariate proportion, the negative side is mostly identified by the topics of learning skills on the platform and training. The positive side there is presented by the valuable characters that the microworker needs "attentive", "logical", "assiduous""). The users there speak about the qualities they need to participate and make money of the platform: "Someone more

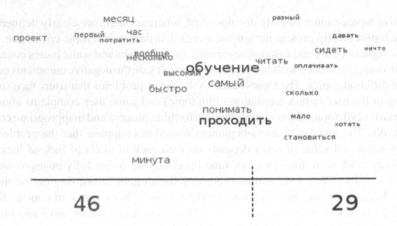

**Fig. 2.** Comparison of negative and positive topics content (Topic 46 and 29)

diligent probably can earn a million here." The negative topics shows the same tendency as described previously, highlighting with the same problems with low payment conditions (Fig. 3).

**Perceived working situation during the period of quarantine measures in the reviews of March-April 2020**

The theme of the work during the quarantine was revealed in the texts of the additionally scrapped text reviews during the period of March-April 2020. Apart from the previously revealed topic with the help of Structural Topic Modeling, now some new themes have appeared. The newly got reviews were analyzed using the Biterm Topic Modelling method for short texts, which finds topics by explicitly modelling word-word co-occurrences. The microworkers in reviews are concerned about the work during Covid19 pandemic and the self-isolation period in Russia, mention lack of money and tasks on the platform nowadays.

Overall, the after the performing STM analysis of the reviews, there were revealed some common practices of using the platform efficiently. Workers mention the qualities that the "Toloker" should have, to perform well at the platform; among them is patience and great concentration. That qualities suggested that for the beginner, as was stated in the reviews, it would be difficult to stay long at the platform from the first attempt, because of the specific training for the task performing, the scale of the task evaluation and mainly the initial low reward. Through the analyses of reviews, it was shown that users deliver their attention to the underpayment problem, to the problems connected with not enough working experience, lacking the skills or personal characteristics such as lacking the patience or assiduity. As the microworkers in the reviews stated that the online work is often for the them is a hobby or only additional source of earning money. The revealed topics put on a question on the estimating extinct and instinct motivations of the users to perform well on the platform and their ability to distribute task and time workload.

**Perceived working situation during the period of quarantine measures in the reviews of March–April 2020**

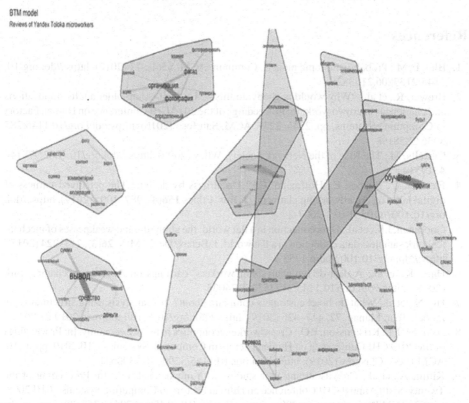

**Fig. 3.** Biterm text model of the microworker's reviews about the Yandex Toloka, scrapped for the period of March–April 2020

## 5  Discussion and Conclusion

The results of this study support evidence from previous observations [4, 11] that such factors as monetary reward, skill enhancement and work autonomy have an impact on the perceived worker's motivations and planning strategies. The ability to work online is perceived not only as a hobby or additional way of earning money, but also as the work opportunity for people unable to be currently employed due to reasons of lack of the work on the market or during the crisis period. The user experience of problems on the Yandex Toloka differ from AMT. The common problems such as low reward system of tasks, that involve high concentration and sufficient time and the task rejection presents on both platforms. Such topics are mostly raised in the negative reviews, that can be sign that the user that posted the review is dissatisfied with the work conditions and either waits for the current improvement or quit the platform and is warning others about the problematic situation. The difference in user's perception of value of money and time can be a sign of experiencing the cognitive dissonance, while the problems often connected by user to the dispositional factor such as lack of experience or concentration.

## References

1. Blei, D.M.: Probabilistic topic models. Commun. ACM. **55**(4), 77 (2012). https://doi.org/10.1145/2133806.2133826
2. Brewer, R., et al.: "Why would anybody do this?": Understanding older adults' motivations and challenges in crowd work. In: Proceedings of the 2016 CHI Conference on Human Factors in Computing Systems, pp. 2246–2257. ACM, San Jose (2016). https://doi.org/10.1145/2858036.2858198
3. Castells, M.: The Rise of the Network Society. Wiley (2009). https://doi.org/10.1002/9781444319514
4. Fieseler, C., Bucher, E., Hoffmann, C.P.: Unfairness by design? The perceived fairness of digital labor on crowdworking platforms. J. Bus. Ethics **156**(4), 987–1005 (2017). https://doi.org/10.1007/s10551-017-3607-2
5. Goodman, J.K., et al.: Data collection in a flat world: the strengths and weaknesses of mechanical turk samples: data collection in a flat world. J. Behav. Decis. Mak. **26**(3), 213–224 (2013). https://doi.org/10.1002/bdm.1753
6. Hara, K., et al.: A data-driven analysis of workers' earnings on Amazon mechanical turk (2018). https://doi.org/10.1145/3173574.3174023
7. Hu, N., et al.: What do hotel customers complain about? Text analysis using structural topic model. Tour. Manag. **72**, 417–426 (2019). https://doi.org/10.1016/j.tourman.2019.01.002
8. Jacques, J.T., Kristensson, P.O.: Crowdworker economics in the gig economy. In: Proceedings of the 2019 CHI Conference on Human Factors in Computing Systems - CHI 2019, pp. 1–10. ACM Press, Glasgow (2019). https://doi.org/10.1145/3290605.3300621
9. Kittur, A., et al.: Crowdsourcing user studies with mechanical turk. In: Proceeding of the Twenty-Sixth Annual CHI Conference on Human Factors in Computing Systems - CHI 2008, p. 453. ACM Press, Florence (2008). https://doi.org/10.1145/1357054.1357127
10. Liu, B., Sundar, S.S.: Microworkers as research participants: does underpaying Turkers lead to cognitive dissonance? Comput. Hum. Behav. **88**, 61–69 (2018). https://doi.org/10.1016/j.chb.2018.06.017
11. Ye, H. (Jonathan), Kankanhalli, A.: Solvers' participation in crowdsourcing platforms: examining the impacts of trust, and benefit and cost factors. J. Strateg. Inf. Syst. **26**(2), 101–117 (2017). https://doi.org/10.1016/j.jsis.2017.02.001

# Author Index